MW01225126

Introduction to C and C++ for Technical Students

A Skill–Building Approach

Timothy S. Ramteke

Pearson Education

Upper Saddle River, New Jersey   *Columbus, Ohio*

Library of Congress Cataloging–in–Publication Data

```
Ramteke, Timothy S.
    Introduction to C and C++ for technical students : a skill-
  building approach / Timothy S. Ramteke.
          p. cm.
    Includes index.
    ISBN 0-13-249608-9
    1. C (Computer program language)  2. C++ (Computer program
  language)  I. Title.
```

QA76.73.C35R359 1998
005.13--dc21   97-39999
                                                             CIP

Cover photo: *Mark E. Gibson / Photophile* ©
Editor: *Charles E. Stewart, Jr.*
Production Editor: *Julie Peters*
Design Coordinator: *Karrie M. Converse*
Text Designer: *Timothy S. Ramteke*
Cover Designer: *Rod Harris*
Production Manager: *Pamela D. Bennett*
Illustrations: *Timothy S. Ramteke*
Marketing Manager: *Debbie Yarnell*

This book was set in Times Roman by Prentice Hall and was printed and bound by Banta Company. The cover was also printed by Banta Company.

© 1998 by Prentice–Hall, Inc.
Upper Saddle River, New Jersey 07458

All rights reserved. No part of this book may be reproduced, in any form or by any means, without permission in writing from the publisher.

Printed in the United States of America

10 9 8 7 6 5

ISBN 0–13–249608–9

Prentice-Hall International (UK) Limited,London
Prentice-Hall of Australia Pty. Limited, Sydney
Prentice-Hall Canada Inc., Toronto
Prentice-Hall Hispanoamericana, S.A., Mexico
Prentice-Hall of India Private Limited, New Delhi
Prentice-Hall of Japan, Inc., Tokyo
Pearson Education Asia Pte. Ltd., Singapore
Editora Prentice-Hall do Brasil, Ltda., Rio de Janeiro

For Daniel, Sarah, and Jonathan,
that they may always walk humbly with their Good Shepherd

Overview

The numbers in parentheses are the number of pages in the units.

Contents

Important: How to Use This Text

What are the main sections that make up each unit?

1. Lesson
2. Drills
3. Experiments
4. Questions
5. Programs

Each page is divided into how many parts?

Every page is divided into a top part that precedes a horizontal bar shown in Figure A. The top part includes the text of the unit (the lessons), experiments, questions, and programs. Below the bar is the bottom part, which includes the drills and their solutions.

How should I follow the flow of the text?

If you are using the top part, follow the text until you come to the horizontal bar. Then skip the bottom part of the page and go to the top of the next page. See Figure B(a). To use the bottom part of the page, follow the same method. See Figure B(b).

Which sections are in which part?

All pages are divided into two parts only so that the drills have their own part on the bottom. Lessons, experiments, questions, and programs are given in the top part.

Briefly, what is the purpose for each section?

Lessons: This is where I give you information, as in a typical textbook.

Drills: First, I give you a brief introduction. Then, on a separate sheet, you should label and answer each of the drills in order. Using the solution provided on the following page, check and correct your answers. Do not use a computer here.

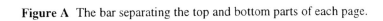

Figure A The bar separating the top and bottom parts of each page.

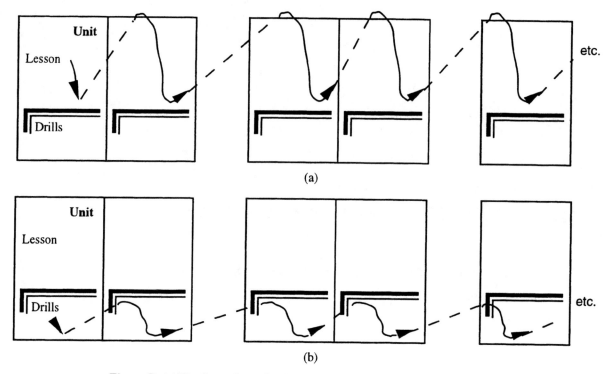

Figure B (a) The flow of text for the top part of the text. (b) The flow of text for the bottom part.

Experiments: For each experiment, type in the program in the computer, run it, and copy the output in the box shown, as in Figure C. Then answer the questions. If you complete the question on separate sheets of paper, you can turn them in as lab assignments.

Questions: Try to answer the questions from what you have learned without first running them on a computer.

Programs: Write programs on separate sheets of paper. Then enter and run them.

In what order should the sections be done in each unit?

If you are adventurous and like to learn things on your own, do the experiments and/or drills first. If you don't feel comfortable "treading unknown waters," study the lesson first. See Figure D.

Figure C The box in which to place the output of each experiment.

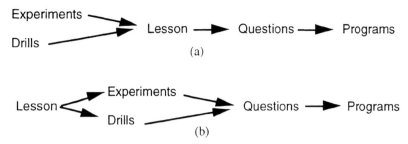

Figure D (a) The exploratory method of studying the units. (b) The "show–me" method of studying the units.

In which sequence should the units be studied?

The answer to this question depends on what you already know and what you want to achieve. Figure E provides a guide.

What should you, the professor, base the lectures on?

Before they go to the lab, many students like to have the programs in the experiments explained, but not necessarily the questions. The lessons can also be covered in class.

What should you, the professor, assign for homework and lab?

To help them take advantage of the drills, collect students' hand–written worksheets for the drills as homework; otherwise, they will not do them and miss out on the practice which they need. You can also assign the questions and programs sections as homework.

For lab, you can collect students' outputs and answers to the questions in the experiments and the listings for their working programs. Remember to get the instructor's manual with a disk with all of the code that is in the text.

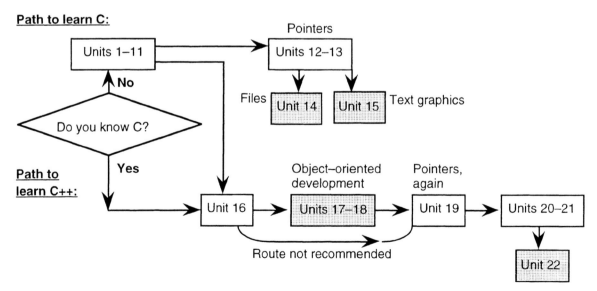

Figure E Sequence of units to cover while learning C and/or C++. The units in the shaded boxes are optional.

Preface

A FRESH APPROACH TO LEARNING C AND C++

A Need for Practice

Everyone in all disciplines agrees that, in mastering a particular discipline, each stage of the learning process must be well developed before continuing to the next stage. When we are taught mathematics in grade school, or taught to swim or play the piano, we are given a lot of repetitive practice in what we need to learn. When studying algebra, a subject related to programming, in high school we are given homework that is repetitious because that is how we will learn the material. We do not learn only one way to factor a quadratic equation, for example, and then without practice start the next topic.

Then why, with so many books on the market in C and C++ programming, doesn't one provide the student with the opportunity to practice what is taught? Even when one of these books has questions or programs at the end of each chapter, they are too sophisticated for the first-time student and thus they are ineffective. Through the use of drills and experiments, this text gives the student the practice needed in one topic before continuing to the next.

However, finding the best book in C and C++ is not enough. I can show you only so many times how to program. Soon you must start writing your own programs. You can't just watch; you have to participate. You must practice, even if it means that you make mistakes.

Less Syntax, More Logic, and More Object–Oriented Concepts

Just as most texts leave no time for practice, they also leave no time to discuss programming logic because they are too busy covering all the syntax of the language. C and C++ are languages rich in features, and shortcuts are almost always possible. Most textbooks explain thoroughly all the details of the language. Little attention, if any, is given to building logic skills.

In the early days of programming, we had time to learn basic logic structures. And over the years, the languages have become more and more complex. We no longer have time to study the different ways of setting up a nested–if statement or to look at the various ways of manipulating arrays. This book will take you back to the basics.

The text, however, gives only what is necessary to move ahead. It just isn't necessary for the first-time programmer to know all the language details. Once the student has written programs using a minimum number of C and C++ components, alternative methods can be learned later and very easily using a handbook on the language. This bare–bones approach allows the students to harness their thinking skills to put a program together, rather than getting mired in learning the complex syntax of the language. For the faster students who can't wait to get an in–depth handbook on C and C++, a section called Optional Topics is provided at the end of some units.

Those who want to learn C++ must pick up one set of books and those who want to learn object–oriented principles must pick up another. Why are these two subjects, which depend on and support each other, presented separately in today's textbooks? Object–oriented design is useless if you don't have a language to implement it. Conversely, a C++ program has nothing new to offer if there is no object–oriented design to precede it. In this text, a balanced view of both will be presented, leaving you with the impression that object–oriented programming is nothing more than an extension of our everyday experiences.

GETTING THE MOST OUT OF THIS TEXT

You have probably noticed that each chapter is called a unit. This word choice emphasizes the fact that the approach of this text is much different than any other text that you may have encountered. Each unit is divided into five or six sections: Experiments, Drills, Lesson, Questions, and Programs, and many also have the Optional Topics section. Each section is a tool that supports the learning process in its own unique way.

Experiments

Students often tell the instructor that they understand when a program is explained in class, but when they go home, their minds go blank. The problem is that the students aren't part of the learning process. They are *told* what happens. The experiments in this book *show* them what happens. In many cases, not only do you see what happens but, by trying alternatives to the code, you can also deduce the reasoning behind it. A student who can interpret the effects of the programming code is becoming part of the learning process rather than remaining an outside observer. The learning becomes part of his or her experience!

We should place much more emphasis on experiments than we do today. Programming lab exercises are usually tacked on to a lecture class. When these experiments are performed in lab on computer systems, they become an integral part of the lecture and reinforce what is taught in lecture. Einstein derived his theory of general relativity mathematically, but it wasn't accepted until it was demonstrated by experiments. All the reasoning in logic is useless unless it can be observed in the lab.

After each experiment, be sure to answer its questions before advancing to the next experiment. Sometimes students rush through the experiments without completing this important step. There are subtle concepts that are best understood by doing the questions directly after observing what was shown on the screen.

Drills

Before I went to Vietnam, I was taught electronics in the army with the use of thick books that merely gave a question on one page and the answer on the next. Complex topics were reduced to small pieces, which made learning fun. I am taking that same idea and using it in the bottom third of each page in this book. Think of the drills on the bottom third of each page as a mini-book inside the main book. In each drill, a quick explanation is given first, then some questions. Answer the questions by writing their answers right in the book. Then look at their solutions on the next page. If you do the drills before the instructor has had a chance to cover the lesson, you will be better prepared for the lesson. After the lesson, you can do the drills a second time. By then, they will be done more quickly.

Do the drills for homework. You don't need a computer. Checking your solutions as you proceed prevents you from acquiring incorrect ideas and will put you back on the right track immediately. Typically, students do homework and don't find the right answers until the teacher reviews it in class. The drill and solution combinations will gently guide you step by step and ensure that the ideas are understood correctly.

Lessons

I try to use concrete examples with which students can relate, such as the gauges on the dashboard of a car. I try to start each lesson with an idea that is common knowledge or something that was covered in a previous unit and extend that topic to introduce new programming principles.

I also introduce complex concepts early in the book so that, when students must explore the concepts in their entirety, they are not totally new. For example, to prepare students for pointers, memory addresses are introduced in Unit 3. Linked lists using arrays are explained in Unit 9. Similarly, functions, which are central to C and C++ programming, are explained in Unit 1 before they are investigated in Units 9 and 10.

Most units have only one or two example problems. This allows the students to concentrate on many of the ideas in one or two examples. I try to keep the instruction in each unit in focus, so the number of examples is kept to a minimum.

Questions

If you know how to use carpentry tools properly, you are in a position to build a beautiful piece of furniture. If you know the function of the various programming tools, then you are ready to write a program. The questions attempt to prepare students for writing a program and should be done after the experiments, drills, and study of the lesson. They can be done very easily for homework. They reinforce the effect of executing the statements in the unit and establish the underlying ground work. The questions reinforce the understanding students need to write their own programs.

Programs

I wish there was an easy way to learn programming. However, if you don't get it the first time, don't be concerned. I didn't learn how to program overnight either. The more you program, the easier it will be for you. The programs can be done either for homework or for lab.

Optional Topics

This section in various units is optional. You can skip this section completely and move to the next unit without losing continuity. Students who are ahead may use this section to do new experiments in lab, giving others a chance to catch up. Others may simply glance over these topics to see if they find anything that interests them.

Flowcharts and Tracecharts

This book provides a lot of exposure to flowcharts and tracecharts throughout. The flowcharts will allow the students to represent programming logic graphically. Tracecharts, which I haven't seen in any other book, will give the students an idea of how the computer executes each step in the programming code. I hope that students make an effort to understand the tracecharts; they give a brand new perspective on how programs execute. Each tool by itself is not sufficient, but together they all form a powerful set of tools that will help students become master programmers.

MY THANKS

My thanks go first to my students, who still find mistakes in my programs. My thanks also go to Charles Stewart, Jr., who one day mailed me the contract for this book and then called me up and asked me if I would sign it. My thanks go to Jennifer King of Borland International who, together with Charles, was able to bundle C++Builder with the text without affecting its cost.

Coming from a Macintosh and UNIX background, I used to tease my students and tell them, "Hey, finally I found a good reason to own a PC; you can run the Linux version of UNIX on it!" After playing with C++Builder, I can now give them an even better reason.

My heartfelt thanks go to JoEllen Gohr, Julie Anderson Peters, Louise Sette, and all their wonderful support staff in production. My thanks go to you too when you work and learn from this book. Then my efforts have made it worthwhile. Please write to me at ramteke@pilot.njin.net. With respect for all faiths, allow me to praise and glorify the Lord Jesus Christ for dying on the cross for everyone's sins, even mine.

LAST THOUGHTS

I have a philosophy in teaching that anyone can master a subject as long as he or she is given enough time. Some people need more time and some need less, but eventually everyone can master a given subject. After teaching for twenty years, I still hold that view. You will find that attitude of mine when you work with this book.

Last, don't give up. When something becomes confusing, don't think of it as a hindrance, but take it as a challenge. Get help. And when you see how a program is done, don't assume that now you can do it also. Redo the program and see if you can make it work, even if you have seen the solution already. Also, no one says that homework can't be done more than once. Keep practicing. Keep experimenting. And when comments are made by others who think you can't, prove that you can. Remember, there is only one difference between what is possible and what isn't: your determination.

COMPILERS

Installing C++Builder

This compiler is provided to us as a courtesy by Borland International, Inc. It is good only for 60 days from the time of its installation. It can be installed on either Windows 95 or Windows NT. To install it, insert the CD–ROM provided in the text in the CD–ROM drive. Then double–click on the following icons in this order: MyComputer, CD–ROM, Setup folder, C++Builder folder, and Readme. Read the license agreement and other instructions. Then double–click on the Setup icon.

Now read the install information and choose full setup. Select the directory where C++Builder should be installed, select the program folder, click on Install, and wait as the files are copied over to your hard drive. Then read the help topics and click on Cancel when done. Now your setup is complete. Click on Finish.

Now you are in position to run a program. Start with the Start button and choose Programs, Borland, and C++Builder, in that order. Read and accept the condition. Click on Yes. When default link state files are created, click on Ok.

Running C++Builder

To write a program, choose New from the File menu. Then double–click on console application. Close the form window. Delete all the lines you see on the screen and type the following:

```
#include <stdio.h>
void main (void)
{
   printf("Wow, we're on a roll!\n");
   getchar();
}
```

Now you can do a File–Save and Run the program using the Run pull–down menu. The output will come up on the screen because the getchar() function stops the program execution until a key is pressed on the keyboard. From this point, you can add and change the program to run the programs in the text.

You can execute one step at a time to see how variables change their values. For example, suppose we have variables *i* and *sum* in a loop and we want to see how their values change. First you select the Add Watch option under the Run menu and add those variables as watch expressions. Then using the Project menu, you select the Build–All option. Now using the Run menu, select Trace to Next Source Line repeatedly and you can watch how the values of *i* and *sum* change, step by step.

Downloading and Running GNU's gcc for DOS

You can download a free, text–based compiler for PCs which runs on DOS. This is a high–quality compiler and is written by the Free Software Foundation. With it you can run all of the programs in this text (except for the programs in Unit 15). It needs about 20 megabytes to install.

First create a directory called gnu in the root directory of the C: drive. From that directory, do all the following steps. Using the site, "ftp://ftp.simtel.net/pub/simtelnet/gnu/djgpp/v2/", download the readme.1st and the djdev201.zip files. Read the readme.1st file. From "ftp://ftp.simtel.net/pub/simtelnet/gnu/djgpp/v2gnu", download these files: bnu27b.zip, gcc2721b.zip, gpp2721b.zip, lgp271b.zip. Now using the site, "ftp://ftp.pkware.com/", download the pkz204g.exe file. After all the files have been downloaded in the gnu directory, run these commands in DOS:

```
C:\gnu>pkz204g              (About 16 files will be self–extracted.)
C:\gnu>pkunzip              (Shows what options are available.)
C:\gnu>pkunzip -d *.zip     (Unzips the five gnu files.)
C:\gnu>edit readygnu.bat    (Create the readygnu.bat file by entering the following two lines.)

        set DJGPP=C:\GNU\DJGPP.ENV
        set PATH=C:\GNU\BIN;%PATH%

C:\gnu>readygnu.bat            (Executes this file which sets up the working environment.)
C:\gnu>edit test.cc            (Create a C or C++ program to test. Use the cc extension.)
C:\gnu>gcc -c -Wall test.cc    (Compile test.cc which creates test.o.)
C:\gnu>gxx -o test.exe test.o  (Link-edit test.o which creates test.exe.)
C:\gnu>test.exe                (Executes the file.)
```

I just found a better way to download this compiler and tomorrow I am sending the final files for this text on disk to production. Try this site first: http://www.delorie.com/djgpp/zip-picker.html. It is much easier to use.

The printf() Function

What Is a Function?

In C and C++, one can't write even a simple program without using functions. Therefore, let us make sure we thoroughly understand the concept of functions. First, we will study the concept of functions as they relate to us in real life.

Functions are quite common in our daily lives, although we may not think of them as such. Consider a parent sending her daughter to a university. See Figure 1.1. Here, the parent is the **calling** function and the university is the **called** function. The parent is calling the university to do a task. The calling function wants the called function to provide a good education for her child. However, the called function requires the calling function to pass what are called **arguments**. The arguments the calling function must provide may be a hard-working student and tuition. When the process of the university is complete, this called function may **return a value**; here the university returns to the parent a student who is well-educated and ready to start her career path.

At this point in the page, skip the bottom part and go to the top of the next page

These drills can be done as homework without the use of a computer. They may be done before the instructor covers the material. This will prepare the student for what will be covered in the lectures. Many of the drills will become redundant, but that is the objective of these drills: that the writing of programs will become second nature to the student. The only way one can achieve proficiency is by repetition. Learning new concepts is more interesting than doing the same exercises over again. However, only by repeating the same exercises can a student master new concepts in programming. Explanations are kept to a minimum so that there will be more time for drills.

For each drill, write your answer in the margins of the text or on a separate sheet (if you need to redo the drills at a later time). Only after you write your answer should you look at the solution on the next page and check your answer.

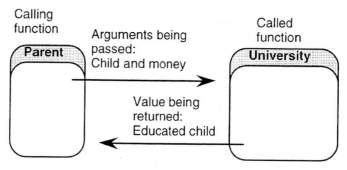

Figure 1.1 A "parent" function calling a "university" function.

How does the university provide its services? It must depend on other functions, such as the English instructor, to help. Now, the university becomes the calling function and the English instructor becomes the called function, as shown in Figure 1.2. The English instructor may require the university to provide her with students who qualify to sit in her class. These are the arguments. In return, the instructor will return to the university a student who is capable of communicating well with others.

In this example we saw how a function may call another and the called function may in turn call another one. In Figure 1.3 we see an example of how four functions may interact with each other.

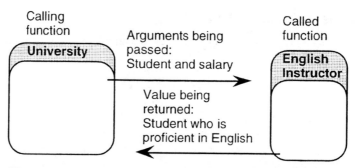

Figure 1.2 A "university" function calling an "instructor" function.

At this point in the page, skip the bottom part and go to the top of the next page

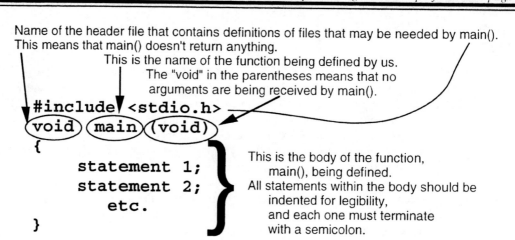

The *printf( )* Function

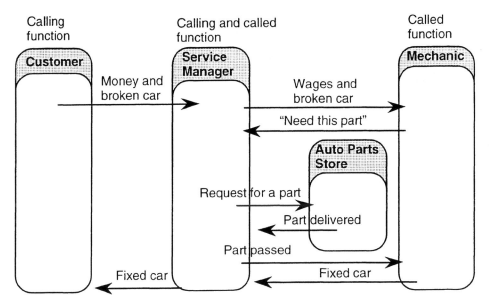

Figure 1.3 An example of various functions calling each other.

Although some concepts in these examples are not real life, such as paying for a broken car before it gets fixed, they will make it easy for us to understand functions as they are used in programming.

The customer provides the service manager with a broken car and the payment as arguments. The service manager passes the broken car as an argument to the mechanic, who returns a value saying that she needs a particular part. The service manager, using the services of the parts store function, obtains the necessary part, calls the mechanic again, and receives from her a fixed car as a returned value. This returned value is then returned to the customer by the service manager.

Functions in C and C++

Example 1.1 illustrates how functions are used in C. When this simple program is executed, it will show on the display what is given under the line labeled "output." The output is the result after running the program. The program is the section of code from '//' to the last closed brace "}."

At this point in the page, skip the bottom part and go to the top of the next page

Drill 1.1 Study the template of a small program on the previous page, and answer these questions:

a. Name the function that must always exist in a program.
b. Should the header file called "stdio.h" be included in the body of main()?
c. What indicates that no arguments are being received by main?
d. What indicates that no values are being returned by main()?
e. How do you know where the body of main() begins? Where it ends?
f. What is used to terminate each statement?

```
//EXAMPLE 1.1
#include <stdio.h>          // header file
void main (void)            /* This line is called the function header */
{
    printf("Isn't this a beautiful day! \n");
    printf("%s is my name \n", "BO");
    printf("Initial: %c. \tAge: %d, \nWeight: %.2f \n", 'Z', 12, 78.75);
}
----- output -----
Isn't this a beautiful day!
BO is my name
Initial: Z.      Age: 12,
Weight: 78.75
```

Before we look at the details of this program, let us take a "bird's eye" view of it. In Figure 1.4, we see the various functions mentioned in the program. We, as programmers, write the main() function and when we run the program, the compiler will start the execution of the program

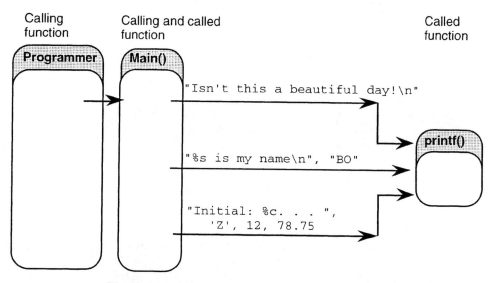

Figure 1.4 An example of how main() calls printf().

At this point in the page, skip the bottom part and go to the top of the next page

Solution 1.1

a. main()

b. No, the header file, called "stdio.h" is included before the header line for main().

c. The "void" inside the parentheses indicates that no arguments are being received by it.

d. The keyword "void" means that nothing is being returned by main().

e. The left brace "{" signals where main() begins and the right brace "}" signals where it ends. They should both be in the same column and all statements between them should be indented.

f. The semicolon ";" is used to terminate each sentence.

beginning with the main() function. The only function that our program defines is the main() function. Hence, a C program must always have a main() function; it is the starting point for running a program. The statements for main() are enclosed between the set of braces "{ }." These statements should be indented as shown so the program is understood easily by those who read it.

We call main() and main() doesn't return any value. If it did, we would see a "return" statement in main(). Since main() doesn't return any value, its header has the keyword "void" in front of it. Furthermore, main() doesn't receive any arguments, so the keyword "void" is placed inside the parentheses after main(). For almost all parts of this text, our main() functions will not receive any arguments or return any values.

What main() must do or what programming code it must execute is specified in its definition. We define main() by coding it, and main() calls printf() three times. The definition of printf() is stored in a separate file called "stdio.h." In order to notify the compiler that the definition for printf() is contained in stdio.h, we provide the include statement for it. "stdio.h" is also called a header file and it contains definitions of other functions as well.

The statements that main() must execute are provided in the **body** of the function. The body of a function is nested inside a pair of braces "{ }." In C++, any characters on a line that follow a pair of slashes "//" are ignored by the compiler and considered as comments. Comments that span many lines are easier to write by enclosing them between "/*" and "*/", as on the function header line. A C program can be executed on a C++ compiler, but not the other way around because the C language is a subset of C++.

The first statement that main() executes is a call to the system defined function, printf(). The item within the parentheses of printf() is the item that main() is passing as an argument. main() is passing only one argument to printf(); it is a character **string**, or more specifically, a **format string**. Characters enclosed within a set of double quotes are called a string in C. This string is passed as an argument by main() to printf(), which simply prints the string. printf() has no value to return back to main(). After the control of execution comes back to main() from the first printf(), main() continues where it left off and calls printf() the second time. Before we look at the second printf(), let us understand the '\n' in the printf() format string.

Although '\n' appears as two printable characters (the '\' and the 'n'), it takes the same amount of memory to store as a single character, such as 'n', would take. The backslash in a format string is a special signal to printf() that the character following it has a special meaning. Hence, it is also called an **escape** character. The special meaning here is to return the carriage and go to a new line. So the items from the next printf() are seen on the following line.

The second time main() calls printf(), it passes two arguments that are separated by one comma within the parentheses. The first argument is the format string and the next one is a string that will be substituted in place of the %s of the format string. Therefore, instead of the %s appearing in the output of the program, we see "BO" in its place. %s is called the **format specifier** to print

At this point in the page, skip the bottom part and go to the top of the next page

Drill 1.2

One kind of statement in main() is a call to a function called "printf()." The first argument that printf() must receive is called a format string and it may receive other arguments. The definition of printf() or how it must work is stored in the file called "stdio.h."

a. If main() calls printf(), do we need the line: "#include <stdio.h>?"
b. Where is printf() defined?
c. Which function may call the printf() function?
d. If printf() is being called, should that statement start at the first column in main()?

character strings. If we had used "DADDY" instead of "BO," then "DADDY" would have been displayed. Finally, the '\n' returns the carriage to a new line to be ready for the next printf().

Last, the printf() is called a third time. This time there are four arguments being passed to the printf() function: the format string and three other items that will be substituted in order, in place of the format specifiers.

As printf() proceeds to print out the format string, it prints all characters it sees until the % is encountered. Hence, "Initial: " gets printed. In place of the %c, the next unused argument gets substituted. In this case 'Z' is printed using a character format. Then the period from the format string is printed. Now our output is "Initial: Z. ".

Then the printf() encounters a backslash, which is a signal for an escape character. This time it is '\t' which stands for a horizontal tab. So "Age:" is displayed on the next horizontal tab. Then at the %d, the format specifier to print decimal integers, the next unused argument, 12, is printed. Now our output is: "Initial: Z.   Age: 12,".

After the 12, we go to the next line because of the '\n' and output "Weight:". Then the next unused argument "78.75" is printed using the %.2f format specifier. This specifier prints numbers with fractions with up to two decimal places. The %f specifier actually stands for a floating point number representation because of the method in which floating point numbers are represented in computer architecture. After that, a final new-line character is placed to go to the next line, in case someone adds another call to a printf() after this one.

Notice that the format specifiers should be chosen to match the type of data they will display: %c is used to display characters, %s for strings, %d for integers, and %.2f for fractional numbers. We will explore these four data types more in the next unit.

Running a Program

A computer's CPU (central processing unit) understands only machine language instructions. Each kind of CPU has its own set of instructions. For example, the instructions for an Intel CPU and a Motorola CPU are different from each other. If a program is written using the machine language for Intel, then we can't run that same program on a Motorola CPU in the future. A nice thing about high–level languages such as C and C++ is that, once such a program is written, it can then be executed on any CPU. All we would need is a special software that converts our C/C++ program into machine language for the particular platform we are using.

In general, this software is called a *compiler*. In Figure 1.5, we see how a C/C++ program is converted into an executable file so that it will run on the machine it is meant for. The program we write is called the source file, as shown on the top of the figure, and the program that is executed on the CPU is called an executable file. Once an executable file is created, the compiler is no longer needed to run it.

At this point in the page, skip the bottom part and go to the top of the next page

---

Solution 1.2

a. Yes, we need that line because it directs the compiler to use the header file called "stdio.h," which contains the definition for printf().
b. printf() is defined in "stdio.h."
c. main() may call printf().
d. No. Only the braces for the body of main() should start in the first column.

Drill 1.3

Does printf() require an argument to be passed to it?

The *printf()* Function

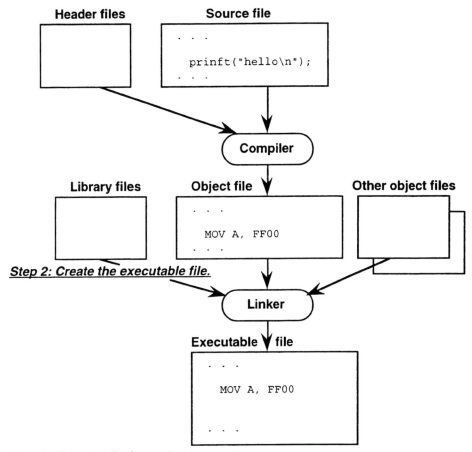

Figure 1.5 Steps that are taken from writing a program to running it.

At this point in the page, skip the bottom part and go to the top of the next page

Solution 1.3 Yes, it needs at least the format string argument to be of any use. For example, calling printf() this way will provide the given output.

```
printf("Come on baby\n");
----- output -----
Come on baby
```

The format string is the string of characters enclosed between the double quotes inside the pair of parentheses. The items inside the parentheses are used to pass arguments.

Drill 1.4 What will be the output of the following?

```
"printf("Go on buster\n");"
```

The *printf()* Function

When we write the source file, it may have a specific extension, such as ".c" for C programs or ".cc" or ".cpp" for C++ programs. Each compiler may require its own extension. When the compiler runs, it converts the source program into a machine language code and at the same time may process some header files required by the program. This is called the compilation step.

Once the object file is generated, it may have to be combined with other object files that have already been created, maybe because the entire project was divided into several programs. The object file will also need to be combined with library routines so that all these separate codes can become one seamless program, ready to execute. This step of connecting and merging the object file with other object and library files is called *linking* and is done by a piece of software called the linker. Now the program is ready to execute.

On many systems, GNU's version of the C++ compiler is available. This high–quality compiler is created by the Free Software Foundation and is available on the Internet. To run a C or C++ program using this compiler on a UNIX system, I use these three steps:

1. `emacs test.cc`   Create and edit the source file called "test.cc."
2. `g++ test.cc`   Compile and link the source file.
3. `a.out`   Execute this executable file that was created in the last step.

EXPERIMENTS

Instead of telling you how the *printf()* works, you should experiment with it yourself on a real computer to see how it works. This is the objective of the experiments. For each one, type in the code exactly as you see it. Watch out for all the details, especially the semicolons. You don't need to save them on a diskette since eventually there will be too many of them to keep track of. Write down the output of each program in the box provided and answer the questions associated with them. If you don't understand what the program is doing or can't answer the questions, don't be overly concerned. By the time you do the drills and study the lesson, those problems should be resolved. If you can at least identify what is unclear, then the lecture portion of the class will become more meaningful. If you are not accustomed to writing in a book, you can place all answers in a notebook, as long as you label your work. If a new experiment is very similar to the previous one, then the new items are shown in bold. The actual method of running a program will vary from compiler to compiler.

At this point in the page, skip the bottom part and go to the top of the next page

Solution 1.4

```
printf("Go on buster\n");
----- output -----
Go on buster
```

The '\n' means "go to the next line." If we don't place it at the end of the format string, the next line will be printed directly after the first one on the same line.

Drill 1.5 Show the output of the following:

```
printf("Come on");
printf("baby \n Go \non buster \n");
```

The *printf()* Function

Exp 1.1 Characters inside a set of double quotes are called a **string**.

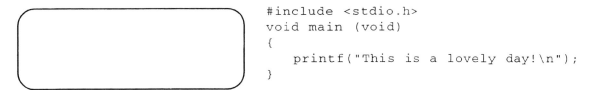

```
#include <stdio.h>
void main (void)
{
    printf("This is a lovely day!\n");
}
```

Note that the slash at the end of the line is a backslash (or a backwack).

Exp 1.2 New additions from a previous experiment are shown in bold.

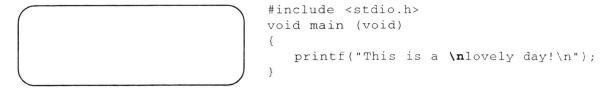

```
#include <stdio.h>
void main (void)
{
    printf("This is a \nlovely day!\n");
}
```

The '\n' is called a **character** and so is 'T'.
a. Does the '\n' get printed as the other characters were printed inside the string?
b. What do you think is its effect?

Exp 1.3 The '\n' is an example of an **escape** character because it provides a means of escaping from printing normal printable characters.

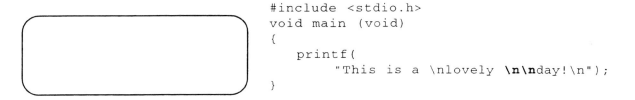

```
#include <stdio.h>
void main (void)
{
    printf(
        "This is a \nlovely \n\nday!\n");
}
```

a. How many '\n's are needed to obtain one blank line?

At this point in the page, skip the bottom part and go to the top of the next page

Solution 1.5

There is no new line character after "on," so the "baby" from the next printf() is printed on the same line as "Come on."

```
printf("Come on");
printf("baby \n Go \non buster \n");
----- output -----
Come on baby
Go
on buster
```

Exp 1.4

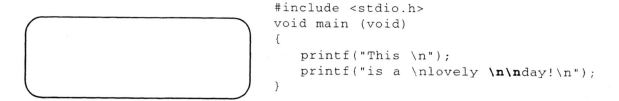

```
#include <stdio.h>
void main (void)
{
    printf("This \n");
    printf("is a \nlovely \n\nday!\n");
}
```

Exp 1.5 Only the last printf() has a '\n'.

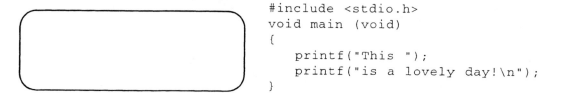

```
#include <stdio.h>
void main (void)
{
    printf("This ");
    printf("is a lovely day!\n");
}
```

a. Why was this printed on one line?
b. How could it have been printed on two lines?

Exp 1.6 Here is an example of another escape character that does something other than print characters.

```
#include <stdio.h>
void main (void)
{
    printf("This \tis a \tlovely day!\n");
    printf("Oh, \tme oh \tmy!\n");
}
```

a. Can you tell what is the effect of the '\t'?
b. Is the 't' from '\t' printed?

At this point in the page, skip the bottom part and go to the top of the next page

Drill 1.6 Just like the special '\n' that goes to a new line, '\t' also does something special like going to the next tab position on the same line. Consider the following:

```
printf("1\t2\t3\n4\t5\n");
----- output -----
1   2   3
4   5
```

What is the output for the following?

```
printf("I\tlove\t");
printf("you\nwhole\tlot\n");
```

The *printf()* Function

Exp 1.7 Let us enter all backslashes as forward slashes.

```
#include <stdio.h>
void main (void)
{
    printf("This /tis a /tlovely day!/n");
    printf("Oh, /tme oh /tmy!/n");
}
```

a. Are the 't's from the '/t's printed?
b. Escape characters have special meanings. Are '/t' and '/n' escape characters?
c. Which slash, the forward or the back, is interpreted in a special way?

Exp 1.8 So far we have been using only one string with the printf() function.
This is called the **format string**. Now let us add other items in the printf() function.

```
#include <stdio.h>
void main (void)
{
    printf("My name's %s and I'm %d.\n",
        "Jim", 45);
}
```

a. Was the %s printed?
b. What was printed in its place?
c. Was the %d printed?
d. What was printed in its place?

Exp 1.9 %s is used to print character strings and %d is used to print whole numbers or decimal integers. They are called **format specifiers**.

```
#include <stdio.h>
void main (void)
{
    printf("My name's %s and I'm %d.\n",
        "Momo", 102);
}
```

At this point in the page, skip the bottom part and go to the top of the next page

Solution 1.6

```
printf("I\tlove\t");
printf("you\nwhole\tlot\n");
----- output -----
I       love    you
whole   lot
```

Drill 1.7 The backslash is a signal to the printf that a special character follows. Similarly, the percent sign % signals that a specific format should be used to print the next argument. In the following example the argument after the format string is substituted for the %c. Show the output.

```
printf("My name is %cin\n", 'T');
```

The *printf()* Function

Exp 1.10 Although placing the "102" and "Momo" out of the format string doesn't serve a useful purpose here, it will become necessary in the next unit.

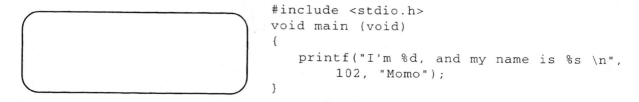

```
#include <stdio.h>
void main (void)
{
    printf("I'm %d, and my name is %s \n",
        102, "Momo");
}
```

Exp 1.11 Let us see what happens if we mix up the format specifiers:

```
#include <stdio.h>
void main (void)
{
    printf("I'm %s, and my name is %d \n",
        102, "Momo");
}
```

a. If the format specifiers don't match the type of items being printed, does it matter?
b. In conclusion, one should use what format specifier to print a string?
c. One should use what format specifier to print an integer or a whole number?

Exp 1.12 Now let us consider fractional numbers or numbers with decimal points.

```
#include <stdio.h>
void main (void)
{
    printf("%f \t %.3f \n %.2f\n",
        1.7835, 1.7835, 1.7835);
}
```

a. %f shows how many places after the decimal point?
b. %.2f shows how many places after the decimal point?
c. %.3f shows how many places after the decimal point?

At this point in the page, skip the bottom part and go to the top of the next page

Solution 1.7

```
printf("My name is %cin\n", 'T');
----- output -----
My name is Tin
```

Drill 1.8 Show the printout.

```
printf("%c can \tdrive \n%cy", 'U', 'm');
printf(" %cruck\n", 't');
```

The *printf()* Function

Exp 1.13 Now let us print single characters instead of strings of characters.

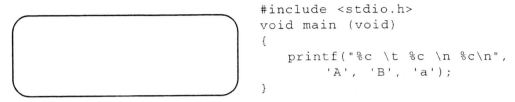

```
#include <stdio.h>
void main (void)
{
    printf("%c \t %c \n %c\n",
        'A', 'B', 'a');
}
```

a. What format specifier is used to print only one character?

Exp 1.14

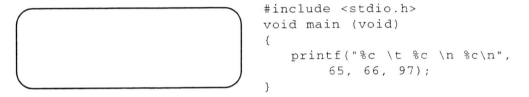

```
#include <stdio.h>
void main (void)
{
    printf("%c \t %c \n %c\n",
        65, 66, 97);
}
```

a. Printing 65 using the %c format specifier prints what character?
b. Printing 66 using the %c format specifier prints what character?
c. Printing 97 using the %c format specifier prints what character?

Exp 1.15

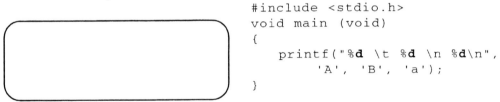

```
#include <stdio.h>
void main (void)
{
    printf("%d \t %d \n %d\n",
        'A', 'B', 'a');
}
```

a. An A is printed as what decimal integer?
b. An a is printed as what decimal integer?

At this point in the page, skip the bottom part and go to the top of the next page

Solution 1.8

```
----- output -----
U can    drive
my truck
```

Drill 1.9 The %s is a format specifier like the %c, except that it prints a string of characters instead. In general, a character is one symbol or letter or number seen on a screen and enclosed in single quotes, and a string is one or more characters enclosed in double quotes. Show the output of the following.

```
printf("this is a %s\n", "string");
printf("this is a one character string: %s\n", "x");
```

c. In conclusion, although the format specifiers may not match the type of data being printed, what format specifier should one use when printing a character?

d. One should use what format specifier when printing a whole number?

e. One should use what format specifier when printing a number with a decimal point? When printing a string?

f. Rerun the program exactly as shown. Is there any difference in how it is executed? Which way do you like better? Why?

```c
#include <stdio.h>
void main (void) { printf(
"%d \t %d \n %d\n", 'A', 'B', 'a');   }
```

QUESTIONS

1. How should the header line for main() be written?
2. Is the main() defined by the system or the programmer?
3. Is the printf() defined by the system or the programmer?
4. In this example,

```c
printf("Hello, %c \tneed you \n", 'I');
```

a. How many arguments are being passed?

b. Which function is passing the arguments? Which one is receiving?

c. What is the name of the first argument?

d. How many escape characters are being used?

5. Give the appropriate escape character or the format specifier for each of the following operations:

a. printing a string

b. printing an integer

c. going to a new line

d. doing a horizontal tab

e. printing a single character

f. printing a number with two decimal positions

6. Show the printout for each of the following:

```c
a. printf("Give me %d \n tickets \n", 2);
   printf("\n\n**\n");
```

At this point in the page, skip the bottom part and go to the top of the next page

Solution 1.9

```c
printf("this is a %s\n", "string");
printf("this is a one character string: %s\n", "x");
----- output -----
this is a string
this is a one character string: x
```

Drill 1.10 %d and %.2f are the format specifiers to print decimal integers and fractional numbers, respectively. Show the output of the following.

```c
printf("I worked %d hours\n", 20);
printf("My wage was $%.2f\n", 1.25);
printf("I made %.2f dollars\n", 25.00);
```

The *printf()* Function

```
        b.  printf("QTY = %d \n", 3);
            printf("PRICE = %.2f\n TOTAL = %.2f\n", 1.25, 3.75);

        c.  printf("*\t*\t\n");
            printf("\n*\t**\n");

        d.  printf("**%c*\n*", 'Z');
            printf("%s*\n", "LO");

        e.  printf("%s is the ", "yellow");
            printf("color %.2f\n", 11.01);
```

PROGRAMS

For each of these programming problems, write complete programs to get the output shown. Pass the arguments as specified with each problem. Call printf() once for each line that is printed; that is, every time printf() is called, a '\n' should appear at the end of its format string.

1. Pass "kind", 19, and 180.00 as arguments.
```
----- output -----
I am kind,
I am 19,
I weigh 180.00
```

2. Pass 'W' and 314 as arguments.
```
----- output -----
The letter is W
314 is the number
```

3. Pass "freak", 1845, and 1846 as arguments. Notice the tabs.
```
----- output -----
1845    don't    freak    out
but     1846     you      may
```

4. Pass "Joe" and "Jill" as arguments.
```
----- output -----
Today, Joe is blue
and Jill is happy
```

At this point in the page, skip the bottom part and go to the top of the next page

Solution 1.10

```
printf("I worked %d hours\n", 20);
printf("My wage was $%.2f\n", 1.25);
printf("I made %.2f dollars\n", 25.00);
----- output -----
I worked 20 hours
My wage was $1.25
I made 25.00 dollars
```

Drill 1.11 Passing "Justin" and 3 as arguments, write one printf() that will give the following output:
```
----- output -----
Sir Justin has gone out to sea
for 3 months.
```

OPTIONAL TOPICS

Other Ways to Print

The **putchar**() function will print only one character. That character is the only argument passed to the function. It doesn't use a format string.

The **putc**() function also prints only one character, but it allows us to specify where the character should be printed. We can specify whether the character is to be printed to a file or on the screen, as with printf(). If the character is to be printed on the screen, which is called standard output, then one must use "stdout". The statement printf("%c", 'X') has the same effect as putchar('X') or putc('X', stdout).

Another function, **puts**(), will accept only one string as an argument and print it.

In C++, one doesn't have to be as concerned about data types when printing because it uses the **cout** statement. This method requires the iostream.h header file. Consider the following:

```
cout << "I am " << 45 << ", I weigh" << 180.00 << endl; // That is an "end-L."
----- output -----
I am 45, I weigh 180.00
```

Here, no format specifiers are needed and the endl is more readable than the '\n'.

More Escape Characters

Table 1.1 shows more escape characters available in C.

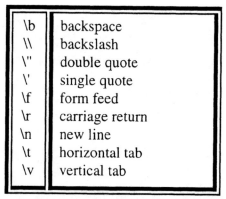

\b	backspace
\\	backslash
\"	double quote
\'	single quote
\f	form feed
\r	carriage return
\n	new line
\t	horizontal tab
\v	vertical tab

Table 1.1 Escape Sequences

Solution 1.11

```
printf("Sir %s has gone out to sea \n for %d months\n", "Justin", 3);
```

Unit 2

Variables and Assignments

LESSON

Data Types

When I am driving my 1966 Plymouth, I see many variables, although I don't call them variables. When the fuel gauge was working, it was a variable that would tell me how much gas was in the tank. The temperature gauge is another type of a variable that indicates how warm the engine is. The odometer is a variable that always increments by one. In programming, variables that increment by one are called counters. Then there are the boolean variables, such as the oil level lamp. Boolean variables can have only two values, either on or off. The traffic lights I see on the road are also variables that may have one of three values. The title of the car has a string variable that used to show the name of the person from whom I bought the car. Now the value of this variable is my name and if I can get someone else even to take the car, it will have that person's name.

In C programming, we will also need variables that communicate with different parts of the program about existing conditions. For our purpose, these programming variables will fall into one

DRILLS

When creating a variable or a location in memory for storing a number, name, or any such item, one must specify the characteristics of that variable. An integer is a data type that stores only whole numbers. Here *n*, *m*, and *k* are declared as integers and *n* is initialized to 40. Then *m* is assigned the value of 10 and *k* is assigned the value of 70 after adding *m*, *n*, and 20.

```
int n = 40, m, k;
m = 10;
k = m + n + 20;
printf("%d %d %d\n", n, m, k);
```

Drill 2.1 Show the output of the programming code given here.

17

of four categories: integer, floating point, character, and character strings. The four categories are called data types. Later, we will define our own data types.

An **integer** data type is used to store whole numbers, positive or negative. There is a limit to how large or how negative the number may be. If 1 is added continually to a variable of type integer, eventually the number will overflow and become the most negative number possible. So one has to be careful that the value of an integer variable doesn't exceed what the variable can hold.

A **floating point** data type holds fractional numbers. One doesn't have to be overly concerned about exceeding the value that this type of variable may hold. Floating point variables are stored in two parts, the mantissa and the exponent. The size of the mantissa in bits determines how accurately the number is represented, and the size of the exponent determines how large or how small, in powers of 2, the number may be.

Variables of **character** data type can hold only one character, such as a printable character. And **character strings** are nothing more than a string of characters with a special character attached to its end. This character is the null character and it is coded as '\0'. Having the null character terminate a string allows one to have variable length strings. Strings don't have to be a fixed length because the '\0' character signals where the string ends.

In Example 2.1, i and j are declared to be integers, and j is given an initial value of 4. However, i is not initialized. Likewise, x and y are declared to be floating point variables, where y is initialized but x isn't. Similarly, a and b are declared as characters, where b is initialized and a isn't.

Figure 2.1 shows how the strings q and r are stored in memory. They each have 11 slots allocated and each slot can hold one character. Since the last character of the string must contain '\0', the length of the longest string that can be stored here is 10, not counting the null character.

The equals sign makes i = 5; an assignment statement. The value on the right–hand side of the equals sign is first evaluated. Then that value is assigned to the variable on the left side. One should have only one variable on the left side of the equals sign because only one variable is being assigned a new value.

11 Slots

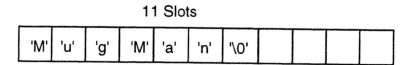

Figure 2.1 Storing the string $r[\ ]$.

Solution 2.1

```
----- output -----
40 10 70
```

Drill 2.2 Show the output of the following programming code:

```
int n, m = 20, k;
n = 10 + m;
k = m + n - 40;
m = m + 1;
printf("%d %d %d\n", n, m, k);
```

Variables and Assignments

```
//EXAMPLE 2.1
#include <stdio.h>          //needed for printf()
#include <string.h>         //needed for strcpy()
void main (void)
{
    int        i, j = 4, k;
    float      x, y = 8.8;
    char       a, b = 'V';
    char       q[11], r[11] = "MugMan";

    i = 5;                          // i becomes 5.
    i = i + j;                      // i becomes 9.
    i = i + y;                      // i becomes 17.
    k = (5 + 6/2) * 3 - 1;
    printf("i=%d, k=%d\n", i, k);

    i = 3;
    x = j / i;                      //integer divided by integer is an integer.
    y = (j * 1.0) / i;
    k = (j * 1.0) / i;
    printf("x=%.2f, y=%.2f, k=%d\n", x, y, k);

    a = 'Z';
    printf("a=%c\nb=%c\n", a, b);

    strcpy(q, r);                   //Can't use "=" sign for assigning strings.
    strcpy(r, "ScatThang");
    printf("q=%s\nr=%s\n", q, r);
}
----- output -----
i=17, k=23
x=1.00, y=1.33, k=1
a=Z
b=V
q=MugMan
r=ScatThang
```

Solution 2.2
```
----- output -----
30 21 10
```
First, n is calculated to be 30 by adding 10 and m. Then k is assigned the value of $20 + 30 - 40$. Finally, 1 is added to m, or 20, making its new value equal to 21.

Drill 2.3 * stands for multiplication and / for division. Show the output of the following:

```
int n = 8, m;
int k = 4;
m = k * 2 - 5;
k = n / k + 3;
n = 2 * (n - 5);
printf("%d %d %d\n", n, m, k);
```

Variables and Assignments   19

Next, we have another three assignment statements before we encounter a printf(). The second assignment statement evaluates the expression on the right side of the equals sign, that is, $i + j$ or 5 plus 4, and assigns the value of 9 to i.

In Figure 2.2(a), we see that the equals sign in C/C++ is treated nothing like an equals sign in algebra. In algebra, this would be an equality, but in programming, this is an assignment statement. The expression on the right–hand side is evaluated and then assigned to the variable on the left–hand side. That means that, on the left–hand side, there must be just one variable and nothing else. This variable is what is being changed. In algebra, items on both sides of the equals sign may be switched, but here that is not the case. The value of the expression on the right–hand side is assigned to the variable that is on the left–hand side.

We add i, which is 9, to y, which is 8.8. The sum of 17.8 is then assigned to i. When arithmetic is done between an integer and a floating point, the result is a floating point value. Therefore, $9 + 8.8$ is 17.8 and not 17. However, when a floating point value is assigned to an integer, the part after the decimal point is truncated so that the 17.8 is turned into 17 when being assigned to i.

When evaluating an arithmetic expression, follow these steps. First, evaluate the parenthetical expressions. Second, evaluate the multiplications and divisions from left to right. Last, evaluate the additions and subtractions from left to right.

Hence, in the statement that evaluates k, we first proceed to evaluate the parenthetical expression, $5 + 6/2$. Here, the division is done before the addition so its value becomes $5 + 3$ or 8. Next, we do the multiplication and obtain 24, and finally subtract a 1 to obtain 23.

In x = j /i; the expression after dividing j (which is 4) by i (which is 3) becomes 1. Doing arithmetic with integers yields an integer result. See Figure 2.2(b). Hence, 1 is assigned to x. x is a float so it becomes 1.0. In the next statement, j is first multiplied by a float, which becomes a floating point value. Dividing a floating point value by an integer makes it 1.33 instead of 1. This 1.33 is assigned to y. In the next statement, the same expression is then assigned to k, an integer; it can't hold the fractional part so k becomes 1. See Figure 2.2(c) and (d).

b was initialized to 'V' and a was assigned 'Z'. When they are printed out, the output is "a=z" and "b=V".

When handling strings, one must realize that they are groups of characters and a simple assignment statement will not suffice. To handle a group of characters, special functions defined in the "string.h" file must be used. Here we are using the strcpy() function to assign r to q, making q "MugMan". The second strcpy() function assigns "ScatThang" to r, and the output reflects that. Remember that each of these strings terminates with a null character.

Solution 2.3
```
----- output -----
6 3 5
```

m is calculated to be 3 by multiplying 4 by 2 and subtracting 5. Then k is calculated to be 5 by dividing 8 by 4 and then adding 3. Finally, n becomes 6 by multiplying 2 by 3.

Drill 2.4 One must be careful when dividing two integers. The result will always be an integer, so that 14 divided by 3 is 4. Show the output of the following:

```
int i, j = 18, k = -20;
i = j / 12;
j = k / 8;
k = k / 4;
printf("%d %d %d\n", i, j, k);
```

The assignment operator.

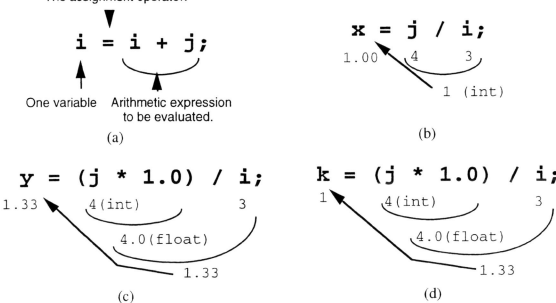

Figure 2.2 (a) The parts of an assignment statement.
(b) Dividing two integers yields an integer.
(c) Assigning 1.33 to a float preserves the decimal point.
(d) Assigning 1.33 to an integer yields an integer.

EXPERIMENTS

Run these exercises, record the outcome, answer the questions, and try to understand why the outcome is the way it is. After the first experiment, the common lines, such as the include <stdio.h>, void main (), and the pair of braces for the main() block, are left out.

Solution 2.4

```
----- output -----
1 -2 -5
```

Drill 2.5 To store fractional numbers, we must declare variables of type float. Show the output for the following.

```
int    i, j = 18;
float x, y = 20.0;
x = y / 8;
y = (y + 18) * 3;
printf("%.2f %.2f\n", x, y);
```

Exp 2.1 The data type for the variable *i* is an integer or a whole number.

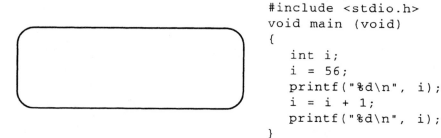

```
#include <stdio.h>
void main (void)
{
    int i;
    i = 56;
    printf("%d\n", i);
    i = i + 1;
    printf("%d\n", i);
}
```

a. What does the statement i = i + 1; do to the value of *i*?

Exp 2.2 Although you will need the #include <stdio.h>, void main (void), and the lines with the braces for the following experiments, they will not be shown.

```
int i;
i = 56;
i = i + 3;
printf("%d\n", i);
i = i + i + 1;
printf("%d\n", i);
```

The lines with the equals signs are called assignment statements.
a. Why is *i* printed as 59 instead of 56 in the first printf()?
b. What is the value of *i* while the last printf() is being called? Why?

Exp 2.3

```
int i = 56, j, k;
j = i + 1;
k = j + 1;
i = k + j;
printf("%d\n", i );
printf("%d\n", j);
printf("%d\n", k);
```

Solution 2.5

```
2.50 114.00
```

Drill 2.6 If an expression divides 10 by 4, then the answer is 2 and not 2.5. If 10/4 is assigned to a float, then the 2 is converted to 2.0 before assignment to the float. Show the output for the following.

```
int    i, j = 18;
float  x, y = 20.0;
x = j / 7;
y = y / 7;
printf("%.2f    %.2f\n", x, y);
```

Variables and Assignments

a. What was the final value of *j* and how did it obtain that value?
b. What was the final value of *k* and how did it obtain that value?
c. What was the final value of *i* and how did it obtain that value?

Exp 2.4

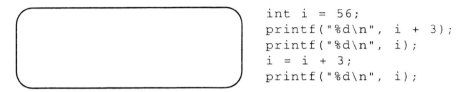

```
int  i = 56;
printf("%d\n", i + 3);
printf("%d\n", i);
i = i + 3;
printf("%d\n", i);
```

a. In which statement is *i* declared as an integer? (An integer is a whole number.)
b. What is the initial value of *i*?
c. Did the first printf() assign a new value to *i*?
d. Did i = i + 3; assign a new value to *i*?

Exp 2.5

```
int  i = 12;
printf("%d\n", i * 3 - 4);
printf("%d\n", i * (3 - 4));
printf("%d\n", i / 2 + 4 * 2);
printf("%d\n", i / (2 + 4) * 2);
printf("%d\n", i );
```

a. After *i* was initialized to 12, was its value ever changed?
b. What is the symbol used to multiply? To divide?
c. In the first printf(), which operation, multiply or subtract, was done first?
d. In the second printf(), which was done first, multiply or subtract? Why?
e. In the third printf(), which operation was done last?
f. Which of the following has the highest, next highest, and the lowest priority?
   That is, which one will be done first, next, and last?
   * and /;   + and −;   ( )

Exp 2.6 Some results you will get may not make sense. A 10 is an integer and a 10.0 is a floating point number (we'll just call it a float).

Solution 2.6 Since both *j* and 7 are integers, their result is an integer, but the second division has a float in it.
```
----- output -----
2.00    2.85
```

Drill 2.7 Try another one.

```
int    i, k = 10;
float  x, y, z = 20.0;
x = z / 6;                  //Statement 1
y = k / 6;                  //Statement 2
i = z / 6;                  //Statement 3
z = k / 6.0;                //Statement 4
printf(" %.2f \t%.2f\t%.2f\t %d\n", x, y, z, i);
```

Variables and Assignments   23

```
printf("%d\n", 10);
printf("%.2f\n", 10);
printf("%.2f\n", 10.0);
printf("%d\n", 10.0);
```

a. Do you use a %d or a %.2f to print an integer?
b. Do you use a %d or a %.2f to print a float?

Exp 2.7 Let us introduce floating point variables.

```
int i = 10;
float x = 10.0;
printf("%d\n", i / 3);
printf("%.2f\n", i / 3);
printf("%d\n", x / 3);
printf("%.2f\n", x / 3);
```

a. To print an integer result, one should use what format specifier?
b. To print a floating point result, one should use what format specifier?

Exp 2.8 Remember that *i* is defined to be an integer or a whole number. It cannot store values with decimals (or fractions). Notice in these printf()'s that some expressions are evaluated as integers and some as floats. Also, some format specifiers are integers and some are floats.

```
int i;
i = 10;
printf("%d\n", i / 2);
printf("%d\n", i / 3);
printf("%.2f\n", i / 3);
printf("%.2f\n", i / 3.0);
printf("%.2f\n", (i + 0.0) / 3);
printf("%d\n", i * 3);
printf("%.2f\n", i * 3.0);
```

Solution 2.7 Statements 1, 3, and 4 have at least one float in their divisions, so the expressions evaluate to floats. *x* and *z* are float variables so they can store floats. *i* isn't a float variable and the whole number 3 is stored in it. Statement 2 uses an integer division, so the fraction portion is truncated.

```
----- output -----
3.33    1.00    1.66    3
```

Drill 2.8 Show the output for the following.

```
int i = 3, j;
float x = 2.0, y;
y = (i + x) * 0.5 - 2.0;
j = y;
printf("%d   %.2f\n", j, y);
```

```
```

a. In C, why do you think 10 divided by 3 is equal to 3 and not 3.33?
b. i/3 evaluates to an integer or a float?
c. i/3.0 evaluates to an integer or a float?
d. How do you think (i * 1.0)/3 will be evaluated?
e. To see the fractional part after dividing two items, what must be true of one of those items?

Exp 2.9

```
int  i  =  10;
float  x  =  10.0;
x  =  i  /  3;
printf("%.2f\n",  x);
x  =  i  /  3.0;
printf("%.2f\n",  x);
```

a. In x = i/3; was the evaluation of i/3 an integer value or a floating point value?
b. Why was the result from the second printf() more accurate than the result from the first printf()?

Exp 2.10

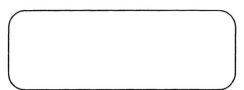

```
int  i  =  10;
float  x  =  10.0;
i  =  x  /  3;
printf("%.2f\n",  i);
printf("%d\n",  i);
i  =  x  /  3.0;
printf("%.2f\n",  i);
```

a. In i = x/3; was the evaluation of x/3 an integer value or a floating point value?
b. Can we store a floating point value in an integer variable?
c. In an arithmetic expression, such as i /2 + 1, if all the items are integers, then the result is of what type?
d. If at least one item is a float, then the result is of what type?
e. When dividing two integers, the result will contain a fractional portion only if it is assigned to a floating point variable. (True or false)
f. When dividing two items and one is a float, the result will be an integer. (True or false)

Solution 2.8

```
0   0.50
```

Drill 2.9

```
int  i  =  5,  j  =  8;
printf("%d\n",  i  +  j);
printf("%d  %d\n",  i  +  1,  j  +  1);
printf("%d\n",  i  -  j  *  (i  -  7));
printf("%d   %d\n",  i,  j);
```

Exp 2.11 Now let us turn our focus to characters and strings. A string is nothing more than a collection of characters. The number in the brackets [ ] minus one gives the length of the string. Here, *t* can store a string that is ten characters long.

```
char a = 'W';
char t[11] = "peace";
printf("%c\n", a);
printf("%s\n", t);
```

a. Name the character variable.
b. Name the string variable.
c. Is a character enclosed between single quotes or double quotes?
d. Is a string enclosed between single quotes or double quotes?

Exp 2.12 This code may not work on your computer, but the next experiment will correct that problem.

```
char a = 'W', b;
char t[11] = "peace", q[11];
b = a;
q = t;
printf("%c\n", b);
printf("%s\n", q);
```

a. Were we able to assign a character to another character?
b. Were we able to assign a string to another string?

Exp 2.13 Since strings are collections of characters, not single items, they need to be treated differently from integers, floats, and characters. Let us try the strcpy() function, which is defined in the string.h header.

Solution 2.9

```
13
6      9
21          Explanation:  i - j * (i - 7)) => 5 - 8 * (5 - 7)
                                => 5 - (8 * -2) = 21
5      8
```

Drill 2.10 Character is another data type, and strings are combinations of characters. Show the output for the following.

```
char b = '$', c = '2', d;
d = c;                        //Statement 1
c = b;                        //Statement 2
b = 'c';                      //Statement 3
printf("%c %c %c\n", b, c, d);
```

```
                                    #include <string.h>
                                    #include <stdio.h>
                                    void main ( )
                                    {
                                        char a = 'W', b;
                                        char t[11] = "peace", q[11];
                                        b = a;
                                        strcpy(q, t);
                                        printf("%c\n",b);
                                        printf("%s\n", q);
                                    }
```

a. How is a character assigned to a character variable?
b. How is a string assigned to a string variable?

Exp 2.14 Let us swap the values of *t* and *r*.

```
                                    #include <string.h>
                                    #include <stdio.h>
                                    void main ( )
                                    {
                                        char t[11] = "peace", q[11], r[11];
                                        strcpy(r, "river");
                                        strcpy(q, t);
                                        strcpy(t, r);
                                        strcpy(r, q);
                                        printf("t=%s\n", t);
                                        printf("q=%s\n", q);
                                        printf("r=%s\n", r);
                                    }
```

a. What value was assigned to *r*?
b. What value was assigned to *q*?
c. What value was assigned to *t*?
d. Now what value was assigned to *r*?

Solution 2.10 In statement 3 the character 'c' is being assigned and not the variable *c*, as it was in statement 1. Also note that in statement 1, *d* is being assigned the character 2 and not the integer 2.

```
----- output -----
c $ 2
```

Drill 2.11 To assign the string *s* to the string *t*, one must use strcpy(t, s); and the equals sign as before. Show the output for the following.

```
char q[11], r[11] = "Jonathan", s[11] = "Daniel";
strcpy (q, s);
strcpy (s, r);
strcpy (r, "Sarah");
printf("%s %s %s\n", q, r, s);
```

QUESTIONS

1. Define an integer called j and initialize it to 12.

2. Define a floating point variable called x and initialize it to 1.0.

3. Define a character variable called a and initialize it to 'Q'.

4. Define a string that can store up to 11 characters and initialize it to "shuttle".

5. Evaluate the following expressions and specify whether the answer is an integer or a floating point value.
   a. 14 / 4 + 7
   b. 14.0 / 4 + 7
   c. 14 / (4 + 7)
   d. (4 − 7) * 12 / 6 − 2
   e. 10 / 2.50 − (15 / 4)

6. If i initially is 5, what is the final value of i after the following statement is executed?

```
printf ("%d\n", i + 1);
```

7. Which can store very large or very small numbers, integers or floats? Which store whole numbers?

8. Identify the data type of each of the following:
   a. 'a'   b. "b"
   c. 2   d. '7'
   e. 7.33   f. "7.33"
   g. '\0'   h. '\n'
   i. "have some c"   j. '/'

9. What is the sequence of steps that swaps the values of x and y, two floats? Also use the variable z.

10. Show the output of each of the following:

Solution 2.11 First "Daniel" is assigned to q, "Jonathan" is assigned to s, and then "Sarah" is assigned to r.

```
----- output -----
Daniel Sarah Jonathan
```

Drill 2.12 Show the output for the following.

```
int i = 45;
printf ("%d %d\n", i + 1, i / 2);
printf ("%d\n", i);
```

```
int i = 3, j = 5;
i = i + 1;
j = j + i + 1;
printf("%d %d\n", i + 1, j - 1);
printf("%d %d\n", i, j);
```

```
float x = 13.0, y = -23.0;
x = (x / 2) * -1 + y;
y = 13 / 2 - 2;
printf("%.2f %.2f\n", x, y);
```

```
char a = 'b', b, s[11]=",", t[11]= "over", r[11]="Roll";
printf("%c %c r=%s s=%s t=%s\n", a, b, r, s, t);
b = a;
a = 'c';
strcpy (s, r);
strcpy (r, t);
strcpy (t, s);
printf("%c %c r=%s s=%s t=%s\n", a, b, r, s, t);
```

PROGRAMS

1. Create three integers and name them *i1*, *i2*, and *i3*. Assign them values of 20, 30, and 50, respectively. Without creating any other variables, print their average. Make sure the answer shows two places after the decimal point.

2. Define *me* as an integer. Assign it the value of 20. Define *you* as an integer and assign it the value of 18. Define *average* as a float and assign it the average of *me* and *you*. Then using one printf() for each line, print the following. The numbers are printed using the values of the variables. The last line starts on a tab position.

Solution 2.12

```
----- output -----
46 22
45
```

Drill 2.13 Characters have single quotes, strings have double quotes, integers are whole numbers and floats contain decimal points. Label the data type of each of the following:

```
3.576
"3401.68"
'2'
3401
```

Variables and Assignments

```
-----output -----
I am 20
You are 18
     We are around 19.00!
```

      3. Define a string called *name* that can hold up to 11 characters including the terminating null character. Define *rate* as a float and *hours* as an integer. Now assign "GooFoo", 10.0, and 20 to these variables, respectively. Without creating any new variables, print the following using the values of *name*, *rate*, and *hours*. Use one printf() for each line that is printed.

```
----- output -----
His name is GooFoo,
Rate is 10.00 and the hours worked was 20
GooFoo made 200.00 dollars.
```

      4. Define an integer *i* and initialize it to 10. Using one printf(), print the remainder after dividing 10 by 7. (Do not use the modulo operator. Use only what was learned up to this point.)

OPTIONAL TOPICS

More on Data Types

      In general, **characters** are stored in a PC using one byte or eight bits. That gives a storage limit of 2^8, or 256, characters. **Integers** use two bytes, which allows 2^{16}, or 65,536, possibilities. The most negative integer is $-32,768$ and the most positive is $+32,767$. If a variable is defined to be **unsigned**, that is, if no negative numbers are represented, then the range of these types of integers is from 0 to 65,535. Four bytes can be allocated to store integers of greater value by using the type **long**. long data type variables have a range of about -2 billion to $+2$ billion.

      Floating point variables may be represented by using 4 bytes: 3 bytes to store the mantissa portion and 1 byte to store the exponent. The size of the mantissa determines the precision of the number. With 3 bytes, only about 7 digits of accuracy are possible and with 1 byte for the exponent, numbers can have values up to $10^{\pm38}$. For example, the number 43,567,889,990,000 is stored as 43,567,890,000,000. The mantissa portion stores 4.356789 and the exponent portion stores 13, to represent 10^{13}.

      To achieve better accuracy in representing floating point numbers, the data type **double** is used. It can store numbers in the range of 10^{-308} to 10^{+308} and provide up to 15 digits of precision.

Solution 2.13

3.576	A floating point number
"3401.68"	A character string
'2'	A character
3401	An integer

Drill 2.14 Show the output for the following.

```
int i = 7;
i = i + 1;
i = i + 2;
i = i + 3;
printf("%d\n", i);
```

Other Format Specifiers

%u is used to print unsigned numbers, **%o** is used to print integers in octal format, and **%x** is used to print numbers in hexadecimal format. If an integer is defined to be long, then use **%ol**, **%dl**, and **%xl** to print the number in long format. These stand for octal–long, decimal–long, and hexadecimal–long formats.

%6d allocates six places to print the integer right justified. **%6.2f** also allocates six places on the printed line to print the float right justified. The six places include the decimal point and the two digits after the decimal point. To print floating point numbers in exponential form, use the **%e** format.

Some Arithmetic Topics

To find the remainder after dividing two integers, use the **modulo operator (%)**. For instance, 7/3 is 2 and 7%3 is 1, the remainder.

An abbreviated way of doing y = y + 1; is y += 1;. Similarly, the + sign here can be replaced by –, *, /, and % signs.

++i; is a short way of writing i = i + 1;. Similarly, – –i is a short way of writing i = i – 1;. One can place the double plus or double minus on either side of the variable. Their position will not matter, unless they are used in conjunction with another statement. In that case, if the signs precede the variable, that operation will be done before the secondary statement. Otherwise, the secondary statement is done first. See the example below. When j = ++i; is executed, first *i* is incremented, then its new value is assigned to *j*. When j = i++; is executed, first *i* is assigned to *j*, then *i* is incremented. Also, with the math.h header file, you can find square roots and powers.

```
// EXAMPLE
#include <math.h>
i = 1;       // i becomes 1.
++i;         // i becomes 2.
j = ++i;     // i becomes 3, then j becomes 3. This is the same as:
             //                              i = i + 1;
             //                              j = i;

j = i++;     // j becomes 3, then i becomes 4. This is the same as
             //(watch the order):           j = i;
             //                              i = i + 1;

printf("Square root of 9 is %.2f\n", sqrt(9));
printf("2 raised to the power of 3 is %.2f\n", pow(2, 3));
```

Solution 2.14 First, 1 is added to 7. Now *i* is 8 and is then added to 2. Now *i* is 10. Last, 3 is added to this 10, giving a final value of 13 for *i*.

```
----- output -----
13
```

Unit 3

The scanf() Function

The Preprocessor Directives

Before we look at the scanf() in Example 3.1, let us explain the #define directive shown in statement 3. This directive, like the #include directive, is a command to the preprocessor that works like nothing more than a simple text editor. The #include <stdio.h> line copied and pasted the stdio.h file before the main() function so that the definitions for printf() and scanf() were available to main(). The #define INIT_BAL 100.00 line simply substitutes 100.00 every time it sees INIT_BAL in the source program. Think of the preprocessor directives as being instructions on how to edit the source code, whereas the compiler converts the source code into machine code instructions that the CPU or the microprocessor can understand. These commands do not end with a semicolon. They must begin with the pound sign (#) and usually at column 1 of each line, and they do not follow the general rules of C/C++ syntax.

DRILLS

Drill 3.1 #include <stdio.h> copies the stdio.h file to the source file before main( ). Show the converted source file if the contents of stdio.h are:

```
/* This is the beginning of stdio.h
(a few lines)
This is the end of stdio.h */
```

and our program looks simply like this:

```
#include   <stdio.h>
void main (void){    }
```

32 Variables and Assignments

The advantage of using a constant such as INIT_BAL instead of a number like 100.00 is that INIT_BAL suggests a meaning to the value other than a plain number would. Also, in the event the INIT_BAL has to be changed to a different value in the future, it has to be changed only once in statement 3 and not in every place it is used. One doesn't have to be worried whether all the occurrences of 100.00 were changed or not. If 100.00 were stored in a variable instead, then every time it was used, the computer would have to go to that variable's location to find its value. A constant takes less time because the number is already substituted in all the places where it is used.

```
//EXAMPLE 3.1
#include <stdio.h>              //Statement 1
#include <string.h>             //Statement 2
#define INIT_BAL 100.00         //Statement 3
void main (void)
{
   float deposit;
   char  initial, name[11];

   printf("What is your name? ");
   scanf("%s", &name);
   printf("Type your first initial: ");
   scanf(" %c", &initial);
   printf("How much did you deposit? ");
   scanf("%f",  &deposit);

   printf("\nREPORT:\n");
   printf("  %c. %s had $%.2f\n", initial, name, INIT_BAL);
   printf("  Now he has $%.2f\n", INIT_BAL + deposit);
   printf("  His initial is stored at %p\n", &initial);
}
----- output -----
What is your name? BoinkyHead
Type your first initial: X
How much did you deposit? 20.50

REPORT:
  X. BoinkyHead had $100.00
  Now he has $120.50
  His initial is stored at FFFE
```

Solution 3.1

```
/* This is the beginning of stdio.h
(a few lines)
This is the end of stdio.h */
void main (void){    }
```

Drill 3.2 If the main() is the same as in Drill 3.1 and the contents of stdio.h are as shown here, then how would our program be converted?

```
/* Starting stdio.h
and ending stdio.h */
```

Variables and Assignments   33

Running the Program

In Example 3.1, we see how data can be obtained from the user of the program. The printf() provides a means to display information to the user (via the monitor), and the scanf() function provides a means to accept data from the user (via the keyboard). The scanf() function is defined in the stdio.h file.

The program starts by prompting the user for her or his name using the printf() statement. Since there is no '\n' at the end, the scanf() statement accepts the name on the same line into the variable *name*. Then the next printf() prompts for the first initial and the scanf() accepts that initial into the variable called *initial*. Again, using a printf() and scanf() pair, the amount of the deposit is accepted into the *deposit* variable. Finally, the last four printf() statements print a report using these read-in items as well as INIT_BAL.

The scanf() function, although it resembles the printf() function, has some peculiarities to it. They both use format strings, but the scanf()'s format string usually doesn't end with a '\n'. The user must press the Enter key for the scanf() to accept any data. Another peculiarity of the scanf(), is that, when passing a variable to it, it must be preceded by the & character. Before we look at the meaning of this special character, let us point out three attributes of a variable.

Three Attributes of a Variable

In addition to its data type, a variable has other attributes: name, value, and address are important for us now. The variable *initial* has a name. It is called "initial." The program can refer to this variable as long as it uses that name.

A variable's value is what is stored in it. The *initial* variable has stored in it, the value of 'X' after it is read in from the user. The value of the *deposit* variable is 20.50 since that is what is stored in it. Last, the address of a variable is the memory location where it is stored. For the most part, programmers don't have to be concerned about variable addresses. They are managed by the compiler. However, here in the scanf() function, variable addresses are used and in later chapters they will become even more important. Review Experiment 3.1.

The memory location of a variable is accessed by preceding it with the '&' character. For example, &*name* provides the address of name while *name* provides the value of that variable. When calling the printf() function, one must provide the value of the variable, such as *name*; but when calling the scanf() function, the function requires that the address of the variable, such as &*name*, be passed to it. In the last printf() of Example 3.1, we are printing the address of the variable *initial*. When printing the address, you can use the %p (for pointer) format specifier; if that doesn't work, use the %u (for unsigned integer) specifier to get an idea of the relative addresses of variables. Pointer variables, which are covered in Units 12 and 19, store addresses of variables. Think of pointers as addresses.

Solution 3.2

```
/* Starting stdio.h
and ending stdio.h */
void main (void){    }
```

Drill 3.3 Like a text editor, #define LIM 11 will convert all occurrences of LIM in the program to the number 11. Show the converted source code once the define directive is applied.

```
#define LIM 11
void main (void)
{    char s[LIM] = "Moonlight";
     char t[LIM] = "Mr. ";              }
```

A string variable contains the address of the location of the first character, so it doesn't matter if we pass *&name* or simply *name* to the scanf() function. Either one provides the starting address of where the string is stored.

Use scanf() Carefully

Use scanf() with care. When reading into a string variable, it reads in only one word and stops reading when it reaches whitespace. Whitespace characters include the space, tab, and the return characters. Therefore, a first name and a last name cannot be read into one string separated by a space. When reading in a single character, if its %c isn't preceded by a space, any whitespace characters could be read into that variable unintentionally. Therefore, use " %c" instead of "%c." This way any leading spaces are bypassed, and the first non-space character is read into the variable. Leading spaces are not necessary in front of the format specifiers when reading integers and floats. In general, use %f instead of %.2f, and do not use '\n' as we normally do with printf().

While scanning for an integer, a character is entered by the user and the scanf() may fail. No error checking is done by this function. Many programmers avoid scanf() altogether and create their own functions instead. See the section called Optional Topics for other alternatives to scanf().

EXPERIMENTS

Exp 3.1 Variables have a name, a value, and an address. Addresses are given in a computer numbering system called hexadecimal notation. You don't need to learn that numbering system. Please note %p's and &'s. If %p doesn't work, try %u.

RAM (or computer memory)

FFE0   7   i   "i" is the name
FFE1   .   ... of the variable.

Some location in   Value of 7
RAM given in hex.   stored in this location.

```
int    i = 7;

printf("variable NAME is %c\n", 'i');
printf("variable VALUE is %d\n", i);
printf("Its ADDRESS is %p\n", &i);
```

a. How do you show the name of a variable that is called *i*?
b. How do you show what value exists in *i*?
c. How do you show where *i* is stored in memory?
d. What format specifier is used to see the address where a variable is stored?

Solution 3.3

```
void main (void)
{    char s[11] = "Moonlight";
     char t[11] = "Mr. ";
}
```

Drill 3.4 Again, show the converted source code after the preprocessor edits this program:
```
#define LENGTH 3.0
#define WIDTH  2.0
void main (void)
{ printf("Length = %.2f\n", LENGTH);
  printf("Area = %.2f\n", LENGTH * WIDTH);
}
```

Variables and Assignments   35

Exp 3.2

```
int    i = 97;
printf("%d %p\n", i, &i);
i = i + 1;
printf("%d %p\n", i, &i);
```

a. Where was *i* stored in Exp 3.1?
b. Where is *i* stored here?
c. When 1 was added to *i*, did the value of *i* change?
d. Did the address of *i* change? Of course, the name of *i*, which is "i," doesn't change.

Exp 3.3 &*i* prints the address of *i*.

```
int i = 23, j = 21;
j = j + 1;
printf("address of i %p\n", &i);
printf("address of j %p\n", &j);
printf("value of   j %d\n", j);
```

a. In which memory location is *i* stored?
b. In which memory location is *j* stored?
c. Is *j*'s value or address being changed?

Exp 3.4 In the next few experiments the computer will stop for you to enter a proper item. Don't think that the computer is dead and reboot it; it's just waiting for your response.

```
int i;
printf("Please enter a whole number ");
scanf("%d", &i);
printf("You entered %d, and ", i);
printf("%d is twice its value\n", 2*i);
```

Solution 3.4

```
void main (void)
{  printf("Length = %.2f\n", 3.0);
   printf("Area = %.2f\n", 3.0 * 2.0);
}
```

Drill 3.5 The float variable *x*, which is initialized to 3.75, is stored in memory location FFF0.
a. What is the name of the variable?
b. What is the address of the variable?
c. What is the data type of the variable?
d. What is the value of the variable?

a. What does the scanf() function do that is different from what the printf() does?
b. Does the scanf() function require a format string, similar to what the printf() required?
c. What is different in the way the format strings end in printf() and scanf()?
d. When passing a variable to scanf(), what is being passed, the variable name, value, or address?

Exp 3.5 When the computer appears to freeze, enter a whole number.

```
int i;
scanf("%d", &i);
printf("You entered %d, and ",  i);
printf("%d is twice its value\n", 2*i);
```

a. Why is Exp 3.4 friendlier to run than Exp 3.5?
b. Normally, each scanf() should be preceded by what kind of statement?

Exp 3.6 In a scanf(), use %f instead of %.2f when reading in a float. Also, don't use the '\n' character.

```
int i;
float  f;
printf("Please enter a whole number ");
scanf("%d", &i);
printf("Please enter a number ");
printf("with a decimal point ");
scanf("%f", &f);
printf("The sum of them is %f\n", i + f);
```

Exp 3.7 When scanning in strings or characters, add a space before the format specifier. Don't use "%s", but use " %s". Use less than 11 characters to read in the string.

```
char x[11];
printf("Enter your name with no spaces ");
scanf(" %s", x);
printf("Your name is %s\n", x);
```

Solution 3.5

a. *x* is the name.
b. FFF0 is the address where it is located.
c. float is the data type.
d. 3.75 is its value.

Drill 3.6 %p is used to print a memory address and the variable is preceded by the character '&' to access its address. How should printf() be called to print the address of *x* and the value that is in it? The output should be:

```
Address = FFF0, Value = 3.75
```

Variables and Assignments

Exp 3.8 When running this program, enter Wingle Wangle for the data.

```
Enter your name:
Wingle Wangle
```

```
char x[11];
char y[11];
printf("Enter your name: \n");
scanf(" %s %s", x, y);
printf("Your name is %s, %s\n", y, x);
```

Exp 3.9 Run this program two times and enter the numbers as shown with spaces and tabs. For the first run, for instance, type these characters in this order:

1, (space), 2, (enter), 3, (tab), 4, (enter)

```
Enter four integers
1 2
3    4
```

```
Enter four integers
1
2 3
       4
```

```
int i, j, k, l;
printf("Enter four integers n");
scanf("%d%d", &i, &j);
scanf("%d%d", &k, &l);
printf("You entered %d and %d:\n", i, j);
printf("You entered %d and %d:\n", k, l);
```

a. What were the values of *i*, *j*, *k*, and *l* during the first run?
b. What were the values of *i*, *j*, *k*, and *l* during the second run?
c. While scanf() is looking for an integer, does it pass over spaces? Over tabs? Over carriage returns?

Exp 3.10 While running this program, enter Q, (tab), R, (enter), S, (space), T.

```
Enter characters
Q    R
S T
```

```
char a, b;
char c, d;
printf("Enter four characters");
scanf("%c%c", &a, &b);
scanf("%c%c", &c, &d);
printf("You entered %c and %c:\n", a, b);
printf("You entered %c and %c:\n", c, d);
```

Solution 3.6

```
printf("Address = %p, Value = %.2f\n", &x, x);
```

Drill 3.7 The function scanf() allows a user to enter a value into a variable. Its format string specifies the data type to be read and after the format string, the address of the variable must be passed. Write the scanf() to read in a float value for *x* and precede it with a printf() to prompt the user as shown below. Bold type is what is entered by the user.

```
----- output -----
Enter the value for x: 3.75
```

a. What were the values of *a*, *b*, *c*, and *d* after the run?

b. While scanf() was looking for a character, did it pass over whitespaces as it did when reading integers in Experiment 3.9?

Exp 3.11 Now force the scanf() to pass over whitespace by preceding the %c with a space (" %c").

```
Enter characters
Q    R
S    T
```

```
char a, b, c, d;
printf("Enter four characters");
scanf(" %c %c", &a, &b);
scanf(" %c %c", &c, &d);
printf("You entered %c and %c:\n", a, b);
printf("You entered %c and %c:\n", c, d);
```

a. If we want to skip over whitespace, that is, spaces, tabs, and carriage returns, and we are scanning for integers, then is it necessary to precede the %d by a space? See Experiment 3.10.

b. What about when we want to read in characters? Should we precede the %c with a space?

Exp 3.12 Precede the %c's with spaces.

```
Enter two char-int pairs
w 6
q    7
```

```
char a, b;
int i, j;
printf("Enter two char-int pairs:");
scanf(" %c %d", &a, &i);
scanf(" %c %d", &b, &j);
printf("%c:%d:\n", a, i);
printf("%c:%d:\n", b, j);
```

a. Did the values get read into the variables as they should have been?

b. Try the same experiment again without the leading spaces in the format strings for the integers. Did you get the same results as before?

c. Try the same experiment again without the leading spaces in the format strings for the characters. Did you get the same results as before?

d. When reading in integers, spaces are not needed. (True or false)

e. When reading in characters, we would add the spaces before the %c's. (True or false)

Format strings for floats behave like integers, and those for strings behave like characters.

Solution 3.7 No '\n' is used after the printf() because the number is to be scanned from the same line. Also, scanf() doesn't take a '\n' in its format string. The %f specifier should be used instead of the %.2f specifier with the scanf().

```
printf("Enter the value for x: ");
scanf("%f", &x);
```

Drill 3.8 Similarly, write a printf() and a scanf() to read a character code into variable *a*, as shown below.

```
----- output -----
What was the sales code? w
```

Variables and Assignments

Exp 3.13 Run this code as shown, then run it by removing one & at a time.

```
int i;
char t[11];
printf("enter an integer and a string:");
scanf("%d %s", &i, &t);
printf("i was %d and t was %s: \n", i, t);
```

a. Do we need the & signs for scanning in integers? For scanning in strings?
b. From the answer to these two questions, do you think the methods of storing strings and integers are different from each other?

Exp 3.14 Last, let us try a couple of #define directives.

```
#include <stdio.h>
#define PI 3.14
#define RADIUS "radius"
void main ( )
{
    float r;
    printf("Give the radius: ");
    scanf("%f", &r);
    printf("The %s is %.2f\n", RADIUS, r);
    printf("The circumference is : %.2f\n",
                    2 * r * PI);
    printf("The area is : %.2f\n", PI*r*r);
}
```

a. If we wanted to add more digits after the decimal point for 3.14 for better accuracy, in how many places would we have to make that change?
b. Do we have to specify the data type with #define directives?
c. Does your compiler allow you to change the value of PI by adding the following statement inside main()? PI = 3.1416;

Solution 3.8

```
printf("What was the sales code? ");
scanf(" %c", &a);
```

Drill 3.9 One can scan in two variables at the same time using one scanf(). Try this one to read an integer into *i* and a character into *a*. Always use a space before the %c in the scanf() format string.

```
----- output -----
Give an integer and a character: 356 w
```

QUESTIONS

1. What is a variable's contents called?
2. What is the location where a variable is stored in memory called?
3. By what is a variable called?
4. When a number is to be read in, which characteristic of a variable is passed to scanf()?
5. Does the format string of a scanf() usually end with a '\n'?
6. If a program uses the same number, say, the percentage of sales commission, in many of its parts, how should that number be stored in the program? Remember: This percentage may need to be changed in the future. Give two more advantages of using this solution.
7. How is the address of the variable *x* specified?
8. Show the screen display for each code segment.
   a. Assume 20 and 4 are entered by the user.
```
printf("Enter length:");
scanf("%d", &length);
printf("Enter width:");
scanf("%d", &width);
printf("The area is %d\n", length * width);
```

   b. Assume "Jackster" and 200.00 were entered by the user.
```
#define COMMISSION 0.08
        :       :
printf("Who is the salesperson?");
scanf("%s", &person);
printf("What were the sales?");
scanf("%f", &sales);
printf("\n\n%s sold $%.2f worth of tickets",
        person, sales);
printf("\nreceived $%.2f in commissions.\n",
        sales * COMMISSION);
```

PROGRAMS

1. Define a directive called TAX_RATE and set it to 0.06. Define a string variable called "part[ ]," a float called "price," and an integer called "quantity." Total sales is equal to *quantity*

Solution 3.9

```
printf("Give an integer and a character:  ");
scanf("%d %c", &i, &a);                         // Don't use "%d%c".
```

Drill 3.10 Using one scanf(), read in the character variable *a* and the integer variable *i*.

```
----- output -----
Give a character and an integer: w 356
```

times *price*, plus the tax on the total sales. On the first line of the screen ask the user to input the name of the part, on the second line ask for the price of the part, and on the third line ask for the number of parts that were sold. After that, print a report that follows this format:

```
Give the part name: washers
Give price: 0.30
How many were sold? 5

   5 washers were sold for $0.30 each.
   The total sales came to $1.59, including tax.
```

2. Define two strings called "employee" and "company" along with a float called "rate" and an integer called "hours." Initialize *employee[]* to "BobDaBlob" and assign "J J Buttons" to *company[]*. Ask for the employee's rate and hours. Calculate his take–home pay as 10 percent less than the product of rate and hours. Display a report similar to what is shown here:

```
Give BobDaBlob's rate, and hours: 8.00   10
BobDaBlob worked 10 hours.
The rate of pay was 8.00 dollars per hour.
The gross pay was $80.00.
And the take-home pay was $72.00.
BobDaBlob works for J J Buttons.
```

OPTIONAL TOPICS

More on the Preprocessor

```
/* This five-line file is called powers.h */
#define SQUARE(x) x*x          // Don't add spaces.
#define CUBE(x) x*x*x
#define FOURTH(x) x*x*x*x
/* End of File */


//Example 3.2A
#include <stdio.h>
#include "powers.h"
#define FORMAT_I "i is equal to %d\n"
#define PRINT_I printf(FORMAT_I, i);  //Also called a macro
```

Solution 3.10

```
printf("Give a character and an integer: ");
scanf(" %c %d", &a, &i);
```

Drill 3.11 Using one scanf(), read in two strings into the variables *first* and *last*. No spaces may be placed within a string because the space marks the separation of fields. Print the names as shown below.

```
----- output -----
Enter your first and last names: Joyster Peacester
Your name is Peacester, Joyster
```

```
void main (void)
{
   int i = 4;
   PRINT_I;
   i = CUBE(i);
   PRINT_I;
   i = FOURTH(4);
   PRINT_I;
}
```

In the file called powers.h, three macros are defined using #define directives. This file is then used in the source code of Example 3.2. This is done by the #include "powers.h" statement. The include statement simply copies the lines of powers.h with the source code so that, instead of using the include, we could have typed in the lines of powers.h there.

Also, at every occurrence of PRINT_I, printf(FORMAT_I, i); is substituted so that Example 3.2A is now converted to Example 3.2B.

```
//Example 3.2B
#include <stdio.h>
#define SQUARE(x) x*x
#define CUBE(x) x*x*x
#define FOURTH(x) x*x*x*x
#define FORMAT_I "i is equal to %d\n"
#define PRINT_I printf(FORMAT_I, i);  //Also called a macro
void main (void)
{
   int i = 4;
   printf(FORMAT_I, i);
   i = CUBE(i);
   printf(FORMAT_I, i);
   i = FOURTH(4);
   printf(FORMAT_I,i);
}
```

Last, for every occurrence of FORMAT_I, the string "i is equal to %d\n" is substituted. And in place of CUBE(i), i * i * i is substituted, since i is used in place of x in the #define CUBE (x) x*x*x directive. Similarly, FOURTH(4) is converted and the final source code that will compile becomes Example 3.2C.

Solution 3.11

```
printf("Enter your first and last names: ");
scanf("%s %s", &first, &last);
printf("Your name is %s, %s\n", last, first);
```

Drill 3.12 Show the output for the following (assume 10.0, 'Z', and −3 are entered):

```
printf("Enter a float, then a character, then an integer ");
scanf("%f %c %d", &x, &b, &j);
printf("ans= %.2f, character=%c.\n", x * j, b);
```

```
//Example 3.2C
#include <stdio.h>
#define SQUARE(x) x*x
#define CUBE(x) x*x*x
#define FOURTH(x) x*x*x*x
#define FORMAT_I "i is equal to %d\n"
#define PRINT_I printf(FORMAT_I, i);  //Also called a macro
void main (void)
{
    int i = 4;
    printf("i is equal to %d\n", i);
    i = i * i * i;
    printf("i is equal to %d\n", i);
    i = 4 * 4 * 4 * 4;
    printf("i is equal to %d\n", i);
}
```

Alternatives to the scanf()

getchar(): A faster function than scanf() is the getchar() function. It doesn't require a format string and reads only one character at a time. One can gain total control over what is read into variables. This function, along with the putchar() function mentioned in Unit 1, is typically defined in stdio.h. This function is commonly used in the UNIX environments. In Turbo C++, this function doesn't receive characters until the Enter key is pressed.

getche(): This function doesn't require the user to press the Enter key to receive characters in Turbo C++. The characters are echoed on the screen. The **getch()** function operates the same way, but no characters are echoed on the screen.

getc(): When one has to specify the file from which the character is to be read in, getc() becomes helpful. When reading from the console or the keyboard, the stdin file is used.

The following three examples are equivalent to each other; they all assign a character to the variable *a*:

```
scanf("%c", &a);
a = getchar();
a = getc(stdin);
```

Solution 3.12

```
----- output -----
Enter a float, then a character, then an integer 10.0 Z -3
ans= -30.00, character=Z.
```

Drill 3.13 As a review, suppose we have an integer called "i."

a. How would you print this integer's name?
b. How would you print its value?
c. How would you print out the address in memory where it is located?

Variables and Assignments

gets(): To read in an entire line of words into one string, use the gets() function. It will place all the characters that are entered into the string until it encounters the new line ('\n') character. In this example, characters up to the first whitespace character are placed in the variable *t*.

```
scanf("%s", &t);
```

In this example all the characters until the first '\n' character are placed into *t*.

```
gets(t);
```

cin >>: Using the iostream.h file, one can read values into a variable easily. This is a C++ construct (which we'll cover in Unit 16). In this example, a character is being read into *a*.

```
cin >> a;
```

Solution 3.13

```
a.    printf("The name of the variable is: %c\n", 'i');
b.    printf("The value of 'i' is: %d\n", i);
c.    printf("The address of 'i' is: %p\n", &i);
```

Unit 4

The for *Loop*

LESSON

Loops are quite common in our daily lives. Consider reading a page of text in a book. We read from left to right and when we reach the end of the line, we start again at the next line. Also consider a driver of a car who must shift gears as she accelerates from a stopped position. The foot has to come off the gas pedal and go on the clutch, the gear has to be shifted into the next position, and the foot has to come off the clutch and go back on the gas. This pattern has to be repeated for each gear as the vehicle is accelerated. We see patterns in music, art, history, and many other areas. We just don't think of them as loops.

Let us look at a loop in the life of a student. The day is initialized to Monday. See Figure 4.1. The student asks the question, "Is it Saturday?" The answer is false so he must wake up at 6 a.m., go to school, go to sleep, and advance the day. On Tuesday morning, the same question is asked. Again, the answer is false, so he must wake up at 6 a.m., go to school, go to sleep, and advance the day. The loop is repeated until Saturday arrives. Then he exits the loop and can sleep late. Just as the student might have to repeat the same loop, a program may have to repeat a loop over and over again. Just as there may be exceptions for the student so that on a holiday, for example, he can sleep late, exceptions may also be included in a loop of a program.

DRILLS

In this unit we start with loops, for loops, in particular. Again, although C and C++ support other types of loops, we will concentrate only on the for loop because that will give us more time to concentrate on the logic of loops rather than on learning more language syntax. The concept of loops makes computer programming powerful.

All loops must start somewhere; this is called the initialization of the loop. They must stop sometime, the termination of the loop, or else they keep going. To terminate a loop, we will need to evaluate conditions, for example, whether a variable is equal to a value or not. Furthermore, while the loop is going through its iterations, it must come closer and closer to the terminal condition.

46

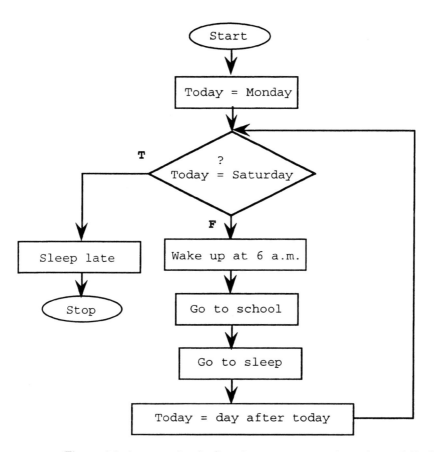

Figure 4.1 An example of a flowchart we may experience in our daily lives.

Flowcharting

Now that we see how common loops are, let us consider a simple loop in programming. Although loops are common in programming, one should not underestimate their power. Because of loops, humans can hand off drudgery work to computers.

In Figure 4.2, we have a flowchart and a tracechart. Flowcharts show the logic of a program graphically and a tracechart shows the sequence of steps taken to execute the flowchart. Flowcharts start at the oval called Start and continue until the oval called Stop is encountered. The numbers in parentheses correspond to the steps shown in the tracecharts.

Drill 4.1

```
main(void)
{
    int i;
    i = 1;              //1
    for(; i <= 2;)      //2
    {
        printf("%d\n", i);  //3
        i = i + 1;          //4
    }
}
```

Step	i	i <= 2?	Printout
(1)	1		
(2)		True	
(3)			1
(4)	2		
(5)		True	
(6)			2
(7)	3		
(8)		False (Loop Stops)	

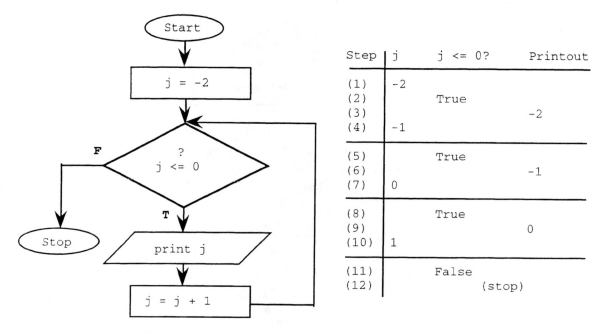

Figure 4.2 A flowchart and its corresponding tracechart.

After the Start, we see an assignment statement (Step 1). Assignment statements are shown in rectangles. Here the variable *j* is assigned a value of −2. Then as we follow the arrow, a decision diamond is encountered. Decisions do not assign any variables but they check a certain condition. Here the condition of j <= 0? is given. There are two ways to exit from a decision diamond: Take either the true or the false path, depending on the condition. Since *j* is −2, which is less than or equal to 0, we fall into the loop by taking the true route (Step 2).

The body of the loop has two statements. The first one says that the value of *j* is printed (Step 3) and the next one adds 1 to *j* (Step 4). Printing and reading of values use parallelograms. After *j* becomes −1, we go back to the diamond. On the tracechart, we draw a horizontal line to show that we are going up in the flowchart. Here we check whether to go into the loop or not. *j*, −1, being less than or equal to 0, makes the flow go into the loop again (Step 5). This time −1 is printed (Step 6) and *j* is incremented to 0 (Step 7). *j* is still less than or equal to 0 (Step 8) so we print the 0 (Step 9) and make *j* equal to +1 (Step 10). Finally, going to the decision, we find that it is false (Step 11) so we exit the loop and stop (Step 12).

The code for Drill 4.1 illustrates a simple loop. The numbers in the comments identify selected statements. A trace is shown alongside the code. Let us walk through the trace.

In step 1 of the trace, line 1 of the code is executed, that is, 1 is assigned to *i*. In step 2, a question is asked. Is *i* less than or equal to 2? Yes, so the loop, which is composed of the two statements inside the set of braces, is executed. Step 3 shows that *i*, with a value of 1, is printed, and then *i* is incremented to 2. Here, we draw a horizontal line in the tracechart to depict that the execution goes up to the for statement.

In step 5, is *i* less than or equal to 2? Yes, so we go through the loop again, printing 2 for *i* and incrementing it to 3. Now we have completed the second iteration of the loop. In step 8, checking to see if i <= 2, we see that it is false and we stop the loop.

Coding the Loop

Converting the flowchart into a program is straightforward. See Example 4.1A. After the Start of the flowchart, the first executable statement is j = −2;. Then the decision diamond is converted into a for loop because we see from the flowchart that the flow is coming back to the diamond, making it a loop. The body of the loop is written inside a pair of braces under the for. Think of the last brace under the main() as the Stop oval in the flowchart.

In general, loops consist of four parts. These parts are labeled in the code. The first one is to initialize the loop. The next one determines how the loop is terminated. Another one brings the loop closer to the terminal condition and the last one is the body of the loop. The purpose of having a loop in the first place determines what should be placed in the body.

```
//EXAMPLE 4.1A
void main (void)
{                                   // Beginning of main()
    int j;
    j = -2;                         // Initialization of the loop
    for(; j <= 0; )                 // Termination
    {
        printf("%d\n", j);          // Body
        j = j + 1;                  // Continuation
    }
}                                   // End of main()
```

Rewriting the Code

The for loop can be simplified so that it takes fewer lines to write. However, by compressing the number of lines, one has to study the for statement more carefully to understand what it is doing. See Example 4.1B. Here, we have taken the initialization statement and placed it before the first semicolon in the for statement. Similarly, we have taken the statement used when continuing the loop and placed it after the second semicolon. So when looking at the three parts of the for statement, which are separated by two semicolons, one sees the first part being executed once when the loop begins. The second part is a condition. If that condition is true, then the body of the loop is executed. If it is false, then the first statement after the loop is executed. In our example, there is no such statement. Every time after the body of the loop is executed and before the condition in the second part is examined, the statement in the third part is executed.

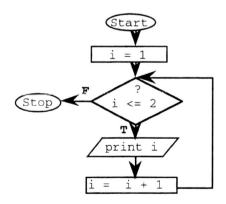

The flowchart for Drill 4.1 is drawn here. The flowchart starts at the oval labeled Start and ends at the one labeled Stop. A rectangle is used for assignments. *i* is assigned 1 to begin. Then we encounter a decision diamond. Here we take the T for the true route and fall into the loop until the condition of i <= 2? becomes false, where we stop.

With a minimum number of changes, convert this flowchart so that all the integers from 3 to 7 are printed. Also write the code.

```
//EXAMPLE 4.1B
void main(void)
{
    int j;
    for(j = -2; j <= 0; j = j + 1)
    {
        printf("%d\n", j);
    }
}
```

Last, if there is only one statement after the for statement, then a set of braces is not required. They are required only if there is more than one statement in the loop. So our code may be reduced to the following:

```
//EXAMPLE 4.1C
void main(void)
{
    int j;
    for(j = -2;   j <= 0;   j = j + 1)
        printf("%d\n", j);
}
```

Conditional Operators

The symbols <= are used together to represent the condition of "less than or equal to." Together they are called a conditional operator. Table 4.1 shows other conditional operators used in C++ programming. The confusing one is the == operator. When assigning a value to a variable, the single = is used; it actually changes the value of the variable that precedes it. However, the double == sign is used to check whether a variable is equal to a certain value.

One Last Example

In Example 4.2, we first obtain the user's name and save it in *name[]*. Then we obtain the number of times the name is to be displayed. In the sample run shown, this number is 2 and it is stored in "times." Then the loop begins. Follow the flowchart and the tracechart in Figure 4.3.

The terminal condition is evaluated. times != 0? (is times not equal to 0?) is true, since times is equal to 2. Then the body of the loop is executed. Since only one statement is in the body of the loop, no set of braces is required and the name is printed.

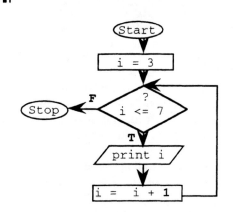

Solution 4.1
```
void main (void)
{
    int i;
    i = 3;                //1
    for(; i <= 7 ;)       //2
    {
        printf("%d\n", i); //3
        i = i + 1;        //4
    }
}
```

Drill 4.2 Write the code and draw the flowchart that will print 3, 5, and 7 instead of 3, 4, 5, 6, and 7.

The *for* Loop

Conditional Operator	Meaning	Conditional Operator	Meaning
<= >= <	Less than or equal to Greater than or equal to Less than	> == !=	Greater than Equal to (not "=") Not equal to

Table 4.1 Conditional Operators

```
//EXAMPLE 4.2
#include <stdio.h>
void main (void)
{
    int times;
    char name[11];

    printf("What is your name in less than 11 characters? ");
    scanf("%s", &name);
    printf("How many times do you want to see it? ");
    scanf("%d", &times);

    for ( ; times != 0; times = times - 1)
        printf("%s\n", name);
}
----- output -----
What is your name in less than 11 characters? TallSally
How many times do you want to see it? 2
TallSally
TallSally
```

Now we go up to the for statement and assign *times* to be 1 less than what it was. Now it is 2 minus 1, or 1. times != 0? is again true so the loop is performed, that is, the name is printed a second time.

We go back up to the for loop and decrement *times* by 1, and it becomes 0. The condition now becomes false because times is equal to 0 and we stop the loop. There is nothing else after the loop so we stop the program as well.

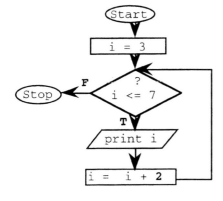

Solution 4.2 For the sake of clarity, the main() block isn't shown.

```
int i;
i = 3;                  //1
for(; i <= 7 ;)         //2
{
    printf("%d\n", i);  //3
    i = i + 2;          //4
}
```

Drill 4.3 As in Example 4.1, do a tracechart for the code shown in Solution 4.2.

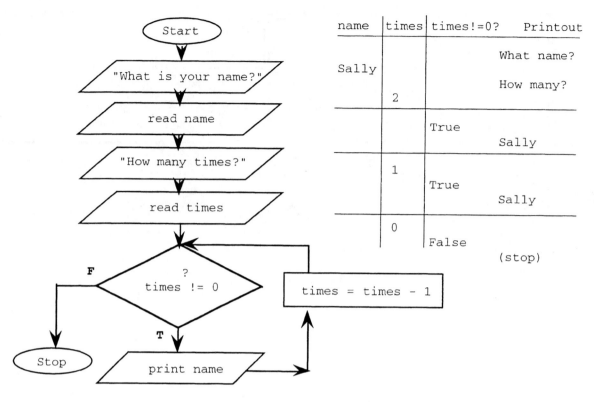

name	times	times!=0?	Printout
Sally			What name?
			How many?
	2		
		True	
			Sally
	1		
		True	
			Sally
	0		
		False	
			(stop)

Figure 4.3 The flowchart and tracechart for Example 4.2.

EXPERIMENTS

You should try to understand what is happening in each experiment before your instructor explains the results in class. Items in experiments that are new are shown in **bold**. We are starting with loops. If you end up getting an infinite loop, be ready to press CTRL–C or else restart your computer. An infinite loop never stops because there is something wrong with the program.

Step	i	i <= 7?	Printout
(1)	3		
(2)		True	
(3)			3
(4)	5		
(5)		True	
(6)			5
(7)	7		
(8)		True	
(9)			7
(10)	9		
(11)		False	(Loop stops)

Solution 4.3 i starts off at 3 and at the decision, we see that i is less than or equal to 7, so we fall into the loop. The first thing done in the loop is that i or 3 is printed and then 2 is added to i, making it 5. Here, we go to the top of the loop and check the condition again. It is true, so we continue with the loop until the condition becomes false.

Drill 4.4 Now switch statements 3 and 4 and draw a tracechart for that code. What is the new printout? Is it the same?

Exp 4.1 You don't need to type in the comments.

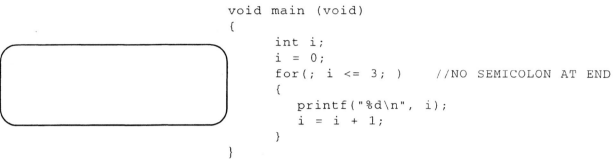

```
void main (void)
{
        int i;
        i = 0;
        for(; i <= 3; )       //NO SEMICOLON AT END
        {
            printf("%d\n", i);
            i = i + 1;
        }
}
```

a. What is the first value of *i*? What is the last value of *i* that is printed?

Exp 4.2 Don't forget main().

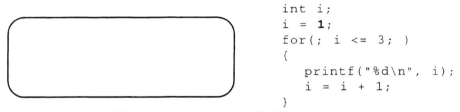

```
        int i;
        i = 1;
        for(; i <= 3; )
        {
            printf("%d\n", i);
            i = i + 1;
        }
```

a. What is the first value of *i*? What is the last value of *i* that is printed?

Exp 4.3

```
        int i;
        i = 0;                             //Statement 1
        for(; i <= 4; )                    //Statement 2
        {
            printf("%d\n", i);
            i = i + 2;                     //Statement 3
        }
```

a. What is the first value of *i*? What is the last value of *i* that is printed?
b. Statement numbers are given after the //. Which statement determines the initial value of *i*?
c. Which statement determines the final value?
d. Which statement determines how the value of *i* is increased?

Step	i	i <= 7?	Printout
(1)	3		
(2)		True	
(3)	5		
(4)			5
(5)		True	
(6)	7		
(7)			7
(8)		True	
(9)	9		
(10)			9
(11)		False	(Loop stops)

Solution 4.4 Notice in Solution 4.4 that the printout is "5, 7, 9" instead of "3, 5, 7." When *i* was 3 in the loop, it was increased to 5 before it was printed. When *i* was 7, it was increased to 9 and then printed, and then at last it was checked to see if the loop should be stopped.

Drill 4.5 Write a for loop that will print "0, 3, 6, 9, 12."

Exp 4.4

```
int i;
i = 0;                          //Statement 1
for(; i <= 4; )                 //Statement 2
{
    printf("%d\n", i);
    i = i + 2;                  //Statement 3
}
printf("*** %d\n", i);   //Statement 4
```

a. What is the first value of *i*?
b. What is the last value of *i* that is printed inside the loop?
c. Is statement 3 inside the loop? What about statement 4?
d. Which statement is done before the loop?
e. Which one is done after the loop?
f. How can we tell which statements are inside the loop?

Exp 4.5 Let us simplify Experiment 4.4:

```
int i;
for(i = 0; i <= 4; i = i + 2)     //Stmt 1
    printf("%d\n", i);            //Stmt 2
printf("*** %d\n", i);            //Stmt 3
```

The for loop now shows three items. We will call the first item as i = 0, the second item i <= 4, and the third item i = i + 2.
a. Which of these three items determines the terminal condition of the loop?
b. Which one determines the incremental value of *i*?
c. Which one determines the initial value of *i*?
d. Is statement 2 in the loop or after it?
e. Is statement 3 in the loop or after it?

Solution 4.5
```
int i;
i = 0;              //1
for(; i <= 12 ;)    //2
{
    printf("%d\n", i); //3
    i = i + 3;         //4
}
```

```
//An equivalent Solution
int i;
i = -3;             //5
for(; i<= 9 ;)      //6
{
    i = i + 3;         //7
    printf("%d\n", i); //8
}
```

Drill 4.6

a. What would happen if Statement 1 were changed to i = 20 in this solution?
b. What would happen if Statement 4 were changed to i = i – 3 in this solution?

Exp 4.6

```
int i;
for(i = 8; i <= 11; i = i + 1)   //Stmt 1
    printf("%d\n", i);           //Stmt 2
printf("*** %d\n", i);           //Stmt 3
```

a. The for loop has three items separated by two semicolons. Which of these parts are assignments, that is, a statement, where a variable is being changed?
b. Which part sets the initial value of *i*?
c. Which part terminates the loop?
d. Which part increments *i*?

Exp 4.7 Change *i* to 1 in statement 2.

```
int i;
for(i = 8; i <= 11; i = i + 1)   //1
    printf("%d\n", 1);           //2
printf("*** %d\n", i);           //3
```

a. How many times did statement 2 execute?
b. Why didn't the values of *i* get printed in the loop?

Exp 4.8 Swap the third part of the for loop with statement 2. The third part could be any valid C statement.

```
int i;
for(i = 8; i <= 11; printf("%d\n",i))//1
    i = i + 1;                       //2
printf("*** %d\n", i);               //3
```

a. Why didn't the 8 get printed this time?
b. Why did 12 get printed twice, once inside the loop and once after the loop?

Solution 4.6

a. If the value of *i* were to start off at 20, then the condition in the for statement would be false to begin with and the loop would not be executed at all. Nothing would be printed.
b. If, on the other hand, the value of *i* became more and more negative, then the condition in the for statement would never become false and we would have what is called an infinite loop.

Drill 4.7 Write a program that will ask the user to give three integers. Call these integers "start," "step_by," and "stop." After these three integers are scanned in, set up the for loop that will start *i* at the value of *start*, make it increase by the value given by *step_by*, and make it stop at the value stored in *stop*. Print these values. Here is an example of the run:

```
----- output -----
Enter three integers: 23 3 32
23    26    29    32
```

Exp 4.9

```
int i;
for(i = 0;  i <= 4;  i = i + 2)    //1
{
    printf("%d\n", i);             //2
    printf("*** %d\n", i);         //3
}
```

a. Why is statement 3 being executed in the loop?

b. We must have a pair of what items if more than one statement is to be executed in the loop?

Exp 4.10

```
int i;
for(i = 0;   i <= 4;   i = i + 2) //1
    printf("%d\n", i);            //2
    printf("*** %d\n", i);        //3
```

a. Why isn't statement 3 being executed in the loop?

b. Can you correct the indentation for statement 3?

Exp 4.11 Add a semicolon at the end of the for and watch what happens.

```
int i;
for(i = 0;   i<=4;   i = i + 2);   //1
    printf("%d\n", i);            //2
    printf("*** %d\n", i);        //3
```

a. Was statement 2 executed inside the loop?

b. Was statement 3 executed inside the loop?

c. What was the only difference between this experiment and the last one?

Solution 4.7

```
int i, start, step_by, stop;
printf("Enter three integers: ");
scanf("%d %d %d", &start, &step_by, &stop);
for(i = start; i <= stop; i = i + step_by)
    printf("%d\t", i);
printf("\n");
```

Drill 4.8 First draw the flowchart for this code. Then do a tracechart, assuming that *small* was scanned in as 7 and *large* was scanned in as 18.

```
int ans, small, large;
printf("Give 2 integers: ");
scanf("%d %d", &small, &large);
for(ans = 0; large >= small; ans = ans + 1)
    large = large - small;
printf("The answers are %d and %d \n", ans, large);
```

Exp 4.12 Now let us try making *i* go backward. Notice the >= operator.

```
int i;
i = 4;
for( ; i >= 2; )
{
    i = i - 1;
    printf("%d\n", i);
}
```

a. Initially, the condition i >= 2? is true or false?
b. With every iteration of the loop, this condition is closer and closer to becoming true or false?

Exp 4.13 The != operator means "not equal to."

```
int i;
for(i = 4; i != 2; i = i - 1)
    printf("%d\n", i);
```

Exp 4.14 Before you run this one, can you tell that it is an infinite loop? How would you correct it?

```
int i;
for(i = 4; i != 2; i = i + 1)
    printf("%d\n", i);
```

QUESTIONS

1. Compress this code as much as possible:

```
i = 1;
for ( ; i < 5;  )
{
    printf("%d\n", i);
    i = i + 1;
}
```

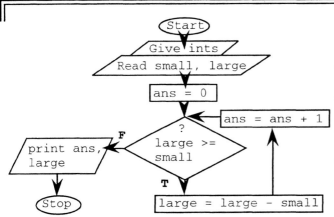

Solution 4.8

small	large	ans	large>= small?	Printout
				Give ints
7	18	0		
			True	
	11			
		1	True	
	4			
		2	False	
				2 4

Drill 4.9 Do a tracechart for Drill 4.8 where *small* was scanned in as 6 and *large* was scanned in as 18. Can you tell what the loop is doing?

2. In the code for Question 1, which part is the terminal condition? Which statement brings the loop closer to the terminal condition with every iteration? Which statement initializes the loop?

3. What is the operator for the assignment statement? What is the conditional operator for equality? Which statement changes a value? Which statement checks only a value?

4. If a loop doesn't approach the terminal condition with every iteration but diverges from it, what kind of loop is it?

5. Show the output of each of the following:

a.
```
for(i = 2; i <= 6; i = i + 2)
    printf("%d\t", i + 1);
```

b.
```
for (i = 2; i != 11; i = i + 3)
    printf("%d\t", i/2);            //Remember integer division.
```

c.
```
for(i = 2; i == 2; i = i + 1)
    printf("%d\t", i);
```

d.
```
for(i = 2; i <=6; i = i + 2); //Notice the semicolon.
    printf("%d\t", i +1);
```

6. Draw the flowchart and the tracecharts for Question 5, a through d.

PROGRAMS

1. Print the times table for 7 in one column.
2. Ask the user for an integer and print out that integer's times table.
3. Ask the user for two integers, first a small one then a larger one. Multiply these two integers by doing repeated addition. For example, if we were to obtain 3 and 5 from the user, then we would find their product by adding the larger one (5) three times.
4. Print out all integers from 10 down to –10.
5. Print out all integers from –10 up to 10.
6. Print out ***** on five consecutive lines.
7. Print out the squares of the first 8 integers.
8. Suppose you are given one cent on day 1 and on day 2 you are given twice as much. If each day you are given twice as much money as on the previous day, then on day 10, how many pennies will you receive? Can you program that?

Solution 4.9 *ans* is the quotient and *large* is the remainder.

small	large	ans	large>= small?	Printout
				Give ints
6	18	0		
			True	
	12			
		1	True	
	6			
		2	True	
	0			
		3	False	
				3 0

Drill 4.10 Write a program that will add up all the integers from 1 to the integer that was scanned into the variable *j*. Store the sum in the variable called "sum," and use *i* to increment the integers from 1 to *j*. Print only *sum*. For example, if 5 were read into *j*, then *sum* would be 1 + 2 + 3 + 4 + 5, or 15. A sample output follows:
```
----- output -----
Give an integer: 6
Sum of integers from 1 to 6 is 21
```

The *for* Loop

OPTIONAL TOPICS

The while Loop

The while loop in C and C++ is very similar to the for loop. The for statement contains two semicolons, which allows placement of the initialization statement, the negation of the termination condition, and the iterative statement in it. However, the while loop allows placement of only the condition so the other two statements must be placed outside the while statement. That is one reason why I prefer the for loop over the while loop, although the while loop is more common.

```
//EXAMPLE 4.3
void main(void)
{
    int j;
    for(j = -2; j <= 0; j = j + 1)
        printf("%d\n", j);
}
```

```
//EXAMPLE 4.4
void main(void)
{
    int j;
    j = -2;
    while(j <= 0)
    {
        printf("%d\n", j);
        j = j + 1;
    }
}
```

Example 4.3 prints out all the integers from −2 to 0, using a for loop. Example 4.4 does the same thing but uses the while loop. Notice that the statements j = −2; and j = j + 1 are removed from the for statement because we converted it to the while loop. Since we now have two statements in the while loop, we needed to add a pair of braces, as we had to with the for loop. Just as the for statement typically doesn't take a semicolon after it, neither does the while statement.

You will see the while loop used often. However, the only difference between a while loop and a for loop is a couple of semicolons. That is, this statement:

Solution 4.10

```
int i, j, sum = 0;
printf("Give an integer ");
scanf("%d", &j);
for(i = 1; i <= j; i = i + 1)
    sum = sum + i;
printf("Sum of integers from 1 to %d is %d\n", j, sum);
```

Drill 4.11 Write a program to do the same calculation as in Drill 4.10, but instead of adding the integers from 1 to *j*, add the integers from *j* down to 1. Also, draw a tracechart for *j* scanned in as 3.

The *for* Loop

```
while ( <condition> )
```

is equivalent to:

```
for  (; <condition> ;)
```

The do–while Loop

Example 4.5 converts the same loop to the do–while loop. The main difference here is that the condition is tested after the body of the loop. With this kind of loop, the body must be done at least once; this is not the case with the other two loops. With the other two loops, if the condition is false at the beginning, then the body of the loop is not executed at all. Notice the semicolon at the end of the "while."

```
//EXAMPLE 4.5
void main(void)
{
   int j;
   j = -2;
   do
   {
      printf("%d\n", j);
      j = j + 1;
   }
   while(j <= 0);
}
```

Solution 4.11

```
int i, j, sum = 0;
printf("Give integer ");
scanf("%d", &j);
for(i = j; i >= 1; i  = i - 1)
     sum = sum + i;
printf("Sum of integers from 1");
printf(" to %d is %d\n", j, sum);
```

j	i	sum	i>=1?	printout
		0		Give integer
3				
	3		True	
		3		
	2		True	
		5		
	1		True	
		6		
	0		False	
				Sum is 6

The *for* Loop

Reading in a Loop

LESSON

This unit reviews many of the topics that we came across in the first four units. It is crucial to understand looping, so here we take some time to do just that.

When combining scanf()'s with loops, there are two types of loops that first should be mastered. I call one the *count* loop and the other the *delimiter* loop. With the count loop, the programmer knows before the loop begins how many iterations that loop will perform. However, with the delimiter loop, the programmer doesn't know that; instead, when a certain data item is encountered, the loop will stop. That certain data item that will terminate the loop is called the delimiter. Here is the general format of the count loop:

DRILLS

Drill 5.1

```
total = 0;
for(i = 1; i <= 3; i = i + 1)
{
    scanf("%d", &k);
    total = total + k;
}
printf("Total = %d\n", total);
```

1. How many times is this loop executed? Does this answer depend on what the data was?
2. How many numbers will the loop read?
3. If 40, 50, and 20 were read in, what would be the value of *total*:
   a. at the end of the first iteration?
   b. at the end of the second iteration?
   c. at the end of the third iteration?
   d. after the loop when it is printed?
4. If 90, 10, and 30 were read in, then what would be printed?

```
//Format of the count loop:
printf("How many data items do you want to enter? ");
scanf("%d", &count);
for(i = 1; i <= count; i = i + 1)
{
   scanf("%d", &data_item);
            :                       //Other statements to process the data item.
}
```

Notice that first the programmer finds out the number of data items to be read. That number is read in a variable called *count*. Then the loop is set up so that it will be performed that many times. The loop could have also been set up this way:

```
for( ; count != 0; count = count - 1)
```

It would have the same effect. However, if for some reason the value of *count* were necessary after the loop, it would not be available as it would be in the first instance. The general format of the delimiter loop is as follows:

```
//Format of the delimiter loop. The delimiter is 0.
printf("Enter data items, when done, enter a 0\n");
scanf("%d", &data_item);
for( ; data_item != 0; )
{
         :                        //Other statements to process the data item.
   scanf("%d", &data_item);
}
```

Here, we have a scanf() before the loop, but it reads in the *data_item* instead of the *count*. If the condition in the for statement is satisfied, then that data is processed and the next data item is read in at the end of the body of the loop. This loop continues as long as the data isn't a 0. Once it reads in a 0, the loop stops.

I would like to draw your attention to the placement of the scanf()'s for the *data_item* in each format. In the count loop, the reading of the data is done at the beginning of the body of the loop. But in the delimiter loop, the reading is done twice—just before the loop and also at the end of the body of the loop.

Solution 5.1
1. 3, No;   2. 3
3a. 40; 3b. 90; 3c. 110; 3d. 110
4. 130

Drill 5.2
```
total = 0;
scanf("%d", &k);
for(i = 1; i <= 3; i = i + 1)
{
   total = total + k;
   scanf("%d", &k);
}
printf("Total = %d\n", total);
```

1. How many times is the loop performed?
2. How many times is each of the statements in the loop performed?
3. How many times is scanf() executed before, during, and after the loop?
4. How many data items are read in?
5. If the data items are 40, 20, 50, and 10, then what is the value of "total" after the first time, second time, and the third time through the loop?
6. Is the first data item added into the loop? What about the last one?

Here is an example that uses both kinds of loops:

```c
//EXAMPLE 5.1
#include <stdio.h>
void main (void)
{
    float sum = 0.0;
    int count, i, data_item;
    printf("How many items do you want to average first? ");
    scanf("%d", &count);
    for(i = 1; i <= count; i = i + 1)
    {
        scanf("%d", &data_item);
        sum = sum + data_item;
    }
    printf("Their average is %.2f\n", sum / count);

    printf("\nEnter data, when done, type in a 0.\n");
    scanf("%d", &data_item);
    for(count = 0, sum = 0.0; data_item != 0; count = count + 1)
    {
        sum = sum + data_item;
        scanf("%d", &data_item);
    }
    printf("Their average is %.2f\n", sum / count);
} // Make sure count doesn't stay 0.

----- output -----
How many items do you want to average first? 3
56    82    70
Their average is 69.33

Enter data, when done, type in a 0.
34    88    45    77    0
Their average is 61.00
```

Solution 5.2

1. 3;
2. 3
3. Once before, three times during, and none after the loop.
4. 4; Once for each time that scanf() was executed.
5. 40, 60, 110
6. Yes; No

Drill 5.3

Draw a flowchart and a tracechart for Drill 5.2.

The data items are 40, 20, 50, and 10. For the tracechart, make columns for *k*, *i*, *total*, and i <= 3?

Reading in a Loop
63

```
//EXAMPLE 5.2
#include <string.h>
#include <stdio.h>
void main ()
{
    float current_temp, previous_temp, total;
    char current_condition[11], previous_condition[11];
    int day;

//Initialize the loop: set up the previous and current values.
    printf("Enter condition and temperature: ");
    scanf("%s %f", &previous_condition, &previous_temp);
    printf("Enter condition and temperature: ");
    scanf("%s %f", &current_condition, &current_temp);
    total = previous_temp;

//Do the loop.
    for(day = 1; current_temp < previous_temp; day = day + 1)
    {
        total = total + current_temp;
            //Now make the current values become the old or previous ones.
        previous_temp = current_temp;
        strcpy(previous_condition, current_condition);
            //And get the new or current values.
        printf("Enter condition and temperature: ");
        scanf("%s %f", &current_condition, &current_temp);
    }

//Print the report
    printf("Lowest temp. before it went up the first time: %.2f\n",
        previous_temp);
    printf("Condition at that time: %s\n", previous_condition);
    printf("Average temperature up to that time: %.2f\n", total / day);
}
----- output -----
Enter condition and temperature: hot      98.5
Enter condition and temperature: balmy    79.1
Enter condition and temperature: mild     68.0
```

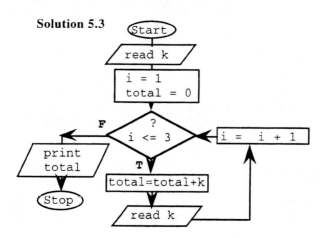

Solution 5.3

k	i	i <= 3?	total
40	1		
		True	40
20			
	2	True	60
50			
	3	True	110
10			
	4	False	

Loop stops and 110 is printed.

Reading in a Loop

```
Enter condition and temperature: windy    65.5
Enter condition and temperature: fair     67.0
Lowest temp. before it went up the first time: 65.5
Condition at that time: windy
Average temperature up to that time: 77.7
```

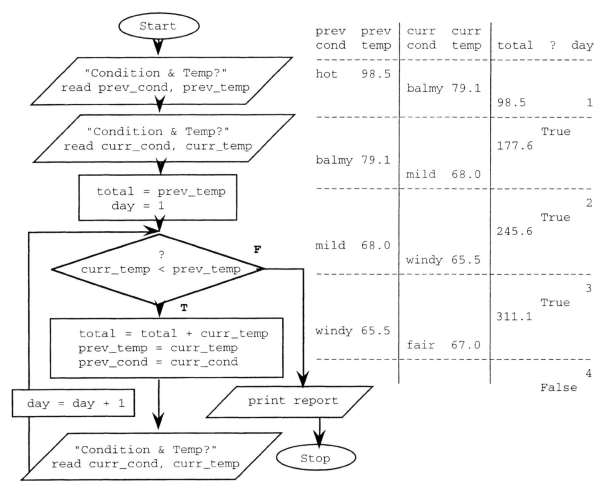

Figure 5.1 The flowchart and tracechart for Example 5.1.

Drill 5.4 The data items are 40, 20, 50, and 10.

```
total = 0;
scanf("%d", &k);
for(i = 1; i <= 3; i = i + 1)
{
    scanf("%d", &k);
    total = total + k;
}
printf("Total = %d\n", total);
```

1. How many times is the scanf() done before, during, and after the loop?
2. After the first iteration of the loop, what is the value of *total*?
3. Was the first data item added into *total*?
4. Was the last data item added into *total*?
5. What will be the final printout?

Reading in a Loop

A Second Example

The temperature was reported as going down each day, so we want to know the first day that it went up. The temperature and the general weather condition for each day are what the program has to read, and it has to report the temperature and the weather condition for the day when the temperature dipped to a minimum before it went up.

The solution for this program is given in Example 5.2. The flowchart and the tracechart are shown in Figure 5.1. (See pages 64 and 65.) As the program is explained, follow the chart.

From the output screen of Example 5.2, we see that the temperature starts at 98.5 and comes down to 65.5 before going up to 67.0. The program detects that the temperature started going up and stops the loop. Then it prints the lowest temperature and the condition at that time. It also prints the average of all the temperatures up to that time. Since we need to find out when the temperature starts to go up, we need to know not only the temperature for the current day, but we also need to save the temperature and the weather condition for the previous day.

The program is divided into three parts: the part before the loop, the loop itself, and the part after the loop. Before the loop we are reading the *previous_condition* and the *previous_temp*. Then we read the *current_condition* and the *current_temperature*. (When reading floats with a scanf(), remember to use %f instead of %.2f.) This means that the program must be provided with two pairs of data items. We need to keep track of the previous values and the current values. The current values always appear after the previous values throughout the program. The value of *total* is set to the *previous_temp*. A sample of the input data is given in bold after the program. Using the input data, the tracechart shows that the previous values are started at "hot 98.5," the current values are shown as "balmy 79.1," and so the total is set to 98.5.

Now we begin the loop. First, *day* is 1. After checking the condition current_temp < previous_temp? we see that it is true and we do the first iteration of the loop. The first statement adds *current_temp* to *total* and in the tracechart, we see that it is 177.6. Then we copy the current variables into the previous ones since now they have become "old." This is because we are reading the next data pair into the current variables. At the end of the first iteration, the previous variables are "balmy 79.1," and the current variables are "mild 68.0."

On our way up to the top of the loop, *day* becomes 2. The condition is still true because 68.0 is less than 79.1. We then enter the loop a second time. *total* becomes 245.6 after 68.0 was added to it; "mild 68.0," instead of being the current values, now become the previous values; and "windy 65.5" is read into the current variables. That ends the second iteration.

At the end of the third iteration, the *current_temp* is 67.0 and *previous_temp* is 65.5. The condition becomes false and we exit the loop. All along we have been saving the current values into the previous ones, so now we have the previous values, including the *previous_condition*, available. We can print the lowest temperature up to that point and the weather condition at that time. Using the values of *total* and *day*, we can print the average temperature.

Solution 5.4
1. Once before, three times during, and none after the loop.
2. 20. 40 was read into *k* but wasn't added to *total*.
3. No, only the second, third, and fourth items were added to *total*.
4. Yes   5. 80

Drill 5.5 Data items are 40, 20, 50 and 10.

```
total = 0;
scanf("%d", &k);
for(i = 1; i <= 3; i = i + 1)
    scanf("%d", &k);    // Stmt 1
    total = total + k; // Stmt 2
printf("Total = %d\n", total);
```

1. Which statement(s) are in the body of the loop?
2. Which statement is indented incorrectly?
3. Will 40 be added to *total*?
4. Which numbers are added to *total*?
5. Out of the numbers that were added to the *total*, which ones were added inside the loop and after the loop?

This example shows one way of controlling a loop that reads in data from the user. There are other methods of controlling a "reading loop," which are illustrated elsewhere in this unit.

EXPERIMENTS

This unit concentrates on using the scanf() function in a for loop. There are many ways to control a loop when reading in values, and here I give you the opportunity to master control of a loop. Remember: == means "is it equal?," != means "is it not equal?," >= means "is it greater than or equal to?" and so on. When running each of the experiments, always enter these values when the program allows you to do so. Enter them one at a time and not all on one line. A program may not need all the values shown here. Write down only the output from the printf()'s. You do not have to write down what was typed in for the scanf()'s. Also, define the variables necessary to run each program.

3   7   8   11   14   10   9   9   6

Exp 5.1 Define the necessary variables for each experiment. Do not show the scanf()'s, only the printf()'s for all experiments.

```
for(i = 1; i <= 2; i = i + 1)
{
    scanf("%d", &k);
    printf("%d \n", k);
}
```

a. How many numbers were accepted by the program?
b. If the <= were changed to <, how many data items would have been processed?
c. If it were changed to !=, how many data items would have been processed?

Exp 5.2

```
for ( i = 1; i <= 0; i = i + 1)
{
    scanf("%d", &k);
    printf("%d \n", k);
}
```

Solution 5.5
1. Only statement 1 or the second scanf() because there are no braces.
2. Only statement 1 should be indented because that is the only statement in the loop. All the others should start at the same column.
3. No. Before 40 is added to *total*, 20 gets read into *k*. However, since statement 2 isn't in the loop, the 20 isn't added either.
4. Only the scanf() is in the loop, so *total* doesn't get anything added to it until the loop is over. When the loop is over, *k* is 10 and only 10 is added to *total*.
5. No numbers will be added to *total* inside the loop; only the 10 is added to *total* after the loop.

Drill 5.6 Using this for loop, for (i = 1; i <= count; i = i + 1), write the program that will first read the variable *count* as a data item, read in that many more data items, and print their total. For example, if the data were 3, 40, 20, 50, 10; *count* would become 3 and the sum of the next 3 data items would be calculated as 110.

a. How many numbers were accepted by the program?
b. How many times was the loop executed?

Exp 5.3 These statements are executed in the following order: 1, 2, 3, 4, 2, 3, 4, 2, etc., until *k* equals 11.

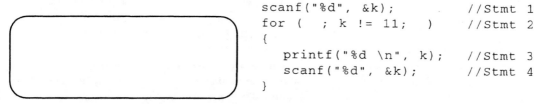

```
scanf("%d", &k);            //Stmt 1
for (  ; k != 11;  )        //Stmt 2
{
    printf("%d \n", k);     //Stmt 3
    scanf("%d", &k);        //Stmt 4
}
```

a. How many numbers were accepted by the program?
b. How many times was the scanf() function called? And the printf()?
c. Was 11 ever read in as data? Why wasn't it printed?
d. Did the program or the data determine the number of times the loop was to be performed?
e. If you wanted all the numbers up to 9 to be printed, how would you have changed the for statement?
f. Draw a flowchart and a tracechart for this experiment.

Exp 5.4

```
scanf("%d", &k);
for ( ; k != 11; )
{
    scanf("%d", &k);
    printf("%d \n", k);
}
```

a. Did the 11 get printed? Why or why not?
b. Did the first number that was read get printed? Why or why not?
c. If you wanted all the numbers up to 9 to be printed, how would you have changed the for statement?

Solution 5.6 Notice in the loop that *k* has to be read in before it can be added to *total*.

```
scanf("%d", &count);
for (i = 1; i <= count; i = i + 1)
{
    scanf("%d", &k);
    total = total + k;
}
printf("%d\n", total);
```

Drill 5.7
1. Was the first data item that was read added to *total*?
2. What was the purpose of the first data item?
3. If the first data item were a 7, how many numbers would the program attempt to add?
4. Complete the for statements, so that the logic is the same as in Solution 5.6, in each case:
   a. for(i =   ; i < count; i = i + 1)
   b. for(i = 1; i <   ; i = i + 1)
        // Do not use "<=."
   c. for(i = count;   ;   )
   d. for(;   ;   )//Do not use *i*.

Exp 5.5

```
k = 0;
for ( ; k != 11; )
{
    printf("%d \n", k);
    scanf("%d", &k);
}
```

a. Did the 11 get printed? Why or why not?
b. Why didn't the first data item, 3, get printed first?
c. Would the 3 have been printed first if the scanf() and the printf() were switched?

Exp 5.6

```
scanf("%d", &m);
for ( ; m != 0; m = m - 1 )
{                                    //Start of body
    scanf("%d", &k);
    printf("%d \n", k);
}                                    //End of body
```

a. How many times was the body of the loop performed?
b. How many times was *k* assigned a new value through the scanf()?
c. What in the data determined how many times the loop was performed?

Exp 5.7

```
scanf("%d", &m);
for (i = 1; i <= m; i = i + 1)
{
    scanf("%d", &k);
    printf("%d \n", k);
}
```

Solution 5.7

1. No. 2. To find out how many data items were to be read in.   3. 7
4. a. for(i = 0; i < count; i = i + 1)
   b. for(i = 1; i < count + 1; i = i + 1)
   c. for(i - count; i != 0; i = i - 1)
   d. for(; count != 0; count = count - 1)

Drill 5.8 What is the output if the input were 4, 2, 9, 11, 4, 0?

```
scanf("%d", &k);
for (i = 1; k != 0; i = i + 1)
    scanf("%d", &k);
printf("%d\n", i);
```

a. Was there any difference between the outputs of Experiment 5.6 and Experiment 5.7?
b. Which of these two experiments preserved the number of times the loop was performed? That is, in which experiment did the value of *m* remain the same?
c. If the <= were changed to !=, then how many times would the loop have been executed? *i* would have gone up to what value?
d. Draw a flowchart and a tracechart.

Exp 5.8

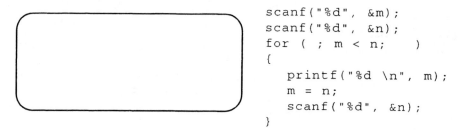

```
scanf("%d", &m);
scanf("%d", &n);
for ( ; m < n;      )
{
    printf("%d \n", m);
    m = n;
    scanf("%d", &n);
}
```

a. The first time that the for loop is encountered, which variable was read in before the other, *m* or *n*?
b. Once inside the loop, there are two numbers available: the one that was read in earlier and the one that was read in later. Inside the loop, which one is printed (the earlier one or the later one)?
c. Inside the loop, does the earlier number now become the later one, or does the later one now become the earlier one?
d. Which one does the scanf() read, the earlier one or the later one?
e. After the scanf(), is *m* the earlier number or the later number?
f. Without using the names of the variables but instead the terms earlier number and later number, state when the loop continues and when it terminates.
g. Draw a flowchart and a tracechart.

Exp 5.9 Now change the conditional operator as shown. Can you determine what will be printed?

Solution 5.8

6. The loop continues until the number that is read in is equal to 0. There are 5 numbers read in until the 0 is encountered.

Drill 5.9

Rewrite Drill 5.8 so that the code will not print the count of data items that were read in, but instead will print out the average of all numbers except the 0. Use *sum* as the variable to add the numbers.

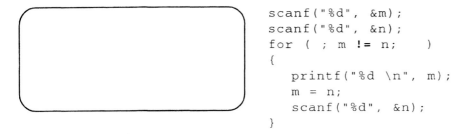

```
scanf("%d", &m);
scanf("%d", &n);
for ( ; m != n;     )
{
    printf("%d \n", m);
    m = n;
    scanf("%d", &n);
}
```

State what numbers are printed and when the loop terminates.

Exp 5.10 Let us continue where we left off in Experiment 5.3.

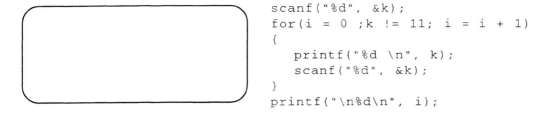

```
scanf("%d", &k);
for(i = 0 ;k != 11; i = i + 1)
{
    printf("%d \n", k);
    scanf("%d", &k);
}
printf("\n%d\n", i);
```

a. What does *i* represent when it is printed after the loop?

Exp 5.11

```
sum = 0;
scanf("%d", &k);
for(i = 0; k != 11; i = i + 1)
{
    sum = sum + k;
    scanf("%d", &k);
}
printf("%d %d %.2f\n", sum, i, sum*1.0/i);
```

a. After the loop, what do the three numbers represent?
b. Draw a flowchart and a tracechart.

Solution 5.9 At the end of the loop, *i* is 6. But we have only 5 numbers to be averaged, so *i* must be decreased by 1.

```
scanf("%d", &k);
for (i = 1; k != 0; i = i + 1)
{
    sum = sum + k;
    scanf("%d", &k);
}
printf("%.2f\n",  (sum * 1.0 ) / (i - 1));
```

Drill 5.10 Now rewrite the code in Solution 5.9 so that the loop stops when the new number is less than the previous one. That is, if the data items were 30, 70, 85, 80, then the loop should stop at 80 but print out the average of all the numbers up to 85, the one before the last one. You will need two variables; call them "last" and "curr." You will also need two scanf()'s before the loop.

QUESTIONS

Using the following numbers as the input data, show the output for each code. You should be able to determine the output without running them. Try using tracecharts to see if they help. All sums are initialized to zero.

2
40
30
90
10
40

1.

```
scanf("%d", &k);
for( i = 1; i <= 4; i = i + 1)
{
    sum = sum + k;
    scanf("%d", &k);
}
printf("%d\n", sum);
```

2.

```
scanf("%d", &k);
for( i = k; i != 0; i = i - 1)
{
    sum = sum + k;
    scanf("%d", &k);
}
printf("%d\n", sum);
```

3.

```
scanf("%d", &k);
for( i = 1; sum < 100; i = i + 1)
{
    sum = sum + k;
    scanf("%d", &k);
}
printf("%.2f\n", (sum * 1.0) / i);
```

Solution 5.10 As long as *curr* is greater than *last*, the loop continues.

```
scanf("%d", &last);
scanf("%d", &curr);
sum = last;
for (i = 1; last < curr; i = i + 1)
{
    sum = sum + curr;
    last = curr;
    scanf("%d", &curr);
}
printf("%.2f\n", (sum * 1.0 ) / i);
```

Drill 5.11 Draw a flowchart and a tracechart for Solution 5.10.

72   Reading in a Loop

4.
```
for(i = 1; i <= 4; i = i + 1)
{
    scanf("%d", &k);
    sum = sum - k;
}
printf("%d\n", sum);
```

5.
```
for(i = 1; i <= 2; i = i + 1)
{
    scanf("%d", &k);
    sum1 = sum1 + k;
    scanf("%d", &k);
    sum2 = sum2 + k;
}
printf("%d %d\n", sum1, sum2);
```

6.
```
scanf("%d", &k);
for( ; k != 10; )
{
    sum = sum - k;
    scanf("%d", &k);
}
printf("%d\n", sum);
```

7.
```
scanf("%d", &k1);
scanf("%d", &k2);
for(i = 1; k1 - k2 < 50; i = i + 1)
{
    sum = sum + k1;
    k1 = k2;
    printf("sum = %d\n", sum);
    scanf("%d", &k2);
}
```

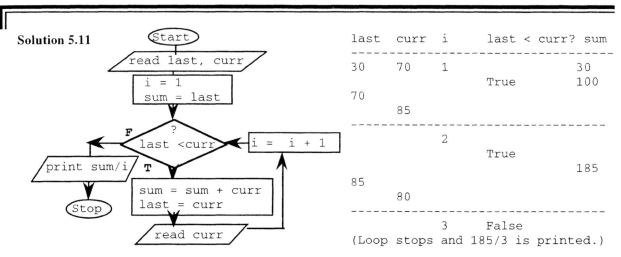

Solution 5.11

last	curr	i	last < curr?	sum
30	70	1		30
			True	100
70				
	85			
		2		
			True	
				185
85				
	80			
		3	False	

(Loop stops and 185/3 is printed.)

PROGRAMS

1. Ask the user how many numbers are to be added. Read in that many floats and print their sum at the end.

2. Read in grades for two quizzes (floats) on each line (for each student) until a –1 is entered for the first quiz. Print the average of each quiz at the end.

3. Read in grades with a value between 0 and 100 until a negative grade is read in. Stop the loop once a negative grade is read in. At the end, print the average of all the other grades except for the negative one.

4. Keep reading in characters until two consecutive characters are equal. Then print the total number of characters except for the last two.

OPTIONAL TOPICS

The EOF Character

A special character called EOF (End Of File) is placed at the end of a file. When a computer system is typing out a file and it encounters this character, it realizes that this is the end of the file and that the typing of the file is complete. In UNIX, this character can be created by pressing CTRL-d. On PC systems, it is created by pressing CTRL-z.

This example shows the use of the EOF character. EOF is a special name defined in the stdio.h file. Its value is –1. The getchar() function was covered in the Optional Topics section of Unit 3. Here we get a character from the user and store it in *i*. If *i* is not equal to EOF, then we use the putchar() function, print it on the screen, and get another one to place it in *i*. This is done until an EOF is encountered, when the loop stops. Notice that the character is read into *i*, an integer. It could also have been a char. In the output a total of 4 is shown because the fourth character, which we cannot see, is the carriage return character.

Drill 5.12 There are two general ways to write loops involving scanning. One is called the count loop and the other is called the delimiter loop. They are shown here. Where in the body should this statement, scanf("%d", &x); be placed in each code?

```
//The Count Loop
printf("How many items? \n");
scanf("%d", &count);
for(i = 1; i <= count; i = i + 1)
{

   //The body of the loop.

}
```

```
//The Delimiter Loop
printf("When done enter a 0\n");
scanf("%d", &x);
for( ;x != 0; )
{

    //The body of the loop.

}
```

```
//EXAMPLE 5.3
#include <stdio.h>        // In here, EOF is defined as -1.
void main (void)          // In UNIX press CTRL-d, in DOS press CTRL-z to signal EOF
{
    int i, j;
    i = getchar();
    for(j = 0; i != EOF; j = j + 1)
    {
        putchar(i);
        i = getchar();
    }
    printf("total = %d\n", j);
}
----- output -----
w7t^dw7t^dtotal = 3
```

Solution 5.12

```
//The Count Loop
printf("How many items? \n");
scanf("%d", &count);
for(i = 1; i <= count; i = i + 1)
{
    scanf("%d", &x);
    //The body of the loop.


}
```

```
//The Delimiter Loop
printf("When done enter a 0\n");
scanf("%d", &x);
for( ;x != 0; )
{

    //The body of the loop.
    scanf("%d", &x);
}
```

Reading in a Loop

The if Statement

The Coin Sorter Example

Figure 6.1 illustrates how a coin sorter sends coins through different chutes so that quarters, nickels, pennies, and dimes are sorted into separate stacks. Quarters have the largest diameter and they are sent first through the rightmost chute, while the others go to the left. Then the nickels are selected to go through one chute while the dimes and pennies go to the right. Dimes and pennies are separated last. You may have seen one of these gadgets in a bank where numerous coins are handled.

Let us use this device to introduce the if–then–else logic used in programming. Figure 6.2 shows the flowchart. Correlate Figures 6.1 and 6.2 as the logic is discussed. At the top, all the coins come through. At the first branch, or the decision diamond, coins with a diameter of 24mm are sent to the true side to be counted as quarters. This condition diameter == 24? is false for the rest of the coins and they go down the false branch of the decision. These coins come to the diameter != 21?

In the first part of our drills we will use the rate table in Table 6.1 to construct the logic for determining the correct rate. "r" will stand for "residential," and "c" will stand for "commercial."

Units Used	Residential	Commercial
0 < units <= 200	0.8	0.6
above 200	0.7	0.3

Table 6.1 Rate table for utility company

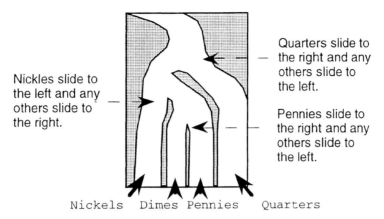

Figure 6.1 A coin sorter.

Quarters slide to the right and any others slide to the left.

Pennies slide to the right and any others slide to the left.

Nickles slide to the left and any others slide to the right.

Nickels   Dimes Pennies   Quarters

decision. For the coins whose diameter is 21mm, this condition is false and they are counted as nickels, while the dimes and pennies go to the true side of the branch. After one last decision, the dimes and pennies are separated.

You should notice that quarters have to go through only one decision diamond, nickels have to go through two, and dimes and pennies have to go through three. Example 6.1 is a program that will separate 20 coins depending on their diameter, count them, and at the end, print how much those coins are worth. Now let's follow the if–then–else statements given in the program. These statements are inside a loop which scans in 20 coin diameters.

If the diameter is 24mm, the first if is true and we add one to the number of quarters. Skipping the else or the false side of that first if, we go around the loop to get the next diameter.

If the diameter is 21mm, the first if is false so we proceed to the else side, or the false side, of the first if. Here, there is another if. It asks if the diameter is not equal to 21. Since this is false, the control goes to the else side and one is added to the number of nickels.

If the diameter is 19mm, the first if is false and we go to the else. Here, the diameter != 21? decision is true, so we go to the next statement following it, which is another if. The decision diameter == 19? is true and in that statement, one is added to the number of pennies. If the diameter were 18mm, one would be added to the number of dimes using the else side (diameter == 19?). After the loop, the number of each coin is printed and the total value of all the coins.

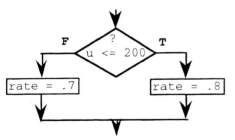

Drill 6.1 Let us first consider the condition for the case where type is equal to "residential" only. If the type is residential and units of consumption are less than or equal to 200, then the rate is 0.8, according to Table 6.1. If the units are not less than or equal to 200, then the rate is made equal to 0.7. Complete the coding for this part of the logic.

```
if (u <= 200)
    rate =        ;
else
    rate =        ;
```

```
//EXAMPLE 6.1  No error checking is done.
#include <stdio.h>
void main (void)
{
    int i, diameter,
        No_of_Quarters = 0, No_of_Dimes = 0,
        No_of_Nickels = 0, No_of_Pennies = 0;

    printf("Enter 20 coin diameters:\n");
    for(i = 1; i <= 20; i = i + 1)
    {
        scanf("%d", &diameter);
        if( diameter == 24)
           No_of_Quarters = No_of_Quarters + 1;
        else
           if( diameter != 21)
              if( diameter == 19)
                 No_of_Pennies = No_of_Pennies + 1;
              else
                 No_of_Dimes = No_of_Dimes + 1;
           else
              No_of_Nickels = No_of_Nickels + 1;
    }
    printf("Total number of Quarters = %d\n",  No_of_Quarters);
    printf("Total number of Dimes    = %d\n",  No_of_Dimes);
    printf("Total number of Nickels  = %d\n",  No_of_Nickels);
    printf("Total number of Pennies  = %d\n",  No_of_Pennies);
    printf("Total amount in Dollars= $%.2f\n", No_of_Quarters  * 0.25 +
                                               No_of_Dimes     * 0.10 +
                                               No_of_Nickels   * 0.05 +
                                               No_of_Pennies   * 0.01);
}
----- output -----(after entering 24, 18, 18, 24, 21, 18, 19, 21, 24,
                     18, 18, 18, 19, 24, 24, 19, 19, 21, 19, 19)
Total number of Quarters = 5
Total number of Dimes    = 6
Total number of Nickels  = 3
Total number of Pennies  = 6
Total amount in Dollars  = $2.06
```

Solution 6.1
```
if(u <= 200)
   rate = 0.8;
else
   rate = 0.7;
```

Drill 6.2 Suppose we wanted the following code instead. What condition would have to be used in the if statement? We want the same result as before, but the if statement is to be constructed differently.

```
if(          )
   rate =  0.7;
else
   rate =  0.8;
```

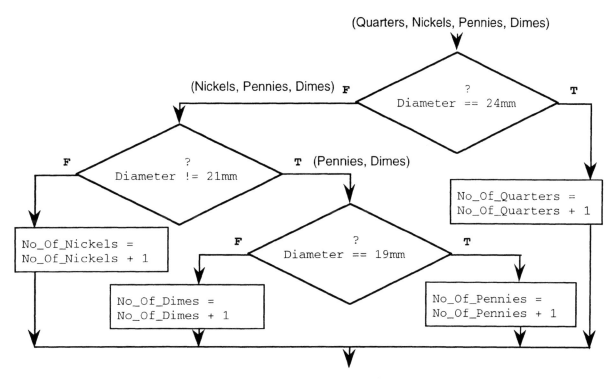

Figure 6.2 Flowchart for the logic of the coin sorter.

The Consecutive Coin Toss Example

As a second example of if–then–else logic, let us look at another coin problem. Two people have decided to flip coins and determine who wins by tossing the maximum number of consecutive tosses. Look at the output of Example 6.2. The h stands for "heads" and t stands for "tails." Even though heads won 7 times and tails won only 5 times, tails won the game because tails had the most number of consecutive tosses. Data is entered until a q terminates it. Follow the program, flowchart, and tracechart in Figure 6.3 (see page 82) as the logic is explained.

First, let us go over the meaning of the variables. *toss* contains the side of the coin that was flipped most recently, and *last_toss* contains the previous coin flip. *count* contains the current number of consecutive flips, whether they be heads or tails. *head_maximum* contains the maximum number of consecutive tosses that were all heads; similarly *tail_maximum* contains the maximum number of consecutive tail flips. As long as the current flip is the same as the previous one, we add

Solution 6.2 If units are equal to 200, we want the rate to be 0.8. In this solution, the condition would be false, which would make rate equal to 0.8 in the else clause. The "reverse" or negative of <= is >, the negative of >= is <, and the negative of != is ==.

```
if(u > 200)
```

Drill 6.3 Now draw the flowchart that will include the two types of customers. First test if t == 'r'. For both the true (residential) and the false (commercial) side of that condition, we must add the condition of units <= 200? Last, use Table 6.1 to determine the rates for each of the four instances.

one to *count*. Once the current flip is different from the last one, we adjust the maximum for the last one if the new *count* is greater than the maximum and start counting from 1 again.

Before we start the loop, we will need to read two tosses, so that the variable *toss* will contain the current coin flip and *last_toss* will contain the previous coin flip. The for loop continues until a q is entered.

Inside the for loop, the first thing that we check is whether or not the current toss is the same as the previous toss. If it is, then we simply add 1 to *count*, save the current *toss* into *last_toss*, and read in the next *toss*.

If the current *toss* is different from the previous one, we find out if the current *toss* is heads. If it is, and *count* is greater than *tail_maximum*, we make *tail_maximum* equal to *count*. We do the same thing if the current toss is tails. In either case, we set the count to 1, set *last_toss* to *toss*, and read the next one.

Let us look at the partial tracechart shown in Figure 6.3. Before the loop, we read in two heads: *toss* and *last_toss*. Inside the loop, the condition toss == last_toss? is true, so we simply add 1 to *count*, and read the next *toss*, which is also heads.

The second time through the loop, the condition toss == last_toss? is again true, so *count* now becomes 3. *last_toss* becomes heads and tails is read into *toss*.

The third through the loop, the condition toss == last_toss? is false. toss != 'h'? is also false. count > head_maximum? is true, so *head_maximum* is set to *count* or 3. *count* becomes 1, indicating that now we are counting the number of consecutive tails.

In the fourth iteration of the loop, we find ourselves with another heads. So toss == last_toss? is false, *toss* is equal to heads, and *tail_maximum* is assigned the value of *count*, this time, making it 1.

```
//EXAMPLE 6.2
#include <stdio.h>
#define HEAD 'h'
void main (void)
{
    char toss;              // Side of the coin for the current toss.
    char last_toss;         // Side of the coin for the previous toss.
    int  count = 1;         // Number of previous consecutive coin tosses.
    int tail_maximum = 0;   // Maximum number of consecutive tail tosses.
    int head_maximum = 0;   // Maximum number of consecutive head tosses.

    printf("Enter h, for heads; t, for tails; q for quit: \n");
    scanf(" %c", &toss);
```

Solution 6.3

Drill 6.4 Now convert the flow-chart into code.

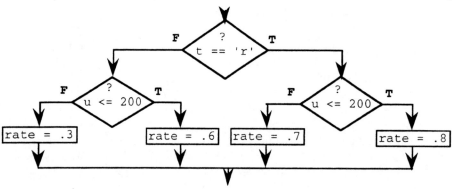

The if Statement

```
   if(toss == HEAD) head_maximum = 1; else tail_maximum = 1;

   last_toss = toss;      // "last_toss" contains the last heads or tails
   scanf(" %c", &toss);   // "toss" contains the current heads or tails

   for(  ; toss != 'q'; )
   {
      if(toss == last_toss)
         count = count + 1;           //No change from the last one, add 1.
      else
      {
         if(toss == HEAD)             //End of string of 't's.
            if(count > tail_maximum)  //If needed, adjust maximum for tails.
               tail_maximum = count;
            else;                     //Line 1. Because of this "else," . .
         else                         //this one matches the correct "if."
            if(count > head_maximum)
               head_maximum = count;
         count = 1;                   //Start counting again.
      }
      last_toss = toss;               //Set "last_toss" to the current one
      scanf(" %c", &toss);            //And get the new one.
   }

   if(last_toss == HEAD) if(count > head_maximum) head_maximum = count;
   if(last_toss != HEAD) if(count > tail_maximum) tail_maximum = count;

   if(tail_maximum == head_maximum) //Print the report of who won.
      printf("It's a Tie!\n");
   else
      if(tail_maximum > head_maximum)
         printf("Heads wins!\n");
      else
         printf(Tails wins!\n");
}

----- output ----- (after entering h h h t h h h t t t h q)
Tails wins!
```

Solution 6.4

```
   if(t == 'r')
      if (u <= 200)
         rate = 0.8;
      else
         rate = 0.7;
   else
      if(u <= 200)
         rate = 0.6;
      else
         rate = 0.3;
```

Drill 6.5 Now draw a flowchart for the same logic, but instead of dividing the logic first by the type of customer, divide it first by the units consumed. Start with u <= 200, then on both sides of the flowchart test for t == 'r'. Also write the code for the flowchart.

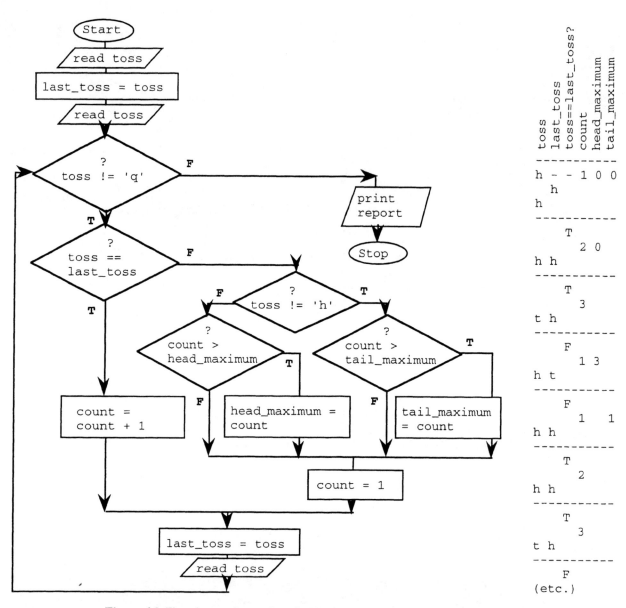

Figure 6.3 Flowchart and tracechart for the consecutive coin toss example.

Solution 6.5

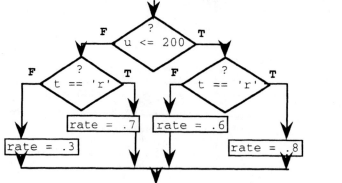

```
if (u <= 200)
    if(t == 'r')
        rate = 0.8;
    else
        rate = 0.6;
else
    if(t == 'r')
        rate = 0.7;
    else
        rate = 0.3;
```

The if Statement

The loop continues until a q is entered. Then the report is printed. If the maximums for heads and tails are equal, then a tie is declared; otherwise, a winner is declared.

Now let us look at the else, on Line 1 in the program. This extra else is needed so that the following else matches the false side of the if(toss == HEAD) statement. The semicolon after the else means do the null statement, or do nothing. Another way to force proper matching of the else is to use braces:

```
if(toss == HEAD)
{
    if(count > tail_maximum)
        tail_maximum = count;
}
else
    if(count > head_maximum)
        head_maximum = count; // . . . and so on.
```

And, Or, Not, and break

In this section, we go a few steps further and explore how to combine two decisions into one, how to negate or reverse a logical expression, and how to terminate a loop in midstream if, for example, an abnormal condition has occurred. Only the for loop of Example 6.2 has been rewritten into Example 6.3 to illustrate these topics.

The condition of toss != 'q'? in the for loop is equivalent to stating !(toss =='q'?). The exclamation mark, !, means a logical not; that is, is toss =='q'? negated? Although here the not or ! makes the logical expression more complicated, in other places, you will find that it simplifies it.

What does Example 6.3 do when characters other than the ones allowed are entered by mistake? Look at the first if inside the loop. The operator || is called the logical or operator and the && is called the logical and operator. If the user entered a q, then the loop would stop and we don't need to test for that condition. We want to abnormally terminate the loop only if the *toss* were something other than an h *or* a t. Notice the or in the last sentence. In the English language it is correct to use "or," but logically, it is necessary to use the and operator instead.

What we want to express logically is this: is toss not equal to 'h' and not equal to 't'? The expression toss != 'h' || toss != 't'? is true for all values of *toss*. For example, if *toss* were equal to 'h', then the first part of the expression would be false but the second part would be true. One should always avoid using the not logical operator in conditional expressions.

If the *toss* isn't an h or a t, then the value of *toss* is printed and the keyword "break" forces the control of program execution to exit out of the loop. In Unit 8, we will review nested loops, that

Drill 6.6 Now we turn our attention to a different type of problem. The more practice we have with a variety of logic problems, the better prepared we will be for whatever we encounter.

We will read in three integers: *a*, *b*, and *c*. We want to construct the logic so that, no matter how these numbers were provided by the user, the output will always be the three numbers printed in order. For example, if we read in 40, 20, 60 into *a*, *b*, and *c*, respectively, then our logic would print *b*, *a*, and *c*, in that order. This will give an output of 20, 40, and 60. Or if we read in 70, 10, 60, then the output would be *b*, *c*, and *a* in that order. This will give an output of 10, 60, and 70.

    1. If *a* is greater than *b* and *b* is greater than *c*, is *a* greater than *c*?

    2. Is there any variable that we can say is the largest?

    3. Is there any variable that we can say is the smallest?

    4. If *a* is greater than *b* and *c* is greater than *b*, is *a* greater than *c*?

    5. Is there any variable that we can say is the largest?

    6. Is there any variable that we can say is the smallest?

is, loops inside loops. In such a case, the break statement would terminate only the inside loop, but the outer one would continue.

```
//EXAMPLE 6.3 This is a variation of Example 6.2.
for( ; !(toss == 'q'); )
{
   if(toss != 'h' && toss != 't')
   {
      printf("%c is not a valid entry\n", toss);
      break;
   }
   if(toss == last_toss)
      count = count + 1;
   else
   {
      if((toss == HEAD) && (count > tail_maximum))
         tail_maximum = count;
      if((toss != HEAD) &&  (count > head_maximum))
         head_maximum = count;
      count = 1;
   }
   last_toss = toss;
   scanf(" %c", &toss);
}
```

Example 6.3 also shows how nested if's from Example 6.2 are combined into one if using the and or the && logical operator. The result is the same in both examples.

EXPERIMENTS

In this unit we experiment with the if statement, which is similar to the for loop because they both test for conditions. The only difference between the two is that the for loop is a loop and the if statement is not. We use a grading system where grades from 0 to 59 are F's, 60 to 69 are D's, 70 to 79 are C's, 80 to 89 are B's, and 90 to 100 are A's. For the first twelve experiments enter the following data and press the Return key after each number:

79	91	80	59	100	60	89	45	90

Solution 6.6
1. Yes, *a* must be greater than *c*.
2. *a* is the largest.
3. And *c* is the smallest. Suppose that you are taller than me and I tell you that I am taller than my child at home, then we know that you are taller than my child.
4. No.
5. Yes, *a* is the largest because it is greater than the other two.
6. No, either *b* or *c* could be the smallest. Suppose that I (a) am taller than you (b) and I tell you that I (a) am also taller than my brother (c) who is at home. Then we know that I am the tallest. However, to determine who is the smallest, we need to compare my brother with you.

Drill 6.7 To begin to develop this logic, draw a partial flowchart that starts with the comparison of a > b?. On its true side, there is another decision diamond that compares b > c? Also, print the order of the three variables for the case when it can be determined.

84   The if Statement

Exp 6.1 With the if statement, if the condition is true, then "fail" is printed; otherwise (or else) "pass" is printed. Show the output; *i* and *k* are integers.

```
for(i = 1; i <= 7; i = i + 1)
{
    scanf("%d", &k);
    if(k < 60)
        printf("Fail\n");
    else
        printf("Pass!\n");
}
```

a. If the grade is less than 60, what is printed?
b. If the grade is 60 or more, what is printed?

Exp 6.2 Here only < 60 is replaced. Complete the program so that the output here is the same as that of Experiment 6.1. No output is necessary here.

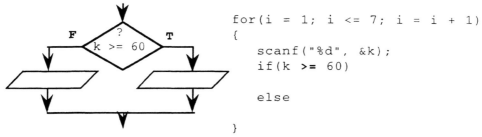

```
for(i = 1; i <= 7; i = i + 1)
{
    scanf("%d", &k);
    if(k >= 60)

    else

}
```

a. If the grade is 60 or more, what is printed?
b. If the grade isn't 60 or more, what is printed?

Exp 6.3 One doesn't have to have a matching else and if. However, you could have two consecutive if's. Again, complete the two if's so that the result would be the same as before.

```
for(i = 1; i <= 7; i = i + 1)
{
    scanf("%d", &k);
    if(k >= 60)

    if(k < 60)

}
```

Solution 6.7 If *a* is greater than *b* and *b* is greater than *c*, then we know that *a* is the largest, followed by *b* and last by *c*.

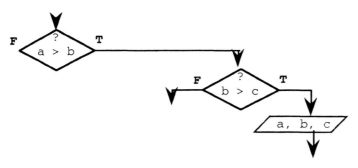

Drill 6.8 On the false side of b > c?, which variable do we know for sure is the largest or the smallest? Add an appropriate diamond there and show a printf() on both sides of the diamond.

Exp 6.4 Again, complete the two if's so that the result will be the same as before.

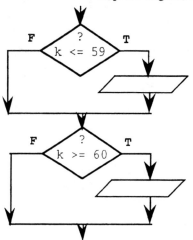

```
for(i = 1; i <= 7; i = i + 1)
{
    scanf("%d", &k);
    if(k <= 59)


    if(k >= 60)


}
```

a. Could you replace the second if with simply else?
b. Could you replace the first if with simply else?

Exp 6.5 This time let us count the number of passes and fails. Place passes = passes + 1; and fails = fails + 1; under the proper if's.

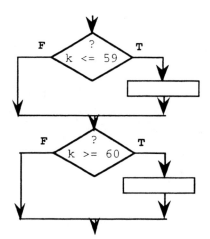

```
int i, k, passes = 0, fails = 0;
for(i = 1; i <= 7; i = i + 1)
{
    scanf("%d", &k);
    if(k <= 59)


    if(k >= 60)


}
printf("Number of passes = %d\n", passes);
printf("Number of fails = %d\n", fails);
```

Exp 6.6 This time let us see who got A's and who didn't. Complete the two if's using either > or <. Remember: Those who received 90 or above receive an A. When you try your solution by running it, you should end up with 2 who received A's and 5 who didn't receive A's.

Solution 6.8 On the false side of b > c?, we know that *a* is greater than *b* and *c* is greater than (or equal to) *b*. Since *b* is the smallest, we need a diamond to determine the relationship between *a* and *c*. On the false side of that diamond, *c* is the largest, *a* is next, and *b* is the smallest. On the true side of it, we have the same order, but the *a* and *c* are switched.

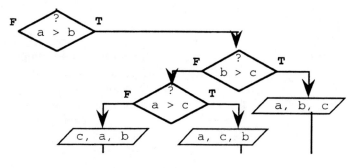

Drill 6.9 On the false side of a > b?, add a diamond that checks b > c?. Then show one printf() on the correct side of the diamond that prints the variables in order without requiring an additional diamond.

The if Statement

```
                          for(i = 1; i <= 7; i = i + 1)
                          {
                              scanf("%d", &k);
                              if(k        )
                                  printf("It's an A!\n");
                              if(k           )
                                  printf("It's not an A\n");
                          }
```

a. How would the if's be written if you had used >= and <= instead?

Exp 6.7 Notice that if *k* is greater than 89, then an A gets printed. Otherwise, out of those who got less than 90, the next if selects the B's and the final else selects those who received less than 80. Show the output and complete the flowchart for only the if statements.

```
                          for(i = 1; i <= 7; i = i + 1)
                          {
                              scanf("%d", &k);
                              if(k > 89)                    // Only A's
                                  printf("A\n");
                              else                          // Non-A's.
                                  if(k > 79)                // Only B's
                                      printf("B\n");
                                  else                      // Others
                                      printf("not an A or B\n");
                          }
```

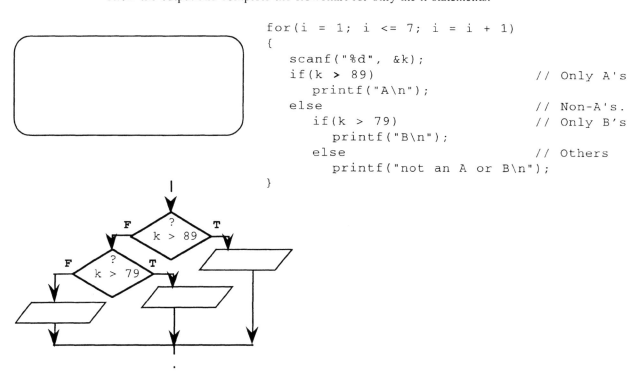

Solution 6.9

Drill 6.10 Complete the flowchart by adding an a > c? diamond on the true side.

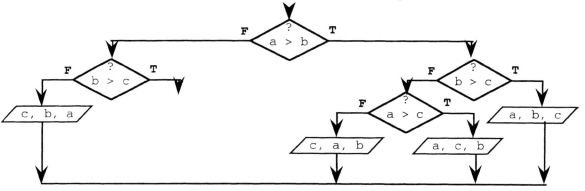

The if Statement

Exp 6.8 This experiment will count the number of A's, B's, and the lower grades. The logic has been rearranged. Complete the flowchart and the program. Place these three statements properly: lower = lower + 1; a = a + 1; and b = b + 1;.

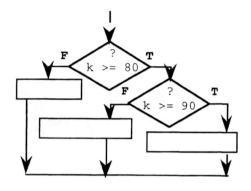

```
int i, k, a = 0, b = 0, lower = 0;
for(i = 1; i <= 7; i = i + 1)
{
    scanf("%d", &k);
    if(k >= 80)
        if(k >= 90)

        else

    else

}
printf("A's= %d\t B's= %d\t Lower= %d\n",
        a, b, lower);
```

Exp 6.9 This experiment should give the same result as Experiment 6.8. Only the logic has been rearranged. Complete the flowchart and the program so that the output is the same as before.

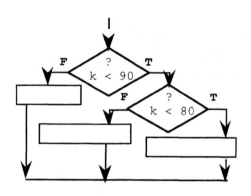

```
for(i = 1; i <= 7; i = i + 1)
{
    scanf("%d", &k);
    if(k < 90)
        if(k < 80)

        else

    else

}
printf("A's= %d\t B's= %d\t Lower= %d\n",
        a, b, lower);
```

Solution 6.10

Drill 6.11 If a = 5, b = 10, and c = 3, through how many decisions would the logic flow? Convert this into code.

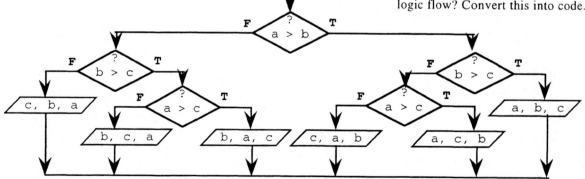

Exp 6.10 Now let us test the conditions for all five grades, namely, A, B, C, D, and F. In the blank spaces, for each grade, place the appropriate statement of this type: printf("A\n");. Each else that is lined up under an if is that condition's false side.

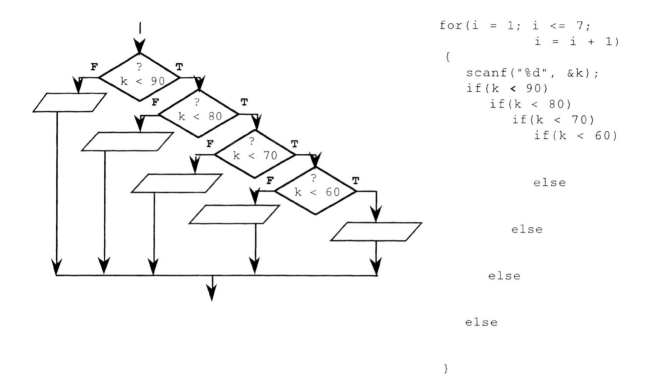

```
for(i = 1;  i <= 7;
              i = i + 1)
{
    scanf("%d", &k);
    if(k < 90)
        if(k < 80)
            if(k < 70)
                if(k < 60)


                else


            else


        else


    else


}
```

a. On the F side of k < 90? only A grades are selected. On the T side of that condition, which grades are selected, A, B, C, D, and/or F?
b. On the T side of k < 80?, which grades are selected?
c. On the T side of k < 70?, which grades are selected? What about on the F side?
d. Grades that end up getting a B must go through how many decision diamonds?
e. Grades that end up getting a D must go through how many decision diamonds?

Solution 6.11 a > b? is false, b > c? is true, and a > c? is true. The answer is 3.

```
if(a > b)
    if(b > c)
        printf("%d %d %d\n", a, b, c);
    else
        if(a > c)
            printf("%d %d %d\n", a, c, b);
        else
            printf("%d %d %d\n", c, a, b);
else
    if(b > c)
        if(a > c)
            printf("%d %d %d\n", b, a, c);
        else
            printf("%d %d %d\n", b, c, a);
    else
        printf("%d %d %d\n", c, b, a);
```

Drill 6.12 Let us reconstruct the same logic differently. For the first diamond, use a > c?. For both sides of that diamond, add an a > b? diamond. Show two places where the order of the variables can be determined without requiring any other decision diamonds.

The if Statement

Exp 6.11 Perform the same steps as in Experiment 6.10. However, since the logic is rearranged, the printf()'s will need to be placed at different locations.

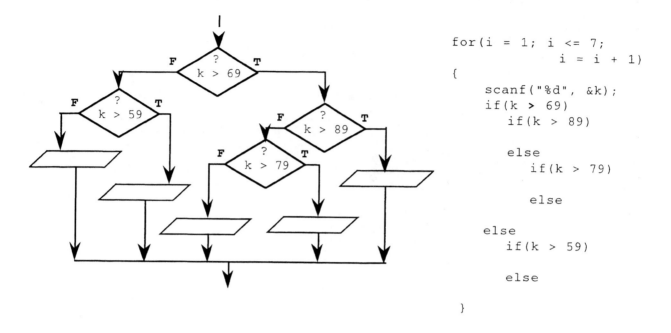

```
for(i = 1; i <= 7;
            i = i + 1)
{
    scanf("%d", &k);
    if(k > 69)
       if(k > 89)

          else
             if(k > 79)

             else

    else
       if(k > 59)

       else


}
```

a. F grades will go through two conditions: k > 69?, which would be false, and k > 59?, which also would be false. D grades go through how many conditions?
b. C grades go through how many conditions?
c. B grades go through how many conditions?
d. If k > 79? were changed to k <= 80?, then what changes would be necessary in the flowchart?
e. When a grade that is read into the variable *k* enters this set of nested if's, it has a choice of going through how many different paths?
f. The control of execution may take how many different paths at any one time?

Exp 6.12 Perform the same steps as in Experiments 6.10 and 6.11. However, count the number of grades in each category instead of printing them.

Solution 6.12 If *a* is greater than *c* and *b* is greater than *a*, then we know that *b* is the largest and *c* is the smallest. On the left side of the flowchart, *c* is greater than *a* and *a* is greater than *b*; hence, the order of the variables is *c, a, b*.

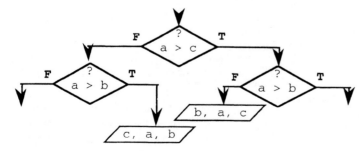

Drill 6.13 Add b > c? at two places in the flowchart and complete it.

The if Statement

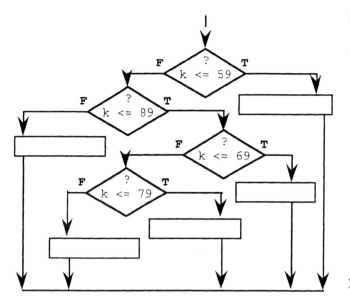

```
for(i = 1; i <= 7;
                  i = i + 1)
{
    scanf("%d", &k);
    if(k <= 59)

    else
        if(k <= 89)
            if(k <= 69)

            else
                if(k <= 79)

                else

            else

}
```

```
printf("A's= %d\t", a);
printf("B's= %d\t", b);
printf("C's= %d\t", c);
printf("D's= %d\t", d);
printf("F's= %d\n", f);
```

For each of these questions, choose from among the grades of A, B, C, D, and F.
a. Which grade(s) are selected on the true side of k <= 59?
b. Which grade(s) are selected on the false side of k <= 59?
c. Which grade(s) are selected on the false side of k <= 89?
d. Which grade(s) are selected on the true side of k <= 89?
e. Which grade(s) are selected on the true side of k <= 69?
f. Which grade(s) are selected on the false side of k <= 69?
g. Which grade(s) are selected on the true side of k <= 79?
h. Which grade(s) are selected on the false side of k <= 79?

In the remainder of the experiments, we will be learning how to find the smallest or the largest number as they are entered by the user.

Solution 6.13

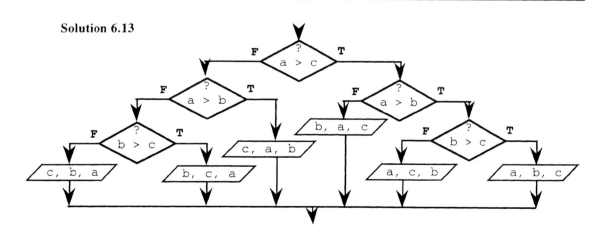

Exp 6.13 When running this program, enter the following integers: 16, 22, 13, 19, 11, –1. The program will determine the smallest number entered.

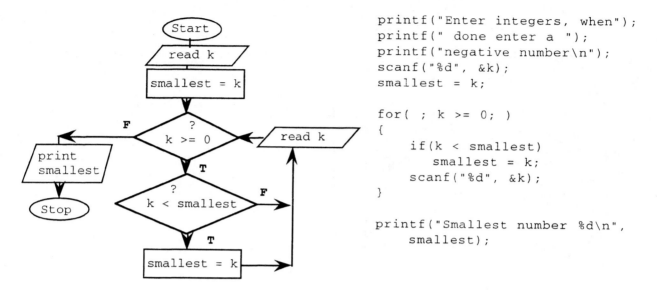

```
printf("Enter integers, when");
printf(" done enter a ");
printf("negative number\n");
scanf("%d", &k);
smallest = k;

for( ; k >= 0; )
{
    if(k < smallest)
        smallest = k;
    scanf("%d", &k);
}

printf("Smallest number %d\n",
    smallest);
```

a. Draw a tracechart.
b. What was the first value of the variable *smallest*?
c. The first time that the condition in the if statement was encountered, what were the values of *k* and *smallest*?
d. The second time that the if condition was tested, what were the values of *k* and *smallest*?
e. The third time that the if condition was tested, what were the values of *k* and *smallest*?
f. During the loop, the value of *smallest* was changed. What were the different values of *smallest*?
g. Does an if statement require a corresponding else statement?
h. Is the scanf() executed inside the loop when the k < smallest is true or false, or irrespective of it?
i. If the data entered were 11, 22, 13, 19, 16, –1, how many times would *smallest* be changed?

Drill 6.14 Below are six sets of values of *a*, *b*, and *c*. For each problem, label the value of each decision (true, false, or N/A). Also, write the order of the variables as they will be printed. The first one is done.

Problem	a	b	c	"a > c"	"a > b"	"b > c"	Order of variables
1	4	1	5	F	T	N/A	c, a, b
2	8	6	5				
3	2	7	1				
4	5	2	4				
5	3	8	9				
6	5	8	6				

Exp 6.14 When running this program, enter the following integers: 16, 22, 13, 19, 11, −1. The program will determine the smallest number entered.

```
printf("Enter integers, when done enter a negative number\n");
scanf("%d", &k);
smallest = k;
for( ; k >= 0; )
{
   if(k < smallest)
   {
      smallest = k;
      printf("smallest has just been changed to %d\n", smallest);
   }
   scanf("%d", &k);
}
printf("Smallest number was %d\n", smallest);
```

    a. Draw the flowchart.
    b. When running this program, how many times did *smallest* change?
    c. When running this program with the following data, 11, 22, 13, 19, 16, −1, how many times did *smallest* change?
    d. Are the braces lined up with the if statement necessary to give the same result?
    e. Now try to alter the program so that it also prints the data item that was entered. For example, with the following data, 11, 22, 13, 19, 16, −1; this should be printed: "the smallest is 11 and it was data item number 1." If you can't do it, don't be concerned. The solution is in the next experiment.

Exp 6.15 When running this program, enter the following integers: 16, 22, 13, 19, 11, −1. The program will determine the smallest number entered.

Solution 6.14

Problem	a	b	c	"a > c"	"a > b"	"b > c"	Order of variables
1	4	1	5	F	T	N/A	c, a, b
2	8	6	5	T	T	T	a, b, c
3	2	7	1	T	F	N/A	b, a, c
4	5	2	4	T	T	F	a, c, b
5	3	8	9	F	F	F	c, b, a
6	5	8	6	F	F	T	b, c, a

```
printf("Enter integers, when done enter a negative number\n");
scanf("%d", &k);
smallest = k;
item_num = 1;
for(i = 1; k >= 0; i = i  + 1)
{
   if(k < smallest)
   {
      smallest = k;
      item_num = i;
   }
   scanf("%d", &k);
}
printf("Smallest number was %d\n", smallest);
printf("and it was data item number %d\n", item_num);
```

Draw a tracechart and note how *i* and *item_num* change.

Now try altering the program so that it prints the smallest and the largest numbers at the end of the loop. You may disregard the variable *item_num*. However, you will now need a variable called *largest*.

Exp 6.16 When running this program, enter the following integers: 16, 22, 13, 19, 11, –1. The program will determine the smallest and the largest numbers entered.

```
printf("Enter integers, when done enter a negative number\n");
scanf("%d", &k);
smallest = k;
largest = k;
for (; k >= 0; )
{
   if (k < smallest)
      smallest = k;
   if (k > largest)
      largest = k;
   scanf("%d", &k);
}
printf("Smallest number was %d\n", smallest);
printf("Largest number was %d\n", largest);
```

Drill 6.15 Now let us combine conditions by using the logical and, or, and not operators. The operator for and is &&, for or it is ||, and for not it is !. For example, x == 1 || x == 2 is true only if *x* is equal to 1 or 2. Likewise, the expression x == 1 && y == 3 is true only if *x* is equal to 1 and *y* is equal to 3. Complete the following chart. Notice that when one condition is false and the other is true, the result of anding them becomes false because both conditions must be true for the result to be true. However, when oring them, only one has to be true for the outcome to be true.

Condition1	Condition2	Condition1 && Condition2	Condition1 || Condition2
F	F		
F	T	F	T
T	F		
T	T		

a. Draw the flowchart.
b. What were the different values of the *smallest* and the *largest* variables?
c. Is it possible for both if statements to be true for a given *k*?
d. When using the following data, 16, 12, 17, 19, 11, –1, what were the different values of *smallest*? What were the different values of *largest*?

Exp 6.17 Now let's try the break command. Run the following program twice. For the first run, use 10 positive integers; for the second, use 5, 12, 7, 2, –3.

```
int sum = 0,   flag = 0;
printf("Enter 10 integers, when done enter a negative number\n");
for (i = 1; i <= 10; i = i + 1)
{
    scanf("%d", &k);
    if(k < 0)
    {
        flag = 1;
        break;
    }
    sum = sum + k;
}
if(flag == 1)
    printf("Unacceptable data\n");
else
    printf("Sum = %d\n", sum);
```

a. When all positive numbers were entered, how many times did the loop execute?
b. When a negative number was entered, did the loop execute the same number of times?
c. What do you think the break statement does?
d. When do you think that it may come in handy?
e. The for and if statements use parentheses. Functions such as printf() and strcpy() also use parentheses. Does break use parentheses?

Solution 6.15 And is true only if both conditions are true; or is false only if both conditions are false.

Condition1	Condition2	Condition1 && Condition2	Condition1 || Condition2
F	F	F	F
F	T	F	T
T	F	F	T
T	T	T	T

Drill 6.16 The condition ! (x == 1) is true as long as *x* is not equal to 1. The ! reverses the logic. It can also be expressed as x != 1. If a condition is true, then "not"ing it makes it false and if it is false, then "not"ing it makes it true. Similar to the table above, show the two–entry table for condition1, which has the values of F and T, and the not of condition1.

QUESTIONS

For all questions and programs it is very important to indent properly. Experienced programmers have said that they would rather have a non-working program that is correctly indented and documented rather than a working program that is sloppy.

Try using the same relational operator throughout a flowchart. For example, use only the >= operator in a given flowchart.

Keep the true on the right side and false on the left side of decision diamonds wherever possible. These rules make the logic easy to follow.

1. Indent correctly and draw the flowchart for the following.

```
if (sex == 'm') if (age > 50) mold = mold + 1; else myoung = myoung + 1;
else if (age > 50) fold = fold + 1; else fyoung = fyoung + 1;
```

2. Indent correctly and draw the flowchart for the following.

```
if (age > 50) { if(smokes == 'y') if (weight > 150) risk_factor = 10;
else risk_factor = 7; else if(weight > 150) risk_factor = 5; else
risk_factor = 2; if (exercises == 'n') risk_factor = risk_factor + 2; }
else printf("forget about it\n");
```

3. Using only the < operator, complete the following flowchart by adding decision diamonds and prints. Like Experiments 6.10 through 6.12, the flowchart is supposed to print the letter grade, given the numeric grade, k.

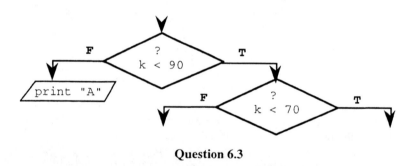

Question 6.3

Solution 6.16

```
          Condition1  !Condition1
          ----------  -----------
              F            T
              T            F
```

Drill 6.17 Complete the truth table for this chart and combine the three kinds of logic. Find the nots of both conditions and then and them.

Cond1	Cond2	!Cond1	!Cond2	(!Cond1) && (!Cond2)
F	F			
F	T	T	F	F
T	F			
T	T			

The if Statement

4. Follow the same procedure as in Question 3, except use only the >= operator.

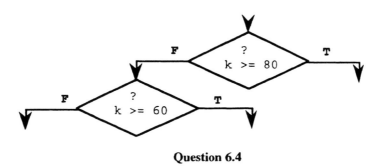

Question 6.4

5. Using Table 6.2, complete the following flowchart to assign the proper value of rate. The procedure is similar to Drills 6.1 through 6.5. Also write the coding.

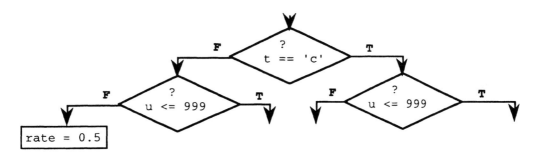

Question 6.5

Units Used	Residential	Commercial
0 < units <= 200	0.8	0.6
200 < units <= 900	0.7	0.3
Above 900	0.5	0.2

Table 6.2 Rate table for Questions 5 and 6

Solution 6.17

Cond1	Cond2	!Cond1	!Cond2	(!Cond1) && (!Cond2)
F	F	T	T	T
F	T	T	F	F
T	F	F	T	F
T	T	F	F	F

Drill 6.18 Complete the following chart and state whether (!Cond1) && (!Cond2)) is equivalent to !(Cond1 || Cond2).

Cond1	Cond2	Cond1 || Cond2	!(Cond1 || Cond2)
F	F		
F	T	T	F
T	F		
T	T		

6. Follow the same procedure as in Question 5.

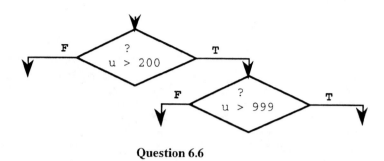

Question 6.6

7. Like the procedures in Drills 6.6 through 6.14, complete the flowchart so that the variables *a*, *b*, and *c* are printed in descending order.

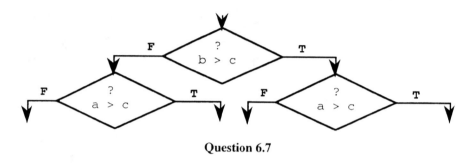

Question 6.7

8. Follow the same procedure as in Question 7.

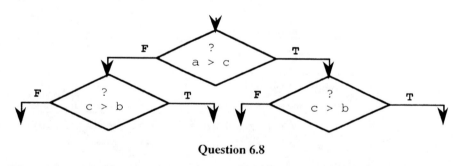

Question 6.8

Solution 6.18 Yes, they are equivalent. They both have the same logic chart.

Cond1	Cond2	Cond1 || Cond2	!(Cond1 || Cond2)
F	F	F	T
F	T	T	F
T	F	T	F
T	T	T	F

Drill 6.19 Now let us do some indenting. Always indent after every if and else, unless there is a brace following them. Match every else with the last unmatched if under the same column. else's and braces should be on lines by themselves. Try indenting the following correctly:

```
if(x == 'y') if(age > 40) ans = 10; else ans = 20; else ans = 30;
```

The if Statement

PROGRAMS

1. Write a complete program that will ask for a person's name and his or her game score. Then it will ask for a second person's score. The program will print the winner's name and also print by how many points that person won.

2. This program will read a float and a character for each scanf(). The character could be d for deposit or w for withdrawl. Starting with a balance of zero, add the deposits and subtract the withdrawals until the balance becomes negative. Then print by how much the balance went negative. Consider the output from the following data:

```
----- output -----
100.0 d
20.0  d
60.0  w
200.0 w
Your account now is -140.00 dollars.
```

3. Men and women are running races. We need to know what was the lowest men's score and the highest women's score. Data are given so that men's scores alternate with those of women: first men's, then women's. The program stops when a time of zero is read for a man's score.

```
----- output -----
7.80
5.70
5.80
8.95
0.0
Lowest men's: 5.80
Highest women's: 8.95
```

Solution 6.19

```
if(x == 'y')
   if(age > 40)      //This line is indented because it follows an if.
      ans = 10;      //This line is indented because it follows an if.
   else              //This else is under the last unmatched if.
      ans = 20;      //This line is indented because it follows an else.
else                 //This else is under the last unmatched if.
   ans = 30;         //This line is indented because it follows an else.
```

Drill 6.20 Rewrite this code using correct indentation.

```
if(x < 0) if (y == 1) printf("a\n"); else if(y == 2) printf("b\n"); else
printf("c\n"); else printf("d\n");
```

The if Statement   99

OPTIONAL TOPICS

Evaluating Conditions

Try running this program:

```
for(i = 1; 5 - i; i = i + 1)
   printf("%d\n", i);
printf("End of loop\n");
```

Notice that the loop runs only 5 times and then stops. What is really strange in the for loop is that 5 – i is not a condition at all; it is an arithmetic expression. How is that interpreted?

Whenever an arithmetic expression evaluates to zero, that expression is considered to have a false value. Conversely, whenever an expression is non-zero, it is considered to be true. Hence, for the first four values of *i*, 5 – i has a non-zero or a true value. When *i* becomes 5, then 5 – i becomes zero, the expression becomes false, and the loop stops.

Writing conditions like this takes fewer instruction cycles from the CPU, and the code runs faster than if conditional operators were used.

The Conditional Operator, ?:

Whenever one value has to be assigned to a variable if a certain condition is true and another has to be assigned to that same variable if it is false, then the conditional operator can be used. Here again the following code is converted to the one below it.

```
if(x == 'y')             // These
   answer = 1;           //    four
else                     //       lines
   answer = 0;           //          are converted to

answer = (x == 'y') ? 1 : 0;  // this one.
```

The switch Statement

An organized way to write if statements that depend on the value of one variable is to use the switch statement. The following code is converted to the switch statement below. The breaks are required for all the cases except for the last one. Also, the default case is optional.

Solution 6.20

```
if(x < 0)
   if(y == 1)
      printf("a\n");
   else
      if(y == 2)
         printf("b\n");
      else
         printf("c\n");
else
   printf("d\n");
```

Drill 6.21 Remember: A standard for indentation is needed to help programmers and not the compilers. Indent this code correctly:

```
if(x == 0) printf("a\n"); if(x < 0) {
printf("b\n"); count = count + 1; } else
if(y == 't) { printf("c\n"); count =
count - 1; } else count = 0;
```

100

The if Statement

```
If(operator == 'd')
   balance = balance + amount;
else
   if(operator == 'w')
      balance = balance - amount;
   else
      printf("%c not allowed\n", operator);
```

This nested if is equivalent to the following switch statement:

```
switch (operator)  //This is the converted code.
{
   case 'd' :
         balance = balance + amount;
         break;
   case 'w' :
         balance = balance - amount;
         break;
   default  :
         printf("%c not allowed\n", operator);
}
```

Solution 6.21

```
if(x == 0)
   printf("a\n");          //Indent after an if.
if(x < 0)                  //This is not part of the previous "if;" it's a new statement.
{                          //Put braces on a line by themselves. Start of an if block.
   printf("b\n");          //Indent after an if.
   count = count + 1;      //Still under the same if and part of the same "if-block."
}                          //Match the closed brace with the last unmatched open brace.
else                       //Match the else with the last unmatched if.
   if(y == 't')            //Indent after an if.
   {                       //Start of an "if-block."
      printf("c\n");       //Indent after an if.
      count = count - 1;   //Another statement under the same if.
   }                       //Match the braces
   else                    //Match the else with the last unmatched if.
      count = 0;           //Indent after an else.
```

1D Arrays

LESSON

Purpose and Basics of Arrays

Probably the most powerful thing about programming is the ability to perform tasks in a loop. One doesn't have to code data items individually. One codes the program once and uses that one code to process all data items through a loop.

Consider Example 7.1, where arrays are not used. Here game scores for four individuals are read in and they are printed in reverse order. Imagine how much more fun we would have coding if scores for a thousand players, say, around the country, have to be read and processed! Just reading and writing would take two thousand lines, let alone doing any other processing, such as finding the highest score.

```
//EXAMPLE 7.1
#include <stdio.h>
void main (void)
{
    float score1, score2, score3, score4;
    printf("Enter four floats: \n");
```

DRILLS

```
int a[5] = {3, 7, 4, 9, 6};
```

Drill 7.1 Here is an array with 5 elements. The name of the array is *a*. It is an array because it is defined with a set of brackets. The 5 inside the brackets indicates that it has 5 elements numbered from 0 to 4. The keyword, "int," means that each of these 5 slots holds an integer. a[0] is initialized to 3, a[1] is initialized to 7, and so on.

How is a[4] initialized?
Is a[5] initialized?

```
   scanf("%f", &score1);
   scanf("%f", &score2);
   scanf("%f", &score3);
   scanf("%f", &score4);
   printf("The scores in reverse order are:\n");
   printf("%.2f\n", score4);
   printf("%.2f\n", score3);
   printf("%.2f\n", score2);
   printf("%.2f\n", score1);
}
```

Instead, consider the solution using the arrays shown in Example 7.2 (the re–coding of Example 7.1 using arrays). Notice that, although the looping structures are slightly more complicated to code, there are fewer lines of coding. Also, if we wanted to extend the program to handle 1000 scores, then only the define statement would have to be changed — only one statement. The savings in the number of programming lines would also be evident every time we needed to process the scores any further.

```
//EXAMPLE 7.2
#define SIZE 4   // The size of the array.
#include <stdio.h>
void main (void)
{
   float score[SIZE];
   int i;
   printf("Enter %d floats: ", SIZE);      // Loop to read in the
   for(i = 0; i <= SIZE - 1; i = i + 1) // scores into the array.
      scanf("%f", &score[i]);

   printf("The scores in reverse order are:\n"); // Loop to write out the
   for(i = SIZE - 1; i >= 0; i = i - 1)           // scores from the array
      printf("%.2f\t", score[i]);
   printf("\n");
}
----- output -----
Enter 4 floats:
3.40     7.50     2.11     9.00
The scores in reverse order are:
9.00     2.11     7.50     3.40
```

Solution 7.1 a[4] is the last slot of the array. The number in that slot is initialized to 6. a[5] is not a valid slot in the array and it should not be referenced because the slots are numbered starting from 0.

Drill 7.2 "Index" is the term used to refer to a slot number.
a. What is the index where 4 is stored in the array?
b. What is the index where 9 is stored?
c. What is the highest index for *a[]*? What is the lowest index for *a[]*?
d. What is the index in the following expression: a[0]? What is the value stored there?

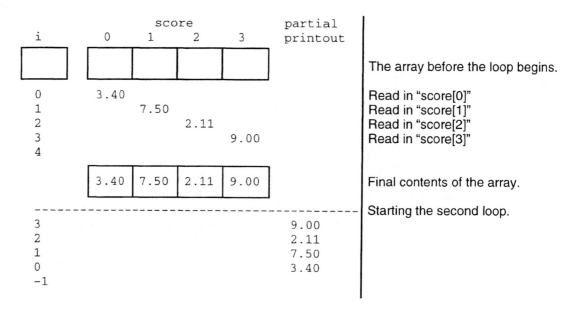

i	score 0	1	2	3	partial printout	
						The array before the loop begins.
0	3.40					Read in "score[0]"
1		7.50				Read in "score[1]"
2			2.11			Read in "score[2]"
3				9.00		Read in "score[3]"
4						
	3.40	7.50	2.11	9.00		Final contents of the array.
						Starting the second loop.
3					9.00	
2					2.11	
1					7.50	
0					3.40	
−1						

Figure 7.1 The tracechart for Example 7.2.

Arrays are identified easily by the brackets following their names, both in their declaration and in their usage. Here, *score[ ]* is an array. The variable *score[ ]* has brackets after it in its declaration. The number in the brackets is 4 because the value of SIZE is 4. This means that *score* has four elements associated with it. I will call them slots. Furthermore, since the array is declared as a float, *score* can store floating points in each of these slots. In Unit 2, we made arrays of type char called strings. Each slot of those arrays stored characters. With strings, a null character at the end signals where the last character is stored. With other kinds of arrays, a variable may be used to hold the number of elements present in the array. In Example 7.2, we use the constant SIZE to store the number of elements available in *score[]*.

One thing that I find confusing in the C and C++ languages is that the counting of elements in arrays starts at 0 and not 1. See Figure 7.1. Here, the *score[]* array is shown and the first slot is numbered 0, the second one is numbered 1, and so on. Therefore, if an array has four slots, as is the case here, the last slot is numbered 3. Since the numbering of slots starts at 0 instead of 1, you have to be careful when working with slot numbers.

The formal name for a slot number is "index." Its plural is either indices or indexes. Sometimes the word "subscript" is also used. The highest index used with an array should always be one less than its size. Here the highest index used with *score* should be 3, which is one less than its size (which is 4).

Solution 7.2

a. 4 is stored at an index of 2.
b. 9 is stored at an index of 3.
c. The highest index should be 4 and the lowest should be 0.
d. The index for a[0] is 0 and the value stored there is 3.

Drill 7.3

```
int a[5] = {3, 7, 4, 9, 6};
```

a. What is a[1] + a[4]?
b. What is a[0] − a[2]?
c. What is a[0] + 2?
d. What is a[1 + a[0]]?

1D Arrays

After the array elements are read in as seen in Figure 7.1, score[0] is equal to 3.4, score[2] is equal to 2.11, score[5 − 4] + 4 is equal to score[1] + 4 or 7.50 + 4 or 11.5. First, the expression in the brackets should be evaluated to find the index. Using that index, one can then see what is in the slot. We are now ready to look at the tracechart of Example 7.2 in Figure 7.1.

The first loop reads numbers into successive slots of the array, and the second one prints them in reverse order. Inside the first loop, *i* starts at 0 and ends at 3. When *i* reaches 4, the loop is not executed. As far as the loop is concerned, *i* has only the values from 0 to 3.

When *i* is 0, score[0] (pronounced "score sub zero") is read in. The first data item of 3.4 is read into score[0]. When *i* is 1, 7.50 is read into score[1]. This is repeated until 9.0 is read into score[3]. When the loop terminates, all the elements of the array are read in and *i* is 4.

Next since we want to print the elements in reverse order, we start the index (*i*) at 3 and make it decrease to 0. This then prints score[3], which is 9.00, then score[2], which is 2.11, and so on, until 3.40 is printed.

More Array Handling Examples

Let us practice working with arrays before we move to a full-blown programming example. Here, we're using the same score[ ] array from Figure 7.1.

```
for(i = 1; i <= 3; i = i + 1)
    printf("%.2f\t", score[i - 1] + i);
----- output -----
4.4    9.5    5.11
```

Here, when *i* is 1, 4.4 is printed. When it is 2, a 9.5 is printed, and finally when *i* is 3, a 5.11 is printed. In Figure 7.2, we see that when *i* is 1, [i − 1] becomes 0 and score[0] is 3.4. Adding *i* or 1 to this makes it evaluate to a 4.4. Hence, 4.4 is printed for the first iteration. Here's another example:

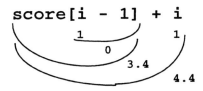

Figure 7.2 Evaluating the expression for *i* equal to 1.

Solution 7.3

a. a[1] + a[4] is 7 + 6, or 13.
b. a[0] − a[2] is 3 − 4, or −1.
c. a[0] + 2 is 3 + 2, or 5.
d. a[1 + a[0]] is a[1 + 3], or a[4], or 6.

Drill 7.4

```
int a[5] = {3, 7, 4, 9, 6};
for(i = 0; i <= 4; i = i + 1)
    printf("%d\t", a[4 - i]);
```

a. In this code, when *i* is 0, the value of a[4 − 0] is printed. What is that value?
b. When *i* is 1, the value of a[4 − 1] is printed. What is that value?
c. When *i* is 4, what is printed?
d. In conclusion, what is the output of this code?

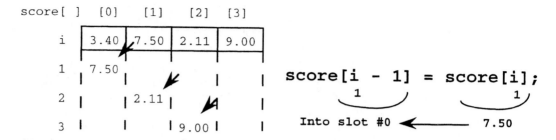

Figure 7.3 Shifting array elements by one to the left.

```
for(i = 1; i <= 3; i = i + 1)
   score[i - 1] = score[i];
```

After the execution of this code, the final contents of the array will become "7.50, 2.11, 9.0, and 9.0." In Figure 7.3, we see that for the first iteration of the loop, when *i* is 1, score[i – 1] = score[i]; reduces to score[0] = 7.50;. Hence, 7.50 is stored in score[0]. When *i* is 2, score[2] is stored in score[1] and when *i* is 3, 9.0 is stored in score[2]. score[3] remains the same.

Searching an Array

As another example of using arrays, let us look at Example 7.3 on page 108. Here the array *score[]* has 12 slots, which are assigned values from input data until a 0 is read in. Therefore, the loop to read data into the array is different from that of Example 7.2. There we had a fixed number of elements to read. Here, we stop reading data into the array when we read in a zero.

The program continues by asking the user what number he or she wants to look up. If the number is found, then it will print where the number was located. If the number isn't found, it will notify the user. The method of doing this search is called a *linear search,* where the number is searched starting from the beginning of the array to the end of it. If the number doesn't appear until the end of the array, this may take some time. For searches involving numerous elements, it is not as efficient as some other methods. A more efficient method of searching is called a *binary search,* which is covered in the Optional Topics section of this unit.

Let us follow Figure 7.4 as we trace through Example 7.3. First, we will see how the array is loaded and then how the linear search is performed.

Solution 7.4
a. When *i* is 0, a[4], or 6, is printed.
b. When *i* is 1, a[3], or 9, is printed.
c. When *i* is 4, a[4 – 4], or a[0], or 3 is printed.
d. In conclusion, the output of the loop is: 6   9   4   7   3.

Drill 7.5 To print the array in reverse order, how should the for statement be written for this printf()? Think about where *i* should start and where it should end.

```
for(          ;              ;                  )
   printf("%d\t", a[i]);
```

i	score[0]	score[1]	score[2]	score[3]	for(?)	max	lookup	if(?)
	3.4							
0					T			
		7.5						
1					T			
			2.11					
2					T			
				0				
3					F			

--------- First loop stops

i	score[0]	score[1]	score[2]	score[3]	for(?)	max	lookup	if(?)
						2		
							2.11	
0					T			F
1					T			F
2					T			T

----------- lookup equals score[2] so break out from the loop

Figure 7.4 The tracechart for Example 7.3.

Before the loop, score[0] is read in and then the loop starts. *i* is 0 and since score[0] != 0, it is 3.4 and the loop proceeds. While *i* is still 0, score[i+1] or score[1] is read in as 7.5. Now *i* becomes 1 in the for statement and we see if score[i] is not 0. score[1] is not 0; it is 7.5. The loop continues and 2.11 is read into score[2]. After *i* becomes 2, it is found not to be a 0 and the loop goes one more time.

Last, 0 is read into score[3] while *i* is still 2. Then in the for statement, *i* is incremented to 3 and found that this number was just read in as 0. The loop stops. *max* is set to *i* – 1, or 3 – 1, or 2. 2 is the highest index that contains a valid number in the array.

Next the program reads in the value for *lookup*, the value to be searched in the array. In our example, that value is 2.11. The loop starts with *i* equal to 0 and ends with *i* equal to *max*. While *i* goes through all the valid indices of the array, each element of the array is checked to see if it equals *lookup*. If it does, then we break out of the loop; otherwise, the loop continues until *i* becomes larger than *max*. In our case, *i* was 2 when a match was found.

After the loop, if i <= max is true, we know the number was found at the index of *i*. Hence, we print i + 1, which is the number in the list of elements. That is, *i* of 2 means that the index is 2, but it is the *third* element in the list. If *i* were larger than *max* after the loop was completed, then that would have meant that *lookup* wasn't found in the array.

Solution 7.5 *i* should start at 4 and step down to 0. Once it becomes –1, the loop terminates.

```
for(i = 4; i >= 0; i = i - 1)
    printf("%d\t", a[i]);
```

Drill 7.6 How would you write the if statement for the code if all the elements greater than 5 are to be printed in order. That is, first see if 3 is greater than 5. Since it is not, don't print it. Then see if 7 is greater than 5. It is, so print it, etc. The final output then should be 7 9 6.

```
int a[5] = {3, 7, 4, 9, 6};
for(i = 0; i <= 4; i = i + 1)
    if(
        printf("%d\t", a[i]);
```

```
//EXAMPLE 7.3
#include <stdio.h>
void main ( )
{
    float score[12],    //An array to store a list of scores.
          lookup;       //The array is searched for this score.
    int   i,            //Used as an index to step through the array.
          max;          //The index of the last score stored in the array.

    //Read in the scores into the array.
    printf("Enter up to 10 floats; when done, enter a 0 \n");
    scanf("%f", &score[0]);
    for(i = 0; score[i] != 0; i = i + 1)
       scanf("%f", &score[i + 1]);
    max = i - 1;

    //Read a score to be searched in the array.
    printf("What score do you want to look up? ");
    scanf("%f", &lookup);

    //Search the array for this score.
    for(i = 0; i <= max; i = i + 1)
       if( score[i] == lookup)
          break; //Abandon the loop if element is found.

    //If it was found, then a break was executed and "i" was <= "max."
    if(i <= max)
       printf("The score of %.2f was number %d in the list.\n",
          lookup, i + 1);

    else //Otherwise, "i" went past the value of "max."
       printf("The score of %.2f was NOT found in the list.\n", lookup);
}
----- output -----
Enter up to 10 floats; when done, enter a 0
3.4
7.50
```

Solution 7.6

```
int a[5] = {3, 7, 4, 9, 6};
for(i = 0; i <= 4; i = i + 1)
   if(a[i] > 5)
      printf("%d\t", a[i]);
```

Drill 7.7 Now instead of printing these numbers, count how many are greater than 5 and print the answer at the end. We will need a variable, call it "count", to add this number. Complete the code by adding two more statements, one to calculate *count* and one to print it. The output should simply be count = 3.

```
int count = 0, a[5] = {3, 7, 4, 9, 6};
for(i = 0; i <= 4; i = i + 1)
   if(a[i] > 5)
```

1D Arrays

```
2.11
0
What score do you want to look up? 2.11
The score of 2.11 was number 3 in the list.
```

Array Initialization

```
int   score[5] = {4, 2, 654, 0, 78};
char name1[5] = {'M', 'i', 'k', 'e', '\0'};
char name2[ ] = "Mike";
```

Above, we see some examples of initializing arrays. Individual elements can be specified using braces and commas, as with score[5] and name1[5]. The two strings, *name1* and *name2,* are initialized to the same value. When initializing arrays as above, one can omit the array size given in the brackets, as in *name2[ ]*. This is because the size of the array can be determined by the number of initial values. Also remember that a string such as "Mike" actually contains five characters because the null character is used to terminate a string.

EXPERIMENTS

Arrays allow programmers to group related items of the same data type in one variable. However, when referring to an array, one has to specify not only the array or variable name but also the slot number of interest. Let us first look at strings that are special types of arrays, since we are more familiar with them.

Exp 7.1 Refer to Figure 2.1 on Page 18 in Unit 2.

```
#include <stdio.h>
void main (void)
{
    char r[11] = "MugMan";
    printf("Slot 0  has %c\n",  r[0]);
    printf("Slot 1  has %c\n",  r[1]);
    printf("Slot 5  has %c\n",  r[5]);
    printf("Slot 6  has %c\n",  r[6]);
    printf("Numerically, it is %d\n",r[6]);
}
```

Solution 7.7

```
int count = 0, a[5] = {3, 7, 4, 9, 6};
for(i = 0; i <= 4; i = i + 1)
   if(a[i] > 5)
      count = count + 1;
printf("count=%d\n", count);
```

Drill 7.8 Now don't print only the *count*, but also print the numbers greater than 5 in the array. (You may want to show just the changes in the above solution for this drill.)

a. The name of the array is r[ ]. How many slots does this array have?
b. How many characters, counting the null character at the end, does this array hold?
c. The number of a slot is also called an index. What is the lowest index?
d. What is the highest index for this array?
e. Is the number for the highest index the same as that for the number of slots?
f. What is stored in the last slot as a character, that is, in slot number 6?
g. What is stored in the last slot numerically? (All strings should have this null character stored in its last slot to signal the end of the string.)

Exp 7.2

```
char a[11] = "sweet girl";
int i;
for(i = 0; i <= 10; i = i + 1)
    printf("Slot %d  has %c\n",  i, a[i]);
```

a. When we wanted to print the index, or the number of the slot, did we print *i* or *a[i]*?
b. When we wanted to print what was stored in a slot, did we print *i* or *a[i]*?
c. Are *i* and *a[i]* the same?
d. Which of the above is the value stored in a slot?
e. Which is the slot number itself?

Exp 7.3 This loop goes up to only "i = 9."

```
char a[11] = "sweet girl";
int i;
for(i = 0; i <= 9; i = i + 1)
    printf("%c", a[i]);
printf("\n");
```

a. Is the '\n' printed inside the loop or after it? Why?
b. If it is printed inside the loop, how would you put it after?

Solution 7.8

```
int count = 0, a[5] = {3, 7, 4, 9, 6};
for(i = 0; i <= 4; i = i + 1)
    if(a[i] > 5)
    {
        count = count + 1;
        printf("%d\t", a[i]);
    }
printf("count=%d\n", count);
```

Drill 7.9 Now add up only those elements in the array greater than 5 and print their sum. We'll need a variable called *sum* to accumulate the additions. First 7 will be added to *sum*. *sum* will be 7. Then 9 will be added, making *sum* equal to 16. Finally 6 will be added, making it 22. You'll need one statement to calculate the sum and one to print it.

c. If it is printed after the loop, how would you put it inside?

d. Can you remember an easy way to write out a string using one printf() and no loop?

Exp 7.4 Can you complete the for loop so that the characters of the array are printed in reverse order, starting from slot number 10 down to slot number 0?

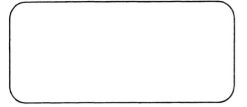

```
char a[11] = "sweet girl";
int i;
for(i = 10;          ; i = i - 1)
   printf("Slot %d  has %c\n",  i, a[i]);
```

a. Did you try to print what was in the –1st slot, which doesn't exist?

b. If so, what kind of error did you get, if any?

Exp 7.5 Remember: In an assignment statement, the value on the right side of the equals sign is stored in the variable shown on its left side.

```
char a[11] = "sweet girl";
int i;
for(i = 0; i <= 9; i = i + 1)
     a[i] = a[1]; //Notice the 'i' and '1'
printf("%s\n", a);
```

Exp 7.6

```
char a[11] = "sweet girl";
int i;
for(i = 0; i <= 9; i = i + 1)
   a[i] = '1';
printf("%s\n", a);
```

Solution 7.9 When adding up *sum*, notice that a[i] should be added, unlike the number 1 that was added when finding the count.

```
int sum = 0, a[5] = {3, 7, 4, 9, 6};
for(i = 0; i <= 4; i = i + 1)
   if(a[i] > 5)
      sum = sum + a[i];
printf("sum=%d\n", sum);
```

Drill 7.10 Now print the sum of the numbers greater than 5 and the count of the elements less than or equal to 5. Use two if's. The count should be printed as 2, since 3 and 4 are less than or equal to 5, and the *sum* should be printed as 22.

a. In Experiment 7.5, what was stored in each slot of the array?
b. In Experiment 7.5, if the array were initialized to "good boy," what would have been printed?
c. In Experiment 7.6, what was stored in each slot of the array?
d. In Experiment 7.6, if the array were initialized to "good boy," what would have been printed?

Exp 7.7 First run this program with the // in front of the printf(), then answer the questions. Finally check your answers by removing the // and rerunning it.

```
char a[11] = "sweet girl";
int i;
for(i = 0; i <= 9; i = i + 1)
{
    a[i] = a[i + 1];
    // printf("i=%d   %s\n", i, a);
}
printf("%s\n", a);
```

a. When *i* was 0, which slot of *a* was changed? To which value?
b. When *i* was 1, which slot of *a* was changed? To which value?
c. When *i* was 2, which slot of *a* was changed? To which value?
d. When *i* was 9, which slot of *a* was changed? To which value?

Exp 7.8 First run this program with the // before the printf(), then answer the questions. Finally check your answers by removing the //.

```
char a[11] = "sweet girl";
int i;
for(i = 0; i <= 9; i = i + 1)
{
    a[i + 1] = a[i];
    // printf("i=%d   %s\n", i, a);
}
printf("%s\n", a);
```

Solution 7.10
```
int count = 0, sum = 0, a[5] = {3, 7, 4, 9, 6};
for(i = 0; i <= 4; i = i + 1)
{
    if(a[i] > 5)
        sum = sum + a[i];
    if(a[i] <= 5)
        count = count + 1;
}
printf("count=%d\n", count);
printf("sum=%d\n", sum);
```

Drill 7.11 Now follow the same procedure as in Drill 7.10, but use only one if statement. Which solution do you prefer?

112

a. When *i* was 0, which slot of *a* was changed? To which value?
b. When *i* was 1, which slot of *a* was changed? To which value?
c. When *i* was 2, which slot of *a* was changed? To which value?
d. When *i* was 9, which slot of *a* was changed? To which value?

Exp 7.9 First run this program with the // before the printf(), then answer the questions. Finally check your answers by removing the //.

```
char a[11] = "sweet girl";
int i;
for(i = 0; i <= 9; i = i + 1)
{
    a[i] = a[9 - i];
    // printf("i=%d  %s\n", i, a);
}
printf("%s\n", a);
```

a. When *i* was 0, which slot of *a* was changed? To which value?
b. When *i* was 1, which slot of *a* was changed? To which value?
c. When *i* was 2, which slot of *a* was changed? To which value?
d. When *i* was 9, which slot of *a* was changed? To which value?

Exp 7.10 So far we have been looking only at character arrays that terminate with a null character, or simply, strings. Now let us turn our attention to numeric arrays. Here, the first loop completes before the second one starts.

```
int i, x[6], y[6] = {3, 8, 2, 9, 4, 1};
for(i = 0; i <= 5; i = i + 1)
    x[i] = y[i];
for(i = 0; i <= 5; i = i + 1)
    printf("%d\t %d\n", x[i], y[i]);
```

Solution 7.11 The following solution is preferred in general because only one condition has to be tested.

```
int count = 0, sum = 0,
    a[5] = {3, 7, 4, 9, 6};
for(i = 0; i <= 4; i = i + 1)
    if(a[i] > 5)
        sum = sum + a[i];
    else
        count = count + 1;
printf("count=%d\n", count);
printf("sum=%d\n", sum);
```

Drill 7.12 Starting with the following lines, find and print the largest number in the array.

```
int largest = a[0],
    a[5] = {3, 7, 4, 9, 6};
for(i = 1; i <= 4; i = i + 1)
```

a. What are the names of the arrays?
b. What are the names of the scalars? (Scalars are the variables that are not arrays.)
c. How many slots do each of the arrays have?
d. What is the lowest index and the highest index for the arrays?
e. Which array is initialized during its declaration?
f. Which array is assigned values in a loop?
g. Are the arrays printed horizontally or vertically?
h. How would you write the code if you had wanted to write the arrays the opposite way?

Exp 7.11 Changes in the code are shown in bold.

```
int i, x[6], y[7] = {3, 8, 2, 9, 4, 1, 0};
for(i = 0; i <= 5; i = i + 1)
    x[i] = y[i + 1]; // Statement 1.
for(i = 0; i <= 5; i = i + 1)
    printf("%d\t %d\n", x[i], y[i]);
```

a. When *i* is 0, which slot of *y* is used? Which slot of *x* is changed?
b. When *i* is 1, which slot of *y* is used? Which slot of *x* is changed?
c. When *i* is 5, which slot of *y* is used? Which slot of *x* is changed?
d. Can you determine what would be printed if Statement 1 were changed to:
   `x[i] = y[i] + 1;`?
e. Can you determine what would be printed if Statement 1 were changed to:
   `x[i] = y[6 - i];`?
f. Can you determine what would be printed if Statement 1 were changed to:
   `x[i] = y[1];`?

Exp 7.12 When running this experiment, enter the following numbers: 6, 4.0, 5.0, 2.0, 55.0, 8.0, 1.0. The first number is the *count* and the rest are the items that go in the array. When scanning a float, use %f and not %.2f.

Solution 7.12

```
int a[5] = {3, 7, 4, 9, 6};
int largest = a[0],
for(i = 1; i <= 4; i = i + 1)
if(a[i] > largest)
    largest = a[i];
printf("largest=%d\n", largest);
```

Drill 7.13 Now print only the index of the largest number in the array. Keeping track of the largest number is not sufficient; we have to keep track of the index. Once we know the index, we know the number in that slot.

```
int largest_index = 0, a[5] = {3, 7, 4, 9, 6};
for(i = 1; i <= 4; i = i + 1)
```

```
int count, i;
float a[6];
printf("How many numbers do you have?\n");
scanf("%d", &count);
for(i = 0; i < count; i = i + 1)
    scanf("%f", &a[i]);
for(i = 0; i < count; i = i + 1)
    printf("%.2f\n", a[i]);
```

a. What was the value of *count*?
b. In the scanf() and the printf(), did *i* ever reach the value of *count*? Why or why not?
c. The 4.0 was read into which slot of the array?
d. The 5.0 was read into which slot of the array?

Exp 7.13 Enter the following numbers: 4.0, 5.0, 2.0, 55.0.

```
int i, j;
float a[30];
printf("Enter floats that are < 10:\n");
scanf("%f", &a[0]);
for(i = 0; a[i] <= 10.0; i = i + 1)
    scanf("%f", &a[i + 1]);
// printf("last value of i was %d\n", i);

for(j = 0; j < i; j = j + 1)
    printf("%.2f\n", a[j]);
```

a. Does the scanf() here change the value of *i*?
b. The first data item was read into which slot of the array?
c. The first time the condition a[i] <= 10.0? was checked, *i* was 0. Was the condition true or false? During the first time through the loop, into which slot did the scanf() place a data item?

Solution 7.13

```
int largest_index = 0, a[5] = {3, 7, 4, 9, 6};
for(i = 1; i <= 4; i = i + 1)
   if(a[i] > a[largest_index])
      largest_index = i;
printf("largest=%d and its index =%d\n",
   a[largest_index], largest_index);
```

Drill 7.14 Let us now change our problem type. Using these data items, read in values into the two arrays, *a[ ]* and *b[ ]*. Show the contents of these arrays. The data items are 3, 8, 2, 9, 1, 5, 7, 6, 0, 4. What happens when *i* is 0?

```
for(i = 0; i <= 3; i = i + 1)
   scanf("%d %d", &a[i], &b[i]);
```

d. The second time that the condition a[i] <= 10.0? was checked, what was *i*? Was the condition true or false? Into which slot did the next scanf() place a new data item during the second iteration of the loop?

e. When the condition a[i] <= 10.0? finally became false, what was the value of i? Run the program again by removing the // to check your answer.

f. In the second loop does *j* ever reach this last value of *i* in the printf()?

QUESTIONS

1. Show the output from each code using the following array and for loop: Remember that the first index is always 0 and not 1. Use the same for loop with each printf().

```
int i, a[ ] = {40, 20, 70, 10, 80, 30, 90};
for(i = 1; i <= 5; i = i + 1)
```

```
a. printf("%d\t", a[i]);
b. printf("%d\t", i);
c. printf("%d\t", a[i + 1]);
d. printf("%d\t", a[i - 1]);
e. printf("%d\t", a[i] + a[i + 1]);
f. printf("%d\t", a[i] + 1);
g. printf("%d\t", a[i] + i);
```

2. Show the contents of the new array after it is changed by each assignment statement. Use the same for loop with each assignment statement. Start with the following array for each. When doing these, remember that during each iteration of the loop, array elements are changing. This is especially important in Questions 2.d, 2.f, and 2.h.

```
int a[ ] = {40, 20, 70, 10, 80, 30, 90};
for(i = 1; i <= 5; i = i + 1)
```

```
a. a[i] = 0;                  //Place this statement in the for loop.
b. a[i] = i;                  //Place this statement in the for loop.
c. a[i] = a[i + 1];           //etc.
d. a[i + 1] = a[i];
e. a[i] = a[i] + a[i + 1];
f. a[i + 1] = a[i] + a[i + 1];
g. a[6 - i] = a[5 - i];
h. a[5 - i] = a[6 - i];
```

Solution 7.14 The contents of *a[ ]* starting at index 0 are "3 2 1 7." The contents of *b[ ]* starting at index 0 are "8 9 5 6." When *i* is 0, 3 is read into a[0] and 8 is read into b[0]. When *i* is 1, 2 is read into a[1], 9 is read into b[1], and so on.

Drill 7.15 Using the following data items again, 3, 8, 2, 9, 1, 5, 7, 6, 0, 4, show the contents of the two arrays after executing the following code:

```
for(i = 0; i <= 3; i = i + 1)
   scanf("%d", &a[i]);
for(i = 0; i <= 3; i = i + 1)
   scanf("%d", &b[i]);
```

3. Show the contents of the arrays, *a[ ]* and *b[ ]*, using this input data. Not all data items may be used.

3 4 9 1 5 2 7 0 8 6

a.
```
scanf("%d", &k);
for(i=0; i <= k; i = i + 1)
   scanf("%d", &a[i]);
for(i = 0; i <= k; i = i + 1)
   scanf("%d", &b[i]);
```

b.
```
scanf("%d", &k);
for(i=0; i <= k; i = i + 1)
{
   scanf("%d", &a[i]);
   scanf("%d", &b[i]);
}
```

c.
```
scanf("%d", &k);
for(i=0; k != 1; i = i + 1)
{
   a[i] = k;
   b[i] = k;
   scanf("%d", &k);
}
```

d.
```
scanf("%d", &k);
for(i=0; k != 8; i = i + 1)
{
   a[i] = k;
   scanf("%d", &b[i]);
   scanf("%d", &k);
}
```

Solution 7.15 The contents of *a[ ]* starting at index 0 are "3 8 2 9." The contents of *b[ ]* starting at index 0 are "1 5 7 6." All four elements of a[4] are read in first, then the four elements of b[4]. a[3] is 9 and b[3] is 6.

Drill 7.16 Show the contents of the arrays after executing the following code. Data items are 3, 8, 2, 9, 1, 5, 7, 6, 0, 4. Notice the k > 1? condition.

```
scanf("%d", &k);
for(i = 0; k > 1; i = i + 1)
{
   a[i] = k;
   scanf("%d", &b[i]);
   scanf("%d", &k);
}
```

1D Arrays

```
                    e.
    scanf("%d", &k);
    for(i=0; k > 1; i = i + 1)
    {
        a[i] = k;
        scanf("%d", &k);
    }
    scanf("%d", &k);
    for(i=0; k > 1; i = i + 1)
    {
        b[i] = k;
        scanf("%d", &k);
    }
```

PROGRAMS

1. Read 10 floats into an array and print their average.

2. Initialize an array with 6 integers. Read another integer and add that number to each element in the array. Then print the array.

3. Initialize an array with 6 integers. Read another integer and print the value of each array element that is less than this read–in integer and print the number of elements that were not printed. For example, if the array were 40, 80, 20, 50, 90, 30, and an 80 were read in, then the output would be:

```
----- output -----
40 20 50 30
count = 2
```

4. Initialize two integer arrays, a[6] and b[6]. First print their elements in two rows, then print them out in two columns.

5. Scan floating point numbers into an array until the sum of those numbers exceeds 100. At the slot where the sum becomes greater than 100, store a −1.0 to denote the end of the array. Now print the number of elements in the array, not including the −1.0.

6. Initialize an integer array with 6 elements. Find the lowest element and swap it with the number in the first slot. For example, if the array is 40, 80, 20, 50, 90, 30, then after the swap the array should become 20, 80, 40, 50, 90, 30.

Solution 7.16 The contents of *a[ ]* starting at index 0 are "3 2." The contents of *b[ ]* starting at index 0 are "8 9." *k* is first read as a 3. Then it is seen to be greater than 1 and the loop proceeds. In the first iteration of the loop, a[0] is assigned the 3 from *k*, b[0] is read in as 8, and 2 is read into *k*. In the for statement, *k* is still greater than 1, so we enter the second iteration of the loop. a[1] becomes 2, b[1] is read in as 9, and *k* is read in as 1. In the for statement, the loop terminates because *k* is not greater than 1.

Drill 7.17 Show the contents of only array a[4] after executing the following code. Data items are 3, 8, 2, 9, 1, 5, 7, 6, 0, 4. Notice that the index is not *i*.

```
scanf("%d", &k);
for(i = 0; i <=2; i = i + 1)
{   scanf("%d", &a[k]);
    scanf("%d", &k);
}
```

OPTIONAL TOPICS

Binary Search

As mentioned before, binary searches are more efficient than linear searches for searches involving many elements. The only problem of a binary search is that the elements must be sorted to begin with. We will discuss sorting of arrays in Unit 8.

The idea behind a binary search is to find the midpoint in the array and see if the number being searched is less than or greater than the number of the mid–point. Suppose there are 1000 elements in the array. Then see if the number being searched is greater or less than the number at index 500. If the number is greater, then search through the top half of the array; otherwise, search through the lower half. Then while searching further, continue to apply this same principle of dividing the number of elements to be searched by two. The number of searches is cut in half with every search. Hence, it is called a binary search.

In Figure 7.5, we see how the number 57 is searched through the given array. First, the number in the middle of the array, 39, is determined to be less than 57, so disregard the first half of the array. The search is thus limited to the range of numbers consisting of the top half of the array. The number in the middle of the top half of the array is 61, which is greater than 57, so the search now is limited to the lower half of that range of the array. This process is continued until the number is found. Now we are ready to trace Example 7.4 using Figure 7.6.

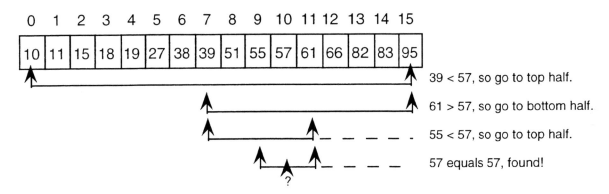

Figure 7.5 Showing the ranges while doing a binary search for 57.

Solution 7.17 The contents of *a[ ]* starting at index 1 are "5 9 8." First *k* is read in as 3, which will be used as the index for a[4]. In the first iteration of the loop, a[3] is read in as 8. Then *k* is read in as 2. The second time through the loop, at this index of 2, a 9 is read in. Last, *k* is read in as 1. For the index, a 5 is read into a[1]. The loop goes through only 3 times because *i* is controlling the loop.

Drill 7.18 There are two teams a and b, each with 5 runners. The first runners of each team ran against each other, then the second runners, and so on, until all 5 runners ran against each other. Find out how many races the a team won. Fill in two statements after the for.

```
float a[5]= {4.6, 7.2, 4.3, 4.9, 8.1},  b[5]= {4.9, 8.1, 6.1, 4.7, 8.2};
int count = 0;
for(i = 0; i <= 4; i = i + 1)
    :                    :
printf("The A team won %d races.\n", count);
```

1D Arrays   **119**

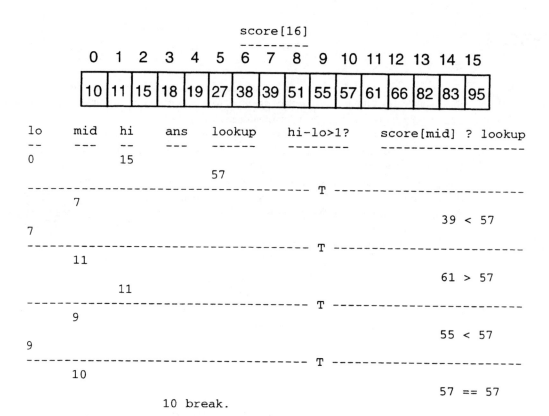

score[16]

0	1	2	3	4	5	6	7	8	9	10	11	12	13	14	15
10	11	15	18	19	27	38	39	51	55	57	61	66	82	83	95

```
lo    mid    hi    ans    lookup    hi-lo>1?    score[mid] ? lookup
--    ---    --    ---    ------    --------    --------------------
0            15
                          57
-------------------------------------------- T ---------------------------
      7
                                                          39 < 57
7
-------------------------------------------- T ---------------------------
      11
                                                          61 > 57
             11
-------------------------------------------- T ---------------------------
      9
                                                          55 < 57
9
-------------------------------------------- T ---------------------------
      10
                                                          57 == 57
        10 break.
```

Figure 7.6 Tracechart for doing a binary search on 57.

```
//EXAMPLE 7.4 BINARY SEARCH
void main(void)
{
    int score[16] = {10,11,15,18,19,27,38,39,51,55,57,61,66,82,83,95};
    int lo = 0,    //Lowest slot index in the range that is being searched.
    mid,            //Index of the middle slot in the range.
    hi = 15,        //Index of the highest slot in the range.
    ans = -1,       //This will be the index if lookup is found.
    lookup;         //This is what we are searching for in score[].
```

Solution 7.18
```
if(a[i] > b[i])
        count = count + 1;
```

Drill 7.19 Write a loop involving only the b team. This loop will determine the score of the fastest runner (which is 4.7). Then write a second loop that will count the number of players from the a team that this player could have beaten. (The player with the 4.7 could have beaten the players of the a that received a score of 7.2, 4.9, and 8.1.) Complete the two for loops.

```
float fastest = b[0];
for(i = 1; i <= 4; i = i + 1)// Loop to find the fastest in team b.

for(i = 0; i <= 4; i = i + 1)//Loop to count the slower ones in a.

printf("The fastest b runner could beat %d of the a runners\n", count);
```

```
//First get the number to be searched.
printf("What number are you looking up? ");
scanf("%d", &lookup);


//Start the binary search.
for(; hi - lo > 1;)
{
    mid = (hi - lo) / 2 + lo;   //Find the middle of the range.
    if(score[mid] == lookup)    //If the number is at the midpoint,
    {                                //set answer and break out of loop.
        ans = mid;
        break;
    }
    if(score[mid] > lookup)     //If the number is not at the midpoint,
        hi = mid;                    // adjust either hi or lo.
    else
        lo = mid;
}

//If the number at hi or lo, set the ans.
if(ans == -1)
    if(score[hi] == lookup)
        ans = hi;
    else
        if(score[lo] == lookup)
            ans = lo;

//If ans is still unchanged, the number was not found in the array.
if(ans == -1)
    printf("%d not found.\n", lookup);
else
    printf("%d was found at slot number %d.\n", lookup, ans);
}
----- output -----
What number are you looking up? 57
 57 was found at slot number 10.
```

Solution 7.19

```
float a[5]= {4.6, 7.2, 4.3, 4.9, 8.1},   b[5]= {4.9, 8.1, 6.1, 4.7, 8.2};
float fastest = b[0];
int i, count = 0;
for(i = 1; i <= 4; i = i + 1)// Loop to find the fastest in team b.
    if(b[i] > fastest)
        fastest = b[i];
for(i = 0; i <= 4; i = i + 1)// Loop to count the slower ones in a.
    if(fastest > a[i])
        count = count + 1;
printf("The fastest b runner could have beaten %d of the a runners\n",
    count);
```

Drill 7.20 For each member of the a team, find out how many b team members were slower.

lo and *hi* mark the lower and upper indexes, respectively, of the range of the array being searched. *mid* is calculated to be the midpoint of the range being searched. *ans* is initialized to −1. If the search is successful, it will contain the index where the number was found. If it stays −1, then the search was unsuccessful. *lookup* contains the number being searched. For this example, the array is fixed and has 16 elements, so *hi* is 15 and *lo* is 0 at the beginning. *lookup* is read in as 57. Now the loop begins.

hi − *lo* is greater than 1, so the loop proceeds. Inside the loop, *mid* is calculated to be (hi − lo)/2 + lo. This is (15 − 0) / 2 + 0, or 15/2. Since both 15 and 2 are integers, this is an integer division and *mid* becomes 7, not 7.5. The condition score[mid]==lookup? or 39==57? is false, so nothing is done there. We go to the next if statement. score[mid] > lookup? is evaluated to be score[7] > 57? or 39 > 57?, which is false. Using the else branch of the if statement, make *lo* equal to *mid,* or 7, and go around the loop again.

The difference between *hi* and *lo* is still greater than 1, so continue with the loop. *mid* changes to 11. In the loop, score[mid]==lookup?, or 61==57?, is false. However, score[mid] > lookup?, or 61 > 57?, is true, so now make *hi* equal to whatever *mid* was (*hi* is now 11). The third time through the loop, the midpoint between 7 and 11 becomes 9 and the number at that location is less than 57, so now *lo* becomes 9.

The fourth time through the loop, *mid* becomes 10. The number at slot number 10 is the number for which we are searching. score[mid]==lookup? is true for the first time, so *ans* is set to *mid,* or 10, and we break out of the loop. The first if(ans == −1) condition is false because *ans* is equal to 10. We skip those nested if's since that if doesn't have a corresponding else. With the second if(ans == −1), a corresponding else exists and according to it, we print *lookup* as found in the slot number specified by *ans.*

The first if(ans == −1) is necessary because the number we are searching may be in either slot 0 or slot 15. This is an exception case. Notice that in the loop, only the numbers referenced by *mid* are checked to see if they equal *lookup.* If the searched number is at either extreme position of the array, then they aren't tested. Hence we need this extra set of if's after the loop. Notice also that if(score[hi] == lookup) and if(score[lo] == lookup) are tested only if absolutely necessary. As in our trace above, we didn't have to do those condition tests. We are assuming that, in general, the searched number will not fall in the 0th or the 15th slot.

Solution 7.20 The solution involves a nested loop which will be covered in Unit 8.

```
float a[5]= {4.6, 7.2, 4.3, 4.9, 8.1},  b[5]= {4.9, 8.1, 6.1, 4.7, 8.2};
int i, j, count;
for(i = 0; i <= 4; i = i + 1)        // Loop to access each member of a.
{
   count = 0;              //This has to be reset for each a team player.
   for(j = 0; j <= 4; j = j + 1) // Loop to access each b team member.
      if(a[i] > b[j])
          count = count + 1;
   printf("Team member %d of a was faster than %d members of b\n",
          i + 1, count);
}
```

Nested Loops and 2D Arrays

LESSON

2D Arrays

Figure 8.1 shows two arrays; name[6][10] is a 2D array and score[6] is a 1D array. They are defined in Example 8.1 (see page 126). *name[ ][ ]* is an array of characters and *score[ ]* is an array of integers. To access a slot in *score[ ]*, only one index has to be specified. But to access a slot in *name[ ][ ]*, two indexes have to be specified. The first index is called *row* and the second one, *column*.

In Example 8.1, *name[ ][ ]* is initialized as shown. During the execution of that program, the values for *score[ ]* will be read in. The name[6][10] array has two subscripts (or indexes). The first subscript specifies that there are 6 players and the second specifies that there are up to 9 characters in the names of these players, not including the null ('\0') character.

name[2][4] has the value of 'p'. That is, in the slot where the row is 2 and the column is 4, the value is 'p'. name[1][2] has the value of 'd'. Here, the row index is 1 and the column index is 2. The names of six game players are stored in this array. They are character strings and so each one ends with a null character. When printing strings, all characters are printed in order until a null

DRILLS

Drill 8.1

In this code, how many of the printf()'s are part of the loop?
Show the output:

```
for(j = 0; j <= 4; j = j + 1)
   printf("%d\t", 4 - j);
printf("\n");
```

	columns											
		0	1	2	3	4	5	6	7	8	9	
	0	'A'	'n'	'n'	'a'	'b'	'e'	'l'	'l'	'e'	'\0'	
r	1	'B'	'o'	'D'	'i'	'd'	'l'	'y'	'\0'			
o	2	'J'	'o'	's'	'e'	'p'	'h'	'\0'				
w	3	'L'	'e'	'o'	'n'	'a'	'\0'					
s	4	'M'	'o'	'l'	'l'	'y'	'\0'					
	5	'O'	's'	'i'	'e'	'\0'						

0	34
1	21
2	89
3	45
4	12
5	67

(a)   (b)

Figure 8.1 (a) The name[6][10] 2D array. (b) The score[6] 1D array.

character is encountered, so name[2] has the value of "Joseph". The *name[ ][ ]* array holds the names of players and the *score[ ]* array holds the scores of the corresponding players. For example, the game score of 89 is stored in score[2] for "Joseph," which is stored in name[2].

Nested Loops

Now that we see how 2D arrays are constructed (with two subscripts), let us see how we can access all of its elements using nested loops. Right after the definitions of variables in Example 8.1, we see nested Loop 1, which counts the number of a's and A's. The first loop varies *i* from 0 to 5 in increments of 1. The nested loop varies *j* from 0 in increments of 1 until the end of the string is encountered. What happens here is that *i* stays fixed at 0, while in the inside loop, *j* varies until a null character is found. After that, *i* stays at 1 and *j* varies from 0 until a null character is found, and so on. While the loops make *i* and *j* vary so that all valid characters are accessed, the if statement counts the number of a's and A's.

Let us trace through the execution of those loops. Starting from the beginning, *i* is 0 and then *j* is 0. The if condition reduces to name[0][0] == 'a' || name[0][0] == 'A'?. This is true because 'A' is in this slot of the array. Hence, the *count* is incremented to 1. Then while *i* stays fixed at 0, only *j* becomes 1. Here, the condition reduces to name[0][1] == 'a' || name[0][1] == 'A'?. This is false because an 'n' is at this location. When *j* is 3, *count* becomes 2; now we have two a's. All 9 characters are checked until the '\0' is found at name[0][9]. Now the *j* loop terminates and *i* becomes

Solution 8.1 Only the first printf() is in the loop. Initially when *j* is 0, 4 − j or 4 − 0 is printed. Next when *j* is 1, 4 − 1, or 3, is printed. Last, when *j* is 4, a 0 is printed.

```
4   3   2   1   0
```

Drill 8.2 Now let us place the *j* loop inside an *i* loop, making the *j* loop nested. We want the *j* loop and the last printf() to be inside the *i* loop, so a pair of braces are needed. When *i* is 0, we start the *j* loop. Here, *j* starts at 0 and goes to 4, each time printing the value of *i* and *j*. For the first line, 0 0   0 1   0 2   0 3   0 4 will be printed because *i* stays fixed at 0. Show the output.

```
for(i = 0; i <= 2; i = i + 1)
{
    for(j = 0; j <= 4; j = j + 1)
        printf("%d %d\t", i, j);
    printf("\n");
}
```

1. Then the *j* loop is restarted with *j* beginning at 0 until *j* becomes 7, where a null character is found for this *i* of 1. Each of the valid cells are accessed in the array, and *count* contains the number of A's and a's in the array. Then it is printed. Now let us turn our attention to sorting these arrays.

Selection Sort

Sorting of data items is a common task that needs to be done when processing data. There are many sorting algorithms, but the ones that are easy to understand are called "natural" sorts. Selection sort is a natural sort because it is one of the algorithms by which sorting is done by humans. Most texts use the bubble sort, but it is not any faster nor is it a natural sort.

In understanding the selection sort, we want to sort out the two arrays so that the scores are in descending (high to low) order, and *name[ ][ ]* is also sorted so that the names and scores stay together. In other words, "Joseph," with a score of 89 (both are in slot number 2), will both be moved to slot number 0 after the sort is complete. Likewise, "Osie," with a score of 67, will be moved from slot number 5 to slot number 1, since he has the second highest score, and so on. While sorting, we need to keep the players' names with their respective scores.

We can see how this sort process works in Figure 8.2. The shaded cells in this figure show how much of the array is sorted during each pass. During the first pass, the person with the highest

	0	1	2	3	4	5
name[ ][ ]	Annabelle	BoDidly	Joseph	Leona	Molly	Osie
score[ ]	34	21	89	45	12	67
name[ ]	Joseph		Annabelle			
score[ ]	89		34			
name[ ][ ]		Osie				BoDidly
score[ ]		67				21
name[ ][ ]			Leona	Annabelle		
score[ ]			45	34		
name[ ][ ]						
score[ ]						
name[ ][ ]					BoDidly	Molly
score[ ]					21	12

Figure 8.2 The selection sort process.

Solution 8.2
```
0 0    0 1    0 2    0 3    0 4
1 0    1 1    1 2    1 3    1 4
2 0    2 1    2 2    2 3    2 4
```

Drill 8.3 Show the output if *i* and *j* are reversed in the printf().

```
for(i = 0; i <= 2; i = i + 1)
{
    for(j = 0; j <= 4; j = j + 1)
        printf("%d %d\t", j, i);
    printf("\n");
}
```

score, "Joseph," is moved to an index of 0. "Annabelle," with a score of 34 and who occupied this position, is moved down to the index of 2. A swap has occurred because "Joseph" needed to be in the first position and "Annabelle" needed a new slot.

Now we find the player with the highest score in the array starting at index 1. "Osie" is swapped into position 1, with "BoDidly" taking "Osie"'s place in index 5. Then for the third pass, "Leona" takes the position at index 2. For the fourth pass, "Annabelle" happens to be in her proper place and no swapping of players occurs. Finally, "BoDidly" takes the position at index 4, with "Molly" at index 5.

```
//EXAMPLE 8.1
#include <string.h>
#include <stdio.h>
void main (void)
{
    char name[6][10] = //Array holds 6 strings, each 9 characters long.
        {"Annabelle", "BoDidly", "Joseph", "Leona", "Molly", "Osie"};
    int   score[6],      //Array holds scores for 6 players of "name[ ][ ]."
          count=0,       //A variable to count the number of a's.
          largest_ndx,   //Index for the largest score while doing the sort.
          i, j,          //Used for "for" loops.
          temp;          //Used to temporarily store a score while swapping.
    char temp_str[10];   //Used to temporarily store a name while swapping.

    //Loop and nested loop to count the number of a's in all the names.
    for(i = 0; i <= 5; i = i + 1)                    // Nested Loop 1
        for(j = 0; name[i][j] != '\0'; j = j + 1)
            if(name[i][j] == 'a' || name[i][j] == 'A')
                count = count + 1;
    printf("Number of a's is %d.\n\n", count);

    //Loop to get the scores of all 6 players.
    for(i = 0; i <= 5; i = i + 1)                     // Loop 2
    {
        printf("Enter score for %s\t", name[i]);
        scanf("%d", &score[i]);
    }
```

Solution 8.3

0 0	1 0	2 0	3 0	4 0
0 1	1 1	2 1	3 1	4 1
0 2	1 2	2 2	3 2	4 2

Drill 8.4 Rewrite only the for loop statements so that the output is as follows:

0 0	1 0
0 1	1 1
0 2	1 2
0 3	1 3

```
//Starting the sort, i is the number of the pass.
for(i = 0; i <= 4; i = i + 1)                              // Nested Loop 3
{

    //Find index that has the largest number for this pass.
    largest_ndx = i;
    for(j = i + 1; j <= 5; j = j + 1)
       if(score[j] > score[largest_ndx])
          largest_ndx = j;

    //Swap the first score and name for this pass with that of the
       largest score.
    temp = score[i];
    score[i] = score[largest_ndx];
    score[largest_ndx] = temp;
    strcpy(temp_str, name[i]);
    strcpy(name[i], name[largest_ndx]);
    strcpy(name[largest_ndx], temp_str);
}

    //Print out the sorted scores and names.                   // Loop 4
    for(i = 0; i <= 5; i = i + 1)
       printf("%d\t%s\n", score[i], name[i]);
}
----- output -----
Number of a's is 3.
Enter score for Annabelle   34
Enter score for BoDidly     21
Enter score for Joseph      89
Enter score for Leona       45
Enter score for Molly       12
Enter score for Osie        67
89 Joseph
67 Osie
45 Leona
34 Annabelle
21 BoDidly
12 Molly
```

Solution 8.4
```
for(i = 0; i <= 3; i = i + 1)
{
   for(j = 0; j <= 1; j = j + 1)
      printf("%d %d\t", j, i);
   printf("\n");
}
```

Drill 8.5 Now instead of printing both *i* and *j*, let us print their sum and remove the braces. Show the output.
```
for(i = 0; i <= 3; i = i + 1)
   for(j = 0; j <= 1; j = j + 1)
      printf("%d\t", j + i);
printf("\n");
```

The largest score has to be found many times as the sort progresses. During each pass, the next largest is found. Finding the largest score is not sufficient, but we need to know the index of the score with the largest value. We need to know where that largest score exists because a swap has to occur. For instance, for the first pass, when "Joseph" is found to have the highest score, we needed to know that he was stored at slot 2 so that "Joseph" and "Annabelle" and their scores could be swapped.

Swapping itself is a little tricky. To make an analogy, How do we swap blue paint in a red bucket with the red paint in the blue bucket? We need a third bucket. In programming, we usually call it "temp." The third bucket is where, say, the blue paint is first emptied, then the free (or empty) red bucket can accept the red paint from the blue bucket, and finally, the free (or empty) blue bucket can accept the blue paint from temp. It is a three–step process.

See the programming code in Example 8.1, which is directly under the comment referring to swapping. This starts at temp = score[i]. Here, we need to swap the values stored at score[i] and score[largest_ndx]. When swapping "Joseph" and "Annabelle," *i* is 0 and *largest_ndx* is 2. We take 34, which is at score[0], and place it in *temp*. Then the 89 in score[largest_ndx] is placed in score[0], the 0th slot, and the 34 that was in *temp* is placed in score[2], the slot from which the largest number was copied.

This three–step swapping process is repeated for the players. Since the players are strings, the strcpy() function must be used rather than the assignment statements, which were used for the scores. Notice again that, with *name[ ][ ]*, only one subscript is used because we are processing strings. When we were counting the number of a's, we were processing individual characters that were in each slot. Then we needed to use both indexes.

Trace

Looking at Figure 8.3, we see that only the array *score[ ]* is shown. *name[ ][ ]* isn't shown. It will be easier to trace the algorithm for only the *score[ ]* array. The scores for this array are read in during the loop that precedes the sort in Example 8.1. Let us now follow the trace.

In nested loop 3, *i* is initialized to 0. *largest_ndx* is set to *i*, or in this case, to 0. Next we start a nested loop with *j* equal to i + 1, or 1. The only statement in this loop is the if statement and it reduces to 21 > 34?. This is false, so *j* now becomes 2. Here, the condition 89 > 34? becomes true and *largest_ndx* becomes *j*, or 2. For the rest of this pass, *largest_ndx* remains 2 because this condition continues to be false.

After the completion of the *j* loop, we swap score[i] with score[largest_ndx]. That is, we swap score[0] with score[2], the largest score. After also swapping the names, we go to the next iteration of *i*, or the next pass.

Solution 8.5

0   1   1   2   2   3   3   4

Drill 8.6 Here we have a 2D array called A[3][5]. The first index is called the row and the second is the column. A[1][3] refers to the slot where the row is 1 and the column is 3. The number here is 90. A[ ][ ] is defined as:

```
int A[3][5];
```

What is A[0][1] and A[2][4]?
If *i* is 1 and *j* is 2, what is A[i][j] and A[j][i]?

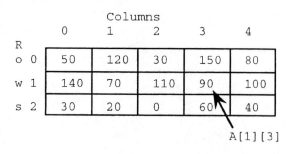

	Columns				
	0	1	2	3	4
R o w s 0	50	120	30	150	80
1	140	70	110	90	100
2	30	20	0	60	40

A[1][3]

Now *i* is 1. *largest_ndx* is *i*, or 1. Then the *j* loop starts again. The condition in this loop is true three times, so *largest_ndx* changes three times. It finally becomes 5 at the end of the *j* loop. Then the score in slot 5 is swapped with the score in slot 1, the value of *i*. This ends the second pass. Now the first two slots of the array are in order and the rest of the array remains to be sorted.

The outer loop continues until the scores in the slots up to index 4 are in order. *i* doesn't have to go to 5 because by that time, the smallest number is already in slot number 5. Besides, if *i* were to go to 5, then the *j* loop wouldn't even start. *i* and *largest_ndx* would both be 5. Now the sort is complete and the arrays are printed using one loop.

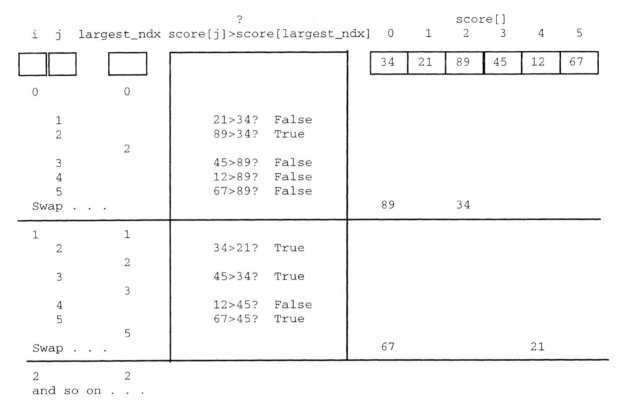

Figure 8.3 A partial trace for the selection sort.

Solution 8.6
A[0][1] is 120 and A[2][4] is 40.
A[i][j] would be A[1][2] or 110.
A[j][i] would be A[2][1] or 20.

Drill 8.7 In this code, when *i* is 0, *j* varies from 0 to 4. While *i* is 0, the output would be 50, 120, 30, 150, 80. Show the complete output.

```
for(i = 0; i <= 2; i = i + 1)
{
    for(j = 0; j <= 4; j = j + 1)
        printf("%d\t", A[i][j]);
    printf("\n");
}
```

EXPERIMENTS

Exp 8.1 When *i* is fixed, *j* varies.

```
int i, j;
for(i = 1; i <= 3; i = i + 1)
{
    for(j = 1; j <= 4; j = j + 1)
        printf("i=%d\tj=%d\n", i, j);
    printf("\n");
}
```

a. There are two loops above, the *i* loop and the *j* loop.
    Which loop is the outer loop?
b. Which loop would you call the nested loop?
c. Which loop is done only once? Which one is repeated?
d. How many times is *i* set to 1? How many times is *j* set to 1?
e. Which variable varies faster than the other?
f. What is the effect of omitting the braces?

Exp 8.2 The part that is different from Exp 8.1 is shown in bold.

```
int i, j;
for(i = 1; i <= 3; i = i + 1)
{
    for(j = 1; j <= 4; j = j + 1)
        printf("%d\t", i * j);
    printf("\n");
}
```

a. First, *i* is 1 and *j* is 1. What is printed at that time?
b. Then, *i* is 1 and *j* is 2. What is printed at that time? Why is it on the same line?
c. Eventually, *i* is 1 and *j* is 4. What is printed at that time?
d. Now that the *j* loop is complete for the first time, what happens before *i* becomes 2?
e. When *i* is 2 and *j* is 3, what is printed?
f. When *i* is 3 and *j* is 4, what is printed?

Solution 8.7

50	120	30	150	80
140	70	110	90	100
30	20	0	60	40

Drill 8.8 Now let us swap *i* and *j* subscripts in the printf(). Here, *j* would be the row subscript and *j* shouldn't go up to 4 because we don't have that many rows. Hence, the for loop statements have to be rewritten as shown. Show the complete output.

```
for(i = 0; i <= 4; i = i + 1)
{
    for(j = 0; j <= 2; j = j + 1)
        printf("%d\t", A[j][i]);
    printf("\n");
}
```

130   Nested Loops and 2D Arrays

Exp 8.3 Can you complete only the for statement for the *j* loop so that the output is as shown below? When *i* is 1, we want *j* to go as far as 1. When *i* is 2, we want *j* to go as far as 2, and so on.

```
1
2    4
3    6    9
4    8    12    16
```

```
2
3    4
4    5    6
5    6    7    8
```

```c
int i, j;
for(i = 1; i <= 4; i = i + 1)
{
    for(j =  ; j <=  ; j = j + 1)
        printf("%d\t", i * j);
    printf("\n");
}
```

a. Can you replace i * j with something else in the printf() to give this output?

Exp 8.4 *a[ ][ ]* is a 2D array. The first index is always the row index and the second one is always the column. *a[ ][ ]* here has 3 rows and 4 columns. *i*, being the first index, is the index for the row. If *j* were the first index, then it would have been the row index. The array is initialized in memory as shown here.

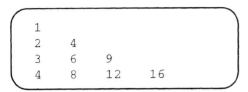

Column indexes

```c
int i, j, a[3][4] = {1, 2, 3, 4, 5, 6, 7,
                        8, 9, 10, 11, 12};
for(i = 0; i <= 2; i = i + 1)
{
    for(j = 0; j <= 3; j = j + 1)
        printf("%d\t", a[i][j]);
    printf("\n");
}
```

a. When *i* is 0 and *j* is 0, the element in the first row and the first column is printed. When *i* is 0 and *j* is 1, the element in which slot is printed?
b. When *i* is 0 and *j* is 3, the element in which slot is printed?
c. When *i* is 2 and *j* is 1, the element in which slot is printed?

Solution 8.8 Initially *i*, the column, is 0 and the first column is printed on the first line.

```
50     140    30
120    70     20
30     110    0
150    90     60
80     100    40
```

Drill 8.9 The following code goes through the entire array. At each slot it checks if the value is greater than 100.
What will be printed?
Are the slots of the array visited row–wise or column–wise?
Why aren't there any braces in the code?

```c
int count = 0;
for(i = 0; i <= 4; i = i + 1)
    for(j = 0; j <= 2; j = j + 1)
        if(A[j][i] > 100)
            count = count + 1;
printf("%d \n", count);
```

Nested Loops and 2D Arrays

Exp 8.5 Answer the following questions as if you had changed the printf() to printf("%d\t", a[j][i]); and reversed the rolls of *i* and *j*.

a. When *i* is 0 and *j* is 0, the element in which slot is printed?
b. When *i* is 0 and *j* is 1, the element in which slot is printed?
c. When *i* is 0 and *j* is 2, the element in which slot is printed?
d. When *i* is 1 and *j* is 0, the element in which slot is printed?
e. What would have been your output? Check your answer by running this version.

Exp 8.6 Change Experiment 8.4 by changing the parts shown here in bold.

```
for(i = 2; i >= 0; i = i - 1)
{
    for(j = 3; j >= 0; j = j - 1)
        printf("%d\t", a[i][j]);
    printf("\n");
}
```

a. When *i* is 2 and *j* is 3, the element in which row and which column is printed?
b. When *i* is 2 and *j* is 2, the element in which row and which column is printed?
c. When *i* is 2 and *j* is 0, the element in which row and which column is printed?
d. When *i* is 1 and *j* is 3, the element in which row and which column is printed?
e. When the last element is printed, what is *i* and what is *j*?

Exp 8.7 In this experiment, the first loop scans characters into a character array and the second prints them. For both loops, *i* stays fixed while *j* varies or the row stays fixed while the column varies. Hence, the data is read in the array row-wise and printed out row-wise. Enter this data: a, b, c, d, e, f, g, h, i, j, k, l. Remember the space preceding the %c in the scanf().

```
int i, j;
char a[3][4];
for(i = 0; i <= 2; i = i + 1)
    for(j = 0; j <= 3; j = j + 1)
        scanf(" %c", &a[i][j]);
```

Solution 8.9

The output is 3. Only three items are found to be greater than 100. The array is accessed column-wise because *i*, the column in this case, is kept constant while *j* is varied.

The *i* loop has only one statement in its body, namely, the *j* loop. The *j* loop has only one statement in its body, namely, the if statement. If the if condition is true, only one statement has to be executed, namely, count = count + 1. Hence, there are no braces needed. The last printf() is independent from all of the above.

Drill 8.10 Write the code to find the largest number in each column. Here's a start:

```
int largest;
for(i = 0; i <= 4; i = i + 1)
{
    largest = A[0][i];
    for(j = 1; j <= 2; j = j + 1)
```

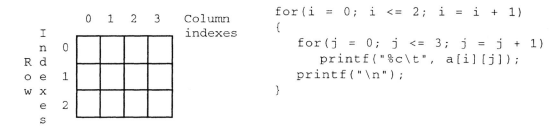

```
for(i = 0; i <= 2; i = i + 1)
{
    for(j = 0; j <= 3; j = j + 1)
        printf("%c\t", a[i][j]);
    printf("\n");
}
```

Questions for the reading loop:

a. Initially when *i* is 0 and *j* is 0, the first character entered is read.

b. In the figure above, write this first character read in the proper slot.

c. Write the second character in its proper slot. What is *i* and *j*?

d. Fill in all the characters that are read into this array properly.

Questions for the printing loop.

e. Initially when *i* is 0 and *j* is 0, which character is printed?

f. What is the second character printed?

g. How many characters are printed before the '\n' is printed?

h. Was the first row or the first column of the array printed first?

Exp 8.8 Use the same array and the data for Experiment 8.7. All changes are shown in bold. Notice that for reading only, *i* and *j* have been reversed.

```
int i, j,
char a[3][4];

for(i = 0; i <= 3; i = i + 1)
    for(j = 0; j <= 2; j = j + 1)
        scanf(" %c", &a[j][i]);

for(i = 0; i <= 2; i = i + 1)
{
    for(j = 0; j <= 3; j = j + 1)
        printf("%c\t", a[i][j]);
    printf("\n");
}
```

Solution 8.10

```
int largest;
for(i = 0; i <= 4; i = i + 1)
{
    largest = A[0][i];
    for(j = 1; j <= 2; j = j + 1)
        if(A[j][i] > largest)
            largest = A[j][i];
    printf("In column %d, the largest is %d \n", i, largest);
}
```

Drill 8.11 Change the code in Solution 8.10 so that for each column, the index of the largest number is printed.

```
----- output -----
1   0   1   0   1
```

Nested Loops and 2D Arrays

a. When reading, notice that *j* and not *i* is the row subscript. This is because *j* is used as the first index with a[ ][ ]. When reading, why did *i* go up to 3 and *j* go only to 2?

b. When reading and when *i* was 0 and *j* was 0, show the character that was read in the correct slot in the figure on the previous page.

c. When *i* was 0 and *j* was 1, show the character that was read.

d. Fill in all elements in the array as they are read in. Does your answer check with your output?

Exp 8.9 Strings are read in by the rows. Each row will have one string. Enter the following data: "you", "my", "luv". Remember that, after each string, a null character is added. We're reading in strings, but printing out only characters.

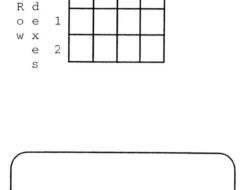

```
int i, j,
char a[3][4];
printf("Give 3 3-characters strings.\n");

for(i = 0; i <= 2; i = i + 1)
    scanf("%s", &a[i]);

for(i = 0; i <= 2; i = i + 1)
{
    for(j = 0; j <= 3; j = j + 1)
        printf("%c", a[i][j]);
    printf("\n");
}
```

a. Show the contents of the array in memory after the three strings are read in the array.

b. Does your output agree?

c. How is the null character, '\0', printed?

d. Is there a garbage character in a[1][3]? If so, why?

QUESTIONS

1. Show the output for each question. Parts of the code that are different from the previous question are shown in bold.

Solution 8.11
```
int largest;
for(i = 0; i <= 4; i = i + 1)
{
   largest = 0;  //For the "i" column, the index of the largest is 0.
   for(j = 1; j <= 2; j = j + 1)//Go through the next two rows.
     if(A[j][i] > A[largest][i])   //If necessary,
        largest = j;                        //adjust the index of the largest.
   printf("In column %d, the largest number's index is %d \n",
          i, largest);
}
```

Drill 8.12 Using *i* for the row index and *j* for the column index, write the code to read the data into the array as shown in Drill 8.6. The data are being entered in this sequence:

50 120 30 150 80 140 70 110 90 100 30 20 0 60 40

a.
```
for(i = 1; i <= 3; i = i + 1)
{
   for(j = 1; j <= 3; j = j + 1)
      printf("%d\t", i - j);
   printf("\n");
}
```
b.
```
for(i = 1; i <= 3; i = i + 1)
{
   for(j = 1; j <= i; j = j + 1)
      printf("%d\t", 2 * i - j);
   printf("\n");
}
```

2. Show the output for each part. Use the following array:
```
int a[3][3] = {10, 20, 30, 40, 50, 60, 70, 80, 90};
```
a.
```
for(i=0; i <= 2; i = i + 1)
{
   for(j = 0; j <= 2; j = j + 1)
      printf("%d\t", a[i][j]);
   printf("\n");
}
```
b.
```
for(i=0; i <= 2; i = i + 1)
{
   for(j = 0; j <= 2; j = j + 1)
      printf("%d\t", a[j][i]);
   printf("\n");
}
```
c.
```
for(i=0; i <= 2; i = i + 1)
{
   for(j = 0; j <= 2; j = j + 1)
      printf("%d\t", a[i][2 - j]);
   printf("\n");
}
```

Solution 8.12

```
for(i = 0; i <= 2; i = i + 1)
   for(j = 0; j <= 4; j = j + 1)
      scanf("%d", &A[i][j]);
```

Drill 8.13 Using the following array, read the strings "I", "do", and "well" into the character array. Notice that for this 2D array, only one subscript is specified. One subscript works because we are reading in strings. Show the contents of the array, including the null character.

```
char A[3][5];
for(i = 0; i <= 2; i = i + 1)
   scanf("%s", &A[i]);
```

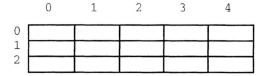

Nested Loops and 2D Arrays   135

d.
```
for(i=0;  i <= 2;  i = i + 1)
{
    for(j = 2;  j >= 0;  j = j - 1)
        printf("%d\t", a[2][j]);
    printf("\n");
}
```

PROGRAMS

1. The following programs are all related to each other, but each can be done without doing the others. Use loops and nested loops whenever possible. Remember that the array could have been much bigger than what is shown, but the programs would be the same. Use the array *bus[ ][ ]* for each part. The rows represent the bus routes and the columns represent the days that the buses run. The numbers in the slots of the array show the number of passengers that were on a given route on a given day.

`int bus[4][5];`

		Mon 0	Tue 1	Wed 2	Thur 3	Fri 4
R o u	0	8	12	9	7	10
t	1	5	7	3	0	4
e	2	20	15	18	21	14
s	3	6	9	5	8	11

Figure 8.4 The bus[4][5] array.

a. Read the data into the array by receiving the data by columns.
```
----- output -----
Give the number of passengers for day 1:  8    5    20    6
Give the number of passengers for day 2:  12   7    15    9
                                                    . . . etc.
```

b. Print the number of passengers as shown in Figure 8.4.
c. Print the total number of passengers for Mon.
d. Print the total number of passengers for the route stored in row 0.
e. Print the maximum number of passengers for the route stored in row 3.

Solution 8.13 The strings are read in row–wise. Each slot contains one character. At the end of the string, there is a null character to mark the end of the string.

	0	1	2	3	4
0	'I'	'\0'			
1	'd'	'o'	'\0'		
2	'w'	'e'	'l'	'l'	'\0'

Drill 8.14 Write a single loop to print the array of strings in Solution 8.13.

Nested Loops and 2D Arrays

f. Print the minimum number of passengers for Thur.

g. Print the average number of passengers for all days and all routes.

h. Find the row with the largest number of passengers and print that number and the index.

2. Rewrite the sorting section of Example 8.1. Instead of a selection sort algorithm, use an insertion sort algorithm. This algorithm takes the next score in the array and inserts it in the proper place in the front part of the array that has been sorted. For example, in Figure 8.5, during the first pass, the score of 34 is compared with only 21 and since they are already in order, nothing is done. However, during the second pass of the sort, the score of 89 appears in the next slot. To make room for this score, 34 and 21 are first moved down and then 89 is placed at index 0. Next, the score of 45 is inserted between 89 and 34. As seen in Figure 8.5, the sort is completed by inserting the next number in its proper place.

3. A doll costs $20, a toy car costs $6, and a yoyo costs $1. What combinations of toys will allow you to buy 100 toys for $200? You will need three nested loops and a break statement.

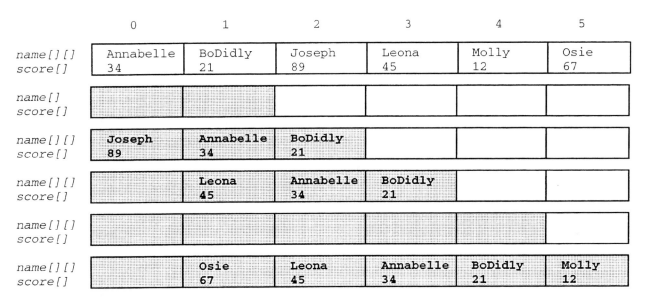

Figure 8.5 The insertion sort process.

Solution 8.14

```
for(i = 0; i <= 2; i = i + 1)
   printf("%s\n", A[i]);
```

Functions with No Returns

LESSON

Advantages of Functions

Functions are very important in C and C++, which is why we started the text with them. We saw how we always call main() and how main() may call other functions, such as printf() or strcpy(). We saw how we passed arguments to functions. Let us now consider the advantages of functions.

For one thing, they make the program more organized and readable. Simply look at main() and see what functions it calls. If good names are given to these functions, we can get a good idea of what the program is doing and how it is divided without actually going into much of its detail. For example, consider this main():

```
void main (void)
{  initialize_settings();
   read_in_data();
   process_data_against_the_settings();
   print_report();
}
```

DRILLS

Drill 9.1 Study the diagram on page 139 where main() is calling a function called testing(). testing(), in turn, calls printf(). When main() calls testing(), no arguments or parameters are passed, which is noted by the empty parentheses. When testing() calls printf(), the argument "nice!\n" is passed. When writing a function other than main(), you should provide a prototype at the top of the program, declaring what the function receives and what it returns. Think of the prototype as a declaration for a variable, such as, int i; where the type of the variable is specified. The prototype is also declaring the function type, void, in this case. Number the events in order starting from 1.

___ testing() calls printf(). ___ We call main() ___ main() begins to execute by calling testing() ___ End of the program. ___ Execution returns to main() from testing().

We can see that this program is divided into four parts and we can get a general idea of what those parts accomplish. If we are concerned about a specific part, we can look at the code for that function and obtain more details. If we don't care, then the coding for that function is not cluttering up main().

Another reason why functions are useful is that they make duplicating of code unnecessary. Consider this code:

```
     :
if(temp_city1 <=32)
   printf("it is freezing in %s\n", "Seattle");
else
   printf("it is not freezing in %s\n", "Seattle");
if(temp_city2 <= 32)
   printf("it is freezing in %s\n", "Oslo");
else
   printf("it is not freezing in %s\n", "Oslo");
     :
```

Contrast it with the following code.

```
print_freezing_or_not(temp1, "Seattle"); //calling the function
print_freezing_or_not(temp1, "Oslo");    //calling the function again.
     :                :
void print_freezing_or_not(int x, char city[ ]); //defining the function.
{
   if(x <= 32)
      printf("it is freezing in %s\n", city);
   else
      printf("it is not freezing in %s\n", city)
}
```

After the initial investment to write the function, it can be called over and over again with only one line. The logic appears in only one place rather than in several places. Without functions, if there is a problem with the logic, it has to be corrected in many places. What if in all the places except one such a mistake was corrected? Then we would have to come back to the same general problem and continue correcting it.

With functions, the logic can be written in only one place: in the function. If there is a problem with the logic, it has to be corrected in only one place. Furthermore, if the logic has to be

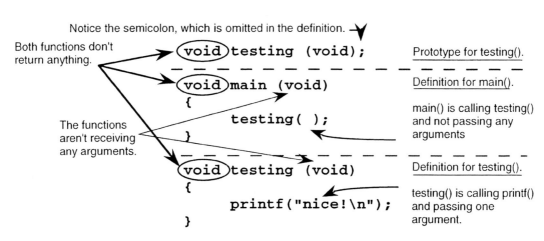

modified later, say, we also wanted to print if the temperature was above 100 degrees, then such a change would have to be done in only one place. The larger the program, the more important it becomes to use functions properly.

Very large programs can be written by a team of programmers rather than by just one person and thus the job can be done faster. Each programmer would be assigned certain functions to write. Of course, this arrangement requires that what each function does, what arguments it receives, and what it returns must be documented accurately. Otherwise, there would be misunderstandings between programmers and how they write the functions.

Functions can be used again by other programmers, if needed, in different programs.

About Functions

The function that is calling another one is called the "calling function." The function that is being called is called the "called function." Functions may receive arguments (also called parameters) or they may not receive any. They may return only one value or none at all. A tricky thing to look out for is that, if an array is being passed by the calling function, the called function may change it and the change could affect the original array in the calling function. This is not true of scalars (non–arrays).

First Example

Example 9.1 shows a simple function. Aside from writing main(), this is the first time we are writing our own function. We have used printf() and others, but they were system–defined functions. The name of this user–defined function is balance_avg(). This name appears in the program four times. It appears first in the function prototype, just before main(). Here, "void" means that this function doesn't return anything and the two int's inside the parentheses mean that this function requires two integers as receiving arguments. This is where the function is said to be declared. If the function is called or defined incorrectly, then this line would signal an inconsistency.

The function name appears the second and third time in main() when balance_avg() is called. At that time, two integers are passed as arguments. The first time, two numbers or constants are provided and the next time, numbers from the two arrays are provided, pair by pair, in a loop.

The fourth time, the function is defined. The first line of the definition mirrors the prototype, but here the names of the arguments, not just their data types, are given. Another difference between the function declaration and its definition is that, in the declaration, a semicolon is placed. In the definition, no semicolon is used, just as when we define main().

Solution 9.1
_3_ testing() calls printf(). _1_ We call main() _2_ main() begins to execute by calling testing()
_5_ End of the program. _4_ Execution returns to main() from testing().

Drill 9.2 Check off the items requiring semicolons at the end of their lines.
____ Calling a function.
____ Heading for a function definition.
____ Prototype for a function.

In the header for a function definition, which void, the first one or the one in the parentheses, means that the function isn't receiving any arguments?_____ Which one means that the function isn't returning any values? _____

```
//EXAMPLE 9.1     Introduction to functions.
#include <stdio.h>
void balance_avg(int, int );                        //Function prototype

void main (void)
{
    int  bal1[5] = {500, 200, 400, 100, 700},  //Balances for one month.
         bal2[5] = {800, 300, 400, 0, 600},    //Balances for another.
         i;                                    //Array index.

    balance_avg(1000, 200);             //Calling the function.
    for(i = 0; i <= 4; ++i)             //"++i" is same as: "i = i + 1"
       balance_avg(bal1[i], bal2[i]);   //Calling the function in a loop.
}


/* balance avg() -------------------------------------------------------
     will print the average of two integers with two decimal points.
     To call this function:
       Pass two integers.
     Upon completion:
       No "return" is executed,
       but the average of the integers will be printed.              */
void balance_avg(int x, int y)
{
    float average;
    average = (x * 1.0 + y ) / 2;   //Multiplying by 1.0 makes it a float.
    printf("%.2f\n", average);
}
----- output -----
600.00
650.00
250.00
400.00
 50.00
650.00
```

Solution 9.2

_Yes__ Calling a function.
_No __ Heading for a function definition.
_Yes__ Prototype for a function.

The void in parentheses means that the function isn't receiving any arguments.
The first void means that the function isn't returning any values.

Drill 9.3 Rewrite only main() in Drill 9.1, which calls testing() two times. Also provide the output.

ball[ ], *bal2[ ]*, and *i* are local variables only to main(). balance_avg() isn't aware of their existence. Similarly, *x*, *y*, and *average* are local variables only to balance_avg(), and main() isn't aware of their existence. In fact, if *x* were also named as *ball* in balance_avg(), the program would execute the same as before. In that case, neither *ball* would know that the other *ball* existed.

Let's walk through the program. We have two initialized arrays that contain the bank balances of five customers. Each array has the balances of the customers at the end of two months. First, we want to find the average of a new customer whose balances are not in the arrays. We pass 1000 and 200 as arguments as we call the function balance_avg(). Now we are executing the code in this function.

Here, *x* becomes 1000 and *y* becomes 200. *average* is calculated by first multiplying *x* by 1.0. This makes the answer a floating point value, so the *average* is calculated to be 600.0 and then it is printed. The function definition shows void, meaning that this function doesn't return anything, and it doesn't. Control of execution comes back to main(), where it was left off. The for loop is next.

In the for loop, *i* varies from 0 to 4. Each time we call the function we pass the next pair of balances to the function, where the average is printed. In this loop, the function is called five times and we return from the function five times. Whenever we return from the function, the value of *i* is remembered so the loop knows how many more times to iterate. Once the loop is over, main() is complete.

Linked List Using Arrays

This section is a good introduction to the topic of pointers. Many students say that this topic is the most difficult in C and C++. I hope when we come to that unit, you won't think so. Example 9.2, the example developed in this section, will make the concept of pointers easier to understand because it uses an array called *link[ ]*, which stores array indexes. Just as each memory location has an address associated with it, so does each array element have an index associated with it. If you become versatile working with array indexes, then working with memory addresses will become much easier. Unit 3 has already introduced memory addresses.

Figure 9.1 shows the names of composers who are played on our radio station. They are stored in an array called *composer[ ]*, starting at an index of 1 instead of 0. Element 0 is not used. Below each composer is the number of listener requests we have received. The requests are stored in an array called *requests[ ]* that is parallel to the *composer[ ]* array. Sometimes we want to have the composer names in order and other times we would like to have the number of requests in order. The problem is that we can't have both arrays in order.

One way we can keep both the composers and their requests in order is by using a linked list. See Figure 9.2. We have added a new array called *link[ ]*. This array starts at index 0. The value stored in *link[0]* always tells where the smallest number of requests is stored. *link[0]* is 3, which means that requests[3], with 70, has the smallest number of requests.

Solution 9.3

```
void main (void)
{
    testing();
    testing();
}
----- output -----
nice!
nice!
```

Drill 9.4 Rewrite only testing() in Drill 9.1 so that the output will be the same as shown in Solution 9.3.

	[1]	[2]	[3]	[4]	[5]
composer[ ]:	"Bach"	"Beethoven"	"Chopin"	"Mozart"	"Schubert"
requests[ ]:	145	150	70	110	95

Figure 9.1 How can we keep both the composers and the number of requests in order?

To find the next smallest number of requests, we access the *link[ ]* slot parallel to requests[3]; that is link[3]. This slot has a 5 in it, which means that requests[5] is the next smallest number of requests. It is 95. To find the next smallest number of requests, we look at link[5]. This is 4. requests[4], or 110, is the next smallest number. Then link[4] points to 1. requests[1] is 145 and link[1] contains 2, meaning that requests[2] is the next one. Last, link[2] is 0. Reaching a 0 means that we are at the end of this ordered chain of indexes. A proper term for this structure is a "linked list."

Each slot in the *link[ ]* array specifies which is the next slot in this linked list. We also need to know where the beginning of the linked list is. We use link[0] to tell us where the beginning of the list is. We also need to know when the list ends. Once a 0 is found in *link[ ]*, then we know this is the end. If link[0] is 0, then there are no elements in the list and the linked list is empty. This would be the case if no elements have been added to the list.

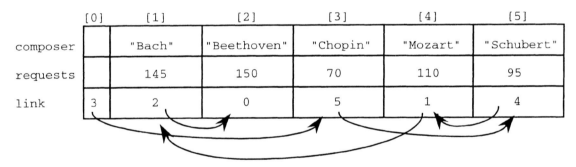

	[0]	[1]	[2]	[3]	[4]	[5]
composer		"Bach"	"Beethoven"	"Chopin"	"Mozart"	"Schubert"
requests		145	150	70	110	95
link	3	2	0	5	1	4

Figure 9.2 A linked list is one way we can keep both the composers and the number of requests in order.

Solution 9.4

```
void testing (void)
{
   printf("nice!\n");
   printf("nice!\n");
}
```

Drill 9.5 Rewrite only the main() in Drill 9.1 so that testing() is called in a loop four times. Use ++i, which is the abbreviated version of i = i + 1. The output will be:

```
----- output -----
nice!
nice!
nice!
nice!
```

Functions with No Returns

```
//EXAMPLE 9.2    A linked list using arrays.
#include <stdio.h>
#define SIZE 6
void link_them (int [ ], int [ ], int);

void main (void)
{
   char composer [SIZE][15] =
           { " ", "Bach", "Beethoven", "Chopin", "Mozart", "Schubert"};
   int requests[SIZE] = {0, 145, 150, 70, 110, 95};
   int i, link[SIZE];

   link_them(requests, link, SIZE);//Call function, create a linked list.

   // Print out the requests in order, using the links.
   for(i = link[0]; i != 0; i = link[i])
      printf("%s\t%d\n", composer[i], requests[i]);
}


/*-------------------------------------------------------------------
   link them()
      will make a linked list so that the requests are in order.
   To call this function:
      R[ ] and max should be initialized and L[ ] is not.
   Upon completion:
      R[ ] and max are unchanged
      L[ ] is a linked list that logically ordered the requests.      */

void link_them (
      int R[ ],   //The number of requests for each composer.
      int L[ ],   //Will become a liked list.
      int max)    //This minus 1 is the number of requests to be ordered.
{
   int  i,       //The index of the next request to be placed in list.
        j,       //The index used to find the correct place in the list.
        prev_j;  //The previous value of j.
   L[0] = 1;     //Initialize the linked list for the first request.
   L[1] = 0;
```

Solution 9.5
```
void main (void)
{
   int i;
   for(i = 1; i <= 4; ++i)
      testing();
}
void testing (void)
{
   printf("nice!\n");
}
```

Drill 9.6 Rewrite only testing() in Drill 9.1 so that printf() is called in a loop four times. The output will be the same as in Drill 9.5.

```
//R[i] is the next request to be placed in the list.
for(i = 2; i <= max - 1; i = i + 1)
{
    prev_j = 0;
    //Find the index j where L[i] should point.
    for(j = L[prev_j]; j != 0; j = L[j])
    {
        if(R[i] < R[j])
        {                   //Found the place to insert L[i] in the list.
            L[prev_j]   = i;
            L[i]        = j;
            break;          //Get the next request to be added to the list.
        }
        prev_j = j;    //Start moving forward in the linked list.
    }

    if( j == 0 )       //If the point to insert L[i] is not found at all,
    {                  // add it to the end of the linked list.
        L[i]        = 0;
        L[prev_j]   = i;
    }
}
}
----- output -----
Chopin       70
Schubert     95
Mozart       110
Bach         145
Beethoven    150
```

main() of Example 9.2

As shown in Figure 9.1, the two arrays *composer[ ]* and *requests[ ]* are initialized in Example 9.2. The first, or the 0th, elements of these arrays are not used. *link[ ]* is not initialized. This array will become a linked list as shown in Figure 9.2 once we call the function link_them(). This is the first executable statement in main(). main() will pass the *link[ ]* and *requests[ ]* arrays. When arrays are passed to a function, that function may alter its contents and those changes will be reflected in the calling function's arrays. That is what will happen here. link_them() will not change

---

Solution 9.6

```
void main(void)
{
    testing();
}
void testing (void)
{
    int i;
    for(i = 1; i <= 4; ++i)
        printf("nice!\n");
}
```

Drill 9.7 In Solution 9.5, testing() is called how many times? Once we are in testing(), printf() is called how many times? In Solution 9.6, testing() is called how many times? printf() is called how many times? What is the total number of times that printf() is called in each solution?

Functions with No Returns   145

```
Statement which
changes "i."          i      i != 0?        printout
--------------        -      -------        ----------------
i = link[0]:          3      True
                                         Chopin       70
i = link[3]:          5      True
                                         Schubert     95
i = link[5]:          4      True
                                         Mozart       110
i = link[4]:          1      True
                                         Bach         145
i = link[1]:          2      True
                                         Beethoven    150
i = link[2]:          0      False
```

Figure 9.3 Using the linked list to print the requests in order.

the *requests[ ]* array; it will be used only to "look" at its numbers. However, the function will place array indexes in the *link[ ]* array, making it a linked list. That is the fun part and we will save it for later. First, let us say that the links have been properly established in link_them() and now we want to print out the responses in order, as done in main().

Let us follow Figure 9.3, which shows the tracechart for the loop for the linked list that appears in Figure 9.2. In the first statement of the for loop, i = link[0], a 3 is assigned to *i*. The condition, i != 0?, is found to be true, so the printf() is executed. This prints composer[3], or "Chopin," and requests[3], or 70.

Now we go up to the for statement. i = link[i] reduces to i = link[3] since *i* is 3. After this statement, the number in link[3], which is 5, becomes the new value of *i*. 5 isn't equal to 0 so we go back into the body of the loop. Here, "Schubert" and 95 are printed and we go back up to the for loop.

i is 5 so link[5] is 4. The new value of *i* becomes 4. Here, "Mozart" and 110 are printed and we go back up to the for statement. *i* is 4 so link[4] is 1. The new value of *i* becomes 1. Here, "Bach" and 145 are printed and we go back up to the for statement.

Likewise, i = link[1] makes *i* equal to 2. Printing the composer and requests for slot number 2 shows "Beethoven" and 150. We return to the for statement and i = link[2] assigns 0 to *i*. This stops the loop and all the composers and their requests are printed in ascending order. If we had wanted to print their names in order, then a loop that doesn't use the *link[ ]* array would suffice.

Solution 9.7 In Solution 9.5, testing() is called four times. Each time we are in testing(), printf() is called only once.

In Solution 9.6, testing() is called only once, but once we are in testing(), printf() is called four times. In either case, printf() is called four times.

Drill 9.8

```
void testing (char [ ]);
void testing (char str[ ])
{
    int i;
    for(i = 1; i <= 4; ++i)
        printf("%s\t", str);
    printf("\n");
}
```

Now we want testing() to accept any string as an argument so that, depending on what string we pass to testing(), that string will be printed in a loop. We wouldn't be restricted to printing only "nice!". I have given you the prototype (notice that the name of the argument is optional) and the definition for testing(). *str[]* is the argument that will be printed four times in a loop. Can you write main() so that when testing() is called, you pass the string "nice!" to it? Also show the output. Notice the brackets have no numbers in them.

Functions with No Returns

link_them() of Example 9.2

Now let us turn our attention back to the function link_them(). This function receives $R[\ ]$, $L[\ ]$, and *max* as arguments from main(). $R[\ ]$ is the same array as *requests[ ]* and $L[\ ]$ is the same array as *link[ ]*. Keeping the brackets empty with the arrays allows us to use a variable length array. One time we can send 5 element arrays and another time send 450 element arrays. One subtracted from the number in *max*, gives us the number of elements in the arrays. Initially, $R[\ ]$ is already set up, but $L[\ ]$ is empty.

Follow Figure 9.4 and the code for Example 9.2. The code places each element of $R[\ ]$ into a linked list, one at a time. Before any loop is encountered, the first element of $L[\ ]$ is placed in the linked list. To do this, L[0] points to 1 (or has a 1 for its value) and L[1] is 0, meaning that we are at the end of the list. We have only one element, 145, in the list right now. See $L[\ ]$ as shown on the first bold line in Figure 9.4.

Now we go into the *i* loop. When *i* is 2, we are placing element 2 in the list; when *i* is 3, we are placing element 3 in the list, and so on. Right now *i* is 2. 2 is not less than 6, so we go into the body of the *i* loop. Here, *prev_j* is made 0 and in the *j* loop, *j* is made equal to the next link in the list (or 1). *j* is not equal to 0 so we enter the *j* loop.

In the *j* loop, we go down the linked list to see where R[i] should go in the list. Once we find out where it goes, then L[i] is placed in the link. *prev_j* is needed to know the position of the previous link.

Inside the *j* loop, we see that R[2] < R[1]? is false. 150 isn't less than 145. Then we march down the link, making *prev_j* equal to *j* and advancing *j* to the next link. However, it is 0. We have gone all the way to the end of the linked list and the number we want to link in, 150, is larger than any number in the list. We have to add 150 at the end of the list.

The *j* loop is complete. Since *j* is equal to 0, we make L[2] equal to 0 or mark it as the end of the list and make L[1] equal to 2. This brings us to the second bold line in Figure 9.4.

i becomes 3. 70 is the next number to be placed in the list. Again, using *j* and bringing *prev_j* just behind *j*, we look for the first number in the list that is greater than 70. The very first number in the list is 145. It is greater than 70. Therefore using *prev_j*, we make slot 0 point to *i*, or 3, and make L[j] or L[3] point to 1, which is the value of *j*.

The loop continues as the next R[i] is placed in the linked list. The tracechart shows what happens when the fourth number is placed in the list and finally when the last one, 95, is placed in the list. Each time a number is added, the list becomes bigger and continues to be a valid linked list. That is, the beginning of the list is pointed to by L[0], and each successive number is placed in the proper place in the list. The last link has a 0 in it, marking it as the end of the chain. You should make a tracechart for a different set of numbers and verify the logic of the function for yourself.

Solution 9.8

```
void main(void)
{
    testing("nice!");
}
----- output -----
nice!    nice!    nice!    nice!
```

Drill 9.9

Now rewrite main() so that it calls testing() twice, once as it passes "nice!" and the next time as it passes "sweet!" as arguments. Show the output again.

Statement:	i	prev_j	j	j!=0?	R[i]<R[j]?	j==0?	L[0]	L[1]	L[2]	L[3]	L[4]	L[5]
R[ ]: ->							145	150	70	110	95	
L[0] = 1;							1					
L[1] = 0;								0				
							1	**0**				
j=L[prev_j]	2	0	1	T								
					F							
prev_j=j		1										
j=L[j]			0	F								
						T						
L[i]=0									0			
L[prev_j]=i								2				
							1	**2**	**0**			
j=L[prev_j]	3	0	1	T								
					T							
L[prev_j]=i							3					
L[i]=j										1		
						F						
							3	**2**	**0**	**1**		
j=L[prev_j]	4	0	3	T								
					F							
prev_j=j		3										
j=L[j]			1	T								
					T							
L[prev_j]=i										4		
L[i]=j											1	
						F						
							3	**2**	**0**	**4**	**1**	

Figure 9.4 A partial tracechart for the link_them() function in Example 9.2.

Solution 9.9

```
void main(void)
{  testing("nice!");
   testing("sweet!");
}
----- output -----
nice!    nice!    nice!    nice!
sweet!   sweet!   sweet!   sweet!
```

Drill 9.10 Write main() so that, when using scanf(), it gets a string from the user and passes that string to testing(). Thus, it can print that string four times. Show the output for the string "kind" being read.

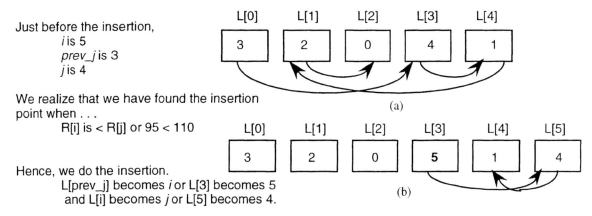

Just before the insertion,
i is 5
prev_j is 3
j is 4

L[0] L[1] L[2] L[3] L[4]
| 3 | 2 | 0 | 4 | 1 |

(a)

We realize that we have found the insertion
point when . . .
R[i] is < R[j] or 95 < 110

L[0] L[1] L[2] L[3] L[4] L[5]
| 3 | 2 | 0 | **5** | 1 | 4 |

Hence, we do the insertion.
L[prev_j] becomes *i* or L[3] becomes 5
and L[i] becomes *j* or L[5] becomes 4.

(b)

Figure 9.5 Inserting the 95 in L[5] in the linked list.

Let us go over how the last number, 95, is inserted into the list. The outer loop starts with *i* being 5. *prev_j* is 0 and *j* is L[prev_j], or 3. R[i], or 95, isn't less than R[j], or 70, so we go through the loop again. Now *prev_j* is 3 and *j* is 4. See Figure 9.5(a). R[i], or 95, is less than R[j], or 110, so we insert the slot five by making L[3] point to 5. An alternative would be to make the number following 70 a 95 and to have L[5] point to 4, or to make the number following 95 a 110. See Figure 9.5(b).

EXPERIMENTS

Exp 9.1

```
#include <stdio.h>
void funny (void); //This is a prototype.
void main (void)    //Always need main().
{
    funny( );              //main() calls funny().
    printf("Yes me!\n");
}

void funny (void)  //Defining funny().
{
    printf("Silly me. \n");
}
```

Solution 9.10

```
void main (void)
{
    char str[10];
    printf("Enter a small string: ");
    scanf("%s", &str);
    testing(str);
}
----- output -----
Enter a small string: kind
kind     kind     kind     kind
```

Drill 9.11

Write the main(), so that, using a loop, three strings are read in and testing() is called each time. Here's a sample output:

```
----- output -----
Enter a small string: kind
kind     kind     kind     kind
Enter a small string: good
good     good     good     good
Enter a small string: cute
cute     cute     cute     cute
```

a. Name two user-defined functions (function bodies which you have typed).
b. Name one system-defined function (a function which is made available to you by the compiler).
c. Execution starts at main(). What is the first function that main() calls?
d. What is the second function that main() calls after the first one is done?
e. What function does funny() call?
f. Number the following events in order from 1 through 3:
___ funny() calls printf()
___ main() calls printf()
___ main() calls funny()
g. How do we know where the definition of main() starts and ends?
h. How do we know where the definition of funny() starts and ends?
i. The (void) after main() indicates that main() doesn't receive any arguments. Does funny() receive any arguments?
j. The void before main() indicates that main() doesn't return any values. Does funny() return any values?
k. All programs must have main(). However, when defining a function other than main(), a prototype should be given, stating the name of the function, what arguments it receives, and what items it returns, if any. A prototype can be given inside or outside main(). Where is the prototype given here? (If these questions were difficult, you may want to review the lesson in Unit 1, where functions were discussed.)

Exp 9.2 The prototype needs a semicolon. Definitions for main() and funny() don't.

```
                                    #include <stdio.h>
                                    void funny (void);
                                    void main (void)
                                    {
                                        funny();
                                        printf("Yes me!\n");
                                        funny();  //Only change from before.
                                    }

                                    void funny (void)
                                    {
                                        printf("Silly me. \n");
                                    }
```

Solution 9.11

```
void main (void)
{
    int i;
    char str[10];
    for(i = 1; i <= 3; ++i)
    {
        printf("Enter a small string: ");
        scanf("%s", &str);
        testing(str);
    }
}
```

150

Drill 9.12

Now let us continue to add more flexibility to testing(). We also want the calling program to determine how many times the string will be printed. The calling program will pass two arguments, a string to be printed and an integer, and determine the number of times that string will be printed. First write the prototype.

a. Number the events in order from 1 to 5.
___ funny() calls printf()
___ funny() calls printf()
___ main() calls printf()
___ main() calls funny()
___ main() calls funny()
b. When main() calls funny(), which function do you think is the calling function?
c. Which function do you think is the called function?
d. When funny() calls printf(), which function do you think is the calling function?
e. Which function do you think is the called function?
f. Which function gets called and also calls another function?
g. When printf() is called from main(), "Yes me!\n" is the argument passed to printf(). What argument is being passed to printf() from funny()?
h. When main() calls funny(), is there an argument passed to funny()?

Exp 9.3 Enter the program only, including funny() but not the diagrams on the right.

```
#include <stdio.h>
void funny (void);
void main (void)                              i
{
    int i = 54;
    printf("i is %d\n", i);
    funny();
    printf("i is %d\n", i);
}

void funny (void)
{                                             i
    int i;
    printf("    i=%d\n", i);
    i = -28;
}
```

a. *i* is a local variable in main(), which means that only main() has access to it. What is the local variable in funny()?

Solution 9.12 Don't forget the semicolon at the end of the prototype.

```
void testing(char [ ], int);
```

Drill 9.13 Now write the definition for testing(). Call the string *str[]* as before and call the integer *num*.

b. main() sets the value of *i* to 54. Then it was printed. Execution then went to funny(). At the beginning of funny() was the value of *i* equal to 54 or just "garbage"?

c. funny() set the value of *i* to –28. After coming back to main(), what was the value of *i*?

d. Was the *i* in main() the same as *i* in funny()?

Exp 9.4

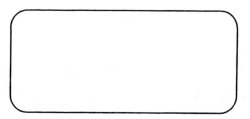

```
#include <stdio.h>
void funny (void);
void main (void)
{
        funny();
}
void funny (void)
{
    int i;
    for(i = 1; i <= 3; i = i + 1)
        printf("*");
    printf("\n");
}
```

Exp 9.5

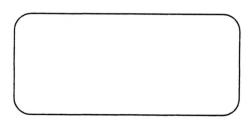

```
#include <stdio.h>
void funny (void);
void main (void)
{
    int i;
    for(i = 1; i <= 3; i = i + 1)
        funny();
    printf("\n");
}
void funny (void)
{
    printf("*");
}
```

a. How many times was funny() called in Experiment 9.4? In Experiment 9.5?

b. Every time that funny() was called, printf() was called how many times in Experiment 9.4? In Experiment 9.5?

Solution 9.13 Remember that there is no semicolon for the function header.
```
void testing(char str[ ], int num)
{ for( ; num != 0; num = num - 1)
     printf("%s\t", str);
   printf("\n");
}
```
-- OR --
```
void testing(char str[ ], int num)
{  int i;
   for(i = 1 ; i <= num; i = i + 1)
     printf("%s\t", str);
   printf("\n");
}
```

Drill 9.14

Write main() to go with our new testing(). Have main() call testing() twice. The first time have it pass "forgiving" and 3. The second time have it pass "patience" and 2. Also show the output.

Functions with No Returns

c. In total, how many times was printf() called in Experiment 9.4? In Experiment 9.5?

Exp 9.6

```
#include <stdio.h>
void funny (void);
void main (void)
{
    int i;
    for(i = 1; i <= 3; i = i + 1)
    {
        printf("i is %d\n", i);
        funny();
    }
}

void funny (void)
{
    int i;
    for(i = 1; i <= 2; i = i + 1)
        printf("    i=%d\n", i);
}
```

a. How many times does main() call funny()?
b. Each time that funny() is called, printf() is called how many times from funny()?
c. The loop in main() is done how many times?
d. The loop in funny() is done a total of how many times?
e. The printf() in main() is done how many times?
f. What is the total number of times that printf() is called from funny()?
g. Tracing the execution of this program, initially, main() sets *i* to 1. Then the control of execution goes to funny(). Here, *i* is also set to 1. From the output, can you determine whether this is the same *i*, or are they different?
h. Starting again, the *i* in main() is set to 1 and then the *i* in funny() goes from 1 to what value? After that, we go back to main() and now *i* is incremented to 2 and we come back to funny(). When we come back to funny(), *i* goes from 1 to what value? The third time we come back to funny(), *i* goes from 1 to what value?

Solution 9.14

```
void main (void)
{
    testing("forgiving", 3);
    testing("patience", 2);
}
----- output -----
forgiving   forgiving   forgiving
patience    patience
```

Drill 9.15

Now let us start working with arrays. main() has two integer arrays called A[3] and B[3]. Have main() send A[1] and B[1] to a function called largest(). This function should print the larger of the two integers. Write the function, the prototype, and the main().

Exp 9.7 Let us now pass arguments to funny(). The differences for the time when a function receives an argument are shown in **bold**.

```
#include <stdio.h>
void funny (int); //receiving an integer
void main (void)
{
        funny(4);       // 4 will go into num.
        printf("\n");
        funny(3);       // 3 will go into num.
}


//num is a formal argument.
void funny (int num)
{
        printf("num=%d\n", num);
}
```

a. main() calls funny() how many times?

b. What is the difference in how funny() is called here compared to how it is called in Experiment 9.6?

c. When funny() is called by main() for the first time, what argument (an integer) is passed?

d. When funny() is called by main() for the second time, what argument is passed?

e. What is the value of *num* when funny() is executed the first time?

f. What is the value of *num* when funny() is executed the second time?

g. In the prototype for funny(), should the data type of the argument be given?

h. In the prototype for funny(), do we have to give the variable name of the argument, that is, *num*?

i. In the definition for funny(), should we give the data type of the argument?

j. In the definition for funny(), is the variable name of the argument given?

k. Number the order of events:

___ funny() starts executing with *num* equal to 3

___ funny() starts executing with *num* equal to 4

___ main() calls printf() and sends one format string as an argument

___ main() calls funny() and sends 3 as an argument

___ main() calls funny() and sends 4 as an argument

___ funny() sends two arguments to printf(), a format string and *num*, which has a value of 3

___ funny() sends two arguments to printf(), a format string and *num*, which has a value of 4

Solution 9.15

```
void largest (int, int);
void main (void)
{
    int A[3] = {30, 20, 60},
        B[3] = {20, 50, 10};
    largest(A[1], B[1]);
}
void largest (int x, int y)
{
    if(x > y)
        printf("%d\n", x);
    else
        printf("%d\n", y);
}
```

Drill 9.16

Now write only the main(), largest() being the same as before. Using a loop, have main() send all three pairs of numbers, one pair at a time, to largest().

```
----- output -----
30
50
60
```

Exp 9.8

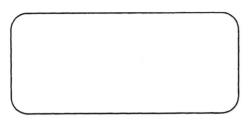

```
#include <stdio.h>
void funny (int);        //Function prototype.
void main (void)
{
        int i;
        for(i = 1;  i <= 5; i = i + 1)
           funny(i);
}

void funny (int num) //Function definition.
{
        int j;
        for(j = 1; j <= num; j = j + 1)
           printf("%d\t", j);
        printf("\n");
}
```

   a. If *j* were also named *i* in funny(), would there have been a problem?
   b. main() calls funny() how many times?
   c. Each time that funny() was called, what were the values that were passed?
   d. What were the values of *num* each time funny() was called?
   e. For every time that funny() was called, how many times was the *j* loop executed?

Exp 9.9

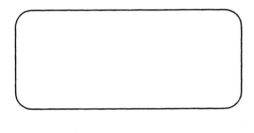

```
#include <stdio.h>
void funny (int, int);
void main (void)
{
        funny(5, 8);
}

void funny (int num1, int num2)
{
        for(; num1 <= num2; num1 = num1 + 1)
              printf("%d\n", num1);
}
```

Solution 9.16

```
void main (void)
{
   int  i, A[3] = {30, 20, 60},
           B[3] = {20, 50, 10};
   for(i = 0, i <= 2; ++i)
      largest(A[i], B[i]);
}
```

Drill 9.17

Now rewrite largest() and main(). Have main() pass the entire array to largest() and have largest() go through a loop, printing the largest in each pair.

a. When two arguments are passed to a function, should data types be given for each one in the prototype?

b. In the definition of funny(), do we need the keyword, int, in front of *num2* as well? Try it.

c. main() passes what two arguments to funny()?

d. In funny(), how do we know which of the passed values will become *num1* and *num2*?

e. How many times does main() call funny()? How many times does funny() call printf()?

Exp 9.10 Let us now pass an array.

```
#include <stdio.h>
void wish (int, char[ ]); //Prototype
void main (void)
{
        wish(5, "Zaire");
}

//Definition of wish().
void wish (int num, char country[ ])
{
        int i;
        for(i = 1; i <= num; i = i + 1)
            printf("I wish I was in %s\n",
                   country);
}
```

num   country

a. What are the two values passed to wish()?

b. In wish(), what becomes the value of *num*? What becomes the value of *country*? Write them in the boxes provided.

c. Notice that in both the prototype and the definition of wish(), there is no number in the brackets, giving the number of cells of country[ ]. Can you think why omitting this number makes the function more flexible for use in other instances?

d. How can we tell that "Zaire" is a character string? How can we tell that country[ ] should also be a character string?

e. If wish() were called from main() with this statement, wish (3, "Bogota");, then what would be the output?

Solution 9.17 When passing entire arrays, no subscripts are provided.

```
void largest (int[ ], int[ ]);
void main (void)
{
   int   A[3] = {30, 20, 60},
         B[3] = {20, 50, 10};
   largest(A, B);
}
```

```
void largest (int x[ ], int y[ ])
{
        int i;
        for(i = 0; i <= 2; ++i)
          if(x[i] > y[i])
            printf("%d\n", x[i]);
          else
            printf("%d\n", y[i]);
}
```

Drill 9.18 Change only largest() so that the array *x[ ]* will have the larger number of each respective pair. In this example, *A[ ]* would become: 30, 50, 60.

Exp 9.11 This diagram is misleading, although it seems correct! There are no loops this time. We are observing how functions handle arrays and scalars (non–arrays).

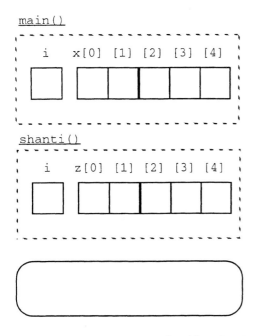

main()

shanti()

```c
#include <stdio.h>
void shanti (int, char[ ]);
void main (void)
{
        int i = 5;
        char x[ ] = "JOJO";
        printf("%d %s\n", i, x);//Stmt 1
        shanti(i, x);
        printf("%d %s\n", i, x);//Stmt 4
}
void shanti(int i, char z[ ])
{
        printf(" %d %s\n", i, z);      //Stmt 2
        i = 0;
        z[0] = 'M';
        printf(" %d %s\n", i, z);      //Stmt 3
}
```

a. The outlined box for main() shows two variables as they appear in memory, *i* and a string called *x[ ]*. Show the contents of each one before main() calls shanti() in Statement 1. Remember that a string is a set of characters with a null character at the end.

b. The outlined box for shanti() shows its two arguments. This representation is incorrect, and in Experiment 9.12 we will clarify it. Show the contents of the variables in shanti() when it is first called, as in Statement 2.

c. In the outlined box for shanti(), cross off the items that are changed and under them show the new values, as in Statement 3. One should be a 0 and the other an 'M'. Is this change confirmed by the last printf() in shanti()?

d. In previous experiments we had already confirmed that *i* in main() is a different variable than the *i* in the function. According to our incorrect diagram, when control comes back to main(), for the last printf(), as in Statement 4, the value of *i* should still be 5 and not the 0 that was assigned in shanti(). Does the printf() confirm that?

e. According to our incorrect diagram, x[0] should still have a value of 'J', and not 'M' that was assigned in shanti(). Does the last printf() in main() confirm that? (Your answer here should be no! We will correct the diagram in the next experiment.)

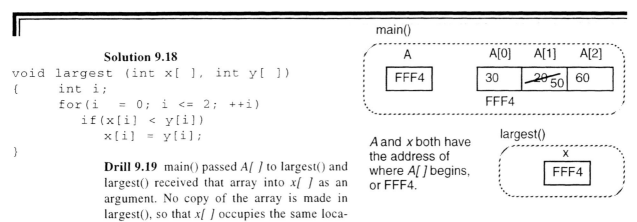

Solution 9.18
```c
void largest (int x[ ], int y[ ])
{     int i;
      for(i  = 0; i <= 2; ++i)
         if(x[i] < y[i])
            x[i] = y[i];
}
```

A and *x* both have the address of where *A[ ]* begins, or FFF4.

Drill 9.19 main() passed *A[ ]* to largest() and largest() received that array into *x[ ]* as an argument. No copy of the array is made in largest(), so that *x[ ]* occupies the same locations in memory as *A[ ]* does. Here, largest() altered *x[ ]* so it would effectively alter *A[ ]* in main(). Rewrite main() so that it will print out the contents of *A[ ]*. Show the output.

Exp 9.12 This diagram is correct! You may want to review the concept of addresses and the & operator explained in Unit 3. We are printing out addresses. If two variables are stored in the same memory address, then it is the same location. Otherwise, they are stored in different locations.

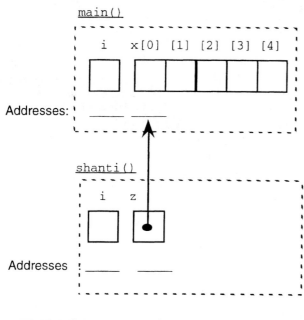

```
#include <stdio.h>
void shanti (int, char[ ]);
void main (void)
{
    int i = 5;
    char x[ ] = "JOJO";
    printf("%d %s %p %p\n",
              i, x, &i, &x[0]);
    shanti(i, x);
    printf("%d %s %p %p\n",
              i, x, &i, &x[0]);
}
void shanti(int i, char z[ ])
{
    printf(" %d %s %p %p\n",
              i, z, &i, &z[0]);
    i = 0;
    z[0] = 'M';
    printf(" %d %s %p %p\n",
              i, z, &i, &z[0]);
}
```

a. In this diagram, inside the outlined box for main():
   Write the value of *i* in its box and its address under it.
   Write the values of x[0] through x[4] in their boxes.
   Write the address of x[0] under its box.

b. In the diagram, inside the outlined box for shanti():
   Write the value of *i* in its box and its address under it.
   Write the address of z[0] under it.

c. Are the addresses of both *i*'s different? If they are, then they are stored in separate locations in memory, just as shown in the diagram.

d. Are the addresses of *x[ ]* and *z[ ]* the same? If so, then they are really the same location, just as shown in the diagram. If z[0] is assigned 'M' in shanti(), then it changes x[0] in main() because they are the same location.

Solution 9.19
```
void main (void)
{
   int i,   A[3] = {30, 20, 60},
            B[3] = {20, 50, 10};
   largest(A, B);
   for(i = 0; i <= 2; ++i)
      printf("%d \t", A[i]);
   printf("\n");
}
----- output -----
30    50    60
```

Drill 9.20 Change the problem and show the trace and the arrays if "child", "ren" are passed to cat().

```
void cat (char x[], char y[])
{
   int i, j;
   for(i = 0; x[i] != '\0'; ++i)
      ;
   for(j = 0; y[j] != '\0'; ++j)
      x[i + j] = y[j];
}
```

Functions with No Returns

e. Why doesn't changing *i* in shanti() change *i* in main()?

f. Is the *i* in main() stored in the same memory address as the *i* stored in shanti()? (Your conclusion here should be no!)

g. Is *x[ ]* in main() stored in the same memory address as is the array *z[ ]* stored in shanti()? (Your conclusion here should be yes! z[0] is the same location in memory as x[0]. If you change one, you change the other.)

Exp 9.13 When passing an array to a function, the changes the function may make will affect the first array because the function has the address of that array. Here's another experiment illustrating that concept. We will call single–element variables such as *i* scalars, to contrast them with arrays. After running the experiment, fill the boxes in the diagram.

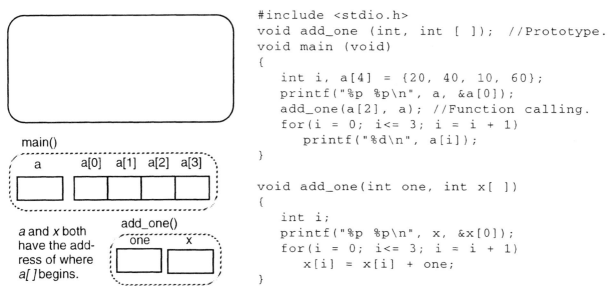

```
#include <stdio.h>
void add_one (int, int [ ]);  //Prototype.
void main (void)
{
    int i, a[4] = {20, 40, 10, 60};
    printf("%p %p\n", a, &a[0]);
    add_one(a[2], a); //Function calling.
    for(i = 0; i<= 3; i = i + 1)
        printf("%d\n", a[i]);
}

void add_one(int one, int x[ ])
{
    int i;
    printf("%p %p\n", x, &x[0]);
    for(i = 0; i<= 3; i = i + 1)
        x[i] = x[i] + one;
}
```

a and *x* both have the address of where *a[ ]* begins.

a. Was a scalar or an array passed when main() passed a[2] to add_one()?

b. Was a scalar or an array passed when main() passed *a* to add_one()?

c. What was the array called in main()?

d. What was the array called in add_one()?

e. When add_one() changed the array *x[ ]* by adding 1 to it, did the array *a[ ]* change in main()? Why?

f. Are the addresses stored in *a* and *x* different or the same?

Solution 9.20

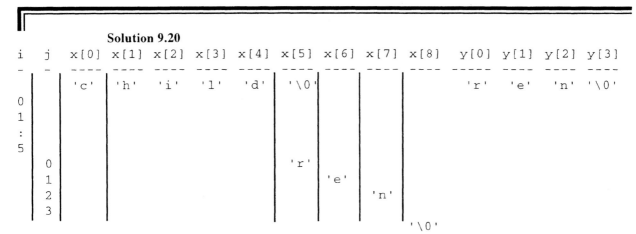

Drill 9.21 In main(), will the first or the second string that is passed be altered?

QUESTIONS

Show the output for Questions 1 to 8.

1.

```
void questions (void);
void main (void)
{  int i;
   for(i = 3; i <= 5; ++i)
      questions( );
}
void questions (void)
{
   printf("Lovely\n");
}
```

2.

```
void questions (void);
void main (void)
{  questions();
   questions();
}
void questions (void)
{
   int j;
   for(j = 1; j <= 3; ++j)
      printf("Lovely\t");
   printf("\n");
}
```

3.

```
void questions (void);
void main (void)
{  int i;
   for(i = 3; i <= 5; ++i)
      questions( );
}
void questions (void)
{
   int j;
   for(j = 1; j <= 2; ++j)
      printf("Lovely\t");
   printf("\n");
}
```

4. Use 4, 1, and 3 for the data in the following.

```
void questions (void);
void main (void)
{  int i;
   for(i = 3; i <= 5; ++i)
      questions( );
}
void questions (void)
{
   int j;
   printf("Enter an integer ");
   scanf("%d", &j);
   for(; j != 0; --j)
      printf("Lovely\t");
   printf("\n");
}
```

Solution 9.21 The function alters the first string so that the first string passed in main() will be altered. The second string stays the same.

Drill 9.22 In Drill 9.20, which loop, the first or the second, looks for the end of the first string? Which loop looks for the end of the second string? Which loop copies characters from one string to the end of the other?

5. Enter 4 for the scanf().
```
void busted (int);
void main (void)
{  int j;
   printf("Enter an integer ");
   scanf("%d", &j);
   for(; j != 0; --j)
      busted(j);
   printf("\n");
}
void busted (int k)
{
   printf("%d\t", k);
}
```

6. Assume the user enters a 4 for the scanf().
```
void rusted (char[ ]);
void main (void)
{
   rusted("choo choo");
   printf("\n");
}
void rusted (char x[ ])
{
   int j;
   printf("Enter an integer ");
   scanf("%d", &j);
   for(; j != 0; --j)
      printf("%s\n", x);
}
```

7.
```
void mustard (int, int);
void main (void)
{
   int i = 50, a[3] = {90, 80,
                       60};
   mustard(i, a[0]);
   printf("i=%d, a[0] = %d\n",
                    i, a[0]);
}
void mustard (int q, int w)
{
   printf("q=%d, w=%d\n", q, w);
   q = 0;
   w = 0;
}
```

8. Draw a diagram to help you.
```
void mustard (int, int[ ]);
void main (void)
{
   int q = 50, a[3] = {90, 80, 60};
   mustard(q, a);
   printf("q=%d, a[0]=%d\n", q, a[0]);
}

void mustard (int q, int w[ ])
{
   printf("q=%d, w[0]=%d\n", q, w[0]);
   q = 0;
   w[0] = 0;
}
```

Solution 9.22
The first loop looks for the end of the first string by searching for the null character '\0'.
The second loop looks for the end of the second string.
The second loop copies characters from the second string to the end of the first one.

Drill 9.23 Write a function called find_len() that will print the length of a string. For example, if main() called find_len() by passing "children", then it will print the integer 8.

	[0]	[1]	[2]	[3]
composer		"Bach"	"Beethoven"	"Chopin"
requests		60	20	50
link	2	0	3	1

9. Suppose before each question, we had only the slots shown above occupied in *requests[ ]* and *link[ ]*. Show the arrays after inserting the following in the linked list:
   a. requests[4] = 10
   b. requests[4] = 30
   c. requests[4] = 80
   d. requests[4] = 30 and requests[5] = 10
   e. requests[4] = 80 and requests[5] = 30
   f. requests[4] = 10 and requests[5] = 55

10. Notice that in the for statement, the two statements before the first semicolon initialize the loop and the two statements after the second semicolon are executed for each iteration. (− − i means i = i − 1.)

```
void drop_in (char [ ], char [], int, int, int);
void main (void)
{
   char a[30] = "Jack Flash";
   drop_in(a, "Jumping ", 5, 10, 8);
   printf("%s\n", a);
}
void drop_in (char str[], char instr[], int start, int len, int ilen)
{
   int i, j;
   str[len + ilen] = '\0';
   for(i - len - 1, j = len + ilen - 1; len - ilen - 1 != i; --i, --j)
      str[j] = str[i];
   for(i = 0, j = start; ilen != i; ++i, ++j)
      str[j] = instr[i];
}
```

Solution 9.23

```
void find_len (char x[])
{
   int i;
   for(i = 0; x[i] != '\0'; ++i)
      ;
   printf("Length of %s is %d\n",
      x, i);
}
```

Drill 9.24 Show the output.

```
void main (void)
{
   int i = 2, A[3] = {5, 9, 4};
   drill_it(i, A);
   printf("%d %d\n", i, A[1]);
}
void drill_it (int j, int B[ ])
{
   j = 0;
   B[1] = 0;
}
```

Functions with No Returns

PROGRAMS

For each of the following questions, write the complete listing that includes the main() as well as the other functions required to test each problem.

1. Have main() read in a string and an integer called *num*. Call a function *num* times, passing the string with it. The function should print the string once each time it is called.

2. Follow the instructions for Program 1, but have main() pass both the string and the num to the function only once. Let the function set up the loop that will print that string *num* number of times.

3. The function should receive three integers and print their average. main() should read in three integers and call the function by passing these integers.

4. The function should receive an array of floats and a scalar float (call it "scalar"). It should then print all the elements in the array greater than "scalar."

5. The function should receive an array of floats and a scalar float called "scalar." The function should add the scalar to each element of the array. Have main() print the array.

6. The function should receive a character string. After counting the characters in the string until it finds the null character, it should print that count. For example, if main() passed "starlight" to the function, it should print its length, 9.

7. The function called swap() should receive two strings and exchange them. For example, if main() has initialized two strings called *a[ ]* and *b[ ]*, then after calling swap(), the string which was in *a[ ]* will be in *b[ ]* and vice versa. Remember that when you pass an array to a function, you are passing its address.

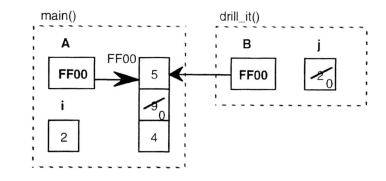

Solution 9.24

```
----- output -----
2   0
```

Functions with No Returns

Functions with Returns

Returning Values from Functions

In the last unit we saw how arguments are passed to a function. We learned the difference between passing a scalar (or a non–array) and passing an array. When passing a scalar, the calling function doesn't have to be concerned that the called function will change its value because the called function has received a copy of the original scalar. Altering the copy doesn't change the original variable in the calling function. However, when passing an array, the array is stored in only one place and no copy has been made. The called function receives the address of the array. Now if the called function changed the array, then that change would reflect the contents of the array in the calling function.

In this unit we will learn how values may be returned from the called function to the calling function. We will also see that only one value can be returned. The return statement will be a new statement for us. With it, we will be able to return values to the calling function upon the completion of the called function.

Many items are different when writing a program with a function that returns a value. These items are outlined in the following code:

DRILLS

Drill 10.1 Will main() be able to get the value of score from get_score() if this program is executed?

```
void get_score(char [ ]);
void main (void)
{
    get_score("Mr. Lollipop");
}
void get_score(char person[ ])
{
    int score;
    printf("What is the score for %s?", person);
    scanf("%d", &score);
}
```

164

```
char just_testing (void);
void main (void)
{
    char x;
    x = just_testing ( );
            :
}
char just_testing (void)
{
    return ('z');
}
```

First, in the prototype as well as in the function heading, we must state the data type of the item that the function returns. Here, we are returning a character. Second, at the end of the function, it should return that type of value using the return statement. Last, when calling the function, the calling function should do something with the item it will receive. Here, main() assigns the received character to the variable x. main() could have also called the function inside a printf(), for instance, and print the received item directly. The calling function can perform other tasks with the received item. Calling the function just_testing(); without assigning it to x or printing it would be wrong.

Figure 10.1 summarizes the various ways of using functions. We can categorize functions by whether or not arguments are passed to them. Or we can categorize them by whether or not values are received from them. Intersecting these two methods of categorizing functions, we come up with four basic methods of writing and using functions. Let us now turn our attention to a complete example using three of these four ways of writing functions.

A Menu-Driven Example

An Overview: I like to start by explaining the output because that shows the purpose of the program. Then it makes sense to look at the tracechart and the code to see how the program works.

Looking at the output of Example 10.1 on page 170, we see that a menu is presented again and again until the user enters the number 4, at which time the program terminates. The user has three other options. If a 1 is entered at the menu, then a number provided by the user is inserted in a list of existing numbers. This list of numbers is kept in ascending order. If a 2 is entered, then a number is deleted, and if a 3 is entered, then the ordered list of numbers is printed for the user.

In the output we see that the user inserts 40, 20, and 60, in that order, in the list. When asked to print the list, the program prints them in order. Then the user asks that 40 be removed from the list. After printing the list, we see that 40 is removed. Only after examining the *num[ ]* array's contents in Figure 10.2 can we see how the list is maintained. Notice that this is not a linked list.

Solution 10.1 No. get_score() read in the score for *person*, but that number will stay only in get_score(). Using the return keyword, we can send that score to main().

Drill 10.2 Let's change the program in Drill 10.1 so that main() can receive a value. First, change the voids for get_score() to int since the data type of the returned value will be of type int. Then add a statement at the end of the definition of get_score() that will be return score;. This will return the value to the calling function. Last, store this returned value in main() in a variable called x. This is done by assigning the function call to x. How does your program look now?

No return — Does not pass arguments

```
void main (void)
{
      funky( );
          :

void funky (void)
{
          :
```

No return — Does pass arguments

```
void main (void)
{
      funky(23);
          :

void funky (int i)
{
          :
```

With a return — Does not pass arguments

```
void main (void)
{
      x = funky( );
          :

int funky (void)
{
      return 20;
}
```

With a return — Does pass arguments

```
void main (void)
{
      x = funky (3);
          :

int funky (int x)
{
      return x * x
}
```

Figure 10.1 Four basic examples of writing and using functions.

In main(), *size* stores the number of elements in the list. Initially, this number is zero. We also have a 20–element integer array called *A[ ]*. First, main() calls the get_choice() function. Nothing is passed to this function. It prints the menu with four choices, reads the menu option from the user, and returns that value. This value is then stored in the variable *selection* in main(). This process of obtaining the value for *selection* is repeated at the bottom of the for loop until an option of 4 or Quit is selected.

Inside the loop, if *selection* is equal to 1, then the function add_num() is called. When calling this function, the array and the size of the array are passed as arguments. The function returns the new size of the array which is then assigned to *size* in main().

If *A[ ]* and *size* were defined, not inside main(), but outside it, as the prototypes are declared, then we would not have to send them as arguments or need to receive *size*. These variables

Solution 10.2

```
int get_score(char [ ]);
void main (void)
{
   int x;
   x = get_score("Mr. Lollipop");
}
int get_score(char person[ ])
{
   int score;
   printf("What is the score for %s?", person);
   scanf("%d", &score);
   return score;
}
```

Drill 10.3 Rewrite only main() so that it prints the value of *x*. Then it calls get_score() again by passing “Mother Dear” and receives and prints her score also.

would be accessible to all functions and they would be called *global*, not *local*, variables. Global variables should be avoided because any function may have access to them and may be inadvertently altered by some function in the program. The larger the program, the more likely this is.

add_num() doesn't check to see if the insertion was successful or not. If it did, then it could return the same *size* as it received. This enhancement can be added later. For now, two equal numbers may coexist in the list.

del_num() is a function similar to add_num(). However, it also doesn't check to see if the deletion was successful or not. If a user wants to delete a number that doesn't exist in the list, the function would not give an error message and *size* would be decremented anyway. This fine tuning can also be added later. The functions are kept simple since this is a first example.

Let us look at the print_nums() function. It receives the array *num[ ]* and its size, *sz*. The for loop goes through all the slots of the array and prints the list of numbers. The numbers are already in order when control of execution comes to this function.

The add_num() function first receives the number from the user and it must be placed in the array. The function uses two loops to insert that number. The first loop looks to find the location where that number belongs in the list, and the second loop shifts to the right all the elements from that point by one slot, making space for the new number. After this loop, the number is inserted using one assignment statement. After incrementing *sz*, the new size is returned.

Let us look at Figure 10.3 to see how the insertion takes place. Here, *sz* is equal to 6 because there are 6 elements in the array. *number* is 70. It is the number that we have to insert in the proper place. Starting from the left, we see if 70 is less than 10 and if 70 is less than 50, and finally we come to the point where 70 is less than 110. In the function, *i* is equal to 2 and we use a break to exit the loop. We now know that the 70 belongs in slot number 2.

Then the second or the *j* loop starts from the other end of the array, sliding its elements by one slot to the right. The 350 is moved to slot 6, the 320 to slot 5, and so on, until the 110 is moved to slot 3. Now there is room for the 70 in slot 2, so it is inserted. Notice that the *j* loop terminates when *j* becomes *i*. You can study the tracechart yourself (with the code) to see how the list is built. Take a few moments to do that; you have to see how it works for yourself.

The del_num() function works similarly. The first loop merely looks for the number to be deleted. When it is found, its location is preserved in *i* by a break. *sz* is decremented. Instead of shifting the elements of the array to the right, the second loop shifts the elements to the left, writing over the element to be deleted. The new size is returned. Remember that in order to complete writing this function, it should handle instances where the number to be deleted doesn't exist in the array in the first place.

Solution 10.3

```
void main (void)
{
    int x;
    x = get_score("Mr. Lollipop");
    printf("The score is %d\n", x);
    x = get_score("Mother Dear");
    printf("The score is %d\n", x);
}
```

Drill 10.4 Now instead of storing the score in *x* each time and then printing out *x*, call get_score() directly from the printf()'s and print the score for each of these people.

```
//EXAMPLE 10.1
#include <stdio.h>
int get_choice ();                //Prints the menu and obtains a selection.
int add_num (int num[ ], int sz);//Inserts a number in the sorted array.
int del_num (int num[ ], int sz);//Removes a number from the array.
void print_nums(int num[ ], int sz);//Prints out the sorted array.

void main ()
{
    int   size = 0,  //The number of elements in array A[ ].
          A[20],     //The array that will keep its numbers sorted.
          selection; //This is the selection made from the menu.

    selection = get_choice();   //Keep doing this loop until a 4 (or Quit)
    for( ; selection != 4; )    //is selected from the menu.
    {
        if(selection == 1)
            size = add_num(A, size);
        else
            if(selection == 2)
                size = del_num(A, size);
            else
                print_nums(A, size);
        selection = get_choice();
    }
}


int get_choice ()  //Assuming that the user will enter only a valid int.
{
    int choice;
    printf("Enter 1 for Insert, 2 for Delete,");
    printf(" 3 for List, and 4 to Quit");
    scanf("%d", &choice);
    return choice;
}
```

Solution 10.4

```
void main (void)
{
    int x;
    printf("The score is %d\n", get_score("Mr. Lollipop"));
    printf("The score is %d\n", get_score("Mother Dear"));
}
```

> **Drill 10.5** Do we need the variable x? If not, can you tell what is the disadvantage of not having it?

```
int add_num (int num[ ], int sz)
{
    int i, j, number;
    printf("What number to insert? ");  //Gets the number to insert.
    scanf("%d", &number);
    for(i = 0; i < sz; ++i)              //Finds the place (i)
        if(number < num[i])              //to put the new number.
            break;
    for(j = sz; j > i; --j)              //Shift the rest of the array by mov-
        num[j] = num[j - 1];             //ing the numbers up by one slot.
    num[i] = number;                     //Place the new number.
    return ++sz;                         //The array size is incremented.
}


int del_num (int num[ ], int sz)//Assuming that the deleted item exists.
{
    int i, number;
    printf("What number to delete? ");  //Gets the number to be deleted.
    scanf("%d", &number);
    for(i = 0; i < sz; ++i)              //Find the place in the array
        if(number == num[i])             //to be deleted.
            break;
    --sz;                                //The array size is decremented.
    for( ; i < sz; ++i)                  //Shift the rest of the array by mov-
        num[i] = num[i + 1];             //ing the numbers down by one slot.
    return sz;
}

void print_nums(int num[ ], int sz)
{
    int i;
    for(i = 0; i < sz; ++i)
        printf("%d\t", num[i]);
    printf("\n");
}
```

Solution 10.5 No, we don't need *x*. The disadvantage of not having *x* is that, once the score is printed, it is not available in main(). If we need that score later for some computation, then we would need to call get_score() again. In that case, it would have been better to have saved the score in *x* at the beginning.

Drill 10.6 Using *x*, rewrite main() so that it prints only the total score of both people.

```
----- output -----
Enter 1 for Insert, 2 for Delete, 3 for List, and 4 to Quit 1
What number to insert? 40
Enter 1 for Insert, 2 for Delete, 3 for List, and 4 to Quit 1
What number to insert? 20
Enter 1 for Insert, 2 for Delete, 3 for List, and 4 to Quit 1
What number to insert? 60
Enter 1 for Insert, 2 for Delete, 3 for List, and 4 to Quit 3
20   40   60
Enter 1 for Insert, 2 for Delete, 3 for List, and 4 to Quit 2
What number to delete? 40
Enter 1 for Insert, 2 for Delete, 3 for List, and 4 to Quit 3
20   60
```

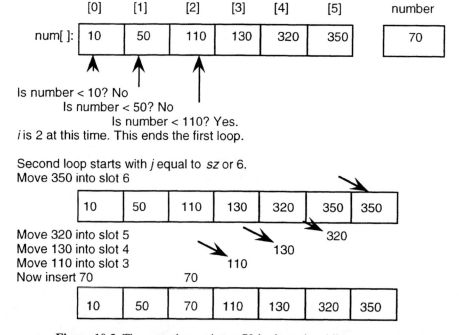

Figure 10.3 The procedure to insert 70 in the ordered list.

Solution 10.6

```
void main (void)
{
    int x;
    x = get_score("Mr. Lollipop");
    x = x + get_score("Mother Dear");
    printf("Total score is %d\n", x);
}
```

Drill 10.7 Rewrite Solution 10.6 so that there is only one assignment statement instead of two. The second time you call get_score(), it must be called from the printf().

Function-Condition	choice	i	j	sz	number	num[0]	num[1]	num[2]
get_choice()	1			0				
add_num()					40			
		0						
i < sz: False								
			0					
j > i: False								
				1		40		
get_choice()	1							
add_num()					20			
		0						
i < sz: True								
number<num[i]: True			1					
j > i: True				2			40	
						20	40	
get_choice()	1							
add_num()		0			60			
i < sz: True								
number<num[i]: False		1						
i < sz: True								
number<num[i]: False		2						
i < sz: False								
			2					
j > i: False				3		20	40	60
get_choice()	2							
del_num()					40			
			0					
i < sz: True								
number==num[i]: False			1					
i < sz: True								
number==num[i]: True			2					
i < sz: True							60	
			2					
i < sz: False						20	60	

Figure 10.2 A partial tracechart for Example 10.1.

Solution 10.7

```
void main (void)
{
   int x;
   x = get_score("Mr. Lollipop");
   printf("Total score is %d\n", x + get_score("Mother Dear"));
}
```

Drill 10. 8 Repeat Solution 10.7 but use no *x* at all.

EXPERIMENTS

Exp 10.1 Review.

```
void average (int, int);           //line 1
void message (void);               //line 2
void main (void)                   //line 3
{
    message();                     //line 4
    average(30, 20);               //line 5
}

void average(int x, int y)         //line 6
{
    printf("%.2f\n", (x + y)/ 2.0); //line 7
}

void message (void)                //line 8
{
    printf("Here is the average:"); //line 9
}
```

a. Give the line number for each of the following descriptions.
   ___ The beginning of the definition for the message() function.
   ___ The beginning of the definition for the main() function.
   ___ The beginning of the definition for the average() function.
   ___ The prototype for message().
   ___ The prototype for average().
   ___ Where main() calls message().
   ___ Where message() calls printf().
   ___ Where main() calls average().
   ___ Where average() calls printf().
b. There are three user-defined functions. Name them.
c. Which function (or functions) does not return anything? How can you tell that?
d. Which function (or functions) does not receive any arguments? How can you tell that?
e. Which function (or functions) receives arguments? How many?
f. If the four lines used to define message() are inserted between main() and average(), would there be any problem running the code?

Solution 10.8

```
void main (void)
{
    printf("Total score is %d\n",
            get_score("Mr. Lollipop") + get_score("Mother Dear"));
}
```

Drill 10.9 Write a function called print_score() that will receive a string and the score, an integer. It will print the string and the score and return nothing. Call the variables *person* and *score*.

Exp 10.2 Now let us have two average() functions, one that returns a value and one that doesn't.

```
void average1 (int, int);            //line 1
float average2 (int, int);           //line 2

void main (void)                     //line 3
{
   float avg;                        //line 4
   average1(30, 20);                 //line 5
   avg = average2(30, 40);           //line 6
   printf("%.2f\n", avg);            //line 7
}

float average2 (int x, int y)        //line 8
{
   return ((x + y) / 2.0);           //line 9
}

void average1 (int x, int y)
{
   printf("%.2f\n", (x + y) / 2.0);
}
```

a. Which function returns a value? What in the prototype indicates that? What in the function definition indicates that?
b. Which function doesn't return a value? What in the prototype and the function indicates that?
c. Which function uses the keyword, return?
d. Notice the difference between line 5 and line 6. Why isn't the function assigned to a variable when average1() is called?
e. Why is the function assigned to a variable when average2() is called?
f. Which function, average1() or average2(), prints the average?
g. Which function, average1() or average2(), returns the average instead of printing it?

Solution 10.9

```
void print_score(char person[ ], int score)
{
   printf("%s's score is %d\n", person, score);
}
```

Drill 10.10 Now write main() that will initialize *person[ ]* to "Mr. Lollipop," and call get_score() by passing *person[ ]* to it. main() will receive the returned score in the variable called *x*. It will then call print_score() by passing *person[ ]* and *x*.

Functions with Returns   173

Exp 10.3 Here are two ways to call average2():

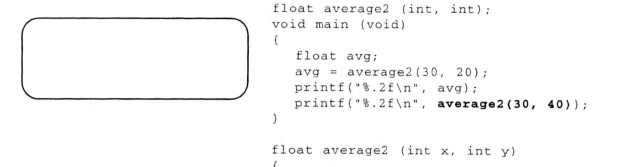

```
float average2 (int, int);
void main (void)
{
    float avg;
    avg = average2(30, 20);
    printf("%.2f\n", avg);
    printf("%.2f\n", average2(30, 40));
}

float average2 (int x, int y)
{
    return ((x + y) / 2.0);     // line 1
}
```

a. How many times does main() call average2()?
b. Is the function assigned to a variable the first or the second time that average2() is called?
c. What happens to the value returned from the function when it is called the first time?
d. What about the second time, when average2() is called? What happens to the value returned from that function if it is not assigned to *avg*?'
e. Add this line between the printf()'s:

```
average2(10, 50);
```

Does the program run? If so, does it print the average of 10 and 50? Why or why not?
f. When calling a function that returns a value, it should be assigned to a variable or printed. (True or false)
g. In line 5 of Experiment 10.2, the value of the function is not assigned or printed in main(). Why not?
h. Replace line1 in average2() with printf("%.2f\n", (x + y)/2.0);. Are there any problems? Why?

Solution 10.10 Notice that get_score() is assigned to a variable; it returns a value. print_score() is not assigned to a variable; it doesn't return a value.

```
void main (void)
{
    char person[20] = "Mr. Lolllipop";
    int x;
    x = get_score(person);
    print_score(person, x);
}
```

Drill 10.11 Now instead of receiving the score into *x*, pass the received score directly to the print_score() function without using *x*.

Exp 10.4 Here are other methods for calling average2(). Watch the parentheses. In this experiment there are three printf()'s.

```
float average2 (float, float);
void main (void)
{
    float avg;
    avg = average2(10.0, 30.0) +
            average2(40.0, 60.0) + 1;
    printf("%.2f\n", avg);

    avg = average2(average2(20.0, 70.0),
            average2(50.0, 90.0));
    printf("%.2f\n", avg);

    printf("%.2f\n",
        average2(10.0, average2(30.0, 50.0)));
}

float average2 (float x, float y)
{
    return ((x + y) / 2.0);
}
```

a. When evaluating the value of *avg* for the first time, the average of 10.0 and 30.0 is returned. What is its value?
b. The average of 40.0 and 60.0 is also returned. What is its value? How is the value of *avg* obtained?
c. The second time that *avg* is assigned a value, the average of 20.0 and 70.0 is received first, then the average of 50.0 and 90.0 is received. How is the value of *avg* obtained?
d. Can you have a function inside another function? If so, which function's result is obtained first, the nested one or the outer one?
e. Are the values received from the nested call (such as the value received from the average of 20.0 and 70.0) used to call the outer one?
f. In the last printf(), printf() calls which function? This function calls which function? Notice that there are multiple nestings of function calls.
g. How is the value received for the printf() to print in the last statement in main()?

Solution 10.11 get_score() returns the score to print_score(), which then prints it.

```
void main (void)
{
    char person[20] = "Mr. Lolllipop";
    print_score(person, get_score(person));
}
```

Drill 10.12 Let us now talk about volumes of cylinders. To do that, we first need to write a function called area(). This function will receive the radius of a circle and return its area. Use all floating point items. The area of a circle is about 3.1416 times its radius squared.

Exp 10.5 Have you wondered if a function may return more than one value? It can't, but here's a trick and it doesn't even have to use a return statement. (We have studied the passing of arrays in Unit 9.) Here, average_hi() calculates the average and the larger of two numbers, and makes these two values available to main() via an array. In the diagram the address FF00 is fictitious. Fill in the values in as many places in the diagram as you can.

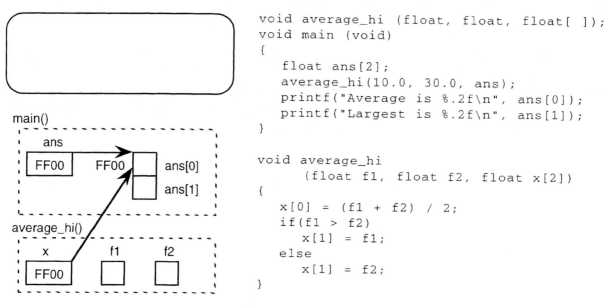

```
void average_hi (float, float, float[ ]);
void main (void)
{
    float ans[2];
    average_hi(10.0, 30.0, ans);
    printf("Average is %.2f\n", ans[0]);
    printf("Largest is %.2f\n", ans[1]);
}

void average_hi
        (float f1, float f2, float x[2])
{
    x[0] = (f1 + f2) / 2;
    if(f1 > f2)
        x[1] = f1;
    else
        x[1] = f2;
}
```

a. How many scalars and how many arrays does main() pass to average_hi()?
b. What are the values of the scalars in main()? In average_hi()?
c. What is the name of the array in main()? In average_hi()?
d. average_hi() calculates the average of *f1* and *f2*. In which index of the array is it placed?
e. average_hi() calculates the larger of *f1* and *f2*. In which index of the array is it placed?
f. Does average_hi() calculate two answers, the average and the largest, and make them available to main()?
g. Since a return is not used in average_hi(), how are these two answers provided for main()?

Conclusion, if more than one answer has to be returned from a function, then those answers can be placed in an array that was passed from the calling function.

Solution 10.12

```
#define PI   3.1416
float area (float radius)
{
    return (PI * radius * radius);
}
```

Drill 10.13 Write a function called volume(). It will receive the "radius" and the "height." It will call area() to receive its area, multiply this area by the height, and return the volume. Use all floating point items.

Exp 10.6 One function can call a second function, which can call a third function. For data, enter 10.0 and 20.0.

```
float average_two ( );
void read_two (float [ ]);
void main (void)
{
    printf("ave of two numbers is %.2f\n",
                average_two());
}

float average_two ( )
{
    float x[2];
    read_two(x);
    return ((x[0] + x[1])/ 2.0);
}

void read_two (float A[ ])
{
    printf("Enter two floats:\n");
    scanf("%f %f", &A[0], &A[1]);
}
```

a. main() calls which function inside its printf()?
b. Does average_two() call read_two() or does read_two call average_two()?
c. There are three functions defined here. Which functions receive arguments?
d. Which function (or functions) returns values?
e. Which function (or functions) places values in an array?
f. Number the sequence of the following events.
___ read_two() scans two numbers in an array
___ average_two() returns the average of floats stored in its array back to main()
___ average_two() calls read_two() passing an array (actually the address of the array)
___ main() prints the average
___ main() calls average_two(), passing no arguments
___ read_two() receives the address of an array into A from the calling function

Solution 10.13

```
float volume (float radius, float height)
{
    return(area(radius) * height);
}
```

Drill 10.14 Write main() that will pass a radius of 3.0 and a height of 5.5 to the volume() function. This will be done within the printf() function in main(). Therefore, without the use of any variables, have main() print the volume of this cylinder. Notice that main() will call volume(), and volume() will call area().

QUESTIONS

For all questions, show the output.

1.
```
char socks (char [ ]);
void main (void)
{
    char x;
    x = socks("black");
    printf("%c\n", x);
}
char socks (char knee[ ])
{
    return(knee [0]);
}
```

2. You are reading in "Yellow", "Red", and "Brown".
```
char socks (char [ ]);
void main (void)
{  int i;
   char x, str[20];
   printf("Enter 3 colors:\n");
   for(i = 1; i <= 3; ++i)
   {
      scanf("%s", &str);
      x = socks(str);      //Line 1
      printf("%c\n", x);  //Line 2
   }
}
char socks (char knee[ ])
{
   return(knee [0]);
}
```

3. For Question 2, show the output if lines 1 and 2 are combined as follows:

```
printf("%c\n", socks(str));
```

4. You are reading in 4, 3, and 7.
```
int more_socks (void);
void main (void)
{
    int x, sum = 0, i;
    for(i = 1; i <= 3; ++i)
       sum = sum + more_socks( );
    printf("%d\n", sum);
}
int more_socks (void)
{  int x;
   printf("Enter an integer");
   scanf("%d", &x);
   return(x);
}
```

Solution 10.14

```
void main (void)
{
   printf("%d\n", volume(3.0, 5.5));
}
```

Drill 10.15 Write a function that will find the length of a string; that is, it will count the characters until a null character is encountered and return the count. Call the function string_len(). The definition for such a function already exists in the string.h header file. Let us write our own. For example, if "Looly Baba" is passed, then 10 should be returned. Here is the beginning of the function:

```
int string_len (char s[ ])
{
   int i;
```

5.

```
int fun_fun (int x);
void main (void)
{
   printf("%d\n", fun_fun(5) );
   printf("%d\n", fun_fun(fun_fun(5)));
   printf("%d\n", fun_fun(5) + fun_fun(5));
   printf("%d\n", fun_fun(fun_fun(fun_fun (5))));
}


int fun_fun (int x)
{
   return(x + x);
}
```

6.

```
int remainder (int a, int b);
void main (void)
{
   int x = 3, y = 8;
   for( ; y >= x; )
      y = remainder(x, y);
   printf("%d\n", y);
}

int remainder (int a, int b)
{
   return(b - a);
}
```

7. For the given main(), calls to functions are given below. These calls will be placed where the comment is shown. By observing how the calls are made in each part, write the function prototypes so that the data types match.

```
void main (void)
{
   int i = 7, a[4];
   float f = 2.0;
   char c = 'Q', b[4];
   // Place call here.
}
```

```
a. testing();
b. testing(i, f);
c. c = testing(a, f);
d. f = testing(b[2], c);
e. printf("%.2f\n", testing(b));
f. printf("%d\n", testing(c));
```

Solution 10.15

```
int string_len (char s[ ])
{
   int i;
   for(i = 0; s[i] != '\0'; ++i)
      ;
   return i;
}
```

Drill 10.16 Write the remove_str() function. It will receive a string, the starting position in the string to be removed, and the count, which is the total number of characters to be removed. For example, if *str[ ]* is "Bethel School" and this call is made, remove_str(str, 2, 3);, then *str* will become "Bel School". Here is some of the code. Fill in the three blanks.

```
void remove_str (char s[ ], int start, int count)
{
   int i, length;
   length = string_len (s);
   for(i = start , j = start + _____; j <= _____; ++i, ++j)
      s[i] = _____  ;
}
```

PROGRAMS

Write the main() as well as the functions needed to test each program.

1. The function largest() is to receive three floats and return the largest of them.
2. The function add_interest() will receive the balance and interest_rate, both floats, from the calling function. It will return the new balance with the amount of interest added to it. For example, if 100.0 and 0.05 are received in the function, then 105.0 will be returned.
3. The function is to receive an array of floats that has a zero in its last slot. It is to return the number of slots preceding the zero. For example, if an array's contents are 3, 7, 2, 7, 1, 0, then it should return 5. Call the function array_len().
4. The function add_array() is to add up all the integers in the array until a 0 is encountered. The sum is to be returned. For example, in the array 3, 7, 2, 7, 1, 0, the returned value should be 20.
5. The function count_array() is to count how many integers in the array are greater than the first number. For example, in the array 3, 7, 2, 7, 1, –7, the two 7's are greater than 3, so 2 is returned. A negative number means that it is the end of the array.
6. The function receives a string and returns the number of characters in it. For example, if the string is "DOODLE", then the function should return 6. Call the function string_len().

OPTIONAL TOPICS

Recursion

It is often necessary for a function to call itself. This procedure is called recursion. So far we have been dealing with iterations in loops, but recursion allows us to reduce a large amount of complex code to a program that is smaller in length. Also, once recursion is mastered, the logic of it is much more simplified. However, one needs to invest the time and energy to understand recursion. LISP is a language that uses recursion extensively. Let us look at an example.

Example 10.2 uses two recursive functions, one is called product() and the other sum(). We can easily tell that they are recursive functions because they call themselves. Within the definition of product(), see that there is a call to product() again. Also sum() calls itself. First let us see how sum() works, then we will look at product(). This example assumes that our computer can only add or subtract the number 1. Using these two primitive operations, the functions can be used to add or multiply two numbers. The idea is not to do something useful but to illustrate recursion using a simple example.

Solution 10.16
```
void remove_str (char s[ ], int start, int count)
{
   int i, length;
   length = string_len (s);
   for(i = start, j = start + count; j <= length; ++i, ++j)
      s[i] = s[j];
}
```

Drill 10.17 Using the example where *str[ ]* is "Bethel School" and the remove_str(str, 2, 3); call is made, answer the following questions:
a. What will be the first value of *i*?
b. What will be the first value of *j*?

```
//EXAMPLE 10.2
#include <stdio.h>
int product(int a, int b);
int sum (int q, int r);

void main (void)
{  int x;
   x = product(3, 4);
   printf("%d\n", x);
}

int product(int a, int b)  //Only adding and subtracting, multiplication
{  if (a == 1)                      //is accomplished.
      return b;
   else
      return(sum(b, product(a - 1, b))); //Calls itself.
}

int sum (int q, int r)  //Only adding and subtracting by 1, "q" and "r"
{  if(q == 0)                       //are added.
      return r;
   else
      return(sum(q - 1, r) + 1 );   //Calls itself.
}
```

Let us look at Figure 10.4 to understand how sum() works. At the top of the diagram, main() calls sum() in its printf() by passing 2 and 3. Inside sum(), q becomes 2 and r becomes 3. Here, the if statement checks if q is equal to 0. It isn't, so sum() is called recursively by subtracting 1 from q. Here, sum() cannot do the return because it is waiting for sum(1, 3) to complete.

Now we are inside sum() a second time. Here, q is equal to 1 and r is again equal to 3. The if statement is false again since q isn't equal to 0, so we must call sum() a third time, this time passing 0 and 3.

This time, q is equal to 0 and we don't call sum() again. Instead we return the value of r, which is 3. This is where the recursion terminates. So far, we have been going into recursion deeper and deeper and we get out of the "hole," so to speak, by following the arrows going up in the figure.

Solution 10.17

a. The first value of i will be 2.
b. The first value of j will be 5.

Drill 10.18
a. What will be the value of *length*?
b. For the first time that s[i] = s[j]; is executed, what character is placed in which position? Or what character takes which character's place in the string?
c. How many times is i incremented? Is it as many times as j is incremented?

The call to sum(0, 3) has been waiting for an answer and now it has received 3. The 3 is added to 1, which is now 4, and 4 is returned to the function call sum(1, 3). This function call has been waiting for its result. It receives the 4, adds 1 to it, and returns the 5 to main(), which has been waiting the longest for its answer. Now that it has the answer, it prints the 5.

This is a very simple illustration of recursion. All previous programs using loops could have been written using recursion. Since we are in the Optional Topics section of the unit, I leave it to you to see how product() works.

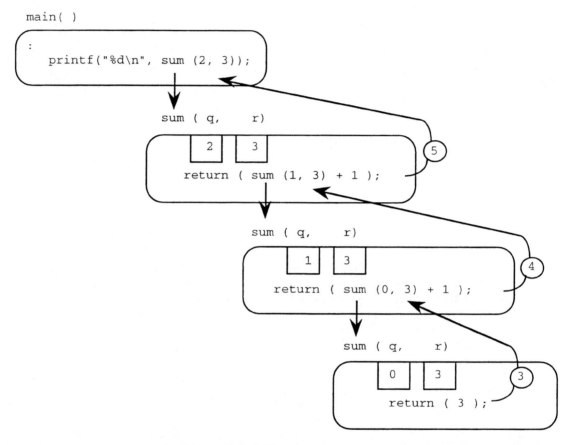

Figure 10.4 Calling sum( ) recursively.

Solution 10.18

a. The value of *length* will be 13.
b. The 'l' of "Bethel" is placed in slot number 2, or the 'l' takes the place of 't'.
c. *i* is incremented as many times as *j* is incremented, that is, 9 times. The last time, that is, the ninth time, the condition j <= length becomes false and the loop is terminated.

Functions with Returns

Unit 11

Structures

In Unit 7, starting on page 102, we discussed the advantages of declaring arrays. We had four game scores from four different players, which we read and printed in reverse order. Instead of defining *score1*, *score2*, *score3*, and *score4*; we defined one array that held all four scores, i.e., score[4]. We grouped them in an array because all items were of the same type and had a similar meaning — they were all game scores.

However, we will need to group data items that are related to each other but aren't of the same type. For example, suppose that along with the game scores, we want to store the name of each player, the country from which they come, and their ages. Here, the score is a float, the player and the country are character strings, and the age is an integer. We would like to store these four items together as one unit. and to handle and process them together as a group. What we need to do is to define a new data type that includes these four items.

DRILLS

Drill 11.1 part_item is a structure template made up of two members. *part* is the variable of type struct part_item. To access the part number, we use part.number. How would you set the price of part as 0.35?

```
struct part_item
{
    char number[10];
    float price;
};
struct part_item part;
```

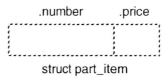

struct part_item

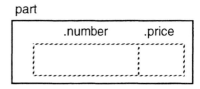

part

183

We have at our disposal a *structure*. For our needs, we can define the structure as:

```
struct participant
{
    char name[15];
    char country[15];
    float score;
    int age;
};
```

struct is a keyword in the language, but participant is a word that I made up. All that we are doing is defining a structure called struct participant. We are not creating a variable; instead, we are creating a new data type that includes other C and C++ data types. Think of this as a *structure template* from which *structure variables* may be defined. Any variable declared as being of this type will have these four parts. Parts of a structure are called *members*. Later in the C++ section of this text we will add more features to structure templates and call them *classes*. Variables defined as classes will be called *objects*, for a lack of a better word. Just as variables are created from data types, or structure variables are created from structure definitions, objects are created from classes.

With arrays, we need to specify the subscript or the index to access one item inside the array. To access one item in a structure, we need to specify the name of the member. The order in which the structure members are defined is not important. This is how structure variables are defined and initialized:

```
struct participant player1, player2 = {"Nashinda", "Uganda", 4.6, 19};
```

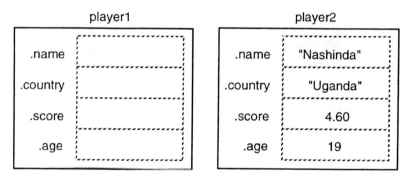

Figure 11.1 Defining two structure variables.

Solution 11.1

```
part.price = 0.35;
```

Drill 11.2 Use Drill 11.1 to answer the following questions.
a. Name the variable.
b. Name the structure template.
c. What are the parts of a structure called?
d. An array uses a set of brackets to specify the index. What do structures use to specify the item inside the structure?
e. Once a structure template and its variables are defined, which name will be used less in the rest of the program?

Structures

player1 is defined and has four members. *player2* is also defined and its four members are initialized. Here, the order is important. They should be initialized in the same order that the structure members are defined. See Figure 11.1. In database terminology, a member of a structure variable is called a *field,* a structure variable with its data is called a database *record,* and a collection of related records is called a *file.*

With arrays, we specify the subscript or an index enclosed in brackets to access one element. With structures, we must follow the variable name by a period, followed by the member name, to access one member. For example, player2.score is equal to 4.60. strcpy(player1.country, player2.country); will copy the country of player2 as the country of player1. Additionally, while player2.country is equal to the string "Uganda," player2.country[3] is equal to the character 'n'. We can always write an array of players like this:

```
struct participant player[2];
```

This will create an array called *player[ ]* with only 2 slots, where each slot is a structure of type struct participant. See Figure 11.2. To read in the name for the player in slot 0, the statement will look like this:

```
scanf("%s", &player[0].name);
```

The & is optional here because array names are actual addresses anyway. We can also create a structure based on other structures. Consider:

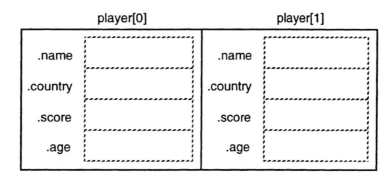

Figure 11.2 An array of structures.

Solution 11.2
a. Variable name is *part.*
b. Template name is struct part_item.
c. Parts of a structure are called members.
d. Structures use the period to separate the structure variable and its member.
e. The name of the structure template is used less in a program. In our case, *part* would be used more than part_item.

Drill 11.3 Add a third member to the structure template called qty, which is an integer. It doesn't matter if it is the first, second, or third member of the structure. Then set the part number to be "SMS0001," the price to be 0.35, and the quantity to be 20. Show the complete structure template and variable definitions.

```
struct team                            //Defining a new structure
{
   struct participant captain;     //struct team contains a structure
   int wins;
   int losses;
   struct participant player[2]; //struct team has an array of structures
};
struct team SweetThings =          //Defining and initializing a variable.
{
   {"Jasmine",  "Cambodia",  3.5,  22},
   5,
   2,
   {{"BoJangle",  "Mexico",  5.2,  20},
    {"Leonard",  "Germany",  4.0,  24} }  // Need the outer braces.
};
struct team RowdyBabies;           //Defining a variable
```

In Figure 11.3 you can see what the variable *SweetThings* looks like. If we want to copy the contents of *SweetThings* to *RowdyBabies*, all we need to do is:

```
RowdyBabies = SweetThings;
```

However, for the sake of obtaining experience in handling structures, let us do the same thing the long way.

```
//Copy the captain values
strcpy( RowdyBabies.captain.name,     SweetThings.captain.name);
strcpy( RowdyBabies.captain.country,  SweetThings.captain.country);
        RowdyBabies.captain.age    =  SweetThings.captain.age;
        RowdyBabies.captain.score  =  SweetThings.captain.score;

//Copy the player values
for(i = 0;  i <= 1;  ++i)
{
   strcpy( RowdyBabies.player[i].name,     SweetThings.player[i].name);
   strcpy( RowdyBabies.player[i].country,  SweetThings.player[i].country);
        RowdyBabies.player[i].age   =  SweetThings.player[i].age;
        RowdyBabies.player[i].score =  SweetThings.player[i].score;
}
```

Solution 11.3

```
struct part_item
{
   char number[10];
   float price;
   int qty;
};
struct part_item part;
strcpy(part.number,
       "SMS0001");
part.price = 0.35;
part.qty = 20;
```

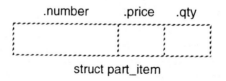

struct part_item

part

Drill 11.4 Remember that when we initialized arrays while defining them, we just placed the items for the array in order, enclosed in a set of braces. With structures, it works the same way. Try to show how to initialize the values of part the same way.

Structures

SweetThings

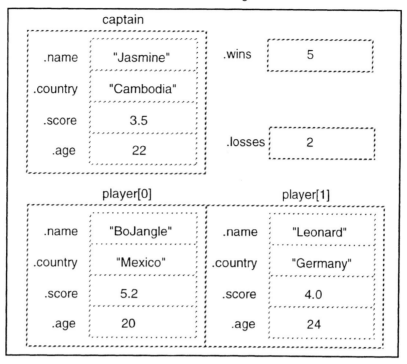

Figure 11.3 A structure of structures.

```
//Copy the wins and losses
RowdyBabies.wins   =   SweetThings.wins;
RowdyBabies.losses =   SweetThings.losses;
```

You can see that, although the first solution is only one statement, the expanded solution illustrates how to handle individual members of structures.

Now let us take a simple structure and use it to illustrate how structures are used with functions. We will do this by writing the entire program. In Example 11.1 we define struct mobile. It is simply made up of two members: one is called make[ ] and the other is year. The structure is defined outside any function, so it is available globally to all functions.

Solution 11.4

```
struct part_item part = { "SMS0001", 0.35, 20};
```

Drill 11.5 To read in a string, we can use the scanf() function. We can also use the gets() function. gets(x); is the statement that reads a string into the character string variable called *x[ ]*. Define another variable of type struct part_item and call it *old_part*. Give the gets() and two scanf() calls that will read the values into *old_part*. Your interactive screen should look like this:

```
----- output -----
What is the part number? OLS0001
The price? 0.60
And the quantity? 30
```

Structures   187 main() defines *car1* and *car2* of type struct mobile. Then main() calls the function find_year() by passing one character string with a value of "Rambler." Execution then goes to that function.

In find_year(), the character string is called *name[ ]*. A local variable of type struct mobile is defined with the name of *car*. find_year() asks for the year of the car given by *name[ ]*, and reads in the year member of *car*. The make member of *car* is assigned the string in *name[ ]*. Then find_year() returns the name and the year of the car as type struct mobile.

This structure is assigned to *car1* in main(). Similarly, the string "Mustang" is passed to find_year(), which returns that string and its year back to main() as a struct mobile. This new structure is assigned to *car2*.

Now main() calls the function print_oldest(). Instead of passing a string, main() passes two structures. Also, instead of assigning the function to a variable like *car1* and *car2*, main() doesn't assign print_oldest() to anything. Hence, there is no return in print_oldest() and its return data type is void.

print_oldest() makes a copy of these two structures into *auto1* and *auto2*. If this function had changed the contents of these structures, the changes would not be reflected in *car1* and *car2* in main(). This is like scalars and unlike arrays. The function proceeds to find the oldest of the two cars and prints its make. Note that there is no return statement here.

```
//EXAMPLE 11.1
#include <stdio.h>
#include <string.h>
struct mobile                                    //Global definition.
{
    char make[15];
    int year;
};

//Function prototypes
struct mobile find_year (char name [ ]);
void print_oldest(struct mobile auto1, struct mobile auto2);
```

Solution 11.5

```
struct part_item old_part;
printf("What is the part number? ");
gets(old_part.number);
printf("The price? ");
scanf("%f", &old_part.price);
printf("And the quantity? ");
scanf("%d", &old_part.qty);
```

Drill 11.6 Now code the program (without the structure template and variable definitions). Have the code simply print the total inventory value of each part. Your output should look like this:

```
---- output -----
SMS0001 0.35 20  7.00
OLS0001 0.60 30 18.00
```

```
void main (void)
{
   struct mobile car1, car2;
   car1 = find_year("Rambler");
   car2 = find_year("Mustang");
   print_oldest(car1, car2);
}

//This function receives one string that is the make of a car,
//  reads in its year, and returns them both as "struct mobile."
struct mobile find_year (char name [ ])
{
   struct mobile car;
   printf("What year is the %s? ", name);
   scanf("%d", &car.year);
   strcpy(car.make, name);
   return car;
}

//This function receives two structures of type "struct mobile"
//  and prints the year of the oldest car. It returns nothing.
void print_oldest(struct mobile auto1, struct mobile auto2)
{
   if(auto1.year < auto2.year)
      printf("The oldest is the %s\n", auto1.make);
   else
      if(auto1.year > auto2.year)
         printf("The oldest is the %s\n", auto2.make);
      else
         printf("They are both the same age\n");
}
----- output -----
What year is the Rambler? 1966
What year is the Mustang? 1964
The oldest is the Mustang
```

Solution 11.6

```
printf("%s\t%.2f\t%d\t%.2f\n", part.number, part.price, part.qty,
                               part.price * part.qty);
printf("%s\t%.2f\t%d\t%.2f\n", old_part.number, old_part.price,
                               old_part.qty, old_part.price * old_part.qty);
```

Drill 11.7 Suppose we had 100 parts. Coding them would be very inefficient. Write a function called print_inv() that will receive a structure variable called *prt* of type struct part_item and print the appropriate report line, as shown in Drill 11.6. The function doesn't return anything.

EXPERIMENTS

Exp 11.1 Let us introduce two new functions intended for strings. First, enter "You're making me blue" and then try to enter "All my loving." When entering song titles, you can enter your favorites. I've given some of mine.

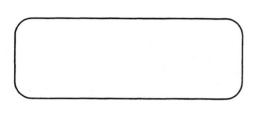

```
#include <stdio.h>
void main ( )
{
    char a[25], b[25];
    puts("name your song");
    gets(a);
    puts("\nname another one");
    scanf("%s", &b);
    printf("%s %s\n", a, b);
}
```

a. Was the scanf() able to read the entire string or only the first word?
b. Was the gets() able to read the entire string or only the first word?
c. Did the gets() stop reading at the first space or the first return that was entered?
d. Did the puts() add a '\n' at the end of the string that is printed?
e. Which function would you prefer to read in a string, scanf() or gets()?

Exp 11.2 First enter "Ooowee Babe" and then 2.40.

```
name your song
Ooowee Babe
How long is it?
2.40
```

```
#include <stdio.h>
void main (void)
{
    struct song   //Definition of structure.
    {
        char name[25];
        float len;
    };             //End of the definition.
```

Solution 11.7

```
void main (void)
{   :     // All statements not shown.
    print_inv(part);
    print_inv(old_part);
}
void print_inv (struct part_item prt)
{
    printf("%s\t%.2f\t%d\t%.2f\n",
        prt.number, prt.price, prt.qty,
        prt.price * prt.qty);
}
```

Drill 11.8 Now add a local variable in print_inv() called *inventory*. Have print_inv() pass *prt* to a new function called find_inv(), which will simply find and return the product of price and qty. In find_inv(), no new variable is needed. print_inv() should give the same output as before, but now it uses find_inv() to find the product. Show the coding for both functions.

Structures

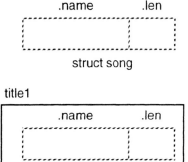

struct song

title1

```
struct song title1; //Declaration of a
                              //variable.
puts("name your song");
gets(title1.name);
puts("How long is it?");
scanf("%f", &title1.len);
printf("Your song is ");
puts(title1.name);
printf("Yours is %.2f min. long.\n",
    title1.len);
}
```

Just as int and float are data types, struct song is a new data type that we have defined.

a. What are the two known data types used to define struct song?

b. struct song is defined with two members. What are their names?

c. Do the words int or float by themselves create new variables or allocate space in memory?

d. Since struct song is also a new data type, do you think that it creates in itself a new variable?

e. Is a semicolon used at the end of the structure definition?

f. Since the definition of the structure doesn't create a new variable, what is the name of the variable declared using the struct song data type?

g. *title1* is a new variable that takes up space in memory. How many parts does it have? What are their names?

h. Show the contents of each member inside the box for *title1*.

i. An array is a collection of many items of the same data type, such as int or char. Similarly, a structure data type is a collection of many items. Do they have to be of the same data type?

j. When accessing a slot in an array, a set of brackets is used, such as a[2] = 0;. When we want to access a member of a structure, what do we use?

k. How would you have assigned the len member of *title1* to 0?

l. How would you have assigned the name member of *title1* to "Mister Moonlight"?

Solution 11.8

```
void print_inv (struct part_item prt)
{  float inventory;
   inventory = find_inv (prt);
   printf("%s\t%.2f\t%d\t%.2f\n",
      prt.number, prt.price, prt.qty,
      inventory);
}
float find_inv(struct part_item prt)
{
   return (prt.price * prt.qty);
}
```

Drill 11.9 Now rewrite only print_inv() and the changes in main(). print_inv() will also return *inventory* to main(), and main() will add the inventories from the two parts and print their sum. Use the variable *sum* in main().

Exp 11.3 Enter "Riders on the Storm" and 3.10 for the input data.

```
#include <stdio.h>
#include <string.h>
void main (void)
{
    struct song
    {
        char name[25];
        float len;
    };
    struct song title1, title2;
    strcpy(title2.name, "Teardrops");
    title2.len = 2.35;
    puts   ("name your song");
    gets   (title1.name);
    puts   ("How long is it?");
    scanf ("%f", &title1.len);
    printf("My song is %s\n Your song is ", title2.name);
    puts   (title1.name);
    printf("Yours is %.2f min. longer \n", title1.len - title2.len);
}
```

a. Can you print out both members of *title2* without specifying the member names? Does this work?

```
printf("%s %.2f\n", title2);
```

b. Can you assign *title2* to *title1* without specifying their members? Does this work?

```
title1 = title2;
```

c. Does this work? Why or why not?

```
title1.name = title2.name
```

Solution 11.9

```
void main (void)
{   :
    float sum;
    :
    sum = print_inv (part);
    sum = sum + print_inv(old_part);
    printf("The total inventory is %.2f\n", sum);
}
float print_inv (struct part_item prt)
{
    float inventory;
    inventory = find_inv (prt);
    printf("%s\t%.2f\t%d\t%.2f\n", prt.number, prt.price, prt.qty, inventory);
    return inventory;
}
```

Structures

Exp 11.4

```c
#include <stdio.h>
void main (void)
{
   struct song
   {
      char name[25];
      float len;
   };

   struct song
      title1 = {"Marvelous Grace", 2.50},
      title2 = {"I Surrender All", 3.0},
      title3;

   title3 = title1;
   title1 = title2;
   title2 = title3;
   printf("1: %s %.2f\n", title1.name,
         title1.len);
   printf("2: %s %.2f\n", title2.name,
         title2.len);
}
```

a. When initializing structures, do you have to provide the value of the first member first or can it be placed second?

b. Can you leave out the value of one of the members? Does this work?

```c
struct song title1 = { , 2.50}, title2 = {"I Surrender All", }, title3;
```

c. How many variables of type struct song were created?

d. What was done to the original values of *title1* and *title2*?

Drill 11.10 Let us leave writing functions aside for now and see what else we can do with structures. We can create an array of structures. See if you can define a structure called part_a[3] that is an array of struct part_item. See also if you can initialize the array so that the members in each cell are as shown in the accompanying figure. When you do that, a nested pair of braces should be used for each array slot and an outer pair of braces should be used for the entire array.

part_a[0]			part_a[1]			part_a[2]		
.number	.price	.qty	.number	.price	.qty	.number	.price	.qty
"SMS0001"	0.35	20	"OLS0001"	0.60	30	"VVU0001"	0.25	50

Exp 11.5

```
#include <stdio.h>
#include <string.h>
struct song              //Start of structure
{                        // definition
        char name[25];
        float len;
};                       //End of structure definition

struct song zero_out (struct song);       //Function prototype

void main (void)
{
   struct song title1 = {"White room", 2.50}, title2;
   title2 = zero_out(title1);                //Call to the function
   printf("1: %s %.2f\n", title1.name, title1.len);
   printf("2: %s %.2f\n", title2.name, title2.len);
}

struct song zero_out (struct song x)//Beginning of function definition
{
   struct song y = {"Have Mercy On Me", 3.20};
   strcpy(x.name, " ");
   x.len = 0;
   return y;
}                                   //End of function definition
```

a. The structure is not defined inside any function. If it were defined inside the main() function, as was done in the previous experiments, will this program work? Why or why not? Try it.

Let us first concentrate on how functions receive arguments that are structures.

b. As shown in the experiment, the definition of the structure is *global*; that is, it is available to all functions. *title1* in main() becomes what variable in zero_out()?

c. zero_out() erased the contents of what was provided through the variable *title1*. Were the contents of *title1* also erased when control went back to main()?

d. When passing a structured variable to a function, can that function change its contents?

e. Do functions make copies of structures like they make copies of scalars?

f. Do functions receive only addresses of structures, as they do of arrays?

Solution 11.10

```
struct part_item part_a[3] =  {  {"SMS0001", 0.35, 20},
                                 {"OLS0001", 0.60, 30},
                                 {"VVU0001", 0.25, 50}
                              };
```

Drill 11.11

For the array above, part_a[2].qty is equal to 50. First, find the name of the variable, *part_a[ ]*; then give its index, part_a[2]; then provide the name of the structure member, part_a[2].qty. Now write a loop to add all the prices in the array.

Let us now consider how functions return structures.

g. What is the data type that zero_out() returns?

h. What variable is returned by zero_out()? What is its data type? What are its values?

i. Which variable in main() accepts the returned structure from zero_out()?

j. Were the values returned by zero_out() received in main()? If so, then into which variable?

Exp 11.6 How about an array of structures!

```
#include <stdio.h>
#include <string.h>
struct song
{
      char name[25];
      float len;
};
void main (void)
{
   struct song title[3] =
      {{"Lone Prairie", 2.50},
       {"Merry England", 3.35}};
   int i;
   puts("Enter a new song");
   gets(title[2].name);
   puts("Enter its time");
   scanf("%f", &title[2].len);

   for(i = 0; i <= 2; ++i)
      printf("%d: %s %.2f\n", i + 1,
         title[i].name, title[i].len);
}
```

a. Remember that indexing starts at 0 and enter the initialized values of the array in the diagram.

b. Show the values that you provided in the array of structures.

c. What is the name of the array? How many slots does it have?

d. What is the name of the structure? What are the names of its members?

e. Why is the index provided next to the array name and not the member name, in all the instances of this experiment? Why isn't the following correct: &title.len[2]?

f. When accessing any item in this array of structures, what must be specified first, second, and last? Choose your answers from: member name, array name, index.

Solution 11.11

```
int i;
float sum = 0.0;
for(i = 0; i <= 2; ++i)
   sum = sum + part_a[i].price;
```

Drill 11.12 Write a loop that sets all the quantities of each array slot to zero.

g. An array slot is specified by using brackets or a period?

h. A structure member is specified by using brackets or a period?

Exp 11.7 Let us have an array of names within a structure. Enter "Satisfied Mind," "Billy," "Jilly," and "Silly" for the input data.

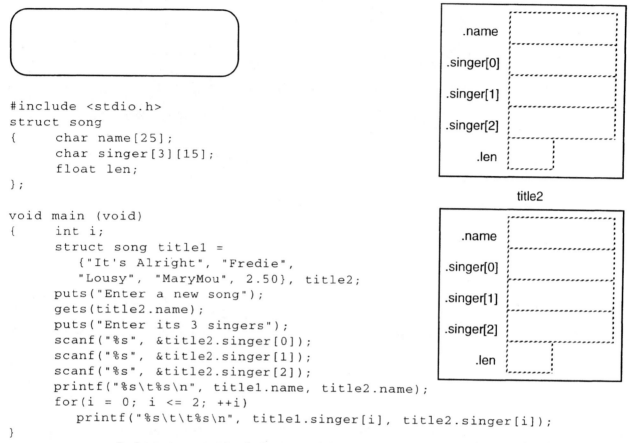

```
#include <stdio.h>
struct song
{      char name[25];
       char singer[3][15];
       float len;
};

void main (void)
{      int i;
       struct song title1 =
           {"It's Alright", "Fredie",
           "Lousy", "MaryMou", 2.50}, title2;
       puts("Enter a new song");
       gets(title2.name);
       puts("Enter its 3 singers");
       scanf("%s", &title2.singer[0]);
       scanf("%s", &title2.singer[1]);
       scanf("%s", &title2.singer[2]);
       printf("%s\t%s\n", title1.name, title2.name);
       for(i = 0; i <= 2; ++i)
           printf("%s\t\t%s\n", title1.singer[i], title2.singer[i]);
}
```

a. So far our structure has had one member that was an array. However, we treated it as a single unit or a string. Here, we have a 3–slot array of strings that hold the names of the singers. When initializing, how do we know which string goes into which slot of the structure?

b. Show the contents of all locations in the figure.

Solution 11.12
```
for(i = 0; i <= 2; ++i)
   part_a[i].qty = 0;
```

Drill 11.13 Let us define a new structure by using a pre–existing structure. For example, see if you can define a structure called struct assembly, which is made up of the parts shown in the diagram. The name of the assembly has 10 characters and uses a 3–element array of struct part_item.

struct assembly

name[ ]	part_a[0]			part_a[1]			part_a[2]		
	.number	.price	.qty	.number	.price	.qty	.number	.price	.qty

Structures

c. When reading in the name member of *title2*, why is no array index given?

d. When reading in the singers for *title2*, why is an index specified?

e. When printing the song names, are array indexes specified? Why or why not?

f. When printing out the singers, are array indexes specified? Why or why not?

g. By looking at the structure definition, how can you tell which member needs an index specified?

h. In Experiment 11.6, was the variable name or the member name specified with an index?

i. By looking at the structure and/or variable definitions, how can you tell if the variable name or the structure member name gets an index?

j. In this experiment, was the variable name or the member name specified with an index? How can you tell which one should be?

k. Show how you would have to change the definition of the structure and/or the variable so that both indexes would have to be given when accessing a singer.

QUESTIONS

For these questions, use the definitions of these structures:

```
struct date
{
    int   yy, mm, dd;
};
struct emp
{
    char  empname[10];
    float salary;
    struct date hired;
};
struct dep
{
    struct emp manager;
    struct emp worker[15];
    float profits;
};
```

1. Define a struct date variable called *date1* and initialize it to February 23, 1934, in the correct format.

2. Define a struct emp variable called *person1* and initialize it to "Roger", with a salary of $30,000, who was hired on February 23, 1998.

Solution 11.13

```
struct assembly
{
    char name[10];
    struct part_item part_a[3];
};
```

Drill 11.14

Define a structure variable called *motor*. Assign its first part number as "SMR0001", its price as 3.57, and the quantity needed as 7. Then read in the three members for the second part. Do not assign any values to the third part.

3. Define a struct dep variable called *toys* whose manager is "Roger", from Question 2 above, and the profits are $80,000. This department has only two employees as shown below:
"Mojax" with a salary of 10,000 and the date of hire being April 12, 1987
"Kojax" with a salary of 8,000 and the date of hire being April 2, 1980
4. Using one printf(), print the contents of *date1*.
5. Using two printf()'s, print the contents of *person1*.
6. Write a function called print_emp() that will receive a structure of type struct emp and print its empname, salary, and date hired. Calling this function three times and using an extra printf(), print the contents of *toys*. You may want to draw a diagram to help you see the components of *toys*.

PROGRAMS

Use the same structure definitions as given in the questions above.
1. Write a function called get_date() that will receive no arguments and ask for the date in numerical format. Then return the date as struct date.
2. Write a function called get_data(). This function will not receive any arguments, but it will ask for the employer's name, salary, and date of hire. It will call get_date() described in Program 1 and assign it to the hire date of the employer. Then it will return this data as a structure of type struct emp.
3. Write a function called print_data(). This function will receive one variable of type struct emp and will print all three members of it on one line. Nothing will be returned.
4. Write main(), which will call get_data() and store the structure in a local variable. Passing this local variable, main() will call print_data() and have this data printed.
5. Write main(), which will define an array called a[10] of type struct emp. main() will then call get_data() in a loop 10 times, each time getting the data in the proper slot of the array. Then main() will call print_data() in a loop so that the data is printed in reverse order.
6. Write a function that will receive one array of type struct emp and an integer that gives the size of the array. Remember that, if the size is 5, then the largest index of the array should be 4. It will then return those employees' average salary.

Solution 11.14

```
struct assembly motor;
strcpy(motor.part_a[0].number, "SMR0001");
motor.part_a[0].price = 3.57;
motor.part_a[0].qty = 7;
printf("Enter a part's name, price, and qty\n");
scanf("%s", &motor.name);
scanf("%f", &motor.part_a[1].price);
scanf("%d", &motor.part_a[1].qty);
```

Pointers

LESSON

A Simple Analogy

When I attended Rutgers, the university post office gave me a post office box. I still remember the number: 396. If at any time someone wanted to send mail to my college address, they had to specify the box number. The college postal employee would place my mail at that location, and I would get the mail at my convenience.

Similarly, when you create a variable, say, with this statement, int i = 54; the compiler assigns an address (or a post office box number) to that variable. i will be stored at one specific address in the computer's memory. This is in RAM (random access memory). I could not tell the post office that I don't want 396, that I want some other number for my box number. What if someone else was already using that number? In the same way, once a compiler stores your variable in a certain memory address, you cannot tell it to now place that variable at some other location in RAM. Its address is fixed.

However, the mail that was placed in my mail box would change from day to day and in the same way, the data placed in your variable can change from time to time. Data is placed in i temporarily

DRILLS

Drill 12.1 Let us first review how computers count: 1, 2, 3, 4, 5, 6, 7, 8, 9, A, B, C, D, E, F, 10, 11, 12, 13, 14, 15, 16, 17, 18, 19, 1A, 1B, 1C, 1D, 1E, 1F, 20, 21, and so on. This method of counting numbers is called the *hexadecimal numbering system*, or *hex* for short.

a. In hex, what number comes after 9, 19, F, and 1D?
b. In hex, what number comes before 10, 20, F, and 2E?
c. In hex, what number comes after 99, 299, 29F, FFEF, and 9FF?

and may be used later. In the same way that my name was associated with box number 396 at the college, the compiler associates the variable *i* with a certain RAM location. The name of the variable and its address is fixed once the program starts executing, but its contents may change.

A Simple Computer

Figure 12.1 shows a simple computer. The CPU (central processing unit), the brains of the computer, has to store the number in its register into the variable *i*. It first figures out that this variable is stored in address location 4 in RAM. Then over the control bus, the CPU signals the RAM that it is placing data in memory. It is the CPU's responsibility to place the correct address, that is, 4, on the address bus and to place the correct data, that is, 54, on the data bus. The RAM, learning the request from the control bus, first reads the address off the address bus and then places the data on the data bus at that location.

Later, after other numbers have come and gone through the register, the CPU may need to read the data that is in *i*. It signals the RAM controller that it needs the data. The CPU places the address of 4 on the address bus. The RAM controller reads the contents of location 4 and places the 54 on the data bus. The CPU then copies it in its register, ready to be processed.

I hope this discussion has helped you understand the role that addresses play for variables.

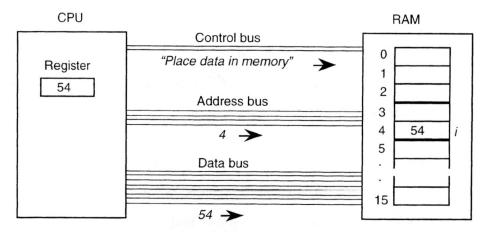

Figure 12.1 Assigning 54 to the variable *i*.

Solution 12.1
a. In hex, after 9 comes A, after 19 comes 1A, after F comes 10, and after 1D comes 1E.
b. In hex, before 10 comes F, before 20 comes 1F, before F comes E, and before 2E comes 2D.
c. In hex, 9A comes after 99, 29A comes after 299, 2A0 comes after 29F, FFF0 comes after FFEF, and A00 comes after 9FF.

Drill 12.2 Each memory location (also called RAM) in a computer has an address so that the system knows which location to access. Each location typically stores one *byte* of data. The amount of data RAM can store is measured in bytes. In this figure, each memory location's address is shown. What is the memory address of the location that is 5 addresses away from FFAE?

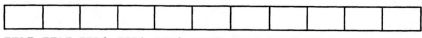

FFAE FFAF FFB0 FFB1 FFB2 FFB3 FFB4 FFB5 FFB6 FFB7 FFB8

The Hexadecimal Numbering System

Computer addresses are usually given in hexadecimal numbers. To understand addresses, we should try to understand the hexadecimal numbering system. Our decimal numbering system, which we learned in kindergarten, uses ten symbols, from 0 to 9. After 9, we go to 10, 11, and so on. In hex (short for hexadecimal) there are 16 symbols, from 0 to 9 and A to F. After F, the next numbers are 10, 11, 12, 13, 14, 15, 16, 17, 18, 19, 1A, 1B, 1C, 1D, 1E, 1F, 20, 21, and so on.

When a car odometer reads 9,999 miles and we go another mile, it will read 10,000 miles. In hex, the number after 9999 is 999A. (Usually we don't use commas in hex numbers.) Similarly, in decimal the number before 45,000 is 44,999 and in hex the number before 4D00 is 4CFF. The F in hex behaves like a 9 in decimal.

If 1 is added to 4CFF, first we add 1 to the rightmost F. This gives us 10. We write down the 0 and carry the 1. Then we add 1 to the second F, which also gives us a 0 and we carry the 1. Then we add 1 to C, which gives us D and we just bring down the 4. Figure 12.2 shows this addition.

What Are Pointers?

Just as we can create variables that store integers, characters, floats, and structures, we can also create variables that store the memory addresses of other variables. Variables that store memory addresses are called *pointers*.

```
int i, *p;
```

Here we have created two variables, *i* and *p*. The similarity between them is that they both have something to do with integers. The difference between them, seen by the asterisk, is that *i* stores integer *values,* whereas *p* stores *addresses* of integer locations. You can store a 54 in *i*, but not in *p*. Similarly, you can store the address of *i* in *p*, but not the address of an integer in *i*. Integer variables store integer values, and integer pointers store the addresses of integers. Both of these statements are legal.

```
i = 54; //Storing an integer value.
p = &i; //Storing an address of an integer variable.
```

$$\begin{array}{r} 4\ C\ F\ F \\ +\quad_{1\ \ 1}\ 1 \\ \hline 4\ D\ 0\ 0 \end{array}$$

Figure 12.2 Adding 1 to 4CFF in hex.

Solution 12.2 FFB3

Drill 12.3 More memory locations are shown here after location FFB8. For those locations, their contents are also shown. In which location is 23 stored? What is the address of the memory location that is 10 addresses before the location where 112 is stored?

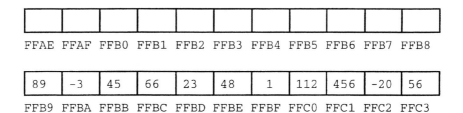

FFAE	FFAF	FFB0	FFB1	FFB2	FFB3	FFB4	FFB5	FFB6	FFB7	FFB8

89	-3	45	66	23	48	1	112	456	-20	56
FFB9	FFBA	FFBB	FFBC	FFBD	FFBE	FFBF	FFC0	FFC1	FFC2	FFC3

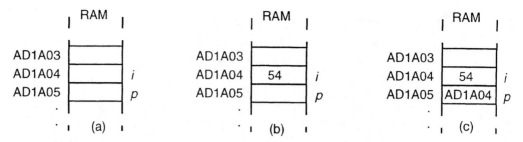

Figure 12.3 (a) Creation of *i* and *p*. (b) Assigning 54 to *i*. (c) Assigning the address of *i* to *p*.

Figure 12.3(a) shows that when the variables are created, *i* is stored at location AD1A04 and *p* is stored at location AD1A05. In Figure 12.3(b), 54 is assigned to *i*, and in Figure 12.3(c), the address of *i*, which is AD1A04, is assigned to *p*.

We can also define pointer variables that store addresses to other data types, such as this:

```
char a[11], *pa;
float x, *px;
```

Here, *pa* can store addresses to character data types and *px* can store addresses to floats. Other combinations are not allowed. Here, both are correct.

```
pa = &a[0];   //Storing a character address in a character pointer.
px = &x;      //Storing a float address in a float pointer.
```

However, here are two statements that are NOT correct.

```
pa = &x;    //This is WRONG! "pa" is not a pointer variable for floats!
px = 3.40;  //This is WRONG! "px" cannot store floating point values!
```

pa is a pointer to characters and can't store addresses of type characters. Also, *x* can store only addresses to floats. 3.40 is not an address.

Names for pointer variables usually begin with the letter p, although they don't have to. Pointer names beginning with p reminds the programmer that this variable may be a pointer and can store only addresses.

54 is an integer *constant*. The value of 54 will always be 54. *i* is an integer *variable*. Its value may be 54 for now, but later it could change. Similarly, AD1A04 is a *pointer constant*; it is the

---

Solution 12.3 23 is stored in memory address FFBD. 112 is stored in FFC0, and 10 locations before that is location FFB6.

Drill 12.4 Here, array *a[ ]* is defined and initialized. Some computers need two bytes of memory to store integers, as shown in the figure. What is the starting address of the location where 28 is stored? How many bytes are needed to store a 4-element integer array?

```
int a[4] = {4, 77, 28, 12};
```

Name of the memory location:	a[0]	a[1]	a[2]	a[3]	
Value in the memory location:	4	77	28	12	

Address of memory location: FFBA FFBB FFBC FFBD FFBE FFBF FFC0 FFC1 FFC2

address of a location in RAM. The address of that location cannot be changed; it will always be AD1A04. However, *p* is a *pointer variable*; the address stored in it may change. Typically, the word "pointer" by itself means a pointer variable.

Pointer Arithmetic

We can add to or subtract from pointer variables. However, we must remember that adding a number to a pointer does not necessarily add that many bytes but adds that number of *storage units*. In this text, we will assume that characters are stored in one byte, integers in two, and floats in four. Bytes are used to measure the amount of memory. On other machines, the number of bytes per storage unit may differ.

```
int i, *p;
```

Using our assumptions above, if 1 is added to a pointer integer, such as *p*, then 2 bytes will be added to the address that is already in it. Similarly if 1 is subtracted from *p*, then 2 bytes are subtracted from its contents. However, for every integer added to *px*, a pointer to floats, four is added to its contents because we are assuming that floats are stored using four bytes. In our case, one storage unit is 4 bytes for floats, 2 for integers, and 1 for characters.

Arrays and Pointers

When arrays are defined, the array name actually holds the starting address of the array. As with mailboxes, this starting address is fixed because we can't move the array to some other location in memory that easily once the array is created

```
int *p, j[ ] = {2, 6, 3, 7, 4};
```

Here, we have a pointer *p* and an array *j[ ]*. As seen in Figure 12.4, the value of *j* is fixed at the address of 1A02 and can't be changed. The integer array is initialized with each slot and the initialization requires two bytes. When we execute this statement:

```
p = &j[2];
```

the value of *p* becomes 1A06, the address of j[2]. We can change the value of *p* because it is a pointer *variable*, but we can't change the value of *j*, a pointer *constant*. Notice that the value of *p* is an address, whereas the value of j[0] is an integer. If we do this,

```
p = p + 1;
```

then the value of *p* will become 1A08, and if we do this:

Solution 12.4 28 or a[2] is stored starting at FFBF. To store a 4-element integer array, we need 8 bytes, 2 bytes per element.

Drill 12.5 If 1 byte is needed to store characters on a certain computer and 4 bytes are needed to store floats, show the starting addresses of each array slot in the diagram for these two arrays. The starting addresses of *b[ ]* and *x[ ]* are given. Also, where does *x[ ]* end?

```
char b[5] = "only";
float x[2] = {44.0, -24.1};
```

b[0]	b[1]	b[2]	b[3]	b[4]		x[0]	x[1]
'o'	'n'	'l'	'y'	'\0'		44.0	-24.1

C1DD

C776

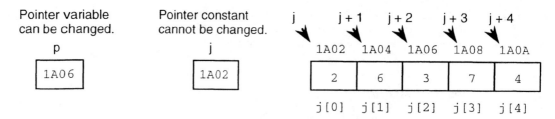

Figure 12.4 The similarity between arrays and pointers.

```
p = j + 1;
```

then the value of *p* will become 1A04 because *j* is fixed at 1A02. However, we can't change *j* like this:

~~j = j + 1;~~   //WRONG

because *j* is an array, and arrays are pointer constants.

Example

Let us summarize many of the concepts of this unit by reviewing Example 12.1. We have an integer array *j[ ]* and an integer pointer *p*, which are both not initialized. There is a floating point array called *x[ ]* and a float pointer *q* initialized to the address of *x*. The starting address of *x[ ]* can be given as *x*, x + 0, &x, or &x[0]. Also, the address of *j* is placed in the pointer *p* in line 1.

```
//EXAMPLE 12.1
#include <stdio.h>
void read_arr (int *x, int y);
void main (void)
{
   int   i, j[5],
         *p;              //p used to store addresses for array j[ ].
   float x[5],
         *q = &x[0];   //q used to store addresses for array x[ ].

   //Printing out the addresses of the two arrays.
   p = &j[0];         //Line 1
   printf("Addresses of j[ ]\tAddresses of x[ ]\n");
```

Solution 12.5 Addresses of the slots of array b[ ] are C1DD, C1DE, C1DF, C1E0, and C1E1. Addresses of the slots of array *x[ ]* are C776 and C77A. The last byte of *x[ ]* is at location C77D.

Drill 12.6
a. How many bytes does each slot of *rupees[ ]* occupy?
b. What is the address of each slot of *rupees[ ]* if the first one starts at FF10?

```
struct money
{
   char country[10];
   int denomination;
   float conversion_factor;
}
struct money rupees[6];
```

```
   for(i = 0; i <= 4; ++i)
      printf("%p \t\t%p \n", p + i, &q[i]);

   //Reading numbers into the integer array.
   printf("Enter 5 integers\n");
   scanf("%d", &j[4]);
   scanf("%d", j);
   scanf("%d", j + 1);         //j can't change, and it hasn't.

   p = &j[1];                  //Same as: p = j + 1;
   p = p + 1;                  //p can change!
   scanf("%d", p);
   read_arr(j, 3);

   //Print the array
   printf("The array is:\n");
   for(i = 0; i <= 4; ++i)
      printf("%d\t", j[i]);
   printf("\n");
}

//Function to read a number into x[y].
void read_arr (int *x, int y)
{
   x = x + y;
   scanf("%d", x);
}
----- output -----
Addresses of j[ ]  Addresses of x[ ]
FE68               FE50
FE6A               FE54
FE6C               FE58
FE6E               FE5C
FE70               FE60
Enter 5 integers
4  2  6  3  7
The array is:
2  6  3  7  4
```

Solution 12.6
   a. Each slot of *rupees[ ]* needs 16 bytes: 10 for the character string, another 2 for the integer, and 4 for the float.
   b. Adding 16 to FF10 gives FF20 in hex. Hence, the slots of the array start at FF10, FF20, FF30, FF40, FF50, and FF60.

Drill 12.7 Pointers are special kinds of variables used to store memory addresses. You use an asterisk in front of the variable when defining a pointer.

```
int i, *p1;
float x, *p2;
```

   a. Which of the four variables above are pointers: *i, x, p1,* and/or *p2*?
   b. Which of these four items can store addresses?

The loop varies *i* from 0 to 4. In each iteration, it prints the address of the next slot in each of the two arrays. It does this by printing the value of *p*, which has the address of *j[ ]*, and adding *i* to it each time. The addresses of the *q[ ]* array are printed by printing &q[i]. This gives the address of each slot. Notice that, in the output, the addresses of the integer array go up by two and that of the float array go up by 4. On your computer, the storage unit of each data type and the actual addresses may be different.

Next, the program uses different ways of specifying the address of each slot in the *j[ ]* array. The addresses are passed to the scanf() function to read in values in the array slots. First, we read 4 into j[4] by passing &j[4]. Then a 2 is read into j[0] because *j* is passed to scanf(). *j* is the same as &j[0]. Similarly, j + 1 is passed to scanf(), which is really &j[1]. This reads in j[1]. Notice that you can add 1 to *j*, which will evaluate the expression to 1A04 in Figure 12.4. However, you can't change *j* to that!

Now, the address of j[1] is stored in *p*, which then *is changed* to p + 1 because *p* is a pointer variable, unlike *j*, which is a pointer constant. Since *p* contains the address of j[2], 3 is read into that slot. Last, *j* and 3 are passed to the function read_arr(). The address given by *j* is now assigned to the pointer variable *x*. We could not change *j* in main(), but here, *x* is a variable and so it can be changed. *y* is 3, so 3 storage units are added to 1A02, and *x* becomes 1A08. Reading a 7 at this address places the 7 in j[3]. Finally, the program prints the array to show its contents.

EXPERIMENTS

Exp 12.1 From Unit 3, remember that &i gives the address of *i*.

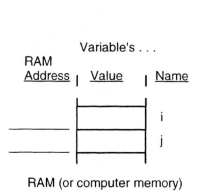

```
#include <stdio.h>
void main (void)
{
    int i = 7, j = 11;
    printf("%d %d\n", i, j);
    printf("%p %p\n", &i, &j);
}
```

As you may recall, each variable has a data type, name, value, and address associated with it. Inside the boxes, under the label of "Value," show the values of *i* and *j*. Likewise, on the lines under the label marked "Address," show the addresses of *i* and *j* in RAM from your output.

Solution 12.7 a. *p1* and *p2* are pointers.
b. Only they can be used to store memory addresses.

Drill 12.8 Not only is *p1* a special kind of a variable (a pointer variable) it is also a special kind of a pointer. *p1* is a pointer to integers **only**. Therefore, if 1 is added to *p1*, then actually 2 is added to it because we are assuming that integers take 2 bytes to store on our computer.

```
int i, *p1;
float x, *p2;
```

a. If we say, p1 = p1 + 3; and the initial value of *p1* is FF18, what will be the final value of *p1*?
b. If the initial value of *p1* were CD1E and we add 5 to it, what will *p1* become?
c. If floats need 4 bytes of RAM to be stored and initially *p2* is 7D50, what will be the value of *p2* after 3 is added to it?
d. If *p2* is initially CABB and 5 is added to it, what will *p2* become?

Exp 12.2

```
int i = 7, j = 11;
printf("%p %p\n", &i, &j);
i = 4;
j = 5;
printf("%d %d\n", i, j);
printf("%p %p\n", &i, &j);
```

a. After the initialization statement, were we able to change the *values* of the variables?

b. After the assignment statements, were we able to change the *addresses* of the variables? Try

```
&i = 4;

j = &i;
```

c. Now at the end of main(), add this statement and try running it:

Were we able to store the address of *i* into *j*?

Exp 12.3 We need a new way to define a variable if that variable will store memory addresses or RAM locations. Notice the declaration of *p1* using an asterisk.

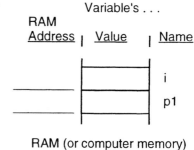

```
int i = 7;       //Stmt 1
int *p1;         //Stmt 2
float x;
printf("%p \n", &i);
p1 = &i;         //Stmt 3
printf("%p\n", p1);
```

RAM (or computer memory)

p1 is a variable that can hold only the memory addresses of integers.

a. In the diagram show the value of *i* inside its box and next to it its address.

b. After statement 3 is executed, what is the value of *p1*? Show the value in the diagram.

c. Can you assign only addresses to *p1*? Can you assign an integer to *p1*?

```
p1 = 4;
```

d. From statements 1 and 2, how can we tell beforehand that *i* can hold only integers and *p1* can hold only the addresses of integers?

e. Try assigning an address of a float to *p1*. Does it work?

```
p1 = &x;
```

Solution 12.8
a. FF1E   b. CD28   c. 7D5C   d. CACF

Drill 12.9 As before, *p1* is a pointer to integers and *p2* is a pointer to floats. Before each part below, assume *p1*'s initial value is F100 and *p2*'s initial value is F2CC. Give the values of *p1* and *p2* after each of these statements:

a. p1 = p1 + 2;

b. p1 = p1 − 2;

c. p2 = p2 + 2;

d. p2 = p2 − 2;

f. Does *p1* have its own memory location in RAM, as shown in the diagram? If so, show the address where *p1* is stored. Try:

```
printf("%p\n", &p1);
```

Exp 12.4 This experiment is a review of the previous three experiments.

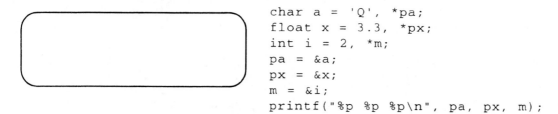

```
char a = 'Q', *pa;
float x = 3.3, *px;
int i = 2, *m;
pa = &a;
px = &x;
m = &i;
printf("%p %p %p\n", pa, px, m);
```

a. Out of the six variables declared, which may store addresses?
b. In the figure below, show the values of *a*, *x*, and *i*.
c. From the output, show the values of *pa*, *px*, and *m* in the figure below.
d. Now that you know the values of *pa*, *px*, and *m*, what are the addresses of *a*, *x*, and *i*? Show them in the figure.
e. Must variables that store addresses begin with the letter *p*? If not, how can we tell from the declarations of these variables that they can store addresses?
f. Which variable(s) may store only (single) characters?
g. Which variable(s) may store addresses to characters?
h. Can you store the address of a float in *pa*? Can you store the address of an integer in *pa*? If not, what error message is obtained?

```
pa = &x;
pa = &i;
```

RAM Address	Variable's... Value	Variable's... Name
____		a
____		pa
____		x

RAM Address	Variable's... Value	Variable's... Name
____		px
____		i
____		m

Solution 12.9

a. F104   b. F0FC   c. F2D4   d. F2C4

Drill 12.10 Assume that *p1* has the address of i[0] and that *p2* has the address of x[0].

```
int i[5], *p1;
float x[5], *p2;
```

a. After this statement (p1 = p1 + 3;) *p1* will contain the address of which slot in the array *i[ ]*?
b. After this statement (p2 = p2 + 3;) *p2* will contain the address of which slot in the array *x[ ]*?
c. In total how many *address locations* were added in a? In b?
d. In total how many indexes were added in a? In b?

```
pa = 'Q';
```
i. Can you store a character in *pa*? If not, what error message is obtained?

j. Can you change the address of a variable? If not, what error message is obtained?
```
&a = 4440;
```
k. Try storing the addresses of *a* and *i* in *px*. Does *px* hold the addresses of floats only?
```
px = &a;
px = &i;
```
l. Try storing the addresses of *a* and *x* in *m*. Does *m* hold the addresses of integers only?
```
m = &a;
m = &x;
```
m. What can you store in *a*? What can you store in *pa*? What in their declarations identifies the difference?

n. What can you store in *x*? What can you store in *px*? What in their declarations identifies the difference?

Exp 12.5

```
char a = 'Q', b = 'X', *pa, *pb;
pa = &a;                              //Stmt 1
pb = pa;                              //Stmt 2
printf("%p %p\n", pa, pb);
pa = &b;                              //Stmt 3
printf("%p %p\n", pa, pb);
```

a. Can we assign a variable that stores addresses to another variable, like in statement 2?

b. Can we store the address of any character variable in either *pa* or *pb*? How can you tell?

c. Where is the variable *a* stored? Where is the variable *b* stored? Fill in the diagram.

d. What is the first address stored in *pa*? Show it in the diagram.

e. Strike out that value you just placed for *pa* and write next to it the new address stored in *pa*.

f. From this experiment, can you tell where *pa* and *pb* are stored? If not, give the statement that will print these addresses and copy those addresses in the diagram.

Address	Value	Name		Address	Value	Name
_____	'Q'	a		_____		pa
_____	'X'	b		_____		pb

Solution 12.10

a. i[3]   b. x[3]   c. 6, 12   d. 3, 3

Drill 12.11 i[0] is stored at F400 and x[0] is stored at BBB0. Assume that *p1* has the address of i[0] and *p2* has the address of x[0].
```
int i[15], *p1;
float x[15], *p2;
```
a. If *p1* contains F410, it has the address of which slot of the array *i[ ]*?

b. If *p2* contains BBC0, it has the address of which slot of the array *x[ ]*?

Exp 12.6 Now let us see what operations we can do with variables that store memory addresses. First, let us have a little lesson in counting memory addresses by 1. Counting is done from 0 to 9, as we do normally. After 9, we count up to A, B, C, D, E, F, and then 10. Here, counting in memory addresses is done as a sample starting at FFDE. Adding 1 to FFDE gives us FFDF, and adding 1 to that gives us FFE0, and so on.

```
...   FFDE  FFDF  FFE0  FFE1  FFE2  FFE3  FFE4  FFE5  FFE6  FFE7  FFE8  FFE9
FFEA  FFEB  FFEC  FFED  FFEF  FFF0  FFF1 ...
```

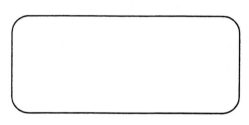

```
char a , *pa;          //Stmt 1
pa = &a;               //Stmt 2
printf("%p \n", pa);
pa = pa + 1;           //Stmt 3
printf("%p \n", pa);
pa = pa + 3;           //Stmt 4
printf("%p \n", pa);
pa = pa - 1;           //Stmt 5
printf("%p \n", pa);
```

  a. Can we add an integer to a variable such as *pa* that stores addresses?

  b. Can we subtract integers from a variable such as *pa* that stores addresses?

  c. Can we multiply integers to a variable such as *pa* that stores addresses? What error do you get?

```
pa = pa * 3;
```

  d. What was the first address stored in *pa* in Statement 2?

  e. After 1 was added to *pa* in Statement 3, what address was stored in *pa*?

  f. After 3 was added to *pa* in Statement 4, what address was stored in *pa*?

  g. After 1 was subtracted from *pa* in Statement 5, what address was stored in *pa*?

  h. Now change only Statement 1 to this:

```
int a, *pa;
```

Rerun the program and answer the same questions, namely:

    (i)   What was the first address that was stored in *pa* in Statement 2?

    (ii)   After 1 was added to *pa* in Statement 3, what address was stored in *pa*?

    (iii) After 3 was added to *pa* in Statement 4, what address was stored in *pa*?

    (iv) After 1 was subtracted from *pa* in Statement 5, what address was stored in *pa*?

Solution 12.11

  a. *p1* is equal to the address of i[8].

  b. *p2* has the address of x[4].

Drill 12.12 Which of the following statements are valid?

```
a. p1 = &i[0];
b. p1 = &x[0];
c. p1 = i[0];
```

i. Adding 1 to a variable that holds character addresses adds what number to that address?

j. Adding 1 to a variable that holds integer addresses adds what number to that address?

k. Since the answer to question i is 1, characters are stored in memory using only 1 BYTE. A byte is a unit of measure of memory. How many bytes are used to store integers on your computer? **Note** that the number of bytes used to store characters, integers, and floats varies depending on the type of computer and the compiler you are using.

Exp 12.7 The compiler knows that if we were to add 1 to a variable that holds addresses to integers, it will actually add 2 because the next integer will be two bytes away. Now find out how many bytes are used to store floating point numbers by observing the number added when 1 is added to a variable that holds the addresses of floats. Change here only the keyword float in Statement 1.

```
float a, *pa;          //Stmt 1
pa = &a;               //Stmt 2
printf("%p \n", pa);
pa = pa + 1;           //Stmt 3
printf("%p \n", pa);
pa = pa + 3;           //Stmt 4
printf("%p \n", pa);
pa = pa - 1;           //Stmt 5
printf("%p \n", pa);
```

a. What was the first address that was stored in *pa* in Statement 2?

b. After 1 was added to *pa* in Statement 3, what address was stored in *pa*?

c. After 3 was added to *pa* in Statement 4, what address was stored in *pa*?

d. After 1 was subtracted from *pa* in Statement 5, what address was stored in *pa*?

e. How many bytes are used to store floats on your computer?

f. Adding 5 adds how much to a variable that holds addresses for a character?

g. Adding 5 adds how much to a variable that holds addresses for an integer?

h. Adding 5 adds how much to a variable that holds addresses for a float?

Exp 12.8 It gets tiring to say "variables that hold addresses of whatever." We need a special term that describes such variables, and "pointer" is the word. However, students get queasy about that word and so we have avoided it. Nonetheless, these variables used to store addresses are a special type of variable and they are called "pointer variables," or "pointers" for short. If you don't like that word, use the phrase "variables that hold addresses of a specific data type." Then you will be reminded of the meaning of these types of variable.

Solution 12.12

a. p1 = &i[0];

   Valid. We can assign the address of an integer to an integer pointer.

b. p1 = &x[0];

   Not valid. We cannot assign the address of a float to an integer pointer.

c. p1 = i[0];

   Not valid. There is no address in i[0].

Drill 12.13

The name of the array is equal to the address of the first slot in that array. If x[5] is stored starting at AA00, then what is the value of *x*? What is the value of &x[0]?

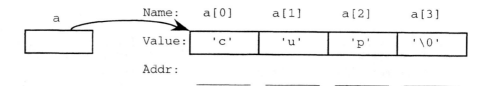

```
struct room
{
    float width;
    float length;
};
struct room dining = {10.5, 12.7},  *d;
d = &dining;
printf("%.2f %.2f \n", dining.width,
                            dining.length);
printf("%p\n", d);
d = d + 2;
printf("%p\n", d);
```

a. What is the name of the pointer variable?
b. This pointer holds addresses of what data type?
c. Variables of this data type take how many bytes to store? How can you tell by the definition of the structure?
d. What is the initial value of *d*, the pointer?
e. What is the value of *d* after 2 was added to it?
f. Do the answers in c, d, and e agree? Explain.

Exp 12.9 Now let us turn our attention to the addresses of array elements.

```
char a[4] = "cup";
printf("%p %p %p %p\n", a, &a[0], &a[1],
                                    &a[2]);
```

a. Does *a* print an address? Show its value in the figure.
b. Fill in the addresses in the figure below.

	Name:	a[0]	a[1]	a[2]	a[3]
a	Value:	'c'	'u'	'p'	'\0'
	Addr:				

Solution 12.13

Since *x[ ]* is an array, the following three are equal:
```
x == &x[0]  == &x or the address of AA00
```

Drill 12.14
If x[15] is stored starting at AA00, then what is the address of each?
a. x + 2
b. &x[2]

c. Is *a* the address of the first slot of the array, namely, &a[0]? Is this equal:

```
a  ==  &a[0]?
```

d. How many bytes is a[1] away from a[0]?
e. Elements in an array are stored next to each other. Hence, how many bytes does it take to store each character in an array of characters?
f. In Question i of Experiment 12.6, what did you conclude about the number of bytes needed to store one character? Does this agree with the answer to the above question?
g. If your answer is yes, then adding 1 to the address of a should give you &a[1], the address of a[1]. Are these two addresses the same?

```
printf("%p %p \n", a + 1, &a[1]);
```

If they are, then this condition a + 1 == &a[1]? is true.
h. And since that is true, this should also be true:

```
printf("%p %p \n", a + 2, &a[2]);
```

Is this also true?

Exp 12.10

```
char a[4] = "cup";
printf("%p %p \n", a, &a);
```

a. In Unit 3, we passed addresses to the scanf() function, and when dealing with character strings, we could send either the name of the string or its address. Then according to this experiment, is the following true?

```
a  ==  &a?
```

b. In conclusion, which of the following are true?

```
a  ==  &a?
a  ==  &a[0]?
a + 1  ==  &a[1]?
```

Solution 12.14
The answer for x + 2 is equal to AA08 for both questions. x + 2 is the same as &x[2].

Drill 12.15 Arrays are similar to pointers. One difference is that we can't change the value of the array address, but we can change the value of a pointer variable. Using the declarations given in Drill 12.11, which of the following are valid?

```
a.  x = x + 1;          b.  x = p2 + 1;
c.  p2 = x + 1;         d.  p2 = p2 + 1;
e.  x[2] = x[2] + 1;    f.  &x[2] = p2;
```

Exp 12.11 Let's change the data type.

```
int a[4];
printf("%p %p %p %p\n", a, &a[0], &a[1],
                                      &a[2]);
```

a. Which of the following are still true?

```
a == &a?
a == &a[0]?
a + 1 == &a[1]?
```

b. How many bytes are used to store an integer on your computer? Does this agree with previous results from Experiment 12.6?

c. Change the int to float in this experiment. Run it. Which of the following are still true?

```
a == &a?
a == &a[0]?
a + 1 == &a[1]?
```

d. How many bytes are used to store a float on your computer? Does this agree with previous results from Experiment 12.6?

e. Can you tell if the following statement is also true without running it? Write down your answer and then try it.

```
a + 1 == &a[0] + 1
```

Exp 12.12 For this experiment the data type used will not affect our conclusions. Here, we see that arrays and pointers are similar! Then we see if there is any difference between them.

```
char a[4] = "cup";                    // Stmt 1
printf("%p %p %p %p %p %p\n",
    a, a + 1, &a, &a[0], &a[0] + 1, &a[1]);
```

Solution 12.15

```
a. x = x + 1;          Not valid. We cannot change the address of an array.
b. x = p2 + 1;         Not valid. We can add 1 to a pointer, but we can't change the address of where
                       x[ ] is stored.
c. p2 = x + 1;         Valid. We can add 1 to x, but as long as we don't change x, we can use that
                       address to assign it to a pointer of type float.
d. p2 = p2 + 1;        Valid. We can, of course, add 1 to the address of a pointer.
e. x[2] = x[2] + 1;    Valid. We can change the value of an element of an array.
f. &x[2] = p2;         Not valid.
```

a. *a[ ]* is an array, so *a* can store addresses. We can also change the array variable into a pointer variable. Replace Statement 1 with these two statements:

```
int *a, b;
a = &b; //Assign an address to a.
```

Is there any difference in the printouts?

b. Between the two printouts, which of the following conditions are true? Complete the table.

Which conditions are true?	"a" is an array int a[5];	"a" is a pointer int *a, b; a = &b;
&a[1] == &a[0] + 1?		
a + 1 == &a[1] ?		

Exp 12.13 We saw in the table above one difference between declaring a variable as a pointer and declaring a variable as an array. Here is one more:

```
float a[4], *b, c;
b = &c;          // Stmt 1
printf("%p\n", b);
```

a. Did Statement 1 execute or did it give an error?

b. Change Statement 1 to this:

```
a = &c;
```

Try running it. Did it give an error? What was that error?

Conclusion: Both *a* and *b* store addresses; that is, they are both pointers. However, the address stored in *b* can be changed; it is a *pointer variable*.

The address of *a* cannot be changed; it is a *pointer constant*.

Drill 12.16 An array can be considered as a pointer constant, and its address can't be changed. A pointer variable such as *p2* can have the address stored in it changed. Which of the two initializations are valid?

a.
```
int *ptr1;
int i[10] = &ptr1;
```

b.
```
int i[10];
int *ptr1 = &i[0];
```

Exp 12.14 This experiment starts with a review of Unit 9.

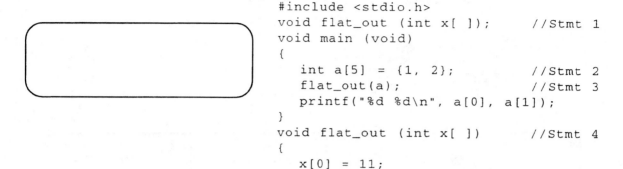

```
#include <stdio.h>
void flat_out (int x[ ]);        //Stmt 1
void main (void)
{
    int a[5] = {1, 2};           //Stmt 2
    flat_out(a);                 //Stmt 3
    printf("%d %d\n", a[0], a[1]);
}
void flat_out (int x[ ])         //Stmt 4
{
    x[0] = 11;
    x[1] = 11;
}
```

a. Did the flat_out() function receive the address of *a[ ]* or copies of its values?

b. Since it received its address, did flat_out() change copies of array *a[ ]* or did it change only the locations where the array elements were stored?
It changed the original locations where the array was stored because the final values of the array that were printed in main() were 11.

c. Change Statement 1 to the following:

```
void flat_out (int *x);
```

Change Statement 4 to the following:

```
void flat_out (int *x)
```

Run the program. Is there any difference in its execution?

d. Change Statement 3 to this:

```
flat_out(&a);
```

Is there any difference in the program's execution?

e. Change Statement 2 to this:
```
int *a;
```

Is there any difference in the program's execution?

Solution 12.16

a. Invalid.
b. Valid. It is okay to define a pointer and initialize it to an address of an integer.

Drill 12.17 Remember from Unit 9 that, when we pass an array to a function, we actually pass the address of that array. Hence, a function that receives an array as an argument can receive it as a pointer. Write a function header for a function called marvin(), where an array is received into a float pointer called *p*. A float pointer is returned.

QUESTIONS

For these questions, use these declarations of variables:

```
int i, j[5] = {4, 5, 6, 7, 8}, *ptr1=&j[0], *ptr3;
float  x[5] = {4.0, 5.0, 6.0, 7.0, 8.0},     *ptr2;
```

1. For each statement below, specify which are valid and which aren't.

a. ptr1 = ptr1 + 3;	b. j = j + 1;
c. ptr1 = j + 1;	d. ptr2 = ptr1;
e. ptr1 = j[1];	f. ptr1 = 2;
g. i = ptr1;	h. ptr3 = ptr1;
i. i = j[2];	j. ptr2 = x;
k. ptr1 = ptr1[2];	l. x = &ptr2[2];
m. j = ptr1 + 3;	n. ptr1 = &j[1];

2. Evaluate the address of each expression. The *j[ ]* array begins at A008 and the *x[ ]* array begins at 9008.

a. &j[0]	b. j
c. j - 2	d. j + 4
e. &x[4]	f. x + 3
g. x - 3	h. &x[2] + 3

3. Using the variables given in Question 1 and the addresses given in Question 2, show the printouts for each of the following.

```
a. for(i = 0; i <= 4; ++i)
   printf("%p %d\n", j + i, j[i]);

b. for(i = 0; i <= 4; ++i)
   printf("%p %p %.2f\n", x + i, &x[i], x[i]);

c. for(ptr2 = x + 4; ptr2 >= x; --ptr2)
   printf("%p %p \n", ptr2, ptr2 - 1);
```

PROGRAMS

1. Define a float array called *t[ ]* with 10 slots. Send the address of the first element of the array to a function called read_em(). Also send 2 and 6 as integers. The function will assign the array

---

Solution 12.17 `float * marvin (float *p)`

Drill 12.18 Write the main() that will pass this array to marvin().

```
float x[5];
```

Also write the marvin() that will print the addresses of the first five elements of the array and return the address of the fifth element. main() will receive that address into a pointer called *q* and it will print it.

Drill 12.19 Last–minute review questions:
a. Is an array a pointer constant or a pointer variable?
b. If *p* is a pointer and *x[ ]* is an array, can we print p[2]?
c. If *p* is a pointer and *x[ ]* is an array, can we print x + 2?
d. What did we assume the storage units (number of bytes) for characters, integers, and floats to be?

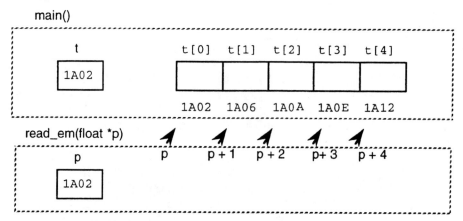

Figure 12.5 The pointer *p* in read_em() accesses the same locations as the *t[ ]* array in main().

address to a pointer called *p* and read floats in all the slots between these two numbers, inclusive. Althogh the read_em() function will read in the *t[ ]* array of main(), the read_em() function should not use brackets [ ] but only the asterisk operator *. When the function is done, have main() print out the entire array. See Figure 12.5.

2. Write a function called find_it(). This function will receive *z[ ]*, a float array; *size*, an integer specifying the number of slots in the array; and *look*, a float. The function will look for *look* in the array and return the *address* where that number was found in the array. Assume that the number will be found. Write main() to go with the function that will pass the appropriate variables and receive the address where the number was found into a pointer. Then print out that address.

Solution 12.18

```
void main (void)              float * marvin (float *p)
{                             {
   float x[5], *q;               int i;
   q = marvin(x);                for(i = 0; i <= 4; ++i)
   printf("%p\n", q);               printf("%p\n", p + i);
}                                return (p + 4);
                              }
```

Solution 12.19

a. An array is a pointer constant. It is stored in fixed locations that can't be moved.

b. *p* is not an array. You shouldn't use a subscript with it.

c. *x* is a pointer constant. You can print 2 more than its value.

d. We took the storage units to be 1, 2, and 4 bytes for characters, integers, and floats, respectively.

Unit 13

The Indirection Operator

LESSON

The Indirection Operator

In the last unit, we learned about pointers and how they store addresses, how they are similar to arrays, and so on. In this unit we will learn how to use pointers. A pointer variable that stores an address needs a method to access the location of that address.

Suppose we have this declaration:

```
int i = 40, j = 60, *ptr1 = &i, *ptr2 = &j;   // Line 1
```

then we know that *i* and *j* are initialized to 40 and 60, respectively. We also know that *ptr1* contains the address of *i*, which is A000, and *ptr2* contains the address of *j*, which is A002. See Figure 13.1. If we print this out,

```
printf("%p %d\n", ptr1, *ptr1);   // Line 2
```

DRILLS

Drill 13.1 The diagram shows four variables and the addresses where they are stored. After the execution of these statements, show the values of the locations that are assigned.

```
int i = 43, j;
int *p1, *p2;
p1 = &i;
p2 = p1;
p2 = p2 + 1;
```

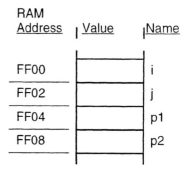

219

Address	Value	Name
A000	40	i
A002	60	j
A004	A000	ptr1
A008	A002	ptr2

Figure 13.1 *ptr1* equals A000 and *ptr1 equals 40.

then *ptr1* will print the address of A000 and *ptr1 will print out the contents of location A000, namely, 40. The asterisks in line 1 are used to declare pointers, *ptr1* and *ptr2*. The asterisk in line 2 is used as an indirection operator. What this means is that, when we print *ptr1, we are de–referencing *ptr1* and printing not the value of *ptr1* but the value of the location whose address is in *ptr1*. Therefore, from Figure 13.1 we see that *ptr1* is A000 while *ptr1 is 40. After the completion of this statement:

```
*ptr1 = *ptr1 + *ptr2 + 1;
```

i will contain 101 because *ptr1 is 40, and *ptr2 is 60, and adding those numbers to 1 gives 101. This number is then assigned to the location of A000, or *ptr1.

The terminology says that the location *pointed to by ptr1* is assigned the number 101. The location *ptr1* is not assigned a new number, but the location pointed to by it, namely, A000, is. We can also say that the location whose address is in *ptr1* is assigned a new number.

Address	Value	Name
A000	3	i
A002	7	j
A004	A000	array[0]
A008	A002	array[1]

Figure 13.2 An array of pointers.

RAM Address	Value	Name
FF00	43	i
FF02		j
FF04	FF00	p1
FF08	FF02	p2

Solution 13.1 *p1* gets the address of *i*. *p2* gets *p1*. *p2* then gets incremented by one storage unit. *p1* and *p2* are pointers to integers.

Drill 13.2 * is the indirection operator. *p1 refers to the location in memory that has its address in *p1*. Or, in other words, the location whose address is given in *p1*. What will this print? (Notice that *p1* uses a %p and *p1 uses a %d.)

```
printf("%p %d\n", p1, *p1);
```

Arrays

We can also store pointers in arrays. Consider this code:

```
int i = 3, j = 7, *array[2];
array[0] = &i;
array[1] = &j;
```

You can see from Figure 13.2 that *array[ ]* is an array of pointers to integers. It has the addresses of *i* and *j*. The content of array[1] is A002, but the value of this expression, *array[1], is 7. *array[ ]* is said to be an array of pointers.

Structures

```
struct node
{
    float value;
    struct node *ptr;
};
struct node x, y, *p;
```

In this code, we have defined a new structure with two parts: value and ptr. value stores a floating point number and ptr stores the addresses of variables which are of type `struct node`. *x* and *y* are variables of type `struct node` and ptr is a pointer to such variables. If we execute these statements:

```
p = &x;
x.ptr = &y;
y.ptr = NULL;
```

we will create a chain of pointers as shown in Figure 13.3(a). The address of *x*, which is A010, is stored in *p*; the address of *y* is stored in the ptr member of *x*; and the NULL pointer, an address that points to no location in memory, is stored in y.ptr. Since the actual addresses are not necessary for programming, only arrows are typically shown, as in Figure 13.3(b).

To access 33.7, we can specify either x.value or (*p).value. *p points you to *x*, but *x* has two members, so the member of interest must be specified. Hence, the value pointed to by *p* is coded as (*p).value. A shorter way of saying "(*p).value," is "p -> value." The value of p -> ptr is A020.

Solution 13.2 *p1* simply prints the address in it, but *p1 prints the value of the location whose address is *p1*. *p1 prints 43 because the address in *p1*, namely, FF00, has 43 stored in its place.

```
FF00    43
```

Drill 13.3 Show the contents of the locations after this code is executed.

```
*p2 = *p1;
j = j + 1;
```

Address	Value	Name
FF00	43	i
FF02		j
FF04	FF00	p1
FF08	FF02	p2

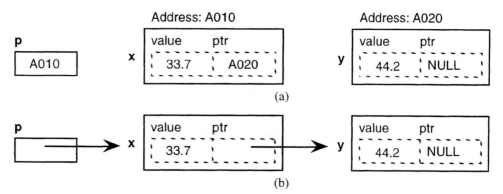

Address: A010   Address: A020

Figure 13.3 (a) How a chain of pointers is created.
(b) How a chain of pointers is represented in figures.

The malloc( ) and free( )Functions

We often need to create storage dynamically. While the program is executing, it may find out that the size of an array needs to be expanded. To allocate storage on–the–fly, malloc() is commonly used. Unfortunately, the syntax of this function is involved. Suppose that we wanted to create another storage place of type struct node; we can do it this way:

```
p = (struct node * ) malloc (sizeof (struct node));
```

The sizeof operator, although it looks like a function, actually finds out for us how many bytes of RAM a location of type struct node takes. Let us say that sizeof (struct node) is equal to 6 bytes on our computer system. Then that many bytes of RAM are given to the program by the operating system using the malloc() function.

However, this space in memory is useless unless the program can access it. What malloc() does is to return the address of the first byte of that location as a pointer to characters. We want to convert the pointer to characters to pointer to struct node, so the pointer type is cast appropriately by preceding the malloc() by (struct node *). Now this address can be assigned to *p*, our pointer to store type struct node.

Typecasting allows one to convert one data type to another. x = (float) i / 3; will convert the integer *i* to a float, divide by 3, and assign the floating point number to *x*. Similarly with the above malloc() example, we are converting pointer types.

A function called free() will simply return the chunk of memory pointed to by the address given in free(). This should be done every time memory is no longer needed.

Solution 13.3 The contents that *p1* points to are stored in the location that *p2* points to. Then 1 is added to *j*.

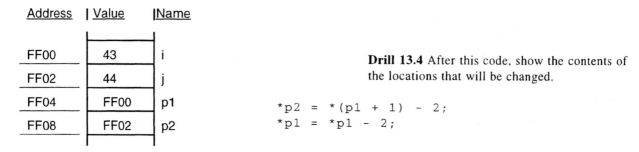

Address	Value	Name
FF00	43	i
FF02	44	j
FF04	FF00	p1
FF08	FF02	p2

Drill 13.4 After this code, show the contents of the locations that will be changed.

```
*p2 = *(p1 + 1) - 2;
*p1 = *p1 - 2;
```

Linked Lists

In Unit 9, we introduced linked lists using an array. Here, we will use a linked list and chunks of memory which are created as we need them. With the array example in Example 9.2, it would have been possible to run out of available slots if we had needed more. If we were to make the array too large, it may take away memory needed by other arrays and variables.

Here, we will start the linked list that occupies hardly any memory. As the linked list becomes larger, we will use the malloc() function to obtain more memory. If we delete an item from the linked list, then we will give the memory occupied by that item back to RAM for other variables and uses. Data in our linked list will be stored in items called nodes.

To see how data is added to a linked list, look at Figure 13.4. In Figure 13.4(a), initially there is nothing in the list. Then a new node is added that has line2 in it. At first, the *p_start* pointer, which gives the address of the node where the list starts, is set to NULL. This means that there is nothing in the list. Using malloc(), memory for a new node is taken from RAM. Its address, A100, is stored in the pointer called *p_new*.

To place this node in the list, we first take the data labeled line2 and place it in the str member of the node pointed to by *p_new*. Then we take the pointer stored in *p_start* and place it in the next member of this new node. It is NULL. Finally, instead of the *p_start* pointer pointing to NULL, we make it point to this node stored at A100. Now the first node is added to the linked list.

In Figure 13.4(b), we add another node that will be added to the beginning of the list. First we grab some memory and get its address, A200, stored in *p_new*. The data of line1 is placed in the str member of the new node. The address of *p_start*, A100, is placed in the next member of the new node and *p_start* now points to A200.

Let us follow the linked list we have so far in order. Starting from *p_start*, we go to A200 which has line1 stored in it. Then following the next pointer we go to A100, which has line2 stored in it. Finally, following its next pointer, which is NULL, we stop traversing the list.

So far we have added nodes at the beginning of the list. In Figure 13.4(c), we are adding a node at the end. First, *p_new* gets the address of A300, where the new node is located. Then we place the data, line3, in the str member of A300. Now we have to traverse the list to see where line3 should go in the list.

p_start starts us at A200. The pointer, *p*, will be used to go down the list, while *p_start* will hold the address of the beginning of the list. There line1 is stored. Next, we go to A100. Before we change *p* to A100, we store the previous pointer of *p* in *p_last*. *p_last* will contain A200. *p_last* and *p* are needed to add a new link between these two nodes. A100 has line2 stored in it. We need to march forward. Before we advance *p*, we save its value in *p_last*, which becomes A100. Then the next member of A100 becomes NULL. There are no more nodes in the list. The new one must be placed at the end.

Solution 13.4 1 is added to *p1*, which is the address FF02. From the contents of the location pointed to by FF02, 2 is subtracted, making *j* equal to 42. *p1* remains the same. Then the contents pointed to by *p1*, which is actually *i*, has a 2 subtracted from it. Now *i* is 41.

Drill 13.5 Show the values for *x* and *y* in the diagram. From main(), shake_it() is called. Show its effects in memory. Last, what is printed?

```
shake_it(p1, p2);
printf("%d %d\n", *p1, *p2);

void shake_it(int *x, int *y)
{ *x = 0;
  *y = 0;
}
```

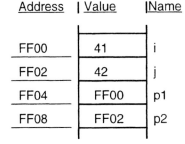

Address	Value	Name
FF00	41	i
FF02	42	j
FF04	FF00	p1
FF08	FF02	p2

Value	Name
	x
	y

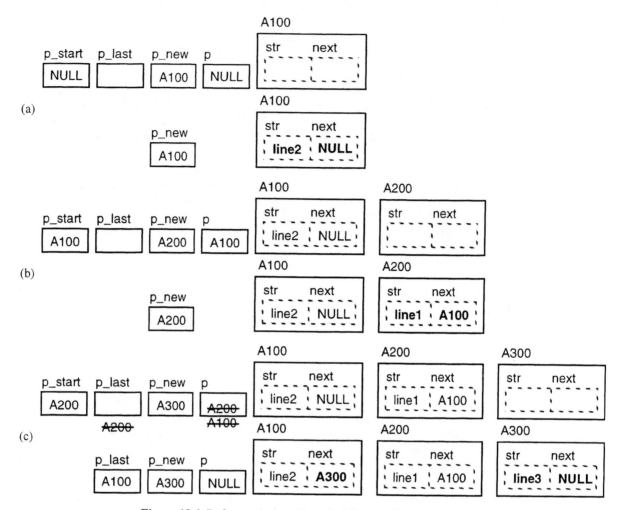

Figure 13.4 Before and after clips of adding to a linked list.

p, or NULL, is stored in the next member of A300. The address in *p_last* gets the address of *p_new*. That is, the next member of A100 gets A300. Now the linked list has three nodes in it. Let us now remove a node.

Solution 13.5
The values for *x* and *y* are FF00 and FF02, respectively. *x is actually *i* and *y is actually *j*. These are set to zero. The two zeros, the values of *i* and *j*, are printed.

Drill 13.6 Show the printout.
```
char x[10] = "Inside", y[10] = "and out";
shake_it(x, y);
printf("%s %s\n", x, y);

void shake_it(char *a, char *b)
{
    *(a + 1) = 'M';
    *b = 'u';
}
```

The Indirection Operator

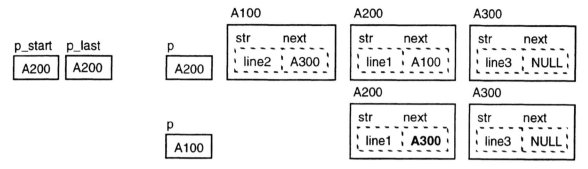

Figure 13.5 Before and after clips of deleting the A100 node from the linked list.

See Figure 13.5. Here we are removing line2 from the list. Starting at *p_start*, with a value of A200, we go down the list, storing the A200 in *p_last*. *p* becomes A100. Here line2, which we want to delete, is stored. We must get the next member of *p*. This is the A300 stored in A100. It must be placed in the next of *p_last*. Hence, the A300 is stored in A200. Last, the memory at A100 is free and the list still starts at *p_start*. When the first node is deleted, then *p_start* has to be moved up to the next node.

The Example

You should understand the maintenance of linked lists as explained above. The program will thus make more sense. You may even want to do Question 4 at the end of the unit now. Example 13.1 is a simple line editor, which allows you to add and delete lines. The program does not do any error checking. Error checking is left out at this stage so that the main logic is easier to understand.

```
//EXAMPLE 13.1
#include <stdio.h>
#include <string.h>
#include <stdlib.h>       //for malloc and free
struct line
{
    char str[40];
    struct line *next;
};
int get_choice (struct line *p);
struct line * add_line (struct line *p);
struct line * del_line (struct line *p);
```

Solution 13.6 Array names are actually array addresses. Hence, the pointer *a* actually has its address at the beginning of *x[ ]*. This is also the case with *y[ ]*. When shake_it() changes the contents of the location pointed to by *a* and *b*, that changes the arrays *x[ ]* and *y[ ]*.

IMside und out

Drill 13.7 Are there any errors here? If not, show the printout.

```
void main (void)
{ char   x[10] = "Inside",
          y[10] = "and out";
  shake(&x[0], &y[0]);
  printf("%s %s\n", x, y);
}
void shake(char a[], char b[])
{
    a[1] = 'M';
    b[0] = 'u';
}
```

The Indirection Operator

```
void main (void)
{
    struct line *head;              //Address of the first node of the list.
    int x;
    head = NULL;                    //Initially the list is empty.
    x = get_choice (head);
    for( ; x != 3; )
    {
        if(x == 1)
            head = add_line (head); //Add a line and adjust head if needed.
        else
            head = del_line (head); //Delete one and adjust head if needed.
        x = get_choice (head);
    }
}




struct line * del_line
            (struct line *p)    //Initially, address of first node.
{
    struct line *p_start,           //Address of the first node.
                *p_last;            //This follows p as p moves forward.
    int i, number;
    printf("\tWhich line number? ");
    scanf("%d", &number);           //Get a line number to delete
    if(number == 1)                 //If deleting first node, adjust p_start
        p_start = p -> next;
    else                            //Otherwise, find p, the node to remove.
    {
        for(p_start = p, i = 1; i < number; ++i, p = p -> next)
            p_last = p;
        p_last -> next = p -> next;
    }
    free(p);                        //Return p to RAM
    return(p_start);                //Return starting address to main().
}
```

Solution 13.7 No errors exist. Addresses can be passed to an array and the pointers can be used as arrays. The output is the same.

IMside und out

Drill 13.8 For these questions, take $a[\ ]$ to be an array and specify which are true.

a. a == &a[0]?
b. a + 1 == &a[1]?
c. *a == a[0]?
d. *(a + 1) == a[1]?

```
int get_choice (struct line *p)
{
   int i, choice;
   printf("\n. . . This is the start of your file so far . . .\n");
   for(i = 1; p != NULL; ++i, p = p -> next) //print out the list.
      printf("%d: %s\n", i, p -> str);
   printf(". . . This is the end ");
   printf("(Enter 1 to Insert, 2 to Delete, and 3 to Quit)\n\t");
   scanf("%d", &choice);          //Get a choice and return it to main().
   return choice;
}

struct line * add_line (struct line *p)
{
   int number, i;
   struct line *p_last, *p_new, *p_start;
   char str_new[40];
   p_start = p;
   p_new = (struct line *) malloc (sizeof (struct line)); //Get memory
   printf("What number will this line be? :");
   scanf("%d", &number);                    //Get line number
   printf("\tEnter your line: ");
   getchar();              //Flush out the <return> from last scanf().
   gets(str_new);          //Get line to add.

   for(i = 1; i < number; ++i, p = p -> next)
      p_last = p;          //Find p and p_last, the point of insertion.
   p_new -> next = p;
   strcpy(p_new -> str, str_new);

   if(i == 1)              //If the new node is the first one,
      return (p_new);          //return that as the starting address.
   else                    //Otherwise, complete the link and . . .
   {                            //return the starting address.
      p_last -> next = p_new;
      return(p_start);
   }
}
```

Solution 13.8 All are true. *a* is the address of &a[0]. *a accesses what is stored in a[0], as does a[0].

Drill 13.9 Here we have an array of pointers. Show the values of the memory locations in this diagram.

```
char x[] = "Lawdy", y[] = "Mamma", *t[3];
t[0] = x;
t[1] = y;
```

Address		
A000		x[ ]
A010		y[ ]
A020		t[0]
A030		t[1]
A040		t[2]

	x
	y

```
----- output -----

 . . . This is the start of your file so far . . .
 . . . This is the end (Enter 1 to Insert, 2 to Delete, and 3 to Quit)
    1
    What number will this line be? : 1
    Enter your line: From where does my help come? (Line 2)


 . . . This is the start of your file so far . . .
1: From where does my help come? (Line 2)
 . . . This is the end (Enter 1 to Insert, 2 to Delete, and 3 to Quit)
    1
    What number will this line be? : 1
    Enter your line: Unto the hills I will lift up my eyes (Line 1)


 . . . This is the start of your file so far . . .
1: Unto the hills I will lift up my eyes (Line 1)
2: From where does my help come? (Line 2)
 . . . This is the end (Enter 1 to Insert, 2 to Delete, and 3 to Quit)
    1
    What number will this line be? : 3
    Enter your line: My help comes from the Lord (Line 3)


 . . . This is the start of your file so far . . .
1: Unto the hills I will lift up my eyes (Line 1)
2: From where does my help come? (Line 2)
3: My help comes from the Lord (Line 3)
 . . . This is the end (Enter 1 to Insert, 2 to Delete, and 3 to Quit)
    2
    Which line number? 1


 . . . This is the start of your file so far . . .
1: From where does my help come? (Line 2)
2: My help comes from the Lord (Line 3)
 . . . This is the end (Enter 1 to Insert, 2 to Delete, and 3 to Quit)
    1
    What number will this line be? : 3
    Enter your line: Who made heaven and earth (Line 4)
```

Solution 13.9

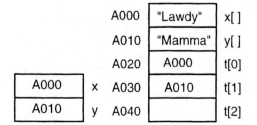

Drill 13.10 For the scanf(), "Hey" is read in. Show the contents of the memory locations after the execution of this code:

```
t[2] = t[1];
strcpy(t[2], t[0]);
scanf("%s", t[0]);
```

```
.. . . This is the start of your file so far . . .
1: From where does my help come? (Line 2)
2: My help comes from the Lord (Line 3)
3: Who made heaven and earth. (Line 4)
 . . . This is the end (Enter 1 to Insert, 2 to Delete, and 3 to Quit)
   3
```

Let us start at the screen, or the section labeled "output" in Example 13.1, to see how the program works. The program first shows your file. Initially, there is nothing in the file. From the options provided, we pick 1, indicating we want to add a line. We also state that we want to add line number 1. The program doesn't allow the user to type in a wrong line number by mistake. That kind of logic should exist in a program.

We enter the first line of our file, the file with one line is shown, and then the three options are given. Again, we decide to add line number 1, making the previous line of text the second line. Then line number 3 is added to the end, and our file is displayed now with its three lines. Next, we delete line number 2 and add another line. This is just an example of the run. We could add and delete lines to our file all day if we wanted to.

The program does this by using four functions, including main(). In main(), a pointer called *head* stores the starting address of the linked list. The function called get_choice() is called in a loop, until a 3 for "Quit" is entered by the user of the program. If the user types a "1," the add_line() function is called, and if a "2" is typed, then del_line() is called. For both add_line() and del_line(), *head* is passed and the new starting address of the list is received in it. After returning from these functions, the starting address of the linked list could be different.

get_choice(): This function also receives *head* from main(), and *head* is copied into *p*, a pointer to type struct line. This function prints the entire file before asking for the choice. *p* goes through the for loop, each time printing the line number called *i* and the str member of the line. When doing the next iteration of the loop, *i* , or the line number, is incremented and *p* is advanced to the address of the next node in the list. Finally, the choice is obtained from the user and that is returned to main().

add_line(): This function also receives the beginning address of the list in *p*. *p* is assigned to *p_start*. Using malloc(), a pointer to type struct line is obtained in *p_new*. Then the string and the line number for inserting the string is obtained from the user. *number* contains the line that this new line will be. In the for loop, *i* is incremented until it is one less than *number*. As *i* is incremented, *p* is advanced to point to the address of each of the nodes of the list. Also, *p_last* comes right behind *p*, making available the address of the previous node when we find the insertion point in the list.

Solution 13.10

A000	"Hey"	x[ ]
A010	"Lawdy"	y[ ]
A020	A000	t[0]
A030	A010	t[1]
A040	A010	t[2]

Drill 13.11 In this structure, rev and fwd are pointers to type struct node. Draw a diagram of each of the four variables. Which have three members and which have only one?

```
struct node
{
    int qty;
    struct node *rev;
    struct node *fwd;
};
struct node x, y, *head, *tail;
```

Once we find the *i* where it is equal to *number*, *p* will point to the address of the node that will follow the new node. This is done using the p_new -> next = p; statement. The string containing the line of data is also copied into p_new.str. If the node is at the beginning of the list, then *p_new* is returned as the address of the start of the list. Otherwise, we have the last node point to the new node and return the same starting address of the list as what we received.

del_line(): If the node to be deleted is the first one in the list, then *p_start* is made to point to the second node in the list. The first node is freed and returns the new starting address.

If the node to be deleted is not the first one, then *p* and *p_last* are obtained using the same for loop as the add_line() function. *p* is the address of the node to be removed. Before it is removed, its next member, which has the address of the next node, is copied into the next member of *p_last*. Then the node is freed and the starting address of the list is returned.

EXPERIMENTS

In the last unit, we studied pointers and how to store and manipulate addresses of memory locations. In this unit we will see how we can use pointers; that is, once we have the address of a location, we will access its contents. The asterisk in the declaration indicates that the variable is a pointer, but the next time the asterisk is used in the program it is called the *indirection operator*.

Exp 13.1 *i* is a variable. Its data type is an integer or a whole number.

```
#include <stdio.h>
void main ( )
{
        int i = 56, *p1;              //Stmt 1
        p1 = &i;                      //Stmt 2
        printf("%p %d\n", p1, *p1);   //Stmt 3
}
```

a. What is the address of *i*?
b. What does *p1* print?
c. What does *p1* print?
d. Does *p1* or *p1* print the address stored in *p1*?
e. Does *p1* or *p1* print the value of the location whose address is stored in *p1*?
f. Why is *p1* printed with a %p format specifier and *p1 printed with a %d format specifier?
g. In which statement is the indirection operator used?

Solution 13.11 Addresses are shown only because we will need them in future drills.

x (Address = A100)   y (Address = A200)

head   rev qty fwd   rev qty fwd   tail

Drill 13.12 Which of the following statements are valid?
a. head = &x;   b. x = &head;   c. head = tail;   d. head = &tail;
e. x = &y;   f. x.rev = 30;   g. x.rev = &head;   h. x.rev = &y;
i. x.rev = &x;   j. x.qty = 30;   k. x.qty = &y;   l. x = y;

Exp 13.2 An easy way of saying "the value of the location whose address is stored in *p1*" is saying "the value pointed to by *p1*." Don't forget main().

```
int i = 56, j, *p1, *p2;          //Stmt 1
p1 = &i;                          //Stmt 2
p2 = p1;                          //Stmt 3
j = *p2;                          //Stmt 4
printf("%d %d %d %d\n", i, j, *p1, *p2);
```

a. In Statement 1, which variable is initialized and to what value? Write it in the diagram.
b. In Statement 2, which variable is assigned and to what value? Write it in the diagram.
c. In Statement 3, which variable is assigned and to what value? Write it in the diagram.
d. In Statement 4, which variable is assigned and to what value? Write it in the diagram.
e. Replace Statement 4 with the following:

```
j = *p2 + 1;
```

and run it. Was 1 added to the address or to the value that was pointed to by *p2*? Which operation had the most priority, the asterisk or the addition?

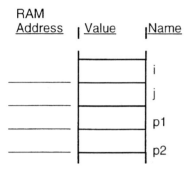

RAM
Address | Value | Name

i
j
p1
p2

Exp 13.3

```
int i = 56, *p1;                  //Stmt 1
p1 = &i;                          //Stmt 2
*p1 = *p1 + 1;                    //Stmt 3
printf("%d %d %p\n", i, *p1, p1);
```

a. *p1* has what address in it?
b. *p1* points to which variable?
c. *p1* points to what value?
d. In Statement 3, the value in which address is changed?
e. In Statement 3, 1 is added to the value in which address?

Solution 13.12 *head* can store only an address of a struct node, so (a) and (c) are true and (d) is false. x.rev also can store only an address of a struct node, so (h) and (i) are true but (f) and (g) are false. In (l), we assign one entire structure to another.

a. head = &x; **T**	b. x = &head; **F**	c. head = tail; **T**	d. head = &tail; **F**
e. x = &y; **F**	f. x.rev = 30; **F**	g. x.rev = &head; **F**	h. x.rev = &y; **T**
i. x.rev = &x; **T**	j. x.qty = 30; **T**	k. x.qty = &y; **F**	l. x = y; **T**

Drill 13.13 In the diagram for Solution 13.11, fill in the values that this code will assign:

```
head = &x;
x.fwd = &y;
y.fwd = NULL; //A NULL means that this address doesn't point to anything.
x.qty = 500;
y.qty = 800;
```

Exp 13.4

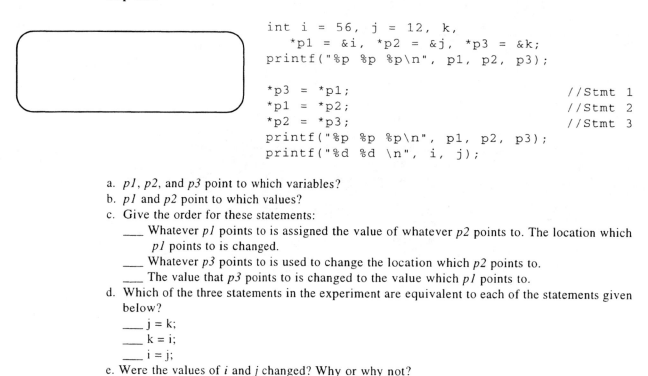

```
int i = 56, j = 12, k,
    *p1 = &i, *p2 = &j, *p3 = &k;
printf("%p %p %p\n", p1, p2, p3);

*p3 = *p1;                              //Stmt 1
*p1 = *p2;                              //Stmt 2
*p2 = *p3;                              //Stmt 3
printf("%p %p %p\n", p1, p2, p3);
printf("%d %d \n", i, j);
```

a. *p1*, *p2*, and *p3* point to which variables?
b. *p1* and *p2* point to which values?
c. Give the order for these statements:
  ____ Whatever *p1* points to is assigned the value of whatever *p2* points to. The location which *p1* points to is changed.
  ____ Whatever *p3* points to is used to change the location which *p2* points to.
  ____ The value that *p3* points to is changed to the value which *p1* points to.
d. Which of the three statements in the experiment are equivalent to each of the statements given below?
  ____ j = k;
  ____ k = i;
  ____ i = j;
e. Were the values of *i* and *j* changed? Why or why not?
f. Were the values of *p1* and *p2* changed? Why or why not?

Exp 13.5 Don't forget the prototypes.

```
void main (void)
{   int i = 56, j = 12, k = 99,
            *p1 = &i, *p2 = &j, *p3;
    p3 = &k;
    printf("%p %p %p\n", p1, p2, p3);
    fun_stuff(&i, p2, p3);
    printf("%d %d %d\n", i, j, k);
    printf("%p %p %p\n", p1, p2, p3);
}
```

Solution 13.13 The address of *x*, which is A100, is stored in head. The address of *y*, which is A200, is stored in x.fwd, and so on.

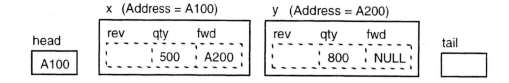

Drill 13.14 Write the statements to set up the following pointers: Have tail point to *y*, have the rev member of *y* point to *x*, and have the rev member of *x* point to nothing.

```
void fun_stuff(int *q, int *r, int *s)
{
    *q = *r + *s;                       //Stmt 1
    *r = *s;                            //Stmt 2
    *s = 0;                             //Stmt 3
    r = r + 1;                          //Stmt 4
    s = s + 1;                          //Stmt 5
}
```

a. In the diagram below, show the addresses and initial values of i, j, and k. Also, show the values of $p1$, $p2$, and $p3$.
b. In fun_stuff() can q, r, and s store integers? Can they store the addresses of integers?
c. In the diagram, show the values received in q, r, and s.
d. In Statement 1, the value at which address is changed? This is the same location of which variable in main()?
e. In Statement 1, the values from which two hex addresses are added?
f. In Statement 2, the value at which location is changed? This is the same location of which variable in main()?
g. Similarly, the location of which variable in main() is set to zero?
h. In Statements 4 and 5, when s and r were changed, were any of the values in main() changed? Why or why not?

Solution 13.14
```
tail = &y;
y.rev = &x;
x.rev = NULL;
```

Drill 13.15 One way to access the qty member of x is to state "x.qty." Another way of doing that now is to state "(*head).qty." *head will bring us to the location of A100, or x. And (*head).qty will bring us to the qty member. A more common way of coding this is to state: "head -> qty." Give three ways to access the fwd member of x.

Exp 13.6 Don't forget the prototypes.

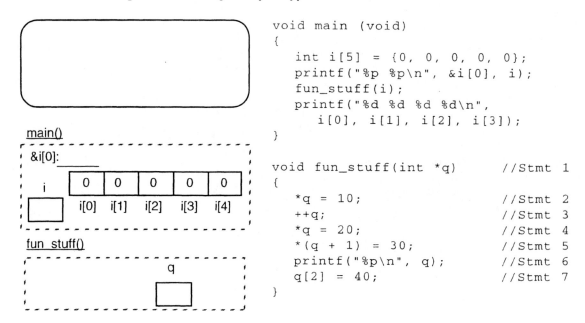

```
void main (void)
{
    int i[5] = {0, 0, 0, 0, 0};
    printf("%p %p\n", &i[0], i);
    fun_stuff(i);
    printf("%d %d %d %d\n",
        i[0], i[1], i[2], i[3]);
}
```

```
void fun_stuff(int *q)        //Stmt 1
{
    *q = 10;                  //Stmt 2
    ++q;                      //Stmt 3
    *q = 20;                  //Stmt 4
    *(q + 1) = 30;            //Stmt 5
    printf("%p\n", q);        //Stmt 6
    q[2] = 40;                //Stmt 7
}
```

Show the address of i[0] and the values of *i* and *q* in the diagram.

a. In Statement 2, what was the value of *q*? Which slot of *i[ ]* was changed here?

b. In Statement 4, what was the value of *q*? Which slot of *i[ ]* was changed here?

c. In Statement 7, what was the value of *q*? Which slot of *i[ ]* was changed here?

d. Change Statement 1 (and the prototype) as follows. Is there any difference in the execution?

```
void fun_stuff(int q[ ])
```

e. If *q* is a pointer, as it was initially, is the following true?

```
*(q + 3) == q[3] ?
```

f. If *q* is an array, as it was in question d, is the following true?

```
*(q + 3) == q[3] ?
```

Solution 13.15
```
x.fwd
(*head).fwd
head -> fwd. We could also say, y.rev -> fwd,
```

Drill 13.16 Try writing the loop that starts with a pointer *p*, which is initialized to *head*, and then traverses the chain by following the fwd pointers until it becomes NULL. Have the loop simply write out the values of *p* and the qty members of each node as it traverses the chain. To advance the pointer *p* to the next link, *p* would have to be set equal to (*p).fwd. Here is how your printout may look:

```
A100  500
A200  800
```

Exp 13.7

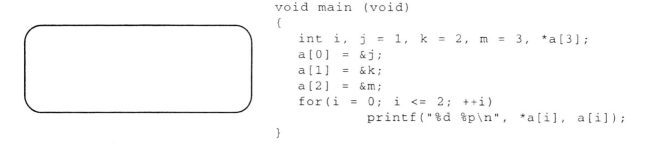

```
void main (void)
{
    int i, j = 1, k = 2, m = 3, *a[3];
    a[0] = &j;
    a[1] = &k;
    a[2] = &m;
    for(i = 0; i <= 2; ++i)
            printf("%d %p\n", *a[i], a[i]);
}
```

Address	Value	Name	Address	Value	Name
		j			a[0]
		k			a[1]
		m			a[2]

a. Fill in all the values you can in the diagram.
b. If the asterisk weren't used when defining *a*, then *a[ ]* would be an array of what?
c. Because there is an asterisk when defining *a[ ]*, *a[ ]* is an array of pointers to what?
d. Why is a %p format specifier used when printing a[i]?
e. Why is a %d format specifier used when printing *a[i]?

Solution 13.16
```
for(p = head; p != NULL; p = p -> fwd)
   printf("%p %d\n", p, p -> qty);
```

Drill 13.17 Now try reversing the traversal, starting *p* with *tail* and following the rev pointers.

Exp 13.8

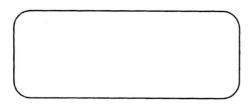

```
void main (void)
{
    int i;
    char j[15] = "I",
         k[15] = "Ain't",
         m[15] = "Retaliating", *a[3];
    a[0] = j;
    a[1] = k;
    a[2] = m;
    printf("%s %p %s %p\n",
        j, j, &j[0], &j[0]);
    for(i = 0; i <= 2; ++i)
        printf("%s %p\n", a[i], a[i]);
}
```

a. Fill in all the values you can in the diagram.
b. *a[ ]* is an array of pointers to what type of data?
c. Which of these conditions is true?

```
j == &j[0]?
j == a[0]?
```

d. The array *j[ ]* holds characters or addresses?
e. The array *a[ ]* holds characters or addresses?
f. When printing *j* or a[0] using a %s format, what is printed?

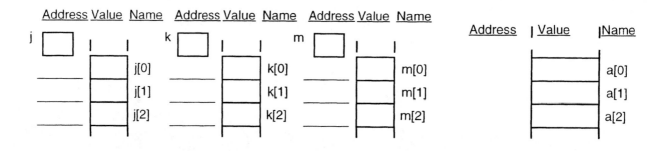

Solution 13.17

```
for(p = tail; p != NULL; p = p -> rev)
    printf("%p %d\n", p, p -> qty);
```

Drill 13.18 Using malloc(), we have created a new node that has no name, like *x* and *y*, but it has an address and it is stored in *p*. Let us pretend that the address stored in *p* is B100. How would you write the code so that this new node is placed between *x* and *y*. That is, *x* and *y* should point to the new node. First, show the values in the diagram that need to be changed.

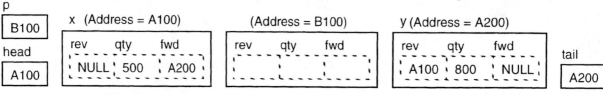

g. When printing *j* or a[0] using a %p format, what is printed?

h. When printing the address of a character string, what format specifier is used to print its hex address? The string characters?

Exp 13.9 When you run this experiment, first make it only executable. Get to the prompt of your operating system and type "ex139 only one life," where "ex139" is the name of your executable file.

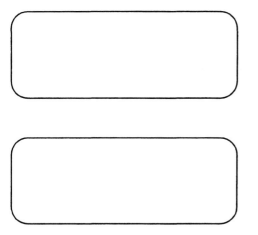

```
int main (int argc, char *argv[ ])
{
    printf("argc = %d\n", argc);
    printf("%p %s \n", argv[0], argv[0]);
    printf("%p %s \n", argv[1], argv[1]);
    printf("%p %s \n", argv[2], argv[2]);
    printf("%p %s \n", argv[3], argv[3]);
    return 0;
}
```

a. Fill in all the values you can in the diagram.

b. Remove the last printf() statement from this experiment. After recompiling it, run it this way:

"ex139 soon past?".

c. What is the data type of *argc* and what does it represent?

d. What is in argv[0] and to what value does it point?

e. What is in argv[1] and to what value does it point?

f. Does main() receive any arguments? How many?

g. Does main() return any values to the operating system?

Address	Value			Value	Name
	"ex139"				argc
	"only"				argv[0]
	"one"				argv[1]
	"life"				argv[2]

Solution 13.18

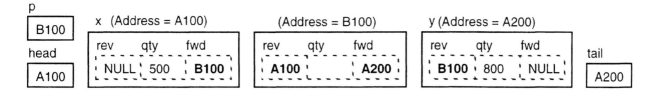

Drill 13.19 I see four addresses assigned or changed in this diagram. Give the four statements that will do that. Does the order of these statements matter? Do not use the pointers *head* or *tail*.

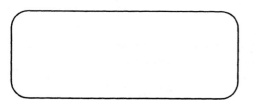

```
struct branch
{
    int value;
    struct branch *left;
    struct branch *right;
};
struct branch x, y, z, *p = &y;
printf("%p %p %p %p\n", &x, &y, &z, p);
x.value = 100;
y.value = 200;
z.value = 300;
x.left  = (struct branch *) 0;
x.right = &z;
z.left  = NULL;
z.right = &y;
y.left  = &x;
y.right = &z;
printf("%p: %d %p %p\n",
        &x, x.value, x.left, x.right);
printf("%p: %d %p %p\n",
        &y, y.value, y.left, y.right);
printf("%p: %d %p %p\n",
        &z, z.value, z.left, z.right);
```

a. How many items each do *x*, *y*, and *z* hold?
b. For each item that they hold, how many are pointers? And pointers to what data type?
c. How many items does *p* hold? It can store addresses to what data type? What is its value?
d. Where are the variables *x*, *y*, and *z* stored? Give their addresses.
e. Fill in all the addresses and boxes in the diagram on the following page.

Solution 13.19 The first or the last two statements can be switched. However, the first two statements should come first. The fwd and the rev members should be used first before new pointers are copied in them.

```
p -> rev = x.fwd;
p -> fwd = y.rev;
x.fwd = p;
y.rev = p;
```

Drill 13.20 Now do the same as above except do not use *x* or *y*. Instead, use *head* and *tail*. Let us also place a quantity of 600 in the new node.

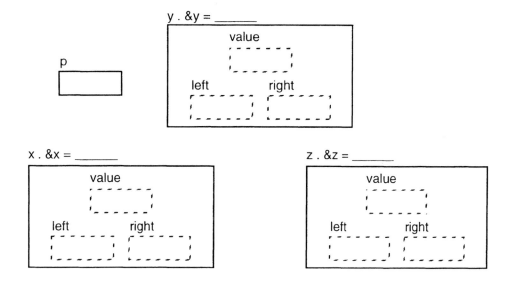

y . &y = _____

p

value

left   right

x . &x = _____

value

left   right

z . &z = _____

value

left   right

Exp 13.11 For this and the next experiment, add the code below to the code given in Experiment 13.10.

```
printf("&y=%p y.value=%d \n", &y, y.value);
printf("y.left=%p y.right=%p \n",
        y.left, y.right);
printf("%p %d \n", p, (*p).value);
printf("%p %p\n", (*p).left, (*p).right);
```

a. When printing y.value, why was a %d used for the format string?
b. When printing y.left, why was a %p used for the format string?
c. What is the address in *p*? This is the address of which variable?
d. Can you print p.value?
e. Why do you need an asterisk in front of the *p* when printing (*p).value?
f. In the three places that this appears, "(*p).", change it to this: "p->". Use no periods or spaces. Is there any difference in the expressions? For instance, try this:

```
printf("%p %d \n", p, p->value);
```

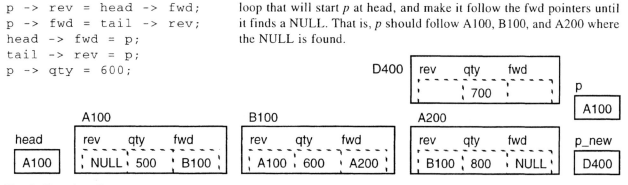

Solution 13.20

```
p -> rev = head -> fwd;
p -> fwd = tail -> rev;
head -> fwd = p;
tail -> rev = p;
p -> qty = 600;
```

Drill 13.21 We will add a new node whose address is in *p_new*. Its quantity is 700 and we are to add it in the list. To start, first write the for loop that will start *p* at head, and make it follow the fwd pointers until it finds a NULL. That is, *p* should follow A100, B100, and A200 where the NULL is found.

D400	rev	qty	fwd
		700	

p
A100

A100	rev	qty	fwd
	NULL	500	B100

head
A100

B100	rev	qty	fwd
	A100	600	A200

A200	rev	qty	fwd
	B100	800	NULL

p_new
D400

The Indirection Operator

g. (*p).left gives the address stored in the left member of which variable?
h. Why does (*p).left give the address stored in the left member of y?
i. The address stored in (*p).left is the address of which variable?
j. Now add the following to the bottom of all the code you have so far:

```
p = (*p).left;
printf("%p %d \n", p, (*p).value);
printf("%p %p\n", (*p).left, (*p).right);
```

k. Now p has the address of which variable?
l. Convert this new line to the notation that uses the arrow. Is the result the same?
m. Now add the following to the bottom of all the code you have so far:

```
p = (*p).right;
printf("%p %d \n", p, (*p).value);
printf("%p %p\n", (*p).left, (*p).right);
```

n. Convert these three lines to the arrow notation and test your code.
o. Now the address stored in p is the address of which variable?
p. Now add the following to the bottom of all the code you have so far:

```
p = (*p).right;
printf("%p %d \n", p, (*p).value);
printf("%p %p\n", (*p).left, (*p).right);
```

q. Convert these three lines to the arrow notation and test your code. Is there an address or a member name on the left side of the arrow? What about on the right side?
r. Now the address that is stored in p is the address of which variable?
s. Can you do any of these assignments? Why or why not?

```
p = (*p).value;
p = &p;
y.left = &y;
```

Exp 13.12 Add the code on the following page to the original code for Experiment 13.10. Here, the keyword, "malloc," meaning "memory allocation," creates space in memory that is the size of one struct branch. The address of this new memory area is assigned to the left member of x. You will need "#include <stdlib.h>" for malloc and free.

Solution 13.21

```
p = head;
for(; p != NULL;
        p = p -> fwd)
```

Drill 13.22 Now add an if statement to this loop that will break out of it when the quantity pointed to by p is greater than the quantity pointed to by p_new. In this example, the loop will break out when p becomes A200. That is, when p is A200 the 800 pointed to by p is greater than the 700 pointed to by p_new.

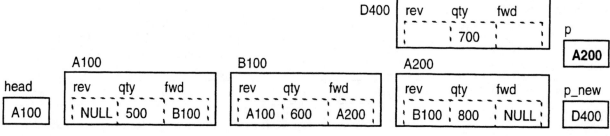

The Indirection Operator

```
                            x.left = (struct branch *) malloc
                               (sizeof(struct branch));
                            printf("%p\n", x.left);
                            (*(x.left)).value = 400;
                            (*(x.left)).left = NULL;
                            (*(x.left)).right = NULL;
                            for(p = &y; p != NULL;  p = p->left)
                                printf("%p   %d \n", p,   p -> value);
```

a. In this part of the coding, convert the arrow notation to the indirection operator notation, and vice versa. Does your code produce the same results?
b. Complete the rest of the figure for Experiment 13.10.
c. Before the for loop, *p* was set to the address of *y*. Inside the loop, how many times was *p* changed?
d. Add the following code to the end of your code and run it.

```
                            (*(x.left)).left = &z;
                            for(p = &y; p != NULL;  p = p->left)
                                printf("%p   %d \n", p, p -> value);
```

e. Give the order in which the branches were traversed.

_____ x
_____ y
_____ z
_____ new branch created with malloc.

f. Now add the following code to the bottom of your program and run it.

```
                            p = x.left;
                            x.left = &z;
                            free (p);
                            for(p = &y; p != NULL;  p = p->left)
                                printf("%p   %d \n", p, p -> value);
```

g. Before, x.left had the address of the new struct branch. Now it has the address of which struct branch?
h. Can we get to the new struct branch from *x*, *y*, or *z*?
i. What do you think free does?

Solution 13.22

```
p = head;
for(; p != NULL; p = p -> fwd)
   if(p->qty > p_new->qty)
      break;
```

Drill 13.23 Since we know the rev pointer from *p*, assign the address of the previous node from *p* into a pointer called *p_last*. That is, *p_last* should now be set to B100 after the loop. Then using *p_last* and *p*, change and assign the needed pointers so that the new node is linked between B100 and A200 in both directions. Also fill in the diagram.

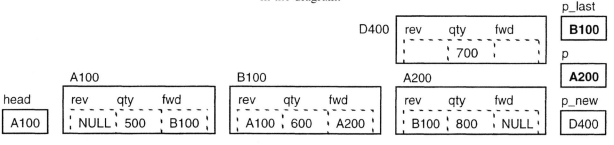

The Indirection Operator

QUESTIONS

For all questions and their parts, start with these definitions:

```
struct ball
{
    int radius;
    struct ball *last;
    struct ball *next;
};
struct ball x, y, *p5=&x, *p6=&y;

int i = 0, m[5] = {3, 6, 9, 12, 15}, *p1, *p3, *q[5];
float j, a[5] = {20.0, 30.0, 40.0, 50.0, 60.0}, *p2 = a;
```

1. Show the contents of the variables that have changed after executing each of the following codes.

a.
```
p1 = &i;
*p1 = 8;
```

b.
```
p1 = &m[0];
p1 = p1 + 2;
*p1 = *p1 + 8;
```

c.
```
p1 = &i;
p3 = m;
*(p3 + 1) = *p3 + *p1;
```

d.
```
p1 = m + 2;
p3 = p1 + 1;
i = *p1 + *p3;
```

e.
```
for(i = 0; i <= 4; ++i)
    q[i] = m + i;
for(i = 0; i <= 4; ++i)
    *(a + i) = *q[i] + a[i];
```

f.
```
for(i = 4; i >= 0; --i)
{
    q[i] = &m[4 - i];
    *p2 = *q[i] + *(a + i);
}
```

2. Which of the following are valid?

a. `last = next;`
b. `x = y;`
c. `p5 = p6;`
d. `x = 10;`
e. `x.last = 10;`
f. `x.radius=10;`
g. `p5.radius = 10;`
h. `p5->radius = 10;`
i. `(*x).radius = 10;`

Solution 13.23

```
p = head;
for(; p != NULL; p = p -> fwd)
    if(p->qty > p_new->qty)
        break;
p_last = p -> rev;
p_new -> fwd = p;
p_new -> rev = p_last;
p -> rev = p_new;
p_last -> fwd = p_new;
```

Drill 13.24 Now assume that our nodes didn't have the rev pointers. Rewrite the code so that the pointer *p_last* follows one node behind *p* inside the loop. When we need to link up the pointers, we will know where the previous node is. Your new code should make no reference to rev pointers because now they are not needed.

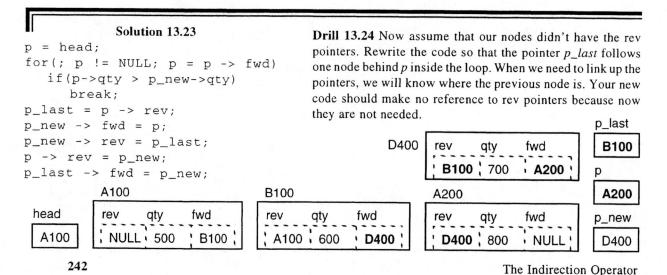

The Indirection Operator

```
j.  *(x.radius) = 10;      k.  *(x.last) = &y;       l.  (*x).last = &y;
m.  (*p5).last = &y;       n.  *(p5.last) = &y;      o.  p5 -> last = &y;
p.  *p5 = y;               q.  p5 -> last = NULL;    r.  p5 -> next = 10;
```

3. *p5* and *p6* are already initialized. Using only *p5* and *p6* in your code and omitting *x* and *y*, set up the pointers and values as shown in Figure 13.6.

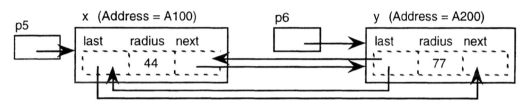

Figure 13.6

4. Figure 13.7(a) shows how the linked list is set up. *p_start* points to A300, or line2. After that comes line4 in A100 and then line8 in A200. Show the contents of all the pointers after each of the following operations. This is a sequence.

   a. Add line1 as shown in Figure 13.7(b).
   b. Remove line4 as shown in Figure 13.7(c).
   c. Add line9 as shown in Figure 13.7(d).
   d. Remove line1 as shown in Figure 13.7(e).

PROGRAMS

1. Write a function called add_two(). It will receive three pointers to floats. It will add the numbers pointed to by the first two pointers and store their sum in the location pointed to by the third pointer. In main(), define *j*, *k*, and *m*. Scan in *j* and *k*, send their addresses to add_two(), and have main() print the address of *m* and its value that is in it from add_two().

2. Define an integer array called a[10]. Initialize it to some values. Then assign the address of the slot whose index is 4 to an integer pointer called *p*. Print the contents of the array and the address of each slot using the name *a* but no brackets. Now do the same using the name *p*.

Solution 13.24

```
p = head;
for(; p != NULL; p = p -> fwd)
   if(p->qty > p_new->qty)
      break;
   else
      p_last = p;
p_new -> fwd = p;
p_last -> fwd = p_new;
```

Drill 13.25 What changes are needed in this code to accommodate each of these special conditions?

a. The new quantity is greater than the quantity in the last node of the list.

b. The new quantity is greater than the quantity in the first node of the list.

c. The linked list is empty; that is, to begin with, *head* is NULL.

The Indirection Operator   243

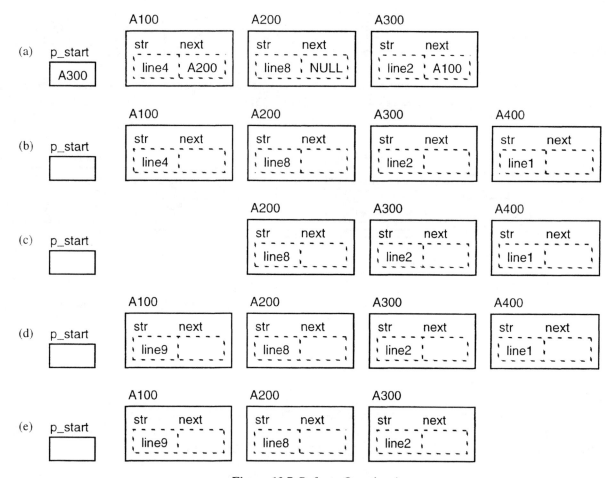

Figure 13.7 Refer to Question 4.

3. a. Write a function called get_node() that doesn't receive anything. It will get 10 bytes of memory using malloc(). It will read in a character string from the user and store that string into this 10-byte chunk of memory. Then it will return the address of this chunk.

Solution 13.25 No changes are needed for part a. Answers for b and c are as follows:

```
p = head;
for(; p != NULL; p = p -> fwd)
    if(p->qty > p_new->qty)
        break;
    else
        p_last = p;
p_new -> fwd = p;

if(p == head)
    head = p_new;
else
    p_last -> fwd = p_new;
```

Drill 13.26
Which of the following are advantages of a double linked list and which are advantages of a single linked list?

a. Takes less memory space.

b. Easier to use if you are dumped in the middle of the linked list and need to go back one node.

c. Easier to traverse in both directions.

d. Less pointer maintenance.

The Indirection Operator

b. Write a function called print_thing(). It will receive the address of a string and print that address as well as the string. Nothing is returned.

c. main() will define an array of pointers to character strings called a[10]. It will call get_node() in a loop, each time placing the address that was returned in the next available slot of *a[ ]*. After this loop, main() will call print_thing() in another loop.

4. Create a structure called struct index with two members; one is an integer called *id* and the other is a pointer to a character string, called *ptr*. See Figure 13.8. Create an array called *a[ ]* of type struct index and read in 5 id–name pairs in order. For each pair read in, malloc a 20–byte chunk of memory whose address is stored in the corresponding ptr member of the correct slot of *a[ ]*, as shown in Figure 13.8. After reading in the 5 pairs of data, call a function that will receive the address of *a[ ]*. The function will print the data from this index structure. (It should be the same thing that was read in.)

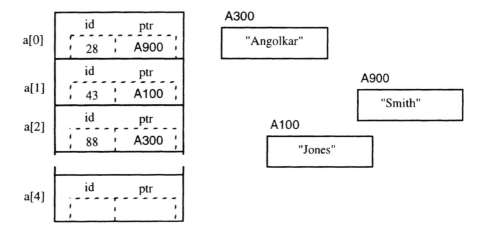

Figure 13.8

Solution 13.26

a. Single

b. Double

c. Double

d. Single

File I/O

In this unit we introduce file I/O functions, and how to store data on a disk and read it back. This is necessary so that the data is still available when the power to the computer is turned off. Although we will be working with small files, file I/O is necessary when the amount of data becomes too much to fit in the available RAM.

Buffering and Types of Processing

Reading data from a disk and writing to it is called file I/O. Getting data to and from a disk takes a long time compared to the amount of time it takes for data to go between RAM and the CPU because disk drives depend on physical movement of mechanisms, while the transfer of data between the CPU and RAM is done at electronic speeds. To get data to the CPU quickly from a disk, buffering is used.

Buffering is a small amount of RAM that is set aside for such purposes as file I/O. In Figure 14.1 we see that the operating system brings in chunks of data from the disk even before it is required by the program run by the CPU. When the program needs to read from the file, it doesn't have to wait until the disk turns around and comes to the right spot where the data is located. The data is

Drill 14.1 Let us study the diagram on page 247 to see the different ways that numbers are represented. On the left, the number 52000.0 is being entered on the keyboard, one character at a time, for a total of 7 characters. These characters are sent to the CPU in ASCII codes. The character '5' is a 35 in ASCII and since the ASCII code is given in hex, we show a 0x in front of it. The remaining 6 characters are also converted as this number goes to the CPU.

The CPU will represent this number as a float by breaking it into two parts: the mantissa and the exponent, or as 5.2 times 10^4. To show the 5.2 requires 3 bytes and the 4, one byte. When the number is to be displayed on the monitor, the binary representation is converted back to ASCII codes. The ASCII codes signal the monitor which characters to display.

a. The keyboard transmits ASCII text codes or binary numbers? What does the CPU use for computation?

b. How many bytes are needed to store the number 8.0 in ASCII and in binary?

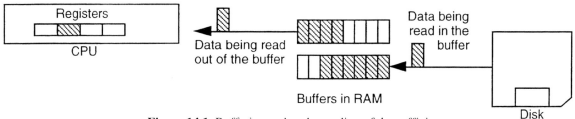

Figure 14.1 Buffering makes the reading of data efficient.

already waiting in one of the buffers and it is transferred to the CPU quickly. While the CPU reads in data from one buffer, the operating system can bring in the next blocks of data from the disk into another buffer. This proves to be efficient only if the program is processing the file sequentially. If the program is processing the records randomly, then we can't bring in blocks of data before they are needed because we have no idea beforehand which ones will be needed next.

Buffering also makes the writing of records to files efficient. Instead of writing one record at a time directly to the disk, the program can execute the following statements while the operating system writes the buffers to the disk.

When all records need to be processed, for instance, when printing out the paychecks for a company, sequential processing of records becomes the best method. The job can be run at night. However, when only one record needs to be processed, such as a reservations update program, then processing records randomly is the preferred method. As you can see, both sequential and random access processing methods have their advantages and disadvantages.

Binary and Text Files

When data is stored in files as characters as we see them on a screen or as we type them on a keyboard, the file is called a *text file*. For instance, if we store the string "hello" or a number as 0.0115, we are storing it in a text file. Here, the number would be stored as six characters: '0', '.', '0', '1', '1', and '5'. These six characters would occupy six bytes on the file. A number that we would see on a screen or that we type on a keyboard would use those six characters.

However, if we were to store the number 0.0115 as the computer would store it when it performs any calculations on it, we would store it as a binary item. A *binary file* typically stores numbers as a CPU would use them. The computer stores floating point numbers as a mantissa (1.15) and an exponent (-2). 1.15 times 10 to the negative 2 is 0.0115. Typically, the mantissa requires 3 bytes and the exponent 1. Together 4 bytes are needed to store a floating point number. Executable files are also called binary files.

We will be using only fprintf() and fscanf() functions when working with text files. When working with binary files, we will be using fwrite() and fread() functions.

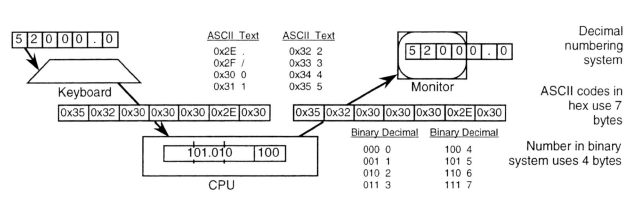

Opening and Closing Files

Here, we have a segment of code that shows how a file may be opened and closed. The variable *ptr* is a pointer to a type called FILE, defined in the stdio.h header file. *ptr* is also called a file handle and it has the address of the package of information about the file: where the buffer is, where the file is found, and so on.

```
FILE *ptr;
ptr = fopen("fileA", "r");
if(ptr == NULL)
     exit(1);
//Code that reads and processes the file would go here.
//And at the end . . .
fclose(ptr);
```

The fopen() function opens the file whose name is given as the first argument. In this case it is fileA. The r as the second argument specifies that the file is being opened for reading. See Table 14.1 for codes for opening files in other modes. The function will return a pointer, which in this code is received in the variable *ptr*. Once the file pointer is set up, the rest of the program does all references to the file by specifying only that pointer name.

If the file cannot be opened, then the operating system returns a NULL value as it is defined in the stdio.h file. The code here exits the program altogether by returning a value of 1. The operating system, if told to do so, can check this error code and be programmed to act upon it. In the simple case, it is the same as terminating the program or doing a return 0 out of main().

If the execution bypasses the exit() function, the file pointer is set up properly and we can start processing that file. That is, in this example we can read from it. Once the file is no longer needed, it should be closed using the fclose() function. Closing the file will flush out any buffers that may be open and allow the file to be used by other programs that may need it.

I/O Functions

When writing to text files in text mode, we'll be using fprintf(). When reading from them, we'll use fscanf() functions. These functions are very similar to the printf() and the scanf() functions that we have been using all along. The only difference is that with the f–functions, we must specify the file pointer with them. For example, to read from the file mentioned above, we can use the following statement:

```
fscanf(ptr, "%s %d", x, &j);
```

Solution 14.1
a. The keyboard transmits ASCII text codes while the CPU prefers the binary format.
b. It takes 3 bytes to send the number 8.0 in text format. Each character ('8', '.', and '0') takes up one byte. In binary, however, it would take 4 bytes. See the diagram from Drill 14.1. The mantissa of 8 will take 3 bytes and the exponent of 0 will take one byte. The number of bytes for one floating point number is fixed, regardless of its size or sign.

Drill 14.2
a. Why do monitors and keyboards convert text into ASCII codes?
b. Why don't CPUs like ASCII codes and instead use binary numbers?

Text mode	Binary mode	Purpose
r w a	rb wb ab	Reading Writing Appending (writing to the end of the file)
The following modes are for reading and writing simultaneously:		
r+ w+ a+	rb+ wb+ ab+	Simple updating If file exits, overwrite its contents Reading and appending

Table 14.1 Modes for opening files

stdin is a file pointer available to us through the stdio.h file. It allows us to get a handle on standard input, such as the keyboard. Similarly, stdout is the file pointer for standard output, such as the display screen. The statement scanf("%f", &p); is equivalent to fscanf(stdin, "%f", &p);. Similarly the statement, printf("%f\n", p); is equivalent to fprintf(stdout, "%f\n", p);.

When working with binary files, we'll be using the fwrite(), fread(), and fseek() functions. The uses of these functions are given in Experiments 14.9 through 14.11 and the drills. If the fread() function is unsuccessful, it will return a 0. This fact can be used to go through the entire file. Every time we read from a file, we read from the next place in the file. The fseek() function allows us to advance to any position in the file, thus allowing us to do random access.

Sequential File Update

A common business application using files is the sequential file update program. In Figure 14.2 we have an old master file and a transaction file. The program is to read these two files and create a third one called the new master file. For the sake of simplicity, the record structure of all files is the same: an account number and an amount. The old master file contains all bank accounts that exist, and the transaction file contains the deposits, which were made by account number. The purpose of the program is to generate a new master file that has the updated balances of all accounts. The old master and the transaction files must first be sorted. Notice that the old and the transaction files are opened for reading while the new master file is opened for writing.

Solution 14.2

a. The keyboard needs some coding method to *communicate* with the CPU what keys were pressed by the user. Similarly, if the monitor displayed a floating point number in binary using a mantissa and an exponent, humans would have a difficult time interpreting it. Hence, ASCII codes tell the monitor which characters to display for humans to understand.

b. CPUs are digital devices and do calculations only in binary.

Drill 14.3 If we want to store data on a file on a disk, we have two choices. One is to store data in text format and the other is to store it "CPU style," or in binary format. Let us suppose that we have three numbers to store: 52000.0, 8.0, and 41.7.

a. How many bytes will be needed to store them in each format?

b. Which format will need less space for storage? Can we tell which one?

c. Which format will store them at regular intervals? That is, how easy is it to tell at which byte, say, the tenth number, would begin?

In Figure 14.2, we read the first records in the old and the transaction files. The "1100" in the old file is not in the transaction file; that account didn't deposit any amounts during this period so that record is simply written to the new file. Next, we read the record for account "1130" from the old file and find the same thing to be true, and that record is also copied to the new file.

Now we read the third record in the old file, "1142," and that matches the transaction record account as well. Hence, the amounts for these records are added and 650.00, the new balance, is written over to the new file.

Next we read account "1241" from the transaction file and realize that this account doesn't have a record in the master file. An error is printed. We continue updating the master file until we run out of records in the transaction file, at which time we need to copy the remainder of the old master records to the new master file.

The Tracechart for Example 14.1

When executing Example 14.1, you should first compile and link, and make it executable. If you name the executable program ex14, then at the command line you may enter:

```
$ex14 mastfile tranfile newfile
```

Then from the heading line for main(), we can see that *argc*, which is the number of arguments on the command line, should be 4. Also, argv[0] would point to the address where the path and the program name, "ex14," are stored. argv[1] would contain the address where the word "mastfile" is stored. argv[2] would contain the address of the next argument, "tranfile," and argv[3] would have the address of the word, "newfile."

The program is self–contained. It creates its own master and transaction files. Typically, they would be created by a separate program. We have three file pointers corresponding to these

Old master file:

"1100" 500.00	"1130" 600.00	"1142" 500.00	"1341" 450.00	"1342" 100.00	"1380" 700.00

Transaction file:

"1142" 150.00	"1241" 150.00	"1342" 50.00

New master file:

"1100" 500.00	"1130" 600.00	"1142" **650.00**	"1341" 450.00	"1342" **150.00**	"1380" 700.00

Figure 14.2 Performing a sequential file update.

Solution 14.3 The representation of the three numbers, 52000.0, 8.0, and 41.7, are shown here using both formats.

a. As a text file, they will need 14 bytes (0 to 13) and as a binary file, they will need 12 bytes.

b. Text files take up less space if there are fewer digits. In general, we can't tell which one is more efficient.

c. Binary files store numbers at regular intervals. Record number 1 starts at byte 0, record number 2 starts at byte 4, and so on. Record number 10 would start at byte 36, or 9 times 4.

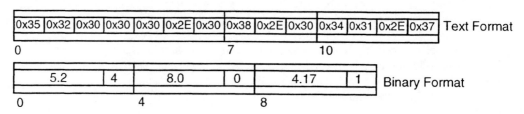

File I/O

three files that the program will be using: *masf, transf,* and *newf.* If *argc* is not 4 (the number of items on the command line), then the program prints an error message and exits. Otherwise, it calls two functions, create_test_masterfile() and create_test_transfile(), by passing the appropriate file names to them. Those functions then create the two necessary files that must exist before the update can occur. Then the three files, master and transaction files for reading and new file for writing, are opened.

   Before we start the loop that goes until the end of the transaction file, we have to read one record from each file. Since their record formats are the same, we use the function called read_rec(). read_rec() uses an fscanf() and reads in one record into the appropriate structure. *mastrec* and *transrec* are two local structure variables that will hold one record from their corresponding files. *mflag* will contain an EOF (end of file) if the end of the master file is reached. Similarly, *tflag* will contain an EOF if the end of the transaction file is reached. Let us follow Figures 14.2 and 14.3 as we discuss Example 14.1.

Position in program	mastrec	transrec	To new master file:	Error messages:
Before the tflag loop:	"1100" 500	"1142" 150		
strcmp loop:			"1100" 500	
	"1130" 600			
			"1130" 600	
strcmp if:	"1142" 500			
	650			
			"1142" 650	
	"1341" 450	"1241" 150		
Second time in the tflag loop:				"1241" Not in master file
		"1342" 50		
Third time in the tflag loop:			"1341" 450	
	"1342" 100			
	150			
			"1342" 150	
		(EOF)		
	"1380" 700			
mflag loop:				
			"1380" 700	
	(EOF)			

Figure 14.3 Making a tracechart for Example 14.1.

Drill 14.4 Not all of the statements are shown:

```
struct drug
{
    char type[10];
    float cost;
};
struct drug medicine;
printf("Enter 10 drug names and their prices:\n");
for(i = 1; i <= 10; ++i)
{
    scanf("%s %f", medicine.type, &medicine.cost);
    fwrite(&medicine, sizeof(struct drug), 1,
                      drug_file);
}
```

The loop reads in the ten drug names and costs from the monitor into the structure and, using fwrite(), writes them to the drug_file. The fwrite() writes from the medicine variable. It writes 14 bytes because that is the size of the structure. It writes one (1) record to the drug_file at a time. The first record begins at byte 0 in the file.

a. Where does record 2 begin?
b. Where does record 3 begin?
c. Given "x," where does record "x" begin?
d. Which byte is the last byte for "x"?

```
//EXAMPLE 14.1
//Assumptions;
// The master and the transaction files are presorted with no errors.
// There is only one transaction record per account number.
#include <stdio.h>
#include <string.h>
#include <stdlib.h>
struct record
{
    char acct[5];
    float amt;
};
int read_rec(FILE *ptr, struct record *x);
void create_test_masterfile(char *filename);
void create_test_transfile(char *filename);
void create_file(char *filename, struct record x[ ], int j);


int main (int argc, char *argv[ ])
{
    struct record mastrec, transrec;
    int mflag, tflag;
    FILE *masf, *transf, *newf;
    if(argc != 4)
    {
        printf("Type %s, old, trans, and new filenames \n", argv[0]);
        exit(1);
    }

    //Create the master and transaction files for testing
    create_test_masterfile(argv[1]);
    create_test_transfile(argv[2]);

    //Open all files and initialize loop
    masf = fopen(argv[1], "r");
    transf = fopen(argv[2], "r");
    newf = fopen(argv[3], "w");
    mflag = read_rec(masf, &mastrec);
    tflag = read_rec(transf, &transrec);
```

Solution 14.4

a. Record 1 is in bytes 0 to 13, that is, 14 bytes, so record 2 begins at byte 14.

b. Record 2 ends at byte 27, and record 3 begins at byte 28.

c. Deriving a formula from these two examples, the byte where record "x" begins is byte number $14 * (x - 1)$. For example, if "x" is 2, then $14 * (2 - 1)$ becomes $14 * 1$, or just 14.

d. Similarly, record "x" ends at $14 * x - 1$. For record 2, this gives us $14 * 2 - 1$, or 27.

Drill 14.5 The fseek() function is used to bring us to the beginning of any record in a file. The fread() function will read that record in the structure similar to how fwrite() wrote it to the file. fseek() takes three arguments. The first is the name of the file, the next argument is how many bytes to advance from the current position in the file, and the last argument gives the byte number of the current position, which typically is 0 to denote the beginning of the file. Can you write the fseek() and the fread() functions so that you will have record number 5 in the variable *medicine*? The format of fread() is like that of fwrite().

```
//Process all transaction records first
for( ; tflag != EOF; )
{
    //Find the next master record for this transaction record
    for(; strcmp(mastrec.acct, transrec.acct) < 0;)//If mastrec < trans
    {
        fprintf(newf, " %s %f", mastrec.acct, mastrec.amt);
        mflag = read_rec(masf, &mastrec);
    }

    //If master record is found, write to the new master file.
    if( strcmp(mastrec.acct, transrec.acct) == 0)    //If they are equal
    {
        mastrec.amt = mastrec.amt + transrec.amt;
        fprintf(newf, " %s %f", mastrec.acct, mastrec.amt);
        mflag = read_rec(masf, &mastrec);
    }
    else //If not there, then there is an error in the trans file.
        printf("%s not in  master file\n", transrec.acct);
    tflag = read_rec(transf, &transrec);
}

//Copy over the rest of the master records, if there are any
for( ; mflag != EOF; )
{
    fprintf(newf, " %s %f", mastrec.acct, mastrec.amt);
    mflag = read_rec(masf, &mastrec);
}
fclose(masf); fclose(transf); fclose(newf); return 0;
}

//Given file pointer and address of the record, fscanf() one record
int read_rec(FILE *ptr, struct record *x)
{
    float *fp;
    int i; fp = &(x -> amt);
    i = fscanf(ptr, " %s %f", x -> acct, fp);
    return i;

}
```

Solution 14.5 sizeof(struct drug) could be replaced by 14 but if, at a later time, another member is added to struct drug, then the 14 would also have to be changed.

```
fseek(drug_file, 4 * (sizeof (struct drug)), 0);
fread(&medicine, sizeof(struct drug), 1, drug_file);
```

Drill 14.6 Before we can use a file, the file pointer must be declared and the file opened.

```
FILE *fptr;
fptr = fopen("disk_file", "wb");
```

In this example, the name of the file on the disk is called disk_file. It is opened for writing because of the w in the fopen() function. The b specifies the binary mode. How do you think you would open the file so that you can read from it?

```
//Create a test master file
void create_test_masterfile(char *filename)
{
    struct record x[6] = {{"1100",500.0}, {"1130",600.0}, {"1142",500.0},
                           {"1341",450.0}, {"1342",100.0}, {"1380", 700.0}};
    create_file(filename, x, 6);
}

//Create a test transaction file
void create_test_transfile(char *filename)
{
    struct record x[3] = {{"1142",150.0}, {"1241",150.0}, {"1342",50.00}};
    create_file(filename, x, 3);
}

void create_file(char *filename, struct record x[ ], int j)
{
    FILE *ptr;
    int i;
    ptr = fopen(filename, "w");
    if(ptr == NULL)
    {
        printf("You don't know how to follow directions, just kidding\n");
        exit (1);
    }
    for(i = 0; i <= j - 1; ++i)
        fprintf(ptr, " %s %f", x[i].acct, x[i].amt);
    fclose(ptr);
}
```

As we said, the first record from each file is read in. *mastrec* contains "1100 500" and *transrec* contains "1142 150." It is not the end of the transaction file, so we go into the loop that we call the *tflag* loop. Here, we encounter a nested loop or the strcmp loop. The strcmp() function returns a value of –1 if the first argument passed to it is alphabetically less than the second one passed to it. It returns a 0 if they are equal and returns a positive number if the second argument is less than the first one. This function is available through the string.h header file.

Since "1100" in *mastrec* is less than "1142" in *transrec*, the record for "1100" is written to the new file and the next record is read into *mastrec*. Again, the account in *mastrec* ("1130") is

Solution 14.6
```
FILE *fptr;
fptr = fopen("disk_file", "rb");
```

Drill 14.7
If the file can't be opened, then the fopen function returns a NULL. How would you execute the exit(1) command after printing an error message if a NULL is actually returned by fopen()?

File I/O

less than the account in *transrec* ("1142"), so the "1130" record is written to the new file and "1142" is read into *mastrec*. Now the two accounts are equal, so we stop the strcmp loop and check the strcmp if statement.

This if statement is true, so the 150 from *transrec* is added to the 500 in *mastrec*, and its updated value is written to the new file. Before we go on to the next iteration of the tflag loop, the next master file and transaction file records are read in.

The "1341" in *mastrec* is not less than the "1241" in *transrec*, so the strcmp loop is not done. Neither are they equal, so we go to the else and print an error message saying that this account in the transaction file doesn't have a record in the master file. Now only the next transaction record is read and we go in the third iteration of the tflag loop.

The "1341" in *mastrec* is less than the "1342" in *transrec*, so the *mastrec* is written to the new file while "1342" is read in for *mastrec*. This record is updated as usual and the next two records are read in. However, we get an EOF (end of file) signal for the transaction file, so the tflag loop terminates and we go to the mflag loop. Here, we copy the rest of the master file records over to the new file. There is only one, so we get an EOF signal for the master file as well. Now the program stops. We can go over to the operating system and type out the new master file to see if the updating is done correctly. This means that we would do the cat newfile command in UNIX or do the type newfile command in DOS. In Windows we would open newfile by starting Notepad.

EXPERIMENTS

Exp 14.1 Before we start with files, let us explore the difference between return and exit().

```
#include <stdio.h>
#include <stdlib.h>//Needed for exit().
int show_me(void);
void main (void )
{
    int i;
    i = show_me();
    printf("Done = %d\n", i);
}
int show_me(void)
{
// exit(0);      // Line 1
    return 0;
}
```

Solution 14.7

```
FILE *fptr;
fptr = fopen("disk_file", "rb");
if(fptr == NULL)
{
    printf("File can't be opened.\n");
    exit(1);
}
```

Drill 14.8 Hashing is a technique commonly used to store records randomly. Accessing records randomly allows programmers to access one particular record without having to access all the others that preceded it. Let us say that we need to store a maximum of 89 prescriptions in our file. First, we allocate space in the file to store 100 records. When we need to access the record for a particular drug, we will divide its number by 89, and find the remainder. The remainder will be the record number where that record will be found. For example, the hashing address, or the record number, is 11 for the drug whose *id* is 100. That is, 100 divided by 89 is 1. We disregard the quotient but use the remainder (11) as the address. Find the hashing addresses for 269 and 94.

a. With line 1 commented, does execution return from show_me() to main()?
b. Uncomment line 1. Does the execution return from show_me() to main()?
c. Change exit(0) to exit(1). Does the execution return from show_me() to main()?
d. Change main() as shown below. What does exit() do?

```
void main (void)
{       printf("Done\n");
        exit(0);
        printf("Still here?\n");
}
```

Exp 14.2 stdout is a pointer to a file defined in stdio.h. This typically refers to your screen.

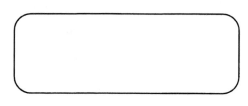

```
#include <stdio.h>
void main ( )
{
    int i = 56;
    printf("%d\n", i);
    fprintf(stdout, "%d\n", i);
}
```

a. Does the fprintf() function require the file pointer where the printing is to be done?
b. Does the printf() function require the file pointer as well?

Exp 14.3 stdin is a pointer to a file defined in stdio.h. This typically refers to your keyboard.

```
#include <stdio.h>
void main ( )
{
    int i, j;
    fprintf(stdout, "Enter two integers ");
    scanf("%d", &i);
    fscanf(stdin, "%d", &j);
    fprintf(stdout, "i = %d, j = %d\n",
                      i, j);
}
```

a. Does the fscanf() function require the file pointer from where the input is to be taken?
b. Does the scanf() function require the file pointer?

Solution 14.8 We are assuming that *id* is an integer member of struct drug. Dividing 269 by 89 gives 3; 89 times 3 is 267; 267 from 269 leaves us with a remainder of 2. So the hashing address for 269 is 2 using our method of hashing. The hashing address of 94 is 5. That is the remainder after dividing 89 into 94.

Drill 14.9 In this diagram, write in the *id*'s where they would be stored in our file. A key is a field in a record by which records are stored. An identification number is typically the key. Show the records where these *id*s would be stored: 100, 269, 94, 8, 893, and 178. To begin, all empty records are initialized to 0, an invalid *id*.

Address	0	1	2	3	4	5	6	7	8	9	10	11
Key	0	0	0	0	0	0	0	0	0	0	0	0

Exp 14.4 Instead of using file pointers defined in stdio.h, let us define our own. For data, enter 511 and 890.50.

```
#include <stdio.h>
void main ( )
{
   char acct[10];
   float bal;
   FILE *acct_file;                                          //Stmt 1
   acct_file = fopen("master_f", "w");                       //Stmt 2
   fprintf(stdout, "Enter account number and balance: ");
   fscanf(stdin, " %s %f", acct, &bal);                      //Stmt 3
   fprintf(stdout, " %s %f\n", acct, bal);                   //Stmt 4
   fprintf(acct_file, " %s %f", acct, bal);                  //Stmt 5
   fclose(acct_file);                                        //Stmt 6
}
```

a. In Statement 1, a pointer to type FILE is created, what is that pointer's name?
b. Is the file being opened or closed in Statement 2? How can you tell?
c. If the file is being opened in Statement 2, where is it being closed? Or if it is being closed, where is it being opened?
d. Is a file opened before it is used or after?
e. Is a file closed before it is used or after?
f. What is the name of the file pointer that we declared?
g. What are two other file pointers used here?
h. Do we have to open or close those files, or is that done for us automatically?
i. In Statement 2, is the file going to be read from or written to? How can you tell?
j. In Statement 2, how is the file called master_f on the disk accessed by the program? By what pointer's name?
k. The string, "Enter account number and balance: " is printed by fprintf(). To which pointer is it printed?
l. *acct* and *bal* are read using which file pointer?
m. In Statement 4, *acct* and *bal* are printed to which file?
n. In Statement 5 *acct* and *bal* are printed to which file?
o. Go to your operating system. Find the file called master_f. What is stored in that file? Type it out from your operating system. Which statement placed those items in master_f?

Solution 14.9 The hashing addresses of 100, 269, and 94 have already been calculated. Dividing 8 by 89 gives a quotient of 0 and the remainder of 8, so 8 is the address. Dividing 893 by 89 gives a remainder of 3, and dividing 178 by 89 gives a remainder of 0.

Address	0	1	2	3	4	5	6	7	8	9	10	11
Key	178	0	269	893	0	94	0	0	8	0	0	100

Drill 14.10 Refer back to Drill 14.4. If *id*, an integer, is read in from the terminal, write an assignment statement to calculate *rec_num* using our hashing algorithm. Also write the fseek() and the fread() functions so that the record identified in *id* is read into the *medicine* variable.

p. Step A in the diagram below shows data being sent from RAM to the screen. What statement in the program does this? Match the other three steps with their corresponding steps in the experiment. Also, show as many as possible of the bytes being written to the file.

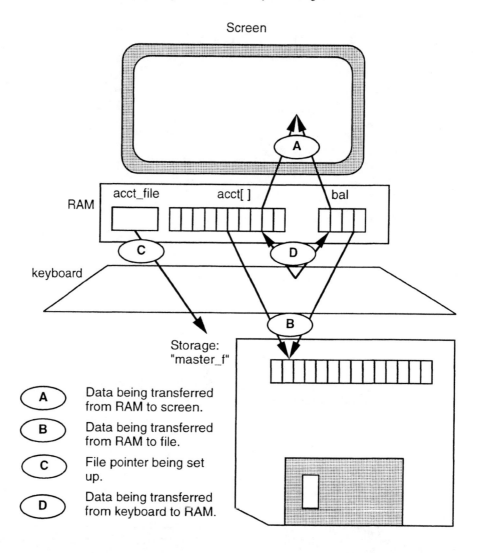

A — Data being transferred from RAM to screen.

B — Data being transferred from RAM to file.

C — File pointer being set up.

D — Data being transferred from keyboard to RAM.

Solution 14.10 Using concepts of integer division, we obtain the following:

```
rec_num = id - id / 89 * 89;      //or this could simply be: id % 89
fseek(acct_file, 14 * (rec_num - 1), 0);
fread(&medicine, sizeof(struct drug), 1, drug_file);
```

Drill 14.11 Conversely, if a new *id* is given to us, how do we write the three statements so that the new record is written in our random access binary file?

File I/O

Exp 14.5 Now can we read the data from master_f into our program?

```
#include <stdio.h>
void main ( )
{
    char acct[10];
    float bal;
    FILE *acct_file;                        //Stmt 1
    acct_file = fopen("master_f", "r");                         //Stmt 2
    fprintf(stdout, "Here is your account number and balance: ");
    fscanf(acct_file, "%s %f", acct, &bal);                     //Stmt 3
    fprintf(stdout, "%s %f\n", acct, bal);                      //Stmt 4
    fclose(acct_file);                                          //Stmt 5
}
```

a. Was there any difference in the statement that opened the file to read from the statement that opened the file to write? How many differences were there? What were those differences?

b. Is there any difference between how you close a file opened for writing and how you close a file opened for reading?

c. Why did the string "Here is your account number and balance: " get printed to the screen?

d. Why didn't *acct* and *bal* get read from the keyboard in statement 3?

e. Why didn't they get printed to the file in statement 4?

Exp 14.6 Suppose that you wanted to enter more than one record. Type this for your data precisely with 3 characters for accounts and 6 characters for each balance, as shown:

```
422 105.00
811 134.25
922 450.00
711 250.50
111 307.75
0   0
```

Solution 14.11 Get to the record you want quickly without going through a loop.
```
rec_num = id % 89;
fseek(acct_file, 14 * (rec_num - 1), 0);
fwite(&medicine, sizeof(struct drug), 1, drug_file);
```

Drill 14.12 What if two *id*'s have the same hashing address, or remainders, in our case? We have to accommodate instances where multiple records have the same remainder. This part of the hashing algorithm is called *collision handling*. If our remainder technique works well, we won't have many records that collide, but we would still have to do something when they do collide. For collision handling, let us use an overflow area starting at record number 89 and ending at 99. Each time there is a collision, we enter the record in the next available record number in the overflow area. We will use the variable, *overflow_rec*, to specify where the next empty record is available. When there are no records in the file at all, what should *overflow_rec* be initialized as? Every time a record is thrown in the overflow area, what should be done with this variable?

```
#include <stdio.h>
void main ( )
{
        char acct[10];
        float bal;
        int i;
        FILE *acct_file;
        acct_file = fopen("master_f", "w");
        fprintf(stdout, "Enter account numbers and balances: \n");
        fprintf(stdout, "When done, enter a zero twice \n");
        fscanf(stdin, " %s %f", acct, &bal);
        for(i = 0; acct[0] != '0'; ++i )
        {
            fprintf(acct_file, " %s %f", acct, bal);          //Stmt 1
            fscanf(stdin, " %s %f", acct, &bal);
        }
        fclose(acct_file);
        fprintf(stdout, "There were %d records entered\n", i);
}
```

a. When the file was opened for writing, was it opened once or several times inside a loop? Was the file closed once or several times?

b. Rewrite two of the fscanf()'s to scanf()'s. Did the program work the same way?

c. How many records were entered?

d. The first fscanf() read how many records? The fscanf() in the loop was executed how many times?

e. The first record was written by which fprintf()? Subsequent records were written by which one?

f. Go to your operating system. Type out the file. What happened to the data that was in that file from the previous experiments? Was it overwritten, or was the new data added after?

g. Why is all the data printed on one line next to each other rather than under each other?

h. How would you write to the file so that the pairs of data, the account and the balance, appear under each other when printed? Try it. Then revert the program to what it was before. Run it. You will need to have this file created the original way for doing the next experiments.

overflow_rec	Address 0	1	2	3	4		88	89	90	91
89	Key 178	0	269	893	0		0	0	0	0

Solution 14.12 *overflow_rec* should be initialized as 89 and it should be incremented by 1 every time a new collided record is added.

Drill 14.13 The *id*'s of 178, 269, and 893 have already been added. Show the file after the *id*'s of 181, 360, and 890 are added to the file, in that order.

Exp 14.7 Now after creating the file as it was done originally in Experiment 14.6, let us try to read that file into our program. EOF is a constant defined in the stdio.h file.

```
#include <stdio.h>
void main ( )
{
      char acct[10];
      float bal;
      int i, flag;
      FILE *acct_file;
      acct_file = fopen("master_f", "r");
      fprintf(stdout, "Enter account numbers and balances: \n");
      fprintf(stdout, "When done, enter a zero twice \n");
      flag = fscanf(acct_file, " %s %f", acct, &bal);

      for(i = 0; flag != EOF; ++i )
      {
         fprintf(stdout, " %s %f\n", acct, bal);          //Stmt 1
         flag = fscanf(acct_file, " %s %f", acct, &bal);
      }
      fclose(acct_file);
      fprintf(stdout, "There were %d records read\n", i);
}
```

   a. The fscanf() function actually returns a value. If the scanning is not successful because there are no more records in the file, then the function will return an EOF (end of file) integer code. This code is then stored in an integer called *flag*. If there are five records stored in the file, how many fscanf()s will be executed before the EOF signal is received?
   b. Change the *flag* to a character data type. Is there any difference in how the program executes? EOF should be considered as an integer.
   c. When all the data items are stored in the file next to each other, why are they printed under each other, as they were entered in the previous experiment?
   d. How can we call fprintf() in the last statement when the fclose() was called before it?

Solution 14.13 First, the contents are shown after adding 181 and 360, and then after adding 890.

overflow_rec	Address 0	1	2	3	4		88	89	90	91
90	Key 178	0	269	893	360		0	181	0	0

overflow_rec	Address 0	1	2	3	4		88	89	90	91
91	Key 178	0	269	893	360		0	181	890	0

Drill 14.14 Notice that above, 181 and 893 have the same hashing address, but their physical addresses or record numbers are different. Now add 270 to what we have so far.

Exp 14.8 Precisely enter the data of Experiment 14.6 to create the file master_f. The position of each byte in the file is critical in this experiment. What if I want just one random record in the file and not all of them? For data, type any integer from 1 to 5.

```
#include <stdio.h>
void main ( )
{
      char acct[10];
      float bal;
      int i, rec_num;
      FILE *acct_file;
      acct_file = fopen("master_f", "r");
      fprintf(stdout, "Assuming the data in the file was entered \n");
      fprintf(stdout, "using the correct number of characters,\n");
      fprintf(stdout, "What record number do you want? Choose 1 - 5: ");

      fscanf(stdin, "%d", &rec_num);
      fseek(acct_file, 15 * (rec_num - 1), 0);              //Stmt 1
      fscanf(acct_file, " %s %f", acct, &bal);
      fprintf(stdout, " %s %f\n", acct, bal);
      fclose(acct_file);
}
```

a. From your operating system, type out the master_f file. How many characters are used for each account number, including the space before it? How many are used between each account number and its balance? How many are used for the balance (that includes the characters before the decimal point, after the decimal point, and the decimal point itself)?

b. Adding all the characters in the question above, you should obtain the number of characters in one record. In our file, each record takes up how many characters?

c. If you entered a 4 when running the program, which record was printed out?

d. If *rec_num* was 4, then 15 was multiplied by what number in fseek()? Why wasn't it multiplied by 4 when seeking the record stored as the fourth one?

e. Which record is stored starting at byte 0? The first record ends at which byte number? Counting of bytes is done starting at 0.

f. At the fifteenth byte, which record is stored?

g. The zero in statement 1 means to start looking for the record from the beginning of the file. Try placing a 15 there. What is its effect?

Solution 14.14

overflow_rec	Address	0	1	2	3	4			88	89	90	91
92	Key	178	0	269	893	360			0	181	890	270

Drill 14.15 So far we have mostly been adding records to our file. Let us see how we would retrieve them. If we wanted to access the record whose *id* is 893, which of the following steps would we have to do? Number them in order.

____ Check the *id* in record number 3 to see if it is the same as the *id* for which we are searching.

____ fread() record number 3.

____ fread() all the records in the overflow area, starting at record number 89.

____ Calculate the hashing address, i.e., 893 % 89 equals 3.

Exp 14.9 We need a better method of accessing data randomly from a file. We can't expect a user to enter data with precisely so many characters, so we introduce fwrite() and fread(). Use this data:

```
422     105.00
811     134.25
92222   45000.00
7111    25.50
4       1307.75
0       0
```

```c
#include <stdio.h>
void main ( )
{
     char acct[10];
     float bal;
     int i, rec_num;
     FILE *acct_file;
     acct_file = fopen("file1", "wb");                    //Notice the 'b'
     printf("Enter account numbers and balances: \n");
     printf("When done, enter a zero twice \n");
     scanf("%s %f", acct, &bal);
     for(i = 0; acct[0] != '0'; ++i )
     {
        fwrite(acct, 10, 1, acct_file);
        fwrite(&bal, sizeof(float), 1, acct_file);
        scanf("%s %f", acct, &bal);
     }
     fclose(acct_file);
     printf("There were %d records written\n", i);
}
```

a. Again, go to your operating system, and type out your file, file1. Compare it against master_f. The "422" from the data was represented which way in both files? How many bytes were used for file1 and how many for master_f? Were you able to see all the bytes on the screen when you typed out both files?

b. The 105.00 was represented which way in both files? The 105.00 needed how many bytes in each file? Were you able to see all the data on the screen when you typed out the files?

c. Did fwrite() write data to the file the same way as did fprintf()?

Solution 14.15 The record is not in the overflow area so it doesn't have to be searched there.

 _3_ Check the id in record number 3 to see if it is the same as the id for which we are searching.

 _2_ fread() record number 3.

 ____ fread() all the records in the overflow area starting at record number 89.

 _1_ Calculate the hashing address, i.e., 893 % 89 equals 3.

Drill 14.16 I want to access the record whose *id* is 90, which isn't in the file. I won't know that until I search the file.

a. Would I have to calculate the hashing address?

b. Would I have to do an fread()?

c. Would I have to increment the *overflow_rec* variable?

d. Would I have to do an fread() more than once?

d. Regardless of the number of characters used in each data pair, how many bytes did each record occupy in file1? Which function writes fixed–length records to a file, regardless of the size of the data?

e. Which function do you think is more suitable for writing to files using random access? Why?

f. The fwrite() function writes to the file in binary format and the fprintf() function writes to it in text format. In which mode, binary or text, do you think data is represented in CPUs? In which mode is data represented on a keyboard? What about the screen or the printer?

Exp 14.10 Now let us read that data using random access.

```
#include <stdio.h>
void main ( )
{
        char acct[10];
        float bal;
        int i, rec_num;
        FILE *acct_file;
        acct_file = fopen("file1", "rb");
        fprintf(stdout, "What record number do you want? Choose 1 - 5: ");
        fscanf(stdin, "%d", &rec_num);
        fseek(acct_file, (10 + sizeof(float)) * (rec_num - 1), 0); //Stmt 1
        fread(acct, 10, 1, acct_file);
        fread(&bal, sizeof(float), 1, acct_file);
        fprintf(stdout, "%s %f\n", acct, bal);
        fclose(acct_file);
}
```

a. Randomly access any record. Since each record is fixed, it becomes easy to know where each record begins. How many bytes long is each record?

b. When doing an fread(), why doesn't *acct* need a &? Notice that *bal* does. (Incidentally, *bal* could have been an entire structure in both this fread() as well as the fwrite() in Experiment 14.9.)

c. The fread() function returns the number of items it read. If the read is unsuccessful, then it will return a zero. Rewrite this experiment so that the entire file is printed on the screen. Use the fread() function in a loop until it returns a 0. No fseek() function calls are necessary, since we are not doing a random search but are going through the file sequentially.

Solution 14.16 a. Yes   b. Yes   c. No   d. No, only once.

We would first find the hashing address, which is 90 % 89, or 1. Then we would do an fseek() and an fread() on record number 1. We would notice that the *id* stored there is 0, which means that there are no records in our file whose hashing address is 1. Hence there is no need to look in the overflow area.

Drill 14.17 How many fread()s would have to be done if the record whose *id* is 270 is retrieved? Will the *overflow_rec* change?

Exp 14.11 To do this experiment, go to the operating system and create this small text file using a text editor. Make sure you can type it out from your operating system. Call the file file2.

```
Big Daddy
Smooooth!
```

If you were able to create that file and save it as file2, then run this:

```
char x;
int i, rec_num;
FILE *fileptr;
fileptr = fopen("file2", "r");
i = fscanf(fileptr, "%c", &x);          //No spaces inside the quotes
for( ;i != EOF; )
{
    printf("%c:%x: \n", x, x);          //%x prints the value in hex
    i = fscanf(fileptr, "%c", &x);      //No spaces inside the quotes
}
printf("%d", i);
fclose(fileptr);
```

    a. What is the hex equivalent of the 'a' character?
    b. What is the hex equivalent of the space character (' ')?
    c. What character(s) are stored at the end of each line? Find them in the ASCII chart.
    d. What character(s) are stored at the end of the file?
    e. What is the value of EOF in decimal? Does the EOF signal from your operating system get read into x or is it something that is returned by the scanf() function?
    f. Try to rewrite this experiment so that it opens two files, file2 for reading and file3 for writing. Then copy file2 into file3.

QUESTIONS

1. For each of the following, specify if the description is for sequential access or random access files.
    a. Uses buffers.
    b. Efficient for processing all records.
    c. Efficient for processing one record at a time.

Solution 14.17 The *overflow_rec* will not change. There would be 4 fread()s that would be necessary. We would need to do fread()s starting at location 89 until we find 270 or we reach the end of the overflow area.

The hashing address of 270 is 3. First, we would access record number 3, whose *id* doesn't match the 270 that we are looking for. However, since there is no 0 there, we have to search through the overflow area to be sure that it isn't there. Hence, a total of 4 disk accesses were necessary to find 270.

Drill 14.18 If we were looking for the record whose *id* is 89, how many fread()s or disk accesses would be necessary to determine that the record isn't in the file?

2. For the sequential file update program of Example 14.1, show the new master file and the number of error messages. Initially, the master file is: "1100" 100, "2200" 200, "3300" 700, and the transaction record is: "1100" 50, "1700" 100, "3300" 50.

3. How would you add the records with the *id*s shown below using the hashing technique discussed in Drills 14.10 to 14.17? Assume that initially there are no records in the file as shown in Figure 14.4.

267, 268, 178, 181, 90

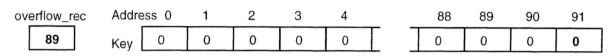

Figure 14.4

Now for each of the following id's, how many accesses would be required either to access the record or to determine that it doesn't exist?
267, 91, 178, 90, 89

4.
```
struct tree
{
   char kind[20];
   int age;
   float height;
};

struct tree x;

for(i =0; i <= 4; ++i)
{
   fprintf(stdout, "Enter age, kind, and height:\n");
   fscanf(stdin, "%d %s %f", &x.age, &x.kind, &x.height);
   fprintf(fptr,  "%d %s %f",  x.age,  x.kind,  x.height);
}
```
   a. Are there 1, 2, or 3 statements here that access the file?
   b. How many records are printed to the file?

Solution 14.18 The answer again is 4. The hashing address of 89 is 0 and record number 0 has an *id* of 178. We have no way of knowing that there were collisions on the hashing address of 0 while creating the file. Therefore, we must go through the overflow area to determine that the *id* isn't there.

Drill 14.19 Update the figure in Solution 14.14 if the record having the *id* of 270 is deleted.

c. How would you define *fptr*?

d. How would you open the file fileA to be pointed to by *fptr*?

e. How would you close the file?

Suppose that each kind member is entered with exactly 5 characters instead of 20.

f. How many characters are written to the file per record?

g. How many characters total are written to the file?

5. Assume that the file in the last question is opened for reading. Write only the for loop that will print the file to the screen one record per line. Do not assume that there are 5 records stored in the file.

PROGRAM

Create a structure with two members: empno (an integer), and wages (a float).

As you read each record, do two things. One, write it to a binary file called main_file using fwrite(), one record or a structure at a time. The first employee is written in the first record of the file; the second, in the second one; and so on.

Two, create this array called *index[ ]*. Each slot of the *index[ ]* array has two integer members, an eno and a recno. Use the insertion sort method discussed in the Programs section of Unit 8 to keep the employee numbers in order. Have the user ask for the wages for any employee. Using the index, find the record number where that employee exists in the file, and using the direct access method, retrieve the record for that employee.

Here's the data:

320	200.00
100	500.00
480	300.00
110	600.00
370	100.00
340	500.00
0	0.00

index[ ]

eno	recno
100	1
110	3
320	0
340	5
370	4
480	2

The "main_file":

record number: 0	1	2	3	4	5
320 200.00	100 500.00	480 300.00	110 600.00	370 100.00	340 500.00

Solution 14.19

overflow_rec	Address	0	1	2	3	4		88	89	90	91
91	Key	178	0	269	893	360		0	181	890	0

Unit 15

Text-Based Graphics on the PC

Registers in the CPU

Since this entire unit is centered around the Intel x86 family of PCs, let us go over some of the basics about its hardware. As seen in Figure 15.1, the Intel CPU has four registers that we will

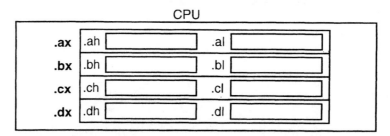

CPU

Figure 15.1 Each of the 16–bit x registers are made up of two 8–bit registers.

Drill 15.1 In this unit we will be considering only simple graphics on Intel-based PCs. The screen is divided into 80 columns called the y axis and into 25 rows called the x axis. See the diagram for Experiment 15.1. Part of RAM, starting at address 0xB8000, is dedicated to store the information of what is to be placed on the screen, two bytes per character. So the information for the character that is in the top left–most position on the screen is stored at address 0xB8000 and 0xB8001.

a. How many characters can be displayed on the screen?
b. In decimal, how many bytes are needed to store all the information that goes on the screen?
c. What two bytes are used to store the character in the first row and the third column?

encounter in our programming. There are others but we don't have to concern ourselves with them now. Registers are super–fast memory locations that the CPU uses to store data temporarily while it needs to process it. Arithmetic and logic operations are performed by first bringing the data into registers.

In the early CPUs these registers were 16 bits long, which were divided into two 8-bit registers. The 16–bit *a* register is called the .ax register, while its higher–order 8 bits are called the .ah register and the lower–order 8 bits are called the .al register. This naming convention is repeated for the *b*, *c*, and *d* registers.

We will need to include the dos.h header file to perform some of the tasks in this unit. Along with other items, these registers are defined here as follows:

```
struct BYTEREGS
{
    unsigned char al, ah, bl, bh, ch, cl, dh, dl;
};
struct WORDREGS
{
    unsigned int ax, bx, cx, dx; //Plus there are others.
};
union REGS
{
    struct BYTEREGS h;
    struct WORDREGS x;
};
```

Unions allow us to access the same area of memory using more than one format. If we want to access only a one–byte–length register, then we use struct BYTEREGS. If we want to use the full 16–bit registers, then we use struct WORDREGS. Unions allow us to access registers either way. What we have to include in our program is:

```
union REGS regs;
```

Then the union variable called *regs*, will be available to us. To access the 8–bit .ah register, we would specify regs.h.ah, and to access the 16–bit *ax* register, we would use regs.x.ax.

The BIOS (Basic Input/Output System)

Along with the CPU, the PC also needs a BIOS to perform all I/O (input/output) functions. Whenever the CPU needs to access a network card, a printer, a floppy drive, or any other I/O device, the services of the BIOS are requested. For instance, whenever you press a key on your keyboard,

Solution 15.1
a. 80 times 25 is 2000 characters that can be displayed.
b. Each text character requires two bytes, so a total of 4000 bytes are needed to store the entire screen in video RAM.
c. Bytes 0xB8002 and 0xB8003 are used to store the second character, so bytes 0xB8004 and 0xB8005 are used to store the third character.

Drill 15.2 The first byte of each character specifies which character to display, and the next byte specifies its attribute. Attribute in this context means the background and foreground colors and whether or not the character is blinking. In the diagram for Experiment 15.4, some codes for characters are shown, and in the diagram for Experiment 15.3, codes for attributes are shown. Using these two charts, can you tell which character is displayed and with what attributes if the memory location 0xB8000 contains 0xCD and 0xB001 contains 0x1F? (0x1F is 0001 1111 in binary.)

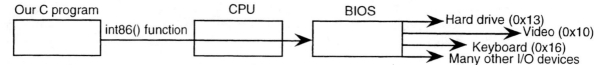

Figure 15.2 Calling the BIOS (basic input/output sytem) interrupt services from a C program. Some interrupt levels are shown.

you are signaling the BIOS to get this character read from the keyboard or its buffer. The signal sent to the BIOS to perform a certain task is called an interrupt.

In your operating system, when you want to print something, the operating system sends an interrupt to the BIOS. Or if you want to print out a document from your word processor, then your word processor may get to the BIOS through the operating system. Or it may signal the BIOS directly. In the dos.h header file, we have the int86() function available if we want to send an interrupt directly to the BIOS. See Figure 15.2.

We will be drawing full–screen menus and we will want to turn off the cursor for that. However, when the user needs to input some data, the cursor will have to be turned back on. To do that, we will have to call the int86() function. Here's how you can turn off the cursor so it doesn't blink on the screen:

```
regs.h.ah = 0x01;
regs.h.ch = 0x20;
int86(0x10, &regs, &regs);
```

The first argument, 0x10, tells the BIOS that we are requesting the video service. The second and third arguments will give the addresses of the *regs* union variables. The 0x01 in the .ah register tells the BIOS that we want to do something with the cursor that is associated with the video service. And the 0x20 in the .ch register indicates that we want to turn the cursor off completely.

Other topics that deal with hardware I/O using C are covered in the drills and experiments.

Example

In this example I have given only the function prototypes and the main() function. The function definitions (other than main) are given in the experiments. The function prototypes in this example have notes specifying in which experiments those functions are defined.

```
#include <conio.h>              //for getch()
#include <dos.h>                //for int86() and union REGS
```

Solution 15.2 The character code of 0xCD is two horizontal parallel lines. This character will be displayed with a blue (001) background and a white (1111) background. Since the first bit of the attribute is 0, this character will not be blinking.

Drill 15.3 What are the codes for a blue on cyan blinking 4? Use the following chart:

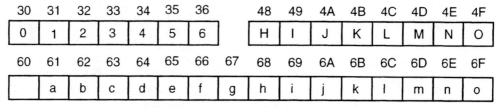

Some of the ASCII character set

Text-Based Graphics on the PC

```
#define C_ATTR 0x3C00          //Light red over cyan
#define VBIOS 0x10
void draw_window(int, int, int, int, unsigned int);    // Experiment 15.4
     //Top left and lower right corners in X & Y coordinates, plus color
void show_menu(int);                                   // Experiment 15.5
void turn_off_cursor(void);                            // Experiment 15.6
void turn_on_cursor(void);                             // Experiment 15.6
void show_name(char [ ]);     //Displays the name      // Experiment 15.8
int enter_name(char [ ]);     //Changes the name       // Experiment 15.9
int far *farptr;
     //farptr is a pointer variable that points to display RAM.
union REGS regs;
     //regs is a union variable that gives us access to the registers.

void main (void)
{
     int row, column, pos = 0;
     char choice, name[11] = "Alice";
     farptr = (int far *) 0xB8000000L;
     turn_off_cursor();
     for(; ;)                      // This loop continues on the next page.
     {
        show_menu(0);
        for(; getch() ==0;) //Continue as long we are getting an
        {                            //extended keyboard character.
            choice = getch(); //This is an extended keyboard character
            if(choice == 80)   //If it is a down-arrow,
               if(pos == 2)     //and we are on the last choice in menu,
               {
                  show_menu(0); //then show the first choice
                  pos = 0;       //set pos to mean
               }                        //we are on first choice.
               else              //if we are not on the last choice,
               {                         //highlight the next choice, and
                  show_menu(pos + 1);
                  ++pos;                 //adjust pos to the next choice
               }
        }                        //Person typed a non-extended keyboard
```

Solution 15.3 The first byte is 0x34 for the character '4,' and the next character, the character for the attribute, is 1011 0001, or 0xB1. The first binary 1 is for blinking, the next 011 is for the cyan background, and the last 0001 is for the blue foreground.

Drill 15.4 We will initialize a pointer called a *far pointer* that can hold large addresses. This will hold the address of the first byte of the display RAM, i. e.,

```
int far *farptr = 0xB8000000L;
```

To store 0x34B1 starting at 0xB8000, we need to specify it backward:

```
*farptr = 0xB134;   //The first byte is placed second and vice versa.
```

How would you store 0xCD1F, from Solution 15.2, into these two bytes?

Text-Based Graphics on the PC

```
      if(pos == 0)              //character. If s/he was on first
         enter_name(name);      //choice, get a new name from user
      else
         if(pos == 1)           //If it was on second choice,
            show_name(name);    //display name in variable
         else
            break;              //Or else, quit altogether.
   }
   turn_on_cursor();
   for(row = 0; row <= 24; ++row)//make the screen normal again.
      for(column = 0; column <= 79; ++column)
         *(farptr + row*80 + column) = 0x0700;
}
```

EXPERIMENTS

This unit is for those who have a PC–compatible computer, or for those who have an x86-based Intel processor. Specifically, it is for those who can run under DOS. If you skip this unit, it will not place you at a disadvantage for future units. Many of the hardware details will not be explained for the sake of brevity. However, they were covered in the lesson part of the unit .

Exp 15.1 In this unit we need to access the part of RAM that stores the information about how the screen on your computer will be displayed. What is to be displayed on the screen is stored in RAM starting at a RAM address of B8000000. This address is given in hex, so it will be preceded with a 0x. 0xB8000000 is too large a number to be stored as a normal integer. It must be specified as a long integer, so we have to end that number with an L. So this address must be written as 0xB8000000L. In fact, since the address of the display memory is so large, we need a special type of pointer that can hold such large addresses. Hence, we need to define a far pointer. We call it *farptr* in the experiment. A normal pointer can hold only 16–bit memory addresses, but a far pointer can hold 32–bit memory addresses, which are needed to access the display portion of RAM.

```
#include <conio.h>
void main (void)
{
      int far *farptr;//Here' the far pointer
      char c;
```

Solution 15.4 *farptr = 0x1FCD;

Drill 15.5 Since usually it is more pleasant to have a uniform set of attributes for the entire screen, in programming, we separate the attribute portion from the characters that are displayed. To do this we use the bit–wise OR operator |. That is, 1100|0101 equals 1101. If one of the two corresponding bits is a 1, ORing them yields a 1; otherwise, the answer is 0.

```
1100  First binary number
0101  Second binary number
----
1101  The OR of these two numbers
```

What are the answers for ORing these numbers: 0110|0011 and 1F00|00CD? (Here, the hex system is used to abbreviate the binary numbers.)

```
        farptr = (int far *) 0xB8000000L;
        *farptr = 0x0700 | 'T'; //Stmt 1
        *(farptr + 1) = 0x0700 | 'U';
             //"0x0700 |" will be explained soon.
        *(farptr + 2) = 0x0700 | 'V';
        *(farptr + 79) = 0x0700 | 'W';
        *(farptr + 80) = 0x0700 | 'X';
        *(farptr + 24 * 80) = 0x0700 | 'Y';
        *(farptr + 24 * 80 + 79) = 0x0700 | 'Z';
        getch();
             //Enter any key to continue
}
```

a. In the diagram show where each character was printed. Typically, you should have 80 columns and 25 rows on your display. How many characters can be displayed on the screen?
b. It turns out that farptr + 0 is equal to 0xB8000, farptr + 1 is equal to 0xB8002, and farptr + 2 is equal to 0xB8004. How many bytes are needed to store each character that is displayed? How many bytes are needed in total (in decimal) for the entire display RAM?
c. In Statement 1, are the contents of *farptr* changed or are the contents of what it points to changed?
d. In the display RAM, are characters for the screen stored by rows or by columns? Is the first row stored first, or is the first column stored first in the display RAM?
e. If we number the first character on the screen as character 0, what is the number of the last character on the screen? Similarly, if we number the first byte in display RAM as byte 0, what is the number of the last byte?

Exp 15.2

```
#include <conio.h>
void main (void)
{
        int far *farptr;
        char c;
        int row, column;
        farptr = (int far *) 0xB8000000L;
        for(row = 0; row <= 24; ++row)
           for(column = 0; column <= 79; ++column)
               *(farptr + row*80 + column)= 0x0700 | 'T';      // Stmt 1
        getch();                                               // or getchar();
```

Solution 15.5

```
0110        1F00 = 0001 1111 0000 0000
0011        00CD = 0000 0000 1100 1101
----        ----   ---- ---- ---- ----
0111        1FCD = 0001 1111 1100 1101
```

Drill 15.6 How do we set the entire first row of characters to an attribute of 0x0700, the attribute showing white on black nonblinking characters? Fill in the for loop.

```
int far *farptr = 0xB8000000L;
int i;
for(i = ? ; i <= ? ; ++i)
   *(farptr + i) = 0x0700; //Adding i will actually add 2*i number of
                           //bytes to farptr.
```

Text-Based Graphics on the PC

a. Initially, *row* is 0 and we fall into the *column* loop. Then the *column* is zero. Where is the 'T' placed?

b. After the first 'T' is placed in the display RAM, is the second 'T' placed in the same row or the same column? In the beginning of the execution, is the first row or the first column filled with the character 'T'?

c. After the first row is filled with the character 'T,' we go to the *row* loop, get the next *row* (which is 1), and fall back into the *column* loop again. This time, do we fill in the second row or the second column?

Exp 15.3 Now change statement 1 in Experiment 15.2 to the following:

```
*(farptr + row*80 + col) = 'T'| 0x2400;                    //Stmt 1
```

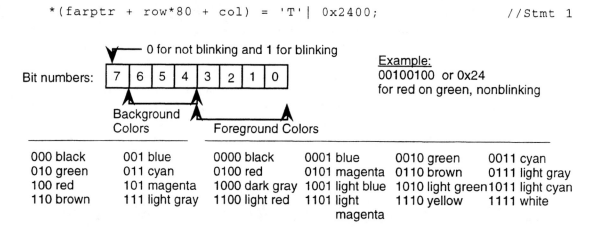

000 black	001 blue	0000 black	0001 blue	0010 green	0011 cyan
010 green	011 cyan	0100 red	0101 magenta	0110 brown	0111 light gray
100 red	101 magenta	1000 dark gray	1001 light blue	1010 light green	1011 light cyan
110 brown	111 light gray	1100 light red	1101 light magenta	1110 yellow	1111 white

a. The left side of the vertical bar determines what character is to be printed, and the right side of it determines the attribute for that character. The attribute of red text on a green background with a nonblinking text makes the attribute byte equal to 0x24. By using this chart, determine the attribute byte for a blinking yellow character on a blue background.

b. If you were able to change the attribute, find an attribute that is both pleasing to look at as well as easy to read.

Solution 15.6

```
for(i = 0 ; i <= 79; ++i)
    *(farptr + i) = 0x0700;  //Adding i will actually add 2 * i number of bytes to farptr.
```

Drill 15.7 How do we change this loop so that we make only the second line cleared to the normal attribute?

Exp 15.4 Now let us write a function that will draw a window, in which we will write a menu. x is the horizontal axis, with 0 being the left–most character. y is the vertical axis, with 0 being the top–most character.

```
void draw_window(int x1, int y1, int x2, int y2, unsigned int
win_color);
#define C_ATTR 0x3C00 //Light red over cyan
#include <stdio.h>
#include <conio.h>
int far *farptr;
void main (void)
{
    char c;
    int row, column;
    farptr = (int far *) 0xB8000000L;
    for(row = 0; row <= 24; ++row)
        for(column = 0; column <= 79; ++column)
            *(farptr + row*80 + column) = C_ATTR; //Blank out the screen
    draw_window(31, 9, 48, 15, 0x2100);
    getch();
}
void draw_window(int x1, int y1, int x2, int y2, unsigned int win_color)
{
    int row, col;
    for(col = x1; col <= x2; ++col) //Draw the horizontal lines
    {
        *(farptr + 80*y1 + col) = win_color | 0x00DB;
        *(farptr + 80*y2 + col) = win_color | 0x00DB;
    }
    for(row = y1 + 1; row <= y2 - 1; ++row) //2 vertical blocks on sides
    {
        *(farptr + 80*row + x1)     = win_color | 0x00DB;
        *(farptr + 80*row + x1 + 1) = win_color | 0x00DB;
        *(farptr + 80*row + x2 - 1) = win_color | 0x00DB;
        *(farptr + 80*row + x2)     = win_color | 0x00DB;
    }
}
```

Solution 15.7 Since there are 80 characters per line, adding 80 to *farptr* brings us another 160 bytes after 0xB8000. Adding *i* to this will make us go across the second line.

```
for(i = 0 ; i <= 79; ++i)
    *(farptr + 80 + i) = 0x0700;
```

Drill 15.8 How would you clear the entire screen? Replace the question marks with the correct items.

```
for(j = 0; j <= ?  ; ++j) //Takes us to the next line down the screen
    for(i = 0 ; i <= 79; ++i) //To the next character across the screen
        *(farptr + 80 * ?   + i) = 0x0700;  //Inserts the attribute
```

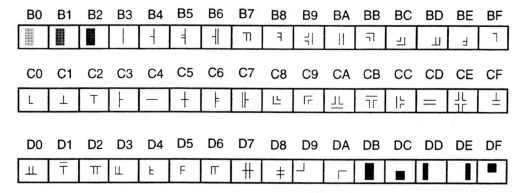

B0	B1	B2	B3	B4	B5	B6	B7	B8	B9	BA	BB	BC	BD	BE	BF
▓	▓	█	│	┤	╡	╢	╖	╕	╣	║	╗	╝	╜	╛	┐

C0	C1	C2	C3	C4	C5	C6	C7	C8	C9	CA	CB	CC	CD	CE	CF
└	┴	┬	├	─	┼	╞	╟	╚	╔	╩	╦	╠	═	╬	╧

D0	D1	D2	D3	D4	D5	D6	D7	D8	D9	DA	DB	DC	DD	DE	DF
╨	╤	╥	╙	╘	╒	╓	╫	╪	┘	┌	█	▄	▌	▐	▀

Some of the IBM character set

```
for(col = x1 + 2; col <= x2 - 2; ++col)
   for(row = y1 + 1; row <= y2 - 1; ++row)
      *(farptr + 80*row + col) = 0x7600;
}
```

a. From the chart for the IBM character set given above, we see that the hex code of DB is the code to fill in one text character on the screen. Using this block we draw a border around the window that we need. In the function draw_window(), *x1* and *y1* give the coordinates for which of the following corners of the window to be drawn: top left, top right, bottom left, or bottom right?
b. *x2* and *y2* give the coordinates of which corner of the window?
c. Now instead of using the DB code to make the border, can you rewrite the function so that it draws a double border around the window? (Hint: 0xBB is the code for the top right corner of the double border.)

Exp 15.5 Now let us write a simple menu in the window that we created.
```
void draw_window(int x1, int y1, int x2,int y2, unsigned int win_color);
#define C_ATTR 0x3C00 //Light red over cyan
#include <stdio.h>
#include <conio.h>
int far *farptr;
void show_menu (int);
```

Solution 15.8
```
for(j = 0; j <= 24; ++j)//Takes us to the next line down the screen
   for(i = 0 ; i <= 79; ++i)  //To the next character across the screen
      *(farptr + 80 * j + i) = 0x0700;   //Inserts the attribute
```

Drill 15.9 We have a string stored in name[11] that is equal to "Adam". We want to print out the name stored in name[11] with a text attribute of 0x21. Complete this code to accomplish this.

```
for(i = 0;    ?    ; ++i)
   *(farptr + 16 * 80 + 47 + i) =     ?    ;
```

```
void main (void)
{
    int row, column;
    farptr = (int far *) 0xB8000000L;
    show_menu(0); //Draw the window and display the menu. The zero as
                  //the argument means highlight the first choice.
    getch();
}


//This function will clear the screen, show the menu with three choices,
// and highlight the choice specified in the input argument selection.
void show_menu (int selection)
{
    int row, col, i, j;
    char menu[3][11] = {"Enter name", "Show name ", "Quit      "};
    for(row = 0; row <= 24; ++row)
        for(col = 0; col <= 79; ++col)
            *(farptr + row*80 + col) = C_ATTR; //Blank out the screen
    draw_window(31, 9, 48, 15, 0x2100);
    for(i = 0; i <= 2; ++i)
        if(i == selection)
            for(j = 0; j <= 9; ++j)                  //white on black
                *(farptr + (11 + i) * 80 + 35 + j) = 0x0700 | menu[i][j];
        else
            for(j = 0; j <= 9; ++j)                  //light red over cyan
                *(farptr + (11 + i) * 80 + 35 + j) = C_ATTR | menu[i][j];
}
```

a. Which choice is highlighted? If *selection* were equal to 2, which choice would have been high-lighted?
b. If we add a fourth choice called Clear name, what changes to the show_menu() function would be necessary?
c. If each of the choices were 13 characters long instead of 11, what changes would be necessary?
d. Can we call draw_window() at the very end of show_menu() without altering the effects?
Try each of these variations to check your answer and then restore the function to the way it was.

Solution 15.9 We have to print all the characters in *x[ ]* until a null character is found. These characters must be ORed with the color attribute to be displayed that way.

```
for(i = 0; x[i] != '\0'; ++i)
    *(farptr + 16 * 80 + 47 + i) = 0x2100 | x[i];
```

Drill 15.10 So far we have been exploring methods of placing information on the screen. Now let us see how we take information from the keyboard. Suppose we have a menu displayed on the screen and we want to allow the user to use the down–arrow key to highlight the different options on the menu. To detect if the user pressed a down–arrow key on the keyboard, we must detect these two bytes in sequence: 0x00 and 0x50. How many times has the down–arrow key been pressed by the user if the CPU has detected the following sequence of bytes? 0x87 0x50 0x34 0x50 0x00 0x50 0x50 0x00 0x50 0x35 0x50

Exp 15.6 Notice that the cursor is still on. Turn off the cursor and turn it back on. This will give us more control over what is placed on the screen. *regs* will refer to the registers or part of the small memory that resides inside the CPU. regs.h.ah is the name of one of those registers. Other items will be explained more in the lesson portion of this unit. Add these three lines before main():

```
#include <stdio.h>
#include <dos.h>         //Needed for the int86() function and for REGS.
#define VBIOS 0x10
union REGS regs;         //Defines regs or registers
void turn_off_cursor();  void turn_on_cursor();
void main (void)
{
      turn_off_cursor();
      getchar();
      turn_on_cursor();
      getchar();
}
void turn_off_cursor (void)
{
      regs.h.ah = 0x01;      //Sets these two registers to certain values
      regs.h.ch = 0x20;           //to turn OFF the cursor
      int86(VBIOS, &regs, &regs);   //Then we call an interrupt routine
}
void turn_on_cursor(void)
{
      regs.h.ah = 0x01;      //Sets these two registers to certain values
      regs.h.ch = 0x00;           //to turn ON the cursor
      int86(VBIOS, &regs, &regs);   //Then we call video interrupt
}
```

    a. Which register of the CPU, *ah* or *ch*, specifies that we want to do something with the cursor on the screen?

    b. Which register of the CPU specifies that we want to turn the cursor on or off?

    c. When calling the int86() function, are we passing the value of the registers or their addresses?

    d. The first argument passed to the int86() function, which is defined in the dos.h file, specifies that we want to do something with the video. This argument is called the interrupt service. What is the interrupt level, in hex and in decimal, that will request video services?

Solution 15.10

The user has pressed the down–arrow key only twice. There are only two times that 0x50 is preceded by a 0x00.

Drill 15.11

The bytes not preceded by a 0x00 are simply ASCII codes. Those that are preceded by a 0x00 are called extended keyboard characters. These are the up– and down–arrow keys, the F–function keys, the insert and delete keys, and many others. Several of the extended keyboard characters are generated by pressing two keys, such as the Ctrl–D keys. In the following sequence of bytes, how many are extended keyboard characters and how many are straight ASCII codes? 0x44 0x00 0x55 0x00 0x40 0x40 0x50 0x34 0x00 0x67

Exp 15.7 Let us now go down the menu by pressing the down–arrow key. Notice that a part of main() is commented out for now. When a down–arrow key is pressed, the keyboard first sends a 0x00 and then the code for the down–arrow key, which is 0x50. If the 0x50 isn't preceded by a 0x00, then the CPU will take that as a simple ASCII character. In this case it would be the letter P. All special–purpose characters are called extended keyboard characters and they all start with a 0x00. See the diagram below.

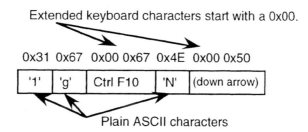

```
//Don't forget to comment out the six lines. We'll add them in later.
void main (void)
{
      int row, column, pos = 0;
      char choice, name[11] = "Alice";
      farptr=(int far *) 0xB8000000L;
      turn_off_cursor();
      for(; ;)
      {
        show_menu(0);
        for(; getch() ==0;) //Continue as long as we are getting an
        {                    //extended keyboard character.
            choice = getch(); //This is an extended keyboard character
            if(choice == 80)  //If it is a down-arrow character,
              if(pos == 2)    //and we are on the last choice in menu,
              {
                show_menu(0); //then show the first choice
                pos = 0;      //set pos to mean
              }                      //we are on first choice.
```

Solution 15.11 There are only three extended keyboard characters. They all start with a 0x00, a pattern that doesn't exist in the ASCII set. And there are four ASCII characters (those that don't begin with a 0x00).

Drill 15.12 If we want to set up a loop so that it continues only as long as an extended character is pressed and terminates if an ASCII character is entered, how should the for statement be written? Use the getch() function to get the next character from the keyboard buffer.

```
            else              //if we are not on the last choice,
            {                      //highlight the next choice, and
                show_menu(pos + 1);
                ++pos;          //adjust pos to the next choice
            }
        }                   //Person typed a non-extended keyboard
//1///  if(pos == 0)            //character. If s/he was on first
//2///      enter_name(name);   //choice, get a new name from user
//3///  else
//4///      if(pos == 1)        //If it was on second choice,
//5///          show_name(name); //display name in variable
//6///      else
            break;             //Or else, quit all together.
    }

    turn_on_cursor();
    for(row = 0; row <= 24; ++row)//make the screen normal again.
        for(column = 0; column <= 79; ++column)
            *(farptr + row*80 + column) = 0x0700;
}
```

a. When you run this program, type in only extended keys, such as the down– and up–arrow keys, F1 key, and insert key. As long as you type in these extended keys (which all begin by sending a 0x00 to the CPU) do you stay in the loop?

b. How can you get out of the loop? Why does that work?

c. The code for the down–arrow extended key is 0x50, or 80 in decimal. Why does the menu change only when the down–arrow key is pressed and not when, say, the F1 key is pressed?

d. Initially *pos* is equal to 0. When is this variable incremented? When is it reset?

e. Can you rewrite this code so that if you press the up–arrow key, the menu changes as well? The code for the up–arrow key is a decimal 72.

Exp 15.8 Now uncomment lines //4//, //5//, and //6// from the previous experiment. Add the following function and its prototype, and run it.

```
void show_name(char x[ ])
{ int i, row, col;
  draw_window(45, 15, 60, 17, 0x2100);
```

Solution 15.12

```
for(  ; getch() == 0;  )
{
```

Drill 15.13

Once we are in the for loop, we want to see if a hex 50 is entered or a down–arrow key is pressed next on the keyboard. How would you check for that condition? Add it inside the for loop.

```
    for(i = 0; x[i] != '\0'; ++i)
        *(farptr + 16*80 + 47 + i) = C_ATTR | x[i];
    getch();
    getch();
}
```

    a. Where in the menu is the name shown?

    b. What type of character do you have to type at this position for the name to be shown? Does pressing any character work? Or do you have to type a non–extended key, or an extended key?

    c. Why does the program quit when pressing Enter at the first position in the menu?

Exp 15.9 Now uncomment all 6 lines, including //1//, //2//, and //3//, from the previous experiment. Add this function and its prototype, and run it.

```
int enter_name(char x[ ])
{
    int i, error_code = 0;
    turn_on_cursor();
    draw_window(5, 5, 30, 7, 0x2100);
    regs.h.ah = 2;
    regs.h.dl = 7;    //Column number 7
    regs.h.dh = 6;    //Row number 6
    regs.h.bh = 0;
    int86(VBIOS, &regs, &regs);//Place the cursor at this position.
    for(i = 0; i <= 9; ++i)
    {   x[i] = getche();
        if(x[i] == '\r')
            break;
        else
            if(x[i] == 0)    //If you obtained an extended keyboard character,
            {                     //flag an error and get out.
                error_code = 1;
                break;
            }
    }
    x[i] = '\0';
    turn_off_cursor();
    return(error_code);
}
```

Solution 15.13
```
for(  ; getch() == 0;  )    //Or 0x00
{
    if(getch() == 0x50)     //Or 80 in decimal
```

Drill 15.14 Will this loop end if we enter the letter 'T'?

a. Does the program work completely? That is, can you change and display the name over and over again?
b. If you press the down–arrow key while entering the name, does the enter_name() function stop accepting characters? What happens to the name if that happens? Does it change or is the new one entered?
c. Why is the cursor turned on and then off in the enter_name() function? Try not calling either of these functions from enter_name(). Does the program still work? Is it better to turn the cursor on and off, or just not bother with it? Why?

QUESTIONS

1. What is the attribute byte for the following colors?
   a. Green on light gray and blinking
   b. Yellow on brown and nonblinking
   c. Light red on green and nonblinking
2. What characters are entered by the user on the keyboard if the following bytes are sent: 0x00 0x50 0x50 0x33 0x63 0x00 0x67? How many are regular ASCII characters and how many are extended keyboard characters?
3. What characters are sent to the display if the following bytes are sent: 0x65 0x4E 0xB3 0x6F 0xBA 0xDB?
4. What is the range of RAM addresses for all the characters on the second line of the screen?
5. What is 0xAD85 | 0xE7CA? This is a bit–wise OR operation.

PROGRAMS

1. Draw two vertical bars up and down the entire screen length at the extreme edges.
2. Rewrite the draw_window() so that a shadow is shown under the drawn window and to its right, thus giving a three–dimensional effect.
3. Change the cursor size by varying the registers .ch and .cl from 0 to 13 in decimal.
4. Write a function called draw_line() that will receive an integer from 0 to 24 and draw a horizontal line at that position on the screen.

Solution 15.14 Yes, the loop continues only as long as extended characters are entered. Typing a 'T' is entering an ASCII character.

Text-Based Graphics on the PC

Unit 16

Abstraction

Object–Oriented Programming – A New Way of Thinking

OOP (object–oriented programming) concepts are introduced in this unit. The next two units explore the analysis and design of problems using OO (object oriented) methods. After that, we will go into the features of the C++ language and incorporate OO techniques.

The hardest part about learning C++ is not learning the language itself but learning how to formulate OO solutions to given problems. There is C++ code in use today that was not properly designed. C programmers were quickly taught C++ features and wrote C++ programs without learning OO concepts. Such programmers think C++ is just a cosmetic extension of C.

Actually it's not their fault. There are many books that are good for C++ but don't emphasize OO concepts. Likewise, there are many books that are good for learning OO concepts but don't show how those concepts are implemented in C++. For the remainder of this text, I will stress OO concepts while showing how those concepts can be developed into C++ code. After all, isn't OO programming the fundamental reason why C++ was created in the first place?

Abstraction is a process that summarizes the essential properties of an object. This process allows us to classify objects by simplifying our view of them.

Drill 16.1 Define an abstraction of a speedometer for a car. That is, what is it about a speedometer that makes it a speedometer?

A good OO design is tantamount to writing a good C++ program. From now on, we will have to change the way we approach programming problems. We will have to change our way of thinking and this will become apparent in how we write programs.

Then Why Learn C in the First Place?

Alan Kay, an early developer of OOP, found that his OOP language, called Smalltalk, was more difficult for programmers than for children to learn. This is because OO concepts are actually more natural to adapt than traditional programming concepts. And children aren't "spoiled" by traditional programming methods. This may lead us to think that beginning students in programming should learn OO concepts from the start rather than have them retrained in OOP.

Many authors do take this approach and do not teach C at all. However, they must present C constructs, C++ constructs, basic programming concepts, and OO concepts (if any) all together. This becomes overwhelming to the beginner, so the first thing to be omitted are OO concepts.

By introducing only the C language first, we were able to study basic programming concepts, such as loops, arrays, and functions. Having covered that, now we can advance to OO concepts and C++ coding and concentrate on that. Conquering one part at a time is easier than attacking all parts simultaneously.

For example, one of the basic building blocks of C++ is the class keyword. To write and use a class, one must know structures, functions, and other C constructs. By now we know how to work with functions and structures, and hence we are ready to combine those features into a class. Furthermore, since C++ evolved from C, it just becomes natural to learn C++ after learning C. The name of the language itself hints that C++ is like enhancing the features of C, just as i++ means to increment *i* by 1.

In any case, every statement you learned in C, you can use in C++. You will be able to do the same coding you did for the if statement and the for loop. Logic won't change. Arrays, functions, pointers, and structures will all be necessary in C++. The only difference will be how they are put together in programs.

The Development of OOP

OOP principles are not new. Plato and the Greek philosophers said that the world could be viewed as objects. In the 1600s, René Descartes, who laid the foundations for calculus, stated that humans view the world in an OO way.

However it was in 1966, only 20 years after the unveiling of the ENIAC, that Ole-Johan Dahl and Kristen Nygaard of the Norwegian Computing Center created the first OOP language,

---

Solution 16.1 My abstraction (which may be different than what you came up with) is this: A speedometer gives the viewer the speed at which the vehicle is moving.

Notice that this definition doesn't specify that the speed be given in mph, that it should be given in arabic numbers, or that the display should be digital. All these things are not the essential properties that make a speedometer a speedometer.

Drill 16.2 What is the abstraction for the mouse of a computer system?

called Simula. This language was primarily used to run computer simulations, such as how a disease may spread in a region, or how the pattern of airplane traffic may congest an area, and so on.

In 1972, Alan Kay at the Xerox Palo Alto Research Center created the Smalltalk language. This language was an effort to make computers easy to use for the masses in general and not just for computer professionals. His work marked the birth of the various windowing interfaces that we all now take for granted.

Bjarne Stroustrup of AT&T Labs felt that the C language had many advantages. Instead of creating a whole new language, in the early 1980s he defined the C++ language as a superset to C. Today out of the many OOP languages that exist, C++ is one of the more widely used.

Benefits of the OO Approach

Advances in computer hardware have always been very rapid compared to the advances in software designs. In searching for a method that will accelerate software development, many ideas were formulated. Some of them were the introduction of subroutines or functions, modular programming, top–down structured programming, and CASE (computer–aided software engineering) tools. Each one had its shortcomings and didn't provide a solution that was fully acceptable for large programs.

The underlying reason that there are many advantages of OOP is that *OOP models the solution very closely to the real–world problem.* In conventional software design, the solution does not reflect the real-world system. Changes appearing in the real-world system must be translated into the solution, and the correct method for translation may not be apparent. In the OO philosophy, the solution space reflects the problem space, and the parts of the solution correspond to the parts of the problem. Because this fundamental principle is central to OOP methods, we derive many benefits from OOP.

When creating a new computer, many chips can be reused. Certain circuits and boards can be reused. When building a chair, screws from a hardware store can be bought ready–made without having to make your own. Computer chips and circuit boards also come ready to use. Why can't we have the same thing in software components? OO methods provide such ready to use parts.

Programming code can be easily *reused* from previously written programs and libraries. Since other programmers have already done the detailed coding, those pieces only need to be "reassembled" or interconnected with programming code. Although the initial writing of the libraries is time consuming, they can be reused later or sold by software houses.

Maintenance of programs is easier with OOP. Traditionally, about 75% of the programming effort is given to maintenance of existing software, leaving less time for new development. If one item had to be changed, it would force changes in other parts of the program. In making changes to an application, there were side effects. This is not the case with OOP. Maintenance is localized to one segment of the code and the effect is easier to predict.

Solution 16.2 By changing the position of this device, we can change the position of the cursor on the computer display. By clicking the button on it, we can select a place or an area of the screen.

Drill 16.3 C++ allows us to abstract essential characteristics of objects of a common type. For the sake of brevity, only a few characteristics are abstracted in the following example:

```
class Part_item
{
   private:
      int qty;
      float cost;
};
```

The keyword, private:, means that qty and cost are members that are not allowed to be accessed by main(). Which items in a speedometer or a computer mouse cannot be accessed by users?

Abstraction

The quality of the OO programs is much higher. Although the cost of coding the actual lines may be higher, the overall cost of the entire development process is much lower. Projects that would never be done on time and within budget can now be done in half the time or better. OOP saves money!

If you are working on a year–long project, the specifications for that project will keep changing during the course of the year. They will keep changing even after the project is complete. No one makes up their mind at the beginning and sticks with it. With OO design, where the solution space models the problem space, changes in the problem specifications can be mapped easily and adjusted in the solution. With procedural style programming, one may have to scrap all the design that was done up to that point and start again. No wonder we once spent 75% of our time maintaining old code. There was hardly any time left to develop new applications.

These are just some of the key benefits of OOP. These advantages can be realized only after we change our view to OOP methods. Managers can no longer afford to demand traditional viewpoints.

Abstraction

In traditional languages, software developers are used to viewing data in terms of its state, that is, what it is. In an OO view, data is viewed not only in terms of what it is but also in terms of what it does.

For instance, a bank account is made up of a name, an account number, a balance, and other such items. Traditionally, programs can do operations on that account, such as draw interest or make deposits. However, those operations or functions are foreign to that bank account. The operations don't define a bank account. Any function can do operations on the bank account, and who does what on the bank account is not controlled. It is open to any function to change data anywhere and any way it pleases.

However, in the OO world, a bank account is defined not only by the data items it holds but also by what operations may be performed on those data items. In other words, a bank account is not only what *it is*, but also what *it can do*. It can have interest added to it, it can have a deposit added to it, and so on.

Data abstraction is a process that helps us understand what an item is and what it can do. Data abstraction is capturing or stating the essential characteristics of something in the real world. If you receive a dime, it doesn't matter where it was minted or how old it is. These are not its essential characteristics. All that matters is that it has a value of ten cents. Where you got the dime or whether it is worn or not is not important for us to determine that it is, indeed, a dime.

However, for a coin collector, this abstraction of a dime may not suffice. His view of dimes and our view of them may be different. Our abstractions of a dime may be different, but defined

---

Solution 16.3 The gears and the inside parts of a speedometer or a mouse cannot be accessed.

Drill 16.4

```
class Part_item
{
   private:
      int qty;
      float cost;
   public:
      void sold (int);
      void arrived (int);
};
```

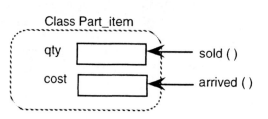
Class Part_item

qty — sold ( )

cost — arrived ( )

a. What members of Part_item do you think are now accessible from main()?

b. What parts of a speedometer or a mouse are we allowed to access?

Abstraction

appropriately for our needs. Each must carefully define her or his abstractions before starting out on the development process.

Properties by which we label the abstraction apply to all instances of the abstraction. That is, all dimes are worth ten cents, or all bank accounts have a primary name, and so on.

A bank account has a primary name associated with it. What color is this account holder's car or what she watches on television is not important to the bank account abstraction.

An abstraction simplifies our view of things. It stresses the characteristics and qualities that are common and essential, and minimizes the characteristics that don't really matter. Data abstractions separate an item into its parts and qualities so that they can be considered by themselves. This is necessary to allow classification.

Consider a common abstraction such as a faucet. What are the essential qualities of a faucet that make it a faucet? I can initially define this abstraction like this: *You turn it on and water comes from it; you turn it off and the water stops.* See Figure 16.1.

If we use this faucet abstraction and a chemical comes out instead, then according to this abstraction, it is not a faucet. If water comes, it doesn't matter if it is hot or cold according to this abstraction. It doesn't matter if the water is drinkable or not. It is still a faucet. If I go to the hardware store and find out that the faucet they are selling doesn't have water coming out of it, then I must change my perspective of what a faucet is, i. e., to conclude that if it is connected to a water source.

However, if water doesn't come or if it doesn't stop when it is supposed to, then it is not a faucet. If we want our abstraction to include these cases, then we must change our abstraction or our view to include properly working faucets. It is necessary to define our abstraction correctly before we look at its instances and study its implementation.

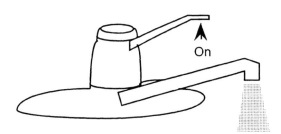

Figure 16.1 The faucet abstraction.

Solution 16.4

a. The members of Part_item listed under public are allowed to be accessed by main(). Hence, they are called public.
b. Similarly, the only thing that we are allowed to do with a speedometer is to look at it, and the only operations we are allowed to do on a mouse are to maneuver or click it. If we start doing anything else, like taking them apart, we may break them.

Drill 16.5 The inside mechanical parts of a speedometer or a mouse are hidden from us. They are also said to be encapsulated. What members of Part_item are hidden or encapsulated?

Instance

A particular item that satisfies all the characteristics defining a specific abstraction is an instance of that abstraction. For example, that dime that my uncle gave me last year to buy some gum is an instance of the dime abstraction. Or the rusty old 1966 Plymouth sitting in my driveway is an instance of the car abstraction.

Interface

The operations that you can perform with an instance of an abstraction are called the interface. Only those operations can be applied to the instance. Buying candy with a dime or changing the oil in the Plymouth are examples of interfaces. With the faucet, I can either turn it on or I can turn it off. These two operations define the interface to the faucet. I am not allowed to do any other operations than what is allowed by the defined interface. You can see this in Figure 16.2.

Encapsulation

For the interface to an abstraction to be simple, the implementation must be hidden from the user. Hiding the implementation of an abstraction is called encapsulation. When I want water from the faucet, I should simply have to turn it on and not have to also jiggle some part in a special way. How the water comes on and how it goes off is an issue I don't want to worry about because there are other, more important issues that I may have to be concerned about, such as filling a bucket of water to put out a fire. However, for me to attend to those important issues, I need that faucet to work properly. I need a simple interface, that is, an implementation that is hidden from me.

In programming, we need a method that will allow us to hide the implementation. In Figure 16.3, the function add_interest() is visible to main(). One part of the program may use one function

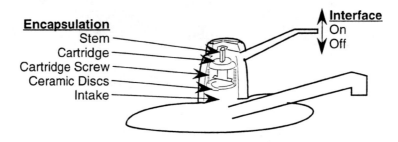

Figure 16.2 Hiding the implementation.

Solution 16.5 The members under private: are hidden from main(). They are encapsulated. Specifically, these members are qty and cost.

Drill 16.6 The items or members accessible to anyone are called the interface.
a. Which section of a class defines the interface?
b. What members of Part_item form the interface for main()?
c. What forms the interface for a speedometer?
d. What forms the interface for a mouse?

to add the interest while another part may use another function to do it, or maybe the program will do it itself without calling a function at all. In such a situation, we have too many programming parts for determining how the interest will be added. If we could just make the function a part of the structure definition and not allow anyone to fiddle with the data items of Account, then we would have full control of how the data items would be changed. All we would need is to provide an interface that is available to all programming parts and, using that interface, do the implementation in one predictable way. It's better if everyone uses the lever to turn on the water rather than allowing some to take the faucet apart to get the water. Being able to hide the implementation is a big advantage!

As another example of the power of encapsulation, consider the abstraction of the data type of int.

```
int i;
```

To instantiate means to make an instance. Here, *i* becomes the instantiation of the abstraction of int. It has an interface and its implementation is hidden from us by its encapsulation. Being able to multiply *i* by 2 is part of the interface. We cannot, however, concatenate *i* with a string; we can only apply arithmetic operators on it. The set of allowable arithmetic operations is thus the interface provided to us. How the actual operations are done is hidden from us. We don't know how integers are manipulated bit–wise when arithmetic operations are done. These procedures are encapsulated. Encapsulation is an advantage because then we can concentrate our efforts on bigger things.

```
struct Account
{
        char name[20];
        float bal;
};
void main (void)
{
        struct Account person1;
        :
        add_interest(person1);
}
```

We need to hide this function here.

Figure 16.3 Searching for an encapsulation technique.

Solution 16.6
a. The public section
b. sold() and arrived() form the actual interface provided to main() or any other function in the program.
c. Looking at it is the only interface that a speedometer provides us.
d. Moving the mouse or clicking it is the interface that a mouse provides to the user.

Drill 16.7 Now that we have determined what should be hidden and what should be the interface, let us implement a method for each of our interfaces. If the speedometer on a car has an interface but doesn't provide a method to implement it, what would be the effect?

The Castle Analogy

Let us go back to the discussion of the advantages of OOP. See the data that exists in procedural–style programming in Figure 16.4(a). It is freely available for any programming module to access or manipulate. Each program must know the characteristics of the data, what its valid values are, how it is updated, how changes in it affect other data, and so forth. Each of these programs must maintain a vast amount of information so that the data isn't corrupted or introduces adverse effects.

Using a castle to represent a hedge of protection, Figure 16.4(b) depicts how data is managed in OO technology. No other program can access data directly and "blow it up" as could be done in Figure 16.4(a). If anyone needs to access the data or do anything with it, she or he must first enter through the "gate." The gate represents the interface provided for others. Since there is only one way to enter into the data, the interface becomes simple. Only through this allowable interface do others have access to the data. Hence, those programs which use the interface don't have to maintain information about the characteristics of the data. All such details are handled by the implementation of the interface and are not duplicated by other programs using the interface. Protecting data, defining it not only by its state but by its behavior as well, is a great advantage. This will become more and more apparent in later chapters.

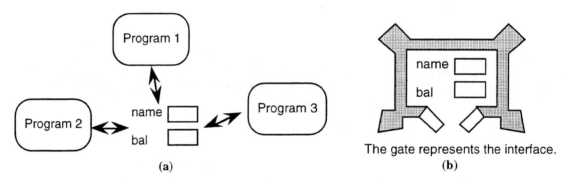

Figure 16.4 (a) In procedural–style programming, many programs can access data directly, each in its own way. (b) In object–oriented programming, data is sacred. Other programs can access data, but only through a well–defined interface.

Solution 16.7 If there were no method to implement the interface for a speedometer, then some of the mechanical parts that make up the speedometer might be broken, or the cable to the wheel used to detect the speed might be broken. In other words, there is something wrong with the speedometer, and if we look at it while we are driving, we wouldn't be provided with an accurate measure of the speed at which we are driving.

Drill 16.8 Similarly, if the mouse feels as if it is working but it doesn't have all of its methods implemented, what would be the effect?

Classes

The benefits of simple data–type abstractions, such as `int`, can be gained on a much wider scale in C++ when we define our own data types. We have already seen how that is done using structures. However, so far we have not used structures where the implementation was hidden from the user and only an interface was provided. In C++, this is accomplished by using the keyword, class instead of struct.

```
class Account
{
   private:                            //This is the implementation section.
      char name[20];
      float bal;
   public:                             //This is the interface section.
      void show();
      void setup(char nm[ ], float b);
};
```

Creating a class, just like creating a structure, does not create an instance. Actually, there is not much difference between a struct and a class. Basically, they differ only in how they are typically used. The way we have used structures so far is much different from how we will use classes. With classes, we will separate the interface from the items that are hidden.

This is done by separating a class into two sections, called private and public. The items listed under each are called *members*. Our example is typical because the data members are private and the member functions are public. Also see Figure 16.5.

The private members are not freely accessible to just any function. Only the functions in the public sections are allowed to access them. However, the public members can be accessed from

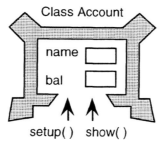

Figure 16.5 For this class, setup( ) and show() are the interfaces, while "name" and "bal" are the encapsulation.

Solution 16.8 If all of the methods weren't implemented, then moving the mouse around may not move the cursor on the screen, or clicking it may not select any spot on the screen. You would deem the mouse broken.

Drill 16.9 Which members in class Part_item need to have their methods implemented in our program?

any part of the program. The public section thus provides the interface to the class, while private members are the hidden implementation.

Objects

To create an instance of the type int, this statement is used:

```
int i;
```

Here, the data type is `int` and the variable is *i*. An instance of a data type is called a variable. Now let us apply the same concepts to classes.

To instantiate a class, that is, to create one instance of it, either of the following two statements can be used:

```
class Account acc;    // or
```

```
Account acc;
```

Here, *acc* is not called a variable but an object. Simply put, an instantiation of a class is called an *object*.

Member Functions

However, the definition of our class is not complete until we define its member functions. The complete program is listed in Example 16.1, which includes the definitions of show() and setup(). In a pure object oriented language, such as Simula or Smalltalk, the definitions of the member functions are all included in the definition of the class to which they belong. C++ is actually a hybrid language; it is a combination of C and OOP, so the definition of member functions seems to be separated from the definition of the class. Hence, I've included the two lines of comments to show that the complete definition of the class includes the definition of member functions.

Vendors of class libraries prefer the visual separation of the class and the function member definitions. This way, they can give you the source code for the class only and give the object code or the compiled code for the member functions.

Let us now take a tour of the program. main() defines an object of class Account called *acc*. Then main() sends two *messages* to the *acc* object. First, it sends the setup() message with "Buggsy" and 30.0 as parameters. Then it sends the show() message with no parameters. When the setup() message is received by the *acc* object, it executes its setup() *method*. In the setup() method, acc.name is assigned "Buggsy" and acc.bal is assigned 30.0. When main() sends the show() message to *acc*, the show() method of the *acc* object is executed and the output is printed. main() can be thought to be the *client* and *acc* to be the *server* when this message is passed.

Notice that in OOP terminology a "call to a function" is described as "passing a message," and a "function definition" is said to be a "method." See Figure 16.6. In plain C, a variable may be

Solution 16.9
```
void sold (int);
void arrived (int);
```

Drill 16.10 Here is how the header line for arrived() would be written:

```
void Part_item::arrived(int i)
```

The double colon means that arrived() "belongs to" or is a member of class Part_item. There is no semicolon at the end. What would be the header line for sold()?

passed as a parameter to a function call. However, in C++, when a message is sent, it has to be sent to a specific object that has the appropriate method defined. Messages can't be sent to a class, only to an object. Messages tell an object *what* to do but not how to do it. Methods specify *how* something is to be done.

```
//Example 16.1
#include <string.h>
#include <stdio.h>
/////////////////////////////////// Starting to define class Account
class Account
{
   private:
      char name[20];
      float bal;
   public:
      void show (void);                   // Prototype for show()
      void setup(char nm[ ], float b);    // Prototype for setup()
};

void Account::show (void)                 // Defining the show() method
{
   printf("%s has $%.2f in the account.\n", name, bal);
}

void Account::setup(char nm[ ], float b) // Defining the setup() method
{
   strcpy(name, nm);
   bal = b;
}
/////////////////////////////////// End of definition of class Account

void main (void)        // main() is permitted to access
{                       // Account is private members only
   Account acc;         // through setup() and show().
   acc.setup("Buggsy", 30.0);       // Sending the setup() message to acc
   acc.show();                      // Sending the show() message to acc
}
----- output -----
Buggsy has $30.00 in the account.
```

Solution 16.10

```
void Part_item::sold(int i)
```

Drill 16.11

Since sold() and arrived() are members of class Part_item, these functions can access the private members of class Part_item.
a. Which function would not be allowed to access the private members?
b. Which members would that function be allowed to access?

Abstraction   293

```
           :
      void Account::show()
      {                              }  Method definition.
            printf( . . . );
      }

      main()
      {
            :
            acc.show();     ◄———————  main() is passing a
                                      message to acc.
```

Figure 16.6 The difference between a message and a method.

Methods (or member functions, as they are called in C++) are declared in the class as shown here:

```
void show();
```

This declaration serves as a prototype. Member functions are defined using a fully qualified function name:

```
void Account::show()
```

The : : symbol is called the scoping operator. It means that the show() method belongs to the Account class. This allows the show() method to access directly the private members of that class.

Once we are executing the lines in the show() method, we can access the name and bal data members of the *acc* object. This is possible because main() has made available the address of *acc* or &acc to show() when it was invoked.

Inheritance and Polymorphism

Two more concepts in OOP are so important that they should be at least mentioned before we end the unit. We have two units about them. The actual implementation of these ideas will be covered later in the text, but I would like you to become accustomed to them. They are called inheritance and polymorphism.

Inheritance is defining a new *subclass* out of an existing class. The class from which the new subclass is *derived* is called a *superclass*, or a *base class*. A subclass is a special case of a

---

Solution 16.11
a. main() would not be allowed to access the private members qty and cost. Only sold() and arrived() are allowed to access these private members.
b. main() would be allowed, however, to access the public members, sold() and arrived().

Drill 16.12 Here is the method for arrived(). Notice that it can directly access qty and cost because it is a member of class Part_item.

```
void Part_item::arrived(int i)
{  qty = qty + i;
   printf("We have to pay the vendor %.2f for these parts.\n", cost * i);
}
```

Now write the method for sold(). This method should decrease the qty by the amount that was sold and display the minimum amount of money that we should have received, that is, if the price of the part were the same as cost.

superclass. For example, two new classes called MortgageAccount and CheckingAccount can be created and have all the features of the class Account. Account is called a superclass and the new derived classes are called subclasses. Deriving subclasses from a superclass is called *inheritance*. The inherited classes can then add new features to themselves or redefine existing ones.

Polymorphism means the implemention of different behaviors for a given interface. The different implementations are hidden behind one interface. Using the inherited classes example above, we can send the same message to instances of either subclass. Each subclass will interpret the message in its own way. A "deduct amount" message may be implemented differently by a receiving object of class MortageAccount than by a receiving object of class CheckingAccount.

The + operator is polymorphic for all variables that are a kind of number. We can execute i = i + 3; or x = 7.1 + 8.63; without regard to the operands' data types. Integers and floats are added using the same + symbol without regard to whether they are integers or floats.

However, our printf() function in the stdio.h header file definitely doesn't provide polymorphism. When we want to print an integer, we must provide the format specifier %d. When we want to print a float, we must specify %f, and so on. We have to be aware of the data items' types and provide the correct specifiers when calling the printf() function.

Fortunately, C++ provides us with a mechanism to scan and print items polymorphically. We use a set of classes made for stream–oriented I/O (input/output). Example 16.2 shows how I/O can be done on strings, integers, and floats without regard to their data types. In fact, we can use the same methods to scan and print data members of objects. All we will need to specify are the object names. Notice the introduction of the iostream.h header file.

```
//EXAMPLE 16.2
#include <iostream.h>
int main (void)
{
    int i;
    float x;
    cout << "Enter an integer and a float: ";
    cin >> i >> x;
    cout << "Their product is: " << x * i << "\n";
    return 0;
}
----- output -----
Enter an integer and a float: 3 10.5
Their product is: 31.5
```

Solution 16.12
Notice that there is no semicolon at the end of the header line or the method.

```
void Part_item::sold(int i)
{
    qty = qty - i;
    printf("We better have received at least %.2f for these parts.\n",
            cost * i);
}
```

Drill 16.13
In the C language, what did we call a method?

Abstraction   295

cout and cin are actually objects of a set of classes pertaining to I/O streams. The << and >> operators are used to shift bits of a memory location to the left or right. However, since they are used with cout and cin, they don't mean to shift bits but to print or scan the variables. Again, << and >> are examples of polymorphism just as the plus and minus signs are. Stream I/O is a complex subject on which entire books have been written. However, since using them is a lot easier than using standard I/O, we will switch to stream I/O for the rest of the book.

A Summary

Let us review many of the object–oriented concepts studied in this unit by exploring a real–world example. Key words are italicized.

Suppose that I take my rusty old car to Joe's Auto Body shop and tell him, "Please paint my car." I go to the shop because I have an *abstraction* of auto body shops. I know that they repair and paint cars, but they don't necessarily have equipment where you can work out and build up your body. Furthermore, I don't go to Joe's because Joe has a dog named Boop. The essential properties about the shop include the fact that they can paint cars. That's why I go to Joe's. This classifies the shop as an auto body shop. I have an abstraction of auto body shops in general and this shop is an *instance* of that abstraction. We could stretch the point and say that Joe's Auto Body is an object of the class called auto body shops.

When I tell him to paint my car, I am sending that *message* to Joe, the owner of the auto body shop. Joe's Auto Body is the *receiver* of my message. The receiver of a message must be an object and not an entire class. I cannot send the message to auto body shops in general, only to a specific one. Neither can I go to an open field at night and send the message to no one. I need to send the message to an object. If I send the message to the wrong object, I may get an error message. For instance, if I send the message, "Please paint my car," to my boss, she may not know what to do with the message, except maybe to fire me.

However, I could give the same message to my daughter, Sarah, and she could send a similar message to Joe or to another object of that same class. The same message is interpreted in two ways. The method that Sarah uses and the method that Joe uses to interpret the message will be different. This is an example of *polymorphism*.

When Joe interprets the message, he will do it in a unique way and invoke a *method* that will suit him. The method may be that he does the job himself or else it may mean that he sends another message to Rob, his assistant, to do the job. What method he *implements* is *hidden* from me. It is *encapsulated*, so that the only *interface* I have to worry about is sending an appropriate message. It is his *responsibility* to use the appropriate method.

The class called shopkeepers has customers. Shopkeepers provide services or products and receive money in return. This information I already know from my experience and I can assume the

---

Solution 16.13 In C, we called it a function. Here, we are calling it a method because it is a special kind of function, a function that belongs to a class.

Drill 16.14 We want to create a real speedometer or a mouse that meets the specifications we described in the abstraction. To create an object that meets the characteristics of a certain class is called instantiation. Then we will have an actual object that will serve as a working example of that class.
a. In a simpler sense, how would you instantiate a data type of `char`?
b. What is an instantiation of a data type called?

same for the class called auto mechanics. There is more information that I can add to the *subclass* of auto mechanics, including the fact that they work with cars. As we become more specialized and consider the class called auto body mechanics, we can add more information to our knowledge base. This is *inheritance*. The class auto body mechanics has inherited the characteristics of the class auto mechanics, and this class has inherited characteristics from the class called shopkeepers.

From this trivial example, you can see that the concepts in OOP relate very closely to our everyday experiences. Although the terminology may be new, the principles by which OOP operates are the same principles we experience in our daily lives. The only challenge now is to see how these ideas can become an integral part of our software design.

EXPERIMENTS

Exp 16.1 Time for a little review! Run this program once by entering "Tired Timmy" when prompted, and once with another name.

```
#include <stdio.h>
#include <string.h>
struct Dept
{
    char manager[15];
    int employees;
};
void main ()
{
    struct Dept toys, mens;
    strcpy(toys.manager, "Tired Timmy");
    toys.employees = 4;
    printf("Manager of toys = %s\n",
            toys.manager);
    printf("Number of employees = %d\n", toys.employees);
    printf("Who is the manager of the mens department? : ");
    gets(mens.manager);
    if(strcmp(mens.manager, toys.manager) == 0)
        printf("Oh, that's the same manager for the toys dept!\n");
}
```

Solution 16.14
a. The variable *a* is an instantiation of a data type `char`.

```
char a;
```

b. The instantiation of a data type is called a variable. C++ will eventually blur the difference between standard data types and classes that we define. Whatever you can do with data types you will be able to do with your own classes.

Drill 16.15 Do you remember how to create a structured variable of a structure that is programmer defined? If so, try creating an instantiation of class Part_item that would be coded in main(). Name the instance *muffler*.

a. What is the name of the structure?
b. What are names of the structured variables?
c. How many members does each structured variable have?
d. Which member of which variable wasn't set to any value? Write a scanf() statement to get its value.
e. Can the if condition be written this way?

```
if(mens.manager == toys.manager)
```

f. What statement must be added at the end of main() if the void before main() is removed? Or can the void be removed without altering any other part of the program?

Exp 16.2 Now let us introduce functions to our simple program. Please don't enter the Stmt numbers. I placed them only for reference.

```
#include <stdio.h>
#include <string.h>
struct Dept set_up_dept (void);    // Stmt 1
void display_dept (struct Dept x,
                   char department[ ]);
struct Dept                                             // Stmt 2
{
   char manager[15];
   int employees;
};

struct Dept set_up_dept (void)                          // Stmt 3
{
   struct Dept x;                                       // Stmt 4
   strcpy(x.manager, "Tired Timmy");
   x.employees = 4;
   return x;                                            // Stmt 5
}
```

Solution 16.15

```
class Part_item muffler;
```

Drill 16.16 The keyword class is not necessary and we will omit it in the future. *muffler* is called an object of class Part_item. Now create another object called *gasket* of class Part_item.

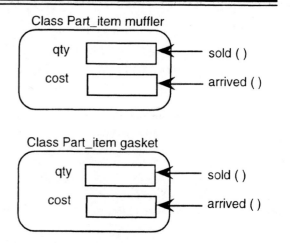

Class Part_item muffler

qty — sold ( )
cost — arrived ( )

Class Part_item gasket

qty — sold ( )
cost — arrived ( )

```
void display_dept (struct Dept x, char department[ ])     // Stmt 6
{
   printf("Manager of %s = %s\n", department, x.manager);
   printf("Number of employees = %d\n", x.employees);
}

int main ()
{
   struct Dept toys;                                      // Stmt 7
   toys = set_up_dept ();                                 // Stmt 8
   display_dept(toys, "toys");                            // Stmt 9
   return 0;
}
```

    a. In which statement is the structure defined?

    b. Is the structure definition local or global? Why is it defined this way?

    c. Is *toys* defined locally or globally?

    d. There are two new functions here. What are their names? Which statement number gives one of their prototypes? (A prototype is also called a function declaration.)

    e. At which statement does the definition of set_up_dept() start?

    f. What data type does set_up_dept() receive as an argument and what data type does it return?

    g. When main() calls set_up_dept() in Statement 8, why is it written as shown? For instance, why isn't Statement 8 written as follows?

```
set_up_dept(toys);
```

    h. Does display_dept() receive any arguments? If so, what are they called in that function?

    i. Does display_dept() return any value to the calling function? If so, what is its data type?

    j. main() calls display_dept() in Statement 9. Can it be called this way?

```
display_dept("toys", toys);
```

    Why or why not?

    k. Describe at least two things wrong with Statement 9 if it were written this way:

```
toys = display_dept( );
```

Solution 16.16

```
Part_item gasket;
```

Drill 16.17 Our eyes must look to get a reading from the speedometer or our hand must operate the mouse for it to fulfill its functions. main() must send a message to an object for it to perform its method. Here is how a message stating that 5 items have arrived can be sent to *muffler*.

```
muffler.arrived(5);
```

Completely rewrite the definition for Part_item and the method called initialize(). This method will receive an integer (*i*) and a float (*x*). It will assign *i* to qty and *x* to cost.

Exp 16.3 Replace struct with class and add the keyword, public. Notice that we have removed all functions for now.

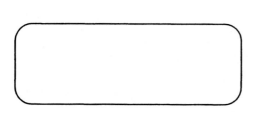

```
#include <stdio.h>
#include <string.h>
class Dept          // Stmt 1
{
    public:          // Stmt 2
        int employees;
};

void main ()
{
    class Dept toys;    //Stmt 3
    toys.employees = 4 ;
    printf("%d", toys.employees);
}
```

a. In Statement 3, will the program work without the keyword class?
b. Except for the keyword, public, is there any difference between a class and a struct that you can tell from this experiment?
c. What happens if you remove the keyword public? What error message do you get?

Exp 16.4 If we don't use the keyword public, the members of the class become private by default. Instead of relying on default settings, let us specifically use the word private. This means that no one, other than the class members, may use the private members.

```
#include <stdio.h>
#include <string.h>
class Dept                      // Stmt 1
{
    private:                     // Stmt 2
        int employees;
    public:                      // Stmt 3
        void set_up();           // Stmt 4
        char manager[15];
};                               // Stmt 5
```

Solution 16.17

```
class Part_item
{
    private:
        int qty;
        float cost;
    public:
        void initialize(int, float);
        void sold (int);
        void arrived (int);
};
```

```
void Part_item::initialize(int i, float x)
{
    qty = i;
    cost = x;
}
```

Drill 16.18 Now write the entire main() function that will initialize muffler to 10 items with a cost of $2.00 each. Also have each of 3 gaskets with a price of $.40 initialized. Then ask the user using printf()s and scanf()s what item was sold and how many. Assume that there are no typing mistakes and the part was either a muffler or a gasket. Also assume that the number of parts sold was less than the number of parts on hand.

Abstraction

```
void Dept::set_up()                                    // Stmt 6
{
   employees = 4;                                      // Stmt 7
}

void main ()
{
   Dept toys;                                          // Stmt 8
   toys.set_up();
// toys.employees = 6;                                 // Stmt 9
// strcpy(toys.manager, "Tired Timmy");   // Stmt 10
// printf("%d", toys.employees);                       // Stmt 11
}
```

a. The class Dept has private members and public members. Which members are private; that is, which ones can't be accessed from, say, main()? Which members are public; that is, which ones can be accessed from main()?
b. Which members of class Dept are data members and which members are functions? Notice that we never defined functions in structures before, although that is allowed.
c. Which statement provides the prototype or the declaration for the set_up() function?
d. At which statement does the definition of set_up() begin?
e. What symbol at that statement means "belongs to"? That is, what shows that set_up() belongs to class Dept after Statement 5?
f. Is the semicolon needed in Statement 5?
g. Uncomment Statement 9. Does it run? Why or why not? Restore the comment.
h. Why does Statement 7 work in set_up()?
i. Why isn't *toys* needed in Statement 7 but in Statement 10 it is?
j. Uncomment Statement 10 and run the program. Why does or doesn't it work? Restore the comment.
k. Uncomment Statement 11 and run the program. Why does or doesn't it work?

Solution 16.18
```
void main (void)
{  char item[15]; int q;
   Part_item muffler, gasket;
   muffler.initialize(10, 2.00);
   gasket.initialize(3, 0.40);
   printf("What item was sold?");
   printf(" and how many");
   scanf("%s %d", item, &q);
   if(strcmp(item, "muffler") == 0)
      muffler.sold(q);
   else
      gasket.sold(q);
}
```

Drill 16.19
One of the most noticeable advantages of C++ is that reading and writing of items are easier than using the printf() and scanf() functions. With these functions we must give the format specifiers, such as %s or %.2f. In C++, we can use I/O streams, which prevents us from having to worry about format specifiers. This statement will print on the screen what is indicated very simply:

```
cout << "It is now:" << 8.50 << "\n";
```

How do you think you could print the character 'x' followed by the value of *x*, a variable?

Exp 16.5 Here is an experiment that puts all these concepts together.

```
#include <stdio.h>
#include <string.h>
class Dept        // Stmt 1
{
   private:
       char manager[15];
       int employees;
   public:
       void set_up(char [ ], int);
       void display();
};

void Dept::set_up(char mgr[ ], int num)
{
   strcpy(manager, mgr);
   employees = num;
}

void Dept::display()
{
   printf("Manager is %s \n", manager);
   printf("Number of employees is %d \n", employees);
}

void main ()
{
   class Dept toys, mens;
   toys.set_up("Tired Timmy", 4);
   mens.set_up("Dan DeMan", 6);
   toys.display();
   mens.display();
}
```

In the diagram on the next page, Dept is a class that summarizes the important characteristics of *toys* and *mens*. *toys* and *mens* are called objects that are of class Dept. Write the data values in the diagram as they are set by the program.

Solution 16.19

```
cout << "x= " << x << "\n";
```

Drill 16.20

In Solution 16.19, do you need to know whether *x* is a float, an integer, or a character? Do you need to know what the data type of *x* is?

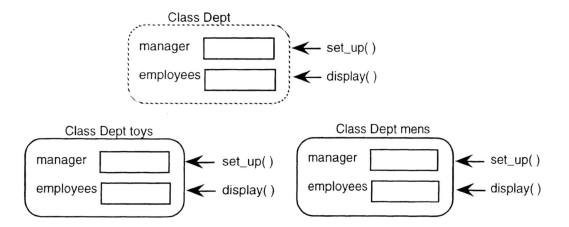

a. How many members does *toys* have? Which are data members and which are member functions? Is this true also for *mens*?
b. What members are public and which are private?
c. Which members can main() access directly?
d. Which members can display() access directly?
e. Are the private members hidden from main()? Are they hidden from display()?
f. Does removing the word private: in the class definition allow the program to compile?
g. Inside main(), in the first line, is the word class necessary?
h. When calling any of the functions from main(), why aren't the functions assigned to any items, as was done in Statement 8 of Experiment 16.2?
i. First restore the program as it is shown here. Then in Statement 1, replace the keyword class with struct. After running the program, do you notice any difference?
j. Change Statement 1 back to class and remove the keyword private. Does the program run fine or does it burp? Now replace class with struct in Statement 1 and remove the keyword private. How does the program run?
k. From the above two questions, can you conclude that classes and structures are almost the same? If so, can you determine the slight difference between the two?

Solution 16.20

No. The compiler knows the data type of *x* and will print it accordingly.

Drill 16.21

You can also scan in variables without using the scanf() function.
a. Instead of cout, what object do you think will do the reading?
b. Instead of <<, what operator do you think will be used?
c. Can you read in a float called *x* and an integer called *i* using this new C++ feature?

Exp 16.6 C++ also provides an easier way to print and scan data without regard to its data type. The compiler has to worry about that, not us. Modify Experiment 16.5. Replace the stdio.h with iostream.h. And use this definition of display():

```
void Dept::display()
{
   cout << "Manager is " << manager << " \n" << endl;        // (end-L)
   cout << "Number of employees is " << employees << "\n";
}
```

   a. Does your program work? If it does, create a string and an integer variable in main(). Have the user enter a string, without any spaces, and an integer. Then send these two items as arguments to set_up() to initialize toys. To scan the data, use the word cin and have the double arrows facing the opposite way from the way they are used with cout.
   b. Did you have to use %s or %d with either cout or cin?
   c. What disadvantage do you foresee? (It's possible to eliminate that disadvantage with another header file.)
   d. What happens if you remove << endl? What is the purpose of endl? (That is an end–L, not an end–l.)

QUESTIONS

1. What OOP concept or term is described by each of the following?
   a. Hiding the details of how operations are performed on an object.
   b. An instance of a class.
   c. Creating a model to represent a real object by selecting certain features and ignoring irrelevant ones.
   d. A given message is responded to in different ways by different objects.
   e. Deriving a special class from an existing class.
   f. Different objects that possess the same behavior are said to be of the same _____ .
   g. The operations that you are allowed to perform on an object.

2. Describe the difference between a message and a method, and between a client and a server.
3. Define an abstraction for a toaster. Using your own words, explain how the following terms can be applied to your abstraction: instance, class, object, encapsulation, interface, and hiding the implementation. Redo this problem for abstractions of a door handle and a vending machine.

Solution 16.21 a. cin   b. >>
            c.
```
cout << "Enter a float and an integer" << "\n";
cin >> x >> i;
```

Drill 16.22 Here are some advantages of object–oriented programming:
1. We can model the real world as we view it into our design and implementation.
2. We can create ready–made software–ICs so that they can be reused, just as chips are reused in building a computer.
3. Changes in the program specifications are easily mapped and implemented in the program.
4. Projects are done on time and on budget, saving time and money.
5. Old C code can be used together with C++ code while a project is undergoing a transition.
6. Programs are more reliable because they contain fewer errors. C++ is easier to debug.

4. Identify mistakes in 7 lines of the following code:

```
class A
{
   private
      int x;
   public
      void init(int);
}
void init (int i)
{
   x = i;
}
void main (void)
{
   class A a;
   int q;
   a.x = 7;
   init(8);
   q = int(8);

}
```

PROGRAMS

1. Define a class called CD. Its private members are a character string of length 20 called title[ ] and an integer called qty. It has three member functions that are public. setup() receives a character string of 20 and an integer, and uses these two arguments to initialize title[ ] and qty. add() receives one integer, which is added to the qty, and returns nothing. show() receives no arguments. It prints the title[ ] using cout, and returns the qty to the calling function.

   Write main() to have an object called *cd1* of class CD. Have the user provide title[ ] and a qty using cin. Initialize *cd1* with those two items. Ask the user if there are any more CDs and using that integer, add it to qty of *cd1*. Finally, print the title[ ] using show() and also print the qty from main().

2. Write a class called Boy. It has two private members called nickels and dimes, both integers. It has five public members. take_em() receives two integer arguments, each representing the

a. Which of the items numbered 1 to 6 is like making a small model of a building instead of creating just a blueprint?
b. Which one is like building an addition to an existing building?
c. Which of the benefits listed in Drill 16.22 is like building a car from a kit?
d. Which benefit is like building a top–quality item?

number of nickels and the number of dimes. It initializes an object of class Boy with these two items. giveN() receives no arguments, returns the number of nickels, and makes its own nickels equal to zero. Similarly, giveD() returns the number of dimes, and makes its own dimes equal to zero. here_is_more() receives two integers as arguments and adds the first integer to the number of nickels and the second one to the number of dimes. Last, what_do_u_have() will display the number of nickels and dimes using `cout`.

Write main() so that it defines *adam* and *seth* as objects of class Boy. Initially, give *adam* 10 nickels and 20 dimes and *seth* 30 nickels and 10 dimes. Then ask *seth* to give his coins to *adam*. Now print the number of coins that *adam* and *seth* have.

If you define these methods as passing appropriate messages between objects, you should be able to appreciate how well OOP can model interactions within the real world as we experience them.

Solution 16.22

a. Item number 1.
b. Item number 5
c. Item number 2.
d. Item number 6.

Analysis

Object-Oriented Software Life Cycle

The most important aspect about C++ is not the C++ language, but the ability to implement an object-oriented design. That is, you don't want to be just a good C++ programmer but a good OO programmer who uses C++.

In developing applications using traditional techniques, such as structured top-down design, a substantial amount of time is spent on implementation, that is, on coding. Relatively speaking, less time is spent on design. In C++, more time is spent on analysis and design than on the programming. Everyone knows that before a house is built or any large project is undertaken, proper planning is more important than the actual building. This is even more true in OO development.

Figure 17.1 shows the four stages in developing an application. These are definition of the user requirements, analysis, design, and implementation (including testing). Analysis models the *problem* and design models the *solution*. Domain experts or business experts are those people who will be using the application system and who know most about what is wanted. They should draft the requirements specification. They direct the OO technology to model the real world. They should

---

In this unit, study and review the sections in this sequence: lesson, drills, experiments, questions, and programs. For these drills I am assuming that you have reviewed the lesson first.

The program for which we will do an analysis in this unit will be designed and coded in Unit 18. The requirements specification for the problem developed in these drills is as follows:

We have a video rental store in which we have only five videotapes and only five valid customers. These tapes and customers are fixed. We can't add or delete. To be able to do that will be part of the requirements for a future project.

Customers can sign out only one tape at a time and there is no penalty for returning the tapes late. In fact, this project doesn't keep track of dates at all. That will be an issue in the next project.

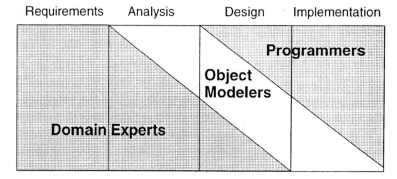

Figure 17.1 Relative involvement of various facilitators during the different stages of OO development.

be involved in the development, at least up to the design stage, to prevent the object modelers from going off track.

Object modelers are the experts in object–oriented technology who help model the physical system and create the design. Implementors or programmers provide feedback to them, stating constraints placed by the programming language.

Notice that, during the analysis phase, how the application will be implemented is not a major concern. During the design phase, all three types of workers should be involved in the process.

One thing to keep in mind is that the analysis and design phases are iterative processes. Again and again we must come back and re–tune our analysis before the design becomes stabilized enough to embark on the actual coding phase. Analysis and design can't be done in a hurry. The natural tendency is to wonder why we have spent so much time on the project and still haven't written one line of code. But that is the nature of OO technology.

If we have to correct mistakes in the implementation of a design, it's not that costly. But correcting a mistake that could have been corrected in the analysis phase can be very costly.

If analysis and design are done with careful thought on each person's part, then implementation will go very quickly. The actual lines of coding may be numerous, but they will be written faster, with fewer bugs, and be easier to maintain and extend (add new features).

Chances are that much of the code may already be written. Classes may have already been written by someone in your group or could be bought from a software house. These could be used as off–the–shelf components to build your application. This is called software *reuse*.

When designing a system, plan carefully so that you don't model only the problem facing you. The current problem is an example of many others not yet modeled. Concern yourself with domain–specific issues: they are fairly stable. Problem–specific issues change constantly, and writing your class libraries based on the current problem means that those classes will be in a

Customer phone numbers are 4 digits long and tape numbers are 3 digits. When seeing the database, the phone numbers are shown in the left column with any tapes that are signed out next to the appropriate phone number. In the column on the right–hand side, the tapes are listed with the phone number of the person who has that tape out (if any).

Here is an example of how the program should behave:

```
1. Check out,    2. Check in,    3. Show data base,    4. Quit : 3
5189            201             // The left column shows the customers' phone numbers.
6065            203             // The right column shows the tape numbers.
7224            207             // Since the column between these two is empty,
3205            202             //   no customers have signed out any tapes.
5552            206             // Since the column on the right–hand side of the tape numbers is empty,
                                //   there are no tapes signed out.
```

308

Analysis

constant state of flux. By keeping this in mind, classes can then be written in a general way, so that they can be reused easily by future applications.

On the other hand, don't attempt to model everything. If a particular property is dropped from a class which other applications depend on, then you could be unpleasantly surprised. It is always easier to add properties to a class than to remove them. Defining a class is like creating a contract with those who will use it.

Because OO development is an iterative process, it becomes artificial to divide it into two parts called analysis and design. However, to concentrate on one item at a time, let us discuss the analysis phase in this unit and the design phase in the next. In the actual development cycle one would go back and forth between these two phases until the model becomes relatively stable. Not being satisfied with the first results of the analysis and design, being flexible, and forever revising are very important concepts in OOP.

Requirements Specification

Before starting an analysis of a software system, a good description of the system requirements must be drafted by the domain experts. They must identify the constraints on the system. They must establish the problem to be solved, the results it must achieve, and basically, what the system must do.

The problem domain should be identified. What are the major entities that we can control? What entities can't we control but interact with? For instance, accounts we can control, but customers we generally can't. This sets up the framework in which a solution must be found.

Additionally, interfaces outside the scope of the problem domain should be identified. They could be graphical user interfaces, database systems, patient monitoring devices, etc. Once identified, these interfaces can be left aside on the back burner until the design phase of the process is fully on its way.

The Sessions

Once the requirements specification and the problem domain are firmly established, brainstorming sessions are scheduled. These sessions could last a week or two and should be conducted off–site. This minimizes typical daily interruptions and gives time for participants to concentrate on the analysis and design phases of the problem.

There should be a total of 5 to 7 participants. One facilitator, if possible from an outside company, should be an OO technology expert who directs the sessions. He or she should be talented in obtaining ideas from the others rather than a person who comes with a preconceived solution in his or her mind.

At least two domain experts who understand the daily operations of the system in place should also be present. Their role is the most important during the analysis phase. They should be able to provide information that is taken for granted in the requirements and should know the operations terminology well.

```
1. Check out,    2. Check in,    3. Show data base,    4. Quit : 1
Give your phone and video numbers: 3205  203

1. Check out,    2. Check in,    3. Show data base,    4. Quit : 3
5189            201
6065            203   3205     // Tape 203 is signed out by customer 3205.
7224            207
3205  203       202            // Customer 3205 has tape 203 signed out.
5552            206

1. Check out,    2. Check in,    3. Show data base,    4. Quit : 4
```

Technical object modelers who know how to write code in more than one OOP language must also be included. They will close the gap between the domain or business experts and the actual software implementors. During the design phase, they will contribute most to the development process. If possible, you should also have a scribe to record all information because some information, if not recorded, will be lost. Only after sufficient preparation has been done for the OO technology sessions should analysis begin.

CRC Cards

In OOP, we must identify objects and the actions for which they will be responsible. We must identify what objects they will need to fulfill their responsibilities. This is called responsibility–driven analysis and is at the heart of OOP.

The best way to accomplish this is with the use of CRC (class, responsibility, collaborator) cards. CRC cards are 3" x 5" index cards that are formatted in a special way. The CRC cards method is an informal technique that is effective for even large programs. You can adapt and change this method to your own liking, and using them can be a lot of fun. They were originally created by Ward Cunningham of Tektronix in 1989. However, because of the books written by Rebecca Wirfs-Brook, Timothy Budd, and Nancy Wilkinson, this technique became popular and widely accepted.

There are also more formal methodologies than the CRC cards method, including Grady Booch's, which uses class, object, state transition, timing, process, and module diagrams. Ivar Jacobson created a method called OOSE (object–oriented software engineering). James Rumbaugh invented the OMT (object modeling technique). However, even in the use of these formal methods, creating CRC cards first can give the development cycle a significant head start.

A blank CRC card is shown in Figure 17.2. On the front, it is divided into three parts: class, responsibilities, and collaborators. On the back, it may contain the description of the class and its attributes or data members.

Under the class name, any derived classes are listed next to the subclass label. Remember from Unit 16 that a derived class occurs due to inheritance. A class that is a special case of another class is called a subclass, while the original class is called a base class or a superclass. Similarly, if a class has a superclass, also called a base class, then it is listed next to the superclass label. In this and the next units, we will not use these parts because inheritance is covered in Unit 20.

The responsibilities of the class are listed on the left side. To their right, classes that will aid in accomplishing those responsibilities are also listed. These classes are called collaborators.

Identifying Classes

The first step in the sessions is to have one person write down class names on a board and as they are suggested by the participants. All class names should be written down. Later they may be discarded or combined into others.

Drill 17.1 The following five messages will be displayed: "Checkout successful," "Tape not available," "Customer already has tape out," "Phone or videoID not in the database," and "Customer and tape do not match." For each of the following cases, the database is as shown above: the customer with a phone number of 3205 has tape number 203 signed out. Give the appropriate message for each case.

a. Customer 3205 brings in tape number 206.
b. Customer 6065 brings in tape number 204.
c. Customer 3205 checks out tape number 201.
d. Customer 7224 checks out tape number 203.
e. Customer 6065 checks out tape number 206.

Class name:	
Subclasses:	
Superclasses:	
Responsibilities	Collaborators

Figure 17.2 The front of a CRC card. Each one shows the class, its responsibilities, and the classes with which they will need to collaborate to fulfill their responsibilities. Subclasses and superclasses, due to inheritance, may also be listed.

Class names should be chosen very carefully because they will be used to convey their meaning through implementation. Don't worry if you are defining a class or an object at this time. During the design phase the difference will become more evident. Use nouns and short names of one or two words, if possible. Think about who is responsible for what actions. Be careful with abbreviations. The class name should communicate what the class represents. It is best to think that each class has a personality.

Some kinds of classes are static data managers, passive data managers, user interfaces, and helper classes. Static data managers maintain a state, that is, information for a significant amount of time. Passive data managers either generate data or process them "on the fly." They hold information for a short duration.

If a GameBoard class is used in an application as a data manager, you may also have a GameBoardView class that is responsible only for graphically displaying the game board and receiving input from the user.

A helper class typically doesn't have information but helps in the execution of message passing.

Once the choice of classes has been agreed upon, then their names are written on the CRC cards, one name per card. The cards are then divided up among the participants, who then write short descriptions of their classes on the backs of the cards. Some examples of class names are GamePiece, PayCheck, Menu, TravelAgent, Aircraft, FundTransfer, and Message.

Solution 17.1

a. Customer 3205 brings in tape number 206.   "Customer and tape do not match."

b. Customer 6065 brings in tape number 204.   "Phone or videoID not in the database."

c. Customer 3205 checks out tape number 201.   "Customer already has tape out."

d. Customer 7224 checks out tape number 203.   "Tape not available."

e. Customer 6065 checks out tape number 206.   "Checkout successful."

Drill 17.2

For which cases will the database be updated? Show the database after each of the valid updates.

On the other hand, Money, CustomerName, and CarModel are not classes because they don't have any behavior. Instead these items may be attributes of classes such as Account, Customer, and Car.

Responsibilities

Now the session participants hold one of their cards up in turn and play the part of their classes as if they have become a living entity of their classes. Each one says what it must be able to do and whether they need another class to help them. For example, the person playing the role of the Registrar class may ask the person who plays the Student class, "I need to know from you if you have taken the course ENG101 as a prerequisite." The Student class then sees if she or he can provide that information or whether she or he needs to collaborate with another class to fulfill this request.

This starts the process of identifying the responsibilities and the corresponding collaborators for the defined classes. During this process, you may need to add more classes or combine them.

Responsibilities should be described using active verbs and short phrases. This section of the card is like a contract with the other classes that use them. Responsibilities describe *what* actions have to be done but not *how* they are to be done. If you start running out of room on the 3" x 5" CRC card, maybe you should create another class or else delegate its responsibilities to other existing classes. If a class is used by other applications, it becomes harder to remove responsibilities. However, adding responsibilities is not a problem.

Defining the responsibilities of a class formulates its behavior or what services it must provide. They specify what actions need to be done by which objects.

Collaborators

The classes required to fulfill the responsibilities are called *collaborators*. A responsibility may not require a collaborator; in such case, the class in question has all the resources to meet that responsibility itself. Other responsibilities may require the services of other classes. These collaborators allow responsibilities to be delegated and the task of the application is divided among different classes.

A collaboration is a request from a *client* object to a *server* object. It is a one–way interaction. The name of the class of the CRC card represents the client object and the name of the collaborator listed represents the server object. The responsibility is the request that connects these two objects together. A server object may reply, stating that the request was successful or not. However, the response of the server object should not be listed as a responsibility in its CRC card.

Collaborators connect objects together. They define how the flow of execution is controlled. More important is that, when a client collaborates with a server, the server should be thought of as becoming "alive." This means that the server not only holds information, but it also has

---

Solution 17.2 Only question e will update the database as follows:

5189		201	
6065	206	203	3205
7224		207	
3205	203	202	
5552		206	6065

Drill 17.3 It is important that you fully understand the problem. Once more, show the messages after each operation done in the given sequence. Then show the state of the database.
a. Customer 3205 brings in tape 203.
b. Customer 6065 brings in tape 202.
c. Customer 5189 signs out tape 203.
d. Customer 5189 signs out tape 202.

Analysis

intelligence and behavior and is now capable of doing something. Contrast this to "dead data" used in structured programming languages, where data just waits to be manipulated. In OOP, objects become alive, become responsible for their own behavior, and provide services to other objects.

Once a server object is invoked, it may then collaborate with other objects, activating them to help it fulfill its responsibility. When the server's task is completed, it then returns the control of execution back to the client, and the server can be thought of as becoming dormant until it is needed again.

Example 17.1 (With Additional Discussions)

Let us now look at a simple problem, give its requirements, and do an analysis using CRC cards. We want to develop a program that will allow two human players to play tic–tac–toe on a computer. This example is chosen not because it will introduce you to writing games but to show you how OO analysis is done. In Chapter 18, we will follow up on this example and do a design and write the code for it as well.

Requirements Specification

Using simple ASCII text characters, display a cleared tic–tac–toe board. Ask the X player to go first. Alternate turns with the O player. Each time, the program should show the state of the board. The program should stop the game when it is over. It should determine the winner or call it a tie if there is no winner. See Figure 17.3 for a sample run of what we want to do.

Correctly understanding requirements and documenting them is crucial to finding a solution. A person from a foreign country who may never have played tic–tac–toe should actually play the game on paper with someone before advancing to the next step of the development process. The domain experts should be bombarded with questions so that everyone will better understand what they want. If there are misunderstandings here then phases of the development process may have to be redone. Hence, it's important that the domain experts are present to ensure that all aspects of the analysis and design are kept on track.

Initial Selection of Class Names

Once the requirements are fully understood by all members of the development team, they may come up with this set of class names: x, o, playerX, playerO, the game, the board, the referee, and board cell (of which there are nine). Typically, this initial list would be larger, but since this is a simple example, the list is relatively small.

When creating this list, look for nouns or simple phrases in the requirements. Look for physical objects such as an employment application or the money dispenser of an ATM. See if there are any conceptual items such as pull–down menus or payroll files. These are also good candidates for class names.

Solution 17.3
a. Customer 3205 brings in tape 203: Check–in successful.
b. Customer 6065 brings in tape 202: Customer and tape do not match.
c. Customer 5189 signs out tape 203: Checkout successful. (Customer 3205 just brought it in.)
d. Customer 5189 signs out tape 202: Customer already has a tape out.

5189	203	201	
6065	206	203	5189
7224		207	
3205		202	
5552		206	6065

Drill 17.4 Now that we understand the requirements specification, it is time to decide on what classes we will need. Give an initial list of class names, whether they are valid or not.

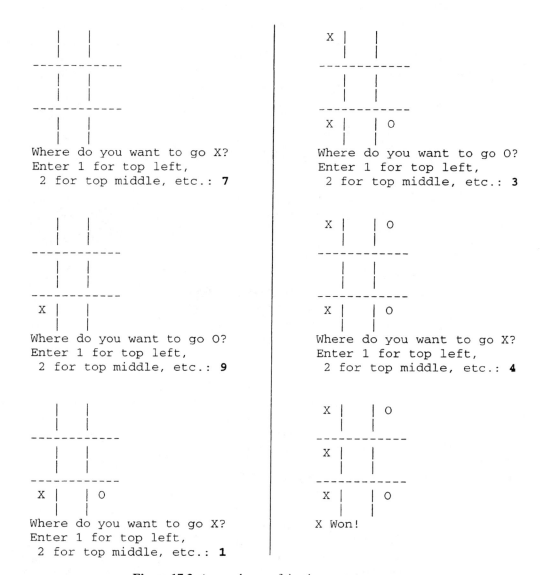

Figure 17.3 A sample run of the tic–tac–toe game.

Solution 17.4 Tape, Video, Customer, Store, CheckoutClerk, Date, Phone, TapeID, Database

Drill 17.5 In a real development process, many early decisions have to be changed as the development progresses. Also, there may be many valid solutions for a given problem. Nonetheless, I will guide you along one of my solutions that wasn't finalized until the entire problem was solved. Re–evaluating the above list, which classes should be kept and which should be deleted? Give your reasons.

Analysis

A graphical user interface, a database, or an operating system are complex subsystems. Treat these kinds of entities as black boxes now. In the design phase start to see how they can be integrated into your application. Look for classes that provide an abstraction to important items exhibiting a definite behavior and remove irrelevant classes.

Intermediate List of Classes

After discussing the virtues of the initial list of classes, the session participants may arrive at this list:

```
Player, Board, and Referee
```

The letters x and o are simply characters. C++ already provides an abstraction of characters in char. There is nothing new that we need to model in x and o that is not already provided in type char, so we eliminate them.

PlayerX and PlayerO exhibit the same behaviors and can be classified as instances of the class Player. In other words, PlayerX and PlayerO will be objects of class Player.

There is one instance of the tic–tac–toe game. It could very well be defined as a class. We eliminate it because we don't think that we can delegate responsibilities to it that are clearly not the responsibilities of the other classes which are chosen.

The nine individual cells of the board are actually the attributes of the board. Knowing the state of the cell doesn't determine if the game is won by anyone or not, but knowing the state of the entire board is more important. During the implementation phase, we will find it easier to treat the Board class as one class rather than to treat the nine cells separately. Therefore, the cell class is also eliminated.

The Final List of Classes

During the phase where responsibilities were assigned to each class, we came up with too many responsibilities for the Referee, so a new class called Facilitator was created. It is a good idea to balance the number of responsibilities if possible. The Facilitator was described as the one who determines the next player, while the Referee was the one who determined a winner. The list of classes may not be finalized until the implementation is well underway. After all the phases of our development were completed, here is our final list of classes which we came up with:

```
Facilitator, Referee, Board, and Player
```

Figure 17.4 shows the backs of the CRC cards, where the class descriptions are written.

Solution 17.5 Tape and Video are different names for the same thing. Pick one; I picked Video. TapeID is an attribute of Video, so drop that one. Similarly, drop Phone because it belongs to Customer. Drop Date because the requirements specification doesn't require it. We need Database to hold all the Video and Customer objects. Store is a valid class name, but our problem domain is limited to one store, so we don't need it. If we need it later, we can always add it. The CheckoutClerk is responsible for interfacing with the customers in the store and processing transactions. Hence, we will keep her, but let's simplify her name to Clerk.

Drill 17.6 What is the new list of class names? Also, in the above solution, hints for two more classes have been made. Can you tell what they are?

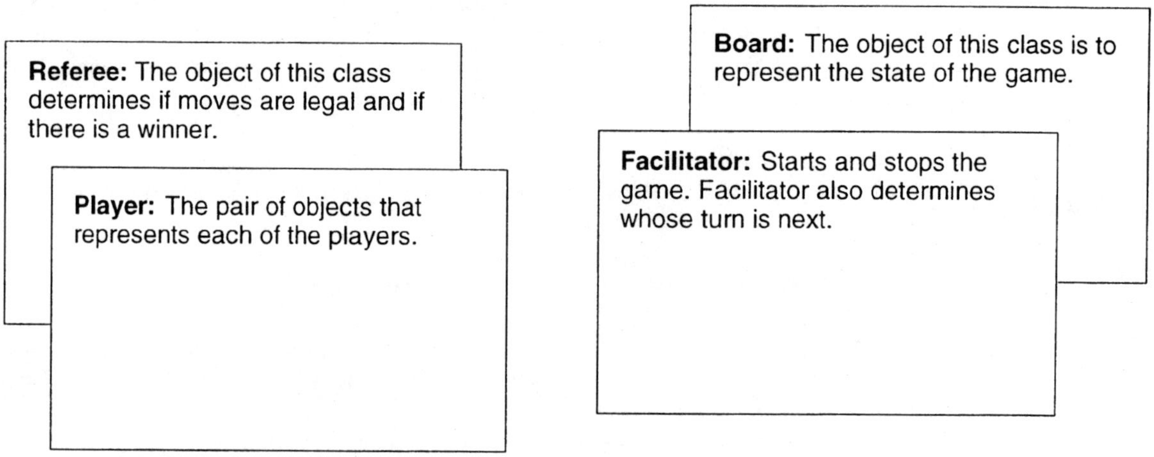

Referee: The object of this class determines if moves are legal and if there is a winner.

Player: The pair of objects that represents each of the players.

Board: The object of this class is to represent the state of the game.

Facilitator: Starts and stops the game. Facilitator also determines whose turn is next.

Figure 17.4 The backs of the CRC cards showing class names and their definitions.

Assigning Responsibilities to the Classes

Once the classes have been decided upon, we need to assign responsibilities to them and list these on the front of the CRC cards. Responsibilities determine why we need the classes in the first place and what behavior they will take upon themselves.

There are two kinds of responsibilities: one is to maintain information about something or be knowledgeable about the state of something. The other responsibility is to determine what actions to do. Responsibilities determine the behavior of objects, that is, what they know and what they do.

This step does not include how they will maintain that knowledge or how they will perform the actions. This information should be hidden from other objects. At this stage we should determine what public services each class will provide to others. Staying with this mind–set, we will not concern ourselves with the list of class attributes that may be needed. They can be listed on the reverse side of the CRC cards when we are well into the design phase of our project or in Unit 18.

Look for verbs in the requirements and in the class descriptions. They will help you identify responsibilities. Try to even out the responsibilities among the classes. This will keep your application more flexible when it is time to modify it. Keep information with the object that will act upon it. This will reduce the number of messages "flying" among objects. One set of knowledge should be kept with one class. If information is duplicated, it is more work to keep it synchronized or keep it up–to–date.

Figure 17.5 shows the fronts of the CRC cards. At the top, we have the class name. In the left column, we list the responsibilities of that class and next to those responsibilities, we give the

Solution 17.6 Out of the original list, Video, Customer, Clerk, and Database are the class names to keep. Transaction and UserInterface will also be added. The Database and UserInterface classes will be quite simple in our solution. However, since they have been made into classes, we can make them more sophisticated later. For example, the Database object could be made to interface with any of the commercial available databases easily. Also, the UserInterface object could be made into a graphical user interface if we write all the input and output statements using the UserInterface.

Drill 17.7 Let us now describe these six classes:

Clerk:	Customer:
Video:	Database:
Transaction:	UserInterface:

classes needed to help fulfill the particular responsibility. These helping classes are called collaborators.

Collaborators

In the following analysis of our problem, you will see how objects collaborate with each other and how the principles of OOP described so far are placed into practice. You should note that this is not the initial analysis, but the one that I arrived at after the entire program was completed as given in Unit 18. Completing of the CRC cards should be done in sessions with the help of several participants as described on page 309. The letter–number combinations, shown in parentheses in the subsequent text discussion, are references made to the responsibilities as labeled in Figure 17.5.

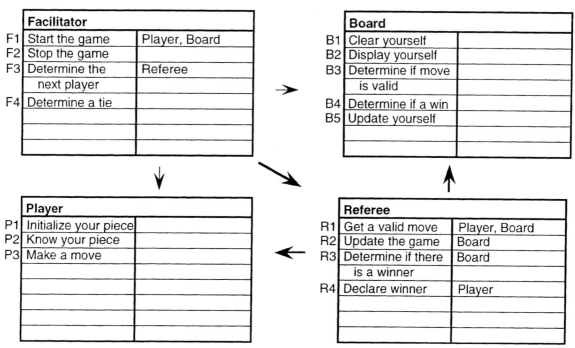

Figure 17.5 The fronts of the CRC cards show the classes, their responsibilities, and the classes with which they will need to collaborate. The responsibilities are labeled for reference, and the arrows show the relative degree of coupling among the classes.

Solution 17.7

Clerk:	The object who serves customers directly in the store.
Customer:	The set of objects that represents customers served by the video rental store.
Video:	The set of objects that represents videotapes lent by the rental store.
Database:	The object that represents the collection of videotapes owned by the store and the list of its customers.
Transaction:	Represents requests made by the clerk to the Database.
UserInterface:	Represents the two–way interface between the Clerk and the Customer.

Drill 17.8 Which of these six classes will not have a state? That is, which classes will not have to store any private variables or information? For the other classes, give one piece of information they will need to keep.

When we start the game, the Facilitator should create and initialize each of the two player objects, making one the X player and the other the O player. To accomplish this, the Facilitator must collaborate with Player (F1). Also, to start the game, the Facilitator must collaborate with the Board to clear it and to display (F1) on the screen. The Board doesn't need the services of any other object to clear and display itself, so no collaborators are listed (B1, B2). The same is true for Player when it initializes itself (P1).

Now the Facilitator "wakes up" the Referee by telling her whose turn it is to play next (F3). In an actual game, a referee doesn't do her job under the control of the players, but the players act out their moves under the supervision of the referee. Hence, we have here the Referee prompting the player when to play (R1). The Player needs no one's help to make a move and no collaborators are listed (P3).

When the Referee gets a move from the player, she must make sure that that board cell is empty on the board. The Referee collaborates with the Board by invoking that service from it (R1). The Board knows its own state, so it can tell the Referee if that cell is occupied or not without anyone's help (B3).

Notice that the Referee asks if the player's move is valid. She doesn't ask if the cell is empty. There is hardly any difference between labeling the responsibility as "Is the move valid?" and "Is the cell empty?" However, asking if the cell is empty would require the Referee to decide that, if this is so, then it must be a valid move. This type of decision involves the affairs of the Board and the Board should be responsible for its own affairs. Therefore, the Referee simply asks the Board whether the move is valid or not, and lets the Board decide.

Now, after the Referee finds out that the move is valid, she asks the Board to finalize the move (R2). The Board updates itself (B5). Then the Referee determines if there is a winner (R3). She does this by collaborating with the Board (B4). If there is a winner, the Referee will ask the Player if she is an X or an O (P2) and declares the winner (R4).

A poor analysis of this problem may have the Referee collaborate with the Board once rather than three times, as shown. The Board could see if the move is valid, update itself, and return a winner to the Referee if there is one. This type of design is tempting for structured programmers because it is simpler and more efficient.

However, there are many reasons why this is not advisable. One is that the definition of the Board class given in Figure 17.4 will be violated. The Board class will be even more burdened with responsibilities, while the Referee class could be eliminated altogether. When a class has one or two responsibilities, it should be reevaluated to see if these responsibilities can be delegated to other classes. If a class has no responsibilities, then it has no reason to exist.

Technically, the entire program can be written using one object, but that defeats the purpose of OOP and voids all its advantages. We want reusable software modules. We want to be able to "plug–and–play" with them. We want to be able to extend or modify our software with as little effort

---

Solution 17.8 One shouldn't think too much about class attributes at first.

Clerk:	No state. When a new customer approaches her, her behavior should not depend on what she did before.
Customer:	Phone number. The Customer needs to know his own phone number.
Video:	Tape number.
Database:	Customer and Video.
Transaction:	Type of transaction. Is a videotape being signed out or returned.
UserInterface:	No state. This object doesn't have to keep track of any information.

Drill 17.9 From our list of six class names, who should be responsible for the following services?
a. set the customer phone number
b. know the customer phone number
c. go to work
d. Give the "in–status." Is the tape in the store?

as possible. Hence, we choose classes with a clear and definite purpose and where responsibilities can be shared among them.

All this time, the Facilitator has been waiting for the turn to finish. He or she is notified by the Referee if there was a winner and if so, he or she will stop the game (F2). Otherwise, he will tell the Referee whose turn it is to play next. If nine turns have been played without the Referee declaring a winner, then the Facilitator will declare a tie and stop the game.

Although this example is small and simple, its analysis had to be revised many times. I have spared you from having to follow all the changes in the analysis that had to be done until it was finalized. When doing OO analysis, one should not be discouraged because the analysis is constantly changing. There are constraints placed even by the language of implementation that will ripple changes back to your design and analysis. Being able and willing to revise is crucial in arriving at a successful solution.

EXPERIMENTS

Before you do these experiments, make sure you study the Lesson and Drill sections of this unit. It is assumed that you have reviewed these sections first.

This section is much different from the previous ones. You won't be running short segments of code here, but you will be guided through the necessary steps of an OO analysis. We will be concentrating on one problem throughout these experiments, so first we will spend a good amount of time understanding what is required.

We want to develop an OO solution to an application that will take incoming customer phone calls and distribute these calls to the agent who has been idle the longest. We have only three agents numbered 1, 2, and 3. Customers have numbers greater than 99. When the day is done, we will show the number of customers handled by each of the three agents.

To simulate this telecommunications application, we will use a series of integers separated by spaces. Data items of 1, 2, and 3 are identified as agents and numbers such as 200 and 700 are identified as calling customers. A data of 0 means that it is the end of the day and the final report for the day is to be printed. For example, if this is the input data:

```
300   1   500   2   100   300   900   400   1   1   200   800   500   2   1   0
```

then the output report should state that agents 1, 2, and 3 served 5, 3, and 1 customers, respectively. Follow the sequence shown in Figure 17.6, which spans the next two pages that will explain how these numbers were obtained in the final report.

Solution 17.9

a. The Customer should be made responsible for setting his own phone number.
b. The Customer should be made responsible for providing his own phone number when requested.
c. The Clerk goes to work
d. The Video should be made responsible to "tell us" if "he" is in the store or has been checked out.

Drill 17.10 Similarly, who should be made responsible for the following services?

a. Is the Customer allowed to sign out a tape?
b. Knowing if the Customer has a particular tape signed out.

(a) Before data is read:

	Agent1	Agent2	Agent3		Agents' queue					Customers' queue			
					[0]	[1]	[2]	[3]		[0]	[1]	[2]	[3]
	0	0	0		1	2	3						

(b) After Customer300 is read:

	Agent1	Agent2	Agent3		[0]	[1]	[2]	[3]		[0]	[1]	[2]	[3]
	1	0	0		2	3							

(c) After Agent1 is read:

	Agent1	Agent2	Agent3		[0]	[1]	[2]	[3]		[0]	[1]	[2]	[3]
	1	0	0		2	3	1						

(d) After Customer500 is read:

	Agent1	Agent2	Agent3		[0]	[1]	[2]	[3]		[0]	[1]	[2]	[3]
	1	1	0		3	1							

(e) After Agent2 is read:

	Agent1	Agent2	Agent3		[0]	[1]	[2]	[3]		[0]	[1]	[2]	[3]
	1	1	0		3	1	2						

(f) After Customer100 and Customer300 are read:

	Agent1	Agent2	Agent3		[0]	[1]	[2]	[3]		[0]	[1]	[2]	[3]
	2	1	1		2								

(g) After Customer900 and Customer400 are read:

	Agent1	Agent2	Agent3		[0]	[1]	[2]	[3]		[0]	[1]	[2]	[3]
	2	2	1							400			

Figure 17.6 The problem to be developed.

Solution 17.10

a. The Customer should be able to tell if he has no tapes signed out, which means that he is allowed to sign out one tape.
b. The Customer should be able to tell if he has a specified tape signed out.

Drill 17.11

Who should be made responsible for the folllowing services? Some are the responsibility of more than one object.
a. Display your own information.
b. Sign the tape in.

(h) After Agent1 is read:

	Agent1	Agent2	Agent3		Agents' queue [0]	[1]	[2]	[3]		Customers' queue [0]	[1]	[2]	[3]
	3	2	1										

(i) After another Agent1 is read:

	Agent1	Agent2	Agent3		Agents' queue [0]	[1]	[2]	[3]		Customers' queue [0]	[1]	[2]	[3]
	3	2	1		1								

(j) After Customer200, Customer800, and Customer500 are read:

	Agent1	Agent2	Agent3		Agents' queue [0]	[1]	[2]	[3]		Customers' queue [0]	[1]	[2]	[3]
	4	2	1							800	500		

(k) After Agent2 and Agent1 are read:

	Agent1	Agent2	Agent3		Agents' queue [0]	[1]	[2]	[3]		Customers' queue [0]	[1]	[2]	[3]
	5	3	1										

(l) After 0 is read, the final report is displayed:

```
Agent1 served 5 customer(s)
Agent2 served 3 customer(s)
Agent3 served 1 customer(s)
```

Figure 17.6 (Continued)

In Figure 17.6(a), we see that, before any data is read, the number of customers served by each of the three agents is zero. Also, they are waiting for customers. Agent1 is at the head of the queue, so he will take the first call. Agent2 will take the next call, and Agent3 will take the third incoming call.

In Figure 17.6(b), Customer300, the first data item, calls and Agent1 serves her; Agent1's count of customers served is now increased by 1. In Figure 17.6(c), Agent1 finishes with his customer and so he goes to the end of the queue.

In Figure 17.6(d), Customer500 is handed over to Agent2 because he is at the front of the queue. Agent3 is moved to the first spot and Agent1 is right behind him. Agent2 has now also served 1 customer.

Solution 17.11

a. UserInterface will be responsible for all displaying and receiving of information.
   The Database should be able to display the database.
   The Video and the Customer should also be able to display their own information.

b. The Transaction should check in the Video.
   The Video should be able to check itself in.
   The Customer should be cleared of having that tape.

Drill 17.12 For the next few drills, let us think about this scenario: Suppose Customer 3205 wants to sign out the tape 203. The Customer has no tapes out and the tape is available.

a. Who should be responsible for displaying the initial menu that receives this request?

b. Who should initialize the transaction that specifies that Customer 3205 wants to sign out tape 203?

(a) Before data is read:

Agent1	Agent2	Agent3		Agents' queue					Customers' queue			
				[0]	[1]	[2]	[3]		[0]	[1]	[2]	[3]

(b) After Customer800 is read:

Agent1	Agent2	Agent3		Agents' queue					Customers' queue			
				[0]	[1]	[2]	[3]		[0]	[1]	[2]	[3]

(c) After Customer600, Customer900, Customer300, and Customer700 are read:

Agent1	Agent2	Agent3		Agents' queue					Customers' queue			
				[0]	[1]	[2]	[3]		[0]	[1]	[2]	[3]

(d) After Agent3 is read:

Agent1	Agent2	Agent3		Agents' queue					Customers' queue			
				[0]	[1]	[2]	[3]		[0]	[1]	[2]	[3]

(e) After another Agent3 is read:

Agent1	Agent2	Agent3		Agents' queue					Customers' queue			
				[0]	[1]	[2]	[3]		[0]	[1]	[2]	[3]

(f) After another Agent3 is read:

Agent1	Agent2	Agent3		Agents' queue					Customers' queue			
				[0]	[1]	[2]	[3]		[0]	[1]	[2]	[3]

(g) After an Agent2 is read:

Agent1	Agent2	Agent3		Agents' queue					Customers' queue			
				[0]	[1]	[2]	[3]		[0]	[1]	[2]	[3]

Figure 17.7 Your turn to process this sequence of data.

Solution 17.12
a. UserInterface
b. Transaction

Drill 17.13 Continuing from the last drill:
a. Who should be made responsible for providing Customer 3205 and Video 203 from the database?
b. Who should be made responsible for setting Customer 3205 to have tape 203?
c. Who should be made responsible for setting the Video 203 to be signed out by Customer 3205?

Agents' queue   Customers' queue

(h) After Customer100, Customer500, and Customer600 are read:

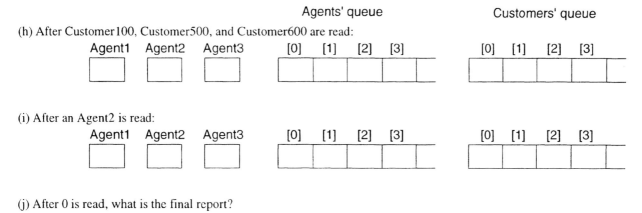

(i) After an Agent2 is read:

(j) After 0 is read, what is the final report?

Figure 17.7 (Continued)

In Figure 17.6(e), Agent2 is now free and he goes to the end of the queue. In Figure 17.6(f), Customer100 and Customer300 call in. Agent3 takes care of Customer100 and Agent1 takes care of Customer300. Each of their counts is incremented by 1. In Figure 17.6(g), Customer900's call can be handled by Agent2, but Customer400 must go to the front of the customers' queue because there are no more free agents left.

In Figure 17.6(h), Agent1 is finished serving Customer300. Since Customer400 is on hold and at the front of the queue, Agent1 can serve him also. Agent1 now has served three customers.

In Figure 17.6(i), Agent1 is free again. Because no customers are in their queue, he can relax and go on the agents' queue. In Figure 17.6(j), three customers call in. Only Agent1 can take care of the first one while the other two go on hold.

In Figure 17.6(k), two agents become free and they serve the two customers on hold. Finally in Figure 17.6(l), the call center closes and the agents' counters are displayed to show how many customers each one served. We hope that Agent1 wasn't brisk with the customers.

IMPORTANT! The first time you do any of these experiments, don't look ahead at the experiments to get an idea of how to answer the questions. Also, don't peek ahead in Unit 18. Only by completing the experiments yourself will you be able to appreciate the thought process needed for OO analysis. After the first pass through these experiments, review them and fill in the answers again to match the session that is described here. When you do the Programs section at the end of this unit, you will have a chance to do your own analysis on new problems. In Unit 18, you will do their designs.

Solution 17.13
a. Database
b. Customer
c. Video

Drill 17.14
a. Who should be responsible for updating the database with the updated Customer and Video?
b. Who should be responsible for providing the phone number of the given Customer? Or the tape number of the given Video?
c. Who should be responsible for displaying the "Checkout Successful!" message.
d. Who should be responsible for deciding on the type of error message to display?

Exp 17.1 Before we can proceed to any analysis or design, we must understand the requirements specification thoroughly. Use Figure 17.7 to show how the following sequence of data would be processed in this telecommunications center. If you have trouble, go over Figure 17.6 again.

800   600   900   300   700   3   3   3   2   100   500   600   2   0

Exp 17.2 After brainstorming, what class names could the session participants list? Write them below.

1.   2.

3.   4.

5.   6.

7.   8.

Exp 17.3 Without looking ahead, answer these questions:
a. Should we create a class called Agent? If so, what behavior should it have?

b. Should we create a class called Customer? If so, what behavior should it have?

c. Should we create a class called PhoneId to read in the input data such as 1, 3, 500, etc.? Why or why not?

Exp 17.4 Without peeking ahead, should we create two classes called AgentQueue and CustomerQueue? Comment. (Someone in my session said that creating these two classes was not a good idea. What reason could she have given?

Exp 17.5 Choosing proper class names is very important in OOP. The names will convey the behaviors of the classes through all phases of the project's development until it is implemented in C++.

In my sessions, participants came up with the following class names. Next to each name, write down "okay" if the class name seems suitable and "no" if it doesn't. For the class names that

---

Solution 17.14
a. Database
b. Customer should provide his own phone number.
   Video should provide its own tape number.
c. UserInterface should display all messages.
d. Transaction should know if it was successful or not. If it was not successful, the Transaction should know why.

Drill 17.15 Compiling information from the previous drills, let us now create our CRC cards. What should the CRC card look like for the Customer? Let's see how closely our answers agree.

Customer	

Analysis

you think are suitable, describe their purpose in one sentence. For the others give your argument against in one sentence.

Manager

CallHandler

Operator

CallDistributor

Coordinator

AgentSupervisor

CustomerSupervisor

QueueController

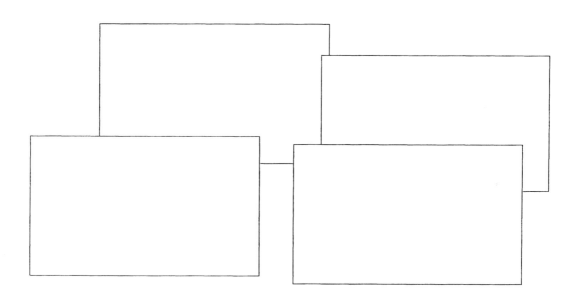

Solution 17.15 No collaborators are needed.
It's okay if my responsibility names do not match.

Drill 17.16 Show the Video card.

Customer	
Set_customer	
Get_phone	
Can_borrow	
Has_tape	
Lend_out	
Returned	
Check_customer	
Show	

Video	

Exp 17.6 We finally agreed to use the following class names: Queue, CallDistributor, Operator, Agent. We placed these names on the front of the four CRC cards. Each person is given one card and will be responsible for it. What description would you write on the backs of these cards if they were assigned to you? (Also label the classes.)

Exp 17.7 For each of the following responsibilities, determine *who* should be made responsible. Think of the objects as being anthropomorphic or "alive" when they are called to provide a service. (That's why I asked "who," rather than "what," should be made responsible. This will help you conceptualize the OO analysis.)

a. Serve a customer
b. Read in data
c. Accept a customer's call
d. Direct a customer call
e. Determine if a free agent should wait or be given a customer to serve
f. Start the workday
g. Stop the workday
h. Add a person to the queue

Solution 17.16

Video	
Set_videoID	
Get_videoID	
Give_in_status	
Sign_out	
Came_in	
Check_videoID	
Check_video	
Show	

Drill 17.17 Fill in the Transaction card.

Transaction	

Analysis

i. Remove a person from the queue
j. Know how many customers an agent has served
k. Print the final report
l. Initialize a queue
m. Notify that a free agent has become available

Exp 17.8 Now label each of the classes and place the responsibilities that we listed on the left side of the appropriate card. Also determine the collaborators, if any, for each one. (Also label the classes.)

QUESTIONS

1. What are the four phases of OO development?
2. State whether the analysis or the design phase is being described for the following:
   a. Domain experts have more influence in this phase than the implementors.
   b. An error made in this phase is not as costly to correct.
   c. This phase models the solution.
   d. This phase models the problem.
   e. Domain experts, object modelers, and programmers should all be involved in this phase.
3. What preparations should be made before OO analysis sessions are started?
4. Draw a CRC card and briefly explain its parts.
5. Which of the following are strong candidates for class names and which aren't: PartDescription, Part, AutoPrice, BookTitle, Document, Baby, BabyAddress?
6. A client requests a server to provide a service. The server responds with either "Successful" or "Failed."
   a. Should the server be listed as a collaborator on the client's CRC card for that service?
   b. Should the client be listed as a collaborator on the server's CRC card for that response?

PROGRAMS

These are not really programs that you have to write, but they require something more important from you: an OO analysis of each. For each problem, create CRC cards and use these cards in the next unit when you will be asked to design and write the programs in C++. It will be more fun if you can team up with at least two of your classmates to go through an OO analysis session as it was described in this unit.

Solution 17.17 Get_choice is a new one. We will need it when the Clerk needs to know the type of transaction to be carried out.

Drill 17.18 Show the Database card.

Transaction	
Set_transaction	
Get_choice	
Check_out	Customer, Video
	Database
Check_in	Customer, Video
	Database

Database	

Analysis

1. ATM Problem

We have only three accounts in our bank. The names on each account are: "Jones," "Brown," and "Smith." Respectively, they each have 500, 200, and 700 dollars, and their PINs are 5390, 4211, and 8607. Our ATM will accept only ATM cards from these customers. No one else will be allowed to use the machine.

When idle, the machine is waiting for the ATM card. If the name on the card matches one of the account names, then the machine will get a PIN from the customer and verify it. If the PIN matches, then the machine will allow the customer to withdraw money, deposit money, or see the balance. The account balance will be updated accordingly.

When you do this analysis, use these two classes (besides others): PinVerifier and ElectronicDrawer. The PinVerifier will get the secret PIN number from the customer and verify it. The ElectronicDrawer will accept cash and dispense it. All input and output amounts should go through this class.

To simulate this machine on the computer, use the following dialog as an example:

```
Insert ATM card: Jackson
Jackson doesn't have an account in this bank

Insert ATM card: Brown
Enter your PIN code: 5390
Sorry,

Insert ATM card: Brown
Enter your PIN code: 4211
Enter 1 for Deposit, 2 for Withdrawal, 3 for Balance, 4 to Exit: 3
You have $200.00
Enter 1 for Deposit, 2 for Withdrawal, 3 for Balance, 4 to Exit: 2
How much? 300.00
Sorry.
Enter 1 for Deposit, 2 for Withdrawal, 3 for Balance, 4 to Exit: 2
How much? 50.00
Remove money from the cash drawer.
Enter 1 for Deposit, 2 for Withdrawal, 3 for Balance, 4 to Exit: 1
How much? 100
Place money in the deposit slot.
Enter 1 for Deposit, 2 for Withdrawal, 3 for Balance, 4 to Exit: 4

Insert ATM card:
```

Solution 17.18

Database	
Initialize	Customer, Video
Get_customer	Customer
Get_video	Video
Update	Customer, Video
Show	Customer, Video

Clerk	

UserInterface	

Drill 17.19 Fill in the Clerk and UserInterface cards.

2. Inventory Problem

When I worked with Northwest Orient Airlines at JFK airport and we needed a piece of equipment, we didn't have parts available from only our own stock. Because many airlines use the same plane, for instance, the Boeing 747, we borrowed parts from other airlines as well. In this problem, create three instances of the class called DB (for database). DB should maintain a simple table of five parts each. Assume that there are only five possible parts in our databases. An airline terminal may handle only one part at a time so that we don't have to ask how many when getting the part information from the user.

If a part is not available in your own terminal, then have your database interrogate other terminals' databases to see if you can borrow one. We won't worry about returning any borrowed parts, for now. Keep the databases as independent or autonomous as possible. Accessing the databases of other terminals should be done only by your own database.

Create CRC cards for this problem. You will be asked to continue its design in the next unit. Here is a sample run:

```
1. Northwest  2. PanAm3. TWA   4. Quit : 2
I am now in the PanAm terminal
   1. Need part, 2. Part came in,  3. See inventory, 4. Leave terminal : 1
   Give part number : A507
   We have it. Take one.
   1. Need part, 2. Part came in,  3. See inventory, 4. Leave terminal : 1
   Give part number : A507
   Northwest lent us one. Take it.
   1. Need part, 2. Part came in,  3. See inventory, 4. Leave terminal : 1
   Give part number : A507
   No one has it. Ground the plane.
   1. Need part, 2. Part came in,  3. See inventory, 4. Leave terminal : 2
   Give part number : X200
   Part placed in stock, thank you.
   1. Need part, 2. Part came in,  3. See inventory, 4. Leave terminal : 1
   Give part number : V009
   No such part
   1. Need part, 2. Part came in,  3. See inventory, 4. Leave terminal :
(and so on)
```

3. Adding Date to the Video Store Problem

Using the solution from the drills, add a class called Date that could be a whole number. The menu should be able to change the current date. When returning a tape, Date should calculate how many days late it is, if any, and this should be simply displayed. No fines are given.

Solution 17.19

Clerk	
Go_to_work	UserInterface
	Transaction

UserInterface	
Run_menu	Transaction
Display_message	
Show_database	Database

Design

Jacobson's Interaction Diagrams

After getting a head start by creating the CRC cards, one faces a choice of many formal methodologies to continue the development of a project. We will primarily focus on Ivar Jacobson's interaction diagrams, which are used in his OOSE (object oriented software engineering) method. These diagrams describe what are called *use cases*. A use case identifies the steps that are executed by the system when it is used in a specific way. It begins with "When . . . ." These diagrams describe a scenario and are sometimes also called event–trace diagrams. They are very easy to follow and to code into a working program — therefore, they are very powerful.

Figure 18.1 depicts the scenario of player X making the first move on the tic–tac–toe board of the example used in Unit 17. Vertically we have dotted lines representing the classes activated in this scenario. On the left of the diagram we have a script explaining the steps taken. This could be written partly in English and partly in C++. The horizontal arrows show what messages are passed between which objects. When an object is "made alive," it must perform some tasks and/or

Before doing these drills, review the lesson and experiments sections of this unit. We will do the design and implementation of the video rental problem presented in the drills of Unit 17. Refer to the CRC cards shown in Solutions 17.15 through 17.19 on pages 325 through 329 while doing these drills. First, let us list the classes and their declarations:

```
#include <string.h>
#include <iostream.h>
/////////////////////// CLASSES
class Clerk
{
    public:
        void go_to_work();
};
```

get services from other objects until "he" fulfills "his" responsibility. At that time "his" services are no longer needed. During the time that an object is alive, "he" is said to have control of the execution flow. The solid vertical lines in the diagram show the time when objects have this focus of control.

The Facilitator obtains the initial control and at first, clears and displays the tic–tac–toe board. The Facilitator will start counting nine turns and if the Referee doesn't declare anyone a winner by then, the Facilitator will terminate the game and declare it a tie.

For the first turn, the Referee is told to let X play. Now the Referee has the focus of control. She asks X to play and from him gets a position. The Board is asked to make sure that no one else is on this spot. If there is, then these steps are repeated until a valid move is obtained from X.

Then the position is added to the Board, the Board is displayed, and the Board is asked if there is a winner. Because this is the first move, no winner is declared and control is handed back to the Facilitator.

Notice from the CRC cards of Unit 17 that each of the classes, responsibilities, and collaborators match what we have in Figure 18.1. They should match because the CRC cards weren't presented until these diagrams and the program was completed. Usually, one has to revise several times until a suitable solution is implemented. Examining the execution of scenarios is very helpful in modeling a system correctly.

When choosing scenarios for interaction diagrams, pick small and simple ones first. Later, scenarios that handle exceptions and errors can be studied. Scenarios should be very specific in nature and once the first ones are studied, additional scenarios become easier.

For instance, consider Figure 18.2. Here we trace the execution of the scenario: O makes the winning move.

First, the Facilitator tells the Referee that it is O's turn to play. The Referee tells that player to move. As before, the steps of this event are executed until the Board notifies the Referee that O has won the game. The Referee declares him the winner and notifies the Facilitator that we have a winner. The Facilitator then ends the game.

The scenario for a tie is very similar except for the last few steps. In a tie, the Facilitator would ask the Referee for the ninth time to manage a move for a player. In this event, the Board would not return a winner and that would make the Referee notify the Facilitator that there is no winner. Knowing that this is the last turn of the game, the Facilitator would declare the game a tie and end it.

Again the CRC cards should be checked against the interaction diagrams to make sure that they are in agreement. Finally, it is time to start coding the programs. However, armed with the CRC cards and a few interaction diagrams, the coding of the program should be straightforward. Don't let the length of the program fool you. A seemingly long program that is well designed in C++ will take much less time to code than a program in straight C. In addition, you will get much better manageability, extensibility, and reusability with your well–designed C++ program!

```
class Customer
{  private:
      char  phone[15];        //Customer identification
      char  cust_vid[15];     //Video Customer has out.
      int   null_flag;        //1 if Customer is null
   public:
      void  set_cust(char p[], char v[]);//Initialize
      void  get_phone(char p[]); //provide the phone
      int   can_borrow( );    //return 1 if ok to borrow
      int   has_tape(char v[]);//1 if cust has this tape
      void  lend_out(char v[]);//cust has borrowed tape
      int   returned(char v[]);//Cust returning this tape
      int   check_cust(char p[]);
      void  show();           //Display phone and cust_vid
      int   is_null();        //1 if null
      void  make_null();  //makes null_flag equal 1
      void  make_valid(); //makes null_flag equal 0
};
```

Before we start, we need to revise our design because C++ doesn't allow us to return an object that is null. When we search the database, for example, for a Customer with a given phone number, and that phone number is not found, how do we return a Customer object that is null? One way to do that without the use of pointers is to have a *null_flag* as a private member of Customer that is set to 1 if the object is null and set to 0 if it is a valid Customer with data.

Design

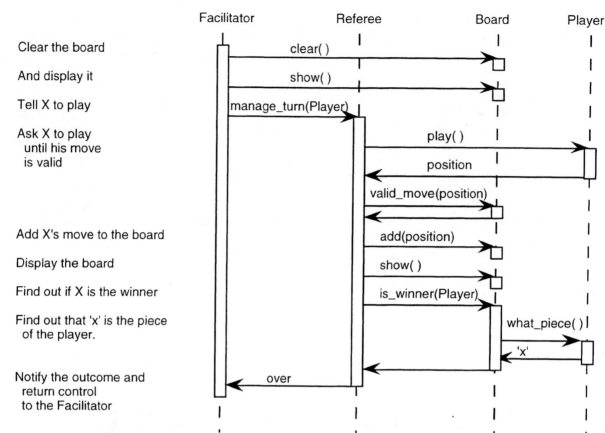

Figure 18.1 The interaction diagram derived from the scenario of X making the first move.

The Implementation Phase

When writing a program in C++, place all class declarations together at the beginning. This tells us, up front, what classes exist and what their interfaces are. The Referee and the Board use Player in their function prototypes in lines 1 and 2, so Player is declared before they are.

After that, any global objects should be declared by placing them toward the beginning of the listing. We have one object called board of class Board. Then the methods used in each class

```
class Video
{  private:
      char   vid[15];
      char   vid_phone[15];
      int    null_flag;
   public:
      void   set_vid(char v[], char p[]);      class Database
      void   get_tape(char v[]);               {  private:
      int    give_in_status( );                      Customer cust[5];
      int    sign_out(char p[]);                     Video    vid[5];
      int    came_in(char p[]);                   public:
      int    check_vid(char v[]);                    void     init_dbase();
      void   show();                                 Customer get_cust(char ph[]);
      int    is_null();                              Video    get_vid (char v[]);
      void   make_null();                            void     update(Customer cust, Video vid);
      void   make_valid();                           void     show();
};                                               };
```

332   Design

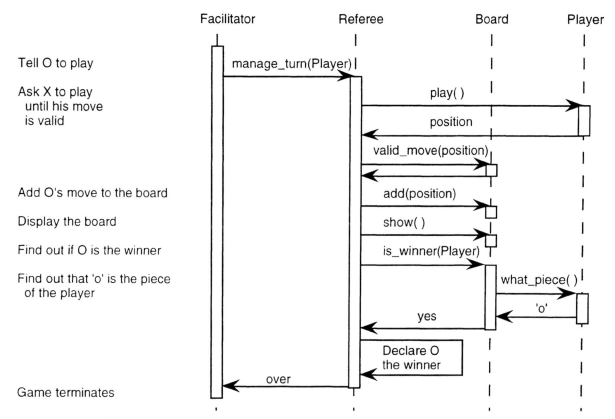

Tell O to play

Ask X to play
until his move
is valid

Add O's move to the board

Display the board

Find out if O is the winner

Find out that 'o' is the piece
of the player

Game terminates

Figure 18.2 The interaction diagram derived from the scenario of O making the winning move.

should be grouped and the classes to which they belong should be highlighted. Last, main() should be listed. Using full–line comments, each of these blocks of code should be clearly identified. If you don't like organizing your code this way, use a consistent method that suits you or is standard in your organization.

   In Example 18.1, execution begins with main(), which immediately obtains the object of Facilitator to play the game. The Facilitator picks the two players and chooses a Referee.

```
class Transaction
{   private:
        int    type;
        char phone[15];
        char vid[15];
    public:
        void set_trans(int sel, char p[], char v[]);
        int   get_choice();
        Database check_out(char msg[], Database dbase);
        Database check_in (char msg[], Database dbase);
};
class UserInterface
{   public:
        Transaction    run_menu(void);
        void           display(char msg[]);
        void           show_db(Database db);
};
```

Drill 18.1 Write the is_null(), make_null(), and make_valid() methods for Customer. These are one–liners and will be similar for Video as well.

Design   333

```
//EXAMPLE 18.1   TIC - TAC - TOE
#include <string.h>
#include <iostream.h>

///////////////////////////////////////// Classes
class Player
{
   private:
         char     piece;
   public:
         void     initialize(char);
         int      play();
         char     what_piece();
};

class Facilitator
{
   public:
         void     play_game();
};



class Referee
{
   public:
         int      manage_turn(Player);                    // Line 1
};

class Board
{
   private:
         char     place[10];   //place[0] is not used
   public:
         void     clear();
         void     show();
         int      empty_cell(int);
         void     add(Player, int);                       // Line 2
         int      three_in_a_row(Player);
};
```

Solution 18.1

```
int Customer::is_null()
{
    return null_flag;
}

void
Customer::make_null()
{
    null_flag = 1;
}

void
Customer::make_valid()
{
    null_flag = 0;
}
```

Drill 18.2 Draw an interaction diagram for the scenario when the Clerk starts to work, initializes the database, and gets the first transaction from the UserInterface.

Clerk	Database	UserInterface	Customer	Video
|	|	|	|	|
|	|	|	|	|
|	|	|	|	|
|	|	|	|	|
|	|	|	|	|

Design

```
///////////////////////////////////// Global Object
Board board;

///////////////////////////////////// Player
void Player::initialize(char c)
{
   piece = c;
}

int Player::play()
{
   int i = 0;
   while(i < 1 || i > 9)
   {
      cout << "Where do you want to go " << piece << "?\n";
      cout << " 1 is top left, 2 is top middle, etc.: ";
      cin  >> i;
   }
   return i;
}

char Player::what_piece()
{
   return piece;
}

///////////////////////////////////// Facilitator
void Facilitator::play_game()
{
   Player  playerX, playerO;
   Referee refer;
   int     turn_count,      // Both players together can go only 9 times.
           over,            // 1 means that someone won, stop the game.
           it_is_Xs_turn = 1;   // 1 means that this is true.
                            //   0 means that it is O's turn.
   playerX.initialize('X');
   playerO.initialize('O');
   board.clear();
   board.show();
```

Solution 18.2

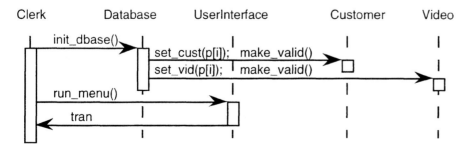

Clerk   Database   UserInterface   Customer   Video

Drill 18.3 Referring to the class declarations, write the init_dbase() method that will set up five Customers and five Videos in two arrays. Also write set_customer() and set_vid() methods. **You will need extra paper for many of the drills in this unit. Remember to use the given class declarations.**

Design

335

```
    for(turn_count = 1; turn_count <= 9; ++turn_count)
    {
        if(it_is_Xs_turn == 1)
            over = refer.manage_turn(playerX);
        else
            over = refer.manage_turn(playerO);
        if(over == 1)                          //if we have a winner, stop game.
            break;
        it_is_Xs_turn = it_is_Xs_turn * (-1); // The other player goes next
    }
    if(turn_count == 10)
        cout << "The game is a TIE! \n";
}


//////////////////////////////////////////// Referee
int Referee::manage_turn(Player p)
{
    int position, valid, won = 0;
    position = p.play();
    for(;board.empty_cell(position) == 0; position = p.play())
        cout << "Not a valid move" << endl ;
    board.add(p, position);
    board.show();
    won = board.three_in_a_row(p);
    if(won == 1)
        cout << p.what_piece() << " WON!\n";
    return won;
}


//////////////////////////////////////////// Board
void Board::clear()
{
    int i;
    for(i=1; i<=9; ++i)
        place[i] = ' ';
}
```

Solution 18.3

```
void Database::init_dbase()                    void Customer::set_cust(char p[], char v[])
{                                              {
    int i;                                         strcpy(phone, p);
    char p[5][15] = {"5189", "6065", "7224",       strcpy(cust_vid, v);
                     "3205", "5552"};          }
    char v[5][15] = {"201", "203", "207",
                     "202", "206"};            void Video::set_vid(char v[], char p[])
    for(i=0; i<=4; ++i)                        {
    {                                              strcpy(vid, v);
        cust[i].set_cust(p[i], "");                strcpy(vid_phone, p);
        cust[i].make_valid();                  }
        vid[i].set_vid(v[i], "");
        vid[i].make_valid();
    }
}
```

Design

```
void Board::show()
{
   int i, j;
   for(i = 0; i <= 2; ++i)
   {
      for(j = 0; j <= 2; ++j)
      {
         cout << ' ' << place[i * 3 + j + 1];
         if(j != 2)
            cout <<"|";
      }
      if(i != 2)
         cout << "\n----------\n";
   }
   cout << "\n\n";
}
```

```
int Board::empty_cell(int i)
{
   if(place[i] == ' ')
      return 1;            // If place is empty, a player can move here.
   else
      return 0;            // Otherwise, there is already someone here.
}
```

```
void Board::add(Player p, int j)    //Add the player's move to the board
{
   place[j] =  p.what_piece();
}
```

Drill 18.4 When the Clerk wants to see the database, to whom does she send what message? What messages are sent by whom because of this initial request? Draw the interaction diagram and write these methods. Again, you will need extra paper.

Clerk	Database	UserInterface	Customer	Video
|	|	|	|	|
|	|	|	|	|
|	|	|	|	|
|	|	|	|	|
|	|	|	|	|

Design

```
int Board::three_in_a_row(Player p)  //See if the player is the winner.
{ char c;
   c = p.what_piece();
   if(place[1] == c)
      if(place[2] == c && place[3] == c)
         return 1;
      else
         if(place[5] == c && place[9] == c)
            return 1;
         else
            if(place[4] == c && place[7] == c)
               return 1;

   if(place[5] == c)
      if(place[2] == c && place[8] == c)
         return 1;
      else
         if(place[3] == c && place[7] == c)
            return 1;
         else
            if(place[4] == c && place[6] == c)
               return 1;

   if(place[9] == c)
      if(place[3] == c && place[6] == c)
         return 1;
      else
         if(place[7] == c && place[8] == c)
            return 1;
   return 0;
}


////////////////////////////////////////// main()
int main (void)
{ Facilitator fac;
   fac.play_game();
   return 0;
}
```

Solution 18.4

```
void UserInterface::show_db(Database db)
{  db.show();
   cout << "\n";
}
```

Clerk   Database   UserInterface Customer   Video

```
void Database::show()
{   int i;
    for(i = 0; i <= 4; ++i)
    {   cust[i].show();
        vid[i].show();
    }
}


void Customer::show()
{   cout << phone << "\t" << cust_vid;
}


void Video::show()
{   cout << "\t" << vid << "\t" <<
                    vid_phone << "\n";
}
```

Design

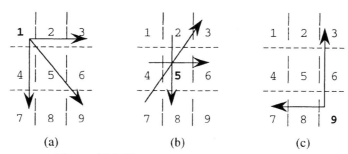

Figure 18.3 Eight ways of winning at tic–tac–toe.

In Facilitator::play_game(), Facilitator counts the nine turns by varying *turn_count* in a for loop. Inside the loop, Facilitator will send playerX or playerO, depending on whose turn it is, to play their turn. If the Referee returns a 1, then a winner is declared. Facilitator will break out of the loop and stop the game.

If no winner is declared, then *over* will not be a 1 and the Facilitator continues with the loop after switching the players.

This logic is quite evident in the interaction diagrams we created earlier. Using the same diagrams, Referee::manage_turn() can be coded easily.

The methods defined in Board are straightforward. In the Board::is_winner() method, the player is identified first as either 'x' or 'o'. Then using that character, a winner is identified. The logic here is that only the person who just played can be the winner. Also, notice how the if's are constructed. If there isn't a winner, then only three if's will be executed. Otherwise, it's possible to get a maximum of eight if's.

In Figure 18.3, the three primary if's are outlined. If the player is in position 1, then there are three ways to win: 1, 2, 3; or 1, 5, 9; or 1, 4, 7. See Figure 18.3(a).

In Figure 18.3(b), the player is in position 5. If this is so, he or she could be a winner if he or she is in position 2, 5, 8; or 4, 5, 6; or 7, 5, 3. In Figure 18.3(c), the last two possibilities are investigated. These combinations make up the eight ways in which one can win at this game.

EXPERIMENTS

The primary objective of the experiments in this unit is to formulate a design and implement the call center problem that was analyzed in the experiments of the previous unit. First, let us review and take care of some C++ syntax.

Drill 18.5 Now let us study the following scenario: "Customer with a phone ID of 3205 who has no other videos out wants to check out video 203, which is in the store."

a. What message will the Clerk pass to whom?
b. What are the arguments that will be sent by the Clerk and which will be returned to her?
c. In Transaction::check_out(), a local object called *cust* will be the customer whose phone number is 3205. Also, a local object *tape*, whose videoID is 203, will be set up. What messages sent to whom will allow *cust* and *tape* to be created?
d. What messages will Transaction send to make sure these two objects are valid?
e. In this case, these two objects are in the database. By which message will Transaction know that this Customer may borrow a tape?
f. By which message will Transaction know that this tape is available for sign out?
g. With which message will Transaction update the *cust* object? And the *tape* object?
h. With which message will Transaction update the database?

Design

Exp 18.1 In this experiment, we have a class called Invoice that has an array of objects of class LineItem. When running this program, there is no output; but enter the following data:

```
5 belts
2 caps
4 pins
```

```
#include <iostream.h>
#include <string.h>

class LineItem
{
    private:
        int qty;
        char description[15];
    public:
        void set_it(int, char [ ]);
};

void LineItem::set_it(int q, char descrip[15])
{
    qty = q;
    strcpy(description, descrip);
}

class Invoice
{
    private:
        LineItem x[3];
    public:
        void generate(void);
};

void Invoice::generate()
{
    int i, qty;
    char descrip[15];
```

Solution 18.5

a. check_out() will be sent to Transaction.
b. A string that I will name *msg*, and *db*, the database, will be sent by the Clerk. The updated database will be received into *db*.
c. The get_cust(phone) and get_vid(vid) messages to the database will create *cust* and *tape*.
d. The is_null() messages will be sent to *cust* and to *tape*.
e. The can_borrow() message to *cust* will determine that.
f. The give_in_status() message to *tape* will determine that.
g. cust.lend_out(vid) and tape.sign_out(phone) will update those objects.
h. The dbase.update(cust, tape) will update the entire database.

Drill 18.6 On a separate sheet draw the interaction diagram for the scenario in Solution 18.5.

Design

```
   cout << "Enter quantity and description three times:\n";
   for(i = 0; i <= 2; ++i)
   {
      cin >> qty >> descrip;
      x[i].set_it(qty, descrip);
   }
}


void main (void)
{
   Invoice march;
   march.generate();
}
```

    a. Can the definition of Invoice be placed before the definition of LineItem in the program listing? Why or why not?

    b. What is the name of the object defined in main()?

    c. In main(), why can't you call generate() without *march*?

    d. In main(), are any arguments passed to the function Invoice::generate()? Is any value returned from there?

    e. In main(), can you access *x[ ]*? Why or why not?

    f. In main(), can you access generate()? Why or why not?

    g. In main(), can you access set_it()? Why or why not?

    h. In main(), what data members are accessible? What member functions are accessible?

    i. In Invoice::generate(), what data members are accessible? What member functions are accessible?

    j. In Invoice::generate(), is set_it() accessible? Why or why not?

    k. What arguments does LineItem::set_it() receive? What value does it return?

    l. Now we want to modify this code so that main() prints the contents of *march*. First, make a copy of the original listing; you may find it helpful to do the next experiment.

Write two functions both named as show_it(), one for Invoice and one for LineItem. In LineItem::show_it(), print only the *description* and return the *qty*. In Invoice::show_it(), print the quantity received from LineItem. Once you get your modification working, copy the lines of code that were added next to the code given above.

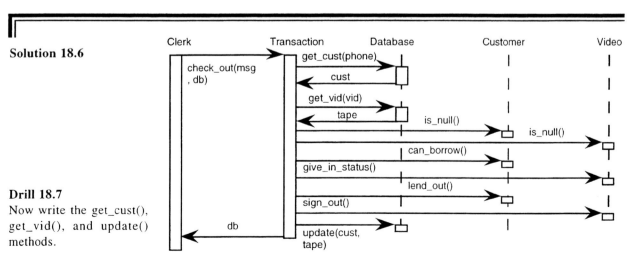

Solution 18.6

Drill 18.7
Now write the get_cust(), get_vid(), and update() methods.

Exp 18.2 Now we want to see how objects are returned by a function. Modify Experiment 18.1 as shown below. Lines shown in bold have been added or changed.

```
#include <iostream.h>
#include <string.h>

class LineItem
{
   private:
      int qty;
      char description[15];
   public:
      void set_it(int, char [ ]);
};

class Part
{
   private:
      int q;
      char d[15];
   public:
      LineItem generate(void);
};

void LineItem::set_it(int q, char descrip[15])
{
   qty = q;
   strcpy(description, descrip);
}

LineItem Part::generate()
{
   LineItem line;
   cout << "Enter quantity and description: ";
   cin >> q >> d;
   line.set_it(q, d);
   return line;
}
```

Solution 18.7

```
Customer Database::get_cust(char ph[])
{  int i;   Customer customer;
   for(i=0; i<=4; ++i)
      if(cust[i].check_cust(ph) == 1)
         return cust[i];
   customer.make_null();
   return customer;
}
Video Database::get_vid(char v[])
{  int i;   Video video;
   for(i=0; i<=4; ++i)
      if(vid[i].check_vid(v) == 1)
         return vid[i];
   video.make_null();
   return video;
}
```

```
void Database::update(Customer customer,
Video video)
{  int i;
   char p[15], v[15];
   customer.get_phone(p);
   video.get_tape(v);

   for(i=0; i<=4; ++i)
      if(cust[i].check_cust(p) == 1)
         cust[i] = customer;
   for(i=0; i<=4; ++i)
      if(vid[i].check_vid(v) == 1)
         vid[i] = video;
}
```

Drill 18.8 Now write can_borrow(), lend_out(), give_in_status(), and sign_out().

Design

```
void main (void)
{
   LineItem march[3];
   Part p;
   int i;
   for(i = 0; i <= 2; ++i)
      march[i] = p.generate();
}
```

a. In Experiment 18.1, main() declared how many objects of class Invoice? What was its name?
b. In Experiment 18.1, one object of class Invoice was made up of how many objects of class LineItem? How were they stored and what was the object's name?
c. In this experiment, main() declared how many objects of class Invoice?
d. In this experiment, main() declared how many objects of class LineItem? Give their names and describe how they are stored.
e. In this experiment, main() declared how many objects of class Part? What are their names?
f. Here, one LineItem has how many data members? Are any of the data members also objects?
g. Does the class Part have any private objects? If so, what are their names?
h. Does the function Part::generate() have any local objects? If so, what are their names?
i. The following questions pertain to how main() sends messages.
    1. main() sends a message to the object of class Part how many times?
    2. What is the name of that message?
    3. Each time that this message is sent to the object, what data type is returned by that object?
    4. What does main() do with that returned object?
j. When an object receives a message, that object uses a _____ to fulfill that request. In straight C, we call this a function definition.
k. Now that you see how objects are returned, try modifying this experiment to see how objects can be passed as arguments. Write Part::display(), which will receive an object of class LineItem and print the two members of LineItem. If necessary, also write LineItem::display().
l. In a loop, have main() assign the elements of *march[ ]* to *p*, and send the display() message each time. Once your modification is working, copy the lines of code that were added next to the code given above.

Call Center Problem: Now let us turn our attention to the call center problem described in the Experiments section of Unit 17. In the last experiments we filled out the CRC cards. Figure 18.4

Solution 18.8

```
int Customer::can_borrow( )
{
   if(strcmp(cust_vid, "") == 0)
      return 1; //Has no video out
   else
      return 0; //Has a video out
}


void Customer::lend_out(char v[])
{
   strcpy(cust_vid, v);
}
```

```
int Video::give_in_status()
{
   if(strcmp(vid_phone, "") == 0)
      return 1;   //Tape is in
   else
      return 0;   //Tape is out
}


int Video::sign_out(char p[])
{
   if(strcmp(vid_phone, "") == 0)
   {
      strcpy(vid_phone, p);
      return 1;   //Successful
   }
   else
      return 0; //Someone else has tape out
}
```

Operator

Go to work	CallDistributor
†Read data	
†Accept a customer's call	
†Accept an agent's call	

Queue

Initialize	
Push (Add someone)	
Pop (Remove someone)	

Agent

Initialize	
Give count	
Serve customer	
*Notify when free	Operator

CallDistributor

Initialize	Queue
Agent free	Queue
Customer call	Agent, Queue
Stop the show	Agent

Figure 18.4 The CRC cards for the call center application.
* This responsibility is not implemented in our system because the read in data signals the Operator when an Agent becomes free.
† These three responsibilities are included in Go to work.

shows mine. How close are we? In any case, let us use my CRC cards to develop the design so that we have a common base on which to build.

In our final design we will omit the responsibilities marked with a star and the daggers because we don't have a real phone center but one simulated with input data. To do the following experiments, use these class declarations:

```
class Operator
{
   public:
      void go_to_work();//Reads data, calls agent_free or customer_call.
};
```

Drill 18.9 The following method needs four messages copied into "*msg[ ]*." Where do they go? The messages are: Checkout successful, Phone or VideoID not in database, Customer already has a videotape out, and Tape not available.

```
Database Transaction::check_out(char msg[],
                              Database dbase)
{  Customer cust;
   Video    tape;

   cust = dbase.get_cust(phone);
   tape = dbase.get_vid(vid);
```

```
   if(cust.is_null()==1 ||
               tape.is_null() == 1)
      strcpy(msg,"        ");
   else
      if(cust.can_borrow() == 1)
         if(tape.give_in_status() == 1)
         {  cust.lend_out(vid);
            tape.sign_out(phone);
            dbase.update(cust, tape);
            strcpy(msg, "        ");
         }
         else
            strcpy(msg, "        ");
      else
         strcpy(msg, "        ");
   return dbase;
}
```

```
class Queue
{
   private:
      int first_empty_slot; //Location of the first free element in queue
      int Array[10];          //This is the queue itself
   public:
      void initialize();      //first_empty_slot is set to 0.
      void push(int);         //caller is added at the end of the queue.
      int pop();              //Returns first person in queue and moves
};                            //everyone else up in the array.


class Agent
{
   private:
      int count;              //This is the number of customers the agent
   public:                    //has served.
      void serve_customer(int);//The agent increments the count.
      int give_count();       //Returns the number of customers served.
      void initialize();      //Sets count to 0.
};


class CallDistributor
{
   private:
      Queue customer_q;       //A queue to store customers on hold
      Queue agent_q;          //A queue to store waiting agents.
      Agent a1, a2, a3;       //Three agents that are managed
      void serve_customer(int, int);//This method is used in agent_free()
   public:                             //and in customer_call().
      void initialize();      //Initializes the queues and agents.
      void agent_free(int);   //Find a customer or push agent on queue.
      void customer_call(int); //Find an agent or push customer on queue.
      void stop_the_show();   //Display the final report.
};
```

Solution 18.9

```
Database Transaction::check_out(char msg[],
                                Database dbase)
{ Customer cust;
  Video     tape;

  cust = dbase.get_cust(phone);
  tape = dbase.get_vid(vid);

  if(cust.is_null() == 1 || tape.is_null() == 1)
    strcpy(msg,
        "Phone or VideoID not in database");
  else
    if(cust.can_borrow() == 1)
      if(tape.give_in_status() == 1)
```
```
        { cust.lend_out(vid);
          tape.sign_out(phone);
          dbase.update(cust, tape);
          strcpy(msg,
              "Checkout successful!");
        }
        else
          strcpy(msg,
              "Tape not available");
      else
        strcpy(msg, "Customer already
              has a video out");
  return dbase;
}
```

Design

(script)	Operator	CallDistributor	Queue	Agent

Exp 18.3 In the diagram provided, draw the interaction diagram for the following scenario: "When the Operator goes to work and triggers the initialization processes, what happens before the reading of data can take place?" The CallDistributor has to initialize two queues, the agent queue that holds the agents waiting to serve a customer, and a customer queue that holds customers waiting to be served.

a. Can there be someone in each of these queues at any given time?
b. The first_empty_slot specifies where the next available location exists in the queue. Initially, this variable should be set to 0 in each queue.
c. After you draw the interaction diagram, you should be in a position to write the three initialize() methods. Try them.

```
void Queue::initialize()



void Agent::initialize()



void CallDistributor::initialize()
```

Drill 18.10 Now let us study what happens when Customer 3205 returns video 203 that he has signed out. Customer 3205 and Video 203 are in the Database.
a. What choice will be selected by the user? What will be the values of *type*, *phone[15]*, and *vid[15]* in the Transaction to be sent by the UserInterface to the Clerk?
b. How will the Clerk find out that this transaction is a check in?
c. After that, what message will the Clerk send to whom?
d. What will the Clerk send as arguments and what will she receive back from that object?
e. How will the Transaction know that Customer 3205 and Video 203 exist at least in the Database?
f. How can Transaction know that the Customer brought the right tape back?
g. How should the Video object be updated?
h. How should the Customer object be updated?
i. How should the Database object be updated?
j. These last three updates are done by which object? By which method?

(script)	Operator	CallDistributor	Queue	Agent
	|	|	|	|
	|	|	|	|
	|	|	|	|
	|	|	|	|
	|	|	|	|
	|	|	|	|
	|	|	|	|
	|	|	|	|
	|	|	|	|

Exp 18.4 Draw the interaction diagram for the following scenario: "Only Agent1 is serving a customer while Agent2 becomes available or free." Use the method names given in the class declarations.

a. The Operator reads the data and determines that it is an agent who has become available. Which message should the Operator pass to the CallDistributor?
b. How can the CallDistributor determine that no customers are on hold waiting to be served?
c. Write the Queue::pop() method that will return a 0 if there is no one in the queue; otherwise, return the integer that is next in line.

```
int Queue::pop()
```

d. If there are no customers on hold, what method should the CallDistributor invoke?
e. If there is a customer on hold, what method should the CallDistributor have invoked? Now try writing CallDistributor::agent_free().

Solution 18.10
a. 2; *type* will be 2, *phone[15]* will be 3205, and *vid[15]* will be 203.
b. The get_choice() message sent to Transaction will return the type of the transaction.
c. The Clerk will send the check_in() message to Transaction.
d. The Clerk will send a *msg[15]* and the Database and receive the Database in return. *msg[ ]* will contain any user messages that need to be conveyed, such as "successful."
e. Transaction will send get messages to the Database, providing 3205 and 203 as arguments. Customer and Video objects will be received. Sending the is_null() messages to them will determine that they are in the Database.
f. Transaction will send the has_tape() message to Customer and pass 203 as an argument.
g. Transaction should send the came_in() message to Video.
h. Transaction should send the returned() message to Customer.
i. Transaction should send the update() message to Database.
j. These updates are done by Transaction in the check_in() method.

```
void CallDistributor::agent_free(int agent)
```

Exp 18.5 Now draw the interaction diagram for the following scenario: "Customers 300 and 700 are waiting when customer 400 calls."

a. First, the Operator sends which message to CallDistributor?
b. In this method of CallDistributor, how does the CallDistributor know that no agents are available?
c. What method does the CallDistributor send in this scenario and to whom?
d. Now try writing the CallDistributor::customer_call() method.

```
void CallDistributor::customer_call(int cust)
```

(script)	Operator	CallDistributor	Queue	Agent

Drill 18.11 Draw the interaction diagram for the check-in scenario.

Clerk	Database	UserInterface	Customer	Video

Exp 18.6 Draw the interaction diagram for the following scenario: "Customers 300 and 700 are waiting when Agent 2 becomes free." This scenario may not add any new information to your design but may only confirm it. If you have something wrong, don't hesitate to go back and correct it.

a. Try writing the Queue::push() method.

```
void Queue::push(int item)
```

b. Finish the CallDistributor::serve_customer() method. Here is how I started it:

```
void CallDistributor::serve_customer(int agent, int cust)
{
   if(agent==1)
     a1.serve_customer(cust);
   else
```

(script)	Operator	CallDistributor	Queue	Agent

Solution 18.11

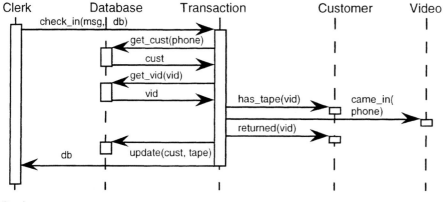

Drill 18.12
We won't bother writing the Transaction::check_in() method this time. It is similar to the check_out() method. However, on a separate sheet, write the Clerk::go_to_work() method.

Design   349

Exp 18.7 Draw the interaction diagram for the following scenario: "The Operator reads a 0."

a. Which message should the Operator send to the CallDistributor?
b. Which messages should the CallDistributor send to the Agent?
c. Now try writing the following four methods:

```
void Operator::go_to_work()
{
   CallDistributor supervisor;
```

```
void CallDistributor::stop_the_show()
{
```

(script)	Operator	CallDistributor	Queue	Agent

Solution 18.12

```
void Clerk::go_to_work()
{
   char            msg[40]="";
   UserInterface ui;
   int             choice;
   Transaction     tran;
   Database        db;

   db.init_dbase();
   tran  = ui.run_menu();
   choice = tran.get_choice();
```

```
   for(; choice != 4; )
   {  strcpy(msg, "");
      if(choice == 1)
          db = tran.check_out(msg, db);
      else
          if(choice == 2)
             db = tran.check_in(msg, db);
      if(strcmp(msg, "") != 0)
          ui.display(msg);
      if(choice == 3)
          ui.show_db(db);
      tran   = ui.run_menu();
      choice = tran.get_choice();
   }
   ui.display("I'm jetting");
}
```

Drill 18.13 Now write the UserInterface::run_menu().

```
void Agent::serve_customer(int customer)
{




int Agent::give_count()
{
```

QUESTIONS

1. What is a use case? What is a scenario?
2. Describe the parts of a Jacobson's interaction diagram and explain how to draw one.
3. When creating a scenario, is it better to study simpler cases first or cases that give errors?
4. Can the implementation phase force the analysis of a problem to be modified? Where in the lesson, experiments, and drills is there support for your answer?
5. Rewrite the nested if logic in int Board::three_in_a_row(Player p) in Example 18.1 on page 338. Is your answer more efficient or less efficient, in general?
6. Using the two classes given below, write set_up() that will create one question and its answer. Write make() that will create an exam with 10 questions. Also write find() that will get a Question with no answer and return that same Question with the correct answer found from the 10 questions of the Exam. Assume that the question exists in the Exam. Write main() to test make() and find(). Add new functions if necessary.

```
class Question                      class Exam
{     char text[50];                {     class Question q[10];
      char answer[50];                  public:
   public:                                  void make();
      void set_up(char t[50],               void find(Question q);
      char a[50]);                   };
};
```

PROGRAMS

For each of the programs for which you wrote CRC cards, create at least two scenarios and draw their interaction diagrams. Then code those designs into C++ code.

Solution 18.13

```
Transaction UserInterface::run_menu()
{
    Transaction tran;
    char p[15], v[15];
    int choice;

    cout << "1.Check out, 2.Check in, 3.Show DB, 4.Quit";
    cin  >> choice;
    if(choice != 3 && choice != 4)
    {
        cout << "Give your phone and video numbers ";
        cin  >> p >> v;
    }
    tran.set_trans(choice, p, v);
    return tran;
}
```

Last note: By now you should be able to code main() and fourteen other functions. Many are small and all of them should be relatively simple.

Dynamic Objects

Learning Pointers

While I was introducing object–oriented concepts in the past three chapters, I was careful not to use any pointers. I did this so that we could concentrate only on OO principles and not have to be sidetracked by implementation details. However, it is difficult to write a program in C or C++ without functions, and it is difficult to write a program with any substance, without pointers. A student once said to me that he doesn't want to learn pointers, he just wants to write games. This is like a farmer saying that he doesn't want to plant and cultivate, he just wants to bring in the harvest. The more you work with pointers, the more fun they will become.

Units 12 and 13 already covered pointers in detail. In this unit I will assume that you skipped those units, but I will move fast. If you have to study this unit twice, do so. If you still find yourself at a loss, then maybe you should go back to Units 12 and 13. In any case, if you want to be proficient with C++, you must be proficient with pointers. And all it takes is a little time!

Drill 19.1 If we declare four variables as follows:

```
int i, j, *q, *p;
```

then *i* and *j* are declared as integer variables that can store only integer values. However, since *q* and *p* have asterisks in front of them, they are called pointer variables. *q* can store only addresses to integer locations, such as &i. &i is the address of *i*. In the diagram on the next page, this is FFF2. Furthermore, *j* is stored at FFF6 and *q* is stored at FFF8. (I just made up these addresses; they could be anything.) The addresses are normally given in hexadecimal.

Understanding Pointers

Maybe the best way to learn pointers is to learn how assembly language works. In Figure 19.1, we have a simple computer system. It shows RAM (random access memory) and a CPU (central processing unit). RAM is simply called memory and this is where computer instructions,

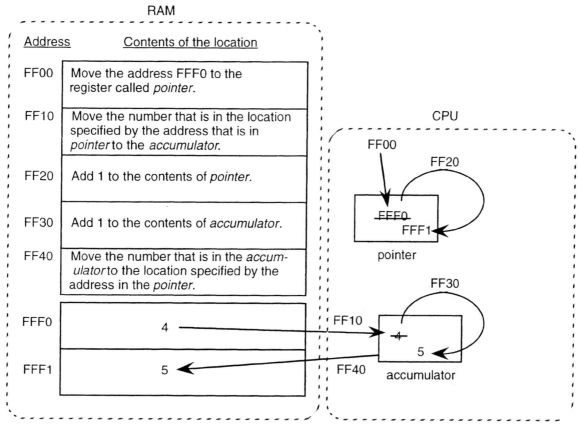

Figure 19.1 An example of the execution of assembly language instructions. Notice the importance of addresses of RAM. The arrows show the effect of executing the instructions stored in the addresses given.

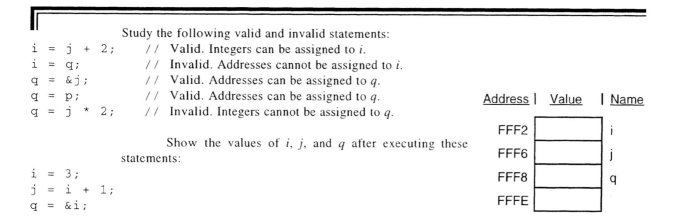

Study the following valid and invalid statements:

```
i = j + 2;      // Valid. Integers can be assigned to i.
i = q;          // Invalid. Addresses cannot be assigned to i.
q = &j;         // Valid. Addresses can be assigned to q.
q = p;          // Valid. Addresses can be assigned to q.
q = j * 2;      // Invalid. Integers cannot be assigned to q.
```

Show the values of *i*, *j*, and *q* after executing these statements:

```
i = 3;
j = i + 1;
q = &i;
```

Address	Value	Name
FFF2		i
FFF6		j
FFF8		q
FFFE		

Dynamic Objects

data, and other items are stored. RAM is made up of locations, and each location is accessed by its address, just as a person's house is found by the address. The intelligence of the computer is in the CPU. It has high–speed registers where arithmetic and other operations can be done.

A sequence of simple assembly instructions are shown in RAM. They are shown in English rather than the real commands. The computer executes the instructions stored in sequence starting at location FF00. The addresses are shown in the hexadecimal numbering system. You don't have to be concerned about this numbering system, only about the fact that it exists. It is used to abbreviate the long strings of 1's and 0's used in the binary numbering system. Let us go through this simple program.

First, the CPU executes the instruction stored at location FF00. This instruction places the RAM address of FFF0 in the CPU's register called the *pointer*. Then the CPU executes the next instruction found in FF10, which says go to the location FFF0, the address that is in the *pointer*, and move the number from there (4) into the accumulator. So now we have a 4 in the accumulator. The next two instructions simply add 1 to the contents of the *pointer* and 1 to the contents of the *accumulator*.

When the CPU is ready to execute the instruction at location FF40, the *pointer* will be equal to FFF1 and the *accumulator* will have a 5 stored in it. Finally, the last instruction will move the number in the *accumulator*, 5, to the location specified by the *pointer*. This location is FFF1.

If you understand what happened in this example, you are well on your way to learning pointers. The only item left is learning the C++ notation that corresponds to the English–like instructions given here. Let us now look at Figure 19.2, where that is done.

Since we know variables in C++ by their names more than by their addresses, I have shown the variable names of *i* and *j* in RAM. *i* is stored at address FFF0 and *j* is stored at address FFF1.

The first instruction, which is at location FF00, is pointer = &i;. The &i symbol means find the address of *i*. This address, which is FFF0, is stored in *pointer*. In the next instruction, *pointer means find the address stored in *pointer* and access what is in that address. In this case, FFF0 is in the *pointer*, and in FFF0 there is a 4. This 4 is then stored in the accumulator. Notice that *pointer* is a one–step access; that is, go to the location called *pointer*. However, *pointer is a two–step access; that is, get the address stored in *pointer*, and then go to that address. Therefore, the * is called the de–reference or indirection operator.

The instructions at FF20 and FF30 simply add 1 to both the *accumulator* and the *pointer*. Now the *accumulator* is equal to 5 and *pointer* is equal to FFF1. In the last statement, the contents of the *accumulator* are stored in *pointer. Hence, 5 is *not* stored in the *pointer*, but in *pointer, which is the location FFF1.

To declare the variables for this example, we need the following statements:

```
int i, j, accumulator,    // These store only integers.
    *pointer;             // This one stores an address to integers.
```

Solution 19.1

Address	Value	Name
FFF2	3	i
FFF6	4	j
FFF8	FFF2	q
FFFE		p

Drill 19.2 The values of *i*, *j*, and *q* are 3, 4, and FFF2, respectively. However, since the value of *q* is an address in RAM, we may want a mechanism to represent the contents of the location whose address is in *q*. We can do this by using an asterisk again. Hence, *q* evaluates to FFF2 and *q evaluates to 3, the contents of the location whose address is FFF2.

When we declare pointers, we can initialize them as well. Using the same figure, show the new values after executing the following statements:

```
int *p = &j;
j = *q;       // Line 2
```

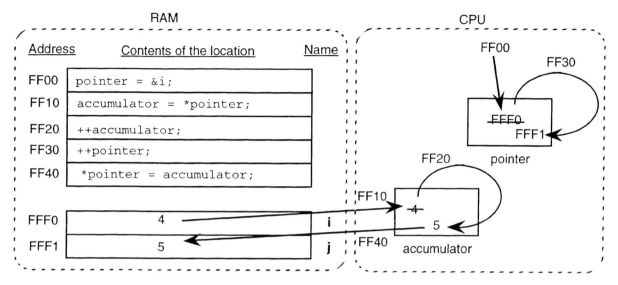

Figure 19.2 The assembly language instructions of Figure 19.1 converted to C and C++ instructions.

One confusing part of declaring *pointer* is that the asterisk is not an indirection operator but a notation to mean that this variable stores addresses. In the statements in Figure 19.2, the * in *pointer refers to the indirection or de–reference operator.

Notice that you may assign *j*, 5, or *pointer to *i*, and you may assign &i or another integer pointer to *pointer*. However, you may not assign *j*, 5, or *pointer to *pointer*, and you may not assign &j or *pointer* to *i*. Pointers may contain only addresses (not integer values) and integer variables may contain only integer values (not addresses). Before moving on to the next topics, you may find it beneficial to do Drills 19.1 through 19.5.

Using Pointers

In this section let us consider the many ways pointers are used and a couple of other C++ features. We will study the topics in this order: const, pointers, inline functions, references, arrays as pointers, and arrays of pointers. First, let us look at Example 19.1.

Solution 19.2 Notice that in int *p = &j; *p* is declared as a pointer variable (or just a pointer). In Line 2, not the value of *q*, but the value of the location whose address is in *q*, is placed into *j*.

$$j = {}^{*}q;$$

Address	Value	Name
FFF2	3	i
FFF6	3	j
FFF8	FFF2	q
FFFE	FFF6	p

Drill 19.3 Change the diagram to show what the following statements will do:
```
*p = 5;
i = *q + 1;
q = p;
```

```
//EXAMPLE 19.1
#include <iostream.h>
inline int minimum(int a, int b)
   { if (a < b) return a; else return b; }
void main (void)
{
   const int SIZE = 8;       // Constant data item
   int i = 3, j = 4,         // Integer variables
        *p1 = &i, *p2;       // Pointers to integers
   int &r = i;               // A reference variable

   p2 = &j;
   *p2 = *p1 + *p2;                              // Stmt 1
   cout << p1 << " " << p2 << endl;
   cout << *p1 << " " << j << endl;
   cout << minimum(SIZE, *p2) << endl;

   r = r + *p2;    // Or i = i + j;             // Stmt 2
   cout << r << " " << &r << endl;
}
----- output -----
FFF4 FFF2
3 7
7
10 FFF4
```

const: This wonderful keyword forces a data item to stay constant. Unlike variables whose values may change during the execution of a program, constants prevent us from inadvertently altering them. Typically, all capital letters are used to name them, so programmers can know that they are constants without having to find their declarations.

You can qualify practically any data type as a constant, including floats, characters, pointers, class members, objects, and so on. When passing an address to a function, the const qualifier can prevent that function from changing the contents of that address. In Example 19.1, SIZE is an integer constant, and it is set to 8. Once it is initialized, its value can't be changed.

Pointers: In the example, i and j are integers, but $p1$ and $p2$ are pointers to integers. The * used in their declarations make them pointers, not the fact that their names begin with the letter p. You cannot store integers in $p1$ and $p2$. In fact, you shouldn't store addresses of other data types in them either. They should contain only addresses of RAM locations where integers are stored.

Solution 19.3 The first statement will assign a 5 into FFF6, the address that is in p. In the second statement, *q is actually i because the address of i, which is FFF2, is in q at that time. Hence, 1 is added to i. In the final statement, not *p, but simply p is assigned to q. That's fine because both are integer pointer types.

Address	Value	Name
FFF2	4	i
FFF6	5	j
FFF8	FFF6	q
FFFE	FFF6	p

Drill 19.4
Show how the values change after the following statements are executed:

```
p = &i;
*p = *q;
*q = j + i;
```

Dynamic Objects

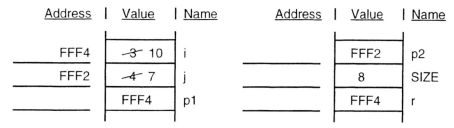

Address	Value	Name	Address	Value	Name
FFF4	~~3~~ 10	i		FFF2	p2
FFF2	~~4~~ 7	j		8	SIZE
	FFF4	p1		FFF4	r

Figure 19.3 Studying the memory locations for Example 19.1.

When they are declared, *p1* is initialized to have the address of *i* or FFF4, but *p2* is not initialized. Later, *p2* is assigned the address of *j*, which is shown as FFF2 in the output. The location addresses are shown in Figure 19.3. On your system, these addresses may be different but they will correspond to whatever is stored in the pointers.

Figure 19.4 shows what happens when Statement 1 is executed. The right side of the assignment is evaluated by first going to *p1* and getting the address stored there, namely, FFF4. Then, at the location whose address is FFF4, a value of 3 is found. This number is added to the 4 found in location FFF2, which is the address stored in *p2*. Finally, 7, the sum, is stored in the location pointed to by *p2*, or into FFF2. FFF2 is the address of *j*, so now *j* has become 7. This is confirmed in the output.

Inline functions: In the third line of the output, we call a function named minimum(). We pass SIZE and *p2, which is now 7, as arguments. The function is declared and defined outside any other function so it can be used by anyone. It has become global. In the function, *a* becomes 8, the value of SIZE, and *b* becomes 7. Since *a* is not less than *b*, the function will return a 7, the value of *b*. Hence, 7 is printed.

The keyword `inline` placed before the function suggests that the compiler make this function inline. This means copy and modify the code every place the function is called. These steps

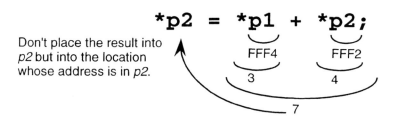

Figure 19.4 Understanding de-reference or indirection.

Solution 19.4 First, the address of *i*, FFF2, is placed into *p*. Next, *q, which is 5, is placed into *p or into *i*. Last, *i* and *j*, which are both 5, are added and placed into *q or into FFF6.

Address	Value	Name
FFF2	5	i
FFF6	**10**	j
FFF8	FFF6	q
FFFE	**FFF2**	p

Drill 19.5 Here's a whole new set of variables and statements. Their addresses are as shown. Again, show the contents of the locations that are changed.

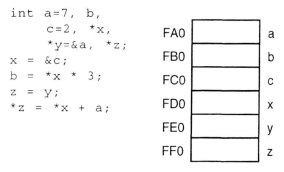

```
int  a=7,  b,
     c=2,  *x,
     *y=&a,  *z;
x  =  &c;
b  =  *x  *  3;
z  =  y;
*z  =  *x  +  a;
```

will make the execution of the program efficient because in a typical function call, the flow of execution jumps to the function and back. With the inline function, the code for the function is substituted right into the lines where the function is called. The code needed to execute the function is right in–line. In this example, the compiler may substitute the following code for the inline function:

```
if(SIZE < *p2)
   cout << SIZE;
else
   cout << *p2;
```

Small functions that are called many times are good candidates for inline functions. If you have too many inline functions, your program may become long, a situation called "code bloat." On the other hand, without inline functions, you have to set up and take down a function call every time it is invoked, a situation called "context shift." Soon we will see how they can be used in defining member functions, a big time saver for coding.

References: In the example, *r* is declared as a reference variable, or simply reference, for short. A reference variable is nothing more than another name for the variable whose address it has. Here, *r* can be treated simply as an *alias* for *i*.

On the surface that is all one needs to know about references. However, in studying them further, one finds that they are similar to pointers. *r* contains the address *i*, which is FFF4, just as *p1* does. However, we could change the value of *p1*, that is, have it point to another integer, such as *j*; but *r*, being a reference variable, can't be changed once it is initialized. It is like a pointer constant.

Furthermore, to de–reference a pointer we use *, while a reference variable is de–referenced automatically. No * is used. Notice in the following in Statement 2:

```
r = r + *p2;
```

to de–reference the pointer *p2*, *p2 is used. To de–reference the reference *r*, *r is not used. Simply *r* is used. See Table 19.1 on page 360 to compare references and pointers. When we need to pass a complex and large data structure to a function, passing by value or copying is not efficient but passing by reference is. Also, since a reference is nothing more than an alias, a reference is easier to use than a pointer.

Arrays as pointers: Now let us turn to Example 19.2 and Figure 19.5. We see in the figure how *a[ ]* and *b[ ]* are stored with the '\0' character terminating each string. I just made up the address locations so it would be easy to keep track of memory addresses. Again, on your system these

---

Solution 19.5

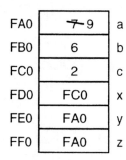

Drill 19.6 Below we have introduced a reference variable called *r*. An ampersand, instead of an asterisk, is placed in front of it while it is being declared. It will contain the address of *j* even though &j is not specified. Also, the last statement will make *j* equal to 1 even though it doesn't state *r = 1;. The & in the declaration and the * in the use of a reference variable are understood. Convert these statements so that *p*, a regular pointer, is used instead of *r*.

```
int i = 10, j = 20;
int &r = j;
r = 1;
```

FFF2	10	i
FFF6	~~20~~ 1	j
FFFA	FFF6	r

Dynamic Objects

```
//EXAMPLE 19.2
#include <stdio.h> // Used to print pointers.
#include <iostream.h>
void main (void)
{
   char a[ ] = "sha";              // An array of characters
   char b[ ] = "boom";             // Another array of characters
   char *c[2];                     // An array of pointers to characters

   printf("%s %s %p %p\n", a, &a[0], a, &a[0]);     // Stmt 1
   c[0] = a;                                        // Stmt 2
   c[1] = &b[0];                                    // Stmt 3
   for(int i = 0; i <= 1; ++i)
      printf("%s %p\n",  c[i], c[i]);
}
----- output -----
sha sha FFA0 FFA0
sha FFA0
boom FFB0
```

addresses may be different, but their behavior will be the same. In Statement 1, we see that, using %s, printing *a* and &a[0] will print the string, while using %p will print the address of where the array begins.

If *a* is an array, then *a* stores the starting address of the array. For that reason, *a* can be thought of as a pointer whose value cannot be changed. Once an array is created in RAM, we can't change its location. It turns out that *a* and &a[0] are equivalent.

Address	Value	Name		Address	Value	Name		Value	Name
FFA0	's'	a[0]		FFB0	'b'	b[0]		FFA0	a
FFA1	'h'	a[1]		FFB1	'o'	b[1]		FFB0	b
FFA2	'a'	a[2]		FFB2	'o'	b[2]			
FFA3	'\0'	a[3]		FFB3	'm'	b[3]		FFA0	c[0]
FFA4		a[4]		FFB4	'\0'	b[4]		FFB0	c[1]

Figure 19.5 Studying the memory locations for Example 19.2.

Solution 19.6
```
int i = 10, j = 20;
int *p = &j;
*p = 1;
```

Drill 19.7 In the following code, convert the pointers to references. Name the references *r1* and *r2*. Also, what will the values of *i* and *j* become? Draw a diagram if you think it may help you.

```
int i = 5, j = 10,
      *p1 = &i, *p2 = &j;
*p1 = *p2 + *p1;
*p2 = 1;
i = *p2 + i;
```

Dynamic Objects

	Pointers	References
To declare	int *p = &i;	int &r = i;
To de–reference	*p	r
Stores the . . .	address of i	address of i
Can this address be changed?	Yes	No
Can what the address points to be changed?	Yes	Yes
To point to a member of a structure	(*p).member	r.member

Table 19.1 Comparing pointers and references

Arrays of pointers: In this same example, the array *c[ ]* is different than the other two arrays. There is an asterisk in front of its declaration which makes it an array of pointers to type character. See Figure 19.6.

In Statement 2, we store the address of *a[ ]*, which is FFA0, into c[0]. Similarly, &b[0], which is the same as *b*, is stored in c[1]. This is FFB0. Refer to Figure 19.5. Last, in a loop, stepping through the array *c[ ]*, we print the two arrays that *c[ ]* points to. For example, FFA0 is the value of c[0], which is the same as the value of *a*, which prints the first string. This is called double indirection; that is, we first need to know where *c[ ]* is stored, then using that address, we need to know where *a[ ]* is stored. When c[0] is printed with %s, the string, "sha," is printed. When it is printed with %p, its address, FFA0, is printed. Study this example and note that *a*, &a[0], and c[0] all have the value of "sha" with a %s format string and that they have the value of FFA0 with a %p format string.

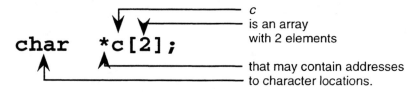

Figure 19.6 Understanding an array of pointers.

Solution 19.7 i will change from 5 to 15, and then to 16. *j* will change from 10 to 1.

```
int i = 5, j = 10, &r1 = i, &r2 = j;
r1 = r2 + r1;
r2 = 1;
i = r2 + i;
```

Drill 19.8 References are really nothing more than aliases in disguise. They can be thought of as renaming a variable because, once they are initialized, what they point to can't be changed. In the following code, define two references. Name *r1* as an alias for *i* and *r2* as an alias for *j*. Then rewrite the following code in terms of these references:

```
int i = 5, j;
j = i + 1;
++i;
```

Pointers and Functions

In Unit 9, we covered the differences between passing a scalar and passing an array to a function. While we review how that works, let us also see how pointers and references are passed to functions.

Figure 19.7 illustrates Example 19.3. Notice that the first line of output is printed in function() and the second and third lines are printed in main(). From the second line of output we find the addresses of i, j, and k to be FFF4, FFF2, and FFF0, respectively. We also see that the value of m is FFEA. This is the starting address where that array is in RAM. The initial values of these locations are simply set by the statements in main(). For the locations in RAM that will be modified by the function, their initial values are crossed off and the new ones are shown next to them. Let us see now how the function changes these values.

When we call the function, i is passed by value. This means that the value of i is copied into w. From the first line of output we see that the address of w is FFE2, which is different from that of the address of i, which is FFF4. Hence, we can say that w contains a copy of i. Furthermore, notice that, although the function changes w to 5, the last line of the output indicates that i remained as 1. The function didn't change i, only its copy: w.

Next, let us review how arrays are passed. They are passed by reference. main() passes m to the function and z gets its address or its reference. Values of array elements are not copied as was done with i. The first line from the output shows us that the value of z is FFEA, which is the same as the value of m. Hence, when the function changes z[0] to 5, m[0], which is the same location, is also changed.

Additionally, since z is nothing more than a pointer, the function heading can be rewritten as:

```
void function (int w, int *x, int &y, int *z)
```

Next, let us look at how main() passes the address of j to function(). This address, FFF2, is copied into x. That is fine because x is declared as a pointer to integers. The first line of the printout confirms that the value of x is FFF2. When the function changes *x or the location that x points to, it also changes j for main() because x points to j. From the last line of the output, we confirm that j has indeed been changed to 5.

Last, when main() passes k to the function, we might think at first glance that k is passed by value, that a copy of k will be made just like a copy of i was made. After all, k is not an array, so we don't have to worry about its value being changed by the function.

Solution 19.8
```
int i = 5, j;
int &r1 = i, &r2 = j;
r2 = r1 + 1;
++r1;
```

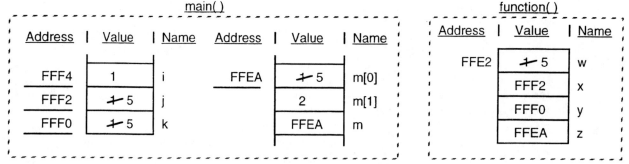

Figure 19.7 Studying the memory locations for Example 19.3.

```
/EXAMPLE 19.3
#include <iostream.h>
void function (int w, int *x, int &y, int z[ ])
{
    w = 5;
    *x = 5;
    y = 5;
    z[0] = 5;
    cout << &w << " " << x << " " << &y << " " << z << " " <<
         y  << endl;
}


void main (void)
{
    int i = 1, j = 1, k = 1;
    int m[2] = {1, 2};
    function(i, &j, k, m);
    cout << &i << " " << &j <<
        " " << &k << " " << m << endl;
    cout << i << " " << j <<
        " " << k << " " << m[0] << endl;
}
----- output -----
FFE2    FFF2    FFF0    FFEA    5
FFF4    FFF2    FFF0    FFEA
1   5   5   5
```

Drill 19.9

```
class Ship
{ private:
     int xpos, ypos;
   public:
     void give_pos() {cout << xpos
        << " " << ypos << endl; }
     void set_pos(int x, int y);
};

void Ship::set_pos(int x, int y)
{  xpos = x;
   ypos = y;
}
```

The set_pos() is a member function here, defined outside the class declaration. We've seen that in Unit 16. However, give_pos() is called an *inline* function and it is defined succinctly within the class declaration.

See if you can rewrite the two functions so that give_pos() is defined outside the class and set_pos() is defined as an inline function.

Dynamic Objects

However, the function does get the address of *k* into *y*. The & symbol used in `int &y` makes *k* an argument passed by reference. Recall that a reference pointer is an alias for another variable. Hence, *y* is another name for *k*. When *y* is changed to 5, it is automatically de-referenced so that *k* is changed to 5. Notice from the first line of the printout that *y* is 5. To print the address stored in it, FFF0, &y is specified.

In the event that you don't want to let the function change the value of the reference, use this function heading instead:

```
void function (int w, int *x, const int &y, int z[ ])
```

This will not allow the function to change *y* because of the keyword const. Now main() can pass a scalar by reference and not have to worry about the function changing it. If a very large structure or object has to be passed, it is more efficient to pass it by reference so that it doesn't have to be copied. With const, you can have that advantage as well as being sure that the original data item will not be modified by the called function.

Dynamic Memory Allocation

Often you don't know how many elements to allocate for an array. If you declare an array with too many elements, you may waste memory. And if you do not allocate enough elements in an array, then sometimes when you run the program, you may run out of them.

A solution for this problem is to create a variable–length array so that you can have long arrays when you need them and conserve memory when you have shorter arrays. Example 19.4 illustrates one way to do this.

Here we have the class LineItem defined. It has two private members. *line* is a pointer to characters or an array of characters with no length defined and *qty* is an integer. It also has three public member functions. show() is an inline function. It is defined within the class. When an inline function is defined within a class, the keyword inline is not needed. All that this function does is print the values of the private members. The ~LineItem() function is also defined as an inline function. However, LineItem() and ~LineItem() are special types of functions. They are called *constructor* and *destructor* functions, respectively.

When a public member function, such as LineItem(), is named after the class to which it belongs, it is called a constructor. A constructor function is called whenever an object of that class is created. Such a function has no return data type and no return statement. We'll return to this constructor in a moment.

If you add a tilde (~) in front of a constructor, you create a destructor function. A destructor is called whenever the object is no longer needed, such as at the end of the function in which it was created. It also has no return data type or return statement. Furthermore, a destructor may not have any arguments.

Solution 19.9

```
class Ship
{  private:
      int xpos, ypos;
   public:
      void give_pos();
      void set_pos(int x, int y)
         {xpos = x; ypos = y; }
};

void Ship::give_pos(void)
{  cout << xpos << " "
      << ypos << endl;
}
```

Drill 19.10

```
void main (void)
{
      Ship bananaboat, *p = &bananaboat;
      (*p).set_pos(2000, 1200);
}
```

FFF2   bananaboat

xpos 2000
ypos 1200   FFF2 p

bananaboat is an object of Ship and *p* is a pointer to objects of class Ship. The last statement sends the set_pos() message to the object whose address is in *p*. Write the statement that would send the give_pos() message.

Dynamic Objects

```
// EXAMPLE 19.4
#include <string.h>
#include <iostream.h>
class LineItem
{
   private:
      char *line;
      int qty;
   public:
      LineItem (char *, int);
      ~LineItem ( ) { delete [ ] line; cout << "destructor\n"; }
      void show ( ) { cout << line << " " << qty << endl; }
};
LineItem::LineItem(char *s, int q)
{
   int len;
   len = strlen(s);               // Find the length of the string
   line = new char (len + 1);     // Create just enough memory for it
   strcpy(line, s);               // Copy the string into it
   qty = q;
   cout << "constructor\n";
}

int main (void)
{
   char string[200];
   int q;
   cout << "Enter line item and qty:";
   cin >> string >> q;
   LineItem item(string, q);      // Constructor is called for item
   item.show( );
   return 0;
}                                 // Destructor is called
----- output -----
Enter line item and qty: carrots 4
constructor
carrots 4
destructor
```

Solution 19.10

```
(*p).give_pos ();
```

This can be rewritten simply as p -> give_pos();

Drill 19.11 Now convert this code using a reference variable, *r*:

```
Ship bananaboat, *p = &bananaboat;
(*p).set_pos(2000, 1200);
p -> give_pos();
```

You may want to review Drill 19.7 and Solution 19.7 for the answer.

main() begins by declaring string[200] to have 200 characters, but this is a temporary location to store the string. When a LineItem object is created, that object will have the necessary amount of allocated memory. There is no loop in this example, but if there were, then each time a LineItem object were created, it would provide it with the exact amount of memory that it needs.

From the user of the program, we obtain the string and the quantity. After that, the LineItem object, *item,* is created. Since an object that has a constructor is created, the constructor is called by passing *string* and *q* as arguments to it.

In the constructor function or in LineItem::LineItem(), *s* has the address of *string[ ]* and *q* is copied. Then the constructor finds the length of the string using the strlen() function. The length, which is 7, is stored in *len.* Using the operator new, enough memory to store 8 characters is allocated and the starting address of that location is stored in *line.* We add one to the length of the string so that we have room to store the null character at the end of it. Next, the string, *s,* is copied into *line* or into the newly created space and *qty* is set. The last thing that we do in the constructor is to print a message to let us know when the constructor was called. Back in main(), *string[ ]* could be reused in a loop to store other character strings and to create more objects of precisely the right lengths.

As seen in Figure 19.8, it's advantageous to know that available memory is divided into two categories. One end of the available RAM is called the *stack* and the other end is called the *heap.* When a function creates new variables, the next available space in the stack is used to store them. The stack holds variables. When the function is finished executing, the memory in the stack is freed automatically.

This is not the case with the heap. When we grab some memory to store data dynamically by using new, we obtain the next available RAM from the heap. This memory is not released automatically to the operating system when we no longer need it, that is, at the end of the program. Hence, we must use the complementary operator, delete, to free the memory from the heap.

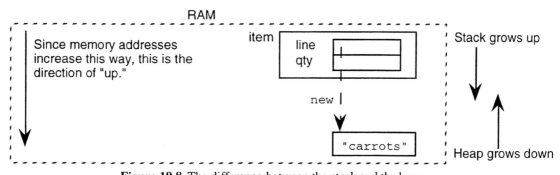

Figure 19.8 The difference between the stack and the heap.

Solution 19.11 De–reference is automatically done when using a reference variable.

```
void main (void)
{
    Ship bananaboat, &r = bananaboat;
    r.set_pos(2000, 1200);
    r.give_pos();
}
```

Dynamic Objects

This can be done very easily with the destructor function. At the end of main(), the compiler starts to remove *item* from the stack, but when it notices that it has a destructor, it executes the destructor first. In our case, this function deletes the entire array to which *line* points with delete [ ] line;. After the memory from the heap is released back to the operating system, the *item* is removed from the stack.

Let us go over Example 19.4 again. First, remember that all program variables are created on the stack, and the compiler is responsible for releasing that memory back to the operating system. However, with dynamic memory allocation, or when using the new keyword, memory is taken off the heap and we, the programmers, are responsible for releasing that memory back to the operating system using the delete keyword.

Let us look at Figure 19.9 and Example 19.4 together. In main(), we see that the variables *string* and *q* are created. *string* stores the starting address of the 200 bytes of memory. We have shown that as address F0. As long as main() is not finished executing, these memory locations shown in Figure 19.9 continue to exist. When main() is done, then the compiler takes care of giving these locations back to the system. In main(), *string* and *q* are read in, then the LineItem constructor is called for the object, *item*.

Inside the LineItem constructor, *s* receives the address of F0, the address where the string is stored. It also receives 4, the value of *q*. Then using strlen(), the length of the string is found to

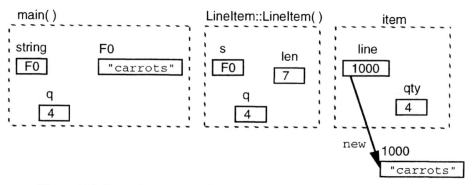

Figure 19.9 Executing the constructor function in Example 19.4. The compiler will delete all the variables, except for the memory pointed to by *line*. We must remember to delete the location starting at address 1000.

Drill 19.12

```
class Ship bananaboat[4];
(*bananaboat).set_pos(2000, 1200);          // We need those outer parens.
(*(bananaboat + 1)).set_pos(2000, 1300);
bananaboat[2].set_pos(2000, 1400);
bananaboat[3].set_pos(2000, 1500);
```

Arrays are like pointers. Here, *bananaboat[ ]* is an array and a pointer. When we declare it as an array, we can think of it as a pointer as well. It holds the address of the first element of the array, so *bananaboat and *(bananaboat + 1) are the same as bananaboat[0] and bananaboat[1], respectively. The above code will set up the array elements as shown. Now convert the lines with pointer notation to array notation, and vice versa.

Dynamic Objects

be 7, which is stored in *len*. While the constructor is executing, these three variables continue to exist and they will be released back to the operating system once *item* is constructed. But first, the new operator in LineItem() grabs 8 bytes of memory, 7 plus 1, and stores its starting address of 1000 into *line*. Using strcpy(), the string is copied into this new RAM and *q* is assigned to *qty*. Now the constructor has done its job. Its variables are no longer needed but *item* starts "living."

item will be de–constructed at the end of main() using the ~LineItem() destructor function. In this destructor we will delete the RAM starting at 1000 (because it's on the heap), but the compiler will release the *line* and *qty* variables (because they're on the stack).

Dynamic Array of Objects

Now that we know how to dynamically create simple arrays, let us now do the same thing with arrays of objects. This will be illustrated using the listing of Example 19.5. Figure 19.10 shows an array called *invoice*. It is an array of class LineItem. When we write the program, we don't know how many elements this array will require, so we cannot do the following:

```
LineItem invoice [ ];
```

An array can't be created without its length being given. We use empty brackets when defining a function because when a function is called, the array length can be determined by the length of the array that is passed. Also, since by default arrays are passed by reference anyway, the array needs only the starting address of the array and not its length.

Here, with the array defined for the first time, no default value can be assumed for its length. Furthermore, arrays are similar to pointers, so we can define an array of unknown length simply by declaring it as:

```
LineItem *invoice;
```

Now we have a place to store the starting address of an array of LineItems, but we still don't have memory set aside to store the actual array.

When our program begins to execute, we will ask the user how many LineItems they will enter and then dynamically create an array of LineItems that will be just the right length. This will be accomplished by the following statement:

```
invoice = new LineItem [num_line];
```

Here, *num_line* will be the size of the array determined at run_time.

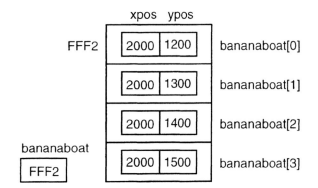

```
// EXAMPLE 19.5
#include <iostream.h>
#include <string.h>

// Start of LineItem class, reused in Example 19.6
class LineItem
{
   private:
      char *line;
      int qty;
   public:
      LineItem(void);
      ~LineItem(void);
      int get_qty(void) { return qty; }
};


LineItem::LineItem (void)
{
   int len;
   char string[200];
   cout << "Enter line item description and quantity:";
   cin >> string >> qty;
   len = strlen (string);
   line = new char [len + 1];
   strcpy(line, string);
}


LineItem::~LineItem (void)
{
   cout << "de-constructing " << " "
        << line << " " << qty << endl;
   delete [ ] line;
}
// End of LineItem class
```

Solution 19.12

```
class Ship bananaboat[4];
bananaboat[0].set_pos(2000, 1200);
bananaboat[1].set_pos(2000, 1300);
(*(bananaboat + 2)).set_pos(2000, 1400);
(*(bananaboat + 3)).set_pos(2000, 1500);
```

Drill 19.13 Now convert these statements to the -> operator. You may want to review Solution 19.10. Also, after converting the statements use a for loop that will print the array elements using the array notation and the give_pos() message.

```
void main (void)
{
    LineItem *invoice;
    int num_line, i, total_qty = 0;
    cout << "How many line items will this invoice have?: ";
    cin >> num_line;
    invoice = new LineItem[num_line];
    for(i = 0; i <= num_line - 1; ++i)
        total_qty = total_qty + invoice[i].get_qty();
    cout << "Total quantity is " << total_qty << endl;
    delete [ ] invoice;
}
----- output -----
How many line items will this invoice have?: 3
Enter line item description and quantity: carrots 4
Enter line item description and quantity: squids 7
Enter line item description and quantity: onions 2
Total quantity is 13
de-constructing onions 2
de-constructing squids 7
de-constructing carrots 4
```

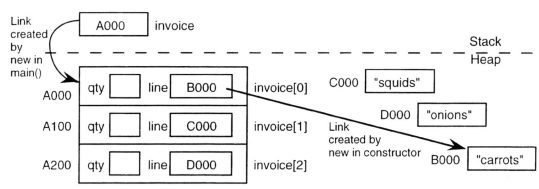

Figure 19.10 Dynamically creating an array of objects.

Solution 19.13

```
int i;
bananaboat -> set_pos(2000, 1200);
(bananaboat + 1) -> set_pos(2000, 1300);
(bananaboat + 2) -> set_pos(2000, 1400);
(bananaboat + 3) -> set_pos(2000, 1500);
for(i = 0; i <= 3; ++i)
    bananaboat[i].give_pos();
```

Let us look at the entire listing given in Example 19.5. I have changed the member functions here to what they were in Example 19.4 to illustrate the different ways they can be handled. The constructor for LineItem doesn't take any arguments but will get the data from the user as soon as a LineItem is created. In other words, just as in Example 19.4, Example 19.5 doesn't allow a LineItem to exist without its description or quantity being initialized.

Example 19.5 doesn't have a show() member function, although the destructor prints the LineItem's data members. We do have a function called get_qty() that will return the quantity of a LineItem. main() uses this function in a loop to add and print the quantities of all the LineItems. Let us trace the program.

Starting in main(), we first find out how many elements our array will need for this run. Using *num_line*, the array Invoice, which is an array of LineItems, is created. As each element in the array is created, its constructor is executed. This constructor uses *string[ ]* as a temporary variable to store the LineItem's description. Then using the new operator, we store the description of the LineItem in *line*, just as we did in Example 19.4. Unlike Example 19.4, however, this constructor gets the data from the user as well as storing it in the LineItem.

Once the array of Invoice has been created, main() requests each element of the *invoice[ ]* array to return its *qty*. This is then accumulated and printed.

Last, main() deletes the *invoice[ ]* array. Since this is an array, the empty brackets must be used with the delete operator. As each LineItem is deleted, its destructor is called, and within the destructor, the *line[ ]* array of characters is also deleted.

Referring to Figure 19.10, we want to make sure that, for every new that was executed, its corresponding delete was executed. For example, we used one new to create one *invoice[ ]* array, so we must use one delete [ ]. On the other hand, we used many new's to create the descriptions stored in *line*. Hence, we should execute that many delete's. One thing we don't want to do is to delete the *invoice[ ]* array and not delete the *line[ ]* arrays by forgetting to place the delete in the destructor. In any case, take a moment to appreciate the simplicity in the coding of this example. This complex data structure is created and deleted dynamically without the use of loops. Properly written classes with constructors and destructors make coding simple for those who use them.

Dynamic Array of Pointers

As a last example of dynamic objects, let us study arrays that can change in length. We will use one array of varying length that will store addresses of LineItems. If *p* is a ten-element array that stores addresses of LineItems, then we can declare it as follows:

```
LineItem *p[10];
```

Drill 19.14 When a program is running, it may need to create another object "on the fly." This is called dynamic memory allocation and is done using the new operator, as follows:

```
Ship *new_ship;
new_ship = new Ship;
```

new_ship is a pointer to objects of class Ship. An area of memory sufficient to store one such object is reserved and its starting address is placed in the *new_ship* pointer.

How could you set the position for this newly created Ship object? You have only the *new_ship* pointer to access it. Give two ways to do this assignment.

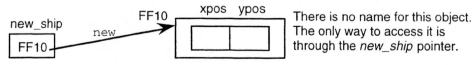

Dynamic Objects

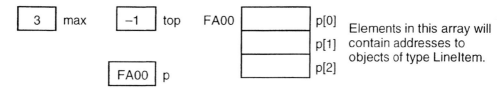

Figure 19.11 Initializing an object of class Invoice.

Here, *p* has ten elements, each of which stores the address of a LineItem object. However, we want to make this a variable length array, as we did in Example 19.5. In that example, we removed the brackets and added an asterisk in front of the array name. Here, we can do the same thing. We'll remove the brackets and add a second asterisk. Now we have this:

```
LineItem **p;
```

Figure 19.11 shows how our variables are initially set up. The pointer *p* will have the address of an array. Each element of this array will have the address of a LineItem object, which we will create dynamically. The variable *max* indicates how many elements are allocated for the array at that time, and the variable *top* indicates the highest index in the array, which is occupied. Initially, *top* is –1, meaning that there are no addresses stored in the array of pointers yet. When we add an address to the array, we will first increment *top* and store the address in that location. The first time we do that, *top* will become 0 and the address will be stored in the "zeroth" element.

Now let us study how the array will increase in size dynamically. In Figure 19.12(a) on page 374, we have already created three LineItem objects using new, and we have stored their addresses in the array. p[0] contains A100, the address of the first LineItem object. Similarly, p[1] and p[2] point to the memory locations where the other LineItem objects were created dynamically. At this point, *max* is 3, the maximum number of elements in the *p[ ]* array; and *top* is 2, the highest index of the array that contains an address. Let us now see how a new LineItem object is added.

```
// EXAMPLE 19.6
#include <iostream.h>
#include <string.h>
//////////////////////////////////////////////////////////////////////////////
// Insert the LineItem class and its functions from Example 19.5 here
//////////////////////////////////////////////////////////////////////////////
const int SIZE = 3;  // Amount by which the "p" array is increased.
```

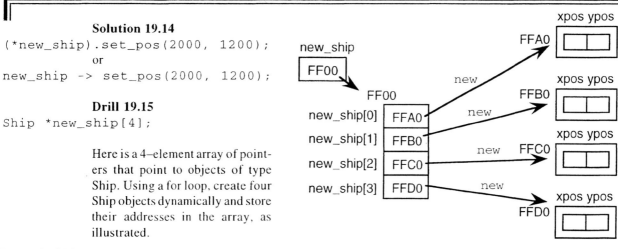

Solution 19.14
```
(*new_ship).set_pos(2000, 1200);
         or
new_ship -> set_pos(2000, 1200);
```

Drill 19.15
```
Ship *new_ship[4];
```

Here is a 4–element array of pointers that point to objects of type Ship. Using a for loop, create four Ship objects dynamically and store their addresses in the array, as illustrated.

Dynamic Objects

```
class Invoice
{
    private:
        LineItem **p;
        int max, top;
    public:
        Invoice() {    p = new (LineItem *[SIZE]);   // Initializing Invoice
                       max = SIZE;                    // See Figure 19.11
                       top = -1;
                    }
        ~Invoice(void);
        void add_another(LineItem *line_ptr);
};

Invoice::~Invoice(void)
{
    int i;
    for(i = 0; i <= top; ++i)            // Delete all the LineItems
        delete p[i];
    delete [ ] p;                        // Delete the Invoice array.
}


void Invoice::add_another(LineItem *line_ptr)
{
    if(top < max - 1)
    {                                        // There is still an unsed
        ++top;                               // element in the "p" array to
        p[top] = line_ptr;                   // add the new LineItem.
    }
    else
    {                                        // The "p" array is full.
        cout << "Please wait while adjusting memory\n";// See Figure 19.12
        LineItem **new_p; int i;
        new_p = new(LineItem *[max + SIZE]);   // First, create a new and
        for(i = 0; i <= max; ++i)              // longer array. Then copy the
            new_p[i] = p[i];       // addresses from the old array, "p[ ],"
```

Solution 19.15
```
int i;
Ship *new_ship[4];
for(i = 0; i <= 3; ++i)
    new_ship[i] = new Ship;
```

Drill 19.16 Now using a for loop, read in four sets of data from the user and send proper messages to these newly created objects so that they are set up properly. Use *x* and *y* to read in the values from the user.
```
int x, y;
```
See if you can do this with and without the -> operator.

```
      max = max + SIZE;          // to the new array, "new_p[ ]."
      ++top;                     // Adjust "max" and increment "top."
      new_p[top] = line_ptr;     // Place the new LineItem there.
      delete [ ] p;              // Delete the old array.
      p = new_p;                 // Set "p[ ]" to the address of new array.
   }
}

void main (void)
{
   Invoice invoice;
   int choice;
   LineItem *ptr;
   cout << "1. To add another item, anything else to quit: ";
   cin >> choice;
   for(; choice == 1; )
   { ptr = new LineItem;
     invoice.add_another(ptr);
     cout << "1. To add another item, anything else to quit: ";
     cin >> choice;
   }
}
----- output -----
1. To add another item, anything else to quit: 1
Enter line item description and quantity: apples 10
1. To add another item, anything else to quit: 1
Enter line item description and quantity: beets 20
1. To add another item, anything else to quit: 1
Enter line item description and quantity: carrots 30
1. To add another item, anything else to quit: 1
Enter line item description and quantity: dill 40
Please wait while adjusting memory
1. To add another item, anything else to quit: 2
de-constructing apples 10
de-constructing beets 20
de-constructing carrots 30
de-constructing dill 40
```

Solution 19.16

```
cout << "Enter four sets of data\n";
for(i = 0; i <= 3; ++i)
{
   cin >> x >> y;
   new_ship[i] -> set_pos(x, y);
   //or (*new_ship[i]).set_pos(x, y);
}
```

Figure 19.12(b) shows that a new LineItem object is created and its address (A400) is temporarily stored in a variable called *line_ptr*. First, we will create a new array of pointers that contains three more elements than the existing array, and place its starting address in *new_p*.

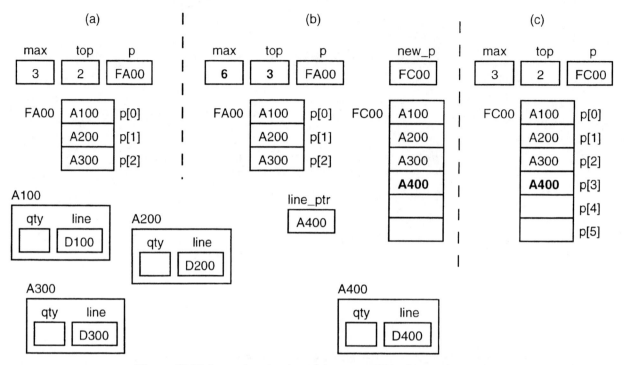

Figure 19.12 Increasing the size of the array of LineItem pointers. (a) The array has reached its maximum length of 3. (b) Making the *new_p* array 3 elements larger to accommodate the extra LineItem's address. Then copying the *p* array addresses into the *new_p* array and inserting the fourth address. (c) Finally, deleting the old array and placing the address of the array, FC00, into *p*.

Drill 19.17 How do you declare and process an array of pointers whose length is only determined at run–time?

If Ship bananaboat[4]; has nearly the same effect as: Ship *bananaboat (since arrays are like pointers), then Ship *new_ship[4]; has nearly the same effect as Ship **new_ship;. Only the length of the array is open–ended.

So far we created objects dynamically. Now we can create dynamically a 5–element array of pointers to Ship objects, like this:

```
Ship **new_ship;
new_ship = new Ship *[5];
```

What if we don't know from the start that the array will have five elements and we need to determine that from the user? Ask the user how many elements there should be in this array of pointers and create that array dynamically. Use an integer *num* to read in the array length.

Dynamic Objects

Then in a loop, we will simply copy the addresses from the *p[ ]* array to the *new_p[ ]* array. Next, we'll copy the *line_ptr* in the next available element of *new_p[ ]*. Then we will delete the *p[ ]* array, copy the address *new_p* into *p*, and we're done. See Figure 19.12(c).

Notice that, although the array has been displaced in RAM, the locations of the objects have not changed. It is easier to move addresses than entire objects. Example 19.6 shows the code for moving addresses. We have decided to create a class called Invoice that will store *max*, *top*, and *p* as just described. Since these data items are related to each other, it makes sense to group them into one class.

Invoice has a constructor that sets up an instance of Invoice as shown in Figure 19.11. LineItem class is the same as it was in Example 19.5, so we reused it here. Invoice::add_another() basically adds another LineItem object address to the array. If there is room in the array, then it is done simply; otherwise, the array size is adjusted first in the else clause.

EXPERIMENTS

Now we want to expand our ability to implement OOP concepts. C++ provides us with almost a limitless way of doing that. However, we won't be spending our time on all the facilities of the language, but instead on a few key ones. It is better to learn a few necessary concepts of C++ well rather than learn *all* of them and end up using them incorrectly!

This unit starts the last part of the text. With this unit, we'll concentrate only on C++ syntax. But before we get to the topic of dynamic objects, we must understand pointers well. Although Units 12 and 13 were based on exploring pointers, we will cover them again here. Even if you have studied pointers, you should still review them here.

Exp 19.1 Notice that Statements 6 and 7 are commented out. &i means the "address of where 'i' is stored." This address is stored in *p1* when it is first declared in: int *p1 = &i;. The *p1 here means that *p1* is a pointer. However, in Statement 4, *p1 means to find the value of *p1*, use it as an address, and find the value stored in that address. Here, the value of *p1 would be 3.

Solution 19.17

```
Ship **new_ship;
cout << "How many ships will you enter?";
cin >> num;
new_ship = new Ship *[num];
```

Drill 19.18 Now create *num* number of objects using new. As you do that in a loop, have the array elements point to these dynamically allocated Ships. Also ask the user to provide *x* and *y* for each of these Ships and set them up using the set_pos() function and the -> operator.

Dynamic Objects

```
#include <iostream.h>
void main (void)
{
    int  i = 3;          // Variable i stores integers.
    int *p2;             // Pointer p2 stores only the addresses of integer variables.
    int *p1 = &i;        // p1 is like p2, but it is initialized with the address of i.
    float *p3;           // Pointer p3 stores the addresses of float variables.
    p2 = p1;                          //Stmt 1
    cout << &i << " " << p1 << " ";   //Stmt 2
    cout << p2 << endl;               //Stmt 3
    cout << i << " "<< *p1 << " ";    //Stmt 4
    cout << *p2 << endl;              //Stmt 5
    // p3 = p1;                       //Stmt 6
    // i = p1;                        //Stmt 7
}
```

a. In the diagram below we see memory locations: their addresses, values, and variable names. Show the value stored in *i* before Statement 1 was executed.

b. In Statement 2 the address of *i,* or &i, is printed. Show this address next to *i,* under the Address heading in the diagram below. You need to show only the last four characters of addresses.

c. When *p1* is declared, it is initialized with the address of *i.* Next to *p1,* under the Value heading, show the value of *p1.* Its value is printed in Statement 2. Are &i and *p1* the same?

d. In the diagram below, show the value of *p2.* This was printed in Statement 3. In which statement was this made equal to &i, that is, the address of *i*?

e. What is the value of *i* as it was printed in Statement 4?

f. Statement 4 also prints *p1. What is the value of *p1 as seen in the printout?

g. From question c, what is the value of *p1*? From question f, what is the value of *p1? If you know *p1,* describe how you would find the value of *p1.

h. Statement 5 prints *p2. Why is it the same as *i*?

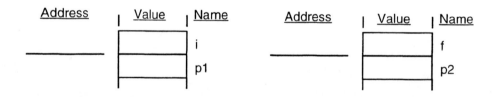

Solution 19.18

```
cout << "Enter  " << num << "pairs of x-y coordinates.\n";
for(i = 0; i <= num - 1; ++i)
{
    new_ship[i] = new Ship;
    cin >> x >> y;
    new_ship[i] -> set_pos(x, y);
}
```

Drill 19.19 Let's change our picture from that of Drill 19.15 and create an array of Ship objects.

```
Ship *ship_array;
ship_array = new Ship[4];
```

How would you read in four sets of data items and set up this array with that data?

i. *p1* and *p2* are both pointers to integers. From Statement 1, can you tell if you can assign an integer pointer to another integer pointer. *p2* has the address of where _____ is stored.
j. Uncomment Statement 6. Can you assign an integer pointer (*p1*) to a float pointer (*p3*)?
k. Restore the comment in Statement 6 and uncomment Statement 7. Can you assign an integer pointer to an integer variable?

Exp 19.2

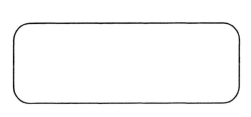

```
#include <iostream.h>
void main (void)
{
    int i = 3, j, *p1 = &i, *p2;   // Stmt 1
    float f = 5.0, *p3 = &f;       // Stmt 2
    cout << &i << &j << &f << endl;// Stmt 3
    p2 = &j;                       // Stmt 4
    *p1 = *p1 + 5;                 // Stmt 5
    *p2 = *p3  + i;                // Stmt 6
    *p3 = *p2 + *p1;               // Stmt 7
    cout << i << j << f << endl;   // Stmt 8
}
```

a. Using Statements 1 through 3, show in the diagram the initial values of the variables and pointer–variables. Don't fill in the addresses of the pointers.
b. Then show the new values of each item by crossing off the old values and placing the new ones next to them as the rest of the program is executed.
c. Will Statement 5 run without the asterisks? These are called indirection operators because they appear after the pointers are declared.
d. Why did *i*, *j*, and *f* change when they weren't directly assigned to anything in Statements 5 through 7?

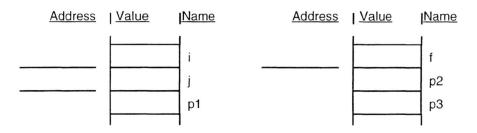

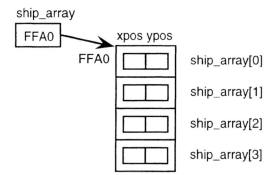

Exp 19.3

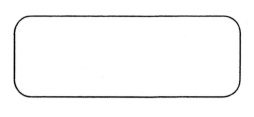

```
#include <iostream.h>
#include <stdio.h>  // To print pointers.
void main (void)
{
    char s[20] = "Pointers!",  *p3;  //Stmt 1
    p3 = &s[2];                       //Stmt 2
    cout << s << &s[0] << endl;       //Stmt 3
    cout << p3 << &s[2] << endl;      //Stmt 4
    cout << p3 << s << endl;          //Stmt 5
    printf("%p %p %s\n", p3, s, s);   //Stmt 6
}
```

a. In the diagram, show the values of *s*, *p3*, and the array *s[ ]*.
b. Will the program work without the * in Statement 1? Why or why not?
c. What is another way of obtaining the address of the first element of an array other than, say, &s[0]?
d. When printing a string using printf(), what format specifier will print the string? What format specifier will print the address of where the string begins?
e. Describe the difference between *p3* and *s*.
f. Which of these two statements is legal? Try adding them one at a time between Statements 5 and 6.

```
p3 = p3 + 1;
s = s + 1;
```

g. Which of these store addresses: *s*, *p3*, and *s[0]*?
h. Which one is a variable and which one is a constant? In other words, which one can be changed and which one can't?

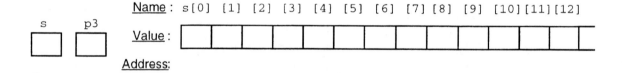

Solution 19.19

```
for(i = 0; i <= 3; ++i)
{
    cin >> x >> y;
    ship_array[i].set_pos(x, y);
}
```

Drill 19.20 When memory is allocated dynamically by a program, the program should also release that memory back to the operating system. This release is done with the delete operator. Here is how an object that was created in Drill 19.14 is deleted:

```
Ship *new_ship;
new_ship = new Ship;
delete new_ship;
```

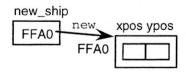

Dynamic Objects

Exp 19.4 Let us now see the difference between passing arrays and scalars to functions.

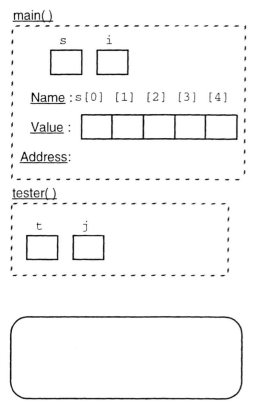

main( )

s   i

Name :s[0] [1] [2] [3] [4]

Value :

Address:

tester( )

t   j

```
#include <iostream.h>
#include <stdio.h> //Used to print pointers
void tester (char t[ ], int j);    //Stmt 1
void main (void)
{
    char s[20] = "Wow!";           //Stmt 2
    int i = 0;
    printf("%s %p %p\n", s, s, &i); //Stmt 3
    tester(s, i);                  //Stmt 4
    cout << s << i << endl;        //Stmt 5
}

void tester (char t[], int j)      //Stmt 6
{
    printf("%p %p\n", t, &j);      //Stmt 7
    t[0] = 'N';
    j = 3;
}
```

a. In the diagram, show the initial contents of *s*, the array *s[ ]*, and i. Write down the memory addresses where *s[ ]* and *i* are stored from Statement 3.

b. Write down what is stored in *t* and the address of *j* using Statement 7.

c. When calling the function, is the array copied? How can you tell?

d. Is a copy of the scalar made? Scalars are non–arrays, like *i* and *j*. How can you tell?

e. Why did changing t[0] change *s[ ]*?

f. Why did changing *j* not change *i*?

g. Run the program again using the following change for Statement 6. Is there a difference? Remember to also change your prototype accordingly.

```
void tester (char *t, int j)
```

Here's the diagram of Drill 19.15 again. How would you delete the 4–element array of Ship objects created this way?

```
Ship *new_ship[4];
for(i = 0; i <= 3; ++i)
    new_ship[i] = new Ship;
```

new_ship

FF00

FF00

| FFA0 |
| FFB0 |
| FFC0 |
| FFD0 |

new

new

new

new

xpos ypos

FFA0

xpos ypos

FFB0

xpos ypos

FFC0

xpos ypos

FFD0

Dynamic Objects

Exp 19.5 Now let us pass an address of a scalar to a function. (Save this source for Experiment 19.8.)

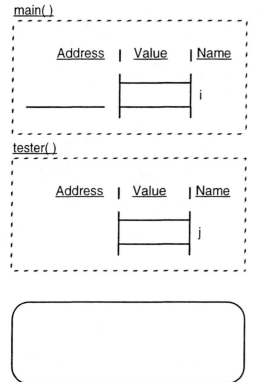

main( )

tester( )

```
#include <iostream.h>
void tester (int *);   //Stmt 1
void main (void)
{
    int i = 0;
    cout << i << &i << endl;    // Stmt 3
    tester(&i);                 // Stmt 4
    cout << i << endl;          // Stmt 5
}


void tester (int *j)            // Stmt 6
{
    cout << j << endl;          // Stmt 7
    *j = 3;                     // Stmt 8
}
```

a. Fill in values and addresses in the diagram. Notice that in Statement 4 we are sending the address of *i*. Are the asterisks necessary in Statements 1 and 6? Why or why not?
b. In tester(), where is the address of *i* stored?
c. Do we need the * in Statement 8? Why or why not?
d. Why did *i* stay the same in the previous experiment and here it was changed after coming back from the function?

Exp 19.6 Let us now place addresses in an array of pointers, such as char *q[ ].

```
#include <iostream.h>
void main (void)
{
    char s1[ ] = "Wow,",
         s2[ ] = " more",
         s3[ ] = " pointers!",
         *q[5];
```

Solution 19.20

```
for(i = 0; i <= 3; ++i)
    delete new_ship[i];
```

Drill 19.21 In the previous drill, objects were created one at a time, so we deleted them one at a time. If an entire array were created dynamically in one step, then such an array would also be deleted in one step.

```
delete [ ] array_name;
```

Now that we have deleted the Ship objects in Solution 19.20, how would we delete the array of pointers called *new_ship*? We had allocated this array as: new_ship = new Ship *[5];

```
    q[0] = s1;
    q[1] = s2;
    q[2] = s3;
    cout << s1 << &s1 << q[0] << endl;
    cout << s3 << &s3 << q[2] << endl;
}
```

    a. Fill in the values and addresses in the diagram. *q* points to q[0], which points to *s1*.
    b. How would you define *q* to be an array of only characters?
    c. How is *q* defined to be an array of the addresses of characters?
    d. How would you define *q* to be an array of pointers to floats?

Name: s1[0] [1] [2] [3] [4] [5] [6] [7] [8] [9] [10] [11] [12]

s1

Value:

Address:

Name: s2[0] [1] [2] [3] [4] [5] [6] [7] [8] [9] [10] [11] [12]

s2

Value:

Address:

Name: s3[0] [1] [2] [3] [4] [5] [6] [7] [8] [9] [10] [11] [12]

s3

Value:

Address:

q

Name: q[0] [1] [2] [3] [4]

Value:

Solution 19.21

```
for(i = 0; i <= num - 1; ++i)
   delete new_ship[i];
delete [ ] new_ship;
```

Drill 19.22
How would you delete the *ship_array* from Drill 19.19?

Dynamic Objects

Exp 19.7 Now let us summarize what we have learned about pointers so far. Use the following statements to answer these questions:

```
int i = 3, j, *p1 = &i, *p2;
char s1[20] = "Wow, more pointers!", s2[20], *p3, *q[5];
```

    a. Name the integers.
    b. In which variables would you place integer values?
    c. In which variables would you place the addresses of integers?
    d. Which statement places the address of *j* in *p2*?
    e. Which statement changes *i* to 5 without using the name *i*?
    f. Give two ways of printing the address where *s1* starts.
    g. The string, "Wow, more pointers!", is 19 characters long. What is the minimum number of characters needed to store that string?
    h. What statement makes *p3* equal to the address of the fourth element of *s1[ ]*?
    i. Precede the following statement with your answer in question h. Describe what will be printed, not the actual values.

```
printf("%p %p\n", s1, p3);
```

    j. For the following, give the answer as either *s1*, *p3*, both, or neither.
        1. stores one character
        2. stores one address
        3. is a constant
        4. is a variable
        5. is a pointer
    k. What are two ways that a function can receive an array of characters as an argument? Let us say that array is called *a[ ]*.
    l. If you call a function and you are passing *i* and *s1* as arguments . . .
        1. When you get control of the execution back from that function, which variable will be unchanged? Which one could be different?
        2. The called function makes a copy of which variable for itself? If the copy is changed, does the original change also?
        3. The called function gets the address of the location of which variable? In this case, how many copies of that variable exist? If the called function changes that location, is the change reflected in the calling function?

Solution 19.22
```
delete [ ] ship_array;
```

Drill 19.23 Suppose that the class Ship had only one private member:
```
char *name;
```
When we create *bananaboat*, an object of class Ship, in main(), we want to initialize its name as "Jamaica Farewell," like this:

```
Ship bananaboat("Jamaica Farewell")
```

To accommodate this, we need a public function named after its class, Ship. A function named after its class is called a constructor. Write a constructor function that receives a character string, called `char *s`, then finds its length using strlen(), dynamically allocates that many characters, and assigns the string to *name.

Dynamic Objects

m. Which statement will store the address of *s1[ ]* in q[2] and the address of *s2* in q[4]?

n. Which statement will store the address that is in q[2] into q[3]?

o. Which statement will print *s1* using the name *q[ ]* instead of *s1*?

p. Which statement will store the string that is in *s1[ ]* into *s2[ ]* using only the *q[ ]* array?

q. Can you execute the following statement?

```
s2 = s1;
```

If not, how can you accomplish this without using *q[ ]*?

r. Can you execute the following statement?

```
p3 = s1
```

Exp 19.8 Redo Experiment 19.5 as shown below. This will be helpful for learning the new concept of reference variables used in C++.

main( )

tester( )

```
#include <iostream.h>
void tester (int *);                //Stmt 1
void main (void)
{
    int i = 0;
    cout << i << &i << endl;         //Stmt 3
    tester(&i);                      //Stmt 4
    cout << i << endl;               //Stmt 5
}


void tester (int *j)                 //Stmt 6
{
    cout << j << endl;               //Stmt 7
    *j = 3;                          //Stmt 8
}
```

a. Why was tester() able to change the value of *i*?

Solution 19.23 Notice that the constructor has no return data type.

```
class Ship
{ private:
    char *name;
  public:
    Ship(char *s)
    {
       name = new char
                [strlen(s)];
       strcpy(name, s);
    }
};
```

Drill 19.24 With this definition of Ship, we are always required to provide its name when creating an object. However, we may want to create a Ship object without initializing its name, as with *spyboat*:

```
Ship bananaboat("Jamaica Farewell");
Ship spyboat;
```

If a constructor wasn't declared, then the compiler would provide an implicit constructor and we would be able to declare *spyboat*. However, since one constructor is defined for Ship, we must now also define the implicit constructor. Write this constructor so that it receives no arguments (as when creating *spyboat*), and inside the body of this constructor, no statements are executed.

b. When main() called tester(), did main() have a hint that tester() might change its *i*? How can you tell?

c. Was *i* passed by value; that is, was a copy of it made when calling tester()?

d. When is it efficient *not* to make a copy of a variable; when the variable is a big structure or a small one?

e. When an argument is passed by value, a copy is made; when it is passed by reference, only the address or its reference is passed. When we pass a scalar to a function, by default we are passing the scalar by value. (True or false) How can we force a scalar to be passed by reference?

f. By default, an array is passed by value or by reference?

Exp 19.9 Now let us introduce the reference variable. Only Statements 1, 4, 6, and 8 have been changed. Instead of *j* being a pointer variable, it is now called a reference variable. See Statement 6. We will see the ways that they are similar to and different from pointers.

```
#include <iostream.h>
void tester (int &);                    //Stmt 1
void main (void)
{
    int i = 0;
    cout << i << &i << endl;            //Stmt 3
    tester(i);                          //Stmt 4
    cout << i << endl;                  //Stmt 5
}

void tester (int &j)                    //Stmt 6
{
    cout << j << endl;                  //Stmt 7
    j = 3;                             //Stmt 8
}
```

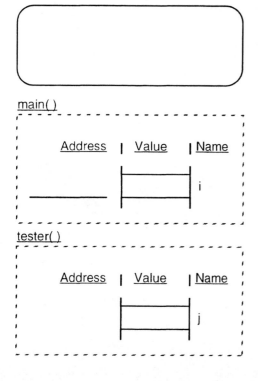

main( )

Address	Value	Name
		i

tester( )

Address	Value	Name
		j

a. Is there any difference in how tester() manipulated *i* in the last experiment and in this one?

b. The & in Statement 6 makes *j* a reference variable. Looking only at Statement 4, can main() tell that tester() may alter *i*?

Solution 19.24

```
public:
    Ship(char *s) // Const'r
    {
        name = new char [strlen(s)];
        strcpy(name, s);
    }
    Ship() {} //Implicit const'r
```

Now *bananaboat* will automatically call the first constructor with an argument. Because *spyboat* isn't declared with an argument, the second constructor would be called automatically.

Drill 19.25 Similarly, the C++ compiler provides a copy constructor that doesn't appear in the class definition. We can override this compiler–supplied copy constructor and write our own. To create a new object by copying members from an old object of the same class, use either of these formats:

ClassName new_object_name = old_object_name;
ClassName new_object_name(old_object_name);

Our *spyboat* doesn't want to look suspicious because it has no name. It wants to copy all its class members from *bananaboat* when it is first created. Show how that can be done.

Dynamic Objects

c. Does *j* contain the value of *i* or its address? From Statement 6, will *j* pick up the address or the value of *i*?

d. Both pointer arguments and reference arguments store addresses. Is *j* a reference argument or a pointer argument in this experiment?

e. In Statement 7, is the value of *i* or its address printed?

f. Change Statement 7 so that it prints &j. Does it then print the value of *i* or its address?

g. In Experiment 19.8, how would you have changed Statement 7 so that it printed the value of *i*?

h. How is Statement 8 of Experiment 19.9 different from that of Statement 8 of Experiment 19.8?

i. Do you need to explicitly de-reference *j*; that is, do you need to use *j?

j. Which lines have been simplified here because *j* is passed by reference?

k. How are a pointer variable (*j* in Experiment 19.8) and a reference variable (*j* in Experiment 19.9) similar?

l. How are they different?

m. When passing a large structure, is it more efficient to pass it by value or by reference?

n. If main() passes *i* by reference, is it possible that the called function may change *i*? Do you have to be concerned that *i* may change?

o. Change Statements 1 and 6 as shown below and explain if Statement 8 is allowed.

```
void tester (const int &);        // Stmt 1
void tester (const int &j)        // Stmt 6
```

p. Name two advantages of using const. (const stands for "constant.")

Exp 19.10 Inline functions are like macros that use the #define construct in straight C. Unlike macros, however, the behavior of inline functions is what one would expect.

```
#include <iostream.h>
inline int add_one (int x) {return x + 1;}
// inline function
void main (void)
{
    int p = 20;
    const int q = 10;          // Notice const
    cout << add_one(p) << endl; // Stmt 1
    cout << p << endl;          // Stmt 2
// cout << add_one(q) << endl; // Stmt 3
// q = add_one(q);             // Stmt 4
}
```

Solution 19.25

```
Ship bananaboat = "Jamaica Farewell";
Ship spyboat = bananaboat;
// Or Ship spyboat(bananaboat);
```

Drill 19.26 Now we want to create a destructor function for Ship. It should deallocate all memory that was created dynamically when a Ship object was declared. A destructor function is identified by a tilde (~) in front of its name, which is the same as its class name. Write the destructor function for Ship that complements its constructors. Let me start it for you:

```
public:
    ~Ship ( ) { . . .
```

a. Here, the inline function is not a member of any class, so the keyword `inline` is used. With inline functions, a function call doesn't take place, but the function is substituted into the code, with the variables renamed accordingly. In Statement 1, what do you think is substituted for add_one(p)? See the output.
b. Try removing the keyword inline. Does the program run?
c. Does *p* change in Statements 1 and 2? Why or why not?
d. Remove the comment for Statement 3 and run the program. Remove the comment for Statement 4 and run the program. Why is Statement 3 valid?
e. Why do you think Statement 4 is invalid?
f. How can you change the program so that Statement 4 will execute uncommented?
g. Add the following statement to the end of main(). Can you pass an inline function as an argument while calling a function?

```
p = add_one(add_one(q));
```

Exp 19.11 Here is an example of an inline function placed inside a class:

```
#include <iostream.h>
class Date
{
    private:
        int dd, mm, yy;
    public:
        void set (int d, int m, int y) { dd = d; mm = m; yy = y;} //Inline
        void see (void);
};

void Date::see (void) //Not an inline function
{
    cout << dd << mm << yy << endl;
}

void main (void)
{
    Date berlin;
    berlin.set(9, 11, 1989); // The wall fell.
    berlin.see();

}
```

Solution 19.26

```
public:
    ~Ship ( ) { delete [ ] name;}
```

Drill 19.27 Now let us turn our attention to regular functions.

```
void funktion(int i, int j[])
{
    i = 0;
    j[0] = 0;
}
```

i ⌐0   j FFA0

```
void main (void)
{ int x = 1,
      y[3] = {1, 1, 1};
    funktion(x, y);
    cout << x << " "
         << y[0] << endl;
}
----- output -----
1 0
```

y FFA0   x 1

FFA0 → 0 y[0]
        1 y[1]
        1 y[2]

In this example, we are passing to the function a scalar, or a non–array, which is *x*, and also the *y[ ]* array. In the function notice how the value of *x* is copied into *i*. This is called passing by value. However, with the array we are

386

a. Is the keyword inline used when the inline function is used within a class?
b. Why do you think inline functions are efficient?
c. Why do you think inline functions are easier to code?
d. Rewrite the class and its member functions so that set() is not an inline function but see() is one. Make the program run.

Exp 19.12 Now let us get acquainted with constructors and destructors. The names of these functions are the same as the names of the classes to which they belong. In this example, it's Date() and ~Date(). A constructor function is called when an object is created, and a destructor function is called when it is no longer needed, for example, at the end of the program. Statements which are commented will be uncommented, one at a time, while doing the questions.

```
#include <iostream.h>
class Date
{
   private:
      int dd, mm, yy;
   public:
//   Date ( ) { }                        // Line 1
     Date (int d, int m, int y)  { dd = d; mm = m; yy = y; } // Line 2
//   ~Date ( ) { cout << dd << mm << yy << endl; }         // Line 3
};

void main (void)
{
// Date x;                              // Line 4
   Date berlin(9, 11, 1989);           // Line 5
   cout << "Is this the end of the pgm?\n";   // Line 6
}
```

a. When a date object is created, we might want to initialize it. This initialization is done with a constructor function. What is the name of a constructor function in this experiment?
b. What is the name of the constructor whose class is called Auto?
c. Does a constructor have a return data type such as void?
d. Rewrite the constructor function of Line 2 so that it is not an inline function. Does it run?
e. Uncomment Line 3 and leave it that way. This is a destructor function and it is executed when the object of that class is no longer needed. Is it executed before Line 6 or at the end of main()?

---

passing the address of y[ ]. This is called passing by reference. No copy is made of the array. Memory used to be precious so arrays were not copied. What this means is that the function can't change x but it can change y[ ], the array.

Hence, the function changes j[0] to 0, which is the same location where y[0] is stored. Therefore, in the output you can see that x is still 1 and not 0, but y[0] was set to 0 by the function.

Now show the output of this program:

```
void pendenis (char c, char d[ ])
{
   cout << c << " " << d << endl;
   c = 'x';
   strcpy(d, "Castle");
}

void main (void)
{
   char x='Q', z[10] = "Cornwall";
   pendenis(x, z);
   cout << x << " " << z << endl;
}
```

Dynamic Objects

f. When were the values for berlin set?

g. Does a destructor have a return data type?

h. Does a destructor have any arguments?

i. Can either a constructor or a destructor have a return statement?

j. Create another object called *south_africa* after *berlin*. Using the constructor, initialize it to 27, 4, 1994, the day they had free elections in South Africa. When is the constructor called, before or after the one for *berlin*?

k. The destructor for which object is called first? How can you tell?

l. Uncomment Line 4. Does the program work or must you also uncomment Line 1? Line 1 is called the implicit constructor.

m. Now make Lines 1, 2, and 5 the only lines with comments. Does the program work? Can *x* be created without any constructors present, that is, without Lines 1 and 2?

n. Uncomment Line 2. Once we define our own constructor as in Line 2, to create *x* must we now also define the implicit constructor as in Line 1?

Exp 19.13 Now we introduce overloading of functions. The term means that you can have different functions with the same name. When calling such a function, the function that matches the number and types of parameters of the call determines which function will be executed.

```cpp
#include <iostream.h>
class Date
{   private:
        int dd, mm, yy;
    public:
        Date (int d, int m, int y) {dd = d; mm = m; yy = y;}      // Stmt 1
        Date (int y) {dd = 1; mm = 1; yy = y;}                     // Stmt 2
        Date (const Date &x) {dd = x.dd; mm = x.mm; yy = x.yy;}   // Stmt 3
        Date ( ) { }
        ~Date ( ) { cout << dd << mm << yy << endl; }
};

void main (void)
{   Date berlin(9, 11, 1989);
    Date india(1947);
    Date hal;
    Date joe(berlin);
    cout << "Is this the end of the pgm?\n";
}
```

Solution 19.27

```
----- output -----
Q Cornwall
Q Castle
```

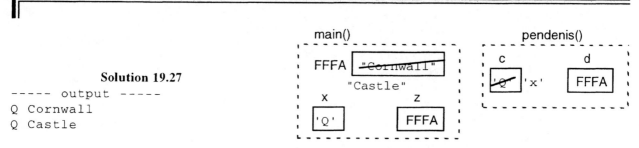

Drill 19.28

a. How else could you write char d[ ]; in the pendenis function header? Hint: Look at *j* in the diagram for Drill 19.27.

b. Show the output for this code. Also, fill in the values in the diagram and show how they are changed.

Dynamic Objects

a. When *berlin* is created, which constructor function is used? Give the statement number. Explain why the constructor from this statement number is called.

b. When *hal* is created, which constructor is used? Explain.

c. When *joe* is created, which constructor is used? Explain. Why is this called a copy constructor? (The const keyword in the constructor protects the *x* object from being altered.)

d. Change Statement 1 to add default arguments as follows to the constructor:

```
Date (int d = 1, int m = 1, int y = 2001) {dd = d; mm = m; yy = y;}
```

Now run the program. Does it work? Why or why not?

e. Leaving Statement 1 with the default arguments, comment out the constructor for Statement 2. Run the program. Does it work? Why or why not?

Moral: Don't get carried away with constructors, especially with default arguments. Keep them simple.

Exp 19.14 Let us now use the new and the delete operators.

```
#include <iostream.h>
class Date
{ private:
      int dd, mm, yy;
   public:
      Date (int d, int m, int y) { dd = d; mm = m; yy = y; }
      Date ( ) {dd = 1; mm = 1; yy =2000; }
      ~Date ( ) { cout << dd << mm << yy << endl; }
      void give_year (void) { cout << yy << endl; }
};
void main (void)
{ Date *p;
  p = new Date;
  cout << p << endl;
  (*p).give_year( ); // Stmt 1
  p -> give_year( ); // Stmt 2
  delete p;
  cout << "Is this the end of the pgm?\n";
}
```

a. If you know the malloc() function from Unit 13, you will notice that the new operator is much simpler. This operator creates memory for an object and returns a pointer to that class. Do you have to specify how much memory the new operator will need, or does the system calculate that?

```
void funky_way(float x, float y, float z[ ])
{
   x = 10.0;
   y = 10.0;
   z[0] = 10.0;
}

void main (void)
{
   float f = 20.0, g[2] = {20.0, 20.0}, h[2] = {20.0, 20.0};
   funky_way(f, g[0], h);
   cout << f << " " << g[0] << " " << h[0] << endl;
}
```

Dynamic Objects

389

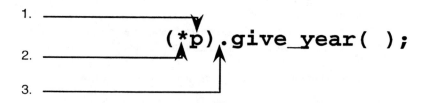

1. ————————

2. ————————

3. ————————

(*p).give_year( );

b. Do we have a name for the object for which memory is allocated?
c. At which address is the object stored?
d. What is stored in *p*?
e. There are three steps necessary to understand the expression in Statement 1. Out of order, they are: go to that location, get this member that is a function and execute it, and find the address. Write in these steps in the diagram above so that the expression is explained in the diagram.
f. From the output, is there any difference between the expressions in Statement 1 and Statement 2?
g. In which statement do you like the expression better? Why?
h. Which expression is easier to understand?
i. Which expression is quicker to type?
j. Is the destructor called when the program terminates, or before that?
k. Is the destructor called when the delete is executed? (If you use new to allocate memory dynamically or "on the fly," then you should use delete to return that memory to the system.)

Exp 19.15 This experiment introduces an array of objects. Fill in all the values that you can in the diagram on page 391. The questions at the end of the next experiment will compare this experiment with the next.

```
#include <iostream.h>
class Date
{
   private:
      int dd, mm, yy;
   public:
      void set (int d , int m, int y)     { dd = d; mm = m; yy = y; }
      Date ( )                      { cout << "constructor called here.\n"; }
      ~Date ( )                       { cout << dd << mm << yy << endl; }
      void give_year (void)            { cout << yy << endl; }
};
```

Solution 19.28
a. char d[ ] can be written as char *d in the function header.
b.
----- output -----
20 20 10

With *g*, only the first element is passed so it is passed by value, as *f* is. However, *h[ ]* is passed by reference, so it can be altered by the function.

Drill 19.29
```
void funsy (int *x, const int *y)
{   int i = 10;
   x[0] = 5;  // Fine.
   y[0] = 5;  // WRONG!
}
```

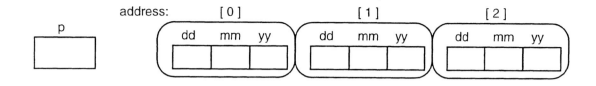

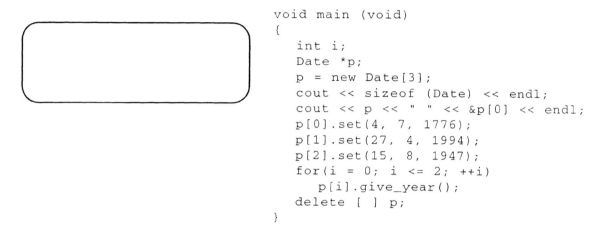

```
void main (void)
{
    int i;
    Date *p;
    p = new Date[3];
    cout << sizeof (Date) << endl;
    cout << p << " " << &p[0] << endl;
    p[0].set(4, 7, 1776);
    p[1].set(27, 4, 1994);
    p[2].set(15, 8, 1947);
    for(i = 0; i <= 2; ++i)
        p[i].give_year();
    delete [ ] p;
}
```

a. Is the following condition true: `"p == &p[0]?"`?

Exp 19.16 Here is an array of pointers to objects. Fill in all the values that you can in the diagram on page 392.

```
#include <iostream.h>
class Date
{
    private:
        int dd, mm, yy;
    public:
        void set (int d, int m, int y) { dd = d; mm = m; yy = y; }
        Date( ) { cout << "constructor called here.\n"; }
        ~Date ( ) { cout << dd << " " << mm << " " << yy << endl; }
        void give_year (void) { cout << yy << endl; }
};
```

If you want to pass an array but you don't want the called function to alter the array, make sure the called function uses `const` in its header. In this example, *x* and *y* both may have the starting addresses of arrays. However, the array *x[ ]* can be changed, while *y[ ]* cannot. In this function, which statements are valid?

```
x[i] = x[0];
i = 5;
y[1] = 20;
x[1] = y[1];
```

```
void main (void)
{
   int i;
   Date *p[3];                    // Stmt 1
   for(i = 0; i <= 2; ++i)        // Stmt 2
     p[i] = new Date;             // Stmt 3
   cout << p << " " << &p[0]   << " " << p[2] << endl;
   cout << p[0] << " " << p[1]   << " " << p[2] << endl;
   (*p[0]).set(4, 7, 1776);
   (*p[1]).set(27, 4, 1994);
   (*p[2]).set(15, 8, 1947);
   for(i = 0; i <= 2; ++i)
     delete p[i];
}
```

Let us now compare Experiments 19.15 and 19.16.

a. In which experiment do you have an array of class Date?

b. In which experiment do you have an array of pointers to class Date?

c. When finding one date object, in which experiment are two references needed? (That is, you have to follow two addresses to get to the object.)

d. A total of how many bytes are allocated dynamically in Experiment 19.15 using the new operator?

e. A total of how many bytes are allocated dynamically in Experiment 19.16 using the new operator?

f. In which experiment do we allocate a whole array with one new and delete a whole array with one delete [ ]?

g. In which experiment do we allocate and free one object at a time?

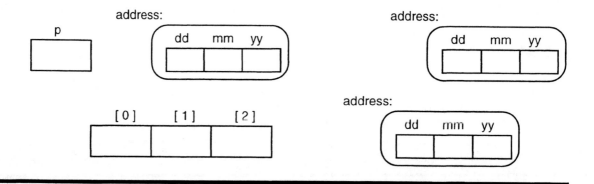

Solution 19.29

All statements are valid except for the third one. This statement is attempting to change *y[ ]* and because of the const keyword in the function heading, that is not allowed.

Drill 19.30

By default, scalars are passed by value and arrays are passed by reference. By using const, we can pass arrays by value as well. In this example, we pass a scalar by reference:

```
void flippity (int *x)
{
   *x = 10;
}
```

h. In which experiment is an entire array deleted using `delete`?

i. In which experiment are objects `deleted` one at a time?

j. Replace Statement 1 with the following two statements:

```
Date **p;
p = new (Date *[3]);
```

And add the following at the very end of main():

```
delete [ ] p;
```

Is there any difference in how the program is executed?

k. In which version of this experiment, the original or the modified, is an array of pointers allocated dynamically?

QUESTIONS

1. Which of the following assignment statements are invalid? For each invalid statement, state why it is invalid.

```
const float PI = 3.14;
class Trial
{  private:
      int x;
   public:
      Trial(void) { return x; }
};

void function (const int &i, int j)
{  i = 3;
   j = 3;
}

void main (void)
{  int i, &r = i, j;
   PI = PI * 2;
   r = &j;
   function(i,j);
}
```

```
void main (void)
{
   int Q = 20;
   flippity(&Q);
   cout << Q << endl;
}
```

Fill in this diagram and show the output.

Dynamic Objects   393

2. Using the given variable declarations, specify whether each statement is valid or invalid. For the valid statements, give the name of the variable being changed and its contents. *x* is stored at FFF0 and *y* at FFE0. Assume that each statement is independent of the others and the changes made by one statement don't affect others.

```
float x=8,  y=3,  *a=&y,  *b = &x;
```

```
a. y = *x;      b. y = *b;      c. b = a;      d. x = a;      e. *a = *a + y;
f. x = *b;      g. *b = *a;     h. x = y;      i. a = &x;     j. y = *a + x;
```

3. In each of the following six parts, what are the final values of the variables in main()? Show also the printouts, if any.

   a. In this problem, also give equivalent statements by converting *x* to *r1* and *y* to *r2*, where *r1* and *r2* are reference variables. Don't convert line 1.

```
void main (void)
{  int i =3,  j = 4,  k,  *x = &i,  *y = &j;
   k = *x + *y + 1;
   y = &k;              // Line 1
   i = *y + *x;
   *y = *x - *y;
}
```

b.
```
void trial (int x, int y[ ],
                  float *z)
{
   y[0] = y[0] + x;
   y[1] = y[1]  + x;
   x = 0;
   *z = 8.0;
}

void main (void)
{
   int i =3,  j[ ] = {4, 5, 6};
   float k = 10.5;
   trial(i, j, &k);
   cout << i << " " << j[0] << " " << j[1] << " " << k << endl;
}
```

c.
```
void try_it (int &x)
{
        x = 8;
}

void main (void)
{
        int a = 7;
        try_it(a);
        cout << a;
}
```

Solution 19.30

----- output -----

10

Drill 19.31

   a. How would you prevent flippity() from changing the value of *Q* in main() by changing the function header?

   b. Review Drill 19.6. Rewrite this code so that *x* becomes a reference variable.

d.

```
class Bag
{ private:
     char contents[20];
   public:
     set(char *x)
        {strcpy(contents, x); }
     Bag () { }
     Bag (char *x)
        {strcpy(contents, x); }
     ~Bag (void)
        {cout << contents; }
};
void main (void)
{ Bag Duffle("Army");
   cout << "GO!\n";
}
```

e. Use the Bag class from part d.

```
void main (void)
{ Bag *p;
   p = new Bag;
   p -> set("paper");
   delete p;
}
```

f. Use the Bag class from part d.

```
void main (void)
{
   Bag *p[2];
   p[0] = new Bag;
   p[1] = new Bag;
   p[0] -> set("laundry");
   p[1] -> set("flour");
   delete p[0];
   delete p[1];
}
```

Is this an array of objects or an array of pointers?

PROGRAMS

1. Write a function called min(). It will receive three integer arrays, each with three elements, into pointers called, x, y, and z. For every corresponding pair of elements of $x[\ ]$ and $y[\ ]$, it will store the smallest of them into $z[\ ]$. main() will initialize two arrays called $a[\ ]$ and $b[\ ]$ to 3, 7, 4 and 5, 2, 6, respectively. main() will also pass an uninitialized array called $c[\ ]$. After min() completes execution, the array $c[\ ]$ should contain 3, 2, and 4: the minimum of 3 and 5, 7 and 2, and 4 and 6 from the first two arrays. Have main() print $c[\ ]$.

To run the rest of the programs for this unit, we will need a class that we can reuse, so write Program 2 before continuing with the others. After Program 2, you can do the other programs in any order.

2. Write a class called Course. It has these two private members: name, which is a string of 20 characters, and credits, which is an integer. For this class create a constructor that asks the

---

Solution 19.31
a. Use this header:
```
void flippity (const int *x)
```

b.
```
void flippity (int &x)
{
   x = 10;
}
void main (void)
{ int Q = 10;
   flippity(Q);
   cout << Q << endl;
}
```

Drill 19.32
What is the advantage of passing an item by reference?

a. The item is copied into the function so that the original item cannot be changed.
b. The item is not copied so that passing of the argument is more efficient than copying, especially if the item is a large structure.

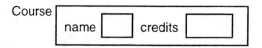

Figure 19.13 Creating a Course class for Program 2.

user for the course's name and the number of credits. Then assign them to the object's private members. Also write a destructor that simply prints out the name and credits. Write an appropriate main() to test the class. See Figure 19.13.

3. In this problem, you will also write a class called Course, as in Program 2. Here, however, have main() ask the user for the data items and pass them to the new constructor function, which will initialize the objects appropriately. Do not use a destructor but have main() send a message called display() that will display the name and credits.

4. Use the class written in Program 2. In main(), create a pointer to Course called *p*. Then dynamically create a new object of class Course. Also, do a delete properly in main(). How can you tell that the constructor and the destructor were called properly?

5. Use the class written in Program 2.
a. Create a new class called Registration. It will have two private members: ptr will be a pointer to Course, and num will be an integer that stores the number of elements in the array. ptr will point to an array of objects. The constructor for Registration will require an integer as an argument that will be assigned to num. The constructor will then dynamically create an array of courses with that many elements that use the constructor and destructor for Course automatically. Also, write a proper destructor for Registration to complement its constructor. See Figure 19.14.

   main() should ask for the number of courses the student is taking and initialize a Registration object by passing that integer to its constructor. At the end of the program, how do you know that all dynamic memory was made free properly?

b. Write a function for the Registration class called total_credits() that will print the total credits a student is taking. The function does not receive any arguments or return any values. Confirm your solution through main().

Solution 19.32
The answer is b.

Drill 19.33 What is the disadvantage of passing an item by reference?
a. The original item in the calling function can be altered by the called function.
b. Since a reference is just an alias for the variable in the calling function, it is inefficient to maintain an extra variable name.
c. There is no disadvantage.

Dynamic Objects

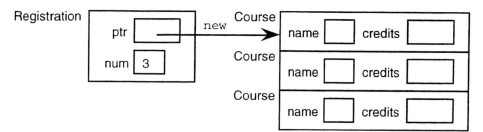

Registration   ptr   new   Course   name   credits

num   3

Course   name   credits

Course   name   credits

Figure 19.14 Creating a Registration class for Problem 5.

6. Use Program 2 again. In main(), create a double pointer to Course called *ptr* and find out from the user the number of courses for which he or she is registering. Dynamically create an array of pointers for that many elements. Then proceed to create dynamically the same number of Course objects and assign their addresses into the array elements.

Then have main() print the total number of credits. Finally, delete properly all memory that was created dynamically. See Figure 19.15.

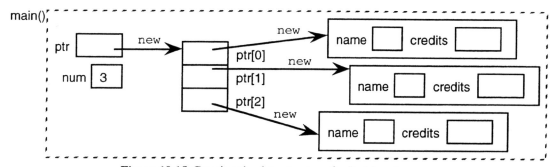

main()   ptr   new   new   name   credits

ptr[0]

num   3   new   name   credits

ptr[1]

ptr[2]   new   name   credits

Figure 19.15 Creating the data structure for Problem 6.

Solution 19.33
The answer is a. However, if const is used with the reference variable, this disadvantage no longer exists.

Inheritance

LESSON

Understanding Inheritance

In Unit 16 we introduced the concept of data abstraction. We saw how it allowed us to extract essential characteristics of objects so we could classify them. In this unit we will take that concept a step further and see how the essential and similar characteristics of two or more classes can be combined into one superclass, also called a base class.

Consider the two classes shown in Figure 20.1. Since the method of calculating the salary for exempt employees is different from that for the non–exempt employees, we have created them as two separate classes. The benefits for each class are also different, and the way we treat these two kinds of employees is much different; we have settled the differences as shown in these two classes.

However, there are other behaviors of these two classes that are identical. For example, the method of updating a name or an address of exempt employees is the same as that for non–exempt employees. Since we observe some characteristics of these two classes to be the same, we factor them out and create a new class called Employee. See Figure 20.2.

DRILLS

Inheritance is applying the knowledge of a general class of objects to a more specialized class of objects. Going back to the example in Unit 16 when I took my car to Joe's Body Shop, I know many things about Joe even before I make the first phone call to him.

Drill 20.1 Which of the following items can I use to formulate my knowledge about Joe?
a. He probably goes to kindergarten.
b. He probably works with cars and trucks.
c. He probably will ask to be paid for his services.
d. He probably does house calls.
e. He probably sells shoes.

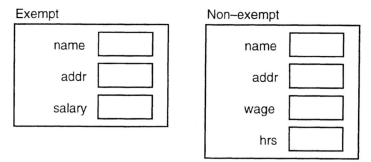

Figure 20.1 Observing two similar classes.

What have we gained by creating a common class? We have abstracted the common elements in each class and grouped them into a class called Employee. Now the functions for updating these common elements have to be written only once, and the Exempt and Non–exempt

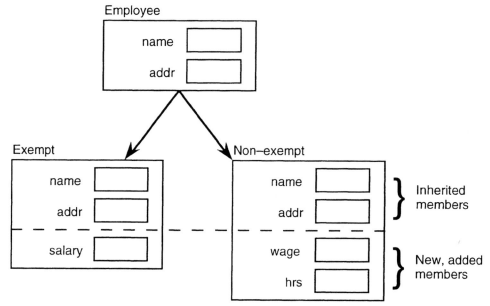

Figure 20.2 Abstraction of the common elements from two classes in Employee.

Solution 20.1 Items b and c are true.

Drill 20.2 Formulating a large knowledge base about Joe without even knowing him personally is a very big advantage. But how do we do that? We do that using inheritance. Inheritance allows us to create a new class simply by adding information to an existing class. The existing class is called the *base* class and the new one is called the *derived* class. In an inheritance diagram, the base class is shown at the top, and the derived class is shown below it. See the example. Draw an inheritance diagram for the following classes: Children, Body_shop_owners, Shoe_store_owners, Humans, Shop_owners, and Auto_shop_owners.

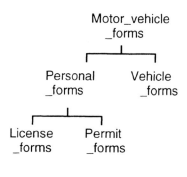

classes can inherit them from Employee. Furthermore, if a new class, such as Consultant, is created, for example, then it can be easily derived from Employee. The new class can reuse the code that already exists for Employee. Here, Employee is called the base class and the others are called the derived classes. The derived classes are inherited from the base class.

Probably the biggest advantage here is not code reuse, but the fact that we have modeled our world the way we view it physically. If there are any future changes in our physical world, then we can easily see how those changes would affect our model, and the changes required in our implementation would be obvious. Basically, our model helps us understand what we are doing. With other programming languages, we can model for inheritance with difficulty, but C++ provides the constructs that make implementation easy and natural.

With inheritance, derived classes can only add members; they can't remove them. In the next unit we'll see how members can be modified.

There are basically two types of relationships we need to contrast and consider: IS–A and HAS–A. IS–A describes inheritance, and HAS–A describes composition. For example, Exempt IS–A Employee, but Employee is composed of name and addr. Therefore, we can say that Employee HAS–A name and HAS–A addr.

Another way to describe these two relationships is by using PART–OF and KIND–OF. PART–OF describes composition and KIND–OF describes inheritance. Rewording the previous example, we obtain Exempt is a KIND–OF Employee and name is PART–OF Employee.

What Is Proper Inheritance?

Inheritance is a two–edged sword; it can help you or hurt you, depending on how skillful you are in using it. If designed properly, inheritance can be very beneficial; otherwise, its disadvantages outweigh all the benefits of object–oriented programming. Most errors in object-oriented design are due to improper inheritance, so let us take some time to define and learn about proper inheritance. What we may intuitively think of as a correct inheritance relationship may not actually be one.

The first rule to remember when reusing code is to rely on its *specification* and not on its *implementation*. When you are given a class or a code to work with, don't be concerned about the actual code and how it is implemented, but rather on its specification. The specification is stable, but the actual coding may change. For example, if part of a function's specification is that it will return a number less than 100, and every time you observed it, it returned a value of less than 10, then don't write your code assuming that this function always returns numbers less than 10. Remember: rely on the specification and not how the specification is implemented.

The second rule is concerned directly with inheritance. It states that the specified behavior for a derived class must be *substitutable* for the specified behavior of its base class. If the specified

---

Solution 20.2

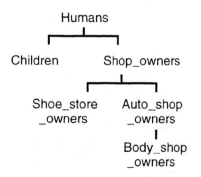

Humans
Children   Shop_owners
Shoe_store   Auto_shop
_owners   _owners
              Body_shop
              _owners

Drill 20.3 Once we learn information about Humans, we can add more information to that and find out about Children or Shop_owners. As we go deeper and deeper in the hierarchy tree, we add more and more information to our knowledge base. For each of the following behaviors, give the highest level class in the Human hierarchy tree that best satisfies it:

a. Sells shoes
b. Paints cars
c. Eats food and sleeps
d. Charges money for goods or services
e. Goes to school
f. Cares about cars

behavior for the derived class is not substitutable for the specified behavior of its base class, then that is not proper inheritance.

How do we determine substitutability? A set of services (or functions) for a derived class is substitutable for the services of its base class if and only if the derived class services' requirements are less than or equal to the base class services' requirements, and the derived class services provide more than or the same amount of its base class services. In simpler terms we can say that a derived class is substitutable if its functions require no more than the same functions in the base class, and the derived class functions promise no less than what the same functions require in the base class. "Require no more and promise no less" is the golden rule of inheritance.

For example, Figure 20.3 shows our Employee–Exempt inheritance relationship. Here, both classes provide the same service called update_name(). The specification for the base class's update_name() service is that the user must provide the old–name and the new–name, and its promise is that it will update the name.

The Exempt class requires only the old–name and using, say, a database, it not only updates the name but also finds that person's new address and updates that also, if necessary. Notice that the derived class did not require more or promise less than the corresponding service of its base class, so this makes for proper inheritance. In fact, the derived class here required less and promised more than its base class. If the Exempt class made the same requirements and promised the same services for that function, that would also be an example of proper inheritance.

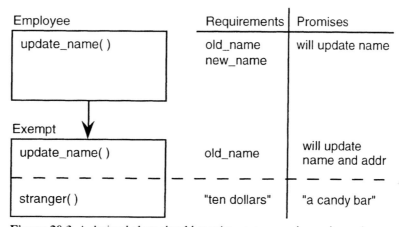

Figure 20.3 A derived class should require no more and promise no less for the same service in its base class. However, a new service can require and promise anything.

Solution 20.3

a. Shoe_store_owners
b. Body_shop_owners
c. Humans
d. Shop_owners
e. Children
f. Auto_shop_owners

Drill 20.4

We use inheritance to our benefit every day without even thinking. Imagine having to learn a new class of objects from scratch without having a base class from which to derive information! Maybe that is why learning the first programming language is more difficult than learning a second.

a. In inheritance, does a derived class add or remove behavior to the base class?

b. We know that humans generally eat and sleep. Does it follow that all objects of classes derived from Humans do the same?

c. What behavior does the Shop_owner class have that Humans in general don't have?

The derived class can specify a brand new function that requires all it wants and promises as little as it wants, and that would also be proper inheritance because that function doesn't appear in the base class. It is a new service. This is illustrated in Figure 20.3 by a stranger asking the exempt employee for his ten dollar bill and providing only a candy bar.

Now let us look at examples of improper inheritance. Figure 20.4 shows a pot representing a base class that provides a service that can hold food objects. The requirement for this service is that the objects be less than eight inches in diameter for the pot to hold them. Under it, a derived

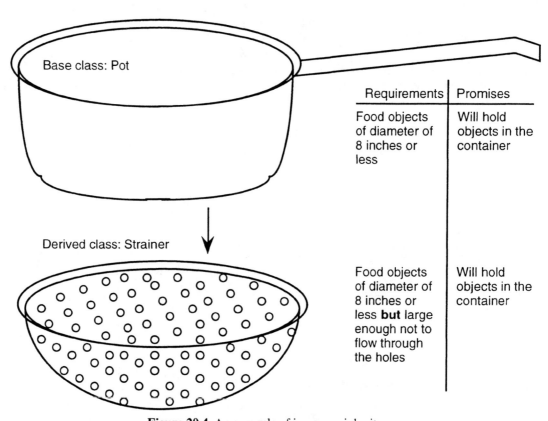

	Requirements	Promises
Base class: Pot	Food objects of diameter of 8 inches or less	Will hold objects in the container
Derived class: Strainer	Food objects of diameter of 8 inches or less **but** large enough not to flow through the holes	Will hold objects in the container

Figure 20.4 An example of improper inheritance.

Solution 20.4 a. A derived class adds behavior to its base class   b. Yes.
c. The Shop_owner class has all the behaviors of Humans plus it also owns shops.

Drill 20.5 Sometimes the behavior of a derived class *overrides* the behavior of its base class. This creates an *exception*. For instance, when I go into the office of an object of class Shop_owners, I don't mind looking around to see what they have placed on their office walls. However, I have learned with Auto_shop_owners to avoid entering their offices. I don't want to see pictures that may be offensive. This can be viewed as an exception because I know that the objects of Shop_owners decorate their walls nicely. However, that is not always true for Auto_shop_owners.
a. The behavior of what Auto_shop_owners hang on their walls _____ the behavior of what Shop_owners, in general, hang on their walls. (Fill in the blank with a new term.)
b. From the description of this knowledge base, does this exception hold true also for Body_shop_owners?
c. Does it hold true for Shoe_store_owners?

Inheritance

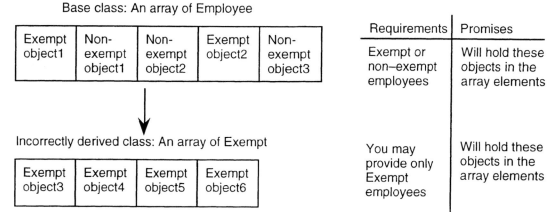

Base class: An array of Employee

Exempt object1	Non-exempt object1	Non-exempt object2	Exempt object2	Non-exempt object3

Requirements	Promises
Exempt or non–exempt employees	Will hold these objects in the array elements

Incorrectly derived class: An array of Exempt

Exempt object3	Exempt object4	Exempt object5	Exempt object6

| You may provide only Exempt employees | Will hold these objects in the array elements |

Figure 20.5 Another example of improper inheritance.

class, represented by a strainer, requires that the objects not be small enough to go through its holes. Since this requirement is more demanding than the requirements for the same service of the base class, we can't model this relationship using inheritance.

To parallel this improper inheritance example, an array that holds objects of a derived class is not properly inherited from an array that holds objects of a base class. See Figure 20.5.

You can derive the Exempt class from the Employee class, but you cannot derive an array of Exempt from an array of Employees. This is because an array of Employee can hold any kind of Employee, either Exempt or Non–exempt. However, an array of Exempt has a more constraining requirement; that is, it can hold only Exempt objects. In fact, this rule isn't restricted only to arrays but to any kind of containers that can hold objects. In general, the rule would be: A container of a derived class cannot be derived from a container of its base class.

Another example of applying this rule is as follows. Shelves of children's books cannot be derived from shelves of any kind of books because shelves of children's books have a stricter requirement. They require that the books they hold be childrens' books.

An Example

Let us study Example 20.1 and Figure 20.6, which illustrates the code in the example. It uses the Employee–Exempt inheritance we have just studied, except for the member called addr, which we have dropped for the sake of simplicity. There are many concepts illustrated in this example, so we will take them one at a time.

Solution 20.5
a. Overrides
b. Yes
c. No

Drill 20.6 In the next unit we'll explore how to code for overridden information. Inheritance is identified by the relationship called KIND-OF, and composition is identified by PART-OF. For example, the class Store_owners is a KIND-OF Humans, whereas the attribute name is PART-OF class Store_owners. For the following pairs of items, state which exhibit KIND-OF relationships, which exhibit PART-OF relationships, and which exhibit neither:

a. footwear — slipper
b. can — soda can
c. animal — horse-like animal
d. brick — cinder block
e. student — teacher
f. planet — planet surface
g. story title — story

```
//EXAMPLE 20.1
#include <iostream.h>
#include <string.h>

class Employee
{
   private:
      char name[20];
   protected:
      char dept[20];       // Accessible by base and derived class members.
   public:
      Employee(char *n)  { strcpy(name, n);}                      // Ctor
      void show (void)   { cout << "Name " << name << endl; }
      ~Employee()        { cout << "Employee destructor \n"; } // Dtor
};


class Exempt : public Employee                              // Line 1
{
   private:
      float salary;

   public:
      Exempt(char *n, float s) : Employee(n)   // Derived ctor calls
      {                                        //    the base ctor first.
         salary = s;
         strcpy(dept, "none");                 // Accessing a protected
      }                                        //    member.
      void show (void)                         // Exempt::show() first
      {                                        //    calls
         Employee::show();                     //    Employee::show()
         cout << "Salary " << salary           //    then it displays its
              << " Dept " << dept << endl;      //    own members.
      }
      ~Exempt()                                // Derived dtor is called
      { cout << "Exempt destructor\n"; }       //    first, then base dtor
};
```

Solution 20.6	Drill 20.7 In the code below, give the relationships between the following pairs of items.
a. KIND–OF	a. Hotel_reservation Reservation b. Hotel_reservation no_of_days
b. KIND–OF	c. deposit no_of_days
c. KIND–OF	class Reservation
d. Neither	{ private: float deposit;
e. Neither	public: void make_deposit(float dep)
f. PART–OF	{ deposit = dep;}
g. PART–OF	};
	class Hotel_reservation : public Reservation
	{ private: int no_of_days;
	public: void set_days (int d)
	{ no_of_days = d;}
	};

```
void main (void)
{
    Employee e1("Jackson"), *p1, *p2;
    Exempt x1("Alexander", 30000.0),  *px = &x1;
    Employee e2 = e1;                   // Line 2
    p1 = &e2;                           // Line 3
    p2 = &x1;                           // Line 4
    e1.show();                          // Line 5
    (*p1).show();                       // Line 6
    p2 -> show();                       // Line 7
    px -> show();                       // Line 8
}                                       // All destructors are called here.
----- output ------
Name Jackson                            // From Line 5
Name Jackson                            // From Line 6
Name Alexander                          // From Line 7, p2 is an Employee ptr
Name Alexander                          // From Line 8
Salary 30000 Dept none                  // Also from Line 8
Employee destructor                     // Destructor for e2
Exempt destructor                       // Derived class destructor for x1
Employee destructor                     // Base class destructor also for x1
Employee destructor                     // Destructor for e1
```

Figure 20.6 (a) The state of the objects and variables before executing
Line 2. (b) The state of the objects and variables at the end of main().

Solution 20.7
a. KIND–OF
b. PART–OF
c. Neither

Drill 20.8
a. From our previous drills, Shop_owners was derived from Humans. In this example, which is the base class and which is the derived class?
b. Which class is inherited from which?
c. If Humans have ears, then Shop_owners also have ears. Which data member exists in both Reservation and in Hotel_reservation?
d. In our example, Shop_owners owned shops but Humans didn't necessarily. Here, which class has data members that the other class doesn't?
e. What is the name of this member?

Inheritance

Declaring Inheritance: First we define the Employee class. Then we define the Exempt class starting at Line 1. This class IS–A Employee, so we use the single colon (:). Now Line 1 can be read as, "Class Exempt IS–A class Employee." The keyword public in this line indicates that anything that is public in Employee is also public in Exempt. In fact, in inheritance we always want that stipulation. We don't want to remove any members; we only want to add them or modify them in the derived class. Hence, always use the keyword public when declaring inheritance. In main(), *e1* is an object of class Employee and *x1* is an object of class Exempt.

Protected Access: The first thing that you may have noticed is the keyword protected in the base class. Employee has a protected member called dept, which means that any member function in a class derived from it may access dept. Exempt is a class derived from Employee, so its member functions may access dept.

For the functions of the derived class, dept acts as if it is public. For anyone else, dept acts as if it is private. This means that other classes not derived from Employee may not access dept. And objects defined in main() cannot access dept. See Table 20.1. For example, in main() this statement would be incorrect:

```
strcpy(e1.dept, "accounting");    // WRONG!
```

It's not a good idea to initialize dept in Exempt and not in Employee. However, to illustrate the behavior of protected, this is done in the example. In general, avoid using protected access. It makes it harder to control the program.

Setting Up Pointers: *p1* and *p2* are pointers to objects of class Employee or to objects of classes derived from Employee. In this example, *px* can point only to *x1*, an object of class Exempt; it can't point to objects of class Employee. A pointer to a base class can point to derived class objects but not the other way around. To help you remember this, think of the direction of the arrows in our diagrams of inheritance trees, such as Figure 20.3. The direction of inheritance arrows is always

	Base class	Derived class	Anyone else
private:	Yes	No	No
protected:	Yes	Yes	No
public:	Yes	Yes	Yes

Table 20.1 Accessibility of base class members from other classes.

Solution 20.8

a. The base class is Reservation and the derived class is Hotel_reservation.
b. The Hotel_reservation class is inherited from Reservation.
c. The deposit member exists in both classes.
d. Hotel_reservation has a member that Reservation doesn't have.
e. This member is no_of_days.

Drill 20.9

Here is the inheritance hierarchy chart. Write in the name of each class and each data member.

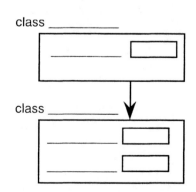

Inheritance

down, and so pointers to base classes can point to base objects or down to derived objects. Services and members for a base class also exist in the derived objects. However, services and members defined in a derived class may not exist in its base class. For example, suppose we have a base class pointer called *pb*, and we initialize it to point to a derived object:

```
Base_class *pb = &Derived_class_object;
```

Then as far as using *pb* is concerned, the members in the derived class don't exist because we think of *pb* as a base class pointer. Of course, we can access the base class members, which are members of the derived class. See Figure 20.7.

Conversely, suppose we have a derived class pointer called *pd*, and we try to point it to an object of a base class object as follows:

```
Derived_class *pd = &Base_class_object; // WRONG!
```

As we use the derived class pointer, we may try to access the members that are unique to the derived class when we de-reference the pointer. However, since the object the pointer is pointing to is actually a base class object, it doesn't have members of the derived class. Hence, this type of assignment is incorrect.

Constructors: When *e1* is created in main(), its name "Jackson" is given in parentheses so the constructor function is called for Employee. Here the name "Jackson" is string-copied into the name member of *e1*. Then *x1* is created from class Exempt. Here, the name and the salary are provided for the initialization and are copied into the *n* and *s* variables of the Exempt constructor function. The single colon (:) after this constructor's header explicitly calls the Employee construc-

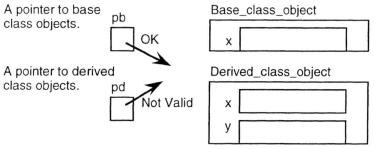

Figure 20.7 A pointer to base class objects can point to derived class objects, but a pointer to derived class objects cannot point to base class objects.

Solution 20.9

Reservation

| deposit | |

Hotel_reservation

| deposit | |
| no_of_days | |

Drill 20.10

a. The make_deposit() member function is available in which class(es)?
b. The set_days() function is available in which class(es)?

tor, which requires only the name and the name is passed. Then the Exempt constructor initializes its salary member and the Employee's dept member because dept has protected access. *px* is created and initialized to point to *x1*. The items created and initialized are shown in Figure 20.6(a).

Copy Constructor: In Line 2, we create a new object of class Employee whose name is *e2*. This object is initialized to the state of *e1*. Since *e1* is copied into *e2*, while *e2* is created, the compiler provides a copy constructor for that class. We don't have to provide one. If we had wanted to write our own version of the copy constructor instead, its header would look like this:

```
public:
   Employee(const Employee &x)
   {
      // etc.
```

In our example, no copy constructor is provided, so using the default copy constructor *e2*'s state would be like using *e1*'s state.

To review what has happened so far, here is the order in which the constructors were called:

e1's Employee constructor
x1's Employee constructor
x1's Exempt constructor
e2's Employee copy constructor

Working with Pointers: In Line 3, the pointer *p1* points to *e2*. This is acceptable because *p1* is a pointer to Employee objects and *e2* is such an object.

In Line 4, the pointer *p2* points to *x1*. This is also acceptable because *p2* is a pointer to Employee objects and *x1* is an Exempt object whose class was derived from Employee. As discussed earlier, *p2* may point to *x1* but *px*, a pointer to Exempt, may not point to *e1*, an object of class Employee. See Figure 20.6(b).

In Line 5, we send the show() message to *e1,* which executes the show() method of Employee. This prints our first line of output, displaying the name "Jackson."

Line 6 sends the show() message to the object pointed to by the pointer *p1*. This object is, in fact, *e2*. The same line is printed again. Line 7 is similar to Line 6, except for the fact that *p2* is pointing to *x1* and we are using the arrow (->) notation.

In Lines 7 and 8, *p2* and *px* are both pointing to *x1*. However, when the show() method is invoked with *p2*, we execute Employee::show() and not Exempt::show(). When the show() method is invoked with *px*, we execute the Exempt::show() method because *p2* is an Employee pointer and *px* is an Exempt pointer. *p2* doesn't know anything about Exempt::show().

Solution 20.10

a. In Reservation and Hotel_reservation.
b. In Hotel_reservation only.

Drill 20.11

In main(), create an object called *r* of class Reservation and an object called *h* of class Hotel_reservation.

Destructors: At the end of main(), we must call the destructors. Destructors are called in reverse order from the order in which the constructors were called. If no destructor exists for a class, the compiler will synthesize one and destroy all the object's members. In our example, we have provided explicit destructors, so they are called.

The last constructor called was *e2*'s default copy constructor, so *e2*'s destructor is called first. Then *x1*'s constructors were called just before *e2*'s constructor was called, so *x1*'s destructors are called next, in reverse order. That is, the Exempt destructor for *x1* is called first, then the Employee destructor is called. Last, *e1*'s destructor is called because its constructor was called first. All this is confirmed from the output.

EXPERIMENTS

Object–oriented programming is based primarily on three key concepts: classes, inheritance, and polymorphism. We have studied classes throughout the last four units. In this unit we will tackle inheritance and in the next we will study polymorphism.

Exp 20.1 Look at the diagram on page 410. We have a class called Course that has two members. From this class we have derived a new class called Lab_course. The two data members in Course become available automatically in Lab_course.

a. The class Lab_course is derived from which class?
b. Which data items does Lab_course have that Course also has?
c. What does Lab_course have that Course doesn't have?
d. Which class inherits features from which other class?
e. Which class would you call the *base class*? Fill in the appropriate blank in the diagram with the word "base."
f. Which class would you call the *derived class*? Fill in the appropriate blank in the diagram with the word "derived."
g. Which class would you call a *subclass*?
h. **Important!** According to the diagram, should the derived class add features to the base class or remove them?
i. Now fill in the table by using the following relationships: HAS–A, IS–A, PART–OF, KIND–OF. One cell should be blank and one should have two relationships. One relationship is already filled in for you. This is, "Course HAS–A credits." To help you with the chart, here are some sample questions. Answer them true or false:

Solution 20.11

```
void main (void)
{
    Reservation r;
    Hotel h;
}
```

Drill 20.12
Now set *r*'s deposit to 100.0, *h*'s deposit to 200.0, and *h*'s days to 3.

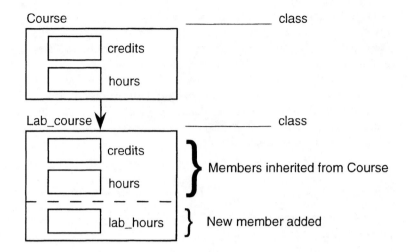

Course _____ class

credits

hours

Lab_course _____ class

credits

hours

} Members inherited from Course

lab_hours } New member added

- 1. Course IS–A Lab_course.
  2. credits is PART–OF Lab_course.
  3. Lab_course IS–A credits.
j. For these questions, fill in the blanks with one of the four relationships. In summary,
  1. If class A HAS–A member M, then member M is _____ class A.
  2. If class D IS–A class B, then class D is a _____ class B.

	Course	Lab_course	credits
Course	–		HAS–A
Lab_course		–	
credits			

Solution 20.12

```
void main (void)
{
    Reservation r;
    Hotel h;
    r.make_deposit(100.0);
    h.make_deposit(200.0);
    h.set_days(3);
}
```

Drill 20.13

a. What data members does *r* have?
b. What data members does *h* have?
c. Is Hotel_reservation a KIND–OF Reservation?
d. Then could you set *r* equal to *h*?

$$r = h;$$

e. If you do this, will *r* have the no_of_days member?

Exp 20.2

```cpp
#include <iostream.h>
class Course
{
   private:
      int   credits,
            hours;
   public:
      void set_up(int cr, int hr)
                        {credits = cr; hours = hr;}
      void show()       {cout << "Credits " << credits << " ";
                         cout << "Hours " << hours << endl; }
      int get_hours ()  {return hours;}
};
class Lab_course : public Course                            // Line 1
{
   private:
      int  lab_hours;
   public:
      void set_up(int cr, int hr, int lab_hr)               // Line 2
               { Course::set_up(cr, hr);
                 lab_hours = lab_hr;                }       // Line 3
      void show(){ Course::show();
                 cout << "Additional hours for lab "
                      << lab_hours << endl;         }
      int get_hours ()
               {return (lab_hours + Course::get_hours());}
};

void main (void)
{  Course eng101;
   Lab_course chem101;
   eng101.set_up(4, 4);
   chem101.set_up(5, 4, 2);
   eng101.show();
   chem101.show();
}
```

Solution 20.13
a. deposit
b. deposit and no_of_days
c. Yes
d. Yes
e. You would lose just the no_of_days member.

Drill 20.14
a. Are all members that are in *h* also in *r*?
b. Do you think that you should be able to set *h* equal to *r*?

$$h = r;$$

Important! Make sure the keyword public, as in Line 1, is always used.

a. While reading Line 1, which of the following relationship(s) from Experiment 20.1 would you substitute for the single colon: IS–A or HAS–A? Lab_course IS–A Course or Lab_course HAS–A Course?

b. When sending the set_up() message to *eng101* in main(), is the method defined in Course invoked or is the one in Lab_course invoked? Why?

c. When sending the show() message to *chem101* in main(), is the method defined in Course invoked or is the one in Lab_course invoked? Why?

d. In the set_up() method of Lab_course, in Lines 2 and 3, how did we ensure that the set_up() method in Course was called?

e. Assume that we didn't write the Course class and that someone else did. We wrote only the Lab_course class. In deriving Lab_course from Course, what advantage do you notice? (The advantage isn't that noticeable because our classes are small. In a larger program, this advantage could be significant.)

f. Besides declaring *eng101* and *chem101*, also declare *eng102* and *chem102*:

```
Course eng101, eng102;
Lab_course chem101, chem102;
```

Then at the end of main(), try the following statements one at a time. Which ones work?

```
eng102   = eng101;      // T or F?
eng102   = chem101;     // T or F?
chem102 = eng101;       // T or F?
```

g. Can you assign one object to another object of the same class?

h. Can you assign an object of a base class to an object of its derived class? Why or why not?

i. Can you assign an object of a derived class to an object of its base class? Why or why not?

j. Which class is reusing methods from which other class?

Exp 20.3

```
// Insert the class Course here from Experiment 20.2
// Also, insert Lab_course here from Experiment 20.2
void find_hours(Course &c)                              // Line 1
{                                                        // Line 2
   cout << "Hours = " << c.get_hours() << endl;          // Line 3
}                                                        // Line 4
```

Solution 20.14

a. No

b. No, *r* doesn't have all the members required by *h*. However, if you set *r* equal to *h*, then all members needed by *r* are available in *h*.

Drill 20.15

If we don't want these objects to exist without being initialized, we need to write constructors for them. Change the functions in Drill 20.7 so that they are constructor functions. Remember that constructors don't have a return type or a return statement.

```
void main (void)
{
    Course eng101;
    Lab_course chem101;
    eng101.set_up(4, 4);
    chem101.set_up(5, 4, 2);
    find_hours(eng101);
    find_hours(chem101);
}
```

    a. In find_hours(), *c* is a reference variable to objects of which class?
    b. Can *c* be an alias to objects of class Course?
    c. Can *c* be an alias to objects of class Lab_course?
    d. If *c* is a pointer to a base class, can it point to objects of its derived class?

Exp 20.4 Now let us explore: if *c* is a pointer to a derived class, can it point to objects of its base class? Change Lines 1 through 4 from Experiment 20.3 as follows:

```
void find_hours(Lab_course &c)                              // Line 1
{                                                           // Line 2
    cout << "Hours = " << c.get_hours() << endl;            // Line 3
}                                                           // Line 4
```

    a. Does the following line in main() compile? Why or why not?

```
find_hours(eng101);
```

    b. Does the following line in main() compile? Why or why not?

```
find_hours(chem101);
```

    c. If *c* is a pointer to a derived class, can it point to objects of its base class? Why or why not?
    d. In the find_hours() function of Experiment 20.3, can you receive *chem101* as an argument? If so, can you call the Lab_course::show() method from find_hours()? Try it.
    e. In the find_hours() function of this experiment, can you receive *eng101* as an argument? If so, can you call the Course::show() method from it? Try it.

Solution 20.15 I abbreviated the class names to make the drills easier to follow. Usually, this abbreviation should be done with care.

```
class Reserv
{ private:    float deposit;
  public:     Reserv(float dep)
                { deposit = dep;}
};
class Hotel   : public Reserv
{ private:    int no_of_days;
  public:     Hotel (int d)    // Line 1
                { no_of_days = d;}
};
```

Drill 20.16 However, now when an instance of Hotel is created, the deposit member isn't initialized. To do that, the Hotel constructor must explicitly call the Reserv constructor. Also, the Hotel constructor must accept two arguments, *d* and *dep*. Change Line 1 in Solution 20.15 so that the Hotel constructor now receives the two arguments, and after a single colon (:), a direct call to the Reserv constructor is made by passing *dep*.

Inheritance

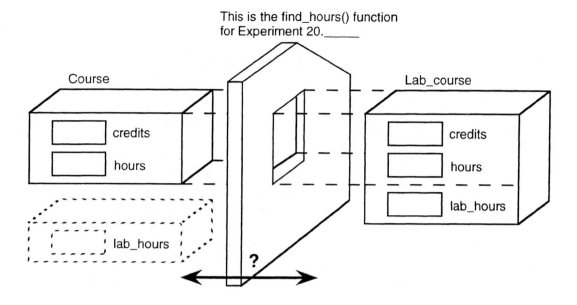

This is the find_hours() function
for Experiment 20._____

Course

credits

hours

lab_hours

Lab_course

credits

hours

lab_hours

?

f. The find_hours() function from which experiment tries to change a Course object into a Lab_course object by adding the lab_hours member: Experiment 20.3 or Experiment 20.4?
g. The find_hours() function from which experiment tries to change a Lab_course object into a Course object by removing the lab_hours member: Experiment 20.3 or Experiment 20.4?
h. The diagram illustrates the conversion of one class into another class as done by find_hours(). This conversion is symbolized by the vertical wall with an opening. Label this wall as the find_hours() function from the correct experiment and also circle one of the arrows indicating which way the conversion is done.

Exp 20.5 Now we want to create a new class called Seminar_course. It should contain the following three data members: credits, hours, and nights_per_wk. The nights_per_wk will store the number of nights a student will be required to go to a musical performance, discussion panel, and so on.
a. Using our classes from the previous experiments, which one would you identify as the base class?
b. Which class would you choose to be the derived class?
c. Modify the diagram of Experiment 20.1 to illustrate the relationship of this new class with the existing ones. Draw arrows in your diagram wherever inheritances are present.

Solution 20.16
```
public:
   Hotel (int d, float dep)   : Reserv (dep)   // Line 1
      { no_of_days = d; }
};
```

Drill 20.17 Create *r* and *h* of Solution 20.12 so that they are initialized using the constructors we have just defined.

Course

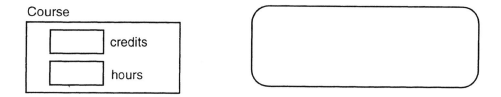

d. Write Seminar_course to include set_up() and show(). Make sure you take advantage of the code reuse principle. Then create an object called *acm101* of class Seminar_course, with members set to 4 credits, 2 hours of lecture, and 1 night per week to attend professional seminars. Does your output confirm the objective of this experiment?

e. This is a very small example illustrating the use of inheritance. However, you can imagine each of these classes and their methods requiring many more lines of code. In C++, what is the biggest advantage when implementing inheritance?

f. What is the advantage of using inheritance in your design? The advantage gained in the design outweighs the advantage gained in the coding for inheritance.

g. Assume that the data members are the only issue to consider and that we're using the inheritances developed so far. Identify the parent class for each of the following two classes:
   1. Class_X : with fields, credits, hours, and recitation
   2. Class_Y : with fields, credits, hours, lab_hours, and recitation

Exp 20.6 Now let us consider constructors and destructors:

```
#include <iostream.h>
class Course
{
   private:
      int   credits,
            hours;
   public:
      Course(int cr, int hr)
                     {credits = cr; hours = hr;
                      cout << "Constructor for Course\n";   }
      ~Course()      {cout << "Credits " << credits << " ";
                      cout << "Hours " << hours << endl; }
};
```

Solution 20.17

```
void main (void)
{
   Reserv r(100.0);
   Hotel h(3, 200.0);
}
```

Drill 20.18 Now that we have created these constructors, we have to use them. Any time we create objects of these classes, we must provide the initialization values. This was not necessary when no constructors were defined. However, with initialization values, all objects of these classes will always begin their "life" in a predefined state.

In any case, we can create a new object out of an old one. The compiler will copy the state of the old object into the new one when creating it. The format for doing this is either of the following:

```
Class_name new_object = old_object;
Class_name new_object (old_object);
```

Now write statements to create a Reserv object called *rr* out of *r*, and a Hotel object called *hh* out of *h*, showing both methods.

Inheritance

```
class Lab_course : public Course
{
    private:
        int   lab_hours;
    public:
        Lab_course(int cr, int hr, int lab_hr) : Course(cr, hr)  // Line 1
                        { lab_hours = lab_hr;
                            cout  <<  "Constructor for Lab course\n"; }
        ~Lab_course()    { cout  <<  "Additional hours for lab "
                            << lab_hours << endl;                   }
};

void main (void)
{
    Course eng101(4, 4);
    Lab_course chem101(5, 4, 2);
}
```

       a. Give the names, in order, of the *constructors* that are called when creating the following objects:
          1. *eng101*
          2. *chem101*
       b. Give the names, in order, of the *destructors* that are called when the following objects are elimi-
nated?
          1. *eng101*
          2. *chem101*
       c. When are the destructors called from main()?
       d. In Line 1 we see the single colon (:) again. While the Lab_course() constructor is called, what other constructor is also called? What arguments are passed to it?
       e. What else does the Lab_course() constructor do besides call another constructor?
       f. Are any destructor functions called explicitly? (**Important!** You should never do this.)
       g. In main(), which object is created first and which is created second?
       h. In main(), which object's destructor is called first?
       i. When constructing a derived class, is the base's or the derived class's constructor called first?
       j. When a destructor for a derived class is called, is the base's or the derived class's destructor called first?

Solution 20.18

```
Reserv rr = r;
    // Or Reserv rr(r);
Hotel hh = h;
    // Or Hotel hh(h);
```

Drill 20.19

In this drill, the objects with an *r* in their names are of class Reserv and those with an *h* in their names are of class Hotel. Also assume in each case that *r* and *h* objects are old, existing objects and *rr* and *hh* are the new ones being created. Using these assumptions, which of the following statements are valid?

```
a. Reserv r = h;         // Redefine r
b. Hotel hh(r);          // Create hh using r
c. Reserv hh = r;        // Create a Hotel object, hh
d. Hotel hh = r;         // Create a Hotel object, hh
e. Reserv rr(h);         // Create a Reserv object using h
f. Hotel hh = h;         // Create a Hotel object from another
```

Exp 20.7 Notice that there are no statements in the body of the classes.

```
class Base { };
class Der1 : public Base { };
class Der2 : public Base { };
class Sub1 : public Der2 { };
class Sub2 : public Der2 { };

void main (void)
{
    Base *pb;
    Der1 *pd1;
    Der2 *pd2;
    Sub1 *ps1;
    Sub2 *ps2;
    // At this point, insert the statements one at a time from
    // Question b.
}
```

    a. Draw the inheritance tree.
    b. Label each of the following statements true or false depending on which are legal or illegal. Try each one in main().

```
pb = pd1;        pb = pd2;        pb = ps1;        pb = ps2;
pd1 = pb;        pd1 = pd2;       pd1 = ps1;       pd1 = ps2;
pd2 = pb;        pd2 = pd1;       pd2 = ps1;       pd2 = ps2;
ps1 = pb;        ps1 = pd1;       ps1 = pd2;       ps1 = ps2;
```

    c. Can pointers to the same class be assigned to each other? Try the following:

```
Base b, *pb = &b, *pbb;
pbb = pb;
```

    d. Can a pointer to a base class point to an object of its derived class?
    e. Can a pointer to a derived class point to an object of its base class?

Solution 20.19

a. Not valid; *r* already exists.
b. Not valid; *r* doesn't have Hotel members.
c. Not valid; *hh* should be of class Hotel.
d. Not valid; same as b.
e. Valid.
f. Valid.

Drill 20.20
When a derived class object is created, first its base class constructor is called, then the derived class constructor is called. The fact that the base class portion should be initialized first makes sense because the derived class is inherited from the base class.

In our case, we have this:
```
public:
    Hotel (int d, float dep):Reserv (dep)// Line 1
             { no_of_days = d; }
```

Exp 20.8 The following introduces protected access:

```
class Top
{
   private:
      Top_priv () { };    // Line 1
   protected:
      Top_prot () { };    // Line 2
   public:
      Top_publ () { };    // Line 3
};

class Under : public Top
{
   private:
      Under_priv () { }; // Line 4
   protected:
      Under_prot () { }; // Line 5
   public:
      Under_publ () { }; // Line 6
};

void main (void)
{
   Top t;
   Under u;
   // Try the statements from Question a here, one at a time.
}
```

a. In main(), which of the following statements compile? Answer yes or no.

```
t.Top_priv ();      t.Top_prot ();      t.Top_publ ();
u.Under_priv ();    u.Under_prot ();    u.Under_publ ();
u.Top_priv ();      u.Top_prot ();      u.Top_publ ();
```

b. For this question, no statement has to be substituted for the comment in main(). For each of the following, state whether it compiles or not. Try the changes one at a time.

Change Line 4 to:
```
Under_priv () { Top_priv(); }
```

Here, the Hotel constructor is explicitly calling the Reserv constructor using : Reserv (dep). Even if we didn't have that explicit call in Line 1 and we simply had this:

```
Hotel (int d, float dep)    // Line 1
```

the Reserv constructor would be called first, this time, implicitly.

In the main() below, name the four constructors and the order in which they are called.

```
void main (void)
{
   Reserv r(100.0);
   Hotel h(3, 200.0);
   Reserv rr(h);
}
```

Can the members shown below call the members shown to the right?	Top_priv()	Top_prot()	Top_publ()
Under_priv () Under_prot () Under_publ ()			

Change Line 4 to:
```
Under_priv () { Top_prot(); }
```

Change Line 4 to:
```
Under_priv () { Top_publ(); }
```

c. Try the same three calls from Under_prot ().
d. Then try the same three calls from Under_publ () and fill in the chart above with yes or no.

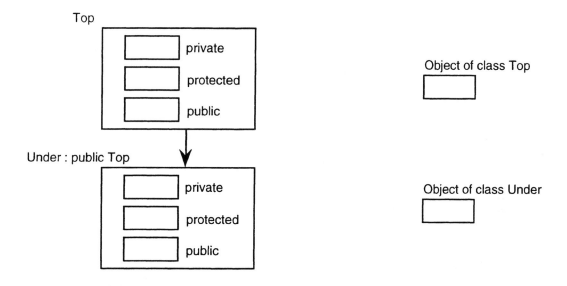

Solution 20.20 Here is the order in which the constructors are called:
1. Reserv constructor for *r*
2. Reserv constructor for *h*
3. Hotel constructor for *h*
4. Reserv constructor for *rr*

Drill 20.21
Now write Reserv::show(), which will print deposit, and write Hotel::show(), which will print the no_of_days and print deposit by calling Reserv::show().

e. Using the information obtained so far, draw arrows in the diagram on the previous page to indicate who can call whom.

f. An object of a derived class can access members with which access of the base class: private, protected, or public?

g. A member function of a derived class can access members with which access of its base class: private, protected, or public?

h. Is there a reason why a class would have protected members if no other class will be derived from it in the future?

QUESTIONS

1. For the following pairs of items, identify the inheritance relationships and composition relationships. Use intuitive judgment without concern for the concept of substitutability. If there is no relationship, then say so.

brush – bristles	brush – paintbrush
brush – toothpaste	building – school
microscope – lens	computer – mouse
rice – brown rice	tricycle – speed
tricycle – vehicle	banana – fruit
banana – mango	shape – pentagon

2. In each of the following four parts, the base class is described first, then its proposed derived classes are listed. For each of the derived classes, which of the relationships are proper? Use the notion of substitutability to determine which are proper.

a. fruit: Can eat it uncooked
                               Is sweet
    tomato (considered a fruit by some)
    lemon
    ripe orange

b. Rectangle   Can position it on its side
                      Has a width and a height
    Cube
    Square

Solution 20.21 Only the pertinent parts are shown.

```
class Reserv
{
   public : void show (void)
   {cout << "Deposit " << deposit << endl;}
};
class Hotel : public Reserv
{
   public : void show (void)
   { cout << "No of days " << no_of_days
        << endl;
      Reserv::show();}
};
```

Drill 20.22 For this main(), show its output:

```
void main (void)
{
    Reserv r(100.0);
    Hotel h(3, 200.0);
    Reserv rr(h);
    r.show();
    h.show();
    rr.show();
}
```

c. Bird: Can fly high
   Sparrow
   Chicken

d. We have determined that Employee is a base class and Manager is a derived class of Employee. Is the following relationship a proper inheritance? A structure that has Employee as a member is the base class. A structure that has Manager as a member is a derived class of a structure that has Employee as a member.

3. Here are some classes and their pointers:

```
class X { };              class W : public X { };
class T : public W { };   class P : public X { };

void main (void )
{
   X *px, *pX;            W *pw;
   T *pt;                 P *pp;
   // Rest of main() would go here.
```

a. Draw the inheritance tree.
b. Which of the following eight assignments are valid?

```
px = pt;    pt = px;
px = pX;    pX = px;
pw = pt;    px = pp;
pp = pw;    pw = pp;
```

4. The program continues on the next page. Show the output with the comment marks and then without them:

```
class Top
{
   public:
      Top ()                  {cout << "Top Ctor\n";}
      Top (const Top &x)      {cout << "Top Copy Ctor\n";}
      ~Top ()                 {cout << "Top Dtor\n";}
};
```

Solution 20.22 Notice that, although a Hotel object was copied into *rr* during declaration, *rr* will not have a Hotel part to it, so Reserv::show() will be executed.

```
Deposit 100.0        // for r.show()
No of days 3         // for h.show()
Deposit 200.0        // also for h.show()
Deposit 200.0        // for rr.show()
```

Drill 20.23
Now convert the show() functions to destructor functions. **Important!** Don't explicitly call any destructors. They are called automatically. Refer to Solution 20.21.

Inheritance   421

```
class Bottom : public Top
{
   public:
      Bottom ()                    {cout << "Bot Ctor\n";}
      Bottom (const Top &x)    {cout << "Bot Copy Ctor\n";}
      ~Bottom ()                   {cout << "Bot Dtor\n";}
};
void main ()
{
   Top t;
// Top tt = t;
   Bottom b;
// Bottom bb = b;
}
```

5. Which of the following class members are accessed incorrectly?

```
class Top
{
   private: int x;
   protected: int y;
   public: int z;
};
class Bottom : public Top
{
   private: int xx;
   public: void mess_up()
      {
         x = 0;
         y = 0;
         z = 0;
      }
};
void main (void)
{  Top t;
   Bottom b;
   cout << t.x  << t.y  << t.z << b.x << b.y << b.z << b.xx <<endl;
   b.mess_up();
}
```

Solution 20.23
```
class Reserv
{  public : ~Reserv() {cout << "Deposit " << deposit << endl;}
};
class Hotel
{  public : ~Hotel ( )   { cout << "No of days " << no_of_days << endl;}
};
```

Drill 20.24 Destructors are called in the reverse order of how the constructors are called. Name the destructors and the order in which they are called. Then show the output. Here is main():
```
void main (void)
{  Reserv r(100.0);
   Hotel h(3, 200.0);
   Reserv rr(h);
}
```

PROGRAMS

1. The following is a sequence of programs. You can write only the first one, if you wish. Or after writing the first one, you can write either the second or the third, or both.

   a. Write a base class called Aircraft. It has one private member called int range that stores the range of the aircraft with fuel tanks full. It has two derived classes called Airplane and Helicopter. Airplane's private member is length, the minimum length of the runway needed for landing and takeoff. Helicopter's private member is clearance, the area needed to land and take off. All variables are integers.

   First, draw a hierarchy diagram for the inheritance. Now write the constructor for each of the three classes that will ask the user for its private member, read it in, and assign it properly. Then write destructors for each that will simply print the associated private members. In main(), create three objects, one of each class. It doesn't matter what you call them. Then simply close main(). The destructors will show you whether or not you constructed the objects properly. Remember that, when a derived constructor is called, its base constructor is first automatically called.

   b. Using the inheritance hierarchy from the above program, create a 5-element array of pointers to Aircraft. Then using the new operator, create dynamically 1 Helicopter, 3 Airplanes, and 1 Aircraft object, all of whose addresses are stored in the array. After that, delete each of these objects using a loop. Then close main().

   c. Redo the above program but instead of creating an array of pointers to objects, create an array of Aircraft objects. Also declare 1 Helicopter, 3 Airplanes, and 1 Aircraft object. Then assign these objects to the elements of the array. No   new or delete operators are needed. Which program is better: this one or the previous one? Why?

2. Write an inheritance hierarchy where Shape is the base class. Its private member is called *col* and it stores the color using 10 characters. Its derived member is Square, which has a private member called side. A constructor for Square receives the color and the length of one of its sides, and explicitly calls the constructor for Shape, which receives the color.

   Shape has a public member called print_col() that merely prints the color, and Square has a public member called print_area() that merely prints the area using the length of the sides.

   Have main() create an object called *flag* of class Square. It provides red and 10 as arguments to its constructor. It also defines a pointer to Shape called *sh_ptr* and a pointer to Square called *sq_ptr*. Have both of these pointers point to *flag*. Using only *sh_ptr*, print the area of *flag*. Using only *sq_ptr*, print the color of the flag. Why or why not does this work?

Solution 20.24

1. Reserv destructor for rr
2. Hotel destructor for h
3. Reserv destructor for h
4. Reserv destructor for r

```
Deposit 200.0
No of days 3
Deposit 200.0
Deposit 100.0
```

Polymorphism

The Three Building Blocks of OOP

Through the last few units we have seen how object–oriented programming models our natural world so nicely. The way we view our physical problem domain has a direct correlation with our programming code. If our problem changes or if it needs enhancements, it becomes obvious where and how the code needs to be changed, even for those who are unfamiliar with the code. Hence, object–oriented code is thought to be extensible. This is not true for programs written in a procedural style.

When we introduced classes in Unit 16, we saw how they allowed us to categorize objects by first abstracting their essential properties. We discussed how the implementation should be hidden so that the user interface could be made simple. This provided a foundation with which we could write programs using object–oriented techniques. See Figure 21.1.

In the process of modeling our real world, we introduced the concept of inheritance. We extended the behavior and states of classes to include additional behavior and classes. We saw how

Drill 21.1 Back in the early 1970s, when I was working for Northwest Orient Airlines, they changed the cockpits of 747s, DC10s, and other airplanes so that they would all look alike. Do you think this was to help the pilots? If so, how could that expensive change help them?

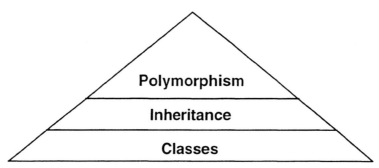

Figure 21.1 The three building blocks of object–oriented programming.

it was natural to derive new classes from an existing base class simply by adding new behavior and states to it.

In our quest to model the world as we experience it, we come across a final concept called *polymorphism*. Using the principles of classes, inheritance, and polymorphism, we can complete our definition of object–oriented programming. Using these three principles, object–oriented programming becomes a powerful extension of our natural world.

Polymorphism in Our Daily Experiences

Polymorphism means simply "many forms." Figure 21.2 is a diagram of a number of places where polymorphism occurs in our daily experiences. Using this diagram, we will introduce new terms so that, when we get to the C++ syntax, we will already be familiar with these ideas. At that time, we will draw a similar diagram and show the categories of polymorphism as it applies to C++.

Polymorphic Objects: This is the first category shown in Figure 21.2. You can think of coal and diamonds as being different forms of carbon. Dogs also come in many varieties. A given word may have different meanings. A word itself could be polymorphic. For instance, the word "base" may have to do with a baseball field, a transistor, an expedition, or paints. All these examples can be thought of as polymorphic objects, or objects with many forms.

Overloaded Operators: This is the next example shown in Figure 21.2. Overloaded operators are like overloaded functions, which we will cover soon. An overloaded operator allows one to use the same operation in different forms. For instance, the verb "add" is polymorphic. We

Solution 21.1 This helped the pilots because they didn't have to re–orient themselves each time they piloted a different aircraft.

Drill 21.2 Recently, when I went to London with my family, I noticed that at many intersections, "LOOK RIGHT" was painted for the pedestrians on the 2–way streets so that the pedestrians would look in the correct direction before crossing. Why wasn't this warning as common in the villages of England as it was in London?

can add numbers, we can add paints, or we can add a person to a list. Likewise, we can find the numbers between 10 and 12, the countries between Thailand and Vietnam, or the elements between helium and carbon in the periodic chart. Even though we don't think of *add* and *between* as overloaded operators, that is what they are.

Overloaded Functions: In the illustration from Unit 16, when I gave the same message, "paint my car," to different objects, they implemented the same message differently. The owner of the body shop implemented it one way and my daughter implemented it a different way. Overloaded functions have different function bodies (or methods) but they all have the same name. We have already seen overload constructor functions in the experiments of Unit 19. In overloading, it is the *name* of the function that has many forms.

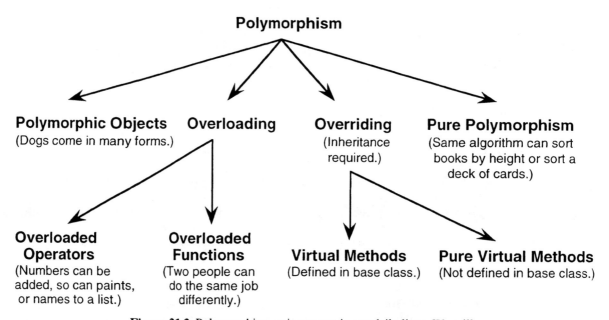

Figure 21.2 Polymorphism as it appears in our daily lives. We will use this same hierarchy to explain polymorphism in C++.

Solution 21.2 London has many foreign visitors from countries where cars are driven on the opposite side of the street, and they are used to looking first to the left before crossing. In the villages, where foreign visitors were fewer, the signs were not needed. Native Englanders are used to looking first in the right direction.

Drill 21.3 In both of these examples, we strive to have a common interface, even though the implementations are different. A pilot likes to have all the controls in the same place, regardless of the number of engines the plane has. Likewise, a pedestrian would like to look first in the same direction before crossing a street, regardless of what country he or she may be visiting. When you sit in an unfamiliar car, what interfaces would you require to be the same as that for other cars?
a. Gas pedal is on the right–hand side and the brake pedal is on the left–hand side.
b. Gas tank is on the right–hand side.
c. The switch for the windshield wipers is labeled and accessible from the driver's seat.
d. The speedometer has a digital display.

```
                              Student
┌──────────────────────────────────────────────────────────┐
│  virtual function: give_slice_of_pizza()                   │
│        { Make it pepperoni. }                              │
│  non-virtual function: give_a_smile()                      │
│        { A cheerful one. }                                 │
└──────────────────────────────────────────────────────────┘
                            V
                       VegetarianStudent
┌──────────────────────────────────────────────────────────┐
│  virtual function: give_slice_of_pizza()                   │
│        { Make it mushroom and onion only. }                │
└──────────────────────────────────────────────────────────┘
```

Figure 21.3 Virtual functions as they appear in my class. A better name for virtual functions would be adaptable, substitutable, or overridable.

Virtual Methods: Virtual methods of functions exist only because of inheritance. Inheritance is a requirement for virtual functions. That is why we covered inheritance in the last unit before doing polymorphism in this one. The word, "virtual," is a poor choice of words. Instead, words such as "adaptable," "substitutable," or "overridable" would be more appropriate. This means that if a base class has a virtual function, then that function may be altered in its derived class so that it is adapted for it. Another way of looking at functions is that the same function may be overridden in the derived class: the virtual function is substitutable in the derived class. When writing a base class, if a function may be redefined in its derived class, then it should be made a virtual function.

For example, suppose that I send a message to my faculty assistant to give everyone in our class a slice of pizza and to make it pepperoni. Let us suppose that he comes back to me and says that there are three vegetarian students in the class who won't eat pepperoni. Therefore, being an instructor in OOP, I analyze my class and draw the inheritance chart as seen in Figure 21.3. Here, Student is the base class and VegetarianStudent is its derived class. I also identify the virtual function, give_slice_of_pizza() and define its method as make it pepperoni.

This virtual method is substitutable, adaptable, or overridable in the derived class. Specifically, the same function now chooses to give a vegetarian slice of pizza to the Vegetarian student. Notice that we look first for the function definition in the derived class. If it isn't in the derived class, then we see if it is defined in the base class. For instance, if I had a function called give_a_smile() in the base class, I don't want to make it virtual. I don't want the derived class to have the ability to change it. In such a case, the non–virtual function is fixed. It can't be overridden by the derived class.

Solution 21.3 I would require choices a and c to be satisfied.

Drill 21.4
a. When you use the interface of "applying the brakes," do you care how the pressure is transferred to the brakes?
b. When you put your foot on the gas, do you care if there is a carburetor or a fuel injection system that accelerates the car?
c. What do you think is the term that is emphasized here?
d. One interface with many ways to implement its service is an example of what?

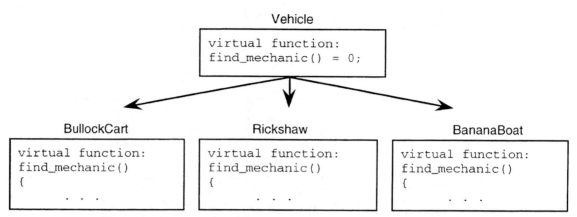

Figure 21.4 A pure virtual function is not defined in the base class but it
is set to zero there. It is defined only in the derived class(es).

Pure Virtual Methods: As seen in Figure 21.2, pure virtual methods are variations of overridden methods. Pure virtual methods occur when the method is not defined in the base class. We can think of these functions as being *deferred methods* because they aren't defined until later, in the derived class. For example, in Figure 21.4 we have a class called Vehicle with three derived classes called BullockCart, Rickshaw, and BananaBoat.

Suppose that the Vehicle class has a function called find_mechanic(), and that this class can't find a mechanic until it knows what kind of vehicle for which we are supposed to find a mechanic. That is, only the derived class can find an appropriate mechanic. Then the function in Vehicle is said to be a pure virtual function because it can't produce a method to satisfy the request, only the derived classes can. However, Vehicle does want to ensure that this function definition is available in all of its derived classes, so it makes the function virtual. In the base class a pure virtual function is set to zero, meaning that it is not defined here but in the derived classes.

Hence, Vehicle is said to be an ABC (abstract base class), and the classes where all of the functions have their definitions available are said to be CDCs (concrete derived classes). An ABC specifies the interface. In our case it is find_mechanic(), but the ABC doesn't provide the implementation. The CDCs must provide the implementation for the interface. An ABC must have at least one pure virtual method. Notice that in Figure 21.3, Student is not an ABC because all of its functions are defined in Student.

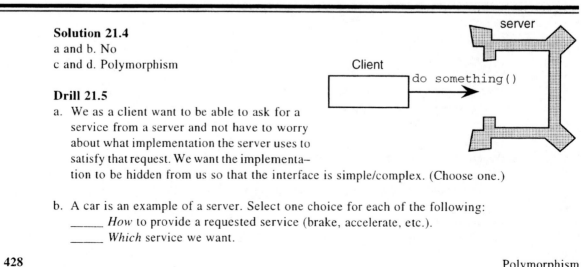

Solution 21.4
a and b. No
c and d. Polymorphism

Drill 21.5

a. We as a client want to be able to ask for a service from a server and not have to worry about what implementation the server uses to satisfy that request. We want the implementa‐ tion to be hidden from us so that the interface is simple/complex. (Choose one.)

b. A car is an example of a server. Select one choice for each of the following:
　　_____ *How* to provide a requested service (brake, accelerate, etc.).
　　_____ *Which* service we want.

A better name for a pure virtual method is a deferred method: a method that is not defined in the base class but its definition is deferred for its derived classes.

Pure Polymorphism: This is the last kind of polymorphism shown in Figure 21.2. Here is one function but its interpretations are many. Sorting in descending order is an example of pure polymorphism. We have a high–level abstraction of how such sorting should be performed, and when we need to apply it, we reuse that high–level abstraction and form a low–level abstraction from it.

For example, arranging books on a shelf by their height, arranging a stack of playing cards by suit, or arranging a stack of personal ID cards by last name are all examples of sorting. As children, we didn't learn separate sorting algorithms for specific objects that needed to be sorted, but we formulated one high–level abstraction of sorting. Then using this high–level abstraction, we created our own low–level abstraction or method that was appropriate for each situation.

Although *polymorphism* is a strange word, we use it every day to our advantage. Hence, polymorphism becomes a major step we must take to understand and correctly model our world as we see it.

Additional Benefits of Polymorphism

Before we learn the various methods of coding polymorphism in C++, let us consider a scenario where the advantages of polymorphism become obvious. In Figure 21.5(a), we think we have an object–oriented design for a windowing drawing program because we are using classes. However, we aren't taking advantage of polymorphism and we will see what problems that creates.

We have a base class called Shape. From it we derive various drawing classes; Square and Line are shown. These classes have their own methods, such as drawSquare() and drawLine(), for drawing themselves on the screen.

On the left–hand side of Figure 21.5(a), we have three other objects of different classes that need to draw the Shape objects. We will simply call the object to be drawn x. Now each of the objects that needs x to draw itself on the screen must go through a nested if statement to figure out which message it should send to x. If the shape of x is a Square, then the drawSquare() message should be sent. If the shape of x is a Line, then the drawLine() message has to be sent, and so on for each kind of shape that our program supports. This long nested if would then have to be written for each class that draws the shapes. This is shown in Figure 21.5(a).

However, such an application would also need to perform other operations on the different shapes. We would also need resizeSquare() and moveSquare() methods and their corresponding methods for each of the objects we support. This would add many more nested if's in our classes that need to invoke the message. These additional nested if's couldn't be shown in the figure because

---

Solution 21.5

a. Simple

b. We want to tell *which* service we want and not have to worry about *how* that service is provided.

Drill 21.6 In previous units we saw how C++ provides methods to simplify our user interface. Another method C++ provides is dynamic binding. Here a base class pointer may point to either a base object or a derived object.

Define *puu* as being a pointer to Upper and *pll* as being a pointer to Lower. Define *U* as an Upper object and *L* as an object of class Lower. Then have *puu* point to *U* and *pll* point to *L*. Use this class hierarchy:

```
class Upper
{ public: void show()
    { cout << "UPPER\n";
    }
};


class Lower :
        public Upper
{ public: void show()
    { cout << "LOWER\n";
    }
};
```

Object 1 of a given class

```
if(x.findshape() == "Square")
      x.drawSquare();
else  if(x.findshape() == "Line")
           x.drawLine();
      else  if( . . .
```

Object 2 of a second class

```
if(x.findshape() == "Square")
      x.drawSquare();
else  if(x.findshape() == "Line")
           x.drawLine();
      else  if( . . .
```

Object 3 of a third class

```
if(x.findshape() == "Square")
      x.drawSquare();
else  if(x.findshape() == "Line")
           x.drawLine();
      else  if( . . .
```

objectX

drawSquare( )
resizeSquare( )
moveSquare( )

class Square

objectY

drawLine( )
resizeLine( )
moveLine( )

class Line

(a)

Figure 21.5 (a) The problems created by using different names for similar methods. Here, drawSquare() and drawLine() are similar methods with different names.

U, a _____ object

```
show()
```
class Upper

puu, a _____ pointer

L, a _____ object

```
show()
```
class Lower

pll, a _____ pointer

Solution 21.6

```
Upper U, *puu;
Lower L, *pll;
puu = &U;
pll = &L;
```

Drill 21.7
Draw arrows in the diagram on the right and write base or derived in the blanks provided.

Polymorphism

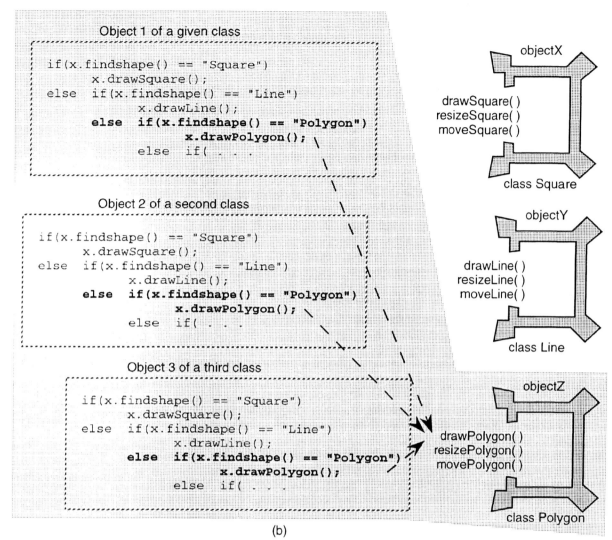

Figure 21.5 (b) The problems multiply if only one new class with a similar method is added. It becomes necessary to update all the code shown in the shaded area. This is shown only for the locations from which versions of draw() are called. The portions of code from which move() and other functions are called must also be updated.

Solution 21.7

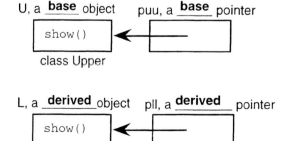

U, a __base__ object   puu, a __base__ pointer

```
show()
```
class Upper

L, a __derived__ object   pll, a __derived__ pointer

```
show()
```
class Lower

Drill 21.8 We as programmers can figure out that *puu* contains an address of an Upper object and that *pll* contains an address of a Lower object. However, the compiler can't tell, at compile–time, to which kind of object these pointers are pointing. Only when the program starts to execute can the compiler tell to which kind of object these pointers are pointing. This is called dynamic binding because only at run–time will the class of the object be determined and the correct version of the show() function be executed. Show the output for the following:

```
pll -> show();
puu -> show();
```

Polymorphism

of lack of room. Imagine having to actually program them! Before OOP, that's what had to be done. In procedural programming, there had to be a different name for each function or procedure, regardless of their similarities. To keep track of the long procedure names and to spell them correctly was a big problem.

But this is only half the problem in procedural style programming! Look at Figure 21.5(b), where we have to add a new kind of shape called Polygon. We must write the methods it needs, like drawPolygon(), resizePolygon(), movePolygon(), and others. If that's all we had to do, our task would be easy. But now all the nested if's for each kind of operation in all the classes have to be rewritten so that the new shape can be supported fully by our program. Instead of making a small change to our program, we must now do a major overhaul. Notice that all the shaded portions of the code in Figure 21.5(b) must be managed and maintained. Furthermore, this major overhaul has to be done every time someone decides to add a new shape.

With polymorphism this is not the case. In Figure 21.6(a), instead of using different names for each method, whether they be drawSquare(), drawLine(), or whatever, we will simply use one name called draw(). Then each of the classes of Shape will respond differently to that same message. This also hides the implementation. The message called draw() will be one simple interface, and we'll leave it up to the receiving object of that message to implement it in its own way. Different implementations are hidden behind a common interface. drawSquare() and drawLine() formed a complex interface to the users of those methods. The users of those methods needed nested if's. However, with polymorphism one simple message name, draw(), can invoke different methods, depending on the class of the receiving object. Which method will be implemented is unknown to the sender of the message. The users of the shapes don't have to worry about what kind of shape x is; they simply tell x to draw itself using a method appropriate to its class. Basically, this is an example of overloading.

In Figure 21.6(b) we see how simple it is to add a new shape. Once the polygon shape and its methods have been defined, then the user doesn't have to worry if x happens to be a Polygon. Adding a new shape doesn't affect the user code. The shaded part of Figure 21.6(b) is different from Figure 21.5(b) because it depicts the reduction in updating the code. In fact, none of the code that is already written has to be updated. That's a big advantage.

Dynamic Binding

In Figure 21.5(a), the compiler uses *static binding*, which means that the function to be called and the point in the programming code at which it is called is determined at compile time. In other words, we know at compile time what function will be called from where. In Figure 21.6(a) the compiler uses *dynamic binding* because at compile time, we don't know what kind of object x

LOWER
UPPER

Solution 21.8

Drill 21.9

a. When was it determined which version of show() to call: at run–time or compile–time?
b. The code in Drill 21.8 is an example of static binding or dynamic binding?
c. When a base pointer points to a base object, which function is selected: the base version or the derived version?
d. When a derived pointer points to a derived object, which function is selected: the base version or the derived version?

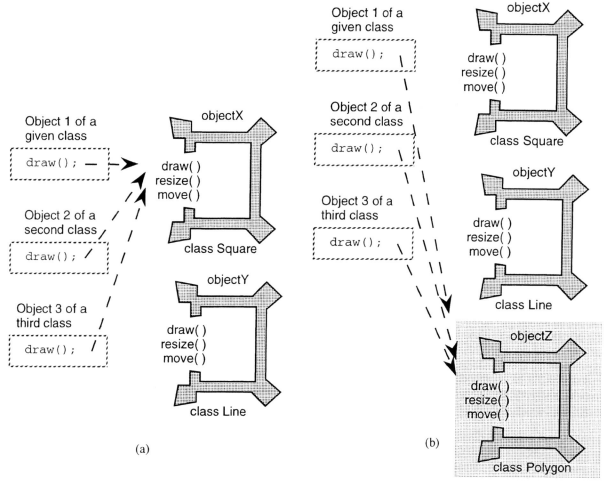

Figure 21.6 (a) Simply by using one method name for similar services, such as draw(), our code is simplified considerably. (b) Adding one new class doesn't require us to update the code we have already written. Only the shaded portion of the code has to be written. It's like writing code that will accommodate classes to be added in the future.

Solution 21.9

a. At run–time
b. Dynamic binding because pointers are used to de-reference the object.
c. Base version
d. Derived version

Drill 21.10

What do you think would happen if show() were not defined in Lower? Are the members defined in the base class still available in the derived class when public inheritance is used?

is. More importantly, we don't know which version of draw() will be invoked at compile time. It's only at run–time, or when the code is actually executing, that we will know what kind of object *x* is and thus know which method is to be bound with *x*.

Dynamic binding allows us to specify *what* service we need rather than *how* it will be implemented. Then a class can improve its services by making its methods more efficient, and the users of that class won't even need to be notified about that change. The users will notice only an improvement in performance. With dynamic binding, the user of services can invoke code for classes which hasn't been written yet but will be added in the future!

Polymorphism in C++

We have seen in Figure 21.2 the various ways that polymorphism occurs in our daily lives. Now using the same hierarchy, shown in Figure 21.7, we will see how those same kinds of

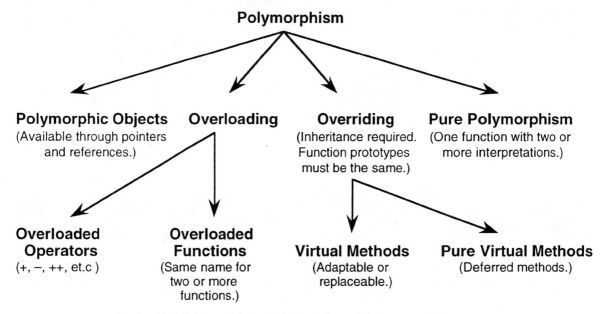

Figure 21.7 Polymorphism and its variations as they appear in C++.

Solution 21.10
We have always emphasized the implemention of public inheritance. For us, members in the base class are always available in the derived class. If show() were not defined in Lower, then the show() version in Upper is always available.

Drill 21.11 What will the program to the right output?

```
class Upper
{  public: void show() { cout << "UPPER\n";
}
};

class Lower : public Upper
{
};

void main (void)
{     Lower L, *pll;
      pll = &L;
      pll -> show();
}
```

Polymorphism

polymorphism occur in C++. As we go through these categories, you may want to refer back to our earlier discussions to understand the terms and the C++ code better.

Polymorphic Objects: The first category shown in Figure 21.7 is polymorphic objects. In languages such as Smalltalk, a variable can contain any type of value. There are no type–declaration statements in Smalltalk. Such languages are called *dynamically typed languages*. The value of a variable may be an integer now, but later it could store a character or any other data type. Values of any type can be stored in objects. In Smalltalk, polymorphic objects are common.

However, C++ is a *statically typed language*. A variable is declared to be of a given type. You can't store a floating point value in an integer variable. If you try to do that, the floating point value will be coerced into an integer value. In C++, polymorphic objects may occur only when using pointers and references.

Example 21.1 shows a class hierarchy that includes TopDog and UnderDog. They both have the same virtual method called show(). We will talk more about virtual methods later. For now, let us say that virtual functions are selected by the type of object to which a pointer points. Which function will be invoked is determined at run time; this is dynamic binding. The actual function that will be invoked depends on the class of the object to which the pointer points at that time.

main() has declared an object called *bernard* of class TopDog and *mutt* of class UnderDog. Then main() calls the coercion() function by passing *mutt* by value. coercion() copies *mutt* into *a*, which is of class TopDog. Here, *mutt* has been coerced into becoming an object of TopDog. See Figure 21.8(a). When this function calls the show() function, it calls the TopDog version of it because *a* is of class TopDog.

Next, main() passes the address of *bernard* to the pointer() function, which stores the address of *bernard* in *b*. Since *b* is pointing to *bernard*, and *bernard* is a TopDog, the TopDog version of show() is invoked from pointer() using *b*. See Figure 21.8(b).

Now main() passes the address of *mutt* to pointer(), which stores it in *b*. *b* is a TopDog pointer so it can point to objects derived from the TopDog class. In this case, it can point to the *mutt* object. See Figure 21.8(c). Hence, when the show() function is called by pointer(), it invokes the UnderDog version of show(). This is an example of a pointer pointing to a polymorphic object. In the previous case, *b* pointed to a TopDog object. In this case, it points to an UnderDog object, and the behaviors of these objects are determined by their classes and not by the kind of pointer.

Last, we pass *mutt* by reference, and *c* is now an alias for *mutt*. Again, as seen in Figure 21.8(d), *c* points to *mutt* so when show() is called, the UnderDog version is called, corresponding to the class of the object to which the reference is pointing. This is another example of a poly-

Solution 21.11

```
UPPER
```

Drill 21.12 Here is one of our conclusions from Solution 21.9:
d. When a derived pointer points to a derived object, the derived version of the function is selected.

How would you extend this conclusion so that it accounts for the possibility when the function is not defined in the derived class?

Polymorphism

```
//Example 21.1
#include <iostream.h>
class  TopDog
{
      public:
                virtual  void show (void)  { cout << "Top Dog \n"; }
};

class UnderDog : public TopDog
{
        public:
                virtual void show (void)  { cout << "Under Dog \n"; }
};

void coercion (TopDog a)
{ a.show(); }

void pointer (TopDog *b)
{ b-> show(); }

void reference (TopDog &c)
{ c.show(); }


void main (void)
{
   TopDog bernard;
   UnderDog mutt;
   coercion (mutt);       // Figure 21.8(a)
   pointer(& bernard);    // Figure 21.8(b)
   pointer(& mutt);       // Figure 21.8(c)
   reference(mutt);       // Figure 21.8(d)
}
----- output -----
Top Dog
Top Dog
Under Dog
Under Dog
```

Solution 21.12 When a derived pointer points to a derived object, the derived version of the function is selected. If the function is not defined in the derived class, then look for it in its base class.

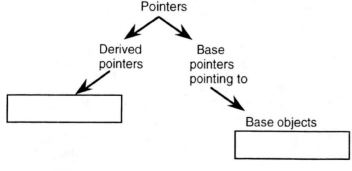

Drill 21.13 Let us summarize what we have learned so far about dynamic binding. Complete this chart by placing "Base only" or "Derived, then Base" in the boxes. These categories will then indicate where to look for the definition of the function being called. We will add another branch to this diagram as we proceed.

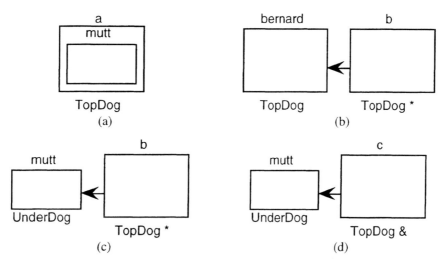

Figure 21.8 (a) The value of object *a* must be of class TopDog. However, a TopDog pointer (b and c) or a reference (d) may point to either a TopDog or an UnderDog object.

morphic object. As we will see later in this unit, if we were to remove the virtual keyword from the classes, then in all of the instances, we would invoke the TopDog version of show().

Operator Overloading: This is the next category of polymorphism in Figure 21.7. In Example 21.2 on page 440, we show how the plus (+) operator is overloaded. Operator and function overloading are very similar. As a reminder, the plus operator is already overloaded by the compiler because it can be used to add integers as well as floats. When we use the + operator, we don't differentiate between adding integers or adding floats. But the compiler must use different implementations to add these data types because integers are stored as single numbers and floats are stored as mantissas and exponents. In the example, we have defined a class called Time with two private members: hr and min. Now the same message, +, will be interpreted three ways: adding integers, floats, and Time, depending on the context. When several functions have the same name (in this case it's addition), it is called *overloading*.

Solution 21.13

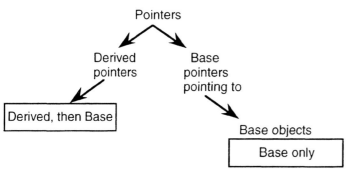

Drill 21.14 Derived pointers may point only to derived objects, but base pointers may point to either base or derived objects. If a base pointer points to a derived object and we need to call its function, then we have to find out if that function is a regular function or a virtual function. With regular functions, the base version of the function is used, even if the object is of a derived class. Virtual functions provide a more powerful method of dynamic binding. In the program on the next page, only normal functions are given. First, show the output as the program is given, then show the output as if show() weren't defined in Lower:

The keyword operator can nearly overload any valid C++ operator, but you cannot define new operators such as **. In our example, operator+() is actually a function. It receives one argument of class Time. In the following statement, *a*, *b*, and *c* are objects of class Time. When the function is called, as in

```
c = a + b;
```

it is the same as calling

```
c = a.operator+(b);
```

Here, *a* is sent the message of operator+() and *b* is passed as an argument. The object returned by operator+() is stored in *c*. Hence, the members of *a* are accessed by using hr and min and the members of *b* are accessed by using y.hr and y.min. Here, *y* is the name of the local receiving object to the function. Notice that the function adds the hr and min members of the arguments, adjusts them if the min member has become greater than 59, and returns the new time to the calling function.

Assume that the class Time and its operator+() function have already been written by someone else and we simply want to reuse that code in main(). All we have to state is a = a + b; and the two times are added automatically by the class's function. Users don't have to worry about how it is implemented. In fact, the class could be compiled by a software house and sold to us as an object file. However, if we have the source code and want to see how it is implemented, then it is better to think of that statement in main() as a = a.operator+(b);.

Lines 1 and 2 in Example 21.2 both begin with the word "Time." But they don't mean the same thing. In Line 1 "Time" represents the class of the object that will be returned by the function operator+(). In Line 2, "Time" is actually the name of the constructor function. Remember that if a function's name is the same as its class, then it is a constructor. See Figure 21.9.

The constructor is an inline function, so the body of that function is defined within the class definition. However, operator+() is not an inline function, so it is defined outside the class. You may want to review such functions by looking back at Example 16.1. We have used mostly inline functions because they are easier to write. But once their definitions become larger than a few lines, it is better to define them outside the class. Line 3 is where the definition of operator+() begins. Line 1 is the prototype for this function, and Line 3 is the header. In Line 3, "Time::" means that the operator+() function belongs to the Time class.

Execution begins in main(), where objects *a* and *b* are created using the constructors for Time. The diagram in Figure 21.9 shows *a* and *b* being initialized in main(). After that, main() invokes and adds these two Time objects, which places us in the operator+() function block. The message is sent to *a*. To access its members, only hr and min need be specified. However, to access

```
class Upper
{ public: void show()
    { cout << "UPPER\n"; }
};

class Lower : public Upper
{
    public: void show()
    { cout << "LOWER\n";
    }
};
```

```
void main (void)
{
    Upper U, *puu;
    Lower L, *pll;
    puu = &L;
    puu -> show();
}
```

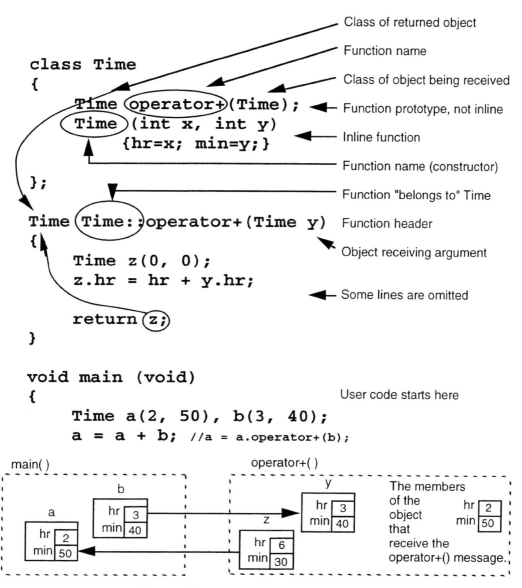

Figure 21.9 Dissecting the parts of Example 21.2.

Solution 21.14

Drill 21.15 As a review, show the output for the following main() and then show the output again as if show() weren't defined in Lower. Use the diagram of Solution 21.13.

```
UPPER // as shown
UPPER // if show() weren't
      // defined in Lower.
```

```
void main (void)
{
    Upper U, *puu;
    Lower L, *pll;
    pll = &L;
    pll -> show();
    puu = &U;
    puu -> show();
}
```

Polymorphism

439

b's members, y.hr and y.min must be used because b was passed by value into y. The function creates a new object called z of class Time. After some arithmetic, it returns the correct value to main(), which copies z back into a. Again, see the diagram in Figure 21.9. Last, the new time is displayed.

```
//Example 21.2
class Time
{  private:
       int hr, min;
    public:
       Time operator + (Time);              // Line 1
       Time (int x, int y)                  // Line 2
                  { hr = x; min = y;}
       void show( ) { cout << hr << ":"<< min << endl; }
};

Time Time::operator + (Time y)              // Line 3
{  Time z(0,0);
   z.hr = hr + y.hr;
   z.min = min  + y.min;
   if (z.min > 59)
   {
      z.hr++;
      z.min = z.min - 60;
   }
   return z;
}

void main(void)
{  Time a(2,50),  b(3,40);
   a = a + b;                    // same as: a = a.operator+(b);
   a.show();
}
- - output<- - -
6:30
```

Message is sent to *a*
b is passed as an argument
Value of *z* is returned to *a*
Function being called

a = a.operator+(b);

Assignment Operator Overloading: To illustrate why operator overloading can be valuable, look first at the following bad example. Here, dynamic data is used and, in such cases, the overloading of the assignment operator (=) can be of great help.

Solution 21.15

LOWER
UPPER

If show() is not in Lower:

UPPER
UPPER

Drill 21.16 Now let us study virtual functions. When a base pointer points to a derived class and the function being called is virtual, then we look for its definition first in the derived class and then in the base class. This method is more powerful because we can have the base pointer point to either a base class or a derived class, and when we request the server to provide a service, we don't have to worry what kind of object that pointer is pointing to. The compiler takes care of that at run–time. If show() is declared as a virtual function, show the output of the following code:

```
puu = &L; puu -> show(); puu = &U; puu -> show();
```

```
//Bad example!
#include <stdio.h>
#include <iostream.h>
void main (void)
{
    char *name1 = new  char[81];
    char *name2 = new  char[81];
    cout << "enter two names\n";
    cin >> name1 >> name2;
    name2 = name1;                    //Line1
    printf("%p %p\n", name1, name2)
    delete name1:
    delete name2;
}
----- output -----
Enter two names
hammer
slammer
FFA0  FFA0
```

This is a bad example. We first declare two pointers to character strings, called *name1* and *name2*. Then we allocate dynamically 81 characters of memory for each and we read names into their locations. At this time, we have the names set up as shown in Figure 21.10(a). Then comes an inappropriate statement:

```
name2 = name1;
```

Instead of copying the name from one location into another, the compiler simply copies the address in *name1* into *name2*. We have the situation shown in Figure 21.10(b). When we print the pointer values, we see that both *name1* and *name2* point to the same memory location, i.e., FFA0.

Now we have lost the address where the second name is stored. More serious, when we delete the memory location, we are attempting to delete the same location (FFA0) twice, a bad idea.

Consider instead Example 21.3. Here *ptr* stores the address of the dynamically allocated memory address. A constructor creates this memory and initializes *ptr*. A destructor prints the value of *ptr* and deletes its allocated memory. Last, we have an overloaded assignment operator function that string–copies one name into the other without changing the pointer values. Only the memory location starting at FFB0 is overwritten. See Figure 21.10(c). Notice also how the constructor properly "delivers the newborn" Name objects and, after their work on earth is done, how the

Solution 21.16 Here, show() is declared as a virtual function. If the base pointer points to a derived object, the derived version of the function is called. If it points to a base version, then the base version of the function is called.

LOWER
UPPER

Drill 21.17 A function is made virtual simply by adding the keyword virtual in front of the function declaration in the base class. It should also be added for the same function in the derived class.

```
virtual void show()
    {  cout << "UPPER\n"; }
```

When a base pointer points to a *virtual* function, what determines the function that will be called? Is it the type of object that it points to or is it the type of pointer?

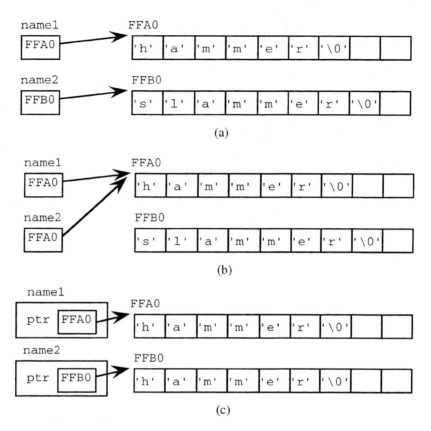

Figure 21.10 (a) Creating two strings, called *name1* and *name2*. (b) Assigning *name1* to *name2* does not copy the string. (c) Example 21.3 shows the correct way of copying strings using operator overloading.

destructor gives them "their proper burials." In summary, the overloading of the assignment operator can be very helpful when working with dynamic data.

```
//Example 21.3
#include <stdio.h>
#include <iostream.h>
#include <string.h>
```

Solution 21.17

With virtual functions, it is the type of object that the pointer points to that determines which function is called.

Drill 21.18

When a base pointer points to a *regular* function, what determines the function that will be called? Is it the type of object that it points to or is it the type of pointer?

Polymorphism

```
class Name
{
   private:
      char *ptr;
   public:
      Name( ) {  ptr = new char [81];
                 cout << "Enter name ";
                 cin >> ptr;}
      ~Name() {  printf("%p %s\n", ptr, ptr);
                 delete [ ] ptr;}
      void operator = (Name &x) {strcpy (ptr, x.ptr);}
};

void main  (void)
{
   Name name1;
   Name name2;
   name2 = name1;
}
----- output -----
Enter name hammer
Enter name slammer
FFB0 hammer                // Name2's destructor
FFA0 hammer                // Name1's destructor
```

Overloading Functions: In the next category of polymorphism in Figure 21.7, we come to overloading of functions. Actually, overloaded operators can be thought of as being similar to overloaded functions. In Unit 19, we already mentioned how constructor functions may be overloaded. In any case, we will cover that concept in more detail here.

Two or more functions with the same name are said to be *overloaded*. Using one name for similar operations simplifies coding. However, overloaded functions must have different *signatures*. A signature includes the number, order, and type of arguments a function receives, but it does not include the return data type. **Important:** Never overload a function by altering only the return data type.

For example, the function called overloaded() in Example 21.4 is defined four times, each time with a different signature. In main() this function is called four times. The first time, a floating point number and a character are passed. From the output, we see that the function receiving a floating point number and a character as arguments is executed.

Solution 21.18

With normal functions, that is, those that are not virtual, the type of pointer determines which function will be called.

Drill 21.19

Now, complete our final chart by placing either "Base only" or "Derived, then Base" in each of the empty boxes.

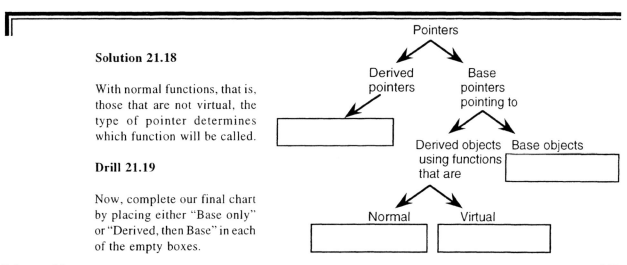

Polymorphism

443

In the second call to a function with the same name, two integers are passed and the function receiving two integers as arguments is executed. With the third call to the function with the same name, a character is passed and the function that has an argument signature that matches the signature of the function call is executed. Last, the function receiving one integer is executed.

In this example, deciding which function will be selected each time is clear. This may not always be the case. To find a match for an argument signature, the compiler will convert a short integer to a regular integer, or an array of characters to a pointer of characters, and so on. However, you should avoid depending on such defaults if at all possible because the rules for resolving signature ambiguities are rather extensive and complicated.

```
//Example 21.4
#include <iostream.h>
void overloaded (int x)
{
    cout << x + 1 << endl;
}
void overloaded (int x, int y)
{
    cout << x + y << endl;
}
void overloaded (float x, char y)
{
    cout << x + 2 << endl;
}
void overloaded (char x)
{
    cout << "x = " << x << endl;
}

void main (void)
{
    overloaded(11.0, 'J');
    overloaded(11, 10);
    overloaded('J');
    overloaded(11);
}
```

Solution 21.19

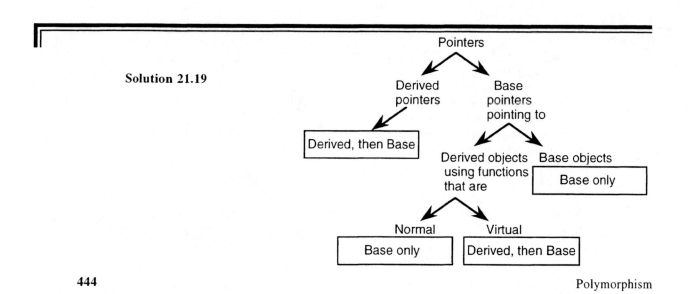

Polymorphism

```
----- output -----
13.0
21
x = J
12
```

Virtual Functions: Now we come to the most important part of this unit. As we have said, the keyword virtual is misleading. "Overridable" would be more appropriate.

Virtual functions appear only where inheritance is present. A base class should declare a function to be virtual only if it may need to be redefined in its derived class(es).

One doesn't need to use the keyword virtual in the derived classes because once a function is declared virtual, it always remains virtual. However, one of the common debugging problems with virtual functions is the omission of the virtual keyword in the base class. Therefore, as a preventive measure for bugs and also to provide documentation to your program, you should always use the keyword virtual in all the classes (base and derived) where the function is virtual.

Another common mistake with virtual functions is making their signatures different. Virtual functions must have the same signatures (that is, the type and the order of the arguments) in the derived class as are in the base class. If two function names are the same and they differ only in their argument signatures, then you have simply overloaded the functions, as seen in Example 21.4. This happens regardless if you have declared the functions virtual.

In Example 21.5 we see how give_bonus() is declared a virtual function in Employee. Exempt, derived from Employee, has its own version of this function. Hence, in main(), when an object of the base class is asked to give a bonus, the base class version of the function is executed. Conversely, when an object of the derived class is asked to give a bonus, the derived class version of the function is executed. Notice that while defining virtual functions, we used the keyword virtual in both classes, the same function name, and the same argument signature. In this example, the output would have been the same if the function wasn't made virtual.

However, consider the situation when we want to give all the employees in our company bonuses. We want to store them all in an array, but what kind of an array? On one hand, if we have an array of Exempt then we can't store objects of class Employee in them because Employee objects don't have the salary member. On the other hand, if we have an array of Employee, then we can store Exempt objects in their elements, but then we would lose their salary members.

The only solution for this dilemma, that is, to try to store both Employee and Exempt objects in an array, is to create an array of Employee pointers. See Figure 21.11. Then each of the Employee pointers may point to either Employee objects or Exempt objects, or, for that matter, to Non–exempt objects or any type of employee that may be derived from Employee. Furthermore, by

Drill 21.20 With static binding, pointers are not used to point to objects. Hence, the compiler knows at compile–time to which class each function is bound. If the message is sent to a derived class object, then the derived version of the function is called (if the message is non–existent, the base version is still available). If the message is sent to a base class object, then the base version of the function is called and this is all determined at compile–time. Show the output for these function calls that use static binding:

```
L.show();
U.show();
```

Polymorphism

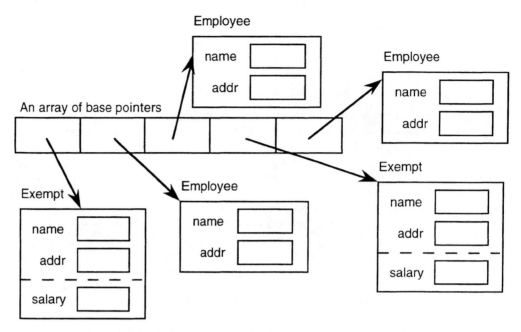

Figure 21.11 Using an array of Employee pointers, we can point to Employee, Exempt, or Non_Exempt objects. This is possible because of virtual functions.

leaving the give_bonus() function virtual, all objects pointed to by the array elements may be given their appropriate bonuses.

In Example 21.6, we reuse the Employee and Exempt classes from Example 21.5. In main() an array of pointers to Employee is declared and called *array[ ]*. In the first loop, we ask the user whether or not we have an Exempt object to create. Depending on the class given, we allocate memory dynamically to create an object of that class. Then we store the address of that new object in array[i]. Once the objects are created and the array contains their addresses, we go through the second for loop and call the give_bonus() function for each pointer in the array. Each time, the correct version of the function is executed because this function is virtual. From the output display, notice that the objects were created in the following order: Exempt, Employee, Employee, Exempt, and Employee. When the function is called, the order of the functions matched the type of object

Solution 21.20

```
LOWER
UPPER
          // Would have been UPPER if show() hadn't existed in LOWER.
```

Drill 21.21 Now let us consider virtual destructor functions. Suppose that I had a virtual function, such as show(), in my inheritance hierarchy. However, the destructors aren't virtual. In this code, only the destructor functions are shown. Using the rules we have learned so far for virtual functions, show the output of the following code. You may want to refer to Solution 21.19.

to which the array element pointed. Last, each of the created objects are deleted. Notice that *array[ ]* was not dynamically allocated, so it should not be deleted.

```
// Example 21.5
#include <iostream.h>
class Employee
{
   private:
      char name [20];
   public:
      //Derived class is given permission to override this function.
      virtual void give_bonus (void)
         {cout << 500 <<"Dollars\n";  }

};

class Exempt : public Employee
{
   private:
      float salary;
   public:
      //Great! I'll give Exempt employees a bigger bonus.
      virtual void give_bonus (void)
         { cout << 700 << "Dollars\n";  }
};

void main (void)
{
   Employee me;
   Exempt you;
   me.give_bonus();
   you.give_bonus();
}
----- output -----
500 Dollars
700 Dollars
```

```
class Upper
{ public:
   ~Upper() { cout << "UPPER\n"; }
};

class Lower : public Upper
{ public:
   ~Lower() { cout << "LOWER\n"; }
};
```

```
void main (void)
{
   Upper *puu;
   puu = new Lower;
   delete puu;
}
```

Polymorphism   447

```
// Example 21.6
#include <iostream.h>

//////////////////////////////////////////////////////////////////////
// Reuse the code for Employee and Exempt classes from Example 21.5 //
//////////////////////////////////////////////////////////////////////

void main (void)
{
    int i;
    char is_exempt;
    Employee *array[5];
    for(i = 0; i <= 4; ++i)
    {
        cout << "If exempt, type 'y', else 'n'   ";
        cin >> is_exempt;
        if(is_exempt == 'y')
            array[i] = new Exempt;
        else
            array[i] = new Employee;
    }
    for(i = 0; i <= 4; ++i)
        array[i] -> give_bonus();
    for(i = 0; i <= 4; ++i)
        delete array[i];
}
----- output -----
If exempt, type 'y', else 'n' y
If exempt, type 'y', else 'n' n
If exempt, type 'y', else 'n' n
If exempt, type 'y', else 'n' y
If exempt, type 'y', else 'n' n
700 Dollars
500 Dollars
500 Dollars
700 Dollars
500 Dollars
```

Solution 21.21 Since the destructor Upper::~Upper() is not virtual and *puu* is a base pointer, there is no reason to execute the derived destructor. Only the base destructor is executed.

UPPER

Drill 21.22 It may be disastrous if the derived destructor is not executed, especially if the derived destructor was supposed to free up some important resource or unlock a record in a database. **Important!** If there is at least one virtual function, make sure that the destructors are also virtual. How would you make the destructors virtual?

```
class Upper
{   public:
    ~Upper() { cout << "UPPER\n";}
};
class Lower : public Upper
{   public:
    ~Lower()  {cout << "LOWER\n";}
};
```

Pure Polymorphism: Recall that pure polymorphism is a high–level abstraction of a process. It is one function with many different interpretations caused by various argument types and classes. In C++ pure polymorphism is available to us in what is called *function templates*.

Think of templates as being high–level classes from which classes, as we know them, are derived. An instantiation of a template is a class (or data type) and an instantiation of a class (or data type) is an object (or a variable). In other words, a group of classes can be generalized using a class template just as a group of objects can be classified by a class. This process is also called *parameterized types*. Likewise, a group of functions can be generalized using a function template. A function template creates a generic function.

In Example 21.7 we define one high–level abstraction of how two objects can be switched. However, we do not provide the class (or data types) of those objects. The class will be determined when we actually make the call to the function. The interpretation of the function is determined when it is implemented.

In Line 1 of Example 21.7, we declare a template in which class T is called the template argument. In Line 2, we call the flip() function, at which time, T is replaced by int since we are passing integers to flip(). In Line 3, when the template function is called, T is replaced by char because of the argument types. We could also pass arguments of user–defined classes for which the assignment operator (=) has proper behavior. Each time, the flip() function switches the values of the arguments passed to it, regardless of their types. We don't have to write separate variations of this function for int, floats, or any classes; the method is defined once and can be reused for each of the different classes or types.

When we had two similar classes with the same interface, such as give_bonus(), but with different implementations, we used inheritance to our benefit. Now we have different interfaces, such as switch two integers or switch two characters, etc., but the same implementation. Now we find function templates useful.

```cpp
// Example 21.7 (Continued on the next page.)
#include <iostream.h>

template<class T>   // Line 1
void flip (T &x, T &y)
{
    T temp = x;
    x = y;
    y = temp;
}
```

Solution 21.22
```cpp
class Upper
{ public:
    virtual ~Upper()
        { cout << "UPPER\n"; }
};

class Lower : public Upper
{ public:
    virtual ~Lower()
        { cout << "LOWER\n";
    }
};
```

Drill 21.23 Now show what the following main() should output, provided that the virtual destructors are defined as shown.

```cpp
void main (void)
{
    Upper *puu;
    puu = new Lower;
    delete puu;
}
```

```
void main (void)
{
    int i = 3, j = 5;
    char a = 'N', b = 'M';
    float r = 1.0, s = 2.5;
    flip(i, j);          // Line 2
    flip(a, b);          // Line 3
    flip(r, s);
    cout << i << " " << j << endl;
    cout << a << " " << b << endl;
    cout << r << " " << s << endl;
}
----- output -----
5 3
M N
2.5 1.0
```

EXPERIMENTS

Exp 21.1 Let's overload functions first. Argument signatures (or simply signatures) are the number of arguments to a function, their types, and their order. They don't include return types.

```
#include <iostream.h>
class Mom
{
    private: int amt;
    public:
        void set( ) { amt = 100; }
        void howMuch(void) { cout << " " << amt << endl; }              //Line 1
        void howMuch(char *s) {cout << s <<" has "<< amt << endl; }//Line 2
        void howMuch(int x, int y) { cout << x + y << endl; }          //Line 3
        int howMuch(int x) { return amt; }                             //Line 4
};
```

Solution 21.23 When constructing, the base is constructed first, then the derived class portion is constructed. Destructors are called in the reverse order.

LOWER
UPPER

Drill 21.24 With virtual functions, you have to be sure that they have the same argument signatures. If the argument signatures are different, then the virtual function is not really the same function that is *overridden* by the derived class, but the function is *overloaded*. Here, Lower has overloaded show(), which means that if, using the classes shown on the next page, we declare these variables:

Lower l;
Upper *p = &l;

then p -> show(); will call the base version of the function because the derived one doesn't exist. The derived version needs an integer passed as an argument. p -> show(32); would cause cause an error because *p*, since it is an Upper pointer, has no record that the function,

```
void main (void)
{
    Mom eve;
    eve.set();
    eve.howMuch("Eve");
    cout << eve.howMuch(32) << endl;
    eve.howMuch(2, 7);
    eve.howMuch( );
}
```

a. Functions with the same name are said to be overloaded. How must overloaded functions differ?
b. Give the name of an overloaded function.
c. If the function names are the same, how do you figure out which function is called and when?
d. From this experiment, do you think an overloaded function may differ only in its return data type?
e. Can *eve* be created without a constructor?

Exp 21.2 Let us add constructors.

```
#include <iostream.h>
class Mom
{
    private: int amt;
    public:
//      Mom(void) { amt = 100; }// Line 1
        Mom(int x) { amt = x; } // Line 2
        int howMuch(void) { return amt; }
};
void main (void)
{
    Mom eve;
    Mom jill(200);
    cout << eve.howMuch( ) << endl;
    cout << jill.howMuch( ) << endl;
}
```

a. Does the program run as shown with Line 1 commented out? It worked in the last experiment. Why doesn't it run now?
b. Uncomment Line 1. Will the program run? Why or why not?

show(int), exists. 1.show(32); will invoke the show(int) function and 1.show(); would cause an error because there are too few arguments provided. Show the output and state errors:

```
class Upper                          void main (void)
{ public:                            {
      virtual void show(void)            Upper *p;
      {cout << "UPPER\n";}              Lower L;
};                                       p = &l;

class Lower : public Upper               L.show();
{ public:                                p -> show(0);
      virtual void show(int x)           p -> show();
      {cout << "LOWER\n";}              L.show(3);
};                                   }
```

Polymorphism   451

Exp 21.3 Let us add inheritance using static binding. Assume that every Son has a Mom.

```
#include <iostream.h>
class Mom
{
   private:
      int amt;
   public:
      Mom(int x) { amt = x; }         // Line 1
      int howMuch(void) { return amt; }  // Line 2
};

class Son : public Mom
{
   private:
      int hisamt;
   public :
      Son(int x, int y) : Mom(x)
         { hisamt = y; }
      int howMuch(void) { return ( Mom::howMuch() + hisamt ); } // Line 3
};

void main (void)
{
   Mom jill(100), lalena(0), *pmom, *pmmom;
   Son abel(200, 300), *pson;
   cout << jill.howMuch() << endl;       // Line 4
   cout << abel.howMuch() << endl;       // Line 5

   pmom = &jill;
   pson = &abel;
   pmmom = &abel;                        // Line 6
   cout << pmom -> howMuch() << endl;    // Line 7
   cout << pson -> howMuch() << endl;    // Line 8
   cout << pmmom -> howMuch() << endl;   // Line 9
   lalena = *pson;                       // Line 10
   cout << lalena.howMuch() << endl;
}
```

Solution 21.24

```
(error)
(error)
UPPER
LOWER
```

Drill 21.25 Show the output for the following:

```
class Upper
{ public:
      void show() {cout << "UPPER\n"; }
      void show(int a, int b) {cout << a <<
                  " " << b << endl; }
      void show(int x) { cout << "***\n"; }
};
void main (void)
{ Upper u;
   u.show(35);   u.show();   u.show(4, 40);
}
```

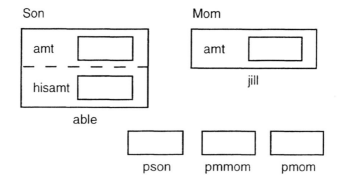

a. When creating a Son object, how many arguments are provided to the Son constructor? Which argument is passed to the Mom constructor? Which is used to initialize hisamt? (The Mom constructor is called before the Son constructor is called.)

b. When the howMuch() function is called in Line 4, which data member is returned?

c. When the howMuch() function is called in Line 5, what value is received from Mom::howMuch() into Son::howMuch()? What value is received from Son::howMuch() into main()?

d. In the diagram above, show all the values of amt and hisamt. Then draw arrows from the pointer variables to the objects to which they point.

e. In Line 4, the function is bound with *jill*, an instance of _____. (Give the class name.)

f. In Line 5, the same function is bound with *able*, an instance of _____ .

g. In Lines 4 and 5, we have what is called *static binding* because at compile time, we can tell which version of the function will be selected with which object. When pointers are used to reference objects, the compiler can't tell which class of objects is referenced. In this experiment, for instance, *pmom* could point to either Son or Mom objects. This is called *dynamic binding* because the type of object that is referenced is determined at run–time. In which lines, from Lines 7 through 10, is dynamic binding used?

h. In Line 9, we have a base pointer point to a derived object. Is this legal?

i. Can a derived pointer pointing to a base object? That is, is this legal? If not, can you tell why not?

```
pson = &jill;
```

j. In Line 9, we have a base pointer pointing to a derived object. Which version of the function is invoked: the base one or the derived one? Does the base pointer realize that it is pointing to a

---

Solution 21.25

* * *
UPPER
4 40

Drill 21.26 Just as functions can be overloaded, operators in C++ can also be overloaded. We have already said that the + operator is overloaded. We can use the same symbol with integers as we can with floats. In both cases, the symbol carries the same meaning. The actual addition of floating point numbers is different from that of integers. Although the implementation is different, the interface is the same.

Let us now start writing a class called Str that will store a character string. We will overload some operators with this class. However, first write the class so that it has one private member called *str* that is 81 characters long. It has one destructor that does nothing and it has two overloaded constructor functions. One receives no arguments but, using strcpy(), it sets *str* to ' \ 0 '. The other receives a character string and sets *str* to this string.

Polymorphism

derived object? Or has the derived portion of the object been "sliced," as in the diagram of Experiment 20.4?

k. With regular functions or functions that are not virtual, what determines which function is selected: the pointer type or the object type to which it points?

l. In Line 10, an object of which class is assigned to an object of what other class?

m. Is the derived class object "sliced," or are members taken away when the derived class object is assigned to a base class?

Exp 21.4 Now add the keyword, virtual, in front of the function declarations in both classes, in Lines 2 and 3. For example,

```
virtual int howMuch(void) { return amt; }  // Line 2
```

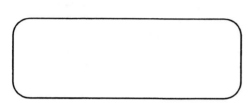

a. Show the new printout. Circle the item(s) that are different here than they were without the virtual keyword.

b. In Line 9, we have a base pointer pointing to a derived object. Which version of the function is invoked: the base one or the derived one?

c. With virtual functions, what determines which function will be called: the pointer type or the object type to which it points? This is a more powerful form of dynamic binding than the kind that was used with pointers as in Lines 7 through 9 in Experiment 21.3.

Exp 21.5

```
#include <iostream.h>
class Mom
{
   private:
      int amt;
   public:
      Mom(int x) { amt = x; }
      virtual int howMuch(void) { return amt; }  // Line 1
};
```

Solution 21.26

```
#include <string.h>
class Str
{
   private:
      char str[81];
   public:
      Str() { strcpy(str, ""); }        // First overloaded constructor
      Str(char *x) { strcpy(str, x); }  // Overloaded constructor
      ~Str() { }                        // Destructor; does nothing
};
```

Drill 21.27 Create objects of Str. Initialize *s1* to "skydive" and *s2* to nothing.

```
class Son : public Mom
{
   private:
      int hisamt;
   public :
      Son(int x, int y) : Mom(x)
         { hisamt = y; }
      virtual int howMuch(void)        // Line 2
         { return ( Mom::howMuch() + hisamt ); }
};

void main (void)
{
   Mom *pmom;
   Son abel(200, 300);
   pmom = &abel;
}
```

a. *Without* the keyword virtual in Lines 1 and 2, which functions will the following lines call from main()?

```
cout << pmom -> howMuch() << endl;
cout << abel.howMuch() << endl;
```

b. *With* the keyword virtual in Lines 1 and 2, which functions will the following lines call?

```
cout << pmom -> howMuch() << endl;
cout << abel.howMuch() << endl;
```

c. Leave the functions virtual for the remainder of this experiment. However, let us say we made a mistake by altering the argument signature in the virtual function in Son. Change Line 2 to the following:

```
virtual int howMuch(int x)        // Line 2
```

Which function will be called from the following line?

```
cout << pmom -> howMuch() << endl;
```

Solution 21.27

```
Str s1("skydive"), s2;
```

Drill 21.28 Since Str is a class, we can easily execute s2 = s1; without executing strcpy(s2, s1); . However, let us overload the assignment operator (=) by writing our own function to do that. This way, we will have the flexibility to do exactly what we want when an assignment is done. operator is a keyword.

Polymorphism

d. By changing the signature in the derived class, did we override the function in the base class? That is, did we redefine it in the derived class?

e. On the other hand, did we overload the function in the base class? That is, did we create a brand new function with the same name?

f. If we overloaded the function, then we should be able to execute all versions of howMuch() in the following statements. Which class's version is called in each case? Did we override or overload the function?

```
cout << abel.Mom::howMuch() << endl;
cout << pmom -> howMuch() << endl;
cout << abel.howMuch(21) << endl;
```

g. How many versions of howMuch() does Son have available?

h. pmom is a base pointer and it has no record that there exists a howMuch() version of the function that accepts an integer. Also, Son::howMuch(void) simply doesn't exist. Which of these give errors?

```
cout << pmom -> howMuch(21) << endl;
cout << abel.howMuch() << endl;
```

i. **Important:** Virtual functions are difficult to debug, but the rules for defining them are simple. When defining virtual functions,
   1. Always use the keyword, _____ .
   2. Always use the same argument _____ .

Exp 21.6 Abstract base classes contain at least one pure virtual function. A pure virtual function is set to zero in the base class, meaning that the function points to the NULL pointer or that it doesn't exist.

We overload the assignment operator by defining the operator=() function as a public member of Str. In main() when we say,

```
s2 = s1;
```

we actually execute the following statement:

```
s2.operator=(s1);
```

s2.operator=(s1);

↑ The object that receives the message.
The name of the function.
The argument being passed.

The only difference is that the first notation is easy to understand. The object on the left–hand side of the operator, *s2*, receives the message so that, in the body of the function, *s2*'s private member is accessible simply by using *str*. However, since *s1* is the receiving argument to the function, its private member is accessible by using x.str, where *x* is the name of the receiving argument in operator=(). Now write the function that will copy x.str into *str*. Nothing is returned.

Polymorphism

```
#include <iostream.h>
class Shape
{
   public: virtual void area (void) = 0; // A pure virtual function
};

class Circle : public Shape
{
   private: int radius;
   public :
      Circle (int r ) { radius = r; }
      virtual void area (void )
         { cout << 6.28 * radius << endl; }
};


void main (void)
{
   Circle round_kind(10);
   round_kind.area();
}
```

a. Is a pure virtual function's method defined in the base class?
b. A pure virtual function is set to 0 in the abstract base class and it should be defined in one of the derived classes. A class where all the function's methods are defined is called a concrete derived class. In this experiment, which is the abstract base class? Which is the concrete derived class?
c. Does this pure virtual function make sense for Shape? Is there a way to find the area of a shape without knowing its kind?
d. Can you create an instance of a concrete class?
e. Can you create an instance of an abstract base class? Does the following compile in main()?

```
Shape x;
```

Solution 21.28
```
void operator = (Str x) {strcpy(str, x.str);}
```

Drill 21.29 Now let us write the equality relational operator (==). Instead of executing:

```
if(strcmp(s1, s2) == 0),
```
we can simply execute:

```
if(s1 == s2).
```
When writing this function, we can think of it as:

```
if(s1.operator==(s2) == 1).
```

To do this, define the operator==() function. It will return a 1 if the two strings are the same and return a 0 if they are not. Use the strcmp() function from the string.h file. It returns a 0 if the two strings are the same.

Polymorphism   457

Exp 21.7 For the last experiment, we will overload operators.

```cpp
#include <iostream.h>
class Vector
{
   private:
      int x, y;

   public:
      Vector (int a, int b)
                      {  cout << "Constructing "<< a << " " << b << endl;
                         x = a; y = b; }
      ~Vector( )     {  cout << "x = " << x << "  y = " << y << endl; }
      Vector operator + (Vector v)
      {  cout << x << y << v.x << v.y << endl;
         Vector sum(0, 0);
         sum.x = x + v.x;
         sum.y = y + v.y;
         return sum;
      }
};

void main (void)
{
   Vector north_west(2, -2), south(-2, 0), answer(0, 0);
   answer = north_west + south;
}
```

a. As the class is written, can you create the vector *answer* without initializing it to 0's?

b. How would you rewrite the class so that you can instantiate an object of Vector without providing any coordinates to it?

c. When the operator function was called, what were the coordinates for *v* and the values for *x* and *y*?

d. At the return statement in the operator function, what were the components for *sum*?

e. At the end of main(), what were the coordinates for *sum*?

f. For each line of the printout, label whether it is from a constructor or a destructor and also label their objects.

Solution 21.29

```cpp
int operator == (Str x)
{
   if(strcmp(str, x.str) == 0)
      return 1;
   else
      return 0;
}
```

Drill 21.30 Writing the operator>() function is very similar to the function in Solution 21.29. The value of `strcmp(a, b)` is positive if *a* is greater than *b*.

1. What are the three building blocks of object–oriented programming? Explain each in your own words using one sentence for each.

2. For the following examples, which form of polymorphism is described? For virtual functions, also describe the inheritance hierarchy. Use Figure 21.2.

   a. When a child first learns what a horse is, she may think that all horses are exactly like the one she sees. The horse may be big and brown and have a saddle. Next time she is shown a horse, the characteristics of that horse will be different and she will have to relearn what a horse is; that is, not all horses are brown and big and they sometimes come without saddles. Soon she forms a high–level abstraction of horses and she is able to identify them, regardless of their color, height, and other characteristics.

   b. Water can exist as vapor or ice.

   c. People in my group are each given a deck of cards to sort. We sort our decks using different sorting algorithms.

   d. I am told to trim the branches of the trees in someone's back yard, but not the branches of the trees bearing fruit.

   e. I am told to add gasoline to vehicles in a fleet, but first find out what kind of vehicle each one is. Maybe some take a different kind of fuel.

3. In your own words, describe the difference between dynamic and static binding.

4. Show the output for the following program. Also, for each function call in main(), specify whether the binding is static or dynamic. The figure of Solution 21.19 may be helpful.

```
class Base
{
   public:
      virtual mvirt()                  { cout << "ONE\n"; }
      virtual mvirt_base_only()        { cout << "TWO\n"; }
              mnormal()                { cout << "THREE\n"; }
              mnormal_base_only()      { cout << "FOUR\n"; }
};

class Der : public Base
{
   public:
      virtual mvirt()                  { cout << "FIVE\n"; }
      virtual mvirt(char x)            { cout << "SIX\n"; }
              mnormal()                { cout << "SEVEN\n"; }
};
```

Solution 21.30 Changes from the function in Solution 21.29 are the two > signs.

```
int operator > (Str x)
{
   if(strcmp(str, x.str) > 0)
      return 1;
   else
      return 0;
}
```

Drill 21.31 Write a main() that will make use of these overloaded operators. Create *s1* and initialize it to "skydive". Create *s2* with nothing in it. Create *s3* and initialize it to "seadive". Then assign *s1* to *s2*. Write an if–else that will state whether *s2* is greater than *s3*. If not, it will test to see if *s2* is equal to *s3*. If so, it will state that the two are equal and if not, it will state that *s3* is greater than *s2*.

```
void main (void)
{  Base  b,  *p;
   Der    d,  *q;
   p = &d;
   q = &d;

   p -> mvirt();
   p -> mnormal();

   d.mvirt();
   d.mvirt('J');
   d.mnormal();
   d.mnormal_base_only();

   b.mvirt();
   b.mnormal();
   q -> mnormal();
   q -> mvirt();
   q -> mnormal_base_only();
   q -> mvirt_base_only();
}
```

5. Use the classes from Question 4.
   a. When a pointer points to an object, can a compiler tell what kind of object it is pointing to? Or is the type of the object determined only at run–time, i. e., q -> mnormal();?
   b. When a pointer points to an object whose non–virtual function is to be executed, a decision has to be made whether to execute the base version or the derived version of the function. Is this decision determined by the *type of the pointer* or the *type of the object* that is referenced?
   c. Refer to Question 5b. What is the answer if the function is virtual?
6. Use the classes from Question 4.
   a. Can you assign Der objects to each element of an array declared as Base x[10];? If so, can you have the entire objects or just their base parts stored in the array?
   b. Suppose you use this declaration instead: Base *x[10];. Determine if each of the following items can be stored in *x[ ]*.
      1. Objects of Der?
      2. Addresses of Der objects?
      3. Addresses of Base objects or addresses of Der objects? That is, can you mix them?

Solution 21.31

```
Str s1("skydive"), s2, s3("seadive);
s2 = s1;
if(s2 > s3)
   cout << "s2 is greater than s3.\n";
else
   if(s2 == s3)
      cout << "s2 is equal to s3\n";
   else
      cout << "s3 is greater than s2.\n";
```

Important! A class with a destructor, an assignment operator, or a copy constructor should include all three.

PROGRAMS

1. Create a class called Fraction. It has two private integer members called numerator and denominator. Write three overloaded constructor functions as shown.

Fraction (void)   This constructor will do nothing. The numerator and denominator will not be set.

Fraction(int x)   This constructor will set x to be the numerator, and the denominator will be set to 1.

Fraction(int x, int y) This constructor will set the numerator to x and the denominator to y.

Also, write the destructor that will simply print the numerator and the denominator. Then run the program with the following main():

```
void main (void)
{
   Fraction one(3, 5), two(5, 2), three, four(4);
}
```

2. For Program 1, write an operator*( ) function that will multiply the corresponding members of the objects but not simplify the fractional answer. Then use the following main():

```
void main (void)
{
   Fraction one(3, 5), two(5, 2), three;
   three = one * two;
}
```

3. Create a class called Car and two derived classes called BoxCar and TankCar as shown in Figure 21.12. Make Car an ABC by declaring find_capacity() as a pure virtual function. BoxCar and TankCar are concrete derived classes. They define the find_capacity() methods. They each have a private member called *used* that stores the amount of capacity already taken up by the car. With BoxCar, capacity is measured in square feet, and with TankCar, it is measured in gallons. Create constructors for the concrete classes that ask the user for the amount used.

In main(), create a 4–element array of pointers to Car called *choochoo[ ]*. Using a loop, the new operator, create objects of either of the derived classes determined by what the user inputs. Now print a report for the train telling how much capacity is left in each case. The maximum

---

Notice how we simplified the C++ language so that we don't have to use the strcpy() and the strcmp() functions with strings. We can now work with strings with the same ease as integers. Sure, we would have loved to have this new class, Str, back in Unit 1. Now however, we can use these techniques to create our own classes and work with them as if they were built–in data types provided by the language. This is powerful!

Drill 21.32 Here are some review questions:
a. When does it make a difference that a function is virtual?
b. What term describes that two functions have the same name but differ only in their signature?
c. What term describes that a method is redefined in the derived class?
d. What kind of class cannot be instantiated?
e. What term means that something has several forms?
f. What term means that a method is defined at a high level of abstraction and that when it must be implemented, its low–level abstraction is formulated?

Polymorphism   461

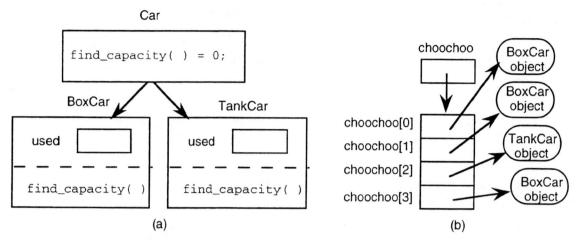

Figure 21.12 (a) The inheritance hierarchy for Program 3. (b) An array of Car pointers managing a train of BoxCar and TankCar objects.

capacity for a BoxCar is 500 square feet, and for a TankCar, it is 1000 gallons. Here is a sample run: Define destructors and find_capacity() correctly-

```
If box car, type 'b' else 't': b
How much square footage is used? 300
If box car, type 'b' else 't': b
How much square footage is used? 100
If box car, type 'b' else 't': t
How many gallons does it hold? 600
If box car, type 'b' else 't': b
How much square footage is used? 200

Car 1: Still has 200 square feet of capacity left.
Car 2: Still has 400 square feet of capacity left.
Car 3: Still has 400 gallons of capacity left.
Car 4: Still has 300 square feet of capacity left.
```

Solution 21.32

a. When a base class pointer points to a derived class object
b. Overloading
c. Overriding
d. Abstract base class
e. Polymorphism
f. Pure polymorphism

Unit 22

Loose Ends

Now that we have covered object–oriented programming using its three building blocks — classes, inheritance, and polymorphism — let us learn some particulars about C++. It should be noted that there are complete books on topics such as streams, templates, etc. However, I thought it was more important to build a solid foundation on the principles of object–oriented programming rather than try to cover all the concepts and syntax that C++ has to offer.

In this unit, we will learn some important topics. This unit will help to make the text more complete.

Function Pointers

We will start with one of the most elegant constructs of C++ and that is the function pointer. This type of pointer does not point to variables or objects but to functions. When we used virtual functions, the system used pointers to functions but we were unaware of them.

DRILLS

Developing a case for Cline–Lomow's Law of the Big Three.

Drill 22.1 Write a class called Customer that has one private member called `char *name`. There are no public members yet. Then write main() that creates an object of Customer called *mycust*.

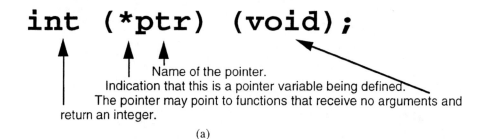

$$\text{int } (\text{*ptr}) \text{ (void)};$$

Name of the pointer.
Indication that this is a pointer variable being defined.
The pointer may point to functions that receive no arguments and return an integer.

(a)

$$\text{ptr} = \text{sharp1};$$

The pointer points to the function sharp1( ).

(b)

$$\text{x} = (\text{*ptr}) \text{ ()};$$

The pointer is dereferenced
using the indirection operator.
Nothing is sent to the function.
And the integer received from the function is stored in *x*.

(c)

Figure 22.1 (a) Declaring a function pointer. (b) Assigning a value to a function pointer. (c) Calling the function by dereferencing the pointer.

In Line 1 of Example 22.1, we defined a function pointer called *ptr* that may point to functions receiving no arguments and returning integers. See Figure 22.1(a).

The example has two such functions defined, sharp1() and sharp2(). First, in Line 2 we assign sharp1() to *ptr*. Now *ptr* points to this function. See Figure 22.1(b). Then we call the function in Line 3, not directly but using the indirection operator, as seen in Figure 22.1(c). While we call this function using *ptr*, we send no arguments and receive the returned integer into *x*. The function prints EINS. In main(), 1, which was received from sharp1(), is printed.

Solution 22.1

```
class Customer
{
    private:
        char *name;
};

void main (void)
{
    Customer mycust;
}
```

Drill 22.2

Since no constructors were defined, the compiler generated a default constructor for us to create *mycust*. Now create your own constructor that will dynamically allocate 25 characters of memory using the new operator and assign it to name. Also write two other functions. Define a destructor to print the name and complement the constructor. Then write the set(char *x) function that will copy the string in *x* into name.

In Line 5 *ptr* is made to point to another function, sharp2(). Hence, in Line 6, when the function is called using `(*ptr) ()`, the returned value is printed directly without storing it in *x* first. The function itself prints ZWEI.

Function pointers can be powerful depending on how they are used.

```
//EXAMPLE 22.1
#include <iostream.h>
int sharp1 (void)
{
   cout << "EINS\n";
   return 1;
}

int sharp2 (void)
{
   cout << "ZWEI\n";
   return 2;
}


void main (void)
{
   int x;
   int (*ptr) (void);              // Line 1
   ptr = sharp1;                   // Line 2
   x = (*ptr) ();                  // Line 3
   cout << x << endl;              // Line 4
   ptr = sharp2;                   // Line 5
   cout <<  (*ptr) () << endl;     // Line 6
}
----- output -----
EINS
1
ZWEI
2
```

Solution 22.2
```
public:
   Customer ( )      { name = new char [25]; }
   ~Customer ( )     { cout << name; delete [ ] name; }
   set (char *x)     { strcpy(name, x); }
```

Drill 22.3
Now write main() that will first create an object called *myCust*. Then it will set the name to "Doofy Duck." Finally, it will create an object called *yourCust* that will receive myCust as an argument.

Friend Functions

In the last unit, specifically in Example 21.2, we saw how operator overloading was done. The Time class had two private members, hr and min, and we used the operator+() function to add two objects of Time. Although we invoked the function as follows:

```
a = a + b;
```

it was equivalent to calling the function like this:

```
a = a.operator+(b);
```

which was unnatural. We wanted to add *a* and *b*. However, the message was sent to the *a* object and *b* was passed as an argument to the function. If we had coded the following:

```
a = b + a;
```

then *b* would have received the message and *a* would have been the argument that was passed. Furthermore, when we actually wrote the following function:

```
Time Time::operator + (Time y)
{  Time z(0,0)
    z.hr = hr + y.hr;
    z.min = min   + y.min;
        . . .
    return z;
}
```

we used hr to access the receiving object's hour member, and we used y.hr to access the argument's hour member. This asymmetry is unnatural. By making the operator+() function a friend function, we can easily restore the symmetry that exists in the addition of two objects.

When a function needs to be operated on the private members of more than one object of the same class, friends become helpful. Simply add the keyword friend before the function declaration in the class. Then define the function as a regular C function outside any class. Example 22.2 repeats Example 21.2 but uses a friend function.

Solution 22.3

```
void main (void)
{  Customer myCust;              // This is initialization
    myCust.set("Doofy Duck");
    Customer yourCust(myCust); // This is initialization
}
```

Drill 22.4 There is a serious problem here. Since we used *myCust* to copy and create a new object called *yourCust*, the compiler generated its own copy constructor. We have no control over how the default copy constructor was defined. It probably created only a name member and didn't actually allocate new memory to store the name. Hence, let us define our own copy constructor that will allocate 25 characters dynamically and then copy the name member into it. Use the following header for the copy constructor:

```
Customer (const Customer &x)
```

```
//EXAMPLE 22.2
#include <iostream.h>

class Time
{
    private:
        int hr, min;
    public:
        friend Time operator + (Time, Time);
        Time (int x, int y)
                    { hr = x; min = y;}
        void show( ) { cout << hr << ":"<< min << endl; }
};

Time operator + (Time x, Time y) // The friend keyword is not used.
{
    Time z(0,0);                    // Also, "Time::" is not used.
    z.hr = x.hr + y.hr;
    z.min = x.min   + y.min;
    if (z.min > 59)
    {
        z.hr++;
        z.min = z.min - 60;
    }
    return z;
}

void main(void)
{
    Time a(2,50), b(3,40);
    a = a + b;
    a.show();
}
- - output<- - -
6:30
```

Solution 22.4

```
Customer (const Customer &x)
{
    name = new char [25];
    strcpy(name, x.name);
}
```

Drill 22.5

Now number these events in the order of execution using the same main() from Solution 22.3:

___ Constructor for *myCust*
___ Destructor for *myCust*
___ Copy constructor for *yourCust*
___ Destructor for *yourCust*

Loose Ends

Enumerated Types

Suppose that we have salespeople who sell cars of four different makes. We want to store the make of the last car sold with the salesperson object. One way to do that is to store the make in a character string, say, of length 10. However, we don't want to waste 10 characters to store the make when we have only four kinds anyway. There will be a lot of repetition in each object.

One thing we can do is store an integer variable called *car_sold*. If the car sold is a Ford, then we will store a 0 in it. If it is a Chevy, we will store a 1 in it, and so on, for the four car makes. Yet this becomes a problem as well. *The program loses its readability.* Imagine having to do an if statement such as the following:

```
if(nancy.car_sold == 0)
   ++ford_count;
else
   if(nancy.car_sold == 1)
      ++chevy_count;
```

The problem with this is that we have to remember that 0 stands for a Ford, 1 stands for a Chevy, etc. It would be better if the programming code were self–documenting, maybe like the following:

```
if(nancy.car_sold == Salesperson::Ford)
   ++ford_count;
else
   if(nancy.car_sold == Salesperson::Chevy)
      ++chevy_count;
```

Then we wouldn't have to keep track of which make is represented by which integer. Example 22.3 shows a complete list using what is called enumerated data types.

```
//EXAMPLE 22.3
#include <iostream.h>
```

Solution 22.5

_1_   Constructor for *myCust*
_4_   Destructor for *myCust*
_2_   Copy constructor for *yourCust*
_3_   Destructor for *yourCust*

Drill 22.6

Rewrite main() so that *myCust* and *yourCust* are created first without any arguments.
Then set *myCust* equal to "Rug Rat" and assign *myCust* to *yourCust*.

```
class Salesperson
{
   public:
      enum make {Ford, Chevy, Chrysler, Packard} car_sold; // Line 1
};

void main (void)
{
   Salesperson nancy;
   nancy.car_sold = Salesperson::Chrysler;                 // Line 2
   cout << nancy.car_sold << endl;                         // Line 3
   if(nancy.car_sold == Salesperson::Chrysler)             // Line 4
      cout << "Chrysler\n";
}

----- output -----
2
Chrysler
```

Using the enum keyword in Line 1, we define an enumerated data type called make. It can have only four values: the names of the four carmakers. Actually, Ford has the value of 0, Chevy has the value of 1, and so on. When we define this enumerated data type, we also declare a data member for the Salesperson class called car_sold. Now car_sold is a data member of Salesperson.

In main(), *nancy* is one object of class Salesperson and we initialize her car_sold member to be a Chrysler in Line 2. When we print the value of this member in Line 3, we print the integer 2. In Line 4, we can use the word Chrysler to see if she has sold this car. This is better than saying whether she has sold the car of type number 2.

If the enumeration were defined outside the Salesperson class, then Lines 2 and 4 would be simplified without requiring Salesperson::, as follows:

```
nancy.car_sold = Chrysler;        // Line 2
if(nancy.car_sold == Chrysler)    // Line 4
```

Solution 22.6

```
void main (void)
{
   Customer myCust, yourCust; // Initialization
   myCust.set("Rug Rat");
   yourCust = myCust;          // Assignment
}
```

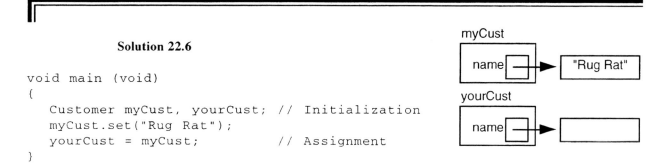

Drill 22.7 Here is a similar problem. The compiler probably just copied the address of name instead of copying the string. Show this effect pictorially by updating the diagram showing the states of the objects right after they are initialized by the constructors. Also, why is this a problem?

Static Members

When you think you need a global variable, you could often probably use a static member in a class. By making a global variable part of a class instead, you modularize your program and place items with the class where they probably belong.

So far we have worked with class members where the members are not static and their scope is the object. Typically, members exist only as long as the object to which they belong are in existence. Sometimes we have a common variable that needs to be shared among all objects of a class. Here, objects of the same class need to share information. In such a case, declare the member to be static using the `static` keyword. A static member is in existence as long as its class is in existence.

Static members can be data members or member functions. Static data members are also called *class variables,* and static member functions are also called *class methods.*

In Example 22.4, *interest_rate* is declared to be `static` in Line 1. In Line 2, we are actually making space for this variable in RAM, and so it is defined outside Account. It is also initialized to 0.0. In Line 3, the rate is changed to 4.5 using the scoping operator (::). Since there is only one copy of *interest_rate*, it is set to 4.5. Last, in Line 4 we add 1.0 to *a*'s interest rate and set that equal to *b*'s interest rate. The interest rates for both objects are in the same location in memory. When their respective *interest_rate*'s are printed, the same number is printed twice.

```
//EXAMPLE 22.4
class Account
{
   public:
       static float interest_rate;                   // Line 1
       float bal;
       char name[20];
};

float Account::interest_rate = 0.0;                   // Line 2

void main (void)
{  Account a, b;
   Account::interest_rate = 4.5;                      // Line 3
   b.interest_rate = a.interest_rate + 1.0;           // Line 4
   cout << b.interest_rate << " " << a.interest_rate << endl;
}
----- output -----
5.5    5.5
```

Solution 22.7 The reference to memory that was first allocated to yourCust was lost, and only the name pointers were made equal by having them point to the same location.

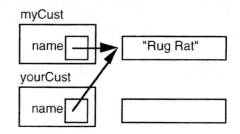

Drill 22.8

a. When the destructors were called at the end of main() from Solution 22.6, how many times was the delete executed on the 25 characters allocated to *myCust*?

b. How many times was the delete executed on the 25 characters allocated to *yourCust*?

Assignment Versus Initialization

Now we come to a delicate subject: the difference between an assignment and an initialization. Their differences are summarized in Table 22.1. If we execute `float w = 30.0;`, then this is an initialization. Here, the variable is declared and initialized at the same time. If we execute the following:

```
float w; w = 30.0; // The second statement is an assignment
```

then first *w* is declared, and after that, 30.0 is assigned to it. Initialization can occur only once during the lifetime of an object, and that is when it is first declared. On the other hand, assignments can be done as many times as needed during the lifetime of an object. One reason why it is easy to confuse them is that they both use the equals sign (=) operator. However, in the first case, it is an initialization, and in the second case, it is an assignment.

In the C language the difference is not that important. But in C++, the difference becomes important because constructors are executed only on initialization, only when an object is first created. Assignment statements do not invoke constructors. When an argument is passed by value to a function in the C language, that argument is *assigned* to the receiving variable. In C++, a copy constructor is called to *initialize* the receiving variable. If the programmer hasn't written a copy constructor, then the compiler will synthesize one. Otherwise, the programmer's copy constructor

	Assignment	Initialization
Operator used for the event	=	=
Example of the event	w = 30.0;	float w = 30.0;
Can this event be part of a declaration?	No	Yes
When can this event occur?	Any time	Only at declaration
How many times can it occur?	Many times	Only once
Does this event invoke a constructor?	No	Yes
Which programming language uses this event to pass values to a function or return values from a function?	C	C++ (using a copy constructor)

Table 22.1 Contrasting two kinds of events.

Solution 22.8
a. Twice, which is *not* recommended.
b. None.

Drill 22.9
Instead of relying on the compiler to assign one object to another when dynamic memory allocation is involved, one should write the proper assignment function to do that. Write the proper operator=() function that will correct the problems we saw in Drill 22.8. Here's the function header:

```
void operator=(const Customer &x)
```

will be used for the initialization. The same thing is true for values returned from a function. The best way to understand all this is by studying some examples. Let us start with a simple one, Example 22.5, and slowly work our way to more complex programs.

```
// EXAMPLE 22.5
#include <iostream.h>
#include <string.h>

class Str
{
   private:
      char str[81];
   public:
      void set_up(char *x)  {  strcpy(str, x);  }
      ~Str()                {  cout << "Dtor   " << str << endl;  }
};

void main (void)
{
   Str s1; // Default constructor is provided by the compiler
   s1.set_up("Feeling alright!");
}     // Destructor called here.

----- output -----
Dtor    Feeling alright!
```

In this example, *s1* is an object of class Str. In main(), when *s1* is created, a compiler–generated constructor is provided and initializes it. This constructor is also called the default constructor. main() then assigns the private member of *s1* a string using the set_up() function. At the end of main(), when the *s1* object is no longer needed, its destructor is called and the string stored in it is printed at that time. We will use the words "Dtor" to mean destructor and "Ctor" to mean constructor.

If we define our own constructor that will initialize an Str object with a string, as follows:

```
Str s1("Feeling alright!");
```

then our compiler–generated constructor will no longer be available. Hence, we will have to define our own default constructor as well. This process is illustrated in Example 22.6.

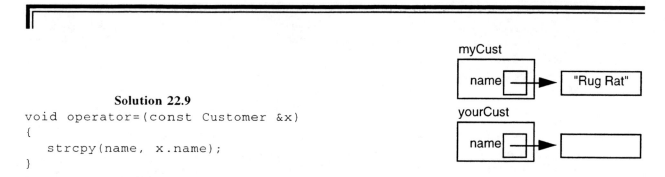

Solution 22.9
```
void operator=(const Customer &x)
{
   strcpy(name, x.name);
}
```

Drill 22.10
Given the initial states, show the state of the two objects after our assignment operator function is executed.

```
// EXAMPLE 22.6
#include <iostream.h>
#include <string.h>
class Str
{
   private:
      char str[81];
   public:
      Str()          {  cout << "Ctor     .\n";
                        strcpy(str, "."); }
      Str(char *x) {  cout << "Ctor    " << x  << endl;
                        strcpy(str, x); }
      ~Str()          {  cout << "Dtor    " << str << endl; }
};

void main (void)
{
   Str s1("Feeling alright!");// Or Str s1 = "Feeling alright!";
   Str s2;                      // Our own default constructor called here.
}                             // Destructors called here.
----- output -----
Ctor    Feeling alright!      // s1's ctor
Ctor    .                     // s2's ctor
Dtor    .                     // s2's dtor
Dtor    Feeling alright!      // s1's dtor
```

The Str(char *x) constructor is called for *s1*, and the Str() constructor is called for *s2*. For *s2*, we initialize *str* to a simple period so when its destructor is called, we see that something is printed from *s2*.

Now if we change the main() to add an assignment statement as follows:

```
void main (void)
{
   Str s1("Feeling alright!");
   Str s2;
   s2 = s1;
}
```

then our output will change to:

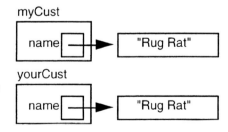

Solution 22.10

The values of name pointers are not changed, only the contents of the locations to which they point.

Drill 22.11

As a review, collect all the parts of the Customer class and rewrite them.

```
----- output -----
Ctor    Feeling alright!
Ctor    .
Dtor    Feeling alright!
Dtor    Feeling alright!
```

This is an indication that no new constructors or destructors are called — this is an assignment statement and not an initialization. Of course, when *s2*'s destructor is called, its new string, which was assigned from *s1*, is printed.

We can overload the assignment operator (=) by defining our own operator=() function. This would be placed in the public section of Str:

```
void operator = (Str x) {  cout << "In=()   " << x.str << endl;
                           strcpy(str, x.str);   }
```

Now this function will handle all our assignments involving Str objects. With this function now added to the Str class, the following main() will print the output shown:

```
void main (void)
{
   Str s1("Feeling alright!");
   Str s2;
   s2 = s1; // Calling the operator=() function
}
```

```
----- output -----
Ctor    Feeling alright! // s1's Ctor
Ctor    .                // s2's Ctor
In=()   Feeling alright! // Now in the operator=() function.
Dtor    Feeling alright! // Whoa, why was this destructor called?
Dtor    Feeling alright! // s2's Dtor
Dtor    Feeling alright! // s1's Dtor
```

We are puzzled by an extra destructor being called, as seen in the output. Because, when we call the operator=() function from main(), we are actually executing the following statement:

```
s2.operator=(s1);
```

Solution 22.11
```
class Customer
{ private:
    char *name;
  public:
    Customer ( ) {name = new char [25]; }              // Constructor
    ~Customer ( ) {cout << name; delete [ ] name; } // Destructor
    set (char *x) { strcpy(name, x); }
    Customer (const Customer &x)                       // Copy constructor
    { name = new char [25];
      strcpy(name, x.name); }
    void operator=(const Customer &x)                  // Assignment operator
    { strcpy(name, x.name); }
};
```

Here, *s1* is passed by value to *x*, the variable in operator=() that receives it. If you remember from the previous discussion and from Table 22.1, in C++ this involves an initialization. The object *x* has to be created first before it can copy *s1* in it. To do this, the compiler synthesizes a constructor called a copy constructor, and the programmer–defined constructor is not called. This copy constructor creates the *x* object and copies all the members of *s1* into it. Hence, when the function is finished executing, it must call the destructor for *x*. We have a destructor already defined for such objects, so it is executed; that is, the first output line with Dtor in it is printed when *x*'s destructor is called.

We can define our own copy constructor and we can place another cout in it. This way we can see if a copy constructor is really used or not. New code in Example 22.7 is shown in bold.

```
// EXAMPLE 22.7
#include <iostream.h>
#include <string.h>
class Str
{
   private:
      char str[81];
   public:
      Str()                      { cout << "Ctor    .\n";
                                   strcpy(str, "."); }
      Str(char *x)               { cout << "Ctor    " << x  << endl;
                                   strcpy(str, x); }
      Str(const Str &x)          { cout << "CpCtor " << x.str << endl;
                                   strcpy(str, x.str); }
      ~Str()                     { cout << "Dtor    " << str << endl; }

      void operator = (Str x) { cout << "In=()   " << x.str << endl;
                                   strcpy(str, x.str);   }
};
void main (void)
{
   Str s1("Feeling alright!");
   Str s2;
   s2 = s1;
}
----- output -----
Ctor    Feeling alright!   // s1's Ctor
```

Static variables and members

Drill 22.12 Now let us turn our attention to static variables. The function drill() on the next page has two local variables. *x* is a regular variable, the kind that we are used to. Every time this function is called, *x* is created and initialized to 0 automatically. Hence, *x* is called an automatic variable.

On the other hand, *y* is a static variable. It keeps its state every time you call the function. The first time you call drill(), *y* will be created and initialized to 0. Then the function will increment the value of *y* and, when the function is called again, *y* will still be the same.

Which variable is created and initialized every time the function is called? Which is created and initialized only once? Which is a static variable and which is automatic?

Loose Ends

```
Ctor         .                     // s2's Ctor
CpCtor  Feeling alright!           // x's copy constructor, copying from s1
In=()   Feeling alright!             // In the operator=() function
Dtor    Feeling alright!           // x's destructor
Dtor    Feeling alright!           // s2's destructor
Dtor    Feeling alright!           // s1's destructor
```

One should note that if a function receives an argument by reference or pointer, then no initialization is done; that is, no copy constructor is called. For example, suppose we change the operator=() function to the following:

```
void operator = (Str &x) { cout << "In=()   " << x.str << endl;
                           strcpy(str, x.str);   }
```

Then the output for the same main() would simply be as follows:

```
Ctor    Feeling alright!           // s1's Ctor
Ctor         .                     // s2's Ctor
In=()   Feeling alright!           // In the operator=()  function
Dtor    Feeling alright!           // s2's destructor
Dtor    Feeling alright!           // s1's destructor
```

x is not constructed so its destructor is not called.

The Cline–Lomow Law of the Big Three

This law was first derived by Cline and Lomow, who maintain a valuable source of C++ information on the Internet in the comp.lang.c++ news group. This important law is also published in their book on page 193.[1] It states that if you find yourself using new and delete in constructors and destructors, you must make sure that you write your own copy constructor and operator=() functions. Do not rely on the compiler to synthesize them for you. Most of the programs which do not follow this law end up eventually reaping disaster. We will cover this law in the Experiments section of this unit.

---

1. Marshall P. Cline and Greg A. Lomow, *C++ FAQs: Frequently Asked Questions*, Addison–Wesley Publishing Company, Reading, Massachusetts, 1995, ISBN 0–201–58958–3.

```
void drill (void)
{
        int x = 0;                 // Automatic variable.
   static  int y = 0;              // Static variable.
   cout << x << "  " << y << endl;
   x = x + 1;
   y = y + 1;
}
```

EXPERIMENTS

Exp 22.1 *print_star* is a variable. Its data type is an integer or a whole number. For now, disregard the warning you may get in this and the next experiment.

```
#include <iostream.h>
enum boolean { FALSE, TRUE };     // Stmt 1
void main ( )
{
      boolean print_star;
      print_star = 0;
      if(print_star)
         cout << "*\n";
      else
         cout << "-\n";
      print_star = TRUE;
      cout << print_star << endl;
      if(print_star)
         cout << "*\n";
      if( !print_star)
         cout << "-\n";
}
```

a. Can you make `print_star` equal to values other than 0 and 1? For example, what happens when you run the following statement?

```
print_star = 2;
```

b. Change statement 1 to the following:

```
enum boolean { FALSE, TRUE, MAYBE};
```

Now what are the values that can be assigned to `print_star`?

c. Restore Statement 1. What do you think is the advantage of declaring boolean as is done in Statement 1 above?

d. If you print out the boolean variable `print_star` using cout at the end of main(), what is printed?

e. What does `!print_star` mean?

Solution 22.12 *x*, an automatic variable, is created automatically and initialized every time the function is called. *y*, a static variable, doesn't change and is created and initialized only once.

Drill 22.13
Using the drill() function, show the output of the following program:

```
void main (void)
{  drill();
   drill();
   drill();
}
```

Loose Ends   477

Exp 22.2

```
#include <iostream.h>
void print_it (boolean x);
enum boolean { FALSE, TRUE };    // Stmt 1
void main ( )
{
     boolean print_star = 0;
     print_it(print_star);
     print_it(TRUE);
}


void print_it (boolean x)
{
   if(TRUE)
      cout << "*\n";
   if(x == FALSE)     // Stmt 2
      cout << "-\n";
}
```

a. Can you pass a variable of boolean type to a function?
b. Can you pass a boolean value to a function?
c. Name two ways Statement 2 can be changed.

Exp 22.3 In the last paragraph of the lesson section of this unit, we mentioned the Cline–Lomow Law of the Big Three. It states that, whenever you use new and delete in constructors and

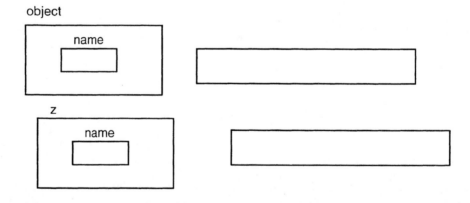

Solution 22.13 Notice that the automatic or normal variable is initialized each time. The static variable is initialized only once.

```
----- output -----
0  0
0  1
0  2
```

Drill 22.14

A static variable keeps its state during the course of the program, and classes can also have static members. This allows objects of the same class to share information or to share states.

a. The shared state of a static member belongs to a class or an object?
b. The scope of a static member is a class or an object?
c. The state of a regular class member belongs to a class or an object?

destructors, you should also write proper versions of the copy constructor and the operator=() function. This experiment explores what happens when you don't do that, and the following experiment shows the benefit of using the rule.

```
#include <string.h>
#include <iostream.h>
class S
{
    private:
        char *name;
    public:
        S()     { name = new char[15];
                  strcpy(name, "Up and");
                  cout << "Ctor Up and\n";
                }
        ~S()    { cout << "Dtor " << name << endl;
                  delete [ ] name;
                }
        void set (char *x) { strcpy(name, x); }
};

void sneeky (S z)
{
    z.set("Away ");
}

void main (void)
{
    S object;
    sneeky(object);
}
```

    a. In the diagram for this experiment on the previous page, draw an arrow from the character pointer of *object* to the long box at the right. What command creates this long box at the right?
    b. What string is stored in this long box for object? Write it in.
    c. When the sneeky() function is called, which object is copied into which?
    d. Is there a programmer–defined copy constructor for the object called *z*?
    e. Who provides a copy constructor?

Solution 22.14
a. Class
b. Class
c. Object

Drill 22.15 Here is an example of a static member for a class:

```
class Hat
{
        private:
                static int counter;
};
```

Remember that a class, like a structure, doesn't require memory. Only when an object is created is memory set aside for it. Here, *counter* is only specified. Outside the class, we still need to allocate memory for it.
a. Inside the class, a static member is only defined or declared?
b. Outside the class, a static member still needs to be defined or declared?

f. When is the *z* object destroyed?

g. Before *z* is destroyed, what string did it point to?

h. When is *object* destroyed?

i. Before *object* is destroyed, what string did it point to?

j. Since *z* and *object* pointed to the same string, was new memory allocated for *z,* as is implied in the program?

k. When *object* was copied into *z* by the compiler–synthesized copy constructor, what did this copy constructor copy? Did it copy simply the address or did it copy the string?

l. Now that you know that only the address was copied from object.name to z.name, show an arrow from z.name to the same string to which object.name points in our diagram.

m. When sneeky() changed the string which *z* pointed to, did it automatically change the string to which *object* pointed? Why?

n. How many times was the `delete` executed? Did it execute once or twice for each time that memory was allocated?

Exp 22.4 Now add the following copy constructor into the class definition and, using the same main(), show the output. The main concept to understand here is the reason why sneeky() can't change the value of *object*. This is a reason to use the Cline–Lomow Law. Of course, we are still missing the operator=() function. You can write it as an exercise.

```
S(const S &x)
{
    name = new char[15];
    strcpy(name, x.name);
}
```

object

name

z

name

Solution 22.15

a. Declared
b. Defined

Drill 22.16
Outside the class, the static member is defined as follows:

```
int Hat::counter = 0;
```

Now write a constructor for Hat so that every time a new Hat object is created, *counter* is incremented.

a. Draw the arrows to represent the pointers in each object that is initialized.

b. When sneeky() changes z.name to something else, does it automatically change object.name for main()? Why or why not?

c. This is an important question. How many times did the `delete` operate on each memory that was allocated?

QUESTIONS

1. State whether an assignment or an initialization is described.
   a. `strcpy(x, " hello");`
   b. Used a constructor
   c. If defined, invokes the operator=() function.
   d. May occur several times during the lifetime of a variable.
   e. In C++, this event is used to pass variables to a function by value.

2. Regarding friend functions:
   a. Do they belong to a class?
   b. When defining them outside a class, is the scoping operator (::) used?
   c. They are most useful when performing an operation between two objects. (True or false)
   d. Is the keyword `friend` used when declaring, defining, or using the function?

3. Declare a pointer called *p* that points to functions receiving a char and a float as arguments and returns a pointer to char.

4. Show the output of the following program:

```
class Car
{
    private:           float gas;
              static   int number;
    public:
       add(int x) { gas = x; number++; }
       show()     { cout << "Gas left " << gas
                    << "\tNumber still in race "<< number << endl; }
};
```

Solution 22.16
```
class Hat
{    private:
          static int counter;
     public:
          Hat() { counter = counter + 1; }
};
int Hat::counter = 0;
```

Drill 22.17

a. If 5 objects of class Hat were declared, how many *counter* members would exist? What would be their final values?

b. What would be the answer to Drill 22.17a if *counter* weren't declared `static`?

```
int Car::number = 0;
void main (void)
{
    Car race[3];
    for(i = 0; i <= 2; ++i)
        race[i].add(20 * i + 1);
    for(i = 0; i <= 2; ++i)
        race[i].show();
}
```

PROGRAMS

1. For Experiments 22.3 and 22.4, write the proper operator=() function.

2. Write three functions, all having the same header but different names. The names of the functions are add(), mult(), and divd(). They return nothing and receive two integers as arguments. Each function prints the operation for which they are named, that is, add, multiply, and divide.

   In main(), declare a pointer to functions that have this argument signature. Then execute these three functions, each time by passing 5 and 7 as arguments. The calling to the functions should be done using the pointer only.

3. Create a class called Movie that has a member called type. type is an enumerated data type with values of Humor, Mystery, Children, and Tragedy. It also has a static integer member called count that, using a constructor, counts the number of Movie objects created. A destructor function prints the value of count and the type of movie each time an object is destroyed.

   In main(), create an array of four elements of class Movie. Assign each of the four types in any order to each of the four elements of the array. Then close main() and let the destructors do the printing.

Solution 22.17
a. Only one *counter* member would exist, and its final value would be five.
b. There would be five *counter* members in existence, and their final values would be 0 or 1, depending on how the constructor was defined.

Index

Symbols

! 83, 94, 95
#define 32, 34, 40, 43, 176, 385
#include 32
% 6
%c 6, 35, 39, 40
%d 6
%f 6
%p 35, 37
%s 6, 37
& 34, 37, 40, 158, 201, 206, 354, 375
&& 83, 94, 97
* 201, 220, 221, 230, 354, 355, 375
** 371, 374
++ 143
-> 221, 233, 239, 364, 368, 375
// 5
:: 292, 294
< 86, 96
<< 296, 301
= 50
== 50, 67
> 86
>> 296, 304
{ } 5
| 272
|| 83, 94, 98
~ 363, 385, 387

A

abstract base classes 456, 462
abstraction 284, 286, 296, 315

add_line() 229
address 35, 158, 199
aliases 360
AND logic 83
argument 138, 140, 147, 150, 154
argument signatures 450
arithmetic 20
array
  2D 128
  addresses 225
  handling 105
  initialization 109, 112, 118
  of objects 376, 390
  and pointers 203, 204, 212, 213, 214, 358, 366
  of pointers 221, 227, 360, 374, 374-375,
      380, 397, 445, 461
  of pointers to objects 391
  purpose of 102
  reading in a 2D 132
  reading in an 114, 115
  searching 106
  of structures 185, 193, 195
  two dimensional 123
  variable-length 363
arrow notation. *See* ->
ASCII 246, 249, 279
assignment 18, 20, 22, 49, 58, 111, 471
assignment versus initialization 471–476, 481
attributes 269, 274, 282, 318
automatic variable 477

B

backslash 6, 9

superclass   294, 310
swap   130, 163
swapping   128
switch   100

T

telecommunications application   319, 339
templates   449
tic–tac–toe   313
tracechart   48, 51, 56, 68
tracecharts   xvi
transaction file   250, 251

U

unions   269
UNIX   8, 74, 255
unsigned   30
use cases   330

V

variable   17
variable address   34
variable attributes   34, 37, 44, 206
video rental application   307, 330
view   287
virtual destructors   446, 448, 449
virtual functions   437, 440, 443, 445–447, 454, 455
   common mistakes   445
   precautions in   456
   pure   457
virtual methods   427
   pure   428–429
void   4, 5, 140, 141

W

while loop   59
whitespace   39
Wilkinson, Nancy   310
window   275, 282. *See also* screen
Wirfs-Brook, Rebecca   310

Imagine your future and make it so.

Try Borland C++Builder today!
The latest C++ compiler is now integrated into a Visual Development Environment.

Borland C++Builder Professional delivers:
- **NEW!** Lighting-fast drag-and-drop development
- **FREE!** 100+ reusable, customizable components
  - **NEW!** Visual Designer and Code Editor—always synchronized!

This CD-ROM contains a full-featured time-locked trial version of Borland C++Builder™ that expires 60 days after installation—try it yourself and experience the power of industry-standard C++!

You can purchase Borland C++Builder Standard for the low educational price of only $49.95* or Borland C++Builder Professional for only $99.95* at any authorized educational reseller. Call 1-800-847-7797 to find the reseller nearest you, or visit our reseller locator on the Web www.borland.com/programs/baer/baer.html/

If you cannot find a local authorized reseller near you, call 1-800-645-4559, ext. 1462 for information on the Borland Scholar Coupon Program.

Real visual development
Real C++
Borland C++Builder Professional

Most complete C++ for 16- and 32-bit development
Borland C++ Development Suite
Targets Windows 3.1, 95, NT, and DOS

The fastest Windows development tool
NEW
Borland Delphi 3 Professional

*Suggested Educational Prices. Prices are in U.S. dollars and may vary by reseller. Instructors who wish to order coupons for their students should send a letter written on school letterhead to: Educational Sales Department, Borland International, Inc., P.O. Box 660001, Scotts Valley, CA 95066-3249. Instructors: please specify the products and number of coupons needed for your class. Photo courtesy of National Aeronautics and Space Administration. Copyright © 1997 Borland International, Inc. All rights reserved. All Borland product names are trademarks of Borland International, Inc. • BI 10188

Borland
www.borland.com